Serverless Beyond the Buzzword

A Strategic Approach to Modern Cloud Management

Second Edition

Thomas Smart

Apress®

Serverless Beyond the Buzzword: A Strategic Approach to Modern Cloud Management

Thomas Smart
Singapore, Singapore

ISBN-13 (pbk): 978-1-4842-8760-6 ISBN-13 (electronic): 978-1-4842-8761-3
https://doi.org/10.1007/978-1-4842-8761-3

Managing Director, Apress Media LLC: Welmoed Spahr
Acquisitions Editor: Susan McDermott
Development Editor: Laura Berendson
Coordinating Editor: Jessica Vakili

Distributed to the book trade worldwide by Springer Science+Business Media New York, 233 Spring Street, 6th Floor, New York, NY 10013. Phone 1-800-SPRINGER, fax (201) 348-4505, e-mail orders-ny@springer-sbm.com, or visit www.springeronline.com. Apress Media, LLC is a California LLC and the sole member (owner) is Springer Science + Business Media Finance Inc (SSBM Finance Inc). SSBM Finance Inc is a **Delaware** corporation.

For information on translations, please e-mail booktranslations@springernature.com; for reprint, paperback, or audio rights, please e-mail bookpermissions@springernature.com.

Apress titles may be purchased in bulk for academic, corporate, or promotional use. eBook versions and licenses are also available for most titles. For more information, reference our Print and eBook Bulk Sales web page at http://www.apress.com/bulk-sales.

Any source code or other supplementary material referenced by the author in this book is available to readers on the Github repository: https://github.com/Apress/Serverless-Beyond-the-Buzzword. For more detailed information, please visit http://www.apress.com/source-code.

Printed on acid-free paper

The Consultant's Purpose

What is a consultant, what is our purpose – why do we exist?
We help organizations in many ways, sometimes even
when they resist.

Some will say they love solving problems, but that isn't a
purpose – it's a skill.
Like engineering, design, or writing, it just takes experience and will.

Our real purpose is to deliver truths; with honesty they are quoted.
Harsh as they often are, they should never be sugarcoated.

We present them diplomatically as needed, with all the
proof and every fact.
That is the commitment to our clients, our guarantee, our pact.

To fulfil that purpose, we never shy away from questioning nor
flinch at digging deep.
We challenge the status quo and overcome distractions;
our focus we must keep.

Pretty PowerPoints are but a medium, not the goal that we pursue.
Our integrity demands each project is given the attention it is due.

While we provide recommendations for our clients to decide,
Sometimes they choose wrongly, but we take that in our stride.

We mustn't take it personally, lest our mental health be assailed.
To the right clients, the best ones, as personal advisors, we will
be hailed.

That is our calling: for our harsh truths to be honest and by our
clients to be trusted.
The experience, capabilities, and medium are but a means
when all is done and dusted.

Thomas Smart, 2022

Table of Contents

About the Author

 **Thomas Smart** has been actively involved with digital projects since 2002. His experience crosses many industries and types and sizes of organizations, giving him a wealth of experience and knowledge to draw upon as part of his consulting services. Since 2020 he has worked as a senior consultant for Sourced Singapore, helping large, regulated enterprises evolve their cloud strategy to productively deliver Serverless applications. This experience has provided many new insights for large enterprises and their unique challenges when adopting modern cloud strategies.

His passion for Serverless comes from a focus on innovation, rapid prototyping, and designing solutions that are as cost-effective as possible. Serverless is a good match for these goals, as will become apparent in this book.

Acknowledgments

A big thank you to my wife, Meiting, whose tolerance and patience with me knows almost no bounds, and to my boys, Blaze, Dash, and Max, who inspire me daily to share my knowledge with the next generation.

Many thanks to my editor, Mary Whitehouse, who helped make the book considerably more readable; Won Jenn Lee, who implemented some of the case studies in the final chapter; and Eden Fall-Bailey, for being an amazing help in researching, assembling, and editing the content for this second edition.

I want to thank KangZheng Li, a Sourced colleague who was instrumental in making the Serverless Training Program a reality. That program was largely based on the first edition of this book, and working with KangZheng to create the program led to many new insights and knowledge gained that have made their way into this edition of the book.

Prologue

Technology is best when it brings people together.

—**Matt Mullenweg, Social Media Entrepreneur**

💼 Who Is This Book For?

This book is for anyone interested in Serverless, regardless of their technical level. I share strategic insights for entrepreneurs and executives, planning and team insights for project managers, and technical insights for architects and team leads. The intent is to provide a deep understanding of Serverless architecture and how it could impact your business and your projects.

This book is not intended to be a Serverless development guide. Because of the sheer number of programming languages and the rapid pace of change in this area, the Internet is the best source of information for finding specific code examples. This book will provide an essential understanding of Serverless, best practices, security guidelines, and other topics that will help an organization productively deliver Serverless applications.

If any of the following scenarios sound familiar, then this is the right book for you:

- You are an executive or manager, and your technical people have been talking about Serverless for some time. You are interested but want to make sure it's the right strategic choice for your business or project.

- You are a project manager or team lead tasked with digital transformation and are looking for a technology strategy that will give you an unfair advantage.

- You are an entrepreneur or innovation manager looking for a way to rapidly prototype ideas using a cost-effective approach.

- You are a software architect or developer who wants to find out more about the broader implications of Serverless, for example, to gain a deeper understanding or to pitch it to your stakeholders.

💼 Technical Levels Used in This Book

As you may have noticed, each section header has a little icon. This icon indicates the **technical** level of that section, helping you to quickly identify if it's suitable for your own technical level and interest.

💼 The briefcase icon indicates a section that is not technical and is appropriate for readers who want a better understanding of the business and strategic implications of using Serverless.

📋 The clipboard icon indicates a section that may contain some technical references relevant to project managers and product owners who want a deeper understanding of the technology so they can improve project planning and communication with developers.

⚙ The gear icon indicates a section containing technical concepts. Some architecture or coding experience is required to fully understand these sections, which are of most value to solution architects, team leads, and developers.

💼 What Will You Learn?

This book will help you understand what colleagues or friends mean when they are talking about *Serverless*.

I want to share the facts about and background of Serverless to help you decide for yourself if it is a technology fad or a technology evolution. You'll be able to determine if it's relevant to you, your career, and your organization and what impact it might have if you were to start using it in your projects.

About a quarter of this book addresses "*why Serverless?*". This includes some history and discusses how the cloud has evolved its Serverless capabilities.

Another quarter explores the *what* of Serverless, providing a deeper understanding of the technology, how it can be used, and the challenges and benefits it can bring to an organization.

The remaining half addresses the *how*. Where do you go from here? How to find the right people and how to enable productive delivery of Serverless applications in your organization?

Chapter 1 introduces Serverless and its challenges and benefits. It will be helpful to anyone looking to understand on a high level what Serverless is and its potential relevance to their business.

Chapters 2–5 delve deeper into the strategic impact of Serverless on cloud management, finance, security, and people within an organization. It answers questions such as

- How can we enable application teams to benefit from Serverless in an enterprise while remaining compliant?

- How are business models, estimates, and budgets evolving with Serverless?

- How does Serverless impact security and GDPR or similar privacy regulations?

- Where do I find and how do I assess the right talent for a Serverless team?

Chapters 6–8 get a bit more technical. We explore DevOps concepts and tooling that can improve the developer experience and automate deployment processes. We will also look at some cloud capabilities such as logging and testing that are essential for Serverless.

Lastly, Chapters 9 and 10 are the most technical, looking at architectural best practices and several examples of Serverless components and entire applications.

Glossary

Before we start, here are some words used frequently throughout the book, along with definitions, for those not entirely familiar with cloud jargon.

Provider, cloud provider, cloud service provider, CSP
A business that makes cloud services available publicly. The top three businesses by market share are Amazon Web Services, Google Cloud, and Microsoft Azure.

Service

Another word for a feature, tool, or software product in the cloud. For example, *Amazon S3* is a storage service. Services are typically owned by the cloud provider and offered through their platform where they can be used by application and cloud teams.

Serviceful

Often an aspect of Serverless architecture, this means to prefer cloud services over writing custom code. For example, instead of writing code to validate user input, we can use a feature of the API Gateway service called *models*. This reduces the amount of custom work that needs to be created and maintained and avoids reinventing the wheel.

Solution

We commonly see an application as an answer to a given problem, so we also call applications *solutions*. In the context of this book, it will usually refer to a cloud-based application.

Architecture

This does not refer to buildings in our industry, although it has some similarities conceptually. Architecture refers to the structure and design of a solution at different levels:

- We call it **software** *architecture* when talking about the application code.

- We call the entire application, including the design and configuration of the cloud services, ***solution*** *architecture*.

- An even higher level, including integration with corporate networks, is called ***enterprise*** *architecture*.

Component

A component typically refers to a piece of a larger Serverless application. It could be a configuration for a single cloud service, a microservice, or an entire user interface. Components are generally considered independent, and they can be shared and reused between different applications.

Solution architect

The title of a person typically responsible for designing the infrastructure of a cloud-based application. Similar to the levels in *architecture*, there are also software architects – who focus more on the application code – and enterprise architects – who focus on broader IT strategies and integrations within the organization.

Instance

This is another word for servers in the cloud. They are not physical servers but a software-defined section of a physical server. In the cloud, physical servers are typically split into multiple sections or *virtual* servers to improve utilization. We will explore this in more detail later in the book.

Provision

This means configuring and activating a particular cloud service for use in your solution. For example, when we *launch a server* in the cloud, the industry terminology would be to *provision an instance*.

Parameters, variables, configurations, settings, options

These all effectively mean the same thing and can usually be used interchangeably. These are used to make services behave in the way required for the solution. For example, the size of an instance can be configured with the *instance type* parameter.

Lambda function vs. Lambda microservice

Lambda is an AWS service for hosting *microservices*, but the official AWS term is Lambda *functions* or even just *Lambdas*. The terms are interchangeable but can cause confusion as microservices can also be deployed on containers. This book will specifically call those *containers* or *container* microservices to avoid confusion, and the term *microservice* on its own will always refer to a Lambda function.

Code base

The code base can include scripts, developed code, unit tests, and infrastructure configuration templates used for an application. With monolithic applications, due to dependencies and how monolithic applications are made, the code base will typically include everything for the entire application. With modern cloud architecture, the entire application could be in a single code base, or each component of the application could be separated in its own code base – depending on how the team structures the project.

💼 Amazon Web Services (AWS)

Most of my experience is on Amazon Web Services, so the cloud services and examples I mention in this book are often for their platform unless otherwise specified. The more strategic aspects of the book and the high-level concepts described can often be applied to all major cloud providers.

Amazon is the largest e-retailer in the world, as well as the largest cloud provider. As cloud services seem to generate more revenue, some people liken it to an IT firm with a gift shop. Joking aside, Amazon's hands-on experience through the e-retail business is one of the reasons that its cloud services are such a success. They have been tried and tested in Amazon's production environments with massive volumes of users and data. 2021 figures reveal that when a service needs to be hosted in the cloud, there is a 33% chance it will be hosted on AWS.

The history of Serverless (discussed in Chapter 1) provides some insights into how AWS started the Serverless evolution. They have been my preferred cloud partner for several years, in part due to their strength in Serverless.

In 2019, in recognition of my Serverless activities, they invited me to join their exclusive AWS Ambassador Partner Program as one of the few independent consultants. I joined Sourced in 2020, where my target audience changed to regulated enterprises. I continued promoting, training, and talking about Serverless and, soon after, rejoined the AWS Ambassador Partner Program as a Sourced employee.

💼 Second Edition

The first edition was published in 2020, and, with the pace of change being as brutal and unforgiving as it is, I started making notes for the second edition within a month of finishing the manuscript. The overall structure has remained the same. We start less technical, more focused on strategy, and work our way up to technical walk-throughs of complex Serverless architectures. However, some of the earlier chapters do have more technical sections where it didn't make sense to split the information.

Almost every chapter has new content added. I go into far more detail on all topics and have added several new topics and entire chapters. There are also considerably more visuals in this edition to help explain some of the more complex concepts.

More attention is paid to the bigger picture strategy of transforming a large organization to be able to deliver Serverless applications productively. This often requires changes to team organizational structures, KPIs, and cloud security and management processes.

One thing that sets this book apart from others in the market is that much of it is written with the limits, challenges, and opportunities of a large enterprise in mind. Often, these are significantly different from those faced by startups and tech companies who find it easier to adopt and experiment with new technologies. Large enterprises, especially regulated ones, need more assurance that a particular cloud strategy is secure, auditable, and resilient before even considering it. This is one of the reasons that it's only now, 6 years after Lambda was launched, that large enterprises are starting to look at Serverless as a potential cloud strategy.

CHAPTER 1

Serverless Basics

The Web as I envisaged it, we have not seen it yet. The future is still so much bigger than the past.

—Tim Berners-Lee, Inventor of the World Wide Web

What Is Serverless Architecture?

Serverless is a means to create software that will run on a server fully managed by a cloud provider instead of a server managed by our organization, and we should only be paying for *actual utilization*, not idle time or availability.

What it really means is that application teams can focus on service configuration, which is not to be underestimated, and application code – in short, the work that should result in a return on investment (ROI) for the application, as opposed to the necessary *plumbing*.

The word "Server**less**" is a bit of a misnomer as there actually are servers involved in storing and running the code. It is called Serverless because the developers no longer need to manage, update, or maintain the underlying servers, operating systems, or software.

Redundancy, load balancing, networking, and, to some extent, security are also largely managed, guaranteed, and monitored by the cloud provider and their dedicated 24/7 operations team.

For a service to be considered *Serverless*, the following should apply:

1. A significant portion of the service is managed by the cloud provider – including the operating system, most software, and any common dependencies. We also expect redundancy, scalability, and, to some degree, security to be managed and automated.

1

© Thomas Smart 2023
T. Smart, *Serverless Beyond the Buzzword*, https://doi.org/10.1007/978-1-4842-8761-3_1

2. We pay only for actual usage, for example, the number of requests, the amount of storage, or the duration for which a service is actually used. If we have to pay for idle time, it would not be considered Serverless. Some cloud services use the term "Serverless" in their name or description but do not satisfy this requirement. If we configure a service but add no data to it and there are no users, then the bill should be zero if it is Serverless.

3. Some services bill for idle time; however, due to their nature or our use case, they can be turned off automatically when not needed and turned back on again automatically when required. This approach helps minimize being billed for idle time and so creates a Serverless experience. However, if this approach compromises the security of the solution in any way or makes it unstable, then it should not be considered Serverless.

There are some related terms that I want to clarify to make sure we are all on the same page.

Cloud-native refers to solutions that have been created **for** the cloud – they are not necessarily Serverless. A cloud-native solution could be running on servers but using cloud capabilities such as autoscaling. As the cloud continues to evolve, the term is becoming more associated with Serverless, but it is not quite interchangeable yet. I use the more specific term *Serverless* in this book to avoid any confusion.

Fully managed is another common term you may have heard. This term can be especially confusing as it can be used to describe a service or a feature of a service. Context and sentence structure is important, and it helps gain a deeper understanding of the various cloud services and their billing models. For example, the *Aurora database is a fully managed service*. In this case, the cloud provider manages the service, but it is still billed based on usage, so we will be paying for idle time. On the other hand, Lambda is a Serverless service, and one of the features of that is that it is fully managed.

Pay for What You Use

Cloud providers like to talk about *"only paying for what you use."* This is a common phrase in marketing materials and basic training, including when the topic is cloud **servers**. This can lead to some confusion when I point out that a benefit of Serverless is that we only pay for actual utilization.

There is a difference. With servers, we pay for **availability**. When cloud providers talk about the benefits of cloud servers, they are typically comparing them against self-managed data center infrastructure. With the latter, organizations need to purchase and maintain hardware, often when it's not needed right away. It is standard practice to have backup hardware for maintenance and predicted future projects.

With cloud servers, organizations can provision the server as and when they need it and discard it when done, only paying for the time it was active. In this context, *"what you use"* means *when a server is running and **available** to use.* Server-based applications expect a server to be running for the application to be available, regardless of whether or not anyone is using the application.

With Serverless, the cloud services powering it are expected to be always available, made so by the cloud provider, and at no cost to us. When we have a user that wants to interact with a Serverless application, the cloud service will respond accordingly and execute the request. We are only billed for the time that the request is **executing**. This request, which may only take a few milliseconds, is what we consider the **actual utilization** - it is driven by actual use and not just availability.

In summary

- With self-managed data center infrastructure, we pay for everything, even when it's not really needed.

- With cloud servers, we pay for availability, even if it's not utilized.

- With Serverless, we only pay when we really use a service.

Server vs. Fully Managed vs. Serverless

Returning to the options we have in the cloud, there are three ways to host an application:

Servers

The organization manages the operating system and software, including all maintenance. The application teams need to configure redundancy and scaling, and we pay a fixed amount every month based on server size and quantity, but regardless of actual utilization.

This is not Serverless because we are paying for idle availability. In a given month, we would pay the same if we had zero visitors or thousands. Due to the nature of servers and, especially, the time needed to start a server, it is not realistic to automatically disable and enable servers in response to visitors.

Fully managed service

The application team is responsible for the code and service configuration, but the cloud provider manages everything else. We still pay a monthly amount regardless of utilization. Some container services and managed databases operate this way in the cloud. Depending on the service and use case, it may be possible to use configuration and custom code to make a fully managed service behave like a Serverless one. For example, we can launch a container on demand for a particular task and then terminate it once the task completes. This way, we are only billing for the *actual* utilization of the fully managed service.

Serverless

And lastly, we have Serverless, which is similar to fully managed, but we only pay for actual utilization. One way to think of this is the service automatically turns off our component between requests and automatically turns it on again with *no noticeable delay* when a user arrives. Because of this, we only pay for each individual request and the time it is running each request.

So far, it's been about understanding the terminology. Let's look at the financial impact that *actual utilization* has on an application. In Figure 1-1, we have a simple registration form. This form is used 20 times a day, and processing a submission takes 1 second.

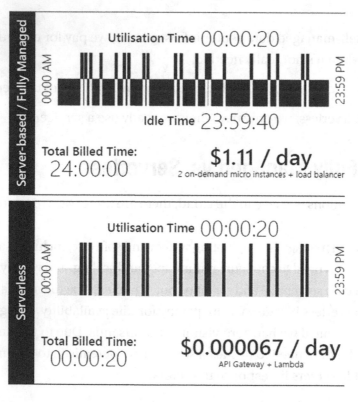

Figure 1-1. *Server and fully managed vs. Serverless utilization*

With a server-based or fully managed approach, we are billed for the full 24 hours of runtime. This means we will have paid for 23 hours, 59 minutes, and 40 seconds of available time and 20 seconds of actual utilization. With Serverless, we will **only** pay for those 20 seconds of utilization. In dollars, that would be over one dollar for an on-demand server-based option for 1 day and less than one-hundredth of a cent for the Serverless option.

This example is purposefully kept simple; 20 requests a day is not a high number compared with most applications. We will look at how Serverless pricing scales and compares with servers for a solution with more users in Chapter 3.

What Serverless Is Not

It is equally important to know what Serverless architecture is **not**.

It will not replace all other ways to build software in the cloud, nor is it suitable for all projects or organizations. As with any tool, we need to pick the right one for the job. Generally speaking, Serverless is usually **not** suitable for

- Computer-intensive applications that need heavy CPU processing power, lots of memory, or Graphic Processing Units (GPUs).

- Migration of existing applications without significant updates or sometimes even a complete rewrite of the application.

- Complex low-latency applications, depending on the specific requirements.

- *Organizations with a multi-cloud policy*: They might be better matched with a container or Kubernetes strategy.

Some organizations may need to restructure their teams and evolve their cloud strategy significantly before they can **productively** deliver Serverless projects.

 # Microservices

Microservices frequently come up when Serverless is discussed, and most Serverless solutions will include them. Microservices are like mini-applications that each handle a specific feature or set of closely related features. Microservices are able to work together to meet an application's full set of requirements.

In a Serverless application, microservices are where we can write our custom code. They make up the compute or intelligence of a solution, effectively replacing the need for servers or containers. Microservices can do calculations, apply algorithms and machine learning models, convert data between different formats, and much more. Microservices are also commonly used as the "glue" between cloud services in a workflow – for example, extracting audio from video in one service (transcode), converting it to text in a second service (transcribe), and then having the text analyzed in a third service (comprehend).

Microservices are what we call *loosely coupled*, meaning that they can function independently of each other. If one microservice fails, the other microservices can still perform their respective tasks.

Let's explain that in more detail. To keep it less technical, I will use a self-service ice cream machine analogy to explain it in Figure 1-2.

Traditionally, software architecture was monolithic, meaning that the application was written as a single collection of code that contained all its functions. In our example, a single ice cream machine will handle the entire request. While well-written monolithic applications are often layered to provide some separation between data, function, and design, the different layers, and the functions within a given layer, are still heavily dependent on each other.

The downside is that if any part of the monolithic machine breaks, the entire machine is essentially unusable. Even worse, any new request for ice cream will simply be met with silence, and any existing request will be lost – including the request's data. We will only find out that something is wrong when a user complains that the machine isn't working or by using external monitoring tools.

Microservices can be thought of as independent mini-applications, each one providing a specific feature. In Figure 1-2, they are represented as four small machines on the right, each one performing a particular part of the request. Below those machines, we have a conveyor belt, representing a workflow-managing service that ensures all our machines are working nicely together to get that final result.

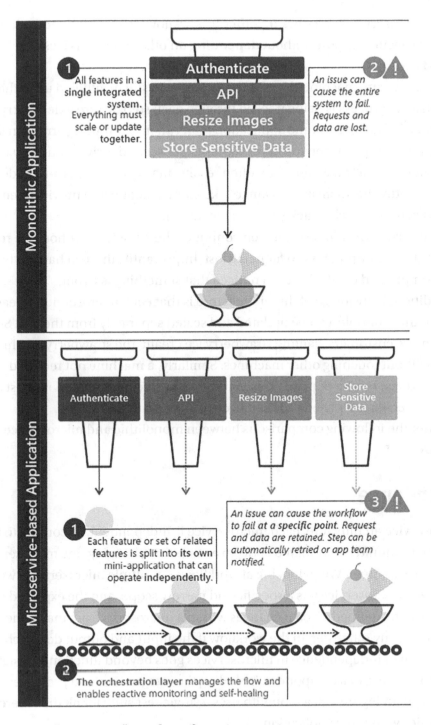

Figure 1-2. *The "ice cream" analogy for microservices*

While microservices can work **together** in workflows, a well-designed microservice can fulfil its specific purpose without **depending** on other microservices or relying on any shared code.

If one of the mini machines breaks, the request can still be fulfilled up to that point, and because the process is being tracked through each step, we are able to retry a failed step automatically. High-volume applications can run into throttling errors on some services, which happen when too many requests per second arrive. Routinely retrying such a request after a small pause can often resolve matters. If the auto-retry doesn't work, it can notify the application team to take manual action and provide them with the details and context to help quickly resolve the matter.

When it's fixed, the request can then continue where it left off without the request, any of its data, or any progress so far being lost. Importantly, this can happen before the user has complained or, ideally, even noticed that something is wrong.

An additional advantage of this architecture is that each microservice, or each machine in this example, can be updated and scaled separately from the rest. So, if we have a lot more customers wanting strawberry ice cream, the strawberry machine can be scaled without touching other machines. Similarly, a machine not required for a particular request can be skipped. This increases the efficiency of each request as the response is specific to its needs and unnecessary steps can be avoided.

Consider the following comparisons between monolithic and microservice architectures.

Independence

In a microservice architecture, each microservice is independent. According to best practice, there should be no shared code, to ensure that changing one microservice does not break another. When looking at workflows – multiple microservices working together, each microservice has a specific and narrow scope, and the expected input and output are clearly defined. Even if changes within a microservice are made, the changes will not impact any other step in the workflow if the input and output do not change.

The notion of independence in microservices goes beyond functional design. It applies to all areas of a component, including the integrations and processes surrounding it. In Figure 1-3, a monolith uses a single test suite for all the different functionalities within the application.

This means that whenever there is a change to any components of our monolith, all components within the application – whether they are affected by the change or not – will need to be tested again.

Figure 1-3 shows how approaches that work initially can become a liability as the application scales over time.

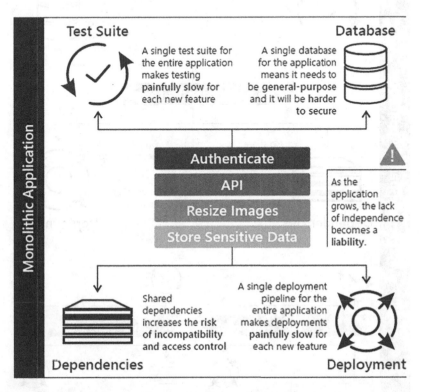

Figure 1-3. *Lack of independence in a monolithic application*

Monoliths tend to use a single database and pick a more general option to support the broad range of different use cases within a single application. While this works, it may not be as efficient as the more purpose-built database options available today.

Monoliths usually share dependencies across layers and features. This can pose a challenge when two features need two different versions of a dependency. This situation will likely force a rewrite of the features to use the same dependency across the application.

For deployments, there is a single deployment process and pipeline for the application's entire code base. Regardless of what has been changed, each deployment will require the entire application to be deployed again, which can be time-consuming.

The independence of microservices means we can have dedicated processes and integrations for each one, as seen in Figure 1-4.

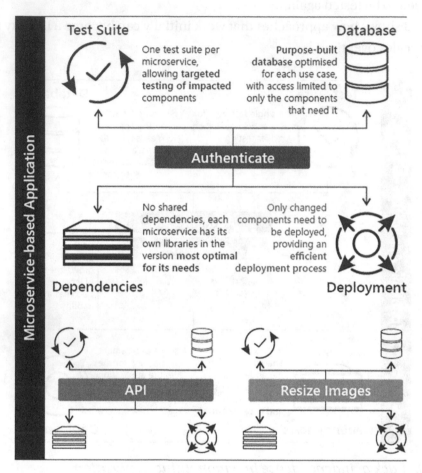

Figure 1-4. *The microservice architecture's independence goes beyond the code*

For testing, we can have a more targeted approach that only tests the changes made to a particular service instead of the entire application. Integration and end-to-end tests can similarly be limited to the updated microservice and any dependencies and dependents.

For databases, we can leverage purpose-built databases to cater to the specific needs of each microservice. For example, we can use Amazon Neptune for a recommendation microservice, Amazon Timestream for an IoT microservice, and Amazon QLDB for a microservice managing financial transactions.

For dependencies, each microservice can have its own set of dependencies in the version that the microservice needs. Version variations will not impact other microservices as they are independent. While this can cause more overhead to manage, programming languages such as NodeJS and Python have dependency and version management features to help with this.

Lastly, for deployment, we only deploy the changed microservice into production, which reduces the impact and speeds up deployment time.

Reusability

A monolithic application might have a function to create thumbnails of images. This same function would be repeated in every other application needing this feature. If the organization wants to upgrade the quality of the thumbnails across its portfolio of applications, the developers will need to update multiple image functions in multiple applications.

If we use a thumbnail microservice, then this would be a stand-alone mini-application for creating thumbnails. Several other applications within the organization can easily use the same microservice. This microservice is given image data and returns thumbnail data, so it does not need to deeply integrate into each solution or access any sensitive resources to be able to perform its task.

Besides shared microservices, the same applies to blueprints and code. Individual components in a Serverless application are stored separately. This makes it easier to share them with the broader organization for use in other projects.

Security

A monolithic application might have a function that stores sensitive transactional information in a database. Because it's a single code base and this function needs access to that database, that means that the entire application, the entire server, and any other applications on the same server will have access to the sensitive database. It is not possible to provide only a part of a monolithic application with access to a database.

In a Serverless solution, there would be a microservice for transactions. This is the only microservice with access to the transactions database – which is exclusively for storing transactions. Other parts of a solution must go via this microservice to interact with transaction data, and all such requests can be more easily monitored, authorized, and audited in this one location.

Separation of Front End (User Interface) and Back End (Processing)

Well-developed monolithic applications can achieve this, too, but it wasn't a typical approach to take. More commonly, well-designed monolithic applications follow the Model View Controller (MVC) approach to achieve separation of front end and back end. However, they would still be within the same code base with shared functions and many dependencies.

With Serverless, the front end and back end are entirely separate and running on different managed services, potentially even developed using different programming languages and by different teams. Multiple front-end interfaces running in a browser, mobile app ,or desktop can all use the same back end, regardless of differences in the programming language, methodology, or even development team.

To facilitate communication, Serverless back ends are typically an API - which we will cover in more detail later in the book. A great benefit of the API approach is that it makes Serverless applications far easier to automate and integrate with other applications.

 **Serverless Example**

Figure 1-5 is a simple Serverless registration form example. We can see the *User Form Frontend* at the top, where a user would fill in some information and upload a photo of themselves. They can then submit this to our Serverless back end.

In this example, the *API Service* takes care of validating and formatting any user input, and it will protect us from attacks such as SQL injection, so we don't need to develop those capabilities in our microservices.

The *Image Handling Microservice* on the right of *Backend* accepts the image uploaded by the user and passes it to the *Shared Image Processing Microservice* in *Shared Services*. This microservice will resize it or perhaps create a thumbnail. An advantage of microservices is that they are very reusable. A single microservice such as this generic image processor can be used by multiple projects and managed centrally as a shared service, as seen in Figure 1-5.

A shared microservice does not necessarily need access to potentially sensitive application resources. An application can pass a task (1) to a microservice, which processes it and returns a result (2) to the application, which can then store it. Nothing needs to be stored or accessed by the shared microservice directly as long as the request contains the information it needs for the task.

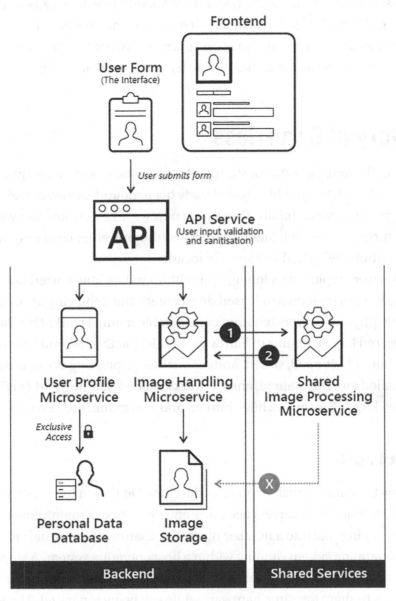

Figure 1-5. *A simple example of a Serverless web application*

The *User Profile Microservice* on the left side of *Backend* handles the sensitive personal data that the user submitted. In a monolithic application, if any feature in the application needs access to a sensitive database, then the entire application will have access to that sensitive database.

Due to the distributed nature of Serverless, each microservice can have its own set of unique permissions. In Figure 1-5, the *User Profile Microservice* has exclusive access to the sensitive *Personal Data Database*. All other microservices, developers, and applications need to go through this microservice to access the sensitive data. That gives us just one location to monitor, audit, and make sure every request is valid and authorized.

 History of Serverless

In the 1990s, as IT rapidly advanced, startups Amazon and Google were quickly catching up with Microsoft and Apple, which had already been around for two decades. The Internet was growing exponentially, thanks to a new wave of websites and web-based applications during this period. Many appreciated the convenience of easy access to applications without being tied to a specific location.

Companies were rapidly developing monolithic applications hosted on physical servers maintained in their own or leased data centers, but deploying applications and data onto these physical servers required considerable manual work. This *bare-metal* approach required large amounts of hardware – both in active use and backup – which needed to be bought, shipped, stored, and maintained. Operating systems and software had to be installed and maintained, and networks needed building and configuring. All of this required large IT teams – a huge burden and cost to the businesses.

Virtual Servers

The technology to enable virtual servers was developed at IBM in the 1970s, but it was in the early 2000s that virtual servers became popular outside of mainframes. Similar to a large house being split into a number of smaller apartments, a virtual server is an independent operating system running within a host operating system. A single hardware server can contain multiple virtual servers, allowing different users, operating systems, and applications to share the same hardware while still being separated. The value was that previously underutilized hardware could be filled with smaller virtual servers to maximize capacity and utilization of the physical servers, as demonstrated in Figure 1-6.

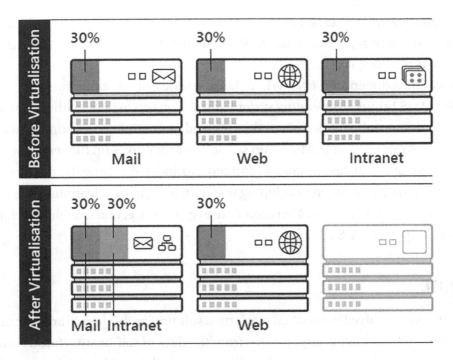

Figure 1-6. *Before and after server virtualization*

Being able to retire one in three hardware servers (in this example) could easily save an enterprise thousands of dollars.

A number of enterprises then got the idea to lease virtual servers to smaller businesses that could not afford their own hardware. Included in this package was the existing networking hardware and configuration. Thus was born the idea of Infrastructure-as-a-Service (IaaS).

The Cloud

Before the launch of AWS's Elastic Compute Cloud (EC2) in 2006, virtual servers and other related services were contracted for 1 year or more. While faster than procuring a physical server, a virtual server could still take hours or even days and required proof of identification, a contract, and up-front payment.

AWS disrupted this model by making their EC2 servers available at a cost per hour (later a cost per second), completely self-managed via their web application and without having to pay anything up front. This became the standard business model of cloud computing as we understand it today. Others followed suit, with Google launching their cloud offering 2 years later in 2008 and Microsoft launching Azure in 2010.

While cloud providers are still often referred to as Infrastructure-as-a-Service (IaaS), most of their modern services can be considered Platform-as-a-Service (PaaS) or even Software-as-a-Service (SaaS).

PaaS was introduced after IaaS. Where IaaS provides all the infrastructure necessities, PaaS brings an operating system and sits on top of IaaS. With PaaS, the business can remove the burden of configuring and maintaining operating systems and sometimes even software. The cloud service provider takes up the responsibility of installation, security patches, upgrades, and monitoring and scaling the platform. The organization can then focus on developing and managing its applications. AWS Elastic Beanstalk and Amplify, Heroku, Microsoft Azure App Service, and Google App Engine are some examples of PaaS.

Software

While technology evolved into virtual platforms, solution and software architectures also evolved. The monolithic applications from the days of self-hosting faced similar challenges in scaling when it came to handling more and more data and users. It became increasingly difficult to run these applications on a single server, so they had to be distributed across multiple servers. This required significant changes to the applications themselves. Both out of necessity and efficiency, applications started to be split into smaller components, with groups of related features moved onto separate servers to distribute the load and enable independent scaling.

Modern Containers

Containers became popular around the same time because they helped simplify the process of splitting applications. A container is similar to a virtual server, except it does not include an operating system. It contains an application and all the dependencies and configuration files that are required to run the application.

Containers are very portable, which makes it easy for a programmer to transfer an application from one platform to another despite any differences in the underlying infrastructure or software. We can develop applications locally and expect a similar experience when moving the container to the cloud. Similarly, containers are more cloud-agnostic as they can be moved between cloud providers if desired.

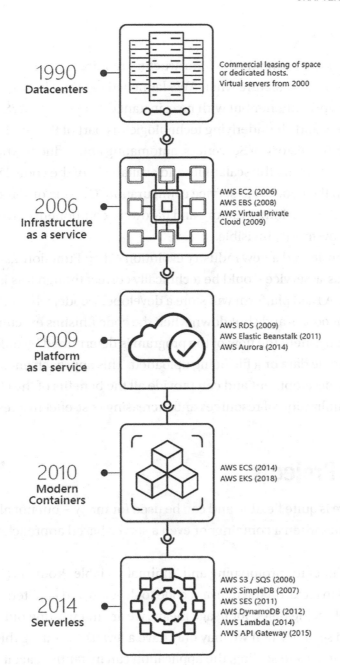

1990
Datacenters

Commercial leasing of space
or dedicated hosts.
Virtual servers from 2000

2006
Infrastructure
as a service

AWS EC2 (2006)
AWS EBS (2008)
AWS Virtual Private
Cloud (2009)

2009
Platform
as a service

AWS RDS (2009)
AWS Elastic Beanstalk (2011)
AWS Aurora (2014)

2010
Modern
Containers

AWS ECS (2014)
AWS EKS (2018)

2014
Serverless

AWS S3 / SQS (2006)
AWS SimpleDB (2007)
AWS SES (2011)
AWS DynamoDB (2012)
AWS Lambda (2014)
AWS API Gateway (2015)

***Figure 1-7.** Timeline of evolving cloud services*

Serverless

Driven by the need to further simplify the infrastructure requirements for developers, Serverless emerged as an architecture when AWS launched Lambda in 2014. Lambda is essentially a temporary container but with near-instant deployment. AWS entirely manages its deployment and all underlying technologies as part of the service. This was a key milestone in the history of Serverless, automating and reducing the speed of deployment while guaranteeing the scalability and availability of the code. Developers could focus entirely on their code and service configuration. Outside of some configuration parameters, the infrastructure and hardware components involved in hosting software are now mostly invisible.

Lambda can be considered a new industry evolution called Function-as-a-Service (FaaS). Microservice-as-a-Service would be technically correct though this is not a commonly used term. A FaaS platform will store a developer's code, which will be run when a specified event occurs and shut down when the code finishes executing. This is also called event-driven, where the flow of the program is determined by different events such as a request for some data or a file being uploaded. This approach encourages fast and agile software development and can provide all the benefits of the cloud while addressing the underutilization of resources and increasing cost-effectiveness.

 # Types of Projects

Serverless architecture is quite flexible and can be used for many – but not all – types of projects. There are times when a container or even a server-based approach may be a better option.

Serverless really shines for prototyping and Minimally Viable Products (MVP) because we only need to focus on the relevant code to develop and can iterate through ideas very rapidly. Only being billed for usage means we are not wasting our budget running underutilized servers when we may only have a few users during this stage of the project. With fully managed scaling, the application can instantly react if we need to do larger tests or have a sudden influx of users.

This makes Serverless especially attractive to startups on a budget. They can develop their solution, and the operational cost is directly proportional to the number of users. This lets them launch without having to carry a high operational cost until their user base grows enough to be self-sustaining.

Serverless can play a role in application migrations and transformation. After migrating an application to a server in the cloud, we can schedule a series of mini-projects, each with its own budget and timeline, and move features one by one out of the legacy system into microservices. The best features are those that need a lot of server resources and are a good fit for an event-driven microservice: image processing, data merging or conversion, and malware scanning, for example.

Moving these features out will result in the server needing fewer resources, enabling us to reduce the size and cost of the server after each update. We can quickly tell if it is viable to convert this solution to Serverless without a major up-front investment and whether it makes commercial and technical sense to do so. The process we use to convert a monolith to microservices is called event storming – which we will cover in more detail in Chapter 2.

Pipelines are another common use case for Serverless. Microservices manage the steps and data between different managed services in the cloud. These can be as simple as generating a thumbnail for an uploaded image to more complex video processing, analysis, and even machine learning pipelines.

Another use case is for small sites and forms. As we saw in our earlier registration form example, it can cost significantly less to take a Serverless approach with these. There are also ways to create search engine–friendly websites with Serverless, which we will look at in more detail later in the book.

Serverless is certainly suitable for larger applications, but such applications are typically very complex with many diverse requirements. As a result, they often end up as hybrids, with a mix of servers or containers and Serverless. A common example would be to meet the popular demand for relational databases, as this type of database is not yet available as a Serverless service. Although Aurora Serverless comes close, it is still considered a fully managed service due to a minimum operating cost, which will inevitably include idle time.

We should avoid being Serverless purists as this is not in the best interests of all applications. Every project can be split into sections - groups of features that belong together more than others. For each such section, we can determine the best architecture optimized for its purpose, increasing the cost-effectiveness and efficiency of the solution as a whole.

💼 Key Challenges

I try to keep this section less technical, focusing on the higher-level challenges and mitigations. In Chapter 9, we will delve deeper into more complex technical challenges and their mitigations.

Vendor Lock-In

Serverless architecture prefers fully managed services over custom development and self-managed third-party solutions. Because of this, there is a high chance we will be using services and features that are unique to a particular cloud provider. While there is overlap in the more common services, the configuration is likely different, and specific features might be different or unavailable. So, without significant rework, an AWS-built fully Serverless solution will not easily port to Google Cloud, for example.

It is possible to make a cloud-agnostic solution that can run on different clouds, but, to achieve this, it needs to be built for the lowest common denominator. As such, it is unlikely to be cost-effective, and we will miss out on many features and services available on more advanced cloud platforms.

Cross-cloud, using the best services from different cloud providers, is possible and not uncommon. Typically, we would still have the primary application running on one cloud. Then we would integrate the specific services that we need from another cloud. Keep in mind that cross-cloud requests will have additional latency, which is already a challenge in Serverless, and data transfer costs between the providers could run up significantly.

Finding Talent

Finding and competing for talent can be challenging and expensive. Serverless is common with startups, but it is still rare in enterprises. Many enterprises still lack in-house Serverless skills, making it challenging to find, attract, and properly assess new Serverless talent. Third-party consultants may be needed to ensure that prospective candidates have the right capabilities and relevant experience.

Less Control

With Serverless, we are building on top of managed services, so many of the underlying configurations normally accessible to the developers are no longer available.

For example, internal or regulatory policies that need a certain server configuration may be challenging or even impossible to achieve with Serverless. There is a need to assess and change such policies before choosing Serverless architecture for a solution.

Some common examples include particular operating system requirements or the use of predetermined hardened and approved server images. Fixed IP addresses or specific ports can also be a requirement. While these exist in Serverless, they are managed by the provider and can change at any time.

Service-Level Agreements (SLAs)

Similarly, SLAs will largely be outside our area of influence. The cloud provider will provide an SLA for the services, and, typically, we will not be able to guarantee much more than that to users or stakeholders. New services, especially, might only have a limited SLA.

If users expect certain SLA guarantees, we may not be able to deliver on those in a Serverless solution if the provider has not included them in their SLA. When migrating existing applications to Serverless, any existing SLAs should be reviewed, and it should not be assumed that they can apply to a new Serverless solution without change.

The availability guarantees of AWS services, as per their SLA, can be found here: www. ernestchiang.com/en/notes/aws/product-list-sla/.

Latency

In broad terms, latency is what we call the delay between a user sending a request and getting a response. Serverless architecture can have more latency per request than a sufficiently sized server because the request needs to go through multiple components and steps.

Microservices are launched on demand and are then kept running for 5–7 minutes to respond to any incoming requests. When a microservice first launches, there is a slightly longer delay before it is ready. This is called a *cold* start. During the following 5–7 minutes, the microservice is considered *warm* and will have a faster response to new requests. This means less-used solutions can seem slower due to frequent *cold* starts in comparison with those with regular active users who will use more *warm* microservices.

The latency challenge makes it crucial to produce highly optimized code and to minimize any requests to other cloud services.

A server's *cold* start is typically 1–10 minutes. However, once servers are up and running, they do not power down between requests. So, while the *cold* start causes delays for developers when deploying or restarting and it factors into the time needed to scale an application, the one-off *cold* start does not impact user requests.

(Almost) Unlimited Scaling

Scaling means automatically growing the capacity of an application to handle larger numbers of users or increasing activity. When user numbers or activity reduces, autoscaling will also reduce the capacity of the solution to minimize wastage and cost.

While server-based solutions can have autoscaling, this is generally a very controlled approach where we specify when and how many additional servers will be deployed with each autoscaling step. Most Serverless solutions have scaling built-in, fully automated, and often without any default limits. The services can scale from 100 to 100,000 users in seconds without any changes needed to the code or configuration, but this can cause problems if not considered during budget estimates and development.

For example, if a user wanted to upload 500 terabytes of data to a cloud storage service, they could. They would be limited only by their Internet connection speed. This sounds like a great benefit until we get the $12,500 bill at the end of the month. So brakes need to be built into the solution to manage the users and their activity. Many services have configuration options that can help with this, and, in Serverless, it is relatively easy to track users and their activity, making it easier to log activity and impose limits when needed.

Calculating Cloud Operational Costs

Estimating the operational cost of a Serverless application can be complex due to the number of variables that need to be considered. There can be several different price points for each managed service included in the solution. We go into more detail on this topic in Chapter 3.

Cloud Management

Traditional ways of managing the cloud can be problematic for Serverless projects because infrastructure and code are closely intertwined and frequently part of the same code base. Changes to Serverless applications often occur in both these areas at the same time.

Organizations that separate provisioning teams from the application teams will struggle to productively deliver Serverless applications. We delve deeper into this topic in Chapter 2.

Service Limits

All Serverless solutions have certain limits imposed on them by the provider for various reasons. Some are called soft limits and are usually in place to prevent abuse of a new cloud account. Soft limits can be raised with a support request and some justification. An example can be found in the SES in new AWS accounts. Initially, it is only possible to send emails to email addresses added and verified in the AWS account. A service request must be submitted and approved by AWS before emails can be sent to any valid email address.

Other limits are hard limits and are often related to the capabilities of the technology or security concerns. These cannot be raised on request, although a service upgrade will sometimes increase them. If we run into hard limits, a better service could be available to address the problem. For example, microservices are not intended to be long-running processes, so a container might be a better solution if we run into timeout limits.

It is important always to know the application requirements and compare them against the limits of a cloud service before using it in a solution design. These limits can be found in the cloud provider's documentation for that service.

 Key Benefits

Near-Zero Wastage

A major benefit of Serverless is that we pay only for what we actually use, not for idle time or underutilization. Even during peak usage, a server should never reach 100% utilization – this would indicate the server is too small. No matter how much it is optimized, some resource margin is always needed to prevent the application from slowing down or crashing and to provide the time needed to scale additional servers.

Underutilization is not only a waste of money. Consider also the environmental impact of all those servers running, consuming electricity but without actually being used.

Reduced Scope of Responsibility and Effort

Because we are building on fully managed services, there is no server to configure, no operating system to configure, and no software to install. There is also no operating system or software that needs to be maintained, with weekly security patches and feature updates that need to be applied, tested, and deployed. Instead, the scope of the project will be limited to

- *Solution architecture*: Having knowledge of and using the right cloud services for the different requirements of the solution

- *Service configuration*: Not to be underestimated, especially optimizing the configuration for both security and efficiency

- Developing the code for microservices

With Serverless, the developers' efforts will be more focused on the deliverables – the return on investment (ROI) – and less on all the tasks necessary to run a solution in the cloud but not specific to the needs of the solution.

Accurate Operational Cost Estimation and Tracking

Making Serverless estimates can be complex due to the many variables. However, if we have the right data, we can create highly accurate estimates for the application and even per type of user. Activity in a Serverless solution can be tracked in detail and linked back to specific users, enabling cloud-like business models for the application, such as billing based on usage and accurate cross-departmental billing.

Highly Reusable Microservices

Microservices are developed with a very specific purpose. For the more generic microservices, this is likely a purpose that is relevant to many different solutions. Think "*app store*" instead of "*project functions*." Every microservice developed across all applications is another app added to our internal store that can potentially be reused by other applications. Over time, this can significantly reduce the development effort for new solutions, increasing productivity and decreasing time to market.

Better Access Security

As described in the Serverless example earlier in this chapter, Serverless offers very fine-grained access controls. For example, a single microservice can have exclusive access to a sensitive database. This same approach can be applied to developers with access to the cloud account: they can be given access just to the services and microservice code they need to access for their development tasks that week.

Agility and DevOps Are Easier to Implement

Serverless with microservices as an architecture choice will force the team to become more agile due to its structure. Microservices should be quite tight in their scope, with between one and five user stories typically applied to create one microservice. This means that individual microservices can be developed, tested, and used in each sprint. Multiple microservices can be developed in parallel by different teams as they can be independently developed and tested. Front-end development can start as soon as the team agrees on how the front end will talk to the back end, and it can be developed in parallel with the back-end development.

Most Serverless services also support automated deployments, and the majority of Serverless frameworks have some amount of DevOps built in. Cloud providers have end-to-end DevOps services that can be integrated with a team's workflows and any services needed within a solution. This allows for automated deployment and greatly reduces the chance of errors.

Easier to Manage Time, Budgets, and Teams

Because the project scope is to develop a series of microservices, it becomes easier to split a single large project into many smaller projects. Each subproject will have its own goals and budget. This independence means dependencies and waiting can be minimized between developers during initial development. With the support of fine-grained access controls, it becomes easier to divide the work between teams and give juniors and external vendors more controlled access to specific portions of code and services. Quality is monitored and controlled through the deployment pipeline.

Microservices tend to have neater code, are easier to test, and are easier to document for similar reasons.

Highly Scalable, Fast Scaling

While we should be aware of the challenge this poses, automated (almost) unlimited scaling is also a great benefit. With most fully managed services, the cloud provider is responsible for ensuring redundancy and scalability. Microservices in the cloud can technically scale to support millions of users in a matter of seconds. In reality, however, code and configuration will often need to be optimized for these numbers. While a service could easily scale to support millions of users, even the slightest bit of unnecessary latency can drastically impact operational costs at these numbers.

The speed at which services such as Lambda can scale is also a benefit. A system that scales slowly needs more margin to support growing numbers while it waits for it to scale. Outside of peak usage, such margins remain largely unutilized but still billable. Fast scaling means the system can scale on demand in amounts that are very close to the actual demand with little margin needed.

Significantly Lower Maintenance Cost

Server-based solutions require monthly maintenance to test and upgrade operating systems and software. Any issues that arise from this or from situations such as drives filling up with logs are also part of maintenance. All this maintenance effort goes away with Serverless solutions because these aspects become the responsibility of the cloud provider.

 Common Objections

The following are some common objections I have heard over the years and my response to them.

Less Stable

Having more nodes or components in a solution means it's less stable.

This refers to Serverless solutions typically having a lot of microservices and integrated cloud services. As mentioned, this can increase latency, depending on how it is designed, but less stability is certainly not true.

As we saw in the ice cream machine example, Serverless and especially microservices have a lot of redundancy built-in and fully managed, making them highly fault-tolerant and even self-healing in some cases.

Less Observable

It's difficult to track what is happening and debug and manage so many microservices.

Logging, and especially proactive logging, is very important for Serverless. Application teams need to build logging into the microservices and configure automated alerts for high-priority events. The cloud provides many services to help with insights, but they need to be configured before we can use them.

A Lot to Configure

It's a lot of work to configure so many services and microservices.

It can be a lot of work to configure and deploy a Serverless application manually. That's why we use automated deployment pipelines and Infrastructure-as-Code (IaC) extensively to fully automate this process, reduce the chance of human error, and make it consistently and easily repeatable between multiple environments.

Architectural Complexity

Another objection is about the perceived complexity when compared with server architecture, but this might be due to how we typically compare architecture diagrams. When we draw server architecture diagrams, we focus on the infrastructure components, which are relatively few because all the complexity is in the application code running on the servers. A basic server architecture can be seen at the top of Figure 1-8.

But with Serverless microservices, much of the code complexity moves into the infrastructure. This makes this architecture seem more complex when compared with a server-based infrastructure diagram (as seen at the bottom of Figure 1-8).

When we diagram the coded functions and the configured redundancy, we end up with a more complete diagram in the middle of Figure 1-8. As the system scales, we may end up with more than just the two servers on the diagram, and the architecture will end up being even more complex.

The microservice architecture at the bottom now seems simpler in comparison. These services are all managed by the cloud provider, so they are able to scale without having to configure or manage any additional resources, and they are often highly available.

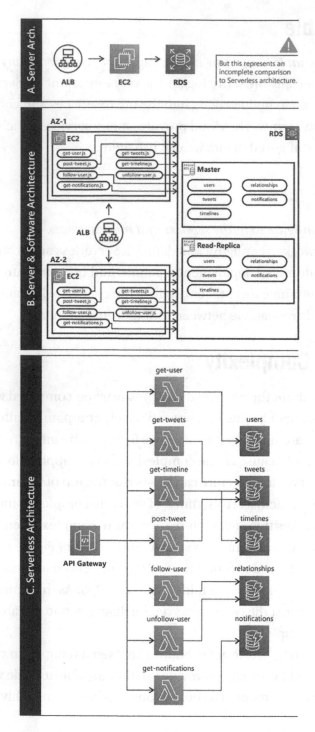

Figure 1-8. *Server architecture diagram compared with Serverless diagram*

💼 Public Case Studies

The following are public case studies that highlight some of the benefits Serverless has brought to these organizations.

NorthOne Bank

This project is a public case study shared by serverlesschats.com on their website. I was not involved in this project or with this organization in any way. The full interview can be found here: www.serverlesschats.com/105/.

The NorthOne Bank industry case study is an interesting perspective into how Serverless has benefited NorthOne Bank's ability to achieve more with less. NorthOne Bank is an online bank for small businesses, freelancers, and startups in the USA and Canada. It has no physical retail outlets. The founding team wanted to build technology that made financial management more accessible and affordable, and, to achieve this, they needed to automate as much of the operations as possible and minimize overheads such as maintenance.

The team was tasked with developing a low-cost and user-friendly banking service that met the strict regulatory compliance requirements. Other objectives included building and deploying the platform in a rapid and agile manner, and they wanted the platform to be highly reliable. They chose Serverless architecture to help them meet these challenges. Serverless and fully managed services minimize overheads, are considered highly reliable, offer far tighter security controls and tracking ability, and greatly reduce the amount of custom code that needs to be developed and maintained.

Their strong automation and DevOps practices enable fast onboarding of new developers, giving each one their own environment to work within, with all necessary infrastructure. Serverless infrastructure only bills actual usage, so having multiple environments, some only used by one developer, does not significantly increase the operational cost. This also made developers free to experiment without worrying about the cost, which helps innovation thrive, resulting in continuous improvement of the platform. The cost-effective billing model also removed the need for an operations team, greatly reducing operational overheads and associated costs.

The platform's customer processes achieved operational efficiency by being entirely online and mobile-first, which greatly lowered the barrier to entry for small businesses and freelancers and supported them in working and banking from anywhere. Being API-driven makes it easy for customers to integrate third-party tools and SaaS solutions commonly used such as accounting systems, ecommerce, and inventory solutions.

Operations and maintenance is a significant cost factor for server solutions. With NorthOne's approach, maintaining servers, operating system and software patching, scaling, and more are all taken care of by the cloud provider.

NorthOne achieved compliance and reliability by building on fully managed and Serverless services and using the tight security controls that they provide. The cloud provider is responsible for redundancy, reliability, scaling, and much of the security of these services, allowing the developers to focus more on customer experience, data security, and delivering value.

Some of the security practices include tokenization to automatically filter out sensitive data. This limits the amount of data flowing through the application. They are also careful to ensure no customer data is included in any application logs. This reduces some capability to debug, but NorthOne considers this an acceptable trade-off to keep user data secure.

Some of the key services that NorthOne bank is using for their platform are shown in Figure 1-9, these include EventBridge, SNS, API Gateway, and Lambda.

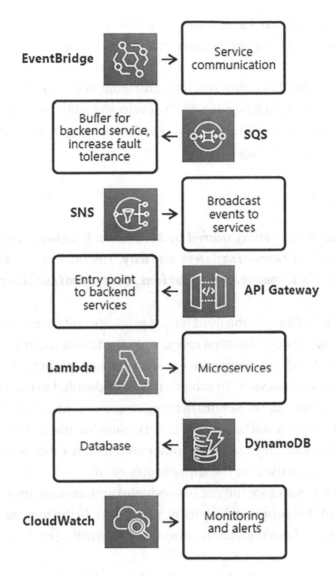

Figure 1-9. *AWS services used by NorthOne bank*

EventBridge is used to communicate between services with events triggering responses and actions from microservices. SQS acts as a buffer and fail-safe for the back-end services. Given the importance of messages, this is a critical part of the overall solution. SNS is used to route certain requests from a source to multiple receiving services. API Gateway is an entry point to back-end services used by web, mobile, and third-party clients. Lambda is the back-end compute service, hosting the many microservices. DynamoDB is a fast and flexible database storing customer transactions and other data fully encrypted. Lastly, CloudWatch is used for monitoring the platform and triggering alarms for errors and other events that potentially need a response from the team.

NorthOne Bank's initial platform was built and launched with only four developers, and, as of June 2021, the team has grown to 25 developers with the success of the business. The platform has faced no bottlenecks when scaling to meet peaks, and more than 190,000 businesses are using it.

Liberty Mutual

This project is a public case study shared by AWS on their website. I was not involved in this project or with this organization in any way. The full case study can be found here: **https://aws.amazon.com/solutions/case-studies/liberty-mutual-case-study/**.

The Liberty Mutual Group is the third largest property and casualty insurer in the USA, with over $40 billion in annual revenue. As the insurance industry becomes increasingly digital, global, and competitive, the challenge for Liberty Mutual was to remain digitally agile and relevant. To achieve this, they decided to pursue a Serverless-first strategy to empower and accelerate their engineering teams. With a Serverless-first mindset, engineering teams will first consider Serverless for new projects. However, if Serverless is not feasible, they can look at other architectures such as containers to ensure the best solution is used for the application's needs.

Liberty Mutual advocates for the use of **serviceful** architecture, preferring managed services over custom development. Internally, they promote the mantra *code is a liability* to discourage engineers from reinventing the wheel and writing custom code when they don't need to.

With a Serverless-first strategy, Liberty Mutual gained an edge over its competitors by reducing their operational burden – since most of the infrastructure, including operating systems and software, is now managed by AWS. In addition, substantial cost savings were achieved due to cutting out billable idle time, which allowed the engineering team to experiment more. This led to new insights faster and more frequently and, combined with modern DevOps practices, increased the frequency of application updates and deployments.

The creation of a software accelerator using AWS Cloud Development Kit (CDK) was integral to Liberty Mutual's strategy. CDK is an open source software development framework that enables engineers to design and provision cloud architecture using familiar programming languages, such as Python and JavaScript. We will cover this in more detail in Chapter 6.

Using CDK, the engineering team could define templates for common Serverless patterns that were reused throughout the organization, helping engineers rapidly deploy new projects and infrastructure that met best practices and other requirements instead of repeatedly writing it from scratch.

In conjunction with the software accelerator, Liberty Mutual also uses the AWS Well-Architected Framework to guide and assess the designs of their applications. The Well-Architected Framework provides key concepts, design principles, and best practices for cloud architecture. By adhering to the principles of the Well-Architected Framework, they ensure that applications are secure, scalable, stable, efficient, and cost-effective. We cover this in more detail in Chapter 9.

One of Liberty Mutual's most successful projects was consolidating the different lines of business around the globe into a centralized general ledger, known as the Financial Central Services (FCS). This project was what we call a lighthouse project, and its learnings and success helped showcase the benefits of a Serverless-first strategy.

The project was deemed too complex to be developed on-premises. Instead, using Serverless on AWS, Liberty Mutual successfully developed the centralized solution with an event-driven approach. Central to the solution were two key services. Lambda is used as the compute service to process new events within the infrastructure. It scales automatically to handle higher demands, and, being Serverless, it does not require any management of infrastructure, operating systems, or software. Redundancy and scalability are similarly fully managed by the service, and Liberty Mutual is only billed for actual execution time, not idle time or availability.

StepFunctions is used to orchestrate the various services and microservices and sequence them to create linear and parallel workflows. With StepFunctions, the engineers write considerably less code since many integrations with services such as Lambda are built-in. StepFunctions is Serverless, meaning no infrastructure to manage and no paying for idle time.

FCS can process 100 million transactions each month, and Liberty Mutual only needs to pay for the days it is running, which is about $60 per million transactions.

With its Serverless-first strategy, the organization has deployed over 3,500 Serverless patterns using CDK in 1 year. Using this architecture to build services has helped decrease the average application build time to just 3 months from what was previously a year on average.

Coca-Cola

This project is a public case study shared by AWS on their website. I was not involved in this project or with this organization in any way. The full case study can be found here: **https://aws.amazon.com/solutions/case-studies/coca-cola-freestyle/**.

This case study provides an insight into how Coca-Cola used Serverless to develop a cost-effective touchless retail solution and launch it within 100 days.

The Coca-Cola Company is a beverage company with products sold in more than 200 countries across the globe. Through the adoption of Serverless, Coca-Cola has reduced infrastructure costs by about 65% to date.

For example, comparing EC2 servers and Lambda, 30 million requests a month for one of their applications cost more than $12,000 on EC2 servers. Using the Serverless service Lambda for the same 30 million requests costs less than $4,500 per month. Coca-Cola has seen a twofold increase in developers' productivity as application teams can spend more time working on the application instead of maintaining infrastructure.

The challenge for Coca-Cola was creating a COVID-safe touchless experience for the Coca-Cola Freestyle machine, a small beverage factor that delivers consumers 200 different drinks. The three objectives Coca-Cola set themselves were to improve customer experience, drive marketing outcomes, and have a low-latency solution so that customers can achieve the *Perfect Pour*.

The Freestyle application needed to provide almost instant feedback when a user clicks the Pour button, and it should stop when the user lifts their finger. To achieve this, the team began to prototype with Serverless. The cost to prototype was very low because they were only billed for the amount of time that the service was executing requests. Since AWS manages the hardware and operating system configuration, the team could focus on developing the prototype instead of creating and recreating infrastructure.

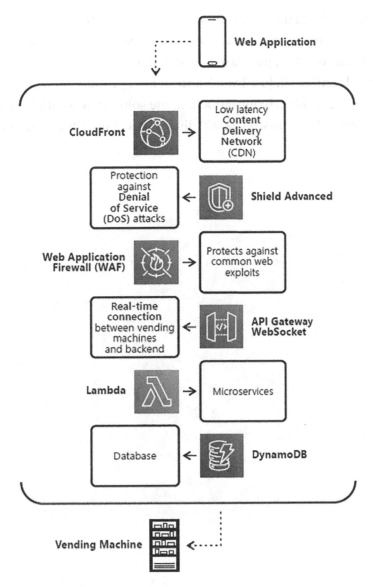

Figure 1-10. *Services used for Coca-Cola's app*

Coca-Cola uses several AWS services in its architecture, as seen in Figure 1-10. These include Amazon CloudFront as a content delivery network (CDN) to provide low-latency access to content around the globe. For security, AWS Shield helps protect the service from Denial of Service attacks, and Web Application Firewall helps protect against common web exploits. API Gateway maintains the connection with the vending machine and interacts with the application through WebSockets. Lambda microservices process the requests and can automatically scale and shrink according to demand. Lastly, DynamoDB is used as a database to store data.

The prototype launched in just 1 week and went to production within 100 days. Within 150 days of the product being launched, the solution was rolled out to 10,000 dispensers, and within 6 months, all 52,000 dispensers in the USA were supported.

CHAPTER 2

Strategy

Innovation is the outcome of a habit, not a random act.

—Sukant Ratnakar, Founder and CEO Quantraz Inc.

 ## Introduction

Serverless architecture is quite unlike the previous evolutions of cloud software. As such, existing cloud management strategies are often incompatible. This is especially a challenge in larger enterprises where for years, the focus has been on optimizing the security, delivery, and operation of server-based applications.

This chapter is about a modern cloud management strategy. There are several options, but this is one I have found very suitable for Serverless application delivery, especially in large enterprises.

The strategy is largely cloud-agnostic; organizations can implement it no matter what their preferred cloud platform is. The content is high level, as transformation strategy details need to be designed for the organization and depend heavily on size, region, industry, and other factors. However, even at a high level, it should still provide guidance and a baseline for designing a Serverless cloud strategy suitable for the organization.

© Thomas Smart 2023
T. Smart, *Serverless Beyond the Buzzword*, https://doi.org/10.1007/978-1-4842-8761-3_2

💼 Traditional Organization Structure vs. Serverless

For organizations that started with on-premises infrastructure or servers in the cloud, *separation of duties* is typically a core security strategy for governing IT infrastructure and ensuring compliance.

With this approach, application responsibilities are split across multiple teams to avoid any single entity holding every permission to the IT environment and application. A high-level organization structure depicting this is shown in Figure 2-1. For example, for a given project, the *application* team will be responsible for developing, customizing, or configuring the application code and software.

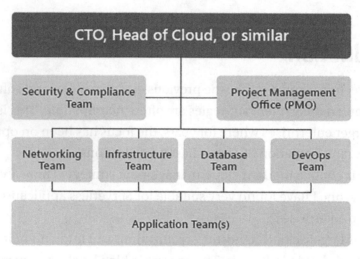

Figure 2-1. *A typical traditional organization's technical team structure*

Provisioning of resources, such as EC2 instances in the cloud, will be done by a separate *infrastructure* team. Once provisioned, limited access to the servers will be provided to the *application* team so they can install the application. Access to the servers is typically via a CI/CD pipeline, a responsibility owned by yet another separate *DevOps* team. The *infrastructure* team would also deploy database servers and then hand over access to a separate *database* team who will configure the database, set permissions, and define the tables and schemas. The network into which the infrastructure team provisioned the servers would be managed by a *network* team, who are often also responsible for opening firewall ports and similar activities. There is a *security and compliance* team that manages user permissions, data classification, and the security rules and policies that other teams must comply with. And lastly, an executive or other decision-maker is involved in stage gate approvals.

All of these teams need to be involved in the application development process, and the separation ensures a limited attack surface in case any individual team or area is compromised.

In some cases, an organization might view separation of duties as an unavoidable regulatory requirement. However, this could be a matter of interpretation, as such regulation tends to be more outcome-driven and not usually so prescriptive. It will depend on the country, but the internal policies of large regulated enterprises are often considerably stricter than the regulator requires. While this is workable for on-premises infrastructure and even servers in the cloud, it is too restrictive for Serverless architecture. This is a common blocker for traditional organizations, preventing them from adopting Serverless, and one of the reasons major innovation projects are often spun out into a separate startup entity that can determine its own policies.

There are two key differences between traditional and Serverless applications that impact cloud management strategy.

Firstly, in traditional applications, there are usually few infrastructure components. For example, a common design would be a three-tier architecture. This consists of one or more front-end servers, one or more back-end servers, and one or more database servers. Each layer with more than one server would have a load balancer to split traffic between the servers in that layer. Support services would be mostly lower-level, such as networking components, firewalls, and domain name management.

Secondly, infrastructure and code are separate parts with no dependencies other than the code needs to run on the infrastructure – typically a server. There will be requirements for server specifications, but these are usually relative to the amount of expected traffic. For example, to process the request of one user, the application needs 25 MB of memory. The application is expected to support up to 100 users at the same time. So the application server will need 2500 MB of memory.

By comparison, applications using Serverless architecture are inherently different in how their architecture works and, as a result, how requirements are determined.

Firstly, much of the code complexity is moved into many different fully managed infrastructure components. These are managed by the cloud provider, greatly reducing the operational burden on the organization. A complex application could easily contain tens if not hundreds of components such as microservices, queue and publish services, storage, and notification and processing services. Similarly, instead of one large relational database, a Serverless application could have several databases of different types, some exclusively linked to a single microservice.

Secondly, the infrastructure is not just a platform the application runs on; it becomes part of the application and is no longer so clearly separated. Serverless developers need to view infrastructure and code as one and the same – fully integrated – and to work on both as part of the application development process.

To go back to our earlier example: An application that needed 25 MB of server memory to process one request is now split. The Serverless equivalent of 20 MB is handled by fully managed cloud services where we just pay for the request and don't have to calculate or worry about how much resources are needed. The remainder is utilized by a microservice to perform its function. Scaling of the microservice is fully managed by the provider. So we only have to calculate that a single code execution needs X MB. We don't have to worry about the total memory required for the potential number of users, as that is all managed by the provider.

A separation of duties strategy can work for server-based applications in the cloud:

- The flow of requesting infrastructure, which is then provisioned by another team, works when the infrastructure consists of just a few servers and is similar across many different applications.

- The infrastructure team also doesn't need to invest much time into understanding the application, at least not outside the server specifications and ports required to run it.

- And lastly, such infrastructure will rarely change, other than the production environment typically using larger servers that have wider margins to handle usage peaks.

The resulting relatively low volume of requests between teams, and the fact that each team fully owns their part of the process, often means that only minimal automation is implemented to help deploy and operate such infrastructure. This is a simple cost-benefit analysis. The effort required to implement complex deployment and operational automation outweighs the value it would provide for only a few servers every couple of months.

But this strategy does not work for Serverless applications:

- The sheer number of infrastructure components and their importance to the application means that architecture designs are a lot more complex.

- The application team is no longer requesting a few servers but possibly hundreds of components and distinct configurations.

- Due to the complexity, such architecture designs are typically an incremental process, with the application team doing proof of concepts and adapting the design as the project is developed.

- This will be during both initial development and ongoing updates to the application.

The application team will frequently be raising a lot of change requests for the infrastructure and other teams to provision and iterate through potentially hundreds of changes during this process. This leads to an overload of support tickets among the different teams, significantly increasing their workload and staffing needs. Due to the often minimal use of automation, the requests stack up and cause congestion, disrupting other projects. Application teams face constant blockers and waiting, dramatically reducing their productivity.

In short, this type of team separation to achieve *segregation of duties* is an anti-pattern for Serverless development. Instead, we want to enable application teams to be self-sufficient and provision cloud resources themselves. Such a strategy is governed by a central team often called the Cloud Center of Excellence (CCoE), and automated controls will be used in the cloud to ensure the compliance of the code and infrastructure deployed by the application teams.

Cloud Center of Excellence (CCoE)

A CCoE is the cornerstone of a successful modern cloud management strategy. A centralized team governing the use of the cloud within the organization, its responsibilities include establishing and enforcing security, regulatory, and other compliance in the cloud through a comprehensive cloud management platform that it operates.

The team collaborates closely with existing departments with opinions about the cloud and creates the rules to be enforced. It owns the cloud platform, including the deployment automation and controls to enforce compliance. The team is an advocate and mentor in the cloud, establishing best practices and providing examples, training, and support to application teams. It is responsible for a technology and capability road map to evolve the organization's use of the cloud.

The CCoE team and the platform together enable the organization's application teams, both in technology and capability.

The team will focus on internal needs, both business and technology. The solutions and platform it builds need to help application teams be more effective in the cloud, not hinder them beyond what is needed for security and compliance – always a challenging balancing act. Teams will be looking to the CCoE for best practices on standards that align with security, compliance, and service policies and, especially, transparency and guidance on the rules being enforced in the cloud. Communication is key; the latest guidance and any changes to the platform should be easy to find and shared directly with those it might impact.

Security policies and operational procedures should be modernized for the cloud, standardized, and, ideally, simplified. Using cloud-native tooling and methodologies can help speed up the onboarding of new team members, especially if they have previous cloud experience. The CCoE should be driving continuous improvement and optimization of the cloud platform, blueprints, and examples as the technology evolves and based on feedback from those using it.

To achieve this, cloud transformation outcomes, purpose, and quantifiable short-, mid-, and long-term goals need to be well-scoped and clearly described. The agreed work scope and responsibilities need to be dedicated to achieving the stated outcomes, and a comprehensive plan must be clearly communicated to the application and other impacted teams. Always consider and address "What's in it for them, or why should they care?" when communicating transformational plans to teams.

Organizational cloud adoption needs top-down support and buy-in. Stakeholders, including C-level, should be aligned and invested in the agreed outcomes. Sufficient time and resources need to be made available to the CCoE roles, with incentives for the broader organization to help bring about change. Organizationally, it will be critical to break down any traditional silos and have joint and collaborative ownership of the cloud platform.

When establishing the CCoE team, there is no single approach that works for all organizations. It is important to have representatives from different domains and viewpoints to ensure a comprehensive and diverse approach to cloud management. The team should include technical members, such as cloud and software architects, data and software engineers, infrastructure and cybersecurity specialists, agile delivery leads, and others, depending on the needs of the organization. However, we also need non-technical members, such as those familiar with relevant regulatory compliance, internal and legal policy, education, and advocacy; community managers; and, of course, specialists in people, culture, and change management.

Ensuring that relevant departments have a voice in the CCoE will help achieve alignment between different stakeholders and reduce the chance of biases and silos forming. It should be clear that the CCoE is not intended to replace the traditional IT or security teams – this is not a political struggle for ownership. Existing teams are invited to be part of the CCoE and will have a say in the strategy and road map being developed and evolved.

A CCoE often includes a mix of full-time team members in the operational teams and advisors or seconded team members from different departments on the Advisory Board. The members work together, meeting at least fortnightly, to propose and agree on compliance goals, best practices, supporting materials, and the direction of the organization's cloud strategy and road map.

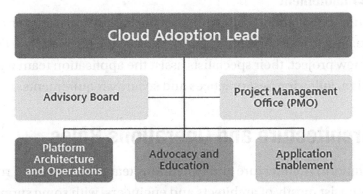

Figure 2-2. *High-level Cloud Center of Excellence structure*

Figure 2-2 offers a high-level view of what a CCoE can look like. At the top, we have the cloud adoption lead, who will be responsible for leadership and governance of the cloud journey. This should be a full-time, dedicated job and not a seconded or part-time role. To achieve a successful cloud adoption, the CCoE needs the undivided attention of the one leading the effort.

The Project Management Office (PMO) and Advisory Board will support the cloud adoption lead in decisions, ensuring standards and the overall design and support of the cloud strategy.

The three operational teams are essential for executing the strategy and its road map:

Platform Architecture and Operations

The purpose of the Platform Architecture and Operations team is to design, implement, and run the cloud management platform. It determines tooling, operational practices, core security and compliance elements, and more. For example, it decides on the application delivery pipeline and sets security standards such as encryption and best practices for cloud architecture.

Advocacy and Education

Advocacy and Education's primary role is to raise awareness, drive cloud fluency, and recruit and retain skilled resources. The team helps garner support for new initiatives, raises awareness of new technology trends, and provides training to different levels within the organization. For example, when adopting Serverless architectures, it educates stakeholders to gain buy-in, trains application teams to follow best practices, and provides architecture designs to help kick off new projects.

Application Enablement

The Application Enablement team embeds with application teams or vendors to share knowledge, mentor best practices, and support using the platform. For example, when starting a new project, their specialists assist the application team with the architecture design, following best practices and security requirements.

Platform Architecture and Operations Roles

Given that the Platform Architecture and Operations team will build and run the cloud platform, it will consist mostly of architects and engineers, with some support roles to track projects and coordinate people.

Three leading roles are the platform, security, and operations architects – together, they are responsible for what we call the *DevSecOps* of the cloud management platform. This industry word is blended from the more common words *development, security*, and *operations*. It infers a breaking down of silos, merging what are traditionally three separate teams into a single collaborative one.

The **platform architect** designs the platform and its core components, such as the AWS account structure, an application delivery pipeline, and capabilities for logging, testing, networking, and other shared services.

They need to be strongly experienced in the cloud to create a comprehensive, efficient, and cost-effective platform. More specifically, their experience should be *broad* – covering many different aspects of the cloud – and *deep*, understanding each of the individual aspects in great detail. This level of expertise requires several years of hands-on design, development, and operation of complex cloud solutions.

They should be comfortable with the top five aspects:

1. Cloud networking, including VPCs, firewalls, security groups, and connectivity services such as PrivateLink.

2. DevOps, including the cloud services in this area or a third-party equivalent.

3. *Monitoring and logging*: In AWS, this means a strong understanding of CloudWatch.

4. *Security*: This knowledge will overlap with the security architect, but understanding at least the cloud side of things will enable them to collaborate more effectively. They should be especially familiar with the security services provided in the cloud, such as GuardDuty and Security Hub.

5. *Data and application architecture*: For Serverless architecture, this means a strong understanding of all of the key services used in Serverless projects, such as Lambda, API Gateway, S3, DynamoDB, and others.

The platform architect will also be designing templates, blueprints, modules, and similar Infrastructure-as-Code assets that the application teams can use, and they will be responsible for the technical road map of the platform, including handling and prioritizing service and feature requests.

A common request will be to enable new features or services application teams want to use. This is a process called *service attestation*, and it is a collaboration between different stakeholders to

1. Understand the request: what it can be used for, how and where it integrates, what are its configuration and security parameters.

2. Perform a risk assessment on the request and design mitigations to address risks.

3. Design the approach that factors in the risk mitigations and estimate the effort required to enable the request in a compliant way – including training, documentation, and examples.

4. Present the proposed approach to the CCoE and obtain approval.

5. Implement the proposed approach to enable the request.

The **security architect** receives input from various departments about the security measures they require in the cloud. The majority of the input will typically come from IT, security, and compliance teams. There may also be a data team with requirements specific to storing and processing data in the cloud, including regulatory requirements, such as those relating to personal data.

The architect will collate the inputs into a single consistent *directives* document covering all of the rules to be enforced in the cloud. They will remove duplicates, seek clarification where needed, and describe the directives clearly and concisely. This document is not a technical scope; it needs to be readable by non-technical stakeholders so they can review and provide approval of the stated directives before implementation starts.

Once the directives are approved, the security architect will design and collaborate with the platform architect to implement the rules in the platform. The details will depend on the platform and the individual directives, but we will cover this in the next section.

Besides the directives, the security architect will also be responsible for reviewing infrastructure from a security perspective, and they will manage and respond to any identified critical risks and cybersecurity incidents.

The **operations architect** designs capabilities to monitor and automate the operation of live applications. Alerts, automated responses, and notifications of events within the cloud fall under their responsibility.

The platform architect will design and implement the *capability to manage* logging, while the operations architect will design *what* to log and how to *respond* to different logs. They will also design and implement dashboards to help with live monitoring and responding to production applications.

Like the security architect, they will design and implement rules. However, these will be about enforcing best practices, sustainability, and cost-effectiveness.

These three architects are purposefully described as *roles*, and a single individual could take up multiple roles, especially in the early days of the CCoE. Usually, each of these roles will initially implement the designs themselves, but, as the CCoE grows, each architect will build an engineering team to help with that implementation, freeing them up to focus on strategy and design.

Finally, it is important that these roles, and indeed the organization, do not operate as an island or spend time reinventing the wheel. Best practices and industry standards are well established. They can be looked at and, where needed, adapted to suit the organization and reduce the risk of gaps and other issues. Similarly, there are many cloud services to consider that specifically address or support some of the responsibilities of the architects. This is especially true for a Serverless cloud strategy where managed services should be used over custom code or managing third-party solutions when possible.

From a Traditional Org Structure to a CCoE

In Figure 2-3, we look at how a CCoE approach to cloud management might impact our earlier example of a traditional organization structure.

Any existing head of cloud or similar role would become the CCoE's cloud adoption lead. If a CTO or similar was leading the cloud adoption effort, then they need to hire or move someone into the CCoE lead role. Either way, the cloud adoption lead needs to give their undivided attention to the cloud transformation efforts. In some cases, a senior consultant provided by the organization's cloud consulting partner can run the CCoE until a suitable hire can be found.

The CTO or executive leadership can assign a representative to the Advisory Board to monitor progress and have a voice in any major cloud decisions. Teams not explicitly noted in this example but who still have an opinion on cloud, such as marketing or data teams, could also assign a representative to the Advisory Board. Depending on the organization's needs and available resources, the Advisory Board could include an external cloud subject matter expert.

The PMO involvement typically remains the same. However, there will be a strong need for an agile approach. If the organization is lacking in that competency, training or new hires may be needed for the PMO to sufficiently support the CCoE's activities and approach.

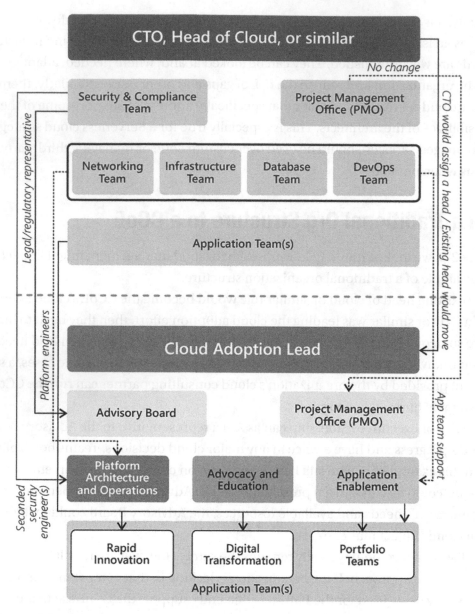

Figure 2-3. *Reorganizing a traditional structure into a CCoE*

Technical security engineers can be moved or seconded to Platform Architecture and Operations. Like the cloud adoption lead, the three lead architects will need to be dedicated to this role and focused solely on their respective teams and responsibilities. Non-technical representatives from the security team, such as legal or regulatory compliance, could be placed on the Advisory Board where they can participate in requirements gathering for the rules, service attestation, security reviews, and other activities needing participation from the security team.

For the various technical teams. involved in the cloud, those previously building and operating infrastructure and components would move to the CCoE's Platform Architecture and Operations. Those supporting the application teams with onboarding and implementation would move into the CCoE's Application Enablement. A consideration here may be to retain some members in the old structure to continue to operate and support existing legacy applications until they can be migrated to the CCoE-managed cloud.

Depending on the organization and broader strategies, application teams might be split into three or more teams under the CCoE, for example.:

1. A rapid innovation team that is focused on prototyping and new ideas

2. A digital transformation team focused on migrating and rearchitecting legacy solutions and digitizing manual workflows

3. Portfolio teams, each responsible for developing and operating a portfolio of applications

Lastly, all application teams will be supported by the CCoE's Application Enablement team.

Cloud Controls as Compliance Guardrails

For Serverless development, the application teams need to be able to provision their own cloud resources as part of the application design and development process. However, the organization still needs to be able to determine *which* resources and *how* they are configured. The directives for security, compliance, and best practices defined by the CCoE need to be applied to the requested resources and, where necessary, enforced. Automating this enforcement will negate the need for a separate provisioning team and many of the manual approvals and stage gates typically in place with enterprises, reducing potential bottlenecks and waiting time.

Modern application teams use Infrastructure-as-Code (IaC) templates to provision the cloud resources they need. Creating resources via the cloud console is not permitted within a controls strategy; application teams must send both IaC templates and code to the cloud via a deployment pipeline. We will cover this in more detail later, but, for now, consider it a kind of pipe through which digital information can travel. Traditionally, this is all that pipelines did; they carried code from point A to point B. However, in the cloud, they have evolved in function and importance.

Besides moving templates and code, modern pipelines include the ability to enforce rules – those CCoE directives we covered earlier. Think of it as a series of sensors and valves throughout the length of the pipe (see Figure 2-4). If a sensor detects something that is not compliant, such as an unapproved cloud service being requested, the pipeline automatically closes the valve, and the deployment fails.

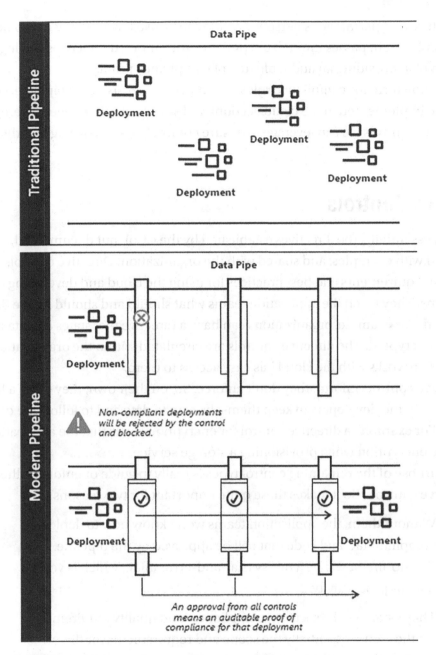

Figure 2-4. *Deployment pipeline with enforced rules*

This means the pipeline is a critical part of the security in many modern cloud management strategies. It provides the organization with a *proof of compliance* for its cloud applications. It guarantees that if an application makes it through the pipeline without being rejected, the application can be considered compliant, at least from an infrastructure and permissions perspective. Pipelines also have logging capabilities. As each deployment passes through the pipeline, the enforced directives will log their evaluation of it, providing an auditable trail of compliance proof.

A common term for compliance rules is *controls*. As well as in the pipeline, controls can also be implemented in the cloud account and several cloud services. There are **four** types of controls we can leverage to ensure comprehensive coverage for the organization.

Directive Controls

These are, essentially, the directives established by the CCoE but documented, augmented with examples, and shared with the organization. Directive controls outline the requirements and best practices for using the cloud and developing cloud applications. They teach the application teams what should and should not be done in the cloud. For example, organizations can have a directive that states all data at rest should be encrypted. The directive controls are circulated within the organization so everyone who works with the cloud has easy access to them.

Directive controls inform; they don't enforce. So, on their own, they place a high level of trust in the developers to keep themselves up to date and to follow the directives correctly. For example, a directive control for encryption trusts that the application team will enable encryption when provisioning a storage service.

The purpose of the remaining control types is really to guide or enforce adherence to the directive controls. So it makes these quite important for two reasons:

1. Without them, the application teams won't know how to deploy compliant IaC and code that will be approved by the pipeline. Development will be a messy trial-and-error affair, which is very bad for productivity.

2. They establish the security, compliance, and quality requirements for the cloud: essentially the scope and requirements for the remaining control types.

Not all controls are created equal. As the directive controls will be the requirements for the remaining types, when we create these controls, we can assign a classification to each of them, which indicates how important they are. The following is a common approach to classification, but this can be adapted to the compliance needs and terminology of the organization:

Class 3: This control protects from *critical* threats to the organization. Implementing, maintaining, and monitoring this control should be given *highest* priority.

Class 2: This control protects from *major* threats to the organization. Implementing, maintaining, and monitoring this control should be given *high* priority.

Class 1: This control protects from *moderate* threats to the organization. Implementing, maintaining, and monitoring this control should be given *medium* priority.

Class 0: This control protects from *minor* threats to the organization. Implementing, maintaining, and monitoring this control should be given *low* priority.

The priority will be especially relevant when budget or resources are limited. Another way to look at this is that for an organization to go to the cloud, class 3 *has* to be implemented, class 2 *should* be implemented, class 1 is *good to have*, and class 0 is *nice to have*.

Preventive Controls

Preventive controls restrict the developers from taking actions that go against the established directives within a cloud environment. For example, preventive controls can block the use of specific cloud services or regions that are not approved.

One way to set up preventive controls is the use of Service Control Policies (SCPs) found in AWS Organizations. With AWS Organizations, we can centrally manage and govern multiple AWS accounts within an organization. SCPs are used to manage permissions at an AWS account level.

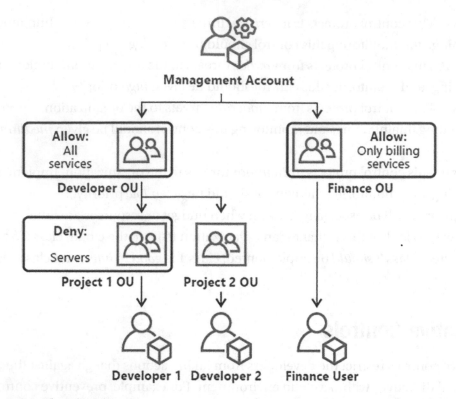

Figure 2-5. *Cloud account management with organization units (OUs) in AWS*

At the top of Figure 2-5, we have the organization management account. In the following, we create two organization units (OUs), one for developers and one for the finance teams. OUs are a grouping of one or more AWS accounts. The grouping might be for a particular department, a functional use case, or anything else the organization deems useful. On the Finance OU in Figure 2-5, we configure an SCP that only permits access to AWS's billing services. SCP permissions are propagated down, meaning that all finance users assigned to the Finance OU can now only access billing services.

The Developer OU is permitted access to all cloud services. Under the Developer OU, we split into OUs for different projects. In Project 1 OU, we add an SCP that prevents the use of servers. Since permissions are propagated down, this means Developer 1 will have access to all cloud services except servers. Since no additional SCP is attached to the Project 2 OU, Developer 2 will still have access to all cloud services, including servers.

The controls added to deployment pipelines will also typically be *preventive*-type controls. They will assess the submitted Infrastructure-as-Code and application code for any non-compliance and block it in the pipeline, preventing it from being deployed.

Detective Controls

Detective controls analyze and monitor the configuration and changes after the fact within a cloud environment for anything that is not compliant with the directives. When a violation occurs, a notification will be sent to alert relevant stakeholders with the details. Any follow-up action will be at their discretion.

Depending on the organization's tolerance for risk, developers may be permitted to experiment with different service configurations in the development or sandbox environment. Detective controls can track non-compliance, but generally, no follow-up will happen. A working design, even if non-compliant, could be used to perform security testing. If it passes, it can be used as a design example to request an exception or policy change. Alternatively, non-compliance in a development environment could indicate a mistake, and the application will need to be made compliant before it can be deployed to the production environment.

AWS Config is a service that can monitor a cloud environment. It can run on a schedule or when it detects any change within the cloud environment. It keeps a record of each change and the outcome of any rules that it was assessed against. The service can be configured to send notifications for any detected non-compliance.

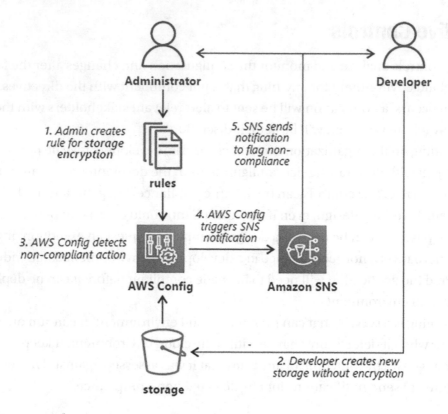

Administrator

1. Admin creates
rule for storage
encryption

5. SNS sends
notification
to flag non-
compliance

Developer

rules

4. AWS Config
triggers SNS
notification

3. AWS Config detects
non-compliant action

AWS Config

Amazon SNS

2. Developer creates new
storage without encryption

storage

Figure 2-6. *Implementing controls with AWS Config*

In Figure 2-6, an admin creates a new rule in Config requiring the use of encryption at rest for storage. Once the rule is added, Config scans the existing infrastructure and flags any existing non-compliant configuration. Later, a developer provisions a new storage resource but has forgotten to enable encryption. Config picks up the non-compliant change soon after the storage resource is created. In this example, Config will trigger the notification service SNS to send a notification about the non-compliant configuration. Detective controls provide the freedom to innovate in the cloud while still ensuring oversight of non-compliance.

Another service that can help implement detective controls is Macie, a fully managed machine learning service for analyzing data stored in the cloud. Macie can identify sensitive information such as personal data, credit card numbers, government IDs, and AWS account keys. Macie can help organizations comply with privacy regulations as it can help flag, detect, redact, or delete sensitive data automatically.

GuardDuty, another machine learning service, is used for threat detection. It can analyze the logs that are collected within a cloud environment and identify abnormalities that could indicate malicious behavior. Automation and notifications can then help with a swift response to potential breaches or other threats.

Corrective Controls

Like detective controls, corrective controls monitor the configuration and changes within a cloud environment after the fact to detect any non-compliance. However, when a non-compliant event occurs, corrective controls go beyond notification and can actually execute appropriate remediation.

AWS Config can be used for corrective controls too. It can be configured to execute a Lambda microservice in response to storage being provisioned without encryption enabled. The microservice can promptly force the encryption setting, disable access to the non-compliant storage, or delete it entirely.

Which Controls to Prioritize?

Preventive controls are the first line of defense, and every effort should be made to implement as many of the directives as possible in preventive controls – certainly for organizations new to the cloud or with a low appetite for risk. Preventive controls will stop non-compliance before it can occur, while detective and corrective controls react after the fact. Preventive controls can be implemented on multiple levels. There are readily available cloud capabilities such as permissions in Identity and Access Management (IAM) policies and service allowlists in SCPs to implement them. Custom controls can be developed in Lambda microservices or CloudFormation Guard that enforce more specific organizational policies. These controls are typically implemented in the deployment pipeline, where they can assess all new IaC and application code being submitted before it is deployed.

Detective controls serve two purposes. Firstly, they can catch any non-compliance that circumvents the preventive controls – for example, changes that are made directly in the account by administrators. Secondly, as organizations with a high tolerance for risk evolve and achieve high maturity in the cloud, they can evolve their cloud strategy and shift from primarily preventive controls to detective – at least in the development environment. This approach places more trust in the developers, giving them the freedom to innovate in the cloud while still tracking any non-compliance.

Corrective controls are used sparingly in practice. The perceived risk of automated rules wrongly changing production infrastructure makes it challenging for many organizations to trust them. By the time the organization has achieved a level of maturity to develop and trust such controls, there may no longer be a need for them – certainly not if the maturity brings with it a shift in strategy from preventive to detective controls.

Corrective controls can still be a good option for data protection where the stakes may be higher. For example, when a data store is wrongly created with public access, corrective controls can immediately rectify the issue and block access to it. False positives in this situation are justified by the potential risk of inadvertently exposing sensitive data. Cloud storage wrongly configured for public access has been shown to be the root cause of several high-profile cybersecurity breaches over the last few years.

Supporting Tools

Let's look at some supporting tools that can help with Serverless cloud management.

Self-Service Portal

Onboarding is an important early step for new cloud applications and, traditionally, tends to happen entirely with code examples and documentation. But this often results in the need for a lot of manual interaction from different teams, with clarifications, support requests, and frequently asked questions. It also leads to inconsistent deployments due to misunderstandings and human error and reduced productivity to cope with the learning curves when deploying infrastructure.

A more friendly option is to have an onboarding portal that provides an easier step-by-step process. This would start with adding a project or application. Besides a title and description, it can be useful to track any data categories that are being processed, relevant security policies, type of architecture, and access permissions. For Serverless, the individual components would then be registered under the application entry. Once everything is confirmed, the portal automatically creates the cloud environment, configures the code storage service for each of the components, and attaches the pipelines needed to deploy the IaC and code to the cloud. Team members receive the information needed to work on the components assigned to them.

During development, the portal provides dashboards with statistics, real-time error logs, and other useful data and tools, and application teams can make changes to their project settings themselves. Lastly, once the application is launched, an operational dashboard will provide similar insights, but geared toward live application operations.

Shared Central Library

Serverless application components are independent and highly reusable. This makes them very sharable within an organization, and developing an internal library of components is a great way to share knowledge and increase application team productivity.

We can make this an extensive library of content to help knowledge sharing and advocacy efforts and get the broader organization on board with Serverless. It would be a centralized internal service for sharing architecture examples and best practices, Infrastructure-as-Code templates, and microservice code.

Such a library can also be a great place to keep or reference policy, pipeline, and resource documentation, onboarding guides and FAQs, training materials, and a news feed with the latest service and feature updates from the cloud provider.

Many organizations may already have some informal sharing area on Confluence or SharePoint, which can be evolved to become a formal library. It's important that the library has clear ownership from the CCoE. The content needs to be moderated, and the CCoE will be accountable for keeping it in line with organizational policy and maintaining it as new cloud capabilities are launched.

The CCoE can add pre-approved architecture components to the library. Using such components should offer benefits to the application teams, such as being able to skip some approval steps or compliance reviews. The pipeline and controls should verify that only the permitted settings for the components have been changed so that compliance can be ensured.

We can aim to build a community around this initiative, which means fostering participation and interaction. Incentives can be created through existing KPI strategies, rewarding contributions, support, and ideas. FAQs and documentation should include feedback features and boards to offer opportunities for discussion and improving the content.

Besides recorded training sessions, we can schedule and promote webinars and live Q&As with subject matter experts through the system.

As the platform would be owned by the CCoE, there is an opportunity for them to share the cloud road map and provide facilities for feature requests and priority voting. An up-to-date overview of which cloud services are allowlisted and documentation explaining the active controls will be helpful too.

Lastly, support should be provided for those wishing to share blogs or videos about their cloud experiences and knowledge. Besides the value of knowledge retention and sharing, developing thought leaders within the organization is great for advocacy and attracting new talent.

Developer Tools

There are hundreds of tools available claiming to be the best option for many aspects of application development – frameworks for developing, tools for testing and quality control, development software, and much more. The sheer volume of solutions can be overwhelming, and while it is good to allow some flexibility, it is certainly recommended to propose a baseline of tools that have been assessed for suitability for the organization and the cloud strategy.

Many such tools will be covered in this book, especially in Chapters 6 and 8, but the CCoE will be tasked with assessing options and picking the right tools for the organization.

 Serverless Adoption: Current State

For organizations that want to support application teams in developing Serverless applications, an important first step is to understand the current state. An organization might be evolving an **existing** cloud strategy, or they might be new to the cloud and looking to **start** with a Serverless strategy.

For evolving an existing cloud strategy such as servers or containers, it will help to have had at least 2 years of working experience in the cloud and for the application teams to have shown interest in, and some exposure to, fully managed and Serverless services. A cloud strategy run by a *Cloud Center of Excellence* and a *controls* approach to managing the cloud environment will be essential for productive delivery of Serverless applications. If these are not already in place, then that will be the first step.

Organizations looking to start their cloud journey with Serverless will face a significant learning curve. However, this approach can be practical for organizations with a small IT team. Serverless minimizes the operational overhead, enabling organizations to securely deploy and operate more applications with fewer IT resources.

To assess and document the current state, we want to look at four areas of capabilities:

1. **Cloud experience**

   We need to understand the organization's experience in the cloud. Some things to note in this area are the number of production applications and any training or experience relevant to Serverless, such as early proof of concepts or team members' past or personal projects.

2. **Cloud management and DevOps**

   How the organization manages their cloud environments and the deployment of applications into them. The organizations should be familiar with deployment automation and Infrastructure-as-Code, have a CCoE or be at least open to establishing one, and have or be willing to use a *controls* strategy to manage the cloud environments.

3. **Application architecture**

   The type of applications that the organization typically deploys into the cloud and the most common programming language will indicate if Serverless is going to be a good match – for example, if they are primarily off-the-shelf or custom-developed or if applications are mostly monolithic or distributed. We also want to see if the organization has any experience with capabilities such as autoscaling and containers and if there is a culture of learning, knowledge sharing, and openness to change.

4. **Security and regulatory compliance**

   Lastly, we need to understand if there are any industry or regional regulatory considerations that the organization has to operate within – especially any limitations that might impact the use of Serverless cloud services. Data classifications and policies will also influence how the organization can use the cloud.

Serverless Adoption: Desired State

AWS created the Cloud Adoption Framework and published the third revision (seen in Figure 2-7) in November 2021. The framework identifies specific organizational capabilities that have been shown to increase the likelihood of success in adopting the cloud. It helps organizations evaluate their current state and prioritize their cloud road map in line with proven strategies.

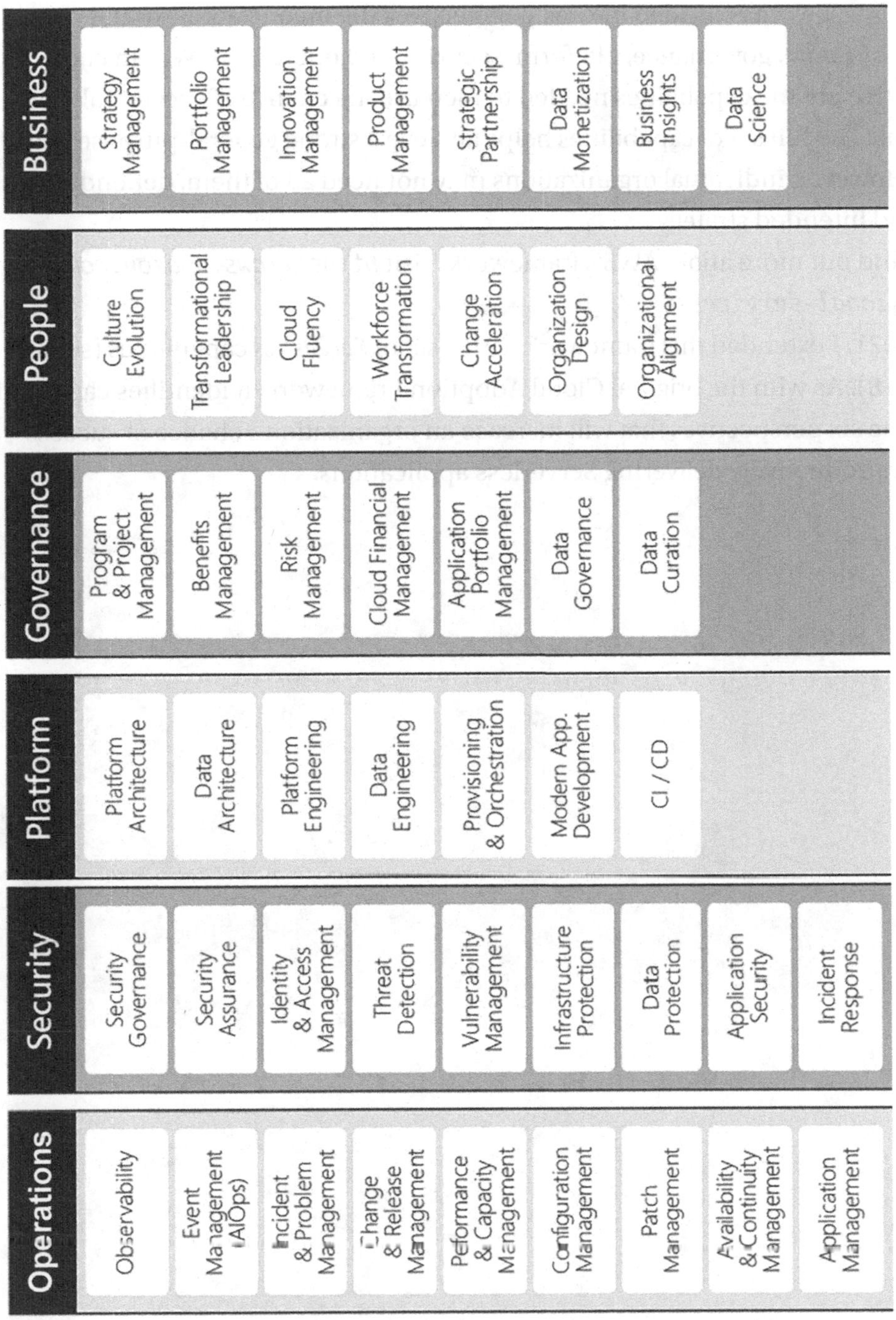

Operations	Security	Platform	Governance	People	Business
Observability	Security Governance	Platform Architecture	Program & Project Management	Culture Evolution	Strategy Management
Event Management (AIOps)	Security Assurance	Data Architecture	Benefits Management	Transformational Leadership	Portfolio Management
Incident & Problem Management	Identity & Access Management	Platform Engineering	Risk Management	Cloud Fluency	Innovation Management
Change & Release Management	Threat Detection	Data Engineering	Cloud Financial Management	Workforce Transformation	Product Management
Performance & Capacity Management	Vulnerability Management	Provisioning & Orchestration	Application Portfolio Management	Change Acceleration	Strategic Partnership
Configuration Management	Infrastructure Protection	Modern App. Development	Data Governance	Organization Design	Data Monetization
Patch Management	Data Protection	CI / CD	Data Curation	Organizational Alignment	Business Insights
Availability & Continuity Management	Application Security				Data Science
Application Management	Incident Response				

Figure 2-7. *Cloud Adoption Framework, as shared by AWS*
https://aws.amazon.com/professional-services/CAF/

The framework is divided into six perspectives the organization should consider: business, people, governance, platform, security, and operations. Within each perspective are the capabilities needed to increase the chance of successful cloud adoption. The full set of capabilities helps achieve a strong general-purpose use of the cloud. However, individual organizations may not need all of them, depending on their goals and intended strategy.

To find out more about AWS's framework, visit *https://aws.amazon.com/ professional-services/CAF/*.

In 2021, I extended this framework with a set of *Serverless* capabilities (seen in Figure 2-8). As with the original Cloud Adoption Framework, it identifies capabilities across the six perspectives that will increase an organization's chance of success – in this case, for productively delivering Serverless applications.

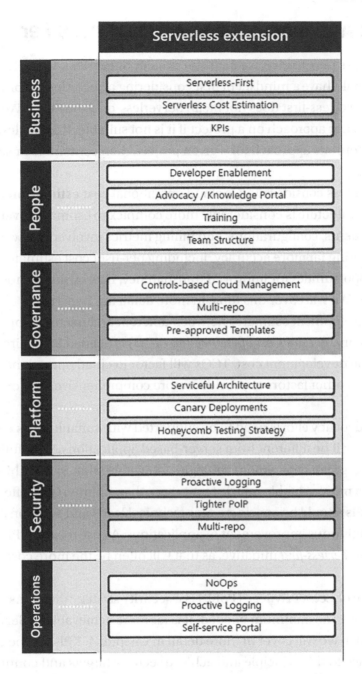

Figure 2-8. *Serverless extension of the Cloud Adoption Framework*

Serverless Adoption Framework: Business Perspective

Under the business perspective, we have the strategy **Serverless-first**. Here, the organization should have a mindset of first considering a Serverless approach for new projects. Serverless-first does not mean Serverless-only, however. We should not force a particular approach on a project if it is not suitable. If Serverless is not deemed an appropriate approach for a given project, then containers or servers can be considered next.

Another business consideration is cloud operational **cost estimation** for Serverless projects. This architecture is considerably more complex to estimate, given the many different components, configurations, and billing metrics involved. However, this complexity can bring far more accuracy, including per-user cost estimates, which can open up new opportunities for improved transparency, new business models, and revenue streams. We will cover this topic in more detail in Chapter 3.

Similarly, development estimates between different architectural approaches do not tell the full story. A *Total Cost of Ownership* (TCO) is needed for a fairer comparison. Besides the initial development cost, TCOs will factor in cloud operational costs, maintenance, and other factors to provide a more comprehensive and long-term cost estimate.

Serverless advocacy efforts need to be supported with suitable **KPIs or OKRs**, and project KPIs will be different from server-based applications. With fully managed services and blue-green deployment strategies, downtime should be a thing of the past, making latency a more valuable metric to measure than uptime. Cost-effectiveness and sustainability KPIs should be considered for technical leads and solution architects to help drive continuous improvement of applications. A cost-related KPI will also strengthen the *Serverless-first* initiative, as that will often be the more cost-effective approach.

The Principle of Least Privilege (PoLP) is a security strategy that aims to limit permissions to only the minimum needed. It is far more achievable in Serverless architecture, which we will cover in more detail in Chapter 4. KPIs can be created to drive adherence to this principle and achieve security targets and continuous improvement of applications.

Serverless Adoption Framework: People Perspective

Under the people perspective, we have **developer enablement**. Separate teams for resource provisioning are not productive for Serverless architecture. Developers need to be willing and able to provision their own cloud resources. Compliance is managed by using controls to add limits where necessary, and deployment automation will be crucial in supporting this.

An **advocacy or knowledge portal** will be important in supporting the different teams on their cloud journey. This may be part of a larger *cloud portal* with other related capabilities, and it can become a community where teams can share patterns and support each other.

Serverless architecture differs significantly from server and container architectures. Besides technology and design differences, mindset is just as important. As such, **training** will be crucial for driving this transformation and achieving successful outcomes.

Lastly, as we covered with CCoE earlier, there may be a need for **team** and organizational **structure** changes to become fully productive with Serverless delivery. New cloud roles, and specialization of existing IT roles for cloud competencies, should be expected too.

Serverless Adoption Framework: Governance Perspective

Under governance, we can find the **controls** that we covered in detail earlier. Secure and compliant developer enablement needs controls to help govern the cloud environment.

Mono-repo provides broad access to an entire application; it's really the only option for monolithic applications. For Serverless architecture, we can use **multi-repo**. We cover this in more detail in Chapter 6, but, in summary, it provides more fine-grained access controls, improved shareability of components, and a more productive deployment experience.

Pre-approved templates and architectural patterns are further boosts to productivity. These are usually approved by the CCoE and can help improve adherence to best practices and standards. As they are pre-approved, they can enable application teams to skip some approval or review steps, reducing onboarding and time to market.

Serverless Adoption Framework: Platform Perspective

Under the platform perspective, we have **serviceful** architecture. This is a common aspect of Serverless projects, where developers should use managed services instead of writing custom code where possible. Managed services enable developers to focus more on adding customer value and less on reinventing the wheel and maintaining common application features.

The next evolution of deployment strategy is **canary deployments**. Blue-green should be supported as a minimum, but with canary, we can select portions of the user base to be routed to the new version of an application. This reduces the impact and blast radius of any potential issues, and we can automatically route the users back to the previous working version if issues do happen.

Unit tests are the de facto standard for testing legacy applications. However, this approach does not sufficiently cover the distributed nature of Serverless applications. As such, we now have the **Honeycomb testing** strategy. This approach prioritizes integration and contract testing, which focuses more on the many connections between components. We cover this topic in more detail in Chapter 8.

As part of testing, a strong logging strategy with automated analysis and notifications will be crucial for Serverless applications. The many components generate too many logs for manual debugging to be productive.

Serverless Adoption Framework: Security Perspective

We also have a **proactive logging** strategy in the security perspective. The same automated approach can greatly benefit security, where we can detect potentially malicious behavior and automatically block a user account, for example.

Furthermore, instead of waiting for users to report a problem, we minimize the impact of any defects by enabling the application to react to them automatically. For example, proactive logging can alert a developer to take action, or it can automatically try and recover from a failure by retrying after a short delay.

The potential for tighter permissions in Serverless architecture needs to be embraced as part of the transformation strategy. Training and KPIs can be used to upskill and motivate the application teams to meet **Principle of Least Privilege** security targets.

Multi-repo, mentioned in governance, is also impactful to the security perspective. The ability to limit access to only the code needed by each team member or any external resources greatly improves application security.

Serverless Adoption Framework: Operations Perspective

Our first item is **NoOps,** where the organization's focus should be on those parts of the infrastructure that will provide a return on investment, such as developing new capabilities and improving customer experience. The mundane operational tasks of maintaining servers, patching operating systems, and scaling should all be offloaded to the cloud provider by using fully managed services.

Proactive logging makes a third appearance here in the operations perspective, where it focuses on monitoring the day-to-day activities of live applications and providing automated responses to events such as errors, resource limits, and spikes in demand.

Related to the aforementioned *knowledge portal*, a **self-service portal** will enable developers to onboard and manage new cloud projects themselves. Such a portal can provide easy access to launching projects with the repos, deployment pipelines, and any blueprints they might need, as well as a monitoring dashboard to get a quick overview of the health of the application and any deployments.

 # Serverless Adoption: Gap Analysis

With the current state established and the desired state understood, we can perform a gap analysis to understand what the organization needs to improve before application teams can productively deliver Serverless applications.

In a spreadsheet, for each desired capability such as *developer enablement* or *proactive logging*, we note the current state and the *gap* between the current and the desired state. As part of this assessment, we will estimate the effort required to achieve the desired state and identify any opportunities and risks.

For example, opportunities can be found in teams that have gained some experience in Serverless architecture and can share lessons learned, case studies, and examples with the wider organization. Risks are areas of concern or perceived blockers to achieving the desired state. For example, Serverless services such as DynamoDB might not be approved by the security team yet, and a lengthy approval process could be expected before application teams can make use of the service.

Figure 2-9 provides a gap analysis spreadsheet with example answers to provide an idea of how to go about this. For the purposes of this book, the answers have been kept simple and short. A real gap analysis would need to capture more detail, sufficient to create a road map and start the transformation process.

Business Perspective		
Serverless Capability	**Current Capability**	**Gap/Opportunity/Risk**
Serverless-first	Server-first, cloud preferred	It is easier to go from servers in the cloud to Serverless than from on-prem to Serverless.
Serverless cost estimation	Server cost estimation	Considerable difference. Training will be needed at all levels in a project team.
KPIs	No cloud-related KPIs	An existing KPI strategy can be adapted to include Serverless KPIs

People Perspective		
Serverless Capability	**Current Capability**	**Gap/Opportunity/Risk**
Developer enablement	Developer segregation	This is a very different approach to cloud that is not compatible with Serverless architecture. Significant strategic, structural, and mindset changes will be needed.
Advocacy/knowledge portal	Confluence information sharing	An existing sharing hub can be evolved to a formal platform owned by a cloud team.
Training	Cloud fluency courses in an existing LMS solution, a team actively managing training for the organization	Serverless training can be added to their scope.
Team structure	Segregated teams, but there is a dedicated cloud management team	Evolving a cloud team to a Cloud Center of Excellence will be easier than starting from scratch.

Governance Perspective		
Serverless Capability	**Current Capability**	**Gap/Opportunity/Risk**
Controls-based cloud management	Segregation of duties management	This is a very different approach to cloud that is not compatible with Serverless architecture. Significant strategic, structural, and mindset changes will be needed.
Multi-repo	Good DevOps and automation capabilities, but all applications are using mono-repo	With training, a multi-repo approach to Serverless applications can be learned.
Pre-approved templates	N/A	This will be a new concept, and it will likely be time-consuming to adapt policies and obtain approvals for these from the various compliance and security stakeholders.

Figure 2-9. *Excel spreadsheet for Serverless adoption gap analysis*

Platform Perspective		
Serverless Capability	**Current Capability**	**Gap/Opportunity/Risk**
Serviceful architecture	Server-based architecture and a lot of custom code	This is a very different way of designing applications but can be addressed by training the technical teams.
Canary deployments	Update in place	This will be a significant shift in deployment strategy, requiring training and platform changes.
Honeycomb testing strategy	Automated unit testing during deployment	The in-place automation that currently facilitates unit testing can be extended to support other types of testing needed for Serverless architecture.

Security Perspective		
Serverless Capability	**Current Capability**	**Gap/Opportunity/Risk**
Proactive logging	Centralized passive logging	Log security and centralization are already well-handled; this can be extended to support automated analysis and reacting to logs.
Tighter PoLP	Server-level access permissions	This can be addressed as part of Serverless training. As we are improving security, there should be limited resistance to this.
Multi-repo	Mono-repo	With training, a multi-repo approach to Serverless applications can be learned.

Operations Perspective		
Serverless Capability	**Current Capability**	**Gap/Opportunity/Risk**
NoOps	Server management	This is a very different way of designing applications but can be addressed by training the technical teams. Careful change management and training will be needed for operational teams.
Proactive logging	Passive logging	Log security and centralization are already well-handled; this can be extended to support automated analysis and reacting to logs.
Self-service portal	App onboarding through a cloud team	This will require the development of a new portal and significant automation and approval of new processes. Careful change management and training will be needed for the cloud team.

Figure 2-9. *(continued)*

Application Suitability for Serverless

When we are talking about the current and desired states, it is typically at an organizational level. The gap analysis will result in a strategy that the organization needs to deliver to enable application teams to use Serverless architecture productively.

Once that has been achieved, teams will need to assess individual applications for their Serverless suitability. While Serverless is quite versatile, there are certainly applications that are not a good fit. Perhaps more challenging is a range of applications where Serverless architecture *could* work, but considerable risks are involved. A cost-benefit analysis should be performed to compare the Serverless approach with other options to identify the best one for the application.

The challenge is in how and when to assess applications. The sooner this can be done, the more accurate the project plan and estimates will be, and less time will be wasted pursuing unsuitable approaches. A solution architect with strong cloud experience can usually assess the risks after a short briefing of the application. However, such a specialist is not always available, or the organization might be new to Serverless. As such, there is value in providing a means for less technical stakeholders to establish early if a given application might be suitable for Serverless or at least within an acceptable risk range.

Serverless Application Risk Assessment

The Serverless Application Risk Assessment aims to address that challenge. It is a simple survey that can be performed on an application to understand if Serverless architecture is potentially a good match. It works for existing applications being considered for redevelopment and new application ideas. I developed this assessment at Sourced, and it was made public via a blog article and video.

The Application Risk Assessment does not directly indicate if Serverless is suitable or not for the assessed application; rather, it provides a risk score and indicates areas of potential risk that can be addressed. Besides the provided risk score, other factors, such as application team experience, timelines, and the Total Cost of Ownership, should be considered when deciding on suitability.

For example, a high risk score from this assessment does not necessarily mean that it would be *impossible* to use Serverless for the application. It indicates that it is likely going to be *difficult,* and there are many *risks* that will need to be mitigated. However, depending on the organization, the long-term benefits of Serverless, such as minimal overheads and maintenance, might justify taking this approach over other options.

Assessment Domains

The assessment covers three key domains. All three domains focus on application requirements that should be knowable for both existing and planning applications:

Business requirements

By using business requirements and making some assumptions, we can uncover technical requirements that can influence the potential application risks. This approach helps reduce the technical proficiency needed by the assessor, making the assessment more accessible.

System requirements

Some technical questions are not entirely unavoidable, however. The remaining ones have been simplified as much as possible and can be found under the system requirements domain. While many product owners and project managers should be able to make an educated guess at these, the accuracy of the assessment will be improved by getting input from someone with cloud and application knowledge.

Data requirements

Lastly are the data-related questions that consider policies and other potential requirements an organization might have for managing data that could impact architectural decisions.

Assessment Guide

The current version of the assessment contains 14 questions: five in business, five in system, and four in data. Each question has three possible answers, and each of those answers has zero, five, or ten points associated with it. These are all provided in Figure 2-10.

The assessment is performed by going through the questions and picking the most appropriate answer for the application. Note that all questions should be answered. Once completed, add up all of the answers' points to get a score between 0 and 140. Divide this score by 1.4 to get an easier-to-understand risk percentage between 0 and 100.

If the risk percentage is between **0 and 20,** it is considered **low** risk. This indicates that the application could be suitable for a Serverless architecture approach.

A risk between **21 and 49** is **medium**. The application has the potential for Serverless, but there are some risks that need to be considered. A possible next step could also be to review the high-risk areas – the answers that had ten points associated with them. Can anything be done to address and mitigate those risks so the score can be lowered?

If the system requirements were too technical, consider performing the assessment again with someone who can help answer the technical questions with more confidence.

A risk **over 50** is considered **high**, and a Serverless approach should be compared with other architecture options using the risks and TCO to find the one most suited to the application.

Keep in mind it might simply be a high-risk application and challenging to develop regardless of architecture choice. This is why other factors such as TCO are just as important to consider when determining the right architecture.

1.1. On a high level, what type of application is it?		
The type of application helps highlight technical requirements that are difficult to support in Serverless, such as those with high resource or GPU requirements. The high-risk answer will be difficult to mitigate as it relates to the technical limitation of the Serverless cloud services.		
1.1.1.	Proof of concept, minimal viable project, an API for a CMS, web or mobile application, IoT related, order workflow or similar, or some form of automation pipeline	0
1.1.2.	Large complex application with many diverse features	5
1.1.3.	Machine learning or heavy data-processing related, or highly sensitive to latency	10
1.2. Is it an existing solution, or will it be custom-developed?		
Custom-developed means it is created to be optimized for Serverless architecture. If it's an existing solution or even existing components, it adds risk to the assessment and may require customization to work in a Serverless architecture.		
1.2.1.	It will be custom-designed and developed for Serverless cloud.	0
1.2.2.	Off-the-shelf or existing solution or key components, confirmed to be suitable for Serverless cloud.	5
1.2.3.	Off-the-shelf or existing solution or key components, not confirmed to be suitable for Serverless cloud.	10
1.3. Are there requirements to control the full tech stack or use a particular OS or software?		
Such requirements add complexity and will usually not be possible in fully managed services.		
1.3.1.	No such requirements.	0
1.3.2.	Yes, but they are confirmed to be compatible with a Serverless approach.	5
1.3.3.	Yes, and it is unknown if this is compatible with a Serverless approach.	10

Figure 2-10. *Serverless Application Risk Assessment questions*

1.4. Expected number of users interacting with this application

More users generally mean more complexity and risk. While scaling is typically managed in Serverless, high numbers of users will require more consideration for areas such as APIGW throttling and Lambda concurrence. Code and architecture efficiency will be crucial to managing costs, and detailed TCO estimates are needed to determine which run mode to use in services such as DynamoDB.

1.4.1.	Up to hundreds	0
1.4.2.	Thousands	5
1.4.3.	Hundreds of thousands and above	10

1.5. Is this a migration or a new build?

While the lessons learned can be useful for migrations, expectations need to be met or exceeded with a new version. Given the significant difference in architecture, this creates additional risk in the project.

1.5.1.	New build	0
1.5.2.	Migration, with a clear scope and flexibility to change features as needed	5
1.5.3.	Migration – the result needs to match the original application very closely	10

2.1. Are there specific programming language requirements for any of the microservices?

Language decisions can be driven by existing experience, existing components, or organizational strategy. For servers, the choice of language will usually have little impact, but Serverless services such as Lambda are limited in the languages they natively support. There are workarounds, such as using custom containers, but this adds complexity and risk to the project.

2.1.1.	NodeJS or Python	0
2.1.2.	Java, Go, PowerShell, C#, or Ruby code	5
2.1.3.	Other languages	10

Figure 2-10. *(continued)*

2.2. Does the application have long-running microservices (more than 10 minutes)?

Lambda is well-known to be limited to 15 minutes of execution time. Microservices that need longer will likely need to be run in a container, adding complexity and overheads to the project and increasing the risk.

2.2.1.	No	0
2.2.2.	Yes, but these could be launched with an on-demand container to process a task and terminated after	5
2.2.3.	Yes, there is a requirement for an always-on microservice that cannot be event-driven	10

2.3. Are there integrations with external systems?

Integrations add complexity to any project. With Serverless architecture, the concern will be on the expected length of external execution time. For example, we do not want a Lambda microservice waiting minutes for a response from an external API. Legacy APIs such as SOAP will also add overheads and latency, which is undesirable.

2.3.1.	No	0
2.3.2.	Yes, the external systems have modern API support. API supports asynchronous for requests that are longer than a few seconds	5
2.3.3.	Yes, the external systems do not have modern API endpoints, or they do not have asynchronous support for requests longer than a few seconds	10

2.4. Does this application need to run on multiple cloud providers?

While Serverless is increasingly supported across clouds, it is still not an ideal requirement and will add risk to the project. For example, services or features in one cloud might not be available in another. This needs to be assessed: alternative approaches may need to be designed, and IaC templates must be created twice.

2.4.1.	No	0
2.4.2.	Yes, but only parts of the application for disaster recovery (DR) or temporary maintenance reasons	5
2.4.3.	Yes, it needs to be fully supported on a second cloud provider	10

Figure 2-10. *(continued)*

2.5. Are there microservices with high resource requirements?

Serverless is not particularly suited to high-resource applications, similar to long-running processes. Lambda offers a maximum of 10 GB of memory and six vCPUs. If more than that is needed, then containers or servers will need to be involved, adding complexity and risk.

2.5.1.	No, all microservices can be achieved within the Lambda compute limits of 10 GB RAM and six vCPUs.	0
2.5.2.	Yes, some microservices will sometimes exceed 10 GB RAM and six vCPUs.	5
2.5.3.	Yes, most microservices will regularly require more than 10 GB RAM and six vCPUs.	10

3.1. Where will application data be stored?

Loading data from another account, region, or on-premises is possible, but it will add risk to the overall solution. It will also add cost and latency, neither of which is ideal in Serverless architecture.

3.1.1.	With the application in a database controlled by the application.	0
3.1.2.	Data will come from another cloud application, account or region.	5
3.1.3.	Data must be stored on-premises but can be processed in the cloud.	10

3.2. What is the format of the application's data schema?

While SQL can run on Aurora Serverless, that database still has a minimum cost. Ideally, we would use one of the Serverless databases such as DynamoDB or Timestream. These do not support SQL, so a hard requirement for SQL will result in a less efficient database choice and added cost and risk.

3.2.1.	Data schema and type of database will be determined as part of the project, expected to be Serverless-friendly.	0
3.2.2.	Existing SQL data format, can be transformed if it needs to be Serverless-friendly	5
3.2.3.	Existing SQL data format, must remain the same format	10

Figure 2-10. *(con tinued)*

3.3. Will the data have a sovereignty requirement?

Data sovereignty needs to be considered for sensitive data such as PII, and a local region needs to be available from the cloud provider to be able to comply with this requirement. While designs with data stored on-premises and only processing in the cloud are possible, these add cost, latency, and complexity to the project, resulting in higher risk.

3.3.1.	No, data is approved for the cloud and can be stored anywhere in the organization's accounts.	0
3.3.2.	Yes, and the required/approved cloud region exists.	5
3.3.3.	Yes, but the required/approved cloud region does not exist.	10

3.4. What is the type of data being moved and processed within the application?

Generally speaking, the more data there is, the higher the risk in managing and processing it. If the application is only working with database records and events, it's well supported in Serverless. Processing larger formats such as video will require additional services or even containers, adding complexity and overheads to the solution and increasing the risk.

3.4.1.	Primarily text data such as database records and event messages	0
3.4.2.	Primarily file data, such as documents and PDFs	5
3.4.3.	Primarily media data, such as images and videos	10

Figure 2-10. *(continued)*

Event Storming

Event storming is a workshop-based approach to transforming a traditional monolithic application into an event-driven Serverless architecture. Earlier, using the ice cream machine analogy, I explained how microservices take a monolith's functionality and split it across multiple mini-applications. However, that example neglected to address **how** we split the monolith into the microservices. Event storming is one approach that can be used to achieve that.

Common Challenges

In Figure 2-11 are some common challenges organizations face when converting a monolith to a microservice design.

Broken integrations are common because it is easy to miss integrations between microservices. Such mistakes might only be discovered later when conducting end-to-end testing or, even worse, by users after the service is live.

There is a risk of creating a **distributed monolith**, especially for application teams less experienced in microservices. A distributed monolith is when microservices are heavily dependent on each other or on shared code. It also describes a microservice with too much functionality, making it behave more like a mini-monolith than a true event-driven microservice.

Given the complexity and number of features in a typical monolith, it is easy to miss functionality buried within it, resulting in **incomplete microservices**. Often, this does not come to light until actual user tests are performed.

It is not uncommon to end up with **duplicate microservices** performing the same or a very similar task, especially if the development tasks are shared between multiple developers working in parallel.

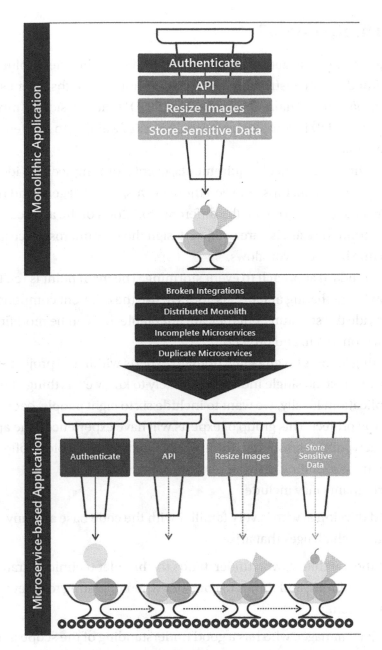

Figure 2-11. *Common challenges of monolith-to-microservice conversion*

To mitigate these challenges, it is important to use an approach that breaks down the monolith in such a way that no details are missed.

Event Storming Basics

Event storming provides a structure for discussing a complex business solution, and it is an effective method for deconstructing and transforming monoliths. Event storming is a simplified approach to Domain-Driven Design (DDD) that is easier for mixed groups to understand. True DDD is complex, requiring hours of training to master, even for seasoned project managers.

Instead of gathering technical requirements, event storming seeks to identify the business events, the relationships between these events, their triggers, and how all these moving parts work together to create the different workflows of the application. The insights derived from the exercise are used to design the new microservice architecture following the same business workflows.

There is no standard approach to event storming. The main point is really to achieve structured knowledge sharing and discussion. We use the different components of event storming to provide the structure, but they are adaptable and can be modified to best suit the organization, team, and project.

Event storming focuses on engaging domain experts within the project – a *group* of participants, because no single individual is likely to know everything about a large monolithic application. Ideally, we want to include six to eight people, each with a distinct role in the project. This group of experts will have experienced the application from different viewpoints and should, through collaboration, be able to offer a comprehensive understanding of the application.

Typical participants may include

- A lead developer, who is very familiar with the code base and any technical challenges that arise

- A solution architect, who understands the broader technical strategy, any integrations, and things to consider when migrating to a new environment

- A project manager, who has a good understanding of the scope and opinions on timeline, resources, and budget

- The product owner, who has a view of the project from a user and business perspective

Some projects might need more specialist participants, such as legal, compliance, marketing, or data specialists, to ensure policies, regulations, and other factors are considered.

End users are generally not involved in this process since their views might be too distinct. The product owner should have a view of confirmed user requirements for the application.

Before we go through a step-by-step workshop example, let's look at the components of event storming in Figure 2-12 and how they work together.

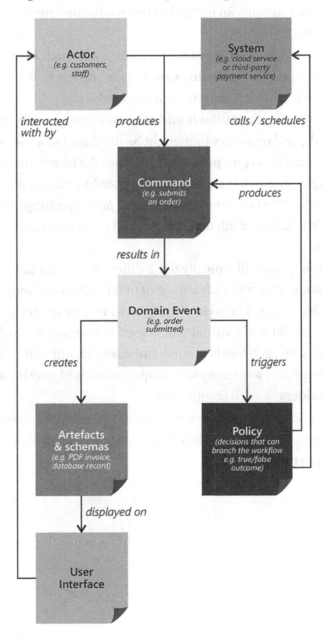

Figure 2-12. *The components of event storming*

Applications have *entities* that interact with them. In event storming, we distinguish two types of entities. At the top right in Figure 2-12, we have **systems**, which are applications, third-party services, and other digital entities. To the left of systems, we have **actors**, who are users - actual humans.

The *actors* and *systems* produce **commands** for the application to do something. In this example, the user submits an order that the application needs to respond to by validating and accepting the order.

Commands result in a **domain event** that is given a title such as *user-submitted order*. Collecting and organizing **domain events** makes up the bulk of an event storming session, and it is these that we will start with in the workshop.

A *domain event* will result in **artifacts** and **schemas** being produced. These include files, database records, and messages that might be displayed in a user interface.

A *domain event* can also trigger **policies**, which are decisions that can branch a workflow. For example, we would validate that the user has included at least one product in their submitted order. The outcome will be *true* or *false*, resulting in two possible branches in the workflow. The result of a *policy* could be to generate a new *command* or interact with a *system*.

During the workshop, we will typically use a different color or pattern sticky note for each component. Patterns have the advantage of making the workshop more inclusive for those with color blindness. The style of each sticky note is arbitrary and typically driven by product availability. If a virtual tool is used to conduct the workshop, any style can be picked; just ensure each one is unique and easily identifiable. For this book, the images need to be grayscale, so I have used unique variants of gray backgrounds with white or black text to identify each component.

We will be using a simple ecommerce website as our example project for this section, and the different components we use will reflect that use case, with actions such as **Place order** and **Process payment**.

Event Storming Steps

Step 1: Identify the *domain events*.

The first step to event storming is identifying the *domain events*.

Here, we want all workshop participants to consider the different workflows in the application that they are familiar with. Then, they should contribute the steps in those workflows they are aware of. These steps are what we call *domain events*. For example, in an image upload workflow, the high-level steps might be the following:

1. Upload image.

2. Validate image format and size.

3. Store image.

4. Resize image.

5. Create a thumbnail from image.

6. Notify user that image upload has completed.

Domain events are written with verbs in the past tense and generally describe an action. For this book, we will be using a very light-gray background with black text for *domain events*, as seen in Figure 2-13.

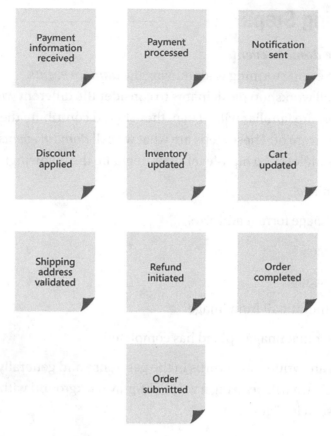

Figure 2-13. *Examples of domain events*

The focus of the first part of the workshop is to collect as many *domain events* as possible. Let the group discuss and brainstorm as it can help in remembering application details, but limit any analysis of individual events as that will distract from collection. We will get to analysis, ordering, and removing duplicates in the next step.

Step 2: Sequence the *domain events*.

Once we have our collection of *domain events*, we sequence them from left to right or top to bottom in chronological order to reflect end-to-end workflows, as seen in Figure 2-14.

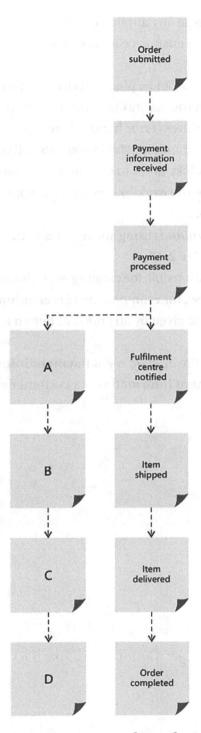

Figure 2-14. *Sequence the domain events in chronological order*

We should remove or merge any duplicate *domain events* and make the terminology consistent in all sticky notes to ensure a common understanding between the participants.

Alternate and parallel flows can be placed above or below the main workflow. For this exercise, we will focus on the *happy* flow, where we have a successful flow of events from start to finish. We will address error handling in a later step.

There is a good chance that missing *domain events* will come to light during this step. Those can be added to new sticky notes to complete the sequence. This step will result in a structured overview of all of the workflows within the application.

Step 3: Identify *commands*.

Next, we identify the *commands* using sticky notes with a very dark-gray background and white text, as seen in Figure 2-15.

These are the triggers responsible for creating each *domain event*. These are written with verbs in the present tense, for example, **Customer submits order**. It can help remember that commands are given by an entity, either an actor or a system, which we will cover next.

In our example, we have the *domain event* **Payment information received**, triggered by the command **Send payment information** – a customer submitting credit card details.

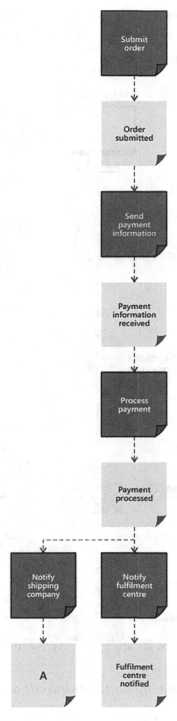

Figure 2-15. *Commands are added to the sequence*

Later, in our architecture, *commands* will usually help define an API endpoint or microservice trigger. Let's digress briefly to look at a slightly technical architecture diagram in Figure 2-16 showing that.

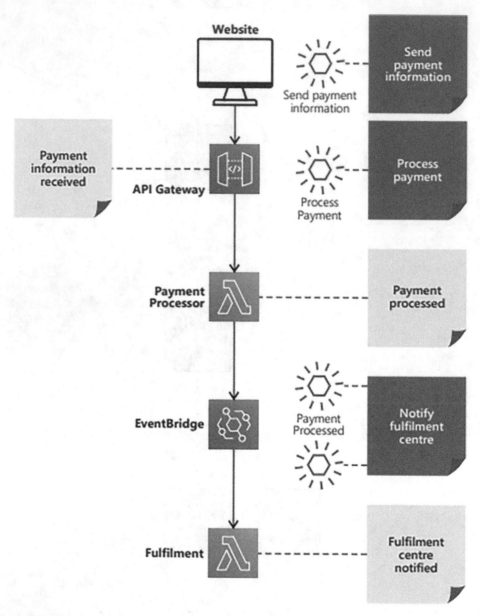

Figure 2-16. *Architecture showing how commands and events can be implemented*

Starting at the top in Figure 2-16, the customer submits their payment information to our API endpoint, which is the implementation of the *domain event* **Payment information received**. The API then issues the *command* **Process payment** to our payment processor microservice. Our microservice, which is the implementation of **Payment processed**, issues the *command* **Notify fulfilment center** to the EventBridge service. This service does exactly that, arriving at another microservice – our implementation of the *domain event* **Fulfilment center notified**.

Step 4: Identify *actors* and *systems*.

Once the commands are added to the board, we can identify the entities responsible for giving those commands.

Actors, such as customers or employees, usually produce *commands* by interacting with a user interface and clicking a button. In this example, we identified customers as *actors* responsible for submitting an order and payment information.

Systems, such as cloud services or an external payment service, can produce *commands* through scheduled events, callbacks, or when policies or actions trigger an event. We have two *systems* here, a third-party payment provider for processing credit card payments and a cloud notification service.

In our example, the *actors* are represented by a sticky note with a light-gray background and black text, while *systems* use a dark-gray background with black text. Uniquely for entities, their sticky notes are attached to *command* sticky notes, which also makes them easier to recognize in Figure 2-17.

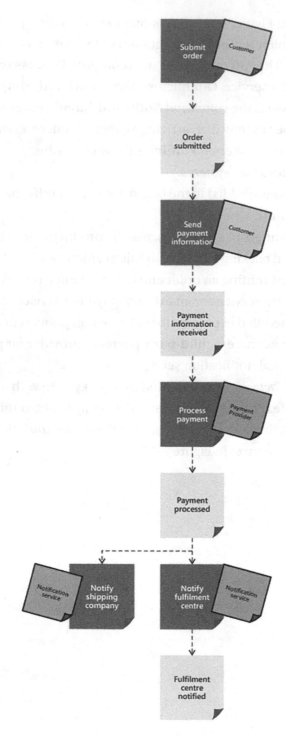

Figure 2-17. *Actors and systems are attached to commands*

Step 5: Identify *policies*.

After we have a happy end-to-end workflow, we can introduce *policies*.

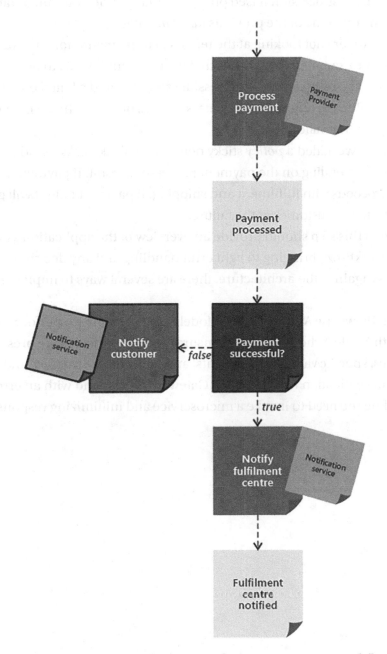

Figure 2-18. *Policies use rules to determine the next step in a workflow*

Polices are applied after a *domain event* and use rules to determine the next step in a workflow. Examples of rules that we can define include performing validation on user input, making an if-else decision based on a particular metric or input, or taking action depending on the outcome of the previous *domain event*.

At this stage, we are not looking at the technical implementation of *policies*, only the possible paths. For example, we establish that the user input needs to be validated, and we need to define the responses to a successful validation and a failed one. However, we do not need to define the required parameters, values, or format that will make up the implementation of that validation.

In Figure 2-18, we added a *policy* sticky note with a black background and white text that takes action depending on the payment processor's result. If payment is successful, the workflow proceeds with fulfilment and shipping. If payment fails, it will generate a message to inform the customer of the failure.

The output of this step should provide an overview of the application's decision logic in the various workflows, bringing to light error handling and any decision trees.

If we digress again to the architecture, there are several ways to implement *policies* in our design.

In Figure 2-19, we use API Gateway's Model Schema feature to perform user input validation. With Model Schemas, we can ensure required variables are present, the format of values, specific value requirements, and many other structure and value-based validations. If the validation fails, then API Gateway will respond with an error directly to the user, avoiding the need to invoke a microservice and minimizing response time.

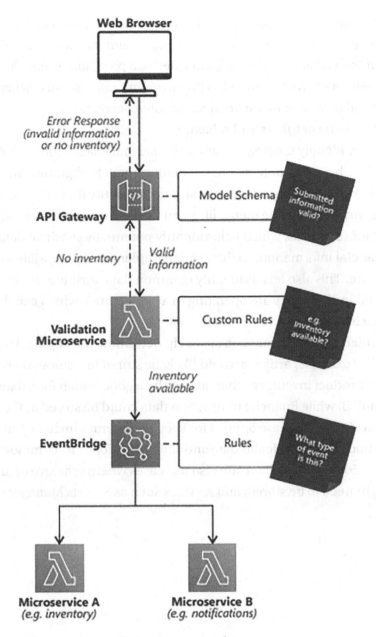

Figure 2-19. *Implementing policies in our architecture*

We can use a Lambda microservice for *policies* that require interaction with databases, other services, or more complex algorithms. In Figure 2-19, we use a microservice to check the available inventory.

95

The EventBridge service is commonly used to distribute events to one or more consumers in a Serverless application. We can implement *policies* here with filter rules to determine which consumers should be notified of a particular event. For example, a *successful* payment event will be routed to the inventory microservice, whereas a *failed* payment event will be routed to the notification microservice.

Step 6: Identify the *artifacts* and *schemas*.

In this step, we identify the *artifacts* and *schemas* that result from each domain event; these are added with a sticky note that has a medium-gray background and white text. The text is a list of bullet points, which may also help identify them in Figure 2-20.

Examples of *artifacts* include media files and documents, while *schemas* define the contents of database records, which helps identify potentially sensitive data such as personal or financial information, so that we can implement appropriate safeguards in our architecture. This also lets us identify common data attributes between domain events: this could indicate they are operating in a similar area, which can drive architectural decisions.

Defining artifacts and schemas can also help determine the appropriate cloud service to use. For example, artifacts would likely be stored in a storage service such as S3 or Glacier. Product inventory schemas may be a good match for a database such as DynamoDB, while financial transaction data could be stored in the Quantum Ledger Database. Other database options for specific schemas include Timestream for data tightly bound to a particular date and time, and Neptune, commonly used for recommendation engines. There are also use cases where sensitive data such as credentials might need to be stored, and services such as Secrets Manager should be considered.

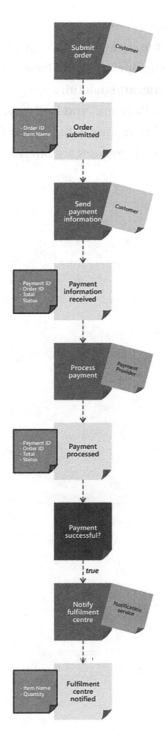

Figure 2-20. *Artifacts and schemas are generated by domain events*

Step 7: Aggregate the *domain events*.

Here, we aggregate or group the sticky notes within each workflow using nouns that define the thing that the sticky note operates on. These aggregates are what *domain events* are creating, reading, writing, and deleting.

In Figure 2-21, we have Order, Payment, and Delivery. **Order submitted** is creating an order; **Payment processed** is interacting with payment; and **Fulfilment center notified** will create a new delivery. *Aggregates* are often business entities and are typically stored in a database.

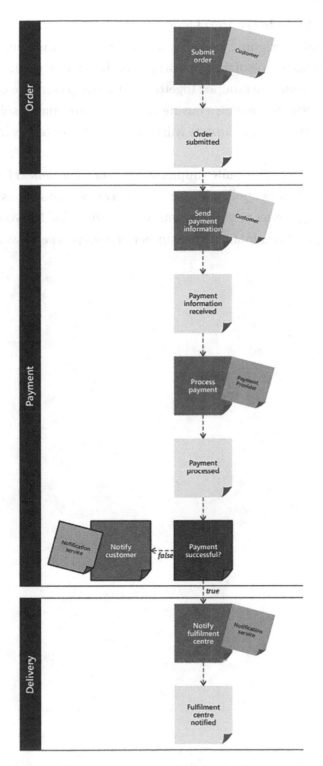

Figure 2-21. *Aggregating the components into logical groups*

Step 8: Create a *bounded context* (scope).

The last step before designing the architecture is to create the *bounded context*, which can represent the scope of the application, as shown in Figure 2-22.

Related *domain events* are grouped together, which helps remove dependencies between them. *Boundaries* separate a business process into smaller subdomains. Later, in the architecture, each *boundary* will often be represented by one or more microservices.

Our ecommerce example is quite simple, so the *bounded context* follows the *aggregates*. In more complex applications, a *bounded context* may consist of more than one *aggregate*, and *aggregates* might span multiple *boundaries*. To avoid microservices becoming too large, try to maintain a low number of *domain events* within a single *boundary*.

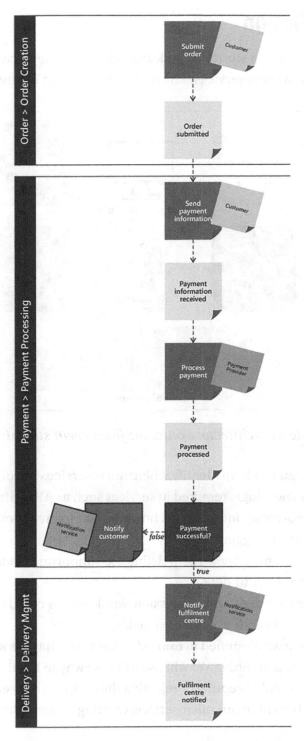

Figure 2-22. *The bounded context often represents one or more microservices*

Architecture Design

When we complete our event storming workshop, cloud architects can use the output to design the event-driven microservice architecture, as shown in Figure 2-23.

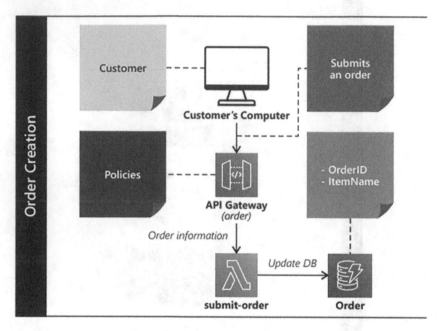

Figure 2-23. *High-level architecture outcome from event storming*

The *bounded context* can help identify where microservices are needed, and the *policies* define the business logic required in services such as API Gateway.

The *commands* provide an indication of how we want to invoke our microservices, such as via an API or event triggers.

Aggregates, artifacts, and *schemas* help define the supporting cloud services and the description and structure of our data.

Actors help define user roles and permissions, and *systems* could highlight any external connectivity that needs to be considered.

Based on what we have identified in examples, we know that the workflow starts when a customer submits an order. We will use API Gateway to handle the user input, verifying the order data and accepting or rejecting the order with an error message. Accepted orders will be sent to our microservice, creating a new order entry in our database.

Final Notes

Event storming can help identify potential problems such as bottlenecks, duplication, or missing integrations, and it can highlight opportunities for improving security, scalability, or other architectural aspects.

In the event of any dispute during the workshop, we should not go into technical details or stray from the primary goal of knowledge sharing and identifying events. Instead, we can place a red sticker on the offending sticky note and come back to it later with a more targeted group.

When designing the architecture, remember that microservices should be tight in scope. A mini event storming session for microservices that may be too large can help break them down into smaller ones.

Event storming can help identify the microservices needed to create a particular workflow within the application. However, microservices shared across multiple applications are not in this scope and should be considered in the architecture design phase.

 **Public Case Studies**

The following public case studies highlight some of the benefits organizations have seen from Serverless.

Toyota

This project is a public case study shared by AWS on their website. I was not involved in this project or with this organization in any way. The full case study can be found here: **https://aws.amazon.com/solutions/case-studies/toyota-connected/.**

Toyota is a multinational car manufacturer, selling almost 10 million cars annually. In 2018, Akio Toyoda, President of Toyota, announced his goal of transitioning Toyota from a car company to a mobility company.

Toyota's cars are equipped with sensors that constantly send data, such as engine metrics, errors, and even when doors or windows are opened. This data is analyzed and used to enhance the customer experience. Data points are collected globally from millions of connected cars. In 2020, Toyota served 18 billion transactions per month, and it was projected to reach 40 billion transactions in 2021.

Due to its need for a **cost-effective** and **scalable** architecture, Toyota decided to adopt Serverless, where scaling is fully managed and billed based on actual utilization. The objective of Toyota's plan was to create new capabilities around safety and convenience, using the data points collected to drive data services that increased customer satisfaction, as well as being compliant with privacy regulation.

When Toyota initially tried servers in the cloud, they found that the platform worked, but it was not cost-effective. An alternative approach they considered was to use spot instances. These are a type of cloud servers that are assigned to the highest bidder at any given time. This makes them less reliable, since anyone bidding more can claim them. Given these challenges with optimizing servers, they decided to adopt a Serverless approach to cloud instead, which achieved cost-effectiveness and minimized wastage.

They also opted for a *serviceful* architecture approach, favoring fully managed cloud services over developing custom code. New applications that were being developed could rely on *purpose-built* services such as Kinesis, increasing productivity and reducing maintenance. This enabled their application team to focus on building capabilities and services, delivering customer value, and less on infrastructure, maintenance, and reinventing the wheel.

As a result, since adopting Serverless, Toyota has seen its cloud operational cost drop by 70–80%, and the cloud provides a single platform where Toyota can find all the services it needs to store, manage, and derive value from the collected vehicle data.

Given the huge volume of data, fully managed services play a critical role in helping simplify their data administration and management tasks. With many overheads removed, Toyota increased its agility and innovated faster to meet customer demands.

Netflix

This project is a public case study shared by AWS on their website. I was not involved in this project or with this organization in any way. The full case study can be found here: **https://aws.amazon.com/solutions/case-studies/netflix-case-study/**.

Netflix streams videos to over 200 million users in over 190 countries. Since 2016, Netflix has fully migrated all its data centers into AWS. By restructuring systems into microservices, Netflix has successfully decoupled architecture and achieved continuous deployment for its platform, improving developers' agility and user experience.

Netflix uses many fully managed AWS services to provide its platform to customers. This includes dealing with petabytes of media data and hundreds of thousands of files changing daily. Netflix needed a way to manage its complex and changing infrastructure by improving operations, automation, monitoring, and logging. Previously, it used *polling* to monitor and react to changes. With polling, one system keeps asking another system if there has been a change. If there has, it responds. If there has not, it ends the request and asks again a short while later.

Netflix changed this approach to an *event-driven* design. With this approach, a changed system informs the environment through a broadcast that a change has happened. Other systems can then react to the broadcast. Event-driven is considerably more efficient, with lower operating costs and faster responses. We will cover event-driven architecture in more detail in Chapter 9.

Netflix was able to implement this approach in several areas. The first was in how media files are processed. When a partner uploads a new file into storage, the event automatically triggers a microservice to process the file, instead of a server constantly polling (asking) storage if there are any new files. Using the parallel processing capabilities of Lambda microservices, the video is sliced into smaller chunks and processed individually before being aggregated again once processing is completed.

Additionally, Netflix uses Lambda to determine whether data needs to be backed up when there is a change in data within the infrastructure and whether it should be moved to an off-site storage facility. When a backup is completed, the event triggers a second Lambda microservice to validate the file to ensure that the backup was completed successfully and retry or raise alarms in case of failures.

For security and conformity, Lambda helps validate the provisioning of new instances within the infrastructure using compliance and readiness rules. For instance, Lambda can check that the services have been set up correctly, and any unauthorized instances can be automatically shut down and an alert sent to the compliance team. These are *corrective controls*, as we covered earlier.

Lastly, to improve operational monitoring, Netflix leverages the events generated within the environment to create dashboards. As Netflix grows and changes are made to the infrastructure, new models and metric exceptions can be generated to adjust and capture new insights.

T-Mobile

This project is a public case study shared by AWS on their website. I was not involved in this project or with this organization in any way. The full case study can be found here: **https://aws.amazon.com/solutions/case-studies/tmobile/**.

T-Mobile is a technology company that is best known for its mobile network with more than 70 million customers. T-Mobile adopted a *Serverless-first* strategy for developing new applications, with services such as Lambda playing a key role in their mission-critical applications, including the company website and the mobile app.

With this approach, T-Mobile enabled the development team to focus on exploration and innovation rather than managing and maintaining infrastructure. Resources are better optimized and simpler to scale, and less updating and patching of operating systems and software are needed. All of this saves developers a significant amount of time and frees them up to respond to customers' requests.

Through the adoption of Serverless, costs are optimized as they are only billed based on actual utilization. On top of that, Serverless removes many time-consuming development and deployment steps, which enables new applications to enter the market faster.

One of the key benefits of Serverless is the ability for developers to quickly and easily provision new resources and experiment with them. With this in mind, the challenge for T-Mobile was to enable development teams to take this approach while ensuring they remained compliant with security, operations, and finance requirements.

T-Mobile needed a solution that

1. Encouraged the adoption of Serverless

2. Ensured compliance with organizational policies

3. Did not hamper the creativity and agility of the developers

T-Mobile's answer to this challenge was for the Cloud Center of Excellence team to create Jazz, an open source platform for building, deploying, and debugging Serverless applications and websites. Jazz automates T-Mobile's operational readiness checklist, reducing development and deployment time while ensuring that the resources that are provisioned are compliant with their organizational policies.

There were potential challenges with existing bespoke approaches, including problems with auditability, ensuring oversight of the configuration, and provisioning of IT resources, alongside cost overruns due to cost-inefficient configurations. There were also issues with oversight – where cloud resources were provisioned and used without control – and service discovery, where it was difficult to locate and reuse existing services.

The following are some of the AWS services that T-Mobile used to power Jazz.

First, Kinesis is used as a scalable data pipeline to collect, process, and analyze streaming data from Jazz integrations such as code repositories and deployment pipelines.

CloudFormation templates are used to standardize, automate, and provision resources in a reliable and consistent manner.

Jazz responds to events within the architecture using Lambda microservices and can perform tasks such as sending a Slack notification or updating a database.

Lastly, Elasticsearch, although not Serverless, is a fully managed service that can be used for log analytics, full-text search, and application monitoring. With Jazz, T-Mobile can provision a new API within minutes, using a simple web interface to select and configure the resource. Behind the scenes, CloudFormation templates ensure that provisioned resources, such as Lambda and API Gateway, are compliant with organizational policies.

Adopting a Serverless approach with Jazz has enabled T-Mobile to now build and deploy steps for developers that are 90% faster. The use of code templates and live feedback helps reduce the number of errors when provisioning resources. This increases developer productivity.

There are significant operational cost savings, as Serverless is billed based on actual usage and eliminates most of the maintenance requirements for infrastructure. In addition, applications created are more robust and stable, which greatly improves the customer experience and feedback.

CHAPTER 3

Finances

Any sufficiently advanced technology is equivalent to magic.

—Sir Arthur C. Clarke, Writer

Total Cost of Ownership (TCO)

In this context, the Total Cost of Ownership (TCO) looks at all costs and cost-offsets incurred in creating and operating an application. These include

- Non-technical costs such as staffing overheads, training, and marketing

- Non-technical offsets such as government and industry grants

- Technical costs such as development, maintenance, and cloud operational costs – including easily overlooked costs such as storage and data transfer

- Technical offsets such as the cloud's free tiers and volume discounts

With a TCO, we seek to understand the full cost of a proposed solution, and it enables fair comparison between different proposals – especially when the architectural approach differs. For a fair comparison, it is important to take into consideration both short-term and long-term costs.

By short-term costs, we are usually referring to one-off development costs. Long-term costs typically refer to predictable recurring costs such as maintenance and cloud fees. Future updates to the application can sometimes be considered as part of long-term costs if they are predictable and required, but they will usually be viewed as a separate, future scope.

© Thomas Smart 2023
T. Smart, *Serverless Beyond the Buzzword*, https://doi.org/10.1007/978-1-4842-8761-3_3

The importance of understanding the different costs becomes apparent when comparing a server-based approach with a Serverless one. Typically, a server-based approach will have a lower short-term development cost, certainly when migrating an existing solution to cloud servers. However, the long-term maintenance and operational costs will be considerably lower with Serverless as there are no servers or operating systems to maintain and patch.

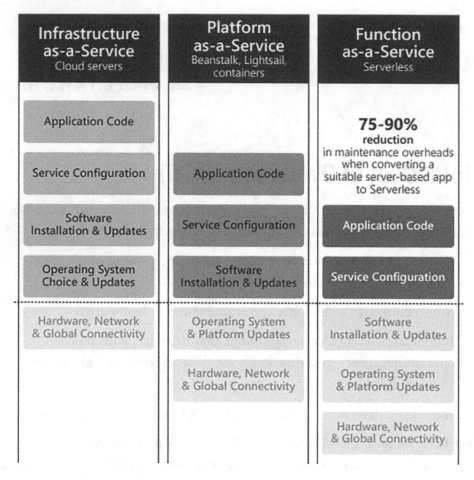

Figure 3-1. *Cloud vs. organization accountability per architecture*

Having all information for both approaches available in a TCO enables a fair comparison and transparently provides all cost-related facts for the project team to make a decision.

Figure 3-1 shows where the accountability of application development and operation between the cloud provider and the organization sits for different types of cloud architecture. This includes the operating system and software updates, monitoring, clearing temporary data, rightsizing, scaling and redundancy, and cost optimization.

With cloud servers, we manage everything except the hardware, some of the network, and connectivity. With fully managed services, the operating system and platform maintenance shifts to the cloud provider.

With Serverless, we only need to maintain microservice code and service configuration. Everything else is fully managed by the cloud provider, which saves significant time and cost. In reality, based on my experience, we typically see a 75–90% reduction in maintenance costs compared with server-based architecture.

The development cost for a Serverless solution is often higher than for a server-based equivalent, especially for teams with limited to no Serverless experience. So, if we only compare two options based on development cost, Serverless will rarely seem like the more cost-effective option.

The cloud operational cost is an important consideration when experimenting with Serverless architecture for projects. Developers find that cloud operational cost significantly differs from server-based cost estimates for three reasons:

1. With servers, it is not necessary to consider the individual functions in the code when calculating operational cost; we simply calculate a lump sum for the server. With Serverless, those functions become individual billable microservices and configured fully managed cloud services.

2. Infrastructure complexity consists of many different managed cloud services, each of which has a distinct billing model and cost parameters that need to be understood. Each parameter will need to be provided with accurate input values for the specific application.

3. Serverless cloud services are billed based on utilization metrics, such as the number of requests, request size, and request duration. Such metrics are more numerous and more complex to provide input values for than an average monthly fee for running a few servers.

The most common challenges presented by organizations in a range of industries and sizes include the following:

1. Understanding the differences between the two architectures and how the estimation approach needs to change to account for those differences.

2. Estimating complex architecture designs with many components that may not even have been designed yet, because the design effort will take time and a ballpark budget may need to be established first.

3. Beyond operational cost estimation, how can we make a fair cost comparison between the two architectures when deciding on the right approach for a new project?

I will answer all of these questions in this section, as well as looking at approaches for effective cost management for our cloud environments and applications.

The Value of Paying for Utilization

As we touched on in Chapter 1, a big advantage of Serverless is far less wastage - especially when it comes to operational budget. With a server-based application, capacity margins need to be maintained on the servers to handle sudden increases in activity, even when using autoscaling, as it can take at least a minute to launch another server.

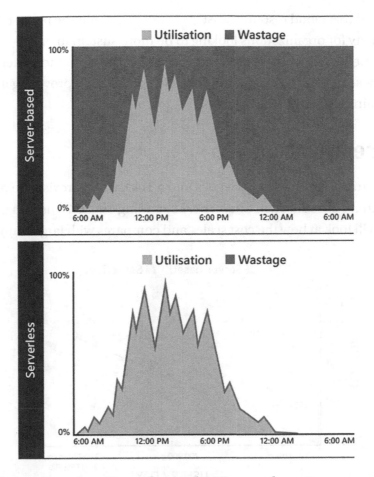

Figure 3-2. *Server-based vs. Serverless utilization and wastage*

Figure 3-2 compares wastage for server-based vs. Serverless utilization for a typical single–time zone business application. Predictably, it is busy during office hours and less busy in the middle of the night. In the server-based example, the light-gray area is billable utilization. The dark-gray area is where the application is available, but nobody is using it. So we can consider it wastage.

With Serverless architecture, that wastage is just a thin gray line. There are always some margins, but these are automatically managed by the cloud provider and considerably less in comparison with the server-based chart.

With Serverless, we pay only for what we use; there is very limited wastage. For example, we pay for the storage we are using, not the total space available for storage. We pay per-millisecond runtime of a microservice responding to an actual request and not for a server running 24/7, even when there are no requests.

Keep in mind that cloud resource wastage is not just about the budget; it is also a waste of electricity for organizations looking to be more sustainable. This has been made more transparent by AWS's new carbon metrics, which can be found under "Billing" in the console. These metrics take 3 months to collect data before providing insights that show how sustainable our infrastructure is.

Scaling User Numbers

Before we get into the specifics of what goes into a TCO, we will revisit the registration form example that I introduced in Chapter 1. Expanding on the 20 users a day it was expecting, we will look at how the cost scales and compares with larger numbers of users.

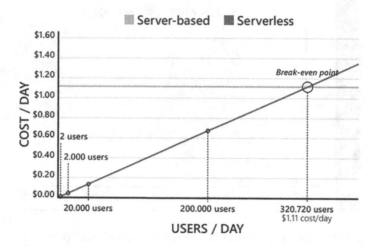

Figure 3-3. *Finding the break-even point by increasing users*

In Figure 3-3, I have charted the costs of the server-based approach – the dotted line in the chart – and the Serverless approach, the solid line, against an increasing number of users on the horizontal axis. The cost on the vertical axis shows us how the cost of the two architectures compares as user numbers increase.

While the server-based cost remains the same – the two fixed servers that we are using – the Serverless cost will increase with the number of users.

The theoretical break-even point on the top right is just over 320,000 users. However, this $1.11 for the server-based version does not tell the full story. Consider the Total Cost of Ownership, such as maintaining and patching the operating system and software on the servers, and the effort required for configuring, operating, and monitoring redundancy, backups, and scaling.

On that point, consider if the two tiny servers we used in this example would even be able to handle over 320,000 users a day. In this architecture, the servers would likely need to scale in size or quantity to meet the peaks, making the server-based solution also increase in cost with more users.

So we can see that, even when scaling to accommodate far larger numbers of users, Serverless often remains the more cost-effective option.

Per-User Cost

Another difference between the budgets of the two architecture approaches lies in the per-user costs.

Server underutilization by a handful of early users makes the per-user cost very high during development and when an application is first launched. In the server-based chart in Figure 3-4, we see that, after the initial peak, the cost per user will decrease over time as user numbers and utilization increase.

Assuming some form of revenue or other value per user, initially, the per-user cost does not match the derived value. This means the organization needs to bear the cost of the underutilized servers during development and in early production when the application only has a few users. Because of this, there is a lot of pressure on the application team to increase user numbers as fast as possible so an application can become cost-effective.

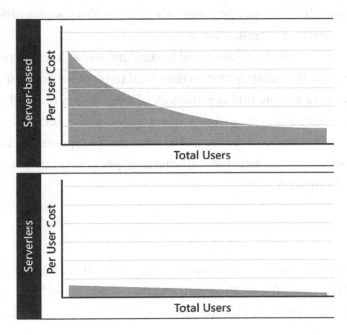

Figure 3-4. *Per-user cost comparison over time*

Per-user cost over time with Serverless is more linear because we are paying for actual utilization. If an application starts with ten users, we are billed for the resources needed for ten users. When our user base grows to 100,000, we pay for 100,000 – usually without the application team needing to change anything.

Not needing up-front operational cost investment is one of the reasons that Serverless is so attractive to bootstrapped startups and innovation teams running many experiments in the cloud. With Serverless, any slight decrease in the cost per user over time would be due to the application team optimizing the application, volume discounts, or cloud service fee reductions.

The Cost to Develop Serverless

When building a new solution, the first focus of a TCO will typically be on the development effort. This section looks at the cost of development for Serverless and server-based applications. To get relevant market data, I did some market research and will provide a breakdown and my views of the results.

The Research

The goal of the research was to obtain proposals from vendors across different regions for both a server-based and a similar Serverless project.

I collected 160 responses from comparable vendors across four regions. The majority of responses were from the Asian region as they tend to be more active on outsourcing websites. It is important to note that the majority of the vendors had little to no previous experience with Serverless. Because of this, the statistics presented here are biased toward those types of vendors. However, this is an accurate representation of the market at this time, so it provides a realistic view of what to expect currently when requesting proposals for a Serverless project.

The Project

The task was to develop a user registration form for an event. The user would access this through a web browser, fill out the form, submit it, and finally be presented with a *"Thank you"* message. In the back end, basic data validation is performed, and the submitted data is sent by email to the site admin. The design was not important, and only a minimal UI was needed to test that the solution worked.

Two separate controlled environments were specified, and different deliverables were expected:

Serverless

Environment:

- AWS Lambda + API Gateway + SES (back end), S3 (front end)

- *Back-end language*: NodeJS 12

- *Front-end language*: Simple HTML/CSS/JS

Deliverables:

1. CloudFormation or CDK to configure the required services in AWS

2. Source code for the Lambda microservice

3. GUI source code for deployment to S3

4. Basic documentation describing the included files

Server-based

Environment:

- Ubuntu 18 running on an AWS EC2 micro-instance

- *Back-end language*: NodeJS 12 or PHP 7

- *Front-end Language*: Simple HTML/CSS/JS

Deliverables:

1. Instructions for setting up the server with the required packages. This should include documentation and a zip with any configuration files for the required packages (to be copied to the server on setup).

2. Zipped code to be deployed to the server's public folder (front and back ends).

3. Basic documentation describing the included files.

For the following report, I did not include or consider the operational or maintenance cost of running either solution - this will be discussed in the next section. Here, I focus only on the development cost that can be expected from an average vendor at this time.

I gave each vendor the option to bid for both or just one of the projects. For those bidding on Serverless, I noted whether or not they had previous experience with Serverless projects.

Comparing the Estimates

In the following graph, across all proposals, a majority estimated the cost of Serverless to be higher than the server-based approach. The average cost for the Serverless project was $449.32, while the server-based project was $380.60, both shown in Figure 3-5.

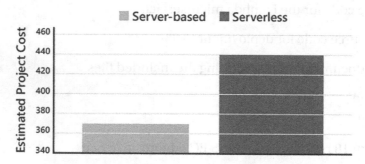

Figure 3-5. *Development cost comparison between server and Serverless*

This higher average cost for Serverless is due to many of the vendors having little or no experience with Serverless development. They were less confident in their ability to estimate such a project and generally expected a considerable portion of the work to be outside of their comfort zone.

For the vendors that I confirmed had Serverless experience, the Serverless proposals were lower than or the same as the server-based proposal. The average estimate from Serverless-experienced vendors was $371.43.

The higher Serverless estimates from vendors with Serverless experience may be related to experienced Serverless developers charging a premium. At the time of writing, average web application developer salaries range from 60k to 110k per year, while average Serverless application developer salaries are in the 90–160k range.

With vendors who shared their hourly rates in the proposal, the rates for the Serverless version were noticeably higher than those for the server-based version from the same vendor or from other vendors in the same region.

I spoke with some of the vendors that had less or no experience with Serverless but had still provided an estimate. I summarized the following responses with my opinions based on those discussions:

- Some vendors were quick to indicate that Serverless requires additional effort for API, network, storage, and many other components that need to be separately configured in the cloud.

- *My view: While there are more services to configure compared with a server-based solution, an experienced Serverless developer will have automated and templated most of these configurations using DevOps tools such as CloudFormation or CDK.*

- Many vendors indicated that a Serverless version would have to be developed from scratch, and they expected and built in a margin to accommodate their developer's learning curve.

- *My view: Experienced Serverless developers will build up a collection of reusable templates, tools, and microservices that can be applied to new projects to reduce effort and cost over time.*

- Others pointed out that deploying a Serverless solution takes many more steps than a server-based solution. They argued that this type of deployment would take more time than deploying a server.

- *My view: While true that there are additional steps, these are there for a reason (testing, quality control, etc.), and they can be fully automated using DevOps tooling. This argument suggests that they do not have, or are not aware of, the automated pipelines that can be built for this.*

Development Time

With the server-based project, I typically saw an equal amount of time go toward setup/deployment and development. With experienced Serverless developers, the development was 80–90% and setup and deployment only 10–20% of the total cost.

In summary, I concluded the following:

- It is still challenging to find vendors experienced in Serverless development, and we need to ask vendors what their level of experience is before asking for a proposal.

- Those that do have the experience will be able to develop Serverless projects faster and with automated deployment and testing strategies that are less prone to mistakes and downtime.

- Serverless can be a cost-effective solution requiring less effort, but the actual cost will always be driven by market forces such as salaries and how cutting-edge a given technology is.

 # The Cost of Migrating Applications

There are three approaches to migrating a server-based application from on-premises into the cloud. Only the last approach is relevant for those considering migrating an application from cloud servers to Serverless.

Rehost, also called lift-and-shift, refers to migrating an application with minimal changes. Typically, the cloud servers will be scoped based on the size of the on-premises servers, and minimal, if any, managed cloud services are used. For example, databases will be self-managed on a cloud server, and storage will be kept on a server or, at best, a shared network disk. This option is often chosen to minimize the initial up-front costs of migration, avoid complex changing and testing of code, and migrate as fast as possible. A common situation demanding this approach is data center evacuation, where an enterprise needs to exit a data center before a given deadline.

The challenge of this approach is that the migrated applications tend to be more expensive to run in the cloud than they are on-premises. There are several reasons for this, and it is important to do an up-front evaluation and estimate to avoid nasty surprises.

On-premises servers tend to be provided based on *availability* rather than application *needs*. Without optimizing the cloud server requirements for what the application *needs*, the provisioned cloud servers are vastly overpowered. In addition, not using autoscaling in the cloud means the application will need the overpowered servers running 24/7 instead of using smaller base servers and adding or removing scaling servers to support the application's needs at any given time. These inefficiencies result in being billed for considerable idle time and unused cloud server resources.

Managed services tend to be more cost-effective than self-managed services, certainly when including the cost of maintenance. For example, the managed database service RDS will be more cost-effective than managing a database on a cloud server, and the storage service S3 will be more cost-effective than using server storage or a shared network disk.

Replatform is similar to rehost in that it will remain a server-based application in the cloud. However, an effort is made to optimize the server architecture for the cloud as much as possible or at least within the available budget. Some strategies considered here are to use managed services such as RDS for databases and S3 for storage. Autoscaling should be implemented and server types optimized for the application needs and autoscaling.

The challenge with replatforming an application is that the architecture changes require at least configuration and often code changes to the application. Some applications might not be able to support such changes at all, in which case the migration will need to revert to a rehost approach. Application changes require time and budget, but this is usually justified by a considerably lower operational cost and burden, and a break-even point can often be reached within just a few months.

Rebuild is as it sounds; the application will be rebuilt from scratch. Usually, a modern architecture such as containers or Serverless is used, as there would be limited value in rebuilding an application for servers compared with replatforming it – unless the application is more than a decade or so old and considerable optimization can be made to the code or the rebuild is also intended to change and add to the application's functionality.

The challenge with a rebuild is the often considerable effort, cost, and risk involved in building and testing an application from scratch, though, in some cases, this might be a new version of a third-party application rather than the organization developing code from scratch. In the long term, the operational cost and maintenance effort of a rebuild can be significantly lower compared with both the rehost and replatform approaches for the same application.

The Cost of Maintenance and Operations

First, let me define what I mean by *maintenance and operations* so we are on the same page.

Maintenance (M)

1. Maintaining the hardware stack needed to keep a given solution online and available – replacing components, keeping additional gear on hand, etc.

2. *Maintaining the operating systems of servers*: This includes hardening for security, monitoring, applying security patches as soon as possible, and major upgrades to the latest supported version every couple of years.

3. *Software updates and patches*: All software running on a server should be monitored and new patches applied as soon as possible. Major version updates are often also a good idea to apply but may have much more impact on a solution requiring code changes. Both typically involve applying the update in a dev environment, testing it with the solution, and then deploying to production once everything checks out.

4. Monitoring and potentially clearing cache, temporary files, and logs and general application maintenance.

Operations (O)

1. Staff and equipment cost for maintenance

2. Space/utility costs

3. Operating system and/or software licenses

4. Network/connectivity management and costs

5. Cybersecurity planning, auditing, and monitoring

6. Supporting service costs

Hardware (M) and space and utility (O) costs are only relevant if an organization is managing its own data center or shared rack space. These are generally not applicable to cloud-based solutions.

Operating system and software maintenance (M) and licenses (O) are relevant to server-based solutions. While we may be able to avoid license costs if using open source products, we still need to track them to ensure we are not breaking the open source license agreements. There are tools and services that can automate and help with this, such as Black Duck.

Serverless does not require operating system upgrades (M) or licenses (O) because the operating system will be fully managed and the responsibility of the cloud provider. Software upgrades (M) and licenses are similarly not relevant in a Serverless environment except for some Software-as-a-Service products such as Amazon QuickSight.

Some managed services, such as Lambda, do update their supported programming languages from time to time, and older versions of a language may be phased out. In this case, any microservices using the older language version will need to be upgraded before they can be deployed again. This can require some work to update the code, especially if the microservices are large and have many included libraries that need to be upgraded too.

Application maintenance (M) really depends on the application, but in most cases, we can design an application that will not need it. Things like logs can be managed and cleaned automatically both in a server and a Serverless environment.

Network and connectivity costs (O) and other supporting service costs (O) are relevant to both server and Serverless solutions, but the billing model will be a bit different.

In short, a secure server-based solution will have an unavoidable maintenance cost, while the cost of a well-designed Serverless application can realistically be zero without compromising quality or security. In real-world situations, a 75–90% reduction in maintenance costs can be expected when comparing a server-based solution with Serverless. Serverless is not *one-size-fits-all*, so hybrid solutions are more common than fully Serverless, and cost optimization will vary considerably between different solutions.

Estimating the Cloud Operational Costs

In this section, I am referring only to the costs billed by the cloud provider or, in some cases, billed by a third-party tool that is part of our solution. I do not include staff or other internal costs here. Knowing these costs up front is vital in determining the right operating budget and business model for an application. Investors or stakeholders will also expect these numbers to be accurate so that an ROI can be calculated.

With server-based applications, estimates are based on the quantity and size of the servers. It's fairly straightforward to calculate a monthly expected cost if we have this information.

One way to ascertain the correct server size is with a stress test, which simulates an increasing number of users interacting with the application server. The resulting metrics can provide a rough indication of the total number of users the server supports before it slows down and eventually crashes. If more users are expected, a larger server will be required, and the stress test is run again to confirm it.

Determining the ideal quantity of servers is a matter of balancing server size, expected sudden spikes of users, autoscaling speed, and other metrics that we won't get into here. Starting with a server in each availability zone is easier and generally accepted as best practice.

In Figure 3-6, we have determined that we need two T3 Xlarge servers for the application and another two of the same for the database.

	Estimates Based On	Per-User Estimates
Servers	**Type and quantity of servers:**	**Rough guesstimates:**
	T3.Xlarge ($0.2112) × 4 = $0.84/hour × 24hours × 30days = $608/month (+10%)	$608 can support 10,000–15,000 users, so approx. $0.06–$0.04/user/month *at capacity*.
Serverless	**Requests/execution time/ request size/storage**	**Precise and as accurate as the information provided:**
	LRx1000 − LFreeTier + LET × 300 ms × 128 MB + LET × 300 ms × 256 MB + APIGWR 1000 + DDBW × 500 + DDBR × 2000 + CFASIA × 30 GB − CFFreeTier + S3S × 250 MB − S3FreeTier =????	1 user (of persona A) = $0.04/month

Figure 3-6. *Estimating server vs. Serverless projects*

The T3 Xlarge server costs just over 21 cents per hour. We multiply that by four to get a total cost of 84 cents per hour. We can then multiply that by 24 (hours) and again by 30 (days) to get an approximate monthly average cost of $608.

The server cloud operating cost will often be the bulk of the cost for a server-based application. Supporting services are a fraction of that, so we can add a small margin to the total to cover them – 10% in the Figure 3-6 example. Storage and data transfer costs will depend on the nature of the application, but we can ignore that for now, as we can assume it will be the same for the Serverless application.

On the right side of Figure 3-6, we look at *per-user* estimates. If these are even possible, they tend to be based on a percentage of the calculated server cost. As a result, these are not very accurate and typically presented in ranges of users. In this example, our stress test has indicated that the two servers can support 10,000–15,000 users. We divide the average monthly cost of $607 by the user range to get a per-user cost range of $0.04–0.06.

In the bottom row of Figure 3-6, we have a Serverless approach where estimates are based on fine-grained utilization metrics. Examples include request quantity, request duration, request size, and the amount stored or transferred. Each service in the architecture will have its own set of relevant metrics, volume discounts, free tiers, and other modifiers on the different utilization metrics.

Serverless architecture consists of many services, so the idea of *supporting services* does not exist when it comes to budget. A Serverless estimate includes many values and subtotals, so no cost will usually be considered unimportant or ignored. As such, there are far more parameters to consider, as seen in Figure 3-6.

Per-user estimates for Serverless can be created the same way but using per-user input values, typically for each type of persona, instead of totals. These estimates can achieve the same level of precision as the total estimates, and, for billable solutions, they can be essential in creating ideal price plans and determining the business model for the application.

The challenge with Serverless really lies in collecting the many parameters needed for an accurate estimate and providing accurate input values for the parameters. However, if those are complete and correct, Serverless estimates can be highly accurate and make it far easier to plan operational budgets and manage expectations.

 ## Collecting the Input Data for an Estimate

There are three categories of parameters that need to be collected: business, technical, and pricing.

Business Parameters

Business parameters are typically provided by the product owner or similar business role. They can be defined based on statistics from existing applications or market research. The main difference with Serverless is that *details* are far more important.

A simple *total expected users* is usually insufficient to get accurate estimates; instead, we need to create personas of the different *types* of users and their behavior and establish the ratio between those types. For example

- User type A uses the application once a week to read data and generate a report. There are 800 type A users per month.

- User type B uses the application several times a day to read and write data. There are 200 type B users per month.

Technical Parameters

Technical parameters are provided by the application team. This can be difficult, especially for teams with limited Serverless experience. It can also be difficult to establish technical parameters when it's still early in the project timeline and there are no detailed requirements available yet.

Three approaches can be taken to find the technical parameters, ranging from *low effort–low accuracy* to *high effort–high accuracy*.

Option 1 is to have reference architectures similar to the planned application that can be used to determine the most likely parameters to include. Such architectures may be found internally if Serverless projects have been delivered in the past or externally from public sources, AWS, or cloud consultants.

	Payment Processor	CRUD Operations	Calling API
Description	Lambda to handle transactions *(credits, debits, and other business logic)* and push status notifications to end-user devices	Executing three DynamoDB calls within a single request	Executing a single API call to an external service
Requests	1 million per day	1 million per day	5 million per day
Memory	1.5 GB (1536 MB)	0.5 GB (512 MB)	0.5 GB (512 MB)
Duration	5 seconds	50 ms	150 ms
TOTAL COST:	$3756.00 per year	$18.50 per year	$217.50 per year

Figure 3-7. *Lambda use case examples for quick ballpark estimates*

Figure 3-7 includes three examples of common Lambda use cases.

1. A Lambda payment processor where each execution runs for 5 seconds. This is quite slow for a Lambda microservice but not uncommon when interacting with complex third-party systems such as credit card processors. It will cost about $3756 a year.

2. A simple API handler with an attached database and no external integrations. Expecting 1 million requests per day, this use case will cost about $18.50 a year.

3. Lastly, a simple proxy API to execute requests with an external service 5 million times per day. Given it only needs 150 ms, the third-party is likely a modern API possible on the same AWS network. This use case will cost just over $217 per year.

These are very basic examples for the purpose of this book. Realistically, full application estimates will be needed as case study examples for cost estimation. As these are harder to find publicly, it is definitely worth ensuring that all internal Serverless projects are documented as a case study with the technical parameters and operational cost information for future reference.

Either way, these examples can provide low-effort ballpark estimates for Serverless projects in the very early stages, especially when it might not yet be justified to spend time designing the full architecture.

In **Option 2,** experienced teams can usually mock up a quick high-level architecture based on a limited project description. This should be sufficient to provide the technical inputs needed for an approximate initial estimate.

Option 3 concerns less experienced teams or highly complex applications. In this case, it will be unavoidable to first design the detailed architecture diagram. This can be a time-consuming process, including creating proof of concepts if any of the requirements are unclear.

Once the technical parameters are identified, we link the persona behaviors to the parameters to determine the most likely values. For example, the 800 type A users read data once per week. That might translate to the following technical parameters and their values:

- *One* API request

- *One* microservice request

- *One* database request

- *200 ms* microservice runtime

- *100 KB* of data transferred via the Internet

Each of these technical parameters is linked to a pricing parameter, and the *value* tells us by how much we need to multiply the pricing parameter.

Pricing Parameters

The last parameter type is pricing. Documented on the cloud provider's service pages or provided by their pricing API, these parameters are relatively easy to find once the relevant technical parameters have been identified. Depending on the service, pricing parameters can include

- Cost per GB of storage

- Cost per request (or per million requests)

- Cost per duration (per millisecond, second, or hour)

- Cost per GB of data transferred

- Possibly tiered pricing for the preceding one depending on configured resources such as memory

- Possibly tiered pricing based on volume, such as total stored or total runtime

- Potentially free tiers to consider

It is important to note any free tiers mentioned on the pricing pages. Free tiers can apply either to all accounts or just to new ones for up to 1 year. For example, many services include some free storage or requests before they start billing. It is not uncommon for these free tiers to cancel out most or even all of the cloud bill in the early days of a new application.

Free tiers typically reduce the technical parameter values, not the individual fees. For example, Lambda has a free tier for *1 million requests per month*. So, in our earlier example, 1 million should be deducted first from the total monthly value of the technical parameter in our example. The standard microservice request *fee* is then multiplied by the remaining value, if it is above zero.

Besides these fixed pricing parameters, there may be other fixed parameters, such as service limits imposed by the cloud provider or limits configured in the application. For example, users might be limited to storing a maximum of 2 GB of data in their profile. It will be important to factor such limits into the estimate as they can apply a ceiling to the potential cost of each user.

Service Pricing

Let's look at the pricing parameters of some popular cloud services. All pricing is in USD and for AWS services in the Singapore region.

	Free Tier (Always Free)	
Lambda Cost (July 2022)	1 million free requests/month	400,000 GB-seconds of compute time/month
	Requests (Monthly)	**Memory (Monthly)**
	$0.20/million requests	$0.0000166667/GB-second
	Compute Savings Plans	
	Commit to a consistent amount of usage measured in $/hour for a 1 - or 3-year term to save up to 17%.	

Assuming a Lambda microservice with 512 MB (0.5 GB) of memory, receiving 3,000,000 requests/month, and running for 400 ms (0.4 seconds) each time
Request Cost
3,000,000 requests – 1,000,000 requests (free tier) = 2,000,000 requests 2,000,000 requests × $0.20/million = **$0.40**
Compute Cost
3,000,000 requests × 0.4 seconds = 1,200,000 compute seconds 1,200,000 compute seconds × 0.5 GB memory = 600,000 compute GB-s 600,000 compute GB-s – 400,000 compute GB-s (free tier) = 200,000 GB-s 200,000 GB-s × $0.0000167/s = **$3.34**
Total Cost: $0.40 + $3.34 = *$3.74*

Figure 3-8. *Lambda service fees (July 2022)*

Lambda has a free tier that provides 1 million free requests and 400,000 GB-seconds of compute time per month. Let's explain that *GB-second* metric first. It means **1** second of execution with **1** GB of memory. However, Lambda can be configured with 128 MB up to 10 GB of memory. If we configure the Lambda with **1** GB of memory, **1** second of execution will be charged the fee noted in Figure 3-8. If we configure the Lambda with **512 MB** of memory, the fee noted in Figure 3-8 will give us **2 seconds** of execution time, and if we configure it with **2 GB** of memory, the fee noted will give us **half** a second of execution time.

After the free tier, the request fee is 20 cents per million requests and seventeen-thousandths of a cent per GB-second. For organizations generating a high enough volume of usage, a compute savings plan can be used to save up to 17% on these costs.

As an example, we have a Lambda with **512 MB** of memory configured, **3 million** requests a month, and an average runtime of **400 milliseconds** per request.

First, requests. We can deduct the 1 million free tier from the 3 million requests leaving 2 million billable requests at 20 cents per million. So a total cost of 40 cents.

Then, request duration. Our microservice only has 512 MB of memory, so we can halve the runtime to 600,000 to give us GB-seconds. Converting our technical parameter value to GB-seconds makes it easier to calculate the free tier. Deduct the 400,000 GB-second free tier, leaving 200,000 billable GB-seconds. Multiply by the per-Gigabyte-second cost to get the request duration total of $3.34.

Add the *requests* total and the *request duration* total to get a total cost of $3.74 for this Lambda microservice example.

S3 Class	Usage	Retrieval Time	Min. Billable Size	Min. Billable Period	Additional Charges
Standard	General-purpose or very small files	Milliseconds	N/A	N/A	N/A
Infrequent access	Infrequently accessed data	Milliseconds	128 KB	30 days	Per GB retrieved
One-zone infrequent access	Infrequently accessed data that can be easily recreated if lost	Milliseconds	128 KB	30 days	Per GB retrieved
Glacier instant retrieval	Long-term archives accessed once per quarter	Milliseconds	128 KB	90 days	Per GB retrieved
Glacier flexible retrieval	Long-term backups and archives accessed yearly	Minutes/hours	40 KB	90 days	Per request and per GB retrieved
Glacier deep archive	Long-term, rarely accessed data	Hours	40 KB	180 days	Per request and per GB retrieved
Intelligent tiering	Unpredictable access patterns or varied throughout the data set. Automatically determines appropriate class for each item	Varied	Varied	30 days	Monitoring and automation fees per item

Figure 3-9. *S3 storage tiers overview*

Next, let's look at the technical parameters of the storage service S3 in Figure 3-9. In S3, there are different classes of storage. There is the S3 standard, S3 infrequent access, and Glacier. S3 standard is recommended for files that are constantly being accessed. Infrequent access is used when files are not frequently accessed, but immediate access is required when the file is requested. This class also has an option to store files in a single availability zone, reducing cost but slightly increasing the risk of losing files. This should only be considered if the files are easily recoverable.

Glacier is used for long-term storage, with three different options. For files that are only accessed once a quarter, Glacier instant retrieval provides retrieval times of milliseconds, whereas flexible retrieval can take up to 12 hours. Deep archive is for archival purposes when the files only need to be accessed once a year, if at all – very similar to the old tape backups. As such, and like the tapes, there is a retrieval delay of up to a few hours after the request. While the storage cost is significantly lower, infrequent and Glacier classes have an additional fee associated with retrieval requests.

S3 offers an intelligent tiering option that analyzes access patterns and automatically moves files to the most cost-effective storage option. While there is an additional cost associated with this feature, it is still a good default option for a cost-effective storage strategy in most cases.

S3 Class	Free Tier (First 12 Months)	Storage Pricing (Per Month)	Data Retrieval (Per 1000 Requests)	Data Retrieval (Per GB)
Standard		**First 50 TB:** $0.025/GB **Next 450 TB:** $0.024/GB **Over 500 TB:** $0.023/GB	N/A	N/A
Infrequent access	5 GB of storage in S3 standard storage class	$0.0138/GB	N/A	
One-zone infrequent access	20,000 GET + 2,000 PUT, COPY, POST, or LIST requests	$0.011/GB	N/A	
Glacier instant retrieval		$0.005/GB	N/A	
Glacier flexible retrieval	15GB of data transfer out/month	$0.0045/GB	**Expedited:** $12.00 **Standard:** $0.06	**Expedited:** $0.036 **Standard:** $0.012
Glacier deep archive		$0.002/GB	**Standard:** $0.12 **Bulk:** $0.03	**Standard:** $0.024 **Bulk:** $0.005

Figure 3-10. *S3 storage tiers cost overview (July 2022)*

The pricing for each of the S3 storage classes differs quite a bit as we can see in Figure 3-10. S3 standard offers a volume-tiered pricing model for data storage. Although storage pricing is lower for the infrequent access classes, we are charged an additional cost per GB of data retrieved. For the Glacier classes, we have the lowest storage pricing but the highest per-GB retrieval cost and a retrieval *request* cost. So, when comparing storage classes, the full cost over a period of time should be calculated for the expected data and its use case to ensure a fair comparison. This will include

- Recurring storage cost per GB

- Total cost of ADD, GET, and DELETE requests

- Retrieval request cost

- Retrieval cost per GB

This can get quite complex, making the intelligent tiering option even more attractive for its simplicity and automation.

Request Fees

With S3 being a storage service, there is a tendency to focus only on storage costs. All requests, such as adding or retrieving a file or changing its storage class, have an associated cost per request, regardless of the file size. For example, uploading 10 million 1 KB files will result in 10 GB of storage, costing 20 cents per month. However, the *act* of uploading these files will incur a one-time cost of $50 for the 10 million upload requests. Uploading ten files that are 1 GB each will result in the same storage cost of 20 cents per month, but the upload request cost will be less than 1 cent in this case. Because of these request costs, there is a benefit in merging or zipping large quantities of smaller files into fewer larger files.

Request fees apply to the Snowball service too. This service ships a physical drive available in several sizes to a given location. We then copy large data sets onto it from a local source before shipping the device back to AWS. The data will be securely imported into S3 in our account from the Snowball device. Renting the device for a week only costs a couple of hundred dollars. However, there are two things to remember when using this service that can significantly impact the total cost of the data import:

1. *The request cost of importing the files into S3*: Merge or zip many small ones to fewer large ones to reduce the cost, and remember to consider the cost of these requests in the cost estimate.

2. Data is imported from the Snowball device to the S3 standard class. Once there, we can move it to the desired class. When importing archive data, there may be an erroneous assumption that it will go directly to archive storage. The cost of storing the data in standard class for a few days and the cost of the requests for changing class need to be considered in the cost estimate.

Data Transfer

Data transfer charges may be one of the most confusing areas to estimate when determining an application's total operational cost. While individual service pages have information about data transfer costs, information about data transfer *between* services is often lacking.

With most server applications, we might ignore or add a small percentage margin for data transfer cost because it will usually only be a fraction of the total operational cost. However, given the high number of integrated components and the low operating cost of Serverless, data transfer can be a sizeable part of the estimate. This makes having *accurate* data all the more critical.

To understand data transfer, we need to understand how data flows between services. For example, a typical request between a microservice and a database would look like this:

1. *Source egress*: A request is sent from the microservice.

2. *Destination ingress*: The request arrives at the database service.

3. *Destination egress*: A response from the database service is sent to the microservice.

4. *Source ingress*: The response arrives at the microservice.

A high-level visual representation of this can be seen in Figure 3-11.

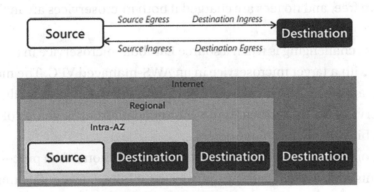

Figure 3-11. *Data flows and environments*

The environment the data transfers through is also important, as different environments have different fees associated with them, whether it's data transferring to or from the Internet, between or within regions, and between or within availability zones. Some services will add a data processing fee, and different network service configurations can impact the total cost too.

Looking at the Lambda service in Figure 3-12, we can see the many integrations and deployment options. For example, when we deploy a new Lambda microservice, we can launch it in our own VPC in the region and availability zone that we choose, or we can use the default AWS-managed VPC. While the AWS-managed VPC is easier in many ways, we have no control over the availability zone that the microservices are launched into.

Let's walk through Figure 3-12 using an example. A common design for a Serverless web application back end is API Gateway integrated with Lambda microservices.

Firstly, when API Gateway invokes a Lambda microservice within the *same* region, there is no charge for data transfer. If it's in a *different* region, the API Gateway egress data transfer will cost 9 cents per GB.

Data transfer between Lambda and most fully managed database services will be free if they are in the *same* region. Data transfer to a *different* region will incur a regional fee of 9 cents per GB for both the Lambda and database egress. Ingress is free for both.

Next, we look at data transfer between two Lambda microservices. If they are in *different* regions, the egress from the source microservice will be billable at the usual regional 9 cents per GB. Ingress and the response egress/ingress are free. If the two microservices are in different availability zones, the ingress and egress from the source microservice will be billable at 1 cent per GB. Ingress and egress on the destination microservice are free, and no fees are charged if both microservices are in the same availability zone.

Slightly more challenging is when a source Lambda microservice in a VPC communicates with a target microservice in an AWS-managed VPC. The most straightforward approach is to invoke the destination microservice directly from the source microservice. For this, the egress-to-Internet data transfer charge of up to 12 cents per GB is billable on the source egress.

Depending on the setup of our VPC, there may be additional data processing charges from components such as NAT gateways, proxies, or similar. Luckily, data transfer between Lambda and these components is free within the same availability zone. If the VPC components are in another availability zone, there will be a 1-cent charge per GB on both the egress and ingress of the source microservice - on top of any data processing charges.

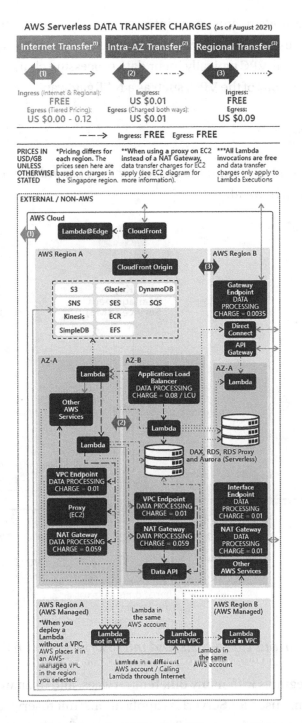

Figure 3-12. *AWS data transfer charges. Copyright Sourced Singapore*
Source: www.sourcedgroup.com/resources/aws-data-transfer-charges-for-*
server-and-serverless-architectur

Lastly, for Lambda microservice integrations, data transfer to most, if not all, other AWS services in the *same* region is completely free. However, remember that microservices *in* our VPC typically incur data processing charges for the components needed to connect *out* of the VPC, such as a NAT gateway.

Other Costs

Besides *data transfer* costs and the cost of *running* Lambda microservices, there are other costs to keep in mind.

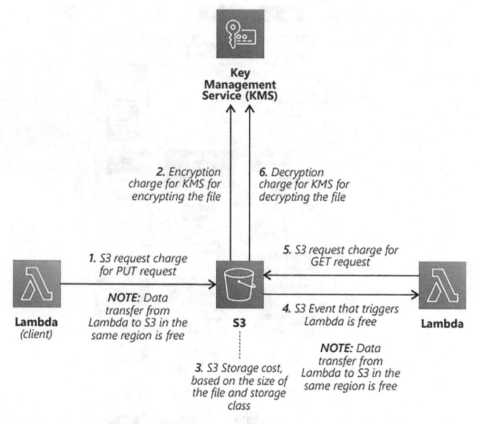

Figure 3-13. *Various cloud costs and microservices to consider*

Lambda integrates with many different services, and in an event-driven architecture, such as commonly used for Serverless applications, microservices are triggered by events in these integrated services. These events can be chargeable, depending on where they originate from.

For example, Serverless applications working with files commonly use S3 to trigger a microservice when a new file is uploaded. There are several costs associated with this as shown in Figure 3-13:

- The S3 cost for the action of adding the file.

- If S3 is configured to encrypt files – a security best practice – there will be an encryption cost from the KMS (Key Management Service).

- The S3 storage cost based on the size of the file.

The following costs need to be considered to retrieve the file for Lambda to process it:

- An S3 action cost for retrieving the file

- A KMS cost for decrypting the file so Lambda can read it

In total, these additional costs would add less than $0.0003 per file. However, these minor costs can quickly add up when processing hundreds of thousands or even millions of files. For example, for processing 100,000 files, the total additional cost would be $26 – on top of data transfer and Lambda service costs.

Architecture Examples

We will get a bit more technical next with two architecture examples. For the less technical, the intent here is not to become an architect or understand exactly what each of these services does. It can be helpful for cost estimation activities to recognize such services in architecture diagrams and find their associated technical and pricing parameters.

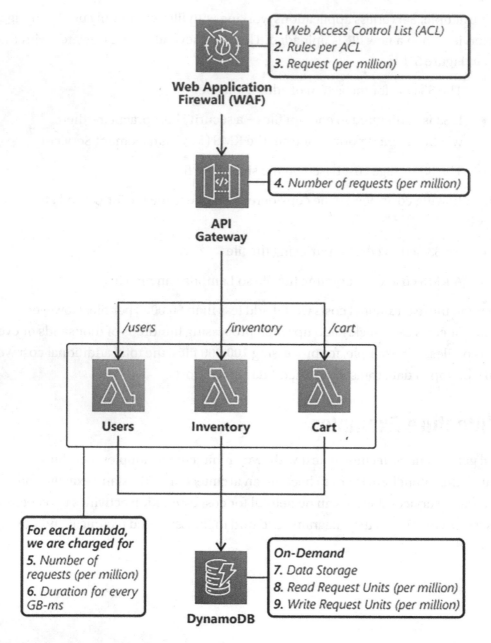

Figure 3-14. *Basic API architecture*

In Figure 3-14, we have a basic API service. At the top is Web Application Firewall (WAF) to protect the API, followed by API Gateway to handle connections. The API is backed by three Lambda microservices for handling requests and a DynamoDB database for the data.

Each service has a distinct set of pricing metrics. With WAF, we are charged for the number of Access Control Lists (ACLs), which determine how much data the WAF can process, the number of rules to enforce on incoming traffic, and the number of requests it can process. Applications with more users will need more ACLs to handle the amount of traffic.

To create a cost estimate, some of the questions we should ask the architect might be the following:

- How many ACLs and how many rules will be configured in the WAF?

- How many users are expected per month?

- How many requests per user on average?

- How much data per request on average?

- What is the memory configuration and expected average execution time for each of the three Lambda microservices?

- What is the number of database read and write queries per execution, again for each of the three microservices?

- What is the average size of each database record?

These questions address each of the technical parameters for the services included in the architecture diagram. The answers to the questions will provide the values needed for those parameters. The parameters are associated with a particular service fee, and the values determine how much we should multiply the fee by.

Figure 3-15 is a basic Step Functions architecture – a service commonly used for managing background workflows. Step Functions charges per run and per transition within a run. We also have three Lambda microservices and SNS – a service used for sending different types of notifications. Predictably, SNS charges per notification.

A key question to ask for Step Functions is the number of times the workflow will be executed per month.

Usually, we can determine the number of transactions from the architecture diagram. In this particular case, we will want to know how many member vs. non-member executions there will be, as this can impact the flow. Assuming no errors, each execution will have six transitions for members due to the *Add points* step and five for non-members.

As with the previous example, we will want to know the execution time and memory setting for each of the Lambda microservices. We can deduce the number of executions from the number of times the workflow will run per member and non-member.

Lastly, assuming SNS sends one email notification for each execution, we can calculate its cost using the provided total workflow executions per month.

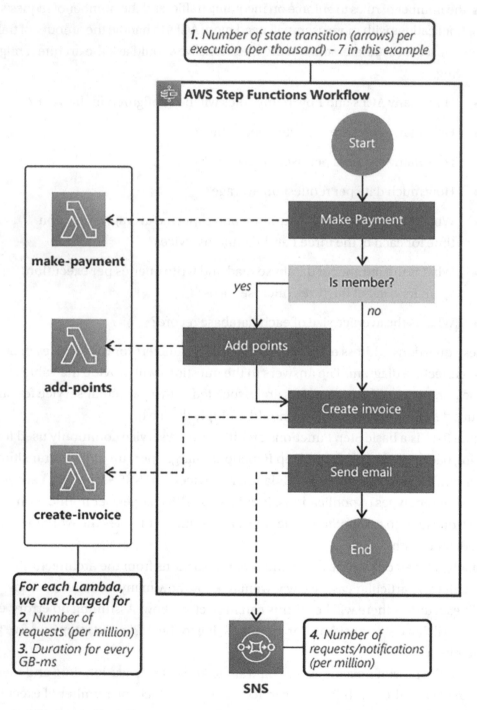

Figure 3-15. *Basic Step Functions architecture*

Calculating the Estimate

The AWS Pricing Calculator is a free tool for creating cost estimates for AWS architecture. Individual services are added to the estimate and configured for the region and relevant parameters. For a Lambda microservice, the relevant parameters will include the number of requests, average request duration, and memory allocated. The tool will then calculate the monthly cost for the microservice and add it to the estimate. Once we have added and configured all the services needed for a given application, the tool will estimate a total operational cost. The created estimates can be saved, exported, and shared with others using a unique link.

While the free tool offers a relatively straightforward way of calculating the operational costs with up-to-date service prices, the focus on technical parameters does make it difficult for non-technical team members to use and try out different scenarios. The calculator does not include all cloud costs; some data transfer costs and different forms of discounts might not be included. It also does not allow adding calculations for revenue or other costs outside of the cloud spend.

Because of these challenges, I usually prefer creating custom spreadsheets for estimates. With this approach, we can create layouts that are easier for stakeholders to work with. It also provides estimates and insights that are more personalized to the needs of the organization, project, and stakeholders. We can include costs outside of the cloud and revenue so that different pricing models and subscription fees can be tried out by stakeholders and compared with the operational costs.

The spreadsheets tend to have three tabs:

Tab 1: Calculator

This is where we can input the business parameters, for example, the number of visits per *persona* (user type) per day. Easily changeable, labeled fields enable product owners and other decision-makers to quickly try different scenarios to produce different estimates. Where appropriate, I will provide drop-down values and similar user experience improvements to make it even easier to use and place limits on the input values. This first tab is also where we show the resulting estimates.

Tab 2: Processing

This is where the intermediary calculations are done before the total is displayed on the first tab. We would include the technical parameters and their values here as these would be determined by the technical team as part of the spreadsheet creation.

Some conversion between business and technical parameters, user input values and calculation values, and some formatting of the result will be done here too. For example, we might ask for storage to be input as MB depending on the application. However, most cloud service fees operate on GB.

Tab 3: AWS service pricing

The last tab will contain the list of AWS service prices for the services we are using in this estimate. Note that with a little bit of development, the parameters on this tab can be automated using the AWS pricing API. This approach will also guarantee that pricing is always up to date.

The following is an example of a spreadsheet to estimate the cost of live streaming webinar videos on AWS. The architecture uses AWS MediaLive and AWS MediaPackage to receive the incoming stream, create three videos at different levels of quality packaged for web broadcast, and archive a copy of the original. Delivery of the streaming packages happens via the CloudFront CDN service. The architecture uses S3 for storing the archive, and it includes a feature to automatically move the file to a low-cost *deep archive* after a desired number of months.

Calculator Tab

Inputs		
Video dimensions	< 1080 × 720	
Bitrate	5	Mbps
Events/month	30	Events
Average event duration	60	Minutes
Average viewers per event	10	Viewers
Archive after	1	Month(s)
Estimates		
Streaming cost	66.82	USD/month
Storage for 1 year (cumulative)	21.23	USD/year

Figure 3-16. *Serverless spreadsheet estimate, calculator tab*

Processing Tab

Original broadcast size/hour		2250	MB/h
Minutes per month broadcast total		1800	minutes
Minutes output to streams (three levels of quality)		5400	minutes
Minutes written to archive		1800	minutes
Average MB per viewer/h (average of three quality levels)		1375	MB
Total MB streamed per viewer/m		41250	MB
Total MB streamed to all viewers/m		412500	MB
Bitrate category	< 10 Mbps		
Combined category	< 1080 × 720 – < 10 Mbps		
	Per Hour	**Total**	
MediaLive input on-demand price/h	0.1368	4.104	$/m
MediaLive output on-demand price/h	0.4068	48.816	$/m
MediaPackage price/h	0.4632568359	13.89770508	$/m
CloudFront data transfer price		56.95266272	$/m
Storage	0.05493164063	1.647949219	$/m
Archive storage	0.00439453125	0.1318359375	$/m
Total broadcast cost		66.81770508	$/m
Total viewers cost		56.95266272	$/m
1-year cumulative storage cost		21.22558594	$

Figure 3-17. *Serverless spreadsheet estimate, processing tab*

AWS Service Pricing Tab

MediaLive Input Hourly Cost for Single-Pipeline Channel		
Resolution – Bitrate	**On Demand**	
< 1080 × 720 – < 10 Mbps	0.1368	/h
< 1080 × 720 – 10–20 Mbps	0.1692	/h
< 1080 × 720 – > 20 Mbps	0.2016	/h
1080 × 720 – 1920 × 1080 – < 10 Mbps	0.27	/h
1080 × 720 – 1920 × 1080 – 10–20 Mbpsx 720	0.3384	/h
1080 × 720 – 1920 × 1080 – > 20 Mbps	0.4068	/h
MediaLive Output Hourly Cost for Single-Pipeline Channel		
Resolution – Bitrate	**On Demand**	
< 1080 × 720 – < 10 Mbps	0.4068	/h
< 1080 × 720 – 10–20 Mbps	0.5076	/h
< 1080 × 720 – > 20 Mbps	0.6084	/h
1080 × 720 – 1920 × 1080 – < 10 Mbps	0.81	/h
1080 × 720 – 1920 × 1080 – 10–20 Mbps	1.0152	/h
1080 × 720 – 1920 × 1080 – > 20 Mbps	1.2168	/h
MediaPackage Price		
Live + packaging	0.115	/GB
CloudFront Price		
Singapore	0.14	/GB
S3 Storage Price		
Standard	0.025	/GB
Archive	0.002	/GB

Figure 3-18. *Serverless spreadsheet estimate, AWS service pricing tab*

Pricing API

AWS also has a pricing API that we can query for the latest service prices. This API is not open to the Internet; it requires AWS credentials to interact with it, but this can be done from any AWS account using a user account with appropriate permissions.

A user account requirement makes it difficult to integrate directly into Excel. Instead, a microservice needs to be developed that interacts with the API, and, typically, it will simplify things by retrieving only the relevant metrics and formatting them for easier consumption. An API Gateway will also be needed before Excel can interact with it. This solution can be created in a private network and only exposed to the business network for internal use.

With the components in place, we can integrate live service pricing into Excel using the *From Web Power Query* feature. This will automatically maintain the latest pricing on the AWS service pricing tab of our estimate spreadsheets.

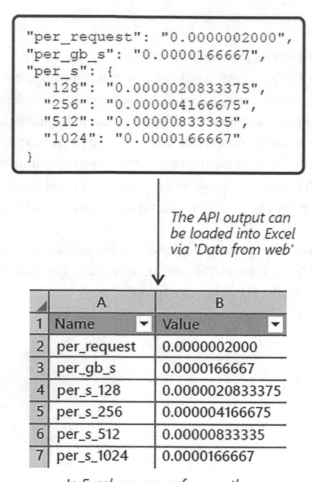

```
"per_request": "0.0000002000",
"per_gb_s": "0.0000166667",
"per_s": {
    "128": "0.0000020833375",
    "256": "0.000004166675",
    "512": "0.00000833335",
    "1024": "0.0000166667"
}
```

The API output can be loaded into Excel via 'Data from web'

	A	B
1	Name	Value
2	per_request	0.0000002000
3	per_gb_s	0.0000166667
4	per_s_128	0.0000020833375
5	per_s_256	0.000004166675
6	per_s_512	0.00000833335
7	per_s_1024	0.0000166667

In Excel, we can reference the values in our calculations

Figure 3-19. *Pricing API to spreadsheet, for automatic up-to-date pricing*

An example can be seen in Figure 3-19. At the top is the output from our API after asking for the latest Lambda pricing. This response can be easily loaded and formatted into Excel cells, as seen at the bottom. Once imported, we can reference the cells in the other tabs to perform the necessary calculations for our estimate.

Cost Management

Tracking individual users in Serverless architecture can be considerably easier and more accurate than in server architecture. Figure 3-20 demonstrates the accuracy that can be achieved and shows that we can use this capability to enable per-user actual usage or cross-departmental billing.

User	Department	Requests	Storage	Cost (USD)
John Smith	Marketing	1446	32GB	$1.42
Vivian Lo	Marketing	2623	61GB	$2.64
Mary Groen	Finance	340	120MB	$0.19
Foo Ying Toh	Legal	2663	68GB	$2.80
			TOTAL:	US $7.05

Figure 3-20. *Tracking and billing individual users in Serverless architecture*

As organizations adopt and expand their use of the cloud, it is crucial to have a suitable cost management strategy. The following case study was shared in a Serverless Guru webinar that can be viewed in full here: www.youtube.com/watch?v=L1t86yna8-M.

In 2019, Dashboard had an unexpected AWS bill of $40,000 for a single month. Given that until then their average bill was $15,000 per month, this came as quite a shock. Combing through their cloud infrastructure, they found that their architecture and provisioned cloud resources had not changed and that the bulk of the cost actually came from a single NAT gateway. This network service allows servers in a private network to communicate with the public Internet.

Upon investigation, they found that a developer had accidentally misconfigured the network, resulting in all of the organization's traffic, such as application logs, database requests, staff requests, and user requests, being sent via the NAT gateway. This service charges $0.06 for every GB of data that it processes. While that may seem low, it can add up very quickly when **all** of an organization's traffic goes through it.

As the configuration change didn't break anything nor result in any noticeable change to the architecture or application experience, no one noticed the mistake until the bill arrived a month later.

A NAT gateway is not the only service that is easily overlooked. Data transfer charges, CloudWatch log storage charges, and service request charges, such as those for S3 and KMS, can easily and quietly rack up considerable costs if misconfigured or misused.

There could be several reasons a month's cost exceeds or is expected to exceed the previous average. It could simply be the cost of success – an increase in users and, with it, resource utilization.

Server applications tend to maintain a similar budget for longer, even as the user base grows. This is due to the underutilized servers slowly becoming more utilized, but without any additional servers needing to be added, yet. Serverless applications, which are billed based on utilization, tend to be more volatile. They will immediately reflect any increase or drop in the number of users.

As illustrated with Dashboard, sudden peaks in resource utilization could be due to a misconfigured service. In this case, the application team should be made aware of the anomaly as quickly as possible, rather than waiting for the bill at the end of the month.

There could also be some form of cyberattack, where, again, the application team should be alerted as quickly as possible to minimize the cost impact.

AWS Cost Management Services

Fortunately, AWS provides us with a suite of cost management services that can help us organize and track cost and usage data, enhance control through consolidated billing and access permission, enable better planning through budgeting and forecasts, and further reduce cost with resource and pricing optimizations. Typical features include service, account, and total costs to date for the current month, predicted total cost for the month, and historical billing data.

The first service we will look at is AWS Budgets. This service can provide insight into past cloud expenditure and forecast the current month based on previous months and the month to date. We can find and analyze the cost of a particular project and configure an alert that can send a notification when cloud spend breaches, or is forecast to breach, a configured budget threshold.

An AWS Budgets *alert* configured with the maximum monthly budget the team is comfortable with will ensure they are immediately made aware of any unforeseen cost spikes and can react accordingly.

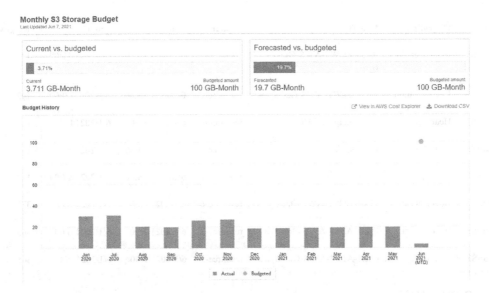

Figure 3-21. *AWS Budgets. Source: AWS console* http://aws.amazon.com/ *2022, Amazon Web Services Inc. or its affiliates. All rights reserved*

AWS Budgets, shown in Figure 3-21, is a detective tool; it only informs and does not stop or restrict services when the configured budget is exceeded. So it is essential to ensure that budget alerts are received and acted on when needed and not lost in the noise of general application logs.

Another AWS service is Cost Explorer, where we can visualize and plan cloud spend. Filtering and grouping features can be used to design a custom dashboard giving essential information for a particular account or application. Cost Explore supports custom reports and simple data analysis that can help identify trends, detect anomalies, and pinpoint the primary cost drivers in a given account for analysis and optimization.

An AWS cost and usage Report contains a cloud account's most detailed cost information. It includes metadata and tags from cloud resources, pricing, and reservations. Resources and tags can be identified and grouped to find the total cost of specific services, applications, users, departments, and portfolios. Service utilization is included by account, IAM user, or tag for each service category. Figure 3-22 provides a few example rows from a cost and usage report.

Service	Operation	UsageType	Resource	StartTime	EndTime	UsageValue
AmazonS3	ReadLocation	APS1-EUW3-AWS-Out-Bytes	resource-1	6/1/2021 10:00	6/1/2021 11:00	142
AmazonS3	ReadLocation	APS1-EUC1-AWS-Out-Bytes	resource-2	6/1/2021 19:00	6/1/2021 20:00	142
AmazonS3	HeadBucket	APS1-Requests-Tier2	resource-3	6/1/2021 3:00	6/1/20214:00	1
AmazonS3	HeadBucket	Requests-Tier2	resource-4	6/1/2021 23:00	6/2/2021 0:00	1
AmazonS3	PutObject	APS1-Requests-Tier1	resource-5	6/1/2021 16:00	6/1/2021 17:00	1
AmazonS3	HeadBucket	USE1-EUC1-AWS-Out-Bytes	resource-6	6/1/2021 7:00	6/1/2021 8:00	375
AmazonS3	HeadBucket	USE1-APS3-AWS-Out-Bytes	resource-7	6/1/2021 5:00	6/1/2021 6:00	365
AmazonS3	HeadBucket	USE1-APS3-AWS-Out-Bytes	resource-5	6/1/2021 5:00	6/1/20216:00	365

Figure 3-22. *AWS cost and usage report example*

The AWS cost management service helps take control of our cost and continuously optimize cloud spend. It comes with a variety of AWS pricing models and resources to choose from. These models and resources measure and improve performance and cost-efficiency with common templates and custom templates that can be created to meet budget goals. The service recommends pricing models based on an application's utilization pattern to help drive down costs without compromising performance.

AWS Cost Categories is a feature of the AWS cost management suite that can group cost and usage information into useful categories based on specific needs.

Custom Tracking

If the provided cost management services don't meet the organization's requirements or if there is a need for something more proactive than just a notification about budget peaks, a Serverless solution for monitoring, tracking, and reacting to costs can be created.

Every service in the cloud has logging capabilities. In many services, advanced or extended logging can and should be enabled. In microservices and containers, custom logging can be added to the code. All these logs are stored in logging and storage services that can be integrated with analytics and notification services. Logs can also be automatically streamed in near real time to a microservice, or a scheduled job can read logs at intervals for less urgent use cases.

Once a log is in a microservice, it can be read and analyzed, and an appropriate reaction can be determined using simple mapping or more complex algorithms such as anomaly detection. This is the same approach used in Serverless cloud management for security and operations to monitor and respond to events in an application. In the context of cost management, we can use the logs to track cost-incurring actions made by individual users throughout a Serverless application. The microservice can identify logs related to cost, associate them with a particular user, and aggregate and store everything in a cost-tracking database.

The following are high-level examples of cost tracking that can be achieved using service logs:

- Microservices log how long they ran at the end of each execution. Knowing the resource configuration for the microservice, we can calculate the cost of that request from the run duration. To link that back to a user, the user ID making the request will need to be logged during the request.

- Logs can be enabled for the storage service S3, which tracks each file upload, download, and retrieval. File metadata in S3 can tag a file to a particular user, enabling us to track metrics such as *total storage* used by one.

- Many cloud services used in a Serverless application are typically launched from a microservice. Accurately tracking such activity is best done by logging the request from the same microservice. Some services bill for the number of requests, others for the specifics of a request, and others for the duration of the request. The microservice can track or calculate and log all these metrics and the associated user ID as part of the workflow.

Resource Tags

Cost allocation tags can be assigned to most resources and are used to organize resources into arbitrary groups such as department, team, application, or individual users. Tags can be used in the cost and usage report to find the total cost of all resources with a particular tag. There are two types of tags: *generated* tags and *user-defined* tags.

Generated tags are created by the cloud provider. For example, AWS can add a *createdBy* tag to provisioned resources that will tell us which AWS account user created them. Generated tags need to be enabled in the Billing and Cost Management console. User-defined tags are assigned by the provisioner to a resource when created via the console, API, or infrastructure template. Tags can also be applied in the deployment pipeline to enforce identification or other information on resources according to organizational policy. Each tag consists of a name and a value, and there are limits on length and characters that can be included, which can be found in the service documentation.

Regional Differences

It's important to remember that each region has its own fees for the services that can be provisioned there. These service fees are not determined by where we are **based** but by where the resources are **provisioned**. Depending on organizational policy, this can allow for the deployment of development environments into cheaper regions such as the USA, while the production environment and customer data are deployed in the local region. The regional fee differences must be considered when estimating the operational cost because local regions often have higher service fees.

 ## Cost Optimization

Where Serverless is concerned, there are two key services where we should start optimizing cost: the storage service S3 and our microservices host, Lambda. With services such as DynamoDB, there is a consideration as to which billing model to pick and where the break-even point is. We will address these cases later in the book when discussing those services in more detail.

S3 Cost Optimization

For S3, having a clear understanding of the different storage classes will help decide on the right one for the data. As a guide, use

- S3 standard for frequently accessed files

- S3 infrequent for files accessed once a month

- Glacier for files accessed once a quarter

- Glacier deep archive for files accessed once a year (at most)

For an easy default, and for files that have varying access patterns, S3 intelligent tiering can automatically move files between the different classes.

Other factors to note are the minimum billable size, the minimum days of storage, and the additional overhead across the different storage classes.

For example, files stored in the infrequent access class are charged for a minimum of 128 KB per file. So a single zipped 10 MB file will cost less than 1000 individual 10 KB files, even though the total stored amount is the same. Files stored in infrequent will also be billed for a minimum of 30 days.

For Glacier and deep archive, an overhead of 40 KB is added per file. 8 KB is charged at standard rates and 32 KB at Glacier or deep archive rates, with a billable minimum of 90 days of storage for Glacier and 180 days for deep archive.

These additional costs and minimums need to be accounted for in estimates. To store smaller files cost-effectively in the infrequent class or Glacier, they should be retained in that class for a longer period. Based on estimates, for 12 months of storing files without accessing them, it is more cost-effective to use the *infrequent* class for files larger than 140 KB and the *Glacier* class for files larger than 230 KB. 12 months of storage for files smaller than 140 KB will be more cost-effective in the S3 *standard* class.

S3 Lifecycle Policies

Organizations can use lifecycle policies to automate the transition of files between storage classes or delete files based on the file's upload date. For example, logs that are unlikely to be accessed after 1 month but need to be retained for audit purposes can be automatically transitioned to Glacier after a month. At the end of the required audit period, they can be automatically deleted with a second lifecycle policy.

Lambda Cost Optimization

For Lambda, memory *rightsizing* is an important activity to manage cost and performance. To do so, the application team should monitor the published CloudWatch metrics to understand the usage pattern of the microservice and ensure that it is not underutilized.

A common misconception is that having a lower memory configuration always results in a lower cost, but this is not always true. The cost of a Lambda microservice is determined by the memory configuration **and** the execution time. Having more memory could lead to a reduction in execution time, potentially providing better performance at the same or lower cost.

Since Lambda execution time is billed per millisecond, we should avoid idle waiting as much as possible. The application team should consider architectural patterns that offload any waiting to services such as SQS or EventBridge. Similarly, bloated libraries and frameworks not intended for this environment should be avoided.

We can also make use of services such as Compute Optimizer, which analyses the configuration and usage patterns of cloud services to provide a rightsizing recommendation.

AWS Cost Reductions

It's important to keep an eye on cloud service cost reductions, especially if we are creating Excel sheet estimates that tend to get reused for future projects. AWS has reduced service fees 80 times since they launched in 2006.

Such reductions can be a simple lowering of price (S3 storage fee reduction, 2022) or a change of billing model (CodeGuru change to repository-size billing model, 2021).

Implementing more granular pricing is another way service billing changes can impact the cost. This happened when Lambda went from billing per 100 ms to 1 ms in 2020. For a microservice that runs for 30 ms, the change resulted in a 70% cost reduction.

AWS Credits

To help organizations with Serverless cost optimization, AWS offers credits that can be used to offset at least some of the cloud spend. There are several channels where organizations can gain access to these credits.

The AWS Migration Acceleration Program (MAP) is offered by AWS to help organizations accelerate their cloud migration journey. Benefits of this service include AWS credits and partner investments to help offset the cost of migrating existing solutions on-premises or with another cloud provider into AWS.

For startups, the AWS Activate program can offer up to $100,000 in credits. Individuals can earn credits by publishing Alexa Skills, attending events such as AWS Innovate, participating in marketing and feedback surveys, or becoming an AWS Ambassador.

Consolidated Billing for AWS Organizations

The AWS cost management service provides a feature called *consolidated billing,* which can merge the cost of multiple AWS accounts. The organization would have a master account that pays for all of the associated member accounts. Permissions, policies, and various types of logging and monitoring can also be centrally managed through organizations.

Consolidated billing works on the principle of blended rates and costs, which can affect overall usage and total costs. Blended rates are the averaged rates of the reserved and on-demand services used by member accounts in an organization. AWS calculates blended costs by multiplying the blended rate for each service with an account's use of that service. When compared with the unblended costs of each linked account, the consolidated prices are far lower.

Another benefit of consolidated billing is the ability to see the unblended costs for each linked account and apply all the consolidated billing benefits such as reservations and tiered prices across all associated accounts in AWS Organizations.

CHAPTER 4

Security

Once a new technology rolls over you, if you're not part of the steamroller, you're part of the road.

—Stewart Brand, Writer

 ## Shared Responsibility

The cloud offers 24/7 security and operations, the cost of which is included in the service fees with economies of scale that are difficult to replicate for a single organization. This is a great benefit and, for many smaller organizations, a higher level of security than they would be able to achieve on their own.

This benefit goes even further with Serverless because the provider's scope includes the security of operating systems, software, and other aspects. The challenge is that cloud services are still very configurable; this makes them flexible but easy to misconfigure.

Many high-profile data breaches in the cloud are due to configuration gaps and not vulnerabilities in the cloud services. To add, poor Serverless architecture design can lead to more potential entry points due to the higher number of components in the architecture and default configurations that include direct access from the Internet.

AWS and other cloud providers all have the concept of *shared responsibility* in the cloud. This refers to how the responsibilities of securing and maintaining the different cloud services are split between the cloud provider and the customer. No single rule applies to all services; each service divides responsibility based on the service nature and scope. One consistent aspect is that the more managed a service is, the more responsibility lies with the cloud provider. Figure 4-1 shows this shifting of responsibility across the three evolutions of cloud services.

© Thomas Smart 2023
T. Smart, *Serverless Beyond the Buzzword*, https://doi.org/10.1007/978-1-4842-8761-3_4

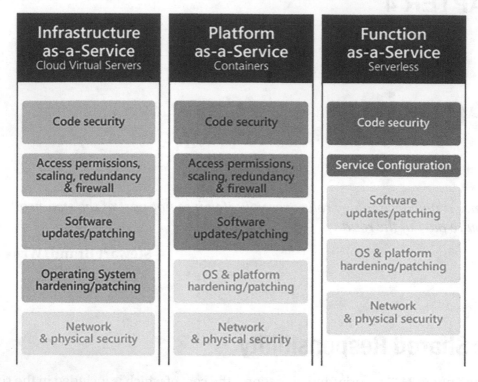

Figure 4-1. *Shifting responsibilities as cloud services evolve*

We touched on the evolutions of cloud services in the "History of Serverless" section in Chapter 1. It refers to the different stages cloud computing has gone through and how each subsequent stage reduced the amount we need to configure for the services.

Examples of Shared Responsibility

EC2 Virtual Servers (IaaS)	
AWS Responsibility	Hardware, data center networking and connectivity, patching and securing the global infrastructure and network
Customer Responsibility	Operating system hardening, maintenance and patching, and software installation, maintenance, and patching. VPC networking and connectivity. Security groups, ports, firewall rules, data encryption, and SSL. User access, IAM roles, and application code
ECS Fargate Containers (PaaS)	
AWS responsibility	Hardware, data center networking and connectivity, patching and securing the global infrastructure and network.Operating system hardening, maintenance, and patching and platform installation, maintenance, and patching. Cluster installation, maintenance, and operations
Customer responsibility	VPC configuration. Container setup, maintenance, and patching. Security groups, ports, firewall rules, data encryption, and SSL. User access, IAM roles, and application code. Scaling and redundancy
Lambda Microservices (FaaS/Serverless)	
AWS responsibility	Hardware, data center networking and connectivity, patching and securing the global infrastructure and network.Operating system hardening, maintenance, and patching; platform and software installation, maintenance, and patching. Cluster installation, maintenance, and operations. Scaling and redundancy
Customer responsibility	Optional VPC configuration with security groups. Service configuration. User access, IAM roles, and application code

Figure 4-2. *Examples of shared responsibilities*

At each level, in Figure 4-2 we see the customer responsibility reducing. While this comes at the cost of infrastructure control and flexibility, the benefits typically far outweigh the cost.

Further information about shared responsibility on AWS can be found here: *https://aws.amazon.com/compliance/shared-responsibility-model/*.

Serverless Security

A common advantage of moving to the cloud is that we can rely on the cloud provider's global, dedicated security team working 24/7 to monitor and improve the security of the platform. Serverless architecture extends the provider's scope to include the operating system and software, further reducing the security scope we are responsible for.

The distributed nature of Serverless architecture is one of its greatest advantages, but this can also pose a significant security challenge in badly designed and configured architecture. Compared with servers, bad Serverless designs can lead to significantly more Internet-facing entry points that malicious users can exploit. It is still a common challenge, especially with budget-strapped teams, that application security only receives minimal attention until the application is up and running. However, with Serverless, application security can be greatly improved with minimal effort by focusing on a few simple but critical areas.

There are several managed security services that can be added to a solution to increase security. For example, Web Application Firewall (WAF) is a fully managed firewall service that comes with several AWS-managed rules that can protect a Serverless back end from attacks such as SQL injection and cross-site scripting (XSS). This service is not fully Serverless as a monthly fee is charged on top of an actual usage fee, but it is fully managed, and, from a security perspective, it is absolutely worth it.

We use services such as Macie to monitor and identify sensitive data in storage, Secrets Manager and Parameter Store can be used to securely store and access credentials, and KMS can be used for all kinds of encryption use cases.

Input validation and sanitization can often be implemented in a fully managed service such as AWS API Gateway. The *model* feature in this service can validate input data against a set of rules that can identify missing required parameters, validate data types, and even perform complex validation of the values using regular expressions. This avoids the need to have to develop these capabilities in the microservices.

An example of using purpose-built solutions to improve security is the Serverless QLDB on AWS. With Serverless, it is not uncommon to use multiple databases of different types, each one the ideal option for a particular data model used by one or more microservices. QLDB is a ledger database where records can be added but never edited or deleted. To change a record, a new record must be added with the change – much like an accountant's ledger. Existing records are fixed in time, and the original and all subsequent updates are verifiable. Those capabilities make this a far more secure choice over a standard MySQL database for fraud-sensitive transactions.

Many past publicly reported cloud security issues were due to misconfiguration of cloud services, not vulnerabilities. Serverless will use far more cloud services than a server-based solution. This means that the application team needs to be deeply familiar with the services, the integrations, and the security options to mitigate the risk of mistakes.

For AWS, this means being very familiar with services such as Identity and Access Management (IAM), including its roles and granular security policies. Familiarity with services such as CloudWatch, CloudTrail, GuardDuty, and Security Hub will be useful too, especially for enterprise and large-scale solutions.

All code and infrastructure templates should be properly tested before deploying to the cloud. This can be automated through DevOps pipelines using cloud-native services such as CodePipeline and CodeBuild, augmented with custom controls running in Lambda.

Finally, always enable encryption on all services for data at rest and in transit. Encryption is available for all Serverless and fully managed services and is enabled by default in most.

 # Principle of Least Privilege

The Principle of Least Privilege (PoLP) is a cybersecurity strategy that is considerably more powerful in Serverless architecture because of its distributed nature with fine-grained access controls.

In a computer security context, privilege refers to our ability to access or modify a given computer resource. For example, on most home computers, we have administrator privileges letting us access and change whatever we want. The Principle of *Least* Privilege (PoLP) limits the privileges of an entity – which could be a person or a program – to only the *minimum* needed to perform its tasks.

PoLP Applied to Teams

PoLP is crucial to managing application security, protecting data, and limiting access to devices, systems, and services. When it comes to applying permissions to team members, considerations include seniority, location, capability, and purpose or goals. For example, while the senior tech lead of an application might have broad access to the application cloud account, an intern or external freelancer would be significantly more limited in what they can access.

Cloud user accounts should follow the Principle of Least Privilege, so consider the following:

- What services does each user need to access daily? Do the developers need full access to the machine learning services? Does finance need access to anything other than billing?

- Consider blocking all users from accessing at least the larger and more expensive servers and services if the organization does not routinely need them.

- It is a good practice to use separate cloud accounts for different purposes – for example, a security account where users and permissions are managed separately from the application accounts. Users with access to the application account do not necessarily need access to the security account. Other commonly created separate accounts are centralized logging, networking, and development and production environment accounts for applications.

- Deployment automation can help further improve adherence to PoLP for cloud users. Instead of the users, advanced deployment pipelines will hold the necessary provisioning permissions. To provision new services, the users must deploy infrastructure templates to the pipeline, which will do the actual provisioning.

PoLP benefits organizations by allowing people to do their job while at the same time minimizing risk exposure by significantly reducing the impact of a compromised account. By blocking access to expensive servers and services, there is less chance of racking up significant unwanted costs if the account is compromised or mistakes are made.

Static vs. Dynamic Privileges

Privileges are often configured statically – a fixed role that does not change very often. But they can also be more dynamic – adjusting to context or changing variables to provide only the access needed for a particular window. This can require more effort to implement or manage, but it can improve security by further limiting access. One way to apply this in an agile project is to implement a privileges review at the start of each sprint. The team members are assigned access rights to the cloud account based on the tasks they need to achieve in the current sprint. For example, if a developer needs to create a database, they will be given permissions to create it in the sprint, but these permissions would be removed in the next sprint, leaving them only with the ability to change the existing database. As the team gains more experience, these changes can become easier to manage through the creation of reusable policies to fit the team's access patterns throughout the development of an application.

Some limitations can also be automated in policies. IAM offers some controls to help with this:

- Policies can be created that change based on date, weekday, and time. For example, this can provide access to developers only during office hours.

- We can assign different limits based on a user's IP address – for example, enabling team members to make changes when accessing the account from the office or over the organization's VPN, but only permitting read access from other IP addresses.

- Limiting users based on whether they are using multi-factor authentication (MFA). MFA is quite an important feature in securing cloud accounts. IAM recognizes if a user is logged in with an MFA, and a policy can be implemented to greatly restrict the user's actions if no MFA is present.

PoLP Applied to Servers

In a monolithic server-based application, we achieve the Principle of Least Privilege by assigning the entire application the permissions needed by each part of the application. There is no way to provide a particular set of permissions to just one part of a monolithic application.

As such, all parts, the entire application, and the server it runs on all have the accumulated permissions needed by each part of the application. This includes *levels* of access as well as permitted *actions*.

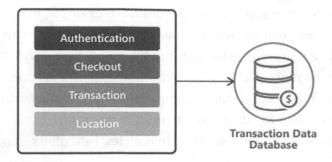

Figure 4-3. *PoLP in servers: broad access for the entire application*

For example, a function responsible for confirming a payment transaction will need read access to the transaction database, as shown in Figure 4-3. So the *retrieve records* permission is provided to the **entire** application. Another function in the application – this one responsible for processing a contact form – would inherit the application permissions and so also have access to the transaction database records, despite having no actual *need* for them. This will apply to all other functions in the application and any other applications running on the same server.

If any of the functions or applications in the server are compromised, the attacker could gain access to retrieve records from the sensitive database – again, despite most of those parts not actually *needing* access to the database in the first place.

PoLP for Serverless

The Principle of Least Privilege is considerably more powerful in Serverless architecture. The distributed nature of this architecture enables us to create a distinct set of permissions for each individual microservice and managed service. It's this that makes the Principle of Least Privilege one of the most powerful security strategies we can leverage in a Serverless application.

In Figure 4-4, the permissions are scoped such that now only the checkout microservice in the application is able to access the transaction database. All other microservices will have *no* access to that database. So, even if they are compromised, they provide no path for the bad actor to retrieve sensitive data.

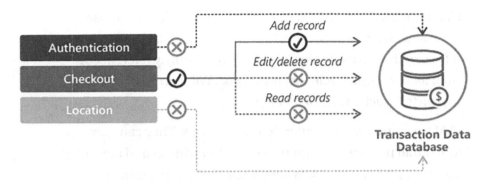

Figure 4-4. *PoLP in Serverless: components can perform specific actions.*

As with most architectures, we can also determine the permitted actions. However, as with access, doing this *per component* offers a far tighter set of permissions. For example, personal data is considered highly sensitive and usually protected by government regulation. A registration form that is open to the public is considered a potential high-risk entry point. Automated scripts and bad actors will be attacking it repeatedly, looking for any vulnerabilities. In a Serverless environment, we will have a microservice that processes each submitted registration form. Such a microservice really only needs to add records to the database; it does not need to edit, delete, or retrieve anything. So we scope the permissions to permit *access* with only the *add* action. If the microservice is compromised with SQL injection or some other attack that attempts to retrieve all our sensitive personal data, it will fail because it simply does not have the permission to do anything other than add a record.

The permissions that we assign for a particular resource can also be exclusive to one component. This means that we can force all requests to a sensitive database to go through a single microservice, reducing the number of potential breach sources. Such a microservice would need to have the permissions needed for different actions, but it provides a single point where requests can be monitored, validated, and audited. It can be faster to lock down the data if any suspicious activity is detected, and it makes it easier to find the source of a breach if one occurs.

⚙ Identity and Access Management (IAM)

AWS offers the free Identity and Access Management (IAM) service to manage access permissions for users and systems – what we call entities. IAM consists of three main parts:

1. IAM policies define the list of resources and actions on those resources that an entity can take. Resources can be broadly referenced, such as *storage service S3*, or narrowly referenced, such as *s3://myfiles/path/to/myfile.doc*. Wildcards are also supported, such as *s3://myfiles/path/*.*

2. IAM users are accounts intended for humans. They can have individual policies or be grouped together with shared group-level policies applied to all users added to a particular group.

3. IAM roles are assumed by trusted entities such as users, applications, and AWS services. Roles are assigned individual policies. Servers in the cloud are typically assigned a role that provides the permissions needed to access storage and databases.

By default, entities do not have *any* permission. To grant access, we attach the relevant policies to them.

IAM policies can be very fine-grained. For example, we can allow users to retrieve a file from a specific path within a specific S3 resource and set a requirement that this must be requested over a secure HTTPS URL with encryption. Any requests that do not meet those requirements will fail.

Each microservice will have its own distinct role instead of one role for the entire server. The policy associated with each role starts with no access but can be configured to access specific services, specific actions within those services, specific data, and many other supported options.

Let's look at some examples:

- A policy to allow access to write a file to a specific path in a storage service but not list or see any of the files on there. This can be used to provide a secure and scalable upload service shared by multiple users. Users could even be restricted to only uploading into a path that includes their own username.

- A policy that allows a microservice to add and retrieve entries but only permits the microservice to modify specific attributes of existing entries. This policy could be useful for managing user profiles, for example. The admin is permitted to view existing users and add new ones, but they can only change specific profile fields of existing users. Traditionally, an application UI would manage this, but with

Serverless policies, we can enforce it at an infrastructure level, which is considerably more secure and less sensitive to coding bugs and vulnerabilities.

- Wildcards (*) are supported in IAM, and while they should be used sparingly and with caution, they can be useful for some situations. As per the example mentioned earlier, we can use a wildcard to provide access to all files within a specific S3 path.

Writing good IAM policies that follow PoLP and other security best practices is hard. It doesn't help that public examples are often very open with the intent to keep things simple for basic tutorials. However, it is common practice to copy-paste such examples, risking the application being rejected on deployment or the open permissions ending up in a production environment.

Using the AWS-managed policies can be a good start, but these are created for fairly generic use cases and so are usually still too open for the needs of specific projects. Managed policies can also be changed at any time without warning by AWS. This recently happened with the managed *read-only* policy, where several permissions were removed, causing a lot of confusion for organizations and users who relied on it.

The main advice here is to study the documentation, understand the different methods and parameters available, start from zero access, and only add the minimum access a microservice or user needs, step by step. It will be a frustratingly slow trial-and-error approach at the start, but instilling this best practice will avoid a lot of problems later on. Custom policies can be stored in the AWS account and reused in the future as a basis for similar microservices.

Wildcards

While wildcards can be useful, as shown earlier for S3, the recommendation is to try and avoid using them in IAM policies unless that is the *only* way to provide the required access. A recent credit card data breach caused by a wildcard left in an IAM policy resulted in a hefty fine of $80 million for Capital One bank. That being said, there are some specific limited instances where a wildcard can be useful. For example, let's say we are creating a policy to allow uploading files to a specific prefix on S3

```
Action: s3:PutObject
Resource: arn:aws:s3:::mybucket/uploads/*
```

or a username prefix:

```
Action: s3:PutObject
Resource: arn:aws:s3:::mybucket/${aws:username}/*
```

When combined with a consistent naming policy on Lambda microservices, a wildcard can also be convenient for allowing API Gateway access to the relevant microservices:

```
Action: lambda:InvokeFunction
Resource: arn:aws:lambda:REGION:ACCOUNT:function:MyAPI*
```

IAM Tips

Here, I have 22 more tips for working with IAM. Most of these tips are for users with higher levels of access to the cloud environment. In a regulated enterprise, these tips will only be relevant to the cloud team or CCoE:

1. IAM is shorthand for Identity and Access Management. It is a service in AWS to manage users, roles, and access permissions.

2. The account (based on the account ID) and the users and roles inside the account are different entities.

3. Users and roles are identities. Users are also known as a *principal*. Roles are used to provide a service with an identity.

4. Roles can also be assumed by users. It is best practice for users to log in with a limited-access user account and then switch to a role that provides more access. Users can also switch to roles that provide access to another account.

5. Policies identify actions that relate to AWS resources and the effect permitted by those actions.

6. Policies can be attached to principals (*identity-based* policies) or resources (*resource-based* policies) such as S3 or KMS.

7. Policies can be created in a single identity or separate and attached to multiple identities. There are also managed policies that AWS provides, such as *administrator,* which provides full admin access to the account.

8. Policies are created either using the create policy interface or by writing a JSON policy template. This can also be automated in CloudFormation, which is the recommended approach.

9. Groups are for managing multiple users. Policies can be applied to groups, and users added to those groups inherit the applied policies. This is the recommended approach; policies created directly on identities should be avoided. Groups cannot be nested.

10. Identities can be federated – users without AWS accounts can be given temporary permissions. Where possible, it is best practice to federate users from services such as AD, Okta, etc., instead of creating individual IAM users.

11. A root user is automatically created along with the creation of the account; it is not the account itself. It can't be deleted, and it is an identity inside the AWS account, not an identity in IAM – it's not listed as a user.

12. After creating a new AWS account, an admin user should be created and the root user locked down using a complex password and MFA. The root account should only be used in emergencies.

13. All users should use MFA. This can be enforced in the policy, blocking all access to new accounts except for attaching an MFA device. After that is done, the user gets the rest of their access automatically.

14. There is a hard limit of 5,000 IAM users per account (each user can be a member of a maximum of ten groups), 5,000 policies per account, 6,144 characters per policy, and ten attached policies per identity.

15. An attempt to access AWS resources is a two-step process: first, the user is AUTHENTICATED inside the account, and then access to resources in that account is AUTHORIZED.

16. All actions in AWS are implicitly denied; granting permissions requires that actions be allowed through policies.

17. There are two types of "deny" – implicit and explicit. All actions are implicitly denied, and an explicit deny can be used to refine allows. For example, *allow * on S3 objects* with a *deny delete action* is fewer lines of code than permitting each individual action except the *delete* action.

18. Roles are used to grant temporary permissions to users or services that exist outside a particular AWS account.

19. Policies can enforce dynamic restrictions such as blocking access on or outside of specific dates, weekdays, times, and IP addresses. Encryption and MFA can also be enforced in policies.

20. Access to programming/CLI-based resources requires the creation of access keys within a user identity.

21. Access to CodeCommit requires the creation of CodeCommit credentials or an SSH key within a user identity.

22. We do not receive the root account when creating a new AWS account in one of the China regions, but a standard IAM user account with admin privileges. The AWS documentation only states that there *is no concept of a root user.* Given that the rest of the platform is largely the same, this has always made me wonder if a root account exists and who might have it.

⚙ AWS Security Services

Next, let's look at a few services specifically intended for enhancing or managing the security of our cloud account and applications. This list is not comprehensive; it covers the services that have some relevance to Serverless architecture.

AWS Organizations

Organizations is an account management service for consolidating multiple accounts into one organization. Along with account management, it offers combined billing capabilities to help stay on track with an organization's budgeting, security, and compliance needs. The organization's administrator can create accounts and invite existing ones to join the organization.

Within this service can be found Service Control Policies (SCPs) that can be used to restrict which AWS services, resources, and API actions can be accessed by the users and roles in each member account. An administrator of *AWS Organizations* can specify the maximum permissions for each member account individually or multiple at once. Conditions such as restricting access to services and resources and limiting actions to specific times or IP addresses can also be defined via SCPs. These restrictions are stringent and override the policies and administrators of member accounts.

A lesser-known policy setting in *AWS Organizations* provides a means to block an organization's user data from being used by managed AI services to improve their algorithms. This activity could be a concern for privacy policies, potentially affecting an organization's relationship with its users and customers. Managed AI services include Rekognition, Comprehend, Polly, and Textract.

Single Sign-On (SSO)

AWS SSO is a cloud-based service that simplifies central management of SSO access to multiple AWS accounts and applications. It includes a user portal so users can find and access all their assigned accounts and permissions. AWS SSO is integrated with AWS Organizations to enable the management of accounts within an organization. To further enhance security for cloud users, SSO supports Security Assertion Markup Language (SAML) 2.0, which enables seamless access to SAML-enabled applications.

AWS Config (Detective Controls)

AWS Config provides a detailed view of the configuration of AWS resources in an AWS account. We can use AWS Config to define rules that evaluate resource configurations for data compliance. AWS Config rules represent the ideal configuration settings for API Gateway resources. If a resource violates a rule and is flagged as non-compliant, AWS Config can alert us using the Simple Notification Service (SNS). For a corrective approach, it can notify a microservice to take more proactive action.

Amazon GuardDuty

A threat detection service that continuously monitors the cloud environment looking for malicious and unauthorized activity. It protects AWS accounts, workloads, and data stored in S3 and automates the process of analyzing CloudTrail logs.

AWS X-Ray

This service helps developers analyze and debug production and distributed applications, including microservices. It is fully integrated with Lambda and easy to enable through the Lambda microservice parameters. Note that some code needs to be added to the microservice for more detailed profiling.

AWS Shield

A managed D-DoS protection service that protects most AWS services for free without having to configure anything. It guards against common network and transport layer attacks such as SYN floods, UDP floods, and reflection attacks.

AWS Shield Advanced is an optional paid service. It provides more visibility on attacks so we can determine a suitable response. Shield Advanced has additional detection and mitigation against network and transport layer attacks. It provides customers 24/7 access to the D-DoS Response Team. And it provides a form of insurance, protecting the organization against spiking costs from autoscaling during a D-DOS attack.

AWS Resource Access Manager or RAM

With this service, we can share resources in an AWS account with other AWS accounts, both within and outside of the organization. For example, we can share a Network Firewall and a VPC to consolidate all services into a single network where we can have centralized control over the ingress and egress traffic of the organization.

Firewall Manager

This offers centralized management of firewall rules and other security components for the organization's accounts.

Amazon Cognito

An authentication and authorization service, typically used for mobile and web applications. Besides login and password, users can authenticate using social identities such as Facebook and Google, as well as enterprise identity providers that use standards such as OAuth or SAML.

AWS Directory Service

Launch a managed Microsoft AD service within a VPC. Leverage AD to manage users, groups, and devices. It can also be useful to extend an existing on-premises AD into the cloud.

Amazon Detective

For incident response services, Detective uses machine learning to analyze collected logs and log insights from AWS services looking for potential security concerns. When it detects anything suspicious, the finding will be displayed in a unified dashboard with relevant data from various sources. This can simplify the investigation process and aid in root cause analysis.

CloudHSM

This encryption service is a fully managed hardware security module for managing encryption keys. It is server-based but managed and an alternative to KMS if its multi-tenancy model does not meet regulatory requirements. CloudHSM provides complete control over the encryption keys – even AWS staff have no access to them. As part of the security considerations, CloudHSM can only be launched into a VPC.

AWS Certificate Manager

Helps to provision and manage SSL and TLS certificates. It provides automatic renewal of certificates, so we do not have to worry about them expiring, and it is integrated into services such as CloudFront, API Gateway, and Application Load Balancer (ALB).

ECR Image Scan

Image Scan is a feature within ECR where we can store container images for deployment into services such as ECS and Fargate. It helps identify software vulnerabilities in those images. Each container image can be scanned once every 24 hours. ECR uses the Common Vulnerabilities and Exposures (CVE) database from the open source Clair project and provides a list of scan findings. Scan findings can be reviewed and remediations determined. The process of scanning and reviewing can also be automated, and critical issues could trigger a rollback or similar response.

Note that it will include a lot of low- or medium-priority issues that likely can't be resolved without breaking the application. As such a risk and cost-benefit analysis should be conducted to determine the likelihood of the vulnerability becoming a problem.

CodeGuru

This is a machine learning code review service. It scans code in a repo to identify vulnerabilities and provide recommendations. Importantly for Serverless, it can also identify potential performance issues and provide recommendations that can help reduce latency. It currently supports Python and Java, though I'm hopeful it will support NodeJS at some point.

API Gateway

For Serverless applications, Lambda is often combined with the API Gateway service, which provides a public access point for mobile and web applications to communicate through to the back-end microservices. This service features heavily in this book, but here we will focus on the security aspects.

APIs are often a target for attacks as they are typically public-facing and, via the microservices, have access to potentially sensitive storage and database facilities used by applications. However, established security best practices can easily mitigate many of the potential risks.

API Authentication and Authorization

There are four mechanisms to authorize an API call within API Gateway. These should be compared for their pros and cons relative to the project's requirements. The available methods are

- AWS IAM authorization

    Managed in an AWS account through users, groups, and policies. The Principle of Least Privilege should be applied here. IAM authorization could be used for internal/private APIs or those intended to be used by other AWS users.

- Amazon Cognito user pool

    A user management and authentication service that can work independently and integrate with social media platforms and Active Directory. This is a great option for public-facing APIs that might be used by mobile and web applications.

- API Gateway custom Lambda authorizer

    Create a custom Lambda microservice that API Gateway will use to authenticate users. Usually, this option will only be used if there is an established user authorization system that needs to be used for the API and can't integrate with Cognito.

- Resource policies

    To enable cross-account access to the API for users in other AWS accounts. As with all policies, the Principle of Least Privilege should be applied here.

It should be noted that API Gateway API keys are **not** recommended for access security. They are intended to be used with *usage plans* to track and limit users' query frequency for a given API.

Security Best Practices for API Gateway

API Gateway provides several security features that should be considered while designing and implementing security policies. The following security best practices can be used as a cheat sheet:

- Principle of Least Privilege.

  IAM policies should be used to implement least-privilege access for creating, reading, updating, or deleting. API Gateway offers several ways to control access to APIs. Make sure to consult the API Gateway documentation for the latest relevant features.

- Implement logging.

  Logging to CloudWatch logs for all requests can be enabled in API Gateway. As with all CloudWatch log groups, they can trigger a Lambda microservice to monitor the logs proactively and send notifications for errors and anything suspicious. Note that the volume of such logs can be considerable for public-facing APIs.

- Implement Amazon CloudWatch alarms.

  CloudWatch alarms are used to monitor a single metric over a specified time. A notification is triggered and sent via Amazon SNS once a metric exceeds a certain threshold. One metric in particular to consider monitoring for API Gateway is throttle events.

- Enable AWS CloudTrail.

  CloudTrail is integrated with API Gateway and, when enabled, will log all calls and activity coming from AWS IAM users and services.

- Enable Web Application Firewall (WAF).

  While not Serverless, the low cost is absolutely worth the fully managed protection it provides out of the box. AWS manages several rulesets that can be enabled to protect APIs against SQL injection, XSS attacks, and other common risks.

Serverless S3 Antivirus Scanning

As with any user data, storing user uploads in the cloud is a risk. Files output from an open source tool or third-party API carry similar risks as there is always a chance that that tool or service can be compromised. The open source ClamAV scanner offers a way to achieve Serverless file scanning in S3 using a Lambda microservice.

An S3 trigger is configured for new files, and ClamAV installed in a Lambda microservice will scan the newly uploaded file. Once the scanning is complete, the function can add two tags to the S3 object, *scan-status* and *scan-time*. The latter tracks the date/time that the file was scanned, and *scan-status* has a result value of either *clean* or *infected*. An S3 bucket policy is created to prevent access to any file where the *scan-status* value is "*infected.*"

S3 Policies and ACLs

To provide security and access control to S3 buckets, Amazon recommends using bucket policies or IAM policies. Before IAM was launched, ACLs were used across S3. An ACL is attached to every bucket and object within and defines the AWS accounts or groups and the types of access provided to each. When we create a bucket or an object, Amazon S3 creates a default ACL that grants the resource owner full privileges over the resource.

ACLs and the behavior of automatically creating default ones can now be disabled since a recent change, and doing so is considered best practice. Once disabled – which can be configured for new and existing buckets – bucket policies are used to share data with users outside of the account. This can greatly simplify permission management and improve auditing. Note that when ACLs are disabled for existing buckets, they can be enabled again at any time, and the previous ACL settings will be restored – useful if an application is broken after ACLs are disabled.

Securing Containers by Decoupling

Containers running third-party software can be a potential security risk if there are open source packages running on them. Containers that are running a one-off or recurring task could have their risk reduced by decoupling them with an SQS queue.

With this approach, the containers do not need direct access to database and storage services such as DynamoDB or S3. Instead, a task is sent to an SQS queue. This task will either contain all of the information needed or, if files are required, signed URLs to retrieve the specific files from the S3 bucket.

The container retrieves the task from the queue, executes it, and sends the result to another SQS queue. If the result is a file, then a signed POST URL can be provided that the task can output to. The output files can then be verified or scanned for malware before being further processed and stored by a Lambda microservice. This minimizes the risk of compromised tools accessing resources beyond their scope. Ideally, these containers should also not have Internet access to help prevent malicious activity.

Security Is Hard!

Security is a vast topic in AWS, covering a broad spectrum of domains.

This is an area that requires considerable planning and effort to ensure the security of our environments, applications, and data. On-premises security tools and policies are rarely suitable for cloud environments. The complexities can make cloud security even challenging for those experienced with on-premises security.

When in doubt, there is no shame in seeking help from security professionals who specialize in cloud security. These experts can bring in their experience and knowledge to help in areas such as reviewing migration plans and existing cloud architecture to determine its security posture and provide any recommendations. They can also help train staff in cloud security and other best practices.

⚙ User Input Validation

The next section focuses on dealing with user input, and while it is certainly not unique to Serverless, there can be some differences in how we can deal with it.

When a service is publicly available, malicious actors can exploit vulnerabilities in the source code to compromise a service. Many vulnerabilities occur because of inexperience or not following best practices. Application security is only as strong as the weakest link. Even a single line of code that introduces a vulnerability could lead to a data breach.

In Serverless, our back-end services are usually fronted by an API Gateway that forwards the users' requests to Lambda microservices. API Gateway offers a few capabilities that can help improve the security posture of an application without having to write a single line of code.

First is Web Application Firewall (WAF), which can be integrated with API Gateway, S3, Application Load Balancer, and AppSync to help protect interfaces against several attacks, including malicious user input.

WAF analyzes each incoming request looking for potential attacks. It can protect against two common attacks related to unsanitized data:

1. SQL injection, which happens when an attacker attempts to modify an SQL query that an application is executing by introducing SQL syntax within their input. For example, they could attempt to retrieve all database records or even delete a database. Note that this is not relevant when using a Serverless NoSQL database such as DynamoDB.

2. Cross-site scripting, also called XSS, is when an attacker submits malicious code that will be displayed to other users or back-end staff, for example, in a comment or feedback feature. The malicious code could introduce unintended behavior, such as redirecting other users to a different website where credentials can be stolen.

After configuring a WAF, we can pick which rules should be included in its assessment of requests. There are rules managed and provided by AWS, we can create custom rules, and there are free and commercial third-party managed rules available in the AWS Marketplace.

WAF also provides the capability to perform text transformations on the request payload. This can help filter and break malicious input that malicious actors attempt to obscure in their request to avoid detection.

Text transformation can do a few useful things:

- It can decode many encoding methods such as Base64, CSS, Hex, and URL to uncover hidden commands an attacker attempted to include within the payload.

- Text transformation can break attempts to inject system-level commands by deleting or replacing potentially dangerous characters within a request.

- The UTF-8-to-Unicode transformation is especially helpful when dealing with non-English input, and this can help convert all the UTF-8 characters to Unicode to minimize any false positives or negatives when applying the rules.

One important thing to note is that only the first 8 KB of content is inspected, as highlighted in the AWS WAF documentation:

> Note that **only the first 8 KB** (8192 bytes) of the request body are forwarded to AWS WAF for inspection by the underlying host service. If you don't need to inspect more than 8 KB, you can guarantee that you don't allow additional bytes in by combining a statement that inspects the body of the web request, such as ByteMatchStatement or RegexPatternSetReference Statement, with a SizeConstraintStatement that enforces an 8 KB size limit on the body of the request. AWS WAF doesn't support inspecting the entire contents of web requests whose bodies exceed the 8 KB limit.

This means that payloads larger than 8 KB will be missed by the WAF checks, potentially allowing a malicious payload to reach the application. The "*Managed Core Rules*" ruleset enforces an 8 KB limit on the size of the content. So enabling this will automatically block any request that exceeds 8 KB.

If Core Rules can't be used for a given application, then another way to mitigate this gap is to create a custom rule that explicitly denies all requests with payloads of more than 8192 bytes, as shown in Figure 4-5.

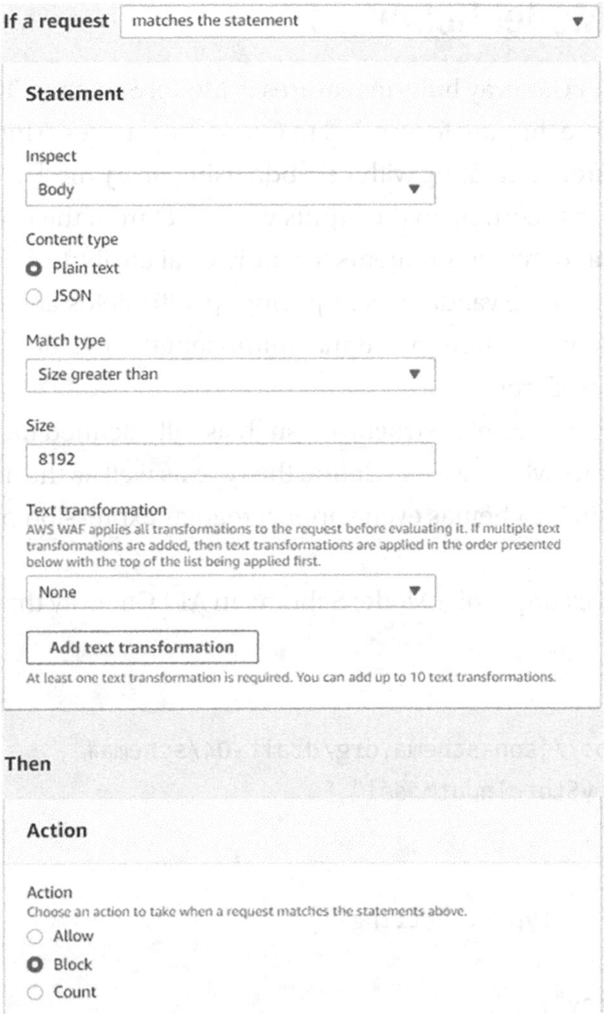

Figure 4-5. *Custom WAF rule. Source: AWS console* http://aws.amazon.com/ *2022, Amazon Web Services Inc. or its affiliates. All rights reserved*

Limiting requests to 8 KB should be carefully assessed first, as it may break functionality common in many applications, such as file uploads or large form submissions.

API Gateway Model Schemas

One of my favorite API Gateway built-in features is Model Schemas. These can validate request payloads before they are forwarded to our microservices. Model Schemas are only available when **not** integrating with Lambda using *proxy* mode.

We create schemas according to the inputs we expect from the front end. We define the overall structure and the requirements for individual attributes.

Schemas support simple validations requiring specific fields and types such as *string* or *number*. We can define minimum and maximum length or value or a specific set of values that can be picked from.

We can also do more complex structures, such as fully defined multidimensional JSON objects and arrays where we can define the type as well as the attributes and types of each element within it. Schemas even support regular expression pattern matching on values.

Here, we have an example of a Model Schema in API Gateway that defines a simple API request:

```
{
  "$schema": "http://json-schema.org/draft-04/schema#",
  "title": "GroceryStoreInputModel",
  "type": "object",
  "properties": {
    "department": { "type": "string" },
    "cart": {
      "type": "array",
      "items": {
        "type": "object",
        "properties": {
          "name": { "type": "string" },
          "price": { "type": "number" },
          "quantity": { "type": "integer" }
        }
      }
    }
  }
}
```

Under the properties field, we have a *department* attribute that expects a string value. We also have a *cart* attribute that expects an array of items with the attributes *name*, a string; *price*, a number that can have decimals; and *quantity*, an integer, so no decimals.

After we define a schema, API Gateway will validate all incoming requests against it. Here we have an example of an invalid request with a couple of mismatches:

```
{
  "category": "produce",
  "cart": [
    {
      "name": 12,
    },
    {
      "name": "bananas",
      "quantity": 5
      "cost": "1"
    }
  ]
}
```

Instead of *department*, the request named this property *category*. We also have missing properties for the items in the cart array, and the types of the *name* and *cost* attribute values are invalid. The request fails the schema validation, and API Gateway will return an HTTP 400 response code to the client. Note that it returns this error without ever invoking the Lambda microservice, which helps minimize latency and cost.

Here we have a valid request that will be forwarded to our microservice:

```
{
  "department": "produce",
  "cart": [
    {
      "name": "apples",
      "price": 1.99,
      "quantity": 3
    },
    {
      "name": "bananas",
```

```
      "price": 0.19,
      "quantity": 5
    }
  ]
}
```

The default configuration of API Gateway for error responses is not CORS compliant. As such, validation error responses can look like CORS failures. The default response templates for API Gateway can be modified to support CORS as well as to include an additional error message that is a bit more informative on the nature of the error. However, the error response is still not great, making it harder to debug issues, and user-facing interfaces should provide a more user-friendly message.

The following are more examples demonstrating the validation capabilities of API Gateway Model Schemas. This is a schema that checks that the account ID attribute is a valid 12-digit string. This can be used to verify if a request comes from an AWS account:

```
"properties": {
  "account_id": {
    "type": "string",
    "pattern": "^\d{12}$"
  }
}
```

ENUM conditions ensure that only specific values are permitted in an attribute's value – in this case *RED*, *GREEN*, or *BLUE*:

```
"properties": {
  "colour": {
    "type": "string",
    "enum": ["RED","GREEN","BLUE"]
  }
}
```

Here is a schema checking for a name with the input length between 1 and 20 characters. The *minLength* and *maxLength* conditions are specifically intended to be used on string types and count the number of characters in the string:

```
"properties": {
  "name: {
```

```
    "type": "string",
    "minLength": 1,
    "maxLength": 20
  }
}
```

For number validation we can use the *minimum* and *maximum* conditions. This example would only permit a value in the 1–100 range:

```
"properties": {
  "name: {
    "age": "number",
    "minimum": 1,
    "maximum": 100
  }
}
```

Lastly, here's a condition that sets the account_id and name as *required* parameters. Note that on its own, this does not prevent the user from submitting an empty value; it only checks that the parameter is present. As such, we should combine this condition with an *enum* or *minLength* condition, for example:

```
"items": {
  "type": "object",
  "required": ["account-id","name"],
  "properties": {
    "account_id": {
      "type": "string",
      "pattern": "^\d{12}$"
    },
    "name": {
      "type": "string",
      "minLength": 1,
      "maxLength": 20
    }
  }
}
```

Storing Credentials

Sensitive information such as access keys, API keys for third-party services, and database credentials should not be stored in Lambda code, environment variables, or code repos where there is a high chance of them being exposed. If a credential ends up in a publicly accessible repo, even for a few seconds, it should be considered compromised and immediately deactivated.

One way to monitor this is to use tools such as Macie to scan S3 buckets for sensitive data. For GIT repos, there is a tool provided by AWS called git-secrets that can be used. Both can be combined with automation to at least notify of any identified issues. More advanced automation can automatically disable compromised AWS keys, lock down S3 buckets, and more.

$45,000 Bill for Losing Credentials

In Figure 4-6 is a use case that nobody should have to experience. In December 2021, Twitter user *@jonnyplatt* had the misfortune of losing the API key for one of his old AWS accounts.

Figure 4-6. *Jonny Platt's unfortunate event. Source: Twitter @jonnyplatt*

The source of the leak is unclear, but the key was picked up by a malicious actor looking to mine crypto coins. The attacker provisioned an AWS Lambda microservice to run a publicly available crypto-mining script for 15 minutes - the maximum duration that a Lambda can run. However, they combined this with a script that kept launching the Lambda microservice, which continued for weeks.

No budget alert had been configured, so *@jonnyplatt* only discovered it when he received a $45,000 cloud consumption bill at the end of the month. During those weeks, the malicious actor had only made $800 in crypto, not exactly an efficient use of cloud resources and a good example of a bad use case for Lambda microservices.

Many people described similar experiences in response to *@jonnyplatt*'s Twitter post, so he is certainly not alone in receiving surprise cloud spend bills. Although users can approach AWS to seek remediation for such incidents, whether AWS waives the fees or not is entirely up to their discretion and certainly not something that should be requested more than once.

Here are a few ways to protect AWS accounts from such a situation:

1. Use appropriate services such as Secrets Manager and Parameter Store to store secrets and manage access. We can use IAM policies to determine exactly which services and users can access the individual secrets for both services.

2. Set up multi-factor authentication for all AWS users and, where possible, third-party credentials. This will help protect leaked keys, though it will make it harder to use the credentials in automated workflows.

3. Control access to credentials stored in services such as Secrets Manager, using IAM policies, and follow the Principle of Least Privilege.

4. Configure monitoring of all stored credentials, and use anomaly detection to trigger an alert for any unusual credential access events.

5. Create AWS user accounts according to the Principle of Least Privilege. Minimize the number of admin accounts and avoid using them on a day-to-day basis.

6. Configure budget alerts as we covered in Chapter 3.

AWS Public Scanning

AWS regularly scans public repositories like GitHub for exposed access keys. AWS will send an email notification about the event when a key is exposed. They will then attach a special quarantine IAM policy to the affected user that greatly restricts their access. A support case will be created to help resolve the matter and minimize any further exposure, and a Health Event and Trusted Advisor finding will be created. Typically, all of this will be brought to the immediate attention of any cloud or security teams within an enterprise.

CloudWatch actions and alerts can be configured to automatically respond to Trusted Advisor alerts with notifications or remediation.

Although AWS does scan public repositories, other public-facing services are **not** covered, such as Pastebin and the many dark web equivalents.

Systems Manager Parameter Store

Systems Manager is a service typically used to help manage server-based infrastructure on AWS. It offers features such as automating maintenance tasks, setting patch baselines, and more.

However, the feature we are interested in is Parameter Store. This feature stores sensitive information fully encrypted in AWS, and microservices can retrieve a secret if they have been granted the appropriate permission to access it. Parameter Store works with KMS to encrypt and secure secrets. This service is not only for credentials; it will store any string data, including JSON, if serialized first. For example, full session data for third-party API integrations can be stored and accessed in Parameter Store.

Access to each secret is controlled via IAM policies. Developers can determine which microservice can access which secret. Fine-grained permissions can limit this to creating secrets or reading secrets.

Standard Parameter Store is a free service, though note that KMS charges $0.03 per 10,000 descriptions of a secret. There is also an *advanced* version of Parameter Store, but that is not required for most use cases.

In Figure 4-7, we have a Lambda microservice that needs to retrieve an API access key in order to call an external API.

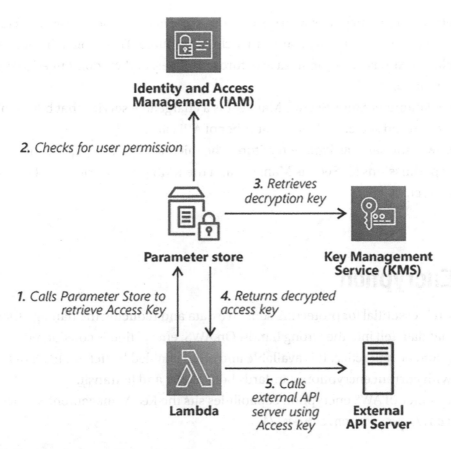

Figure 4-7. *Retrieve sensitive data from Parameter Store*

Since the secret is stored in Parameter Store and encrypted using a customer-managed KMS key, the microservice will require read permission for both the Parameter Store secret and the KMS key.

Once Parameter Store verifies access, it can decrypt the API access key and return it to the microservice.

Secrets Manager

Another service that can store sensitive information is Secrets Manager. Secrets Manager is more powerful than Parameter Store as it has features to generate a new password and automatically rotate credentials, a great benefit for security.

Credential rotation is done with a Lambda microservice where we can configure the new password generation logic and perform any other actions needed.

Secrets Manager integrates with CloudFormation, allowing new passwords to be generated and referenced as with any other cloud resource. This avoids the need to include plain-text passwords in infrastructure templates, and we don't need to create them first manually.

Unlike Parameter Store, Secrets Manager is a chargeable service that bills a monthly rate for each stored secret and for the number of API calls.

The flow is the same as Parameter Store. The microservice will require the necessary permissions for Secrets Manager and the KMS key to retrieve and decrypt the required secret.

 Encryption

Encryption is essential for protecting sensitive data and reducing the damage that could occur if that data fell into the wrong hands. On AWS, encryption is considered a priority capability and best practice. It is available and often enabled by default in all of their services with current encryption standards both at rest and in transit.

At the center of AWS encryption capabilities sits the Key Management Service or KMS (`https://aws.amazon.com/kms/`):

> *AWS Key Management Service (KMS) makes it easy for you to create and manage cryptographic keys and control their use across a wide range of AWS services and in your applications. AWS KMS is a secure and resilient service that uses hardware security modules that have been validated under FIPS 140-2, or are in the process of being validated, to protect your keys. AWS KMS is integrated with AWS CloudTrail to provide you with logs of all key usage to help meet your regulatory and compliance needs.*

Encryption of Data at Rest

For many types of data, encrypting data at rest is critical for regulatory compliance. The goal is to block any user or application from reading the data stored on the disk without a valid key. If physical access to the drive is compromised, it should be as difficult as possible to extract readable data from it.

AWS provides encryption for data at rest on all services that store data. For many services, we can use AES-256 encryption with keys managed by AWS or self-managed keys in the Key Management Service (KMS). Many services also support hardware keys in the CloudHSM service or self-managed keys on our own managed device. Some specific examples include Amazon EBS Volumes – used as drives in virtual servers, S3 buckets, and database services.

Encryption of Data in Transit

To secure data in transit, the connection must be secured with current authentication methods and encryption standards. It is essential to protect the integrity of data being transferred between the public Internet and AWS services as well as between different AWS services. The latter is especially relevant to Serverless due to the number of different services often involved in this type of architecture.

There are best practices to follow that can ensure appropriate security is in place for each type of use case. These can include TLS for HTTPS connectivity, IPSec for VPN connectivity, and LDAP for directory service authentication.

Public/Private Key Encryption

AWS Key Management Service (KMS) provides management and protection of keys for data encryption. It utilizes RSA for this purpose. RSA is an industry-standard algorithm and is currently considered the best option for encryption.

KMS uses public-private keys as the customer master key (CMK). The private portion of the key stays within the service, while the public key can be used for encryption. Public-private key pair encryption is best suited for end-to-end encryption of data in transit. Note that private keys cannot be exported from KMS; this can complicate transferring encrypted data between different AWS accounts.

In modern cryptography, a public/private key pair form a combination taken from a long random number and are mathematically related. Using the key pair, the sender can encrypt the data using the public key, but only the recipient, who holds the private key, will be able to easily decrypt it. One use case is to encrypt data at an edge location, securely transfer it on a USB drive, and then ingest and decrypt it in the cloud where the private key is kept. This is called asynchronous or asymmetric encryption, and it is a great way to protect small amounts of data. An important limitation is that this method does not work for large amounts of data.

Envelope Encryption

Envelope encryption is a method of encryption that combines both asynchronous and synchronous encryption. Asynchronous public/private key algorithms provide easier key management and separation of roles.

Synchronous encryption is not limited by the size of the data being encrypted, and it is often significantly faster at encrypting data. Envelope encryption uses the best of both methods to overcome the limits.

The process is as follows:

1. A key pair is created, and the public key is sent to the data sender.

2. The data sender generates a random encryption key.

3. This key is used to encrypt some data using synchronous encryption.

4. The encryption key is encrypted using the public key. The public key can then be deleted.

5. The synchronous encrypted data and the asynchronous encrypted key are then sent to their destination.

6. At the destination, the private key is used to decrypt the encryption key.

7. The encryption key is used to decrypt the data.

KMS helps with this process by storing and protecting the private key and providing a public key. It can also generate the synchronous encryption key, which it calls a *data key*. Sending data keys over the Internet to the edge device adds risk to the process, however, so it is better to generate them at the edge. As KMS private keys can't be exported, the key pair should be created in the AWS account where the data will be decrypted, or the decrypting user will need to have cross-account access to that key in KMS.

Encryption Exceptions in AWS Cloud

While all AWS services have some form of encryption, which is typically simple to enable, there are some special cases and combinations of services that may require a bit more work, such as assigning a service access to the encryption keys involved. Review the current documentation if implementing any of the following use cases (relevant at the time of writing):

1. When enabling S3 logs, configuring them to be stored on an encrypted S3 bucket can cause problems reading and downloading those logs.

2. Enabling encryption on an S3 bucket may result in the E-tags of files stored in S3 not matching md5 hashes of the same file created elsewhere. This is relevant when trying to checksum data, for example.

3. Moving encrypted snapshots, backups, and images between regions may need special attention to the process to ensure the KMS keys are replicated or otherwise accessible from the other region.

4. SQS needs additional steps for certain scenarios when using encryption, such as S3 events triggering an SQS message.

5. EFS, RDS, and EBS can only have encryption enabled on creation. To enable it later, a new encrypted implementation needs to be created and data migrated into it from the unencrypted implementation.

6. If planning to share an encrypted AMI with another account, then we need to use a customer-managed KMS key to encrypt the AMI, as we will need to share the key with the other account. Sharing a key with another account is not possible with the default account KMS key.

⚙ Protecting Data

In this section, we will be looking at security around managing and storing data. First, securing files in S3 buckets.

S3 is an object storage service that organizations use for a variety of use cases such as user uploads, backups, logs, archives, hosting static sites, and React front ends and as a storage service supporting other cloud services.

By default, all buckets created in S3 are private. Sharing a bucket with other users or making it public requires the explicit granting of permissions. This can be done through different channels such as the S3 Access Control List, the S3 bucket policy, or an IAM policy.

In the following example, we have a sample bucket policy that explicitly allows a particular AWS account to upload or put an object into the DEMO-BUCKET:

```
{
  "Version": "2012-10-17",
  "Statement": [
    {
      "Sid": "AllowUploadFrom111122223333",
      "Effect": "Allow",
      "Principal": {
        "AWS": "111122223333"
      },
      "Action": "s3:PutObject",
      "Resource": "arn:aws:s3:::DEMO-BUCKET/*"
    }
  ]
}
```

Access to the bucket is granted if any of the policies explicitly allow access to the S3 bucket. However, if there is an explicit deny, it takes precedence, and access to the bucket will be denied.

A bucket must be explicitly configured for public access to make it publicly available. Besides configuring the appropriate ACL or bucket policy to allow public access, the Block Public Access Control must also be disabled. This control can be enforced as a blanket rule to prevent a bucket or any object within it from being made public through any of the policies.

For organizations that have a security policy that disallows data from traversing the Internet, developers can use a VPC endpoint to ensure that the S3 traffic stays within the AWS network.

CloudFront

Another way to restrict access to an S3 bucket, especially if we want to make the files within it publicly available, is to put a CloudFront distribution in front of it , as shown in Figure 4-8.

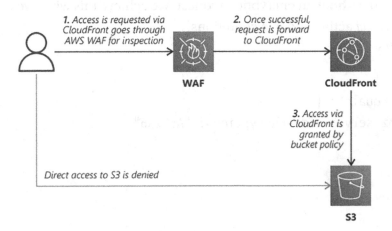

Figure 4-8. *Using CloudFront to secure an S3 bucket*

Using CloudFront, we can create a special user, known as the Origin Access Identity or OAI. This user is given exclusive access to the S3 bucket by configuring the bucket policy to only permit access from that user, as seen in the following example:

```
{
  "Effect": "Allow",
  "Principal": {
    "AWS": "arn:aws:iam::cloudfront:user/CloudFront Origin Access Identity
    A1B2C3D4E5F6G"
  },
  "Action": "s3:GetObject",
  "Resource": "arn:aws:s3:::DEMO-BUCKET/*"
}
```

Note that buckets behind a CloudFront distribution and correctly configured with an OAI do not need to be made publicly accessible for the data to be accessible.

An added benefit of including CloudFront is that we can take advantage of other capabilities, such as caching and integration with other AWS services, such as Web Application Firewall and Cognito, to improve the access security of our bucket further.

Other S3 Features

To protect the data that is being stored in S3, S3 default encryption can be enabled in the bucket configuration. This feature will automatically encrypt all objects added to the bucket. Using IAM or a bucket policy, it is also possible to create a policy that rejects any files being added **without** an encryption request. We achieve this with two deny policies on the *s3:PutObject* action and two conditions:

Deny policy 1:

```
"Condition": {
  "StringNotEquals": {
    "s3:x-amz-server-side-encryption": "AES256"
  }
}
```

Deny policy 2:

```
"Condition": {
  "Null": {
    "s3:x-amz-server-side-encryption": true
  }
}
```

More information on this technique can be found here:

https://aws.amazon.com/blogs/security/how-to-prevent-uploads-of-unencrypted-objects-to-amazon-s3/

S3 has multiple options for data encryption. For server-side encryption, we can let S3 manage the encryption task and keys. This is the easiest and requires no additional effort outside of enabling it in the bucket. We can also supply our own KMS key or even a customer-provided key.

Client-side encryption is, of course, also possible for additional security. This is achieved by encrypting the files **before** they are sent to S3. Third-party tools and encryption options in the AWS SDK or other libraries can be used for this.

Besides encryption, S3 provides features to protect data from being deleted. First, we have *S3 versioning*, which will record all changes made to the files in our bucket. If a file is accidentally deleted, it can easily be recovered by restoring the most recent version.

The *multi-factor authentication* option requires users to provide an additional authentication before they can delete any files. This helps prevent accidental deletes since the second authentication must be explicitly acted upon.

S3 Object Lock enforces a write-once-read-many rule for an S3 bucket. Once configured, a file (also called object) can be written and then read as normal. However, the file cannot be deleted until the configured expiry date.

To ensure that data remains available in the event of a regional disaster, the cross-region replication capability of S3 automatically replicates data into a bucket in another AWS region. Note that depending on the data classification and regions being used, this may cause compliance issues with data sovereignty regulation.

S3 Monitoring

Monitoring can be enabled to help secure and audit S3 buckets and the data and activity within them.

Macie is a service that can monitor data stored in S3 buckets and identify and flag sensitive information such as personal information (PII). Macie can also flag buckets permitting public access and those with no encryption enabled.

Macie can help enforce privacy regulations by detecting user uploads that contain personal data so they can be appropriately managed. Using the insights and some automation, we can automatically redact or delete personal data or simply notify someone to follow up.

GuardDuty is another detective service that analyzes logs to look for any suspicious activity within a cloud environment. For example, if an organization usually only operates out of Singapore, but someone made changes to a cloud service from another region, GuardDuty can detect and flag this as anomalous in case it is malicious. GuardDuty insights can also be automatically responded to via CloudWatch actions and alarms.

GuardDuty offers a feature called S3 protection, which monitors a range of logs and data from S3 buckets looking for any anomalies. Note, however, that it does not monitor any files shared publicly, though, like Macie, it will flag any buckets that have been made publicly accessible.

Some of the suspicious events it can flag include known bad IP addresses, requests from Tor nodes, non-standard API invocations, requests originating from suspicious operating systems, and anyone enabling public access or disabling logs.

S3 access logging is an optional feature that can be enabled to log a detailed record of who accessed S3 objects, including useful information such as the bucket, IP address, and time. These logs are stored in another bucket where they could trigger a Lambda microservice for automatic analysis and response.

AWS Security Hub provides a centralized view of all of the security services such as Macie and GuardDuty within an AWS account. Since October 2021, Security Hub can aggregate findings from multiple regions into a single view.

On-Demand Data Redaction

For a different approach to protecting sensitive data stored in S3 buckets, we can look to S3 Object Lambda. This feature is to analyze and potentially redact files *when they are requested* by a user or system.

In the past, in order to manage different levels of access to sensitive files, organizations would redact files manually when requested, leading to considerable effort and delays. Another approach, one that provides faster responses, is to store multiple versions of the file – for example, the original file for those fully authorized, a version with only personal data redacted, and a fully redacted version without any sensitive information that is used for data science activities.

The challenge with this approach is that it is less cost-effective and difficult to implement without manually reviewing and flagging files for redacting. In a case where the files are user uploads, this will require a lot of effort to moderate.

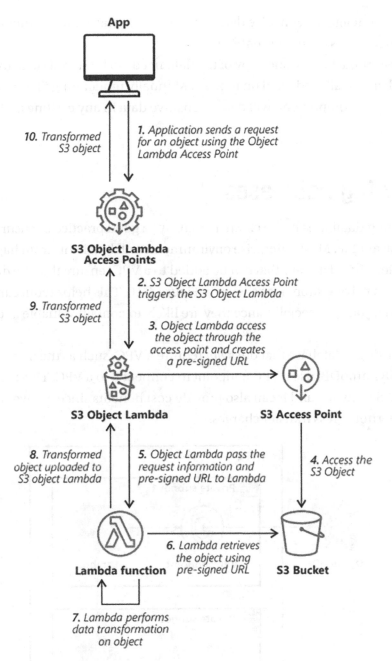

App

10. Transformed S3 object

1. Application sends a request for an object using the Object Lambda Access Point

S3 Object Lambda Access Points

2. S3 Object Lambda Access Point triggers the S3 Object Lambda

9. Transformed S3 object

3. Object Lambda access the object through the access point and creates a pre-signed URL

S3 Object Lambda

S3 Access Point

8. Transformed object uploaded to S3 object Lambda

5. Object Lambda pass the request information and pre-signed URL to Lambda

4. Access the S3 Object

6. Lambda retrieves the object using pre-signed URL

Lambda function

S3 Bucket

7. Lambda performs data transformation on object

Figure 4-9. *Basic S3 Object Lambda architecture*

S3 Object Lambda is a service released in 2021 that can process a requested file in a Lambda microservice after it is requested but before it is returned to the requester. As shown in Figure 4-9, by integrating the Comprehend service in the microservice, we can automatically detect sensitive data in a file. Using the Comprehend analysis result, the Lambda can delete the sensitive data from the file, replace it with random letters or tokens, or refuse access to the file entirely.

With this approach, only one copy of the data needs to be stored since the object can now be dynamically redacted on request. Manually moderating files is also no longer needed, as Comprehend will detect sensitive data in any existing and newly uploaded files.

⚙ Securing Databases

When launching databases in the cloud, it is always a good practice to ensure they are not publicly available. Most enterprise environments will block this from happening. When provisioning a database that *can* be added to a VPC, ensure that the database is launched in a private subnet, as shown in Figure 4-10. This helps reduce the attack surface on a database, especially since they are likely to contain valuable and sensitive information.

If we are using a database that does *not* require a VPC, such as the many Serverless options like DynamoDB, use a VPC endpoint to connect it to a VPC. This keeps all traffic within the AWS network, and it can also provide cost benefits since we avoid the more expensive Internet egress transfer charges.

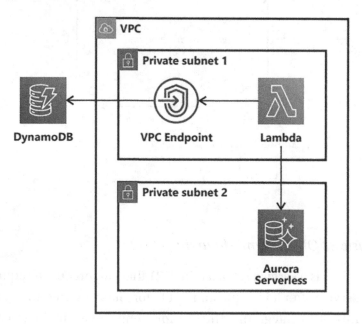

Figure 4-10. *Securing databases in a private subnet or with a VPC endpoint*

Whenever possible, use IAM to authenticate access instead of a username and password. IAM reduces the risk of having credentials compromised. When a particular database only works with a username and password, store the credentials in Secrets Manager, where they are stored encrypted, access is restricted, and the password can be automatically rotated.

To protect data stored in databases, ensure that encryption at rest is enabled. All database services have this option, and the Serverless databases have this enabled by default.

If we are handling data that is sensitive or confidential in nature, consider using client-side protection to add an additional layer of defense to our data. This can add complexity to an application, especially if multiple applications are using the same database, and it can make it challenging to perform search and other advanced queries on the data.

KMS can help provide a centralized location to store encryption keys to encrypt data client-side. Permissions to the individual keys can be granted to only the specific microservices that need access.

In a Serverless environment, we can have a single microservice that has exclusive access to the database. Different applications can use that microservice to interact with the database, providing a single point of contact that can be monitored and audited.

Lastly, we can enable point-in-time recovery and automatic backups on services that support it. This can help minimize the amount of data loss in the event of a disaster but also provide a means to replay the past in an event-driven architecture - more on this in Chapter 9.

Tokenization

Another technique used to protect sensitive data is tokenization. By tokenizing data, we replace sensitive data with randomly generated values. The token by itself does not give any clue as to what the original data was, nor can it be decoded or decrypted to identify the original value. If the token is truly random, then it will be very difficult to *brute-force* it, such as is possible with older forms of data hashing.

The same value throughout an entire data set can be replaced with the same token, which maintains any relationships that might exist between different records.

This is especially useful when we want to perform analysis on the data, such as forecasting or troubleshooting, where the data scientists are looking for statistical insights but do not necessarily need to know the identity of those in the data set.

In Figure 4-11, we have a customer's data record that includes sensitive information, such as their phone number and address.

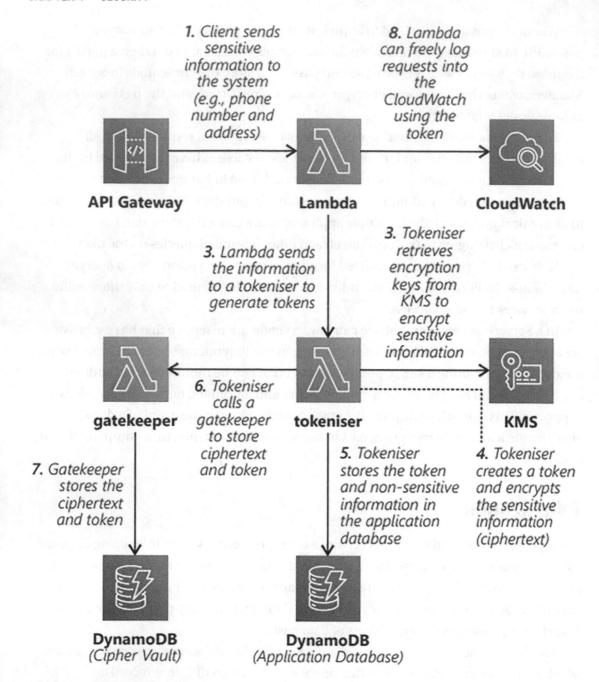

Figure 4-11. *Tokenization basic architecture*

When the back-end microservice receives the record, it generates a token to replace the original sensitive values and stores it in the application database. A data analyst can freely query the application database without being concerned about privacy regulation compliance.

At the same time, the tokenizer encrypts the original data using KMS and stores it in a separate secure database. The secure database is used by explicitly authorized users when the original customer information is required, such as when auditing a transaction. All activities are logged during this process. Ideally, no user data should be stored in logs, but in cases where it is unavoidable, we must only use the tokenized data and not the original.

Database Monitoring

Monitoring is a crucial aspect of security to ensure that the organization has clear visibility on who has access to the data and what they are doing with it. This is important for audit purposes that may require a complete trail of the data movement.

For DynamoDB, we can enable such auditing using the data plane API and for Aurora Serverless through the audit logs sent to CloudWatch.

Database configuration changes can also be monitored using CloudTrail and AWS Config to identify any unauthorized changes and violations. Activities such as attempts to disable logs should be especially flagged and acted upon immediately.

Macie can only scan data in S3. However, with most databases, it is possible to temporarily replicate database records to S3 for scanning if the potential risk justifies the effort of implementing and operating that.

 Privacy and GDPR

When the General Data Protection Regulation (GDPR) came into effect in May 2018, it seemed like it was going to lead to considerable challenges for Serverless architecture and application teams due to enhanced privacy requirements and the need to build data control mechanisms for users.

Nobody likes change, especially when it's regulatory and subject to considerable fines in cases of non-compliance. Codemotion went as far as saying that GDPR will *"kill the Serverless dream."* They questioned how anyone could know for sure where data was stored and how to guarantee that expired data is deleted in a Serverless solution. The assumption was that developers would have a lot more work to do before launching in GDPR markets, such as implementing "*privacy by design*" and additional controls for customers to manage their data.

However, as we can see today, not only is Serverless alive and well but this architecture can actually help meet strict privacy regulations.

What Is Privacy in a Technology Context, and Why Is It Important?

Most of today's online activities are tracked using cookies. Cookies can store a user's activity for a given website. Because cookies can contain enough data to identify a user, they are considered personal data. More details about this can be found at `https://gdpr.eu/cookies/`. When websites just use cookies to track a user's session for a shopping cart, it's not really a problem. However, some organizations are abusing the capabilities of cookies to track users through multiple sites to analyze their habits and interests. The resulting insights from this tracking can be used for targeted advertising or more nefarious purposes such as spam and phishing attacks.

Cookies are just one example of how user data can be collected and how user activity can be tracked without consent. This is why governments across the world are looking to regulate how data is stored, secured, and used. The importance of data privacy regulation is twofold:

1. To ensure that consumer data is safe and that any security breaches are promptly reported to authorities and analyzed.

2. To offer consumers transparency and control over how their information is stored and used. This is also intended to prevent businesses from sharing or using customer data without explicit consent from the customer.

The EU's GDPR is just one example of privacy regulation. Other examples include Singapore's Personal Data Protection Act (PDPA), which passed in 2013, the California Consumer Privacy Act (CCPA), and Brazil's Lei Geral de Proteção de Dados (LGPD) – both passed in 2020. Here I am focusing on GDPR as, at the time of writing, it is still the world's strictest regulation and one of the few posing considerable fines for breaches. If a solution complies with GDPR, it will most likely comply with other national regulations. GDPR is an interesting case study as it came into effect across 31 countries (EEA and UK) at once, many of which are important technology markets.

Complying with GDPR

The following organizations need to comply with GDPR:

- Organizations with any physical presence in an EU country

- Organizations without a physical presence in the EU, but which collect or process the personal data of EU residents

- Organizations with more than 250 employees

- Organizations with fewer than 250 employees but whose data processing impacts the rights and freedoms of data subjects, whose processing is not occasional, or whose data includes certain types of sensitive personal information

The "who" is not always clear, and unless we are actively blocking all EU countries, it is safest to try and comply with GDPR. This will also future-proof the organization and solution in case we decide to expand to the EU region later. As GDPR is the strictest regulation, complying with it will most likely mean we are complying with any local regulation too.

What kind of personal data is subject to GDPR?

- Basic identity information such as name, address, and ID numbers

- Web data such as location, IP address, cookie data, and RFID tags

- Health, genetic, and biometric data

- Financial and other sensitive information specific to a person

A more concise way of thinking about this is "*any data that can be traced back to a specific individual.*" For example, an IP address can often be linked to a person or at least a particular household, but the type of browsers they use, such as Firefox or Chrome, cannot usually be connected to a particular user. If we are tracking website visitor information, we can track which browsers are being used to view our site without revealing personal data, but if we include IP addresses in the logs, then storing and processing these will need to comply with GDPR.

What are the main aspects of GDPR compliance?

- *The right to data portability*: A user has the right to receive a copy of all personal data stored about them.

- *The right to be forgotten*: A user has the right to have their personal data deleted - with some exceptions for audit purposes.

- *Privacy by design*: The security policies should be taken into account from the earliest stages of development.

- *Notifications about breaches*: All breaches must be reported within 72 hours of them being confirmed.

- User consent must be freely given, specific, informed, unambiguous, and revocable.

Cloud and GDPR

A benefit of using cloud services is the *shared responsibility model* mentioned previously. Because of each cloud provider's interest in remaining competitive, they ensured that all their solutions were GDPR compliant as soon as the regulation came into force. AWS, for example, has created a suite of services designed specifically for handling the requirements of GDPR.

Read more about AWS GDPR compliance here:

`https://aws.amazon.com/blogs/security/all-aws-services-gdpr-ready/`

And Azure GDPR compliance is here: *https://azure.microsoft.com/en-gb/blog/ protecting-privacy-in-microsoft-azure-gdpr-azure-policy-updates/*.

To ensure that a cloud provider or a particular service is compliant, we can ask the following:

- Can you select a specific geographical region where the data will be stored and processed, with guarantees that the data will not be stored or copied elsewhere?

- How does their platform protect and anonymize user data as it integrates with external systems?

- What is their protocol for notification in case of a data breach?

- How do they comply with your users' right to data access and erasure?

Why Serverless for GDPR Compliance

Serverless microservice architectures give developers some unfair advantages for ensuring data privacy regulation compliance. These include the following:

Applying the Principle of Least Privilege (PoLP)

As we covered in detail earlier, Serverless architecture provides incredibly fine-grained control over the permissions of each microservice and the data it can access. From a privacy perspective, Serverless greatly lowers the amount of redundant access to data and provides better audit capability over the remaining access.

Gateway microservices

Serverless architecture can enable just one microservice to access a particular database or storage facility. This microservice has exclusive access to the sensitive data stored there, and users or other microservices must go through this one to touch that data. This creates a single point of access – a *gateway* – where data movement can be more easily monitored and audited.

Managed back-end infrastructure

The physical devices and operating systems managed by the cloud providers will likely be more secure than many organizations can afford to achieve on their own. This includes physical data center security, cybersecurity such as firewalls and antiviruses, no legacy equipment, 24/7 monitoring, and frequent security patching. The reason is economies of scale, enabling the cloud provider to invest heavily in security and provide around-the-clock monitoring with restricted access to physical locations and access to highly skilled data center staff.

Ephemerality

Executing Serverless functions entails a provider creating and destroying microservices to react to a particular event. A microservice is triggered and lasts between a few milliseconds and 15 minutes per request. It remains available for up to 30 minutes or until another request activates it again. This makes microservices less vulnerable to long-lived or time-consuming attacks, and it means they cannot be targeted when they are not running.

Automated data encryption

Most cloud services across all cloud providers now have encryption enabled by default for all data at rest and in transit. Most services offer more stringent encryption options, which can be enabled for highly sensitive data. The fact that government entities, financial organizations, and medical institutions are now embracing the cloud indicates that the protection of data has reached a point where it is equal to or better than self-managed data centers.

Data monitoring and auditing

There are several cloud services and features that can help meet GDPR compliance, for example, the previously mentioned Macie and Comprehend services. AWS Connect – a service that provides a call center in the cloud – includes several features to manage GDPR compliance on caller records, including recorded phone calls.

Data storage location

Not all privacy regulation includes data sovereignty – the requirement to keep sensitive data in the country – and, sometimes, this requirement is set as a government policy outside of privacy regulation. Either way, cloud providers allow organizations to choose the region where their data is stored. The available regions should be a consideration when choosing a cloud provider, and it should be noted that even if a provider has a particular region, not all services might be available in that region.

Implementing for Compliance

While managed services offer a lot of support to achieve GDPR compliance, further implementation work is needed for full compliance. This includes developing features that can make it easier to provide users with an adequate level of control over their data, such as the following:

- *Enabling users to request and receive all the information we have about them*: This requires developers to be mindful and design the database and architecture to store all personal data in a single database, for example. A feature to automatically handle customer requests to retrieve or delete their data should be implemented to minimize manual work by staff and delays when such requests are received.

- *Enabling users to correct or update inaccurate or incomplete information*: For example, let users easily modify all their account details themselves, including personal information.

- *Letting users ask to have their personal data deleted*: As with data access, centralizing relevant personal data should be a consideration when designing the database and architecture. For this particular case, some thought should also go into having personal data sets separated from data that is, or can easily be, anonymized if we need to retain it for analytics or audits. Developers must make it easy for users to ask for their data to be deleted, and the request must be honored within 1 month. The user making the request must have their identity authenticated, so a good way for developers to implement this is by providing a function within the user's account management system.

- *Allowing users to ask to stop processing their data*: The distinction here is that a user can ask to stop processing their data within 1 month without their personal data being deleted. This means we can continue to store the customer's data but must ensure that it is not used in any way. In some industries, only this option is available to users when the option to delete data is not available due to regulatory auditing requirements.

- *Enabling users to object to processing their data*: The difference between a request to **stop** processing and a customer **objecting** is that for the latter, we must stop processing data immediately, rather than having 1 month to fulfil the request. This is typically a response when a user does not know how we obtained their data, so it is important to obtain clear and explicit consent from users when collecting data and store the proof of this with the data record. Most people don't bother to read lengthy privacy statements, so it is good practice to put key points on the data collection form to reduce this type of request in the future.

- *Providing customers with a copy of their personal data in a format that can be easily transferred to another company*: This is very solution-specific, but it can be achieved by creating an automated system that can consolidate all data of a particular customer into a readable format, such as a spreadsheet. This point may have implications for how the application's database is modeled and especially how data can be queried to enable everything to be collected for this request. If the application contains media data, such requests could become quite large. Storage, data transfer costs, and the transfer method should all be considered in this case.

- *Having a procedure to protect people's rights if we make decisions about them based on automated processes*: Such a procedure should track every decision for auditing and make it easy for customers to request human intervention and to challenge decisions made by the automated system.

For a comprehensive list of actions that need to be completed for GDPR compliance, visit *https://gdpr.eu/checklist/*.

One final tip: We should be aware that any data we send to AWS-managed AI services, such as Polly and Rekognition, may get used to further improve those services. This is an automatic opt-in, but it could conflict with GDPR depending on the type of data sent to the services. To be safe, we can opt out using a special policy. More information about that can be found on the AWS page here: `https://docs.aws.amazon.com/organizations/latest/userguide/orgs_manage_policies_ai-opt-out_create.html`.

If we are using a different cloud provider, then consult the documentation or a specialist to see how this type of scenario is managed on their platform.

⚙ Security Monitoring with ElectricEye

ElectricEye is a free, open source tool provided by the previous product owner of AWS Security Hub. I wanted to briefly mention it here as it is a great product and fully Serverless. It is a set of Python scripts that runs on a scheduled Serverless Fargate container and scans one or more AWS accounts and regions for any infractions of the 220+ rules that it contains. As it is open source, we can expand and add our own rules. It is fully integrated with Security Hub, so we can combine results with Macie, Firewall, and the managed AWS standards available in Security Hub.

The full documentation can be found here:
https://github.com/jonrau1/ElectricEye

Key Points

- It is integrated with AWS Security Hub and fully Serverless, using only managed services. It has a CloudFormation template to deploy everything we need easily.

- At the time of writing, it contains 220 security and best practice rules, including many services not covered by Security Hub or Config, such as AppStream, Cognito, EKS, ECR, DocDB, and more.

- It offers AWS and third-party integration, including DisruptOps, Config Recorder, Slack, Jira, and Shodan.

- It's highly cost-effective. The schedule can be configured, but if we run it every 3 hours and each run takes 110 minutes, looking at 15 resources with 108 checks 240 times a month, the total cost would be approximately $184 per **year**/region/account.

Deployment and Setup

If nothing goes wrong, this can be achieved in under 20 minutes. However, depending on our system, we may need to troubleshoot or skip steps. More details can be found in the documentation, but this is a quick summary for an Ubuntu workstation.

1. Set up an AWS account with Security Hub and Config enabled. Create and delete a Fargate cluster on ECS to ensure the system role is created by AWS.

2. Set up the local workstation:

```
sudo apt update
sudo apt upgrade -y
sudo apt install -y unzip docker python3 python3-pip
pip3 install boto3

curl "https://awscli.amazonaws.com/awscli-exe-linux-x86_64.zip" -o
"awscliv2.zip"
unzip awscliv2.zip
sudo ./aws/install
```

3. Build and push the Docker image to ECR:

```
aws ecr create-repository --repository-name electriceye --profile
AWSPROFILE --region REGION
mkdir electriceye
cd electriceye
git clone https://github.com/jonrau1/ElectricEye.git
cd ElectricEye
```

```
aws ecr get-login-password --region <REGION> --profile <AWSPROFILE> | sudo
docker login --username AWS --password-stdin AWSACCOUNT.dkr.ecr.REGION.
amazonaws.com
```

```
sudo docker build -t electriceye .
```

```
sudo docker tag electriceye:latest AWSACCOUNT.dkr.ecr.REGION.amazonaws.com/
electriceye:latest
```

```
sudo docker push AWSACCOUNT.dkr.ecr.REGION.amazonaws.com/electriceye:latest
```

Retrieve the ECR container URI from the AWS Console. It will look like this:

```
AWSACCOUNT.dkr.ecr.<REGION>.amazonaws.com/electriceye
```

4. Deploy the AWS resources:

Download the CFM template from here: `https://github.com/jonrau1/ElectricEye/blob/master/cloudformation/ElectricEye_CFN.yaml`

Deploy the template through the AWS console or CLI. The only parameter we need to change is "*ElectricEyeContainerInfo*", which should be set to the container URI we retrieved earlier.

5. Set up a Fargate task.

Manually run the ElectricEye ECS task, and then enter the required params. This is for the first time only. We can find the *ElectricEye2SecurityHubTask* in *ECS/Task Definitions*.

Set the following params; any params not listed here should be left on default:

- *Launch type*: Fargate.

- *VPC*: electric-eye.

- *Subnet*: Any.

- *SecurityGroup*: Edit and select an existing one ("electriceye security").

6. Set a schedule.

In the ECS cluster, go to the Scheduled Tasks tab and edit the only task there to set our preferred frequency for running the rule checks.

7. View results.

If we go to AWS Security Hub in the console, we will be able to find the insights and findings generated by ElectricEye.

And that's it. ElectricEye will run on our configured schedule and keep an eye on things. We can have results trigger a Lambda Microservice if we want to apply some corrective measures to anything critical. If we only want to receive notifications without any automated actions, these can be configured in Security Hub. Given the simplicity of installing this in relation to the level of security it delivers, I generally recommend installing this as soon as possible to keep an **eye** on things.

CHAPTER 5

People

It's not a faith in technology. It's faith in people.

—Steve Jobs, Co-founder of Apple

 Evolving Teams

As we covered in Chapter 2, to productively deliver Serverless architecture, or any modern cloud for that matter, the organization's team structure needs to evolve into a Cloud Center of Excellence. Chapter 2 covered the strategy, key management roles, and the roles responsible for building and running the cloud platform. In this chapter we will look at the more technical roles within the application teams.

The evolution of Serverless technology brought with it a similar evolution in team roles – not necessarily anything new, but a refocusing and specialization of existing roles. For Serverless, a deep understanding of the many available cloud services and their relevant security aspects is crucial. This is different from a traditional IT architect role where the knowledge is focused on technology stacks, operating systems, and networking.

Expectations for developers have similarly moved more toward full-stack capabilities, with JavaScript being a key programming language used in both front and back ends. Knowledge of topics such as DevOps and agility is expected to some degree in all team members.

217

© Thomas Smart 2023
T. Smart, *Serverless Beyond the Buzzword*, https://doi.org/10.1007/978-1-4842-8761-3_5

Build, Buy, or Borrow

The first consideration in a Serverless talent strategy will be to build, buy, or borrow.

Build means upskilling existing teams in Serverless competencies. It can also mean hiring candidates without Serverless experience but with the capacity to learn and then upskilling them in Serverless competencies.

Buy means attracting and hiring talent that already has Serverless experience, headhunting them from competitors or cloud providers, for example.

Borrow means working with vendors, cloud consultancies, freelance cloud architects, development vendors, or resources provided by a cloud provider under a support contract.

For some organizations, a combination of options may be needed to achieve the short- and long-term goals. For example, if there are immediate needs to be solved, such as reducing pressure from competitors or investors, an organization might start with a short-term *borrow* strategy. In parallel, a longer-term *build* strategy can be worked on with the eventual goal of the vendors handing over the work to the newly established internal cloud team.

Enterprises commonly take this approach with cloud consultancies. Consultants are often too costly for long-term engagement, but their deep expertise in the cloud greatly increases the chances of quickly establishing a successful cloud management strategy, team, and platform. Existing staff and new hires will work closely with the consultants to develop the platform. This ensures knowledge is transferred to internal teams and hands-on experience is gained during development under guidance from the more experienced consultants.

Building a Team

Experienced Serverless talent can be hard to find, but Serverless skills can be learned, which makes *build* a great option for organizations that already have application teams.

Depending on the industry and region, it can be hard to find experienced Serverless talent for several reasons:

- The architecture has been popular with startups for some time for the reasons covered in Chapter 3. However, startup staff can be hard to entice into enterprises due to organizational culture differences.

- Most formal education programs have yet to include Serverless architecture and coding practices. It remains a skill that needs to be self-taught with experience gained on the job.

- Most vendors will not propose Serverless if they don't already have experience, and they usually won't learn new skills without a client paying for it, creating a Catch-22 situation. Similarly, at large enterprises, there usually needs to be a strong advocate and business case for Serverless before management will consider this strategy and make resources available for the necessary team and capability adjustments.

- Serverless talent pools tend to be larger in cities where the cloud providers have a strong presence. Outside of these knowledge hubs, skills are still focused on traditional approaches or evolving toward a more cloud-agnostic container architecture.

- The enterprises that typically adopt new technologies first, such as tech companies and those facing strong competition from startups, have aggressively hired the available talent in many markets, especially in the knowledge hubs where such enterprises also tend to be based. Existing salary bands may struggle to compete with such organizations when it comes to experienced Serverless talent.

- It can be difficult for organizations with no established Serverless capabilities to attract experienced talent. There is a concern that such organizations are unable to support the productive delivery of Serverless applications for the reasons outlined in Chapter 2. This is a bit of a chicken-and-egg situation; organizations may struggle to develop Serverless capabilities without experienced people who do not want to join until there are Serverless capabilities.

Given those challenges, it may be more practical for organizations with existing application teams to upskill existing developers. Most teams will have a combination of people interested in learning new skills and those who need to be enticed with KPIs, promotions, and bonuses.

For organizations with limited internal resources, an effective approach can be to hire good developers with an interest in learning and provide the time and resources needed to upskill them in Serverless. This will involve a longer timeline than upskilling existing staff. With both approaches, the risk of staff leaving for a higher salary after being upskilled needs to be addressed. For example, salary bands may have to be adjusted to market rates, and the application pipeline should contain sufficient Serverless work to keep the team interested and motivated.

For upskilling existing and new staff, there are some personality traits and technical backgrounds that will increase the chance of successful training outcomes. Keep in mind that hard skills – the technical knowledge of Serverless architecture – can be learned and certain prior experiences will help reduce that learning curve. What we really want to look for are the soft skills that can ensure candidates will be a natural fit for Serverless and willing and able to learn the hard skills:

- A genuine interest in learning new skills and trying new approaches. Not resistant to change and has no fear of failure (this will largely be determined by the organizational culture, where change may be needed first in some cases).

- Less aversion to risk can help when working with modern architectures and services as they may be unproven and require trial and error to get right. This trait should not put the project or organization at risk; Serverless security should not be underestimated or neglected.

- Prior experience with NodeJS and Python programming languages can be helpful. These tend to be the more common languages used for Serverless microservices.

- With Serverless, developers will be expected to be comfortable with provisioning cloud infrastructure and creating Infrastructure-as-Code templates themselves. They need to be open to learning this, and any previous experience in this area will help.

- DevOps and deployment automation are essential skills for Serverless developers. Look for those team members who are always trying to automate processes and make things more productive.

- While containers are still different from Serverless, they are a step closer to the architecture than servers are. Experience in this area, and especially any microservice container experience, will help developers understand and learn Serverless.

- Developers with a drive to make solutions more cost-effective or sustainable will usually be strongly motivated to learn and use Serverless architecture.

Buying a Team

Hiring new team members and Serverless leads can shorten transformation timelines by reducing the *trial-and-error* approach that inexperienced developers will inevitably go through when exploring a new architecture.

The challenges mentioned earlier remain prevalent, and the organization will need to find ways to mitigate them:

- Cultural change may first need to be implemented in the organization to create a more agile and collaborative environment that supports innovation. Such organizational cultures can help attract Serverless-experienced talent from startups.

- Be vocal about offering learning and growth opportunities in this space and cloud in general. Send team members to major overseas cloud conferences to learn from, and network with, industry thought leaders.

- Find and support an internal advocate and potential thought leader for the organization's Serverless efforts: someone who can talk publicly about successful case studies and attract new talent to the organization.

- Be prepared to relocate talent or consider remote team members if the organization is not located in a tech hub.

- Salary bands, benefits, and relocation packages may need to be adjusted to compete with other organizations in the market hiring this skill set.

- It can help to run an employer branding campaign to promote the organization's new or impending ability to productively deliver Serverless architecture. Similarly, it can help to talk about any exciting in-progress or upcoming Serverless projects that the team will work on.

A tactical approach is to *buy* (hire) a leader with Serverless experience and, ideally, thought leadership. Such a leader can establish the strategy, start working on the platform, and *build* (train) the rest of the team. If the leader is known in the industry, it will be easier for them to attract credible candidates with experience or at least the potential and willingness to learn.

Consider looking globally for remote workers or candidates willing to relocate. Common outsource hubs such as Nepal, Vietnam, Cambodia, the Philippines, and Eastern Europe have many development vendors that are getting more Serverless projects. Their developers are gaining relevant experience and may be open to relocation, given the benefit of obtaining residency in another country. This will greatly increase the size of the talent pool that can be explored for suitable talent.

Besides searching for *Serverless* on LinkedIn, there are several other potential sourcing channels for Serverless talent:

- Headhunt thought leaders and candidates from startups that frequently talk about Serverless, cloud-native, or services such as Lambda, DynamoDB, or Step Functions on social media. This will usually require having an attractive organizational culture.

- Search for relevant Serverless GIT and other code platform project owners and contributors, especially on projects such as AWS CDK, Serverless Framework, and similar. Do be aware of platform rules regarding contacting such individuals.

- Networking circles such as AWS user groups are open to the public; anyone can join, watch presentations, and network with attendees to find potential candidates.

- Hosting and giving talks about Serverless is a way to let the world know you are serious about this architecture and can lead to candidates reaching out.

- There is a good chance that a hired Serverless talent knows other candidates with similar experience or knows groups and sites where others can be found. Offer employee referral bonuses for suitable candidates who remain past their probation.

- Similarly, when working with agencies or freelance recruiters, manage the risk by paying the agent's commission only once the candidate successfully reaches the end of their probation period.

- Like networking groups, industry events are a great place to network and meet potential candidates. Smaller AWS summits are held in several regions once a year, and their major global event *re:Invent* is held once a year in Las Vegas. ServerlessDays is an independent event organized in several cities around the world. As the name suggests, they focus on promoting Serverless technologies and support a global community around that. ServerlessDays events are locally coordinated and nonprofit.

Enterprises with a Serverless-first strategy, training, and a platform that enables developers and strongly supports the productive delivery of Serverless applications are still rare. Establishing these capabilities early will help attract and hire Serverless talent and provide an environment where they can learn and develop solutions following best practices.

Talking publicly about these capabilities will attract talent to the organization – a considerably more affordable approach to talent acquisition. This makes it important to leverage any efforts the organization has made in this area. Mention it in employer branding exercises and job descriptions, and use any opportunity to give public talks at industry events and relevant user groups.

Interviews

General interview guidelines will be an organizational decision. Here, I want to touch on some technical aspects of the interview process that are relevant to Serverless.

First, recruiter shortlisting. Here are some things to look out for in a resume or ask on an initial phone assessment that can indicate a person has some Serverless experience:

Tags

Note that some of these are AWS services. If the organization uses a different cloud provider, then you should look for tags showing the equivalent services on that cloud:

- Serverless/Serverless architecture/AWS Serverless

- (AWS) Lambda

- (AWS) Step Functions

- (AWS) DynamoDB

- Hosted functions

- Function-as-a-Service (FaaS)

- Event-driven architecture

- Microservices

- Service orchestration

- Service choreography

Experiences

For all of these, we want to ask for examples based on actual experience. Hypotheticals are less useful, though if there is no *actual* experience, it can help to at least understand their thinking.

- Have they worked on end-to-end Serverless applications or only individual components and minor background processes?

- What type of applications have they worked on? Often, it will be Serverless processing pipelines or Serverless APIs for mobile or web applications. Look for truly innovative ideas and crazy projects, as that is where most of the learning happens.

- Do they jump in and start developing – common with startups – or do they have experience first designing Serverless solution architecture and including comprehensive documentation?

- Are they competent in the NodeJS and/or Python programming language?

- Have they worked at a company known for digital innovation?

- Have they worked at a company with a Serverless-first strategy?

- Is their experience mostly in implementing tasks given to them, or did they play an active role in designing the solution or even setting organizational strategy? The latter will indicate a more senior candidate.

- Do they understand and can they use deployment pipelines and common tools? Ideally, they will have experience of designing and implementing pipelines and automation.

- Are they experienced with Infrastructure-as-Code (e.g., CloudFormation for AWS) and provisioning resources? It is not uncommon for enterprises trying out Serverless to remain with the traditional team segregation structure. Serverless developers may have been limited to only writing the microservice code or some minimal architecture design in this case.

- Do they have experience with automated testing, unit testing, integration testing, and end-to-end testing?

Personality

- A keen interest in both code and architecture.

- Driven by automation, cost optimization, scalability, and sustainability.

- They are up to date on the latest cloud capabilities and have channels such as the AWS RSS news feed to remain up to date.

- For early hires, we ideally want people who are comfortable with talking publicly and who can be both an advocate for Serverless within the organization and a thought leader outside of it.

- Leadership experience or potential, certainly the ability to mentor early hires.

Given that Serverless hires will mostly be technical candidates, a technical hiring manager should be present. If none is available within the organization, consider engaging a consultant to help with the evaluation.

Most Serverless hires should be asked to whiteboard during the interview. The approach I take is to start with something simple – a secure Serverless API, for example. That is all the instruction I provide, though I will answer any questions they have.

The result should be an API Gateway, protected by a WAF, integrated with Lambda microservices and perhaps a DynamoDB database. This could optionally be placed in a VPC with appropriate use of public and private subnets. For regulated industries, this will certainly be a requirement, and if they have not done so, I will ask them to add what they have to a VPC.

Once the basic design is up, I will then ask them to change things in response to one or more challenges. There are several challenges that can be considered depending on which area of expertise we want to test:

- The organization does not permit direct Internet access. Outbound must go via a proxy, and all inbound comes from a centrally managed VPC.

  - This would require changes to the network, API Gateway, and VPC peering or PrivateLink.

- Operations want to know in near real time when errors happen in the solution.

  - For example, CloudWatch subscriptions with a subscribed Lambda to analyze logs and SNS to notify

- The solution must be as cost-effective as possible. Only 1000 users per month are expected to use it.

  - DynamoDB should use Serverless billing mode. Lambda microservices should be rightsized to pick the ideal memory vs. execution time configuration. Monitoring of metrics related to cost should be configured, and a max budget alert should be enabled.

Many more challenges that can be used in an interview can be found throughout this book.

We will come back to *borrowing* a team in a later section. Before that, we will take a look at the top roles for Serverless teams. Note that we are talking about roles here, not necessarily individuals. Depending on the size and budget of the organization, an individual may need to take on multiple roles. I have described them as we might a job description, and you are welcome to use them as a base for talent acquisition efforts.

Serverless Roles: Solution Architect

The solution architect is one of the highest-demand job roles in Serverless architecture. This role will be expected to have both experience and knowledge breadth and depth across a large number of cloud services. They will be the ones to design complex solution architectures spanning tens of services to meet the project requirements. This can be an independent or leading role in the team. As a consultant, they would be heavily involved at the start of the project before handing over the team but remaining available for questions or changes when needed. As team leaders, they should take charge of the project, leading by example and taking ownership of the solution's overall technical vision. They act as the bridge between business goals and technical capabilities.

Responsibilities of a solution architect include

- Remaining up to date with the latest developments in the cloud

- Designing and often prototyping the best technical solution for a given business problem

- Assessing and monitoring existing systems to decide on improvements

- Describing the system structure, behaviors, opportunities, and risks to the project stakeholders

- Defining features, phases, and solution requirements, providing estimates for design, development, and operations

- Creating and maintaining specifications and documentation for the solution

Requirements for a solution architect include the following:

- Work experience of 8 or more years in one or more IT-related domains, at least five of which are in the cloud. Relevant professional-level certifications are a plus.

- Proven experience in architecting highly available, secure, and fault-tolerant systems in the cloud, with a significant portion built on fully managed and Serverless components. Very familiar with services such as Lambda, Fargate, API Gateway, CloudFront, DynamoDB, SQS, and SNS.

- Deep understanding of IT infrastructure, cloud cybersecurity, and cloud development.

- Knowledge of DevOps strategies, prototyping, and at least two programming languages.

- Business analysis capabilities and the ability to communicate technical concepts effectively to non-technical stakeholders. Solution architects need to be the bridge between stakeholders and developers.

- Technical project and product management experience with complex custom cloud solution projects is a plus.

Serverless Roles: Cloud Security Engineer

A cloud security engineer specializes in providing security systems and tools to manage the security vulnerabilities related to cloud technologies and plays an important role in protecting sensitive business data.

Responsibilities of a cloud security engineer include

- Studying the existing cloud systems and improving the security posture and strategy

- Identifying potential risks and security vulnerabilities and designing and documenting security policies for common design patterns

- Analyzing and identifying possible risks with third-party tools and services

- Actively managing team access roles and supporting the team with the user and microservice policies according to the Principle of Least Privilege

- Monitoring security services and logs for both development and live environments

- Actively engaging the business with guidance, security strategies, security responses, and newly introduced security management technologies

- Providing basic cybersecurity awareness training to the members of the project team at the start of a new project

Requirements for a cloud security engineer include the following:

- At least 5 years of industry experience in cybersecurity. Relevant and internationally recognized certifications are a plus.

- Strong knowledge of different cloud provider ecosystems and security services as well as the security features within commonly used services.

- Practical knowledge of cloud platforms related to computing, network, storage, deployment and delivery, and automation technologies.

- Proven hands-on experience with the Principle of Least Privilege will be especially important for Serverless projects.

- Experience with the programming languages used in the organization and up-to-date knowledge of their vulnerabilities and recommended security standards.

Serverless Roles: Deployment Automation Engineer

Lacking or having a bad deployment pipeline is very inefficient for any project. Using a good deployment pipeline is relatively easy, but building one that is suited for different types and sizes of projects while also being mostly Serverless (ideally) requires hands-on experience and knowledge in this area.

The deployment automation engineer role exists to ensure this competence is included in application teams. This person will be there at the start of every project to understand the needs of the project and design a suitable pipeline, including repository, build and test, and deployment stages.

This role is sometimes called a DevOps expert. However, an important point to note is that for a strong Serverless team, every member should be actively practicing DevOps. It is a shared responsibility. This role is distinct in that it is typically at a higher level than a single project. A good pipeline is an organization-level implementation of development and cloud automation and enablement.

Another reason I have included it as a role here is to make sure new teams with limited DevOps experience get the support they need. Starting a new project with limited or no DevOps practices is going to cause a lot of issues later on, so it's best to get some (outside) help to establish best practices and a DevOps mindset. This role could be a contract or a consultant who will be just as focused on knowledge transfer as they are on setting up the initial deployment pipeline.

Responsibilities of a deployment automation engineer include the following:

- Designing a centrally managed and/or project-specific Serverless deployment CI/CD pipeline according to the business's needs. Cost-effectiveness and security are key points; fully managed services are preferred.

- Transferring knowledge to other team members and training them to be proficient in DevOps so they understand the mindset, best practices, and standards of strong deployment pipelines.

- Ensuring changes to code are tracked and well managed with different repos, sub-repos, and branches. Ensuring appropriate permissions are assigned to different team members for merging and pushing to the different environments.

- Developing security into the pipelines with vulnerability scans, standards, and regulatory compliance scans that automatically notify of any issues and block potential risks.

- Continuous measuring and improving developer productivity. Mentoring and training developers to be self-sufficient in good DevOps practices and strive to continuously improve processes.

- Establishing milestones for necessary contributions from departments and developing processes to facilitate their collaboration.

Requirements for a deployment automation engineer include

- Minimum of 3 years' development cloud automation experience and a high-level understanding of working with various programming languages, systems, and pipelines

- Knowledge of integration technologies, automation tools in the cloud, automation features in common cloud services, and development and testing automation

- Experience with agile methodologies, mentoring technical people, and bringing together people and technology strengths

- Proven experience in developing deployment pipelines in the cloud using fully managed and cost-effective services. Knowledge of third-party common DevOps tools such as Ansible, Chef, Puppet, Docker, Jenkins, and GIT.

 # Serverless Roles: Full-Stack Developer

The modern developer is typically a full-stack developer even though they may have a preference for front or back end. For Serverless, we will typically look for Typescript (JavaScript) developers if we are making web applications, Python if we are working on analytics-driven back-end solutions, or Java in certain sectors where it may be unavoidable. In Serverless, developers will mostly be focused on developing the code for microservices, but they will also need a solid understanding of how to interact with the many cloud services that the solution architect may include in a given project.

Responsibilities of a full-stack developer include the following:

- Translate user stories and requirements into technical tasks, plan the code architecture, and work with the solution architect to plan the overall solution.

- Perform feasibility analysis and develop prototypes for uncertain or high-risk features and take an agile, iterative approach to projects.

- Establish the schemas and standards for communication between different microservices and between microservices and the API, along with the schemas, methods, and parameters for communication between the front end and the API.

- Develop, debug, iterate, and improve microservice code in TypeScript/JavaScript or Python, web interfaces in React or Angular, and mobile and desktop interfaces with React Native.

- Ensure unit tests are developed and work with the DevOps engineer to implement a consistent testing pipeline and approval process.

- Follow best practices, utilize up-to-date technologies in all projects, and ensure that security updates to the code are implemented quickly.

- Monitor microservice analytics and profile logs to detect inefficiencies and optimize them to reduce the cost and improve the speed of the solution.

- Instill consistent documentation standards in the team and ensure that all code is commented on and described in a knowledge sharing solution.

Requirements for a full-stack developer include the following:

- At least 4 years of experience in both front- and back-end development.

- Proven ability to learn new technologies and stay up-to-date with current standards and security recommendations.

- Experience in working with cloud services, Serverless, and microservice architectures.

- Excellent team player, able to work closely with architects, security specialists, DevOps engineers, testers, and other internal or external developers.

- Commercial and business awareness. Technical solutions need to be technically and commercially viable.

Serverless Roles: Database Engineer

For fully Serverless solutions, we often need to work with non-relational databases. These can be complex and need the right data model. Even then, not all data is suitable, but that decision should be made by someone with the appropriate experience and knowledge. The database engineer should be experienced with all kinds of databases in the cloud and know which one is suitable for the solution's data model and expected queries.

Responsibilities of a database engineer include the following:

- Plan and design data models suitable for each solution and match them to one or more best-suited databases.

- Monitor database performance and seek ways to improve it. Work with the development team to optimize queries and improve their understanding of working with a particular database.

- If needed, bring big data capabilities to the team. Design cost-effective and purpose-suitable big data pipelines for ingestion, storage, and access at scale.

- Secure databases by preparing access and control policies and implementing backup and disaster recovery procedures.

Requirements for a database engineer include

- Deep understanding of NoSQL and functional knowledge of specialized cloud databases and the many different relational databases. Knowledge of database fundamentals such as data storage, data modeling, and data access patterns

- Experience designing data models that are fit for purpose, optimizing queries, and monitoring database performance

- Experience designing data pipelines in the cloud, from ingestion to storage to access – all following security, efficiency, scalability, and best practices

Serverless Roles: Project Manager

Project managers assigned to Serverless projects will need to be comfortable managing a large number of mini-projects in parallel. This is a common approach as each component, such as a microservice, can be considered its own project, with an assigned budget, developer, and timeline. Each component is developed, tested, and deployed independently, but toward the end of the project, coordination and collaboration will be needed to perform the end-to-end tests to ensure all the components are working well together and debug any issues arising from that.

Responsibilities of a project manager include the following:

- Manage multiple teams working in parallel on different components (UIs, microservices, etc.).

- Work with business stakeholders to scope project user stories that will become infrastructure configuration and microservice code.

- Work with the teams to estimate the development cost of each microservice and cloud infrastructure, including operational cost estimations.

- Manage stakeholder requirements and expectations.

- Synchronize the individual teams and work toward integrating the different components as they complete.

- Manage the overall workflow from design to development to deployment to testing.

- Manage the end-to-end testing based on business cases.

Requirements for a database engineer include the following:

- At least 5 years of experience in managing projects, with at least 2 years as a scrum master following agile methodology.

- Proven experience managing multiple projects in parallel and organizing large distributed teams in collaboration.

- Detail-oriented where it matters, able to effectively manage timelines and ensure effort is spent where it can add the most value.

- Understanding of change management and digital transformation practices.

- Passing familiarity with at least one programming language is a plus.

- Working knowledge of Jira, Confluence, and any organization-specific project management tools that may be required.

- Knowledge of executing digital project risk assessments and cost-benefit analysis.

- Familiarity and ideally a foundational or business certificate with the relevant cloud provider.

- High-level familiarity with change management concepts, including people and culture change, will be very helpful.

 Serverless Training

Whether we are looking to validate our own or a team's Serverless competency or learn a new skill, Serverless training and certification is a great way to gain and test knowledge.

AWS, being one of the pioneers in Serverless computing, offers several certifications at different levels to validate expertise. While there are no specific *Serverless* certifications yet, most of the existing ones do contain Serverless topics, so they are still worthwhile to pursue.

AWS covers 64% of large-scale enterprises and 68% of small- and medium-scale businesses. This creates a higher demand for those with AWS knowledge and expertise, making their certifications an opportunity-opener for cloud experts. Salary reports by Forbes, Glassdoor, Ambition, and Global Knowledge average the salaries of AWS-certified positions at 10–30% higher than salaries for the same position without certification. Reports even show a 12% difference between the salaries of jobs with an associate-level certification and those of roles with a professional level certification.

While certification can be used as proof of competency and help with salary negotiations, the value of confirming existing knowledge and the experience of gaining the knowledge needed to achieve the certification are equally strong reasons to take this path.

Here are what certificates can do:

- A certificate is proof of capability in a given knowledge area.

- Certificates from reputable organizations open doors for job opportunities, promotions, and salary increases.

- The study needed to fill any gaps in our knowledge is a great learning experience. Note that study efforts should include both theory and practice to be useful.

- Certification leads to a shared and consistent understanding of the topic, which increases efficiency and productivity in teams.

- Certificates can improve our standing with cloud providers and an organization's partner rank, which can lead to more opportunities and other benefits for the organization.

- Achieved certificates can be used as part of salary negotiation, but this will depend on the employer and their hiring policies.

Here are what certification won't do:

- A certificate is not proof of *experience*. We cannot substitute real hands-on experience with a certificate or the theory learned to achieve the certificate.

- A certificate does not guarantee a job. It is an additional qualification and proof of knowledge that may help with shortlisting.

AWS currently offers 12 certifications categorized in four tiers representing different levels of expertise, shown in Figure 5-1.

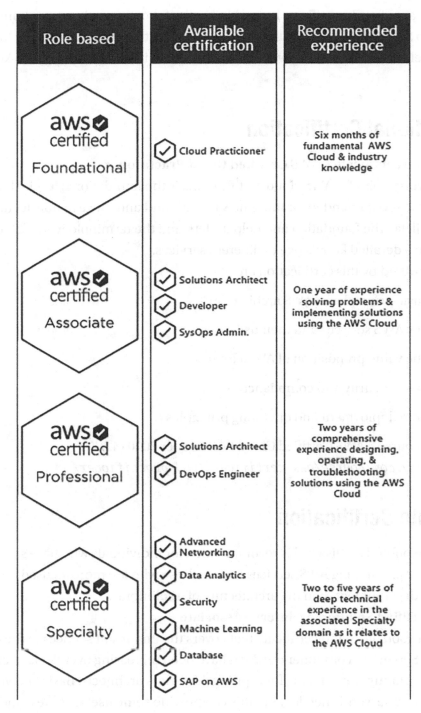

Figure 5-1. *AWS certification paths*

A summary of each certificate is provided in the following with a note about its relevance to Serverless and a link to a Udemy course with its rating. Note that the courses linked are relevant at the time of writing (2022) and the instructors do tend to keep them updated.

Foundational Certification

Foundational certificate – AWS Certified Cloud Practitioner

The starting point for AWS cloud certifications is the foundational level. This certification is recommended for those new to the cloud and those in non-technical roles as it will lay the foundation and help understand the terminology used. It does not go deep into a detailed knowledge of different services.

Areas covered by this certification are

- Basic principles of AWS architecture

- Key AWS services and their use cases

- The value proposition of AWS cloud

- Basic security and compliance

- Core deployment and operating principles

Udemy course – AWS Certified Cloud Practitioner 2020 (4.5/5): *www.udemy.com/course/aws-certified-cloud-practitioner/*

Associate Certification

Certification offered at this level is recommended for individuals who have some experience implementing AWS services and for those who are more focused on application development than the architecture of a solution.

AWS Certified Solution Architect – Associate

This is a good all-round certificate that covers the important services in the cloud. It has some Serverless components, which have been increasing over the last few years, so is certainly worth taking for aspiring Serverless architects. Basic knowledge of networking and servers is needed, but this can provide some useful context and a deeper understanding of what powers Serverless services.

Areas covered by this certification are

- Network technologies and how they work in AWS

- How AWS-based applications work and how client interfaces connect to the AWS platform

- To build secure and reliable applications on the AWS platform

- The design of highly available and scalable systems

- Deploying hybrid systems – with an on-premises data center as well as AWS components

- Data security practices, disaster recovery techniques, and troubleshooting

Udemy course – Ultimate AWS Certified Solution Architect Associate 2022 (4.7/5): *www.udemy.com/course/aws-certified-solutions-architect-associate-saa-c02/*

AWS Certified Developer – Associate

This course focuses on the creation and maintenance of cloud-based applications. Prior experience coding in AWS Lambda and using related services will really help. This certificate is certainly relevant to Serverless, covering services such as Lambda and DynamoDB.

Areas covered by this certification are

- Knowledge of AWS architecture and key features of AWS services

- Hands-on expertise in planning, creating, implementing, and managing applications

- Working awareness of programs that use databases, notifications, workflow, and storage and change management services

Udemy course – Ultimate AWS Certified Developer Associate 2022 (4.7/5): *www.udemy.com/course/aws-certified-developer-associate-dva-c01/*

AWS Certified SysOps Administrator – Associate

Intended for system administrators, so prior experience with networking and other lower-level competencies will be expected. It is less relevant to Serverless, but it can provide some context to how some of the Serverless services work behind the scenes. It is an essential "prep" for the DevOps Professional certificate.

Areas covered by this certification are

- Deployment of apps to the AWS platform

- Exchange of data between on-prem and AWS

- Selecting the appropriate AWS service for a given problem

- Provision, maintenance, and protection of applications in the AWS framework

Udemy course – Ultimate AWS Certified SysOps Administrator Associate 2022 (4.7/5):

www.udemy.com/course/ultimate-aws-certified-sysops-administrator-associate/

Professional Certification

Certification offered at this level is recommended for individuals with extensive experience with AWS services and work on complex end-to-end solutions.

AWS Certified Solution Architect – Professional

Professional solution architects are expected to analyze the user and non-functional requirements and to make design decisions for the development and delivery of complex cloud solutions. Like the Associate certification, it is a mix of server and Serverless competencies. This certification requires hands-on experience with a wide range of cloud services, knowledge of common issues and troubleshooting, and an understanding of how they integrate. It is strongly recommended to achieve the Solution Architect – Associate certificate first.

Areas covered by this certification are

- Best practice for securely and efficiently designing scalable cloud architecture

- Choosing the appropriate service for the requirements of the application and understanding any related integration challenges

- Common issues and troubleshooting

- Migration of enterprise solutions to the cloud

- Knowledge of strategy for cost optimization

- Best practice understanding of multi-application architectural design

Udemy course – Ultimate AWS Certified Solution Architect Professional 2022 (4.7/5): *www.udemy.com/course/aws-solutions-architect-professional/*

AWS Certified DevOps Engineer – Professional

The DevOps certification focuses on provisioning, operating, and managing applications on the AWS platform. This analysis focuses extensively on continuous delivery (CD) and automated process management. It is strongly recommended to pass the SysOps Administrator certification first and have knowledge of and experience with services such as CodeCommit, CodeBuild, and CodePipeline. General experience with DevOps practices, agile methodology, and third-party CI/CD tools will be helpful too. Considering how DevOps-focused Serverless is, this is certainly a worthwhile certification to take for Serverless professionals.

Areas covered by this certification are

- The basics of modern CD methodologies

- Implementation of CD systems

- Setup, monitoring, and logging of systems on AWS

- Implementation of highly available and scalable systems on AWS

- Design and management tools that enable automation of operations

Udemy course – AWS Certified DevOps Engineer Professional 2020 - Hands On! (4.7/5): *www.udemy.com/course/aws-certified-devops-engineer-professional-hands-on/*

Specialty Certification

While the Solution Architect certifications are quite all-round, Specialty certification requires deep hands-on experience in the specific topic that the certificate covers. It is quite difficult to pass these exams with only superficial or theoretical knowledge.

AWS Certified Data Analytics – Specialty

This certification focuses on the topic of big data: ingesting, storing, and analyzing it. It expects knowledge of data analytics and experience using AWS tools for the design and implementation of big data solutions. This certification does cover a number of Serverless big data topics and services, and it is recommended for anyone interested in Serverless data engineering.

Areas covered by this certification are

- Architecting best practices for implementing big data services

- Designing and managing big data

- AWS tools for automating data analysis

- Security best practices for big data solutions

- Security, logging, and integration of the many services

Udemy course – AWS Certified Data Analytics Specialty 2022 - Hands On! (4.6/5): *www.udemy.com/course/aws-big-data/*

AWS Certified Advanced Networking – Specialty

The Advanced Networking Specialty certification is designed to test expertise in and knowledge of performing complex networking tasks on AWS and hybrid IT networking architecture at scale. This course requires deep hands-on experience in the design and deployment of networking technologies and specialized networking awareness on AWS. A background in classical network infrastructure will be helpful too. Beyond providing a deep understanding of how Serverless works behind the scenes, this certificate does not cover many Serverless topics.

Areas covered by this certification are

- Designing, developing, and deploying cloud solutions with AWS

- Implementing core services following architectural best practices

- Automation for AWS tasks for network deployments

- Security and compliance design and implementation

- Network optimization and troubleshooting

Udemy course – AWS Certified Advanced Networking Specialty 2022 (4.6/5): *www.udemy.com/course/aws-certified-advanced-networking-specialty/*

AWS Certified Security – Specialty

The Security certification covers a wide range of security topics in the cloud, including securing services and applications, encryption, logging and auditing, and basic security practices such as incident response and the Principle of Least Privilege. There is a strong focus on the AWS Identity and Access Management (IAM) service. This certification is relevant to server-based and Serverless solutions in the cloud as well as general management of AWS accounts.

Areas covered by this certification are

- Using a range of AWS tools to choose the correct level of protection depending on the installation and sensitivity of the data

- Choosing the most effective data security methods, like encryption mechanisms

- Implementing logging and tracking tools to identify and evaluate protection flaws and deficiencies in the infrastructure

AWS services include AWS Identity and Access Management, AWS CloudTrail, AWS Config, Amazon Inspector, AWS Trusted Advisor, Amazon GuardDuty, Amazon CloudWatch, and Amazon Key Management Service.

Udemy course – AWS Certified Security Specialty 2020 (4.5/5):
www.udemy.com/course/aws-certified-security-specialty/

AWS Certified Machine Learning – Specialty

This certification is a bit different. Around half of the content is not even about AWS services but focuses on open source machine learning tools and algorithms. It expects users to be able to design, apply, and manage machine learning approaches to a range of market problems and is really intended for data scientists. There are some Serverless mentions, but it is predominantly about data scientist activities.

Areas covered by this certification are

- Choosing and justifying the right ML solution for a given problem

- Identifying the relevant AWS solutions for creating and deploying an ML solution (usually SageMaker)

- Developing and deploying cost-optimized, flexible, efficient, and stable ML solutions

Udemy course – AWS Certified Machine Learning Specialty 2022 - Hands On! (4.5/5):
www.udemy.com/course/aws-machine-learning/

AWS Certified Database – Specialty

This certification focuses on AWS database services, especially DynamoDB and Aurora. As such, it is certainly relevant to Serverless. It tests knowledge such as knowing the difference between and when to use different types of databases, database management, and architectural design.

Areas covered by this certification are

- Database design

- Deployment and migration

- Management and operations

- Backup and disaster recovery

- Monitoring and troubleshooting

- Security

Udemy course – Ultimate AWS Certified Database Specialty 2022 (4.4/5):
www.*udemy.com/course/aws-certified-database-specialty-dbs/*
AWS Certified: SAP on AWS - Specialty
Certifies knowledge in designing, implementing, migrating, and operating SAP
workloads on AWS. To take this exam, experience using SAP on AWS is needed, as well as
the ability to design a secure and scalable SAP cloud architecture.

Online Resources to Learn About Serverless

While there are no Serverless certificates yet, there are courses available that focus on
Serverless. The following are relevant courses offered by the popular online course providers:

Udemy

- **Introduction to Serverless (3.9)**

    This course is intended to provide a basic understanding of
    Serverless in a very short 30-minute lunch-and-learn session:

    www.*udemy.com/course/introduction-to-Serverless/*

- **AWS Serverless APIs & Apps - A Complete Introduction (4.6)**

    Learn about building and running a Serverless API and use modern
    techniques to create a scalable and cost-effective web application.
    The course content runs for 6 hours and covers Serverless
    computing in AWS with API Gateway, Lambda, and other services:

    www.*udemy.com/course/aws-Serverless-a-complete-*
    introduction/

- **Basic AWS Architecture Best Practices - Crash Course (4.5)**

  This is a 1.5-hour crash course providing high-level knowledge on AWS design best practices. It covers topics such as scalability, automation, loose coupling, and using services instead of servers:

  www.udemy.com/course/awsbestpractices/

- **Serverless Framework Bootcamp: Node.js, AWS & Microservices (4.6)**

  While I recommend CDK over Serverless Framework, this is an excellent 5.5-hour course that provides knowledge on how to build reliable and scalable Serverless back-end applications. After an introduction to Serverless Framework, it will cover topics such as authentication, extreme scalability, REST API, decoupling using SQS, microservice architecture, and many AWS services. It uses NodeJS as the programming language, so it expects sufficient experience with it as a prerequisite:

  www.udemy.com/course/Serverless-framework/

- **Rocking AWS Serverless - A Real World Guide (4.5)**

  This is another great deep dive into the AWS Serverless stack as well as containers and some hybrid or partially Serverless design patterns. This course is quite broad, covering many related services, background knowledge, and development tools and frameworks. It runs for over 18 hours:

  www.udemy.com/course/aws-serverless-a-complete-guide/

- **Azure Serverless Functions and Logic Apps (4.2)**

  For those interested in Serverless on Azure, this course is designed for senior technical and business professionals who have exposure to Azure. It runs for just over 2 hours and provides an introduction to Serverless on Azure and the relevant services and techniques involved:

  www.udemy.com/course/azure-Serverless/

- **Azure Functions Masterclass (4.4)**

  This is a masterclass for those interested in using Azure to develop real-world applications. The course is also designed for senior technical professionals and runs for over 5 hours, beginning with fundamentals of Azure functions and culminating in seven use case examples.

A Cloud Guru

This platform offers a series of online courses, which has helped over half a million engineers to be experts in AWS, Azure, and Google cloud. It empowers organizations to stay up to date with evolving technologies through its wide range of courses, hands-on labs, and learning paths. Its website can be found here:

https://acloud.guru/

AWS courses offered by A Cloud Guru include

- **AWS certification courses**

- **Coding for Cloud 101**

  This course is a sharp introduction to developing cloud applications for developers and technical managers. No previous experience with coding is needed.

- **Go Serverless with a Graph Database**

  These courses give the requisite know-how to spin a graph database stack and a basic web application by using Serverless architecture and cloud formation to optimize the database info.

- **Create a Serverless Portfolio**

  This course teaches how to build an impressive portfolio that is completely Serverless, using modern programming techniques.

All AWS courses can be found here:

https://acloud.guru/courses/amazon-web-services

Azure-related courses offered by A Cloud Guru include

- **Azure certification courses**

- **AZ-103 Microsoft Azure Administrator 2020**

  This AZ-103 course will teach the latest, redesigned Microsoft Azure Management Test and help one become a qualified Microsoft Azure Manager by developing Azure expertise in storage, protection, networking, and cloud computing.

- **Introduction to Azure**

  This course offers a high-level view of the Azure portfolio of services and its main functions.

- **The Complete Serverless Course**

  This course will provide an introduction to the Serverless landscape. It covers cases of general usage, design trends, and best practices and teaches creating a Serverless solution that works on all of the three major cloud providers.

- **Introduction to Azure DevOps**

  This course offers an understanding of what Azure DevOps is, a short overview of how to set up an instance, what Azure Boards are and how to use them, how to use Azure Repos to store code, how to use Azure Pipelines to set up full-automated builds and releases, Azure Test Plans, and how to use Azure Artifacts to set up customized package management feeds.

All Azure courses can be found here:
https://acloud.guru/courses/microsoft-azure
Coursera

- **AWS Fundamentals: Building Serverless Applications (4.7)**

  This 10-hour course is designed to aid AWS Fundamentals specialization and provides an introduction to Serverless architecture. It shows how to build and deploy Serverless solutions. Hands-on activities include building a Serverless website and chatbot with a focus on taking advantage of modern architectures to improve agility and creativity and lower overall ownership costs across a variety of AWS resources:

www.coursera.org/learn/aws-fundamentals-building-
Serverless-applications

- **Cloud Computing Basics - Azure (4.5)**

  This is an Azure beginner-level course that covers the basics of cloud computing. It explains the Azure services, API and its relationship with cloud computing, cloud deployment models, managed services, and cloud service platforms. This is a 9-hour course provided by LearnQuest - an Apple-authorized global training provider:

  www.coursera.org/learn/cloud-computing-basics

- **Introduction to Cloud Computing - IBM (4.8)**

  This is a course provided by IBM for their cloud. The numerous cloud software architectures (IaaS, PaaS, SaaS), implementation frameworks (public, personal, hybrid), and core elements of a cloud network (VMs, networking, memory document, frame, item, CDN) are covered. Interestingly, it also covers emerging cloud trends and practices, including hybrid multi-cloud, microservices, Serverless, DevOps, native cloud, and modernization of applications. The course lasts 10 hours, and each topic contains two quizzes to complete, while the final lesson contains three quizzes:

  www.coursera.org/learn/introduction-to-cloud

Linux Academy

Linux Academy provides a Serverless learning path that includes a few courses on Serverless from beginner to intermediate. The courses provided are

- Serverless Concepts

- Google Cloud Functions Deep Dive

- Lambda Deep Dive

- Build a Serverless Chatbot with AWS Lex

- Full-Stack Serverless Applications on AWS

A certificate of completion is provided for each of the preceding courses. More information about Linux Academy's Serverless courses can be found here: *https://linuxacademy.com/learning-path/Serverless-computing/*

Annual Serverless Events

With Serverless being a trending topic, different events such as meetups, webinars, and large-scale conferences are held regularly to support and grow the Serverless community.

- **AWS Global Summit**

  AWS Global Summits are free events that are organized to interact, communicate, and learn about AWS, bringing together all those interested in the cloud. We can learn about new service and feature launches, best practices in architecture and security, and, more frequently, how to leverage AI to accelerate business transformations.

  Summits are held in cities across the world, attracting technologists from all sectors and skill levels.

- **AWS re:Invent**

  AWS re:Invent is a conference organized to share knowledge within the global cloud computing community. The event features keynote announcements, opportunities for training and certification, access to more than 2,500 technical sessions, and a partner expo.

- **ServerlessDays**

  ServerlessDays is a worldwide group of events that build and promote a community around Serverless technologies. Every ServerlessDay is unique, locally coordinated, and not for profit. They are run according to three key principles:

  - *Local*: Run by local community organizers.

  - *Accessible*: Financially and physically accessible to the community.

  - *Representative*: Be representative of the broader community within which it exists.

- **Be part of the AWS user community**

  With the growing popularity of AWS with developers, entrepreneurs, and companies, more than 400 AWS interest groups have sprung up around the world. Community groups are peer-to-peer networks that periodically connect to exchange information, address questions, and hear about innovative programs and best practices. Find a user group close to your location and become a part of the community.

  Together with Slash, I launched the Cambodia AWS user group in 2019, and my team members or I can sometimes be found presenting in the Singapore user group.

If English is not your native language and you struggle with accents, then these are three great trainers in three different accents to pick from:

1. The *A Cloud Guru* AWS courses cover most of the certs and are delivered predominantly by an Australian trainer with support from a British trainer on some of the modules.

2. Stephane Maarek is the trainer for most of the Udemy AWS certification courses I have linked previously. He speaks with a French accent. For the Data Analytics and ML courses, he partners with Frank Kane, an American trainer with a very soothing voice, and for the Database course, he partners with Indian trainer Riyaz Sayyad.

3. Zeal Vora is another great Udemy trainer from India who covers a lot of networking, security, and server-based services on AWS in his courses.

There are many other trainers available with different accents but often with very few or poorly rated courses. A good approach is to look for the topic you want to learn about and then watch the preview of the relevant courses to find someone with a voice that works for you.

Lastly, if you are on a learning journey and your employer isn't covering the costs or you are self-employed, be sure to check if your government has any initiatives or grants to support learning. For example, Singaporeans get free access to many Udemy courses via the library board. When purchasing courses from Udemy, note that they frequently have sales, and discount coupons can often be found online for many of the courses.

Serverless Team Structure

Traditionally, an application team would distribute the user stories and tasks between themselves. They would work on a single code base, each downloading the entire application to their system and creating feature branches to work on. Once a feature had been completed, it was committed, and a pull request was created to merge it into the main branch. As with code repositories, Serverless offers a choice between two options when it comes to team structures.

A single team, shown in Figure 5-2, can be collaborative, with developers actively participating in different tasks and more than one on a single task in some cases. A larger collaborative team can include a more diverse set of experiences, which can help in tackling problems that may arise and provide feedback for best practices and other improvements.

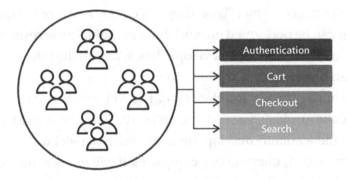

Figure 5-2. *Single collaborative team structure*

Since everyone is working closely together and the development work is more intertwined, there is less chance of silos forming. A larger team has a degree of leeway to handle situations such as team members going on leave.

A disadvantage is the potential for *"too many chefs in the kitchen,"* where clashing ideas can cause team friction or delays due to indecision or code incompatibility. Shared dependencies can be problematic when trying to merge them into the main branch with conflicting changes. Similarly, dependencies between components can cause blockers for one developer while they wait for another to complete their work. Larger teams tend to spend more time on communication, such as standups exceeding 15 minutes.

An alternative option available in Serverless projects is a split team structure, shown in Figure 5-3.

251

Figure 5-3. *Split team structure*

In this structure, the microservices all have an agreed input and output; what happens within the microservice code itself is less important to the wider team.

This means that each developer can work on a different microservice in parallel. They can write the code and test the microservice independently to ensure the expected input/output requirements are met. Then they can deploy it before integration, and end-to-end testing can be performed on workflows of multiple microservices. This works best with a multi-repo setup, so each developer has access to the microservice they are working on and can independently deploy and test it.

This approach applies to user interfaces too. The API schema for the back end should be defined and ideally mocked in a service such as API Gateway. A front-end developer or team can then independently develop the front end in parallel with the microservices. As the development of each microservice completes, it will replace the mock integration in API Gateway with the functional Lambda integration.

This approach offers more freedom to developers; they can determine how to best approach the scope of work as long as the input and output requirements are met. The scope and brief can be tighter, along with the permissions. Each developer only needs access to the code they are working on, and, given the independence of microservices, they only need the scope for their part and the clearly defined input and output requirements. As each microservice has an owner, there is more accountability, and the assigned developers have a sense of ownership.

Dependencies are not an issue until the very end, when end-to-end testing is needed to ensure that multiple components in a workflow can provide the final result. Developers can work and test their components independently without worrying about shared code or dependencies on other components. This also makes it easier for global teams to collaborate as time zone differences are less of a challenge.

But ownership by a single developer can also be problematic if the developer goes on leave or moves to another unit or company. Handover becomes a risk that must be addressed with processes and up-to-date detailed documentation.

Flexibility can lead to mixed adherence to best practices and organizational policies. Communicating these, or even enforcing them in the pipeline, and supporting developers in the development process will be critical.

This approach can easily lead to silos and be difficult for junior developers to adapt to, as a high degree of independence is expected. Efforts must be put in to ensure collaboration across the assigned microservices, and juniors should be paired with experienced developers on a single microservice.

Collaboration will be especially important during the integration of multiple microservices into workflows. Even with the input/output clearly defined, unforeseen issues will often arise that will need multiple developers to work together to find a solution. This takes an experienced project manager to oversee and coordinate.

 Serverless Careers

Serverless developers have a few career paths available to them, depending on their interests and skills. Figure 5-4 shows some potential paths. These may differ based on organizational structures and individual talents and interests, but it provides a general idea of how developer roles could evolve as they gain seniority.

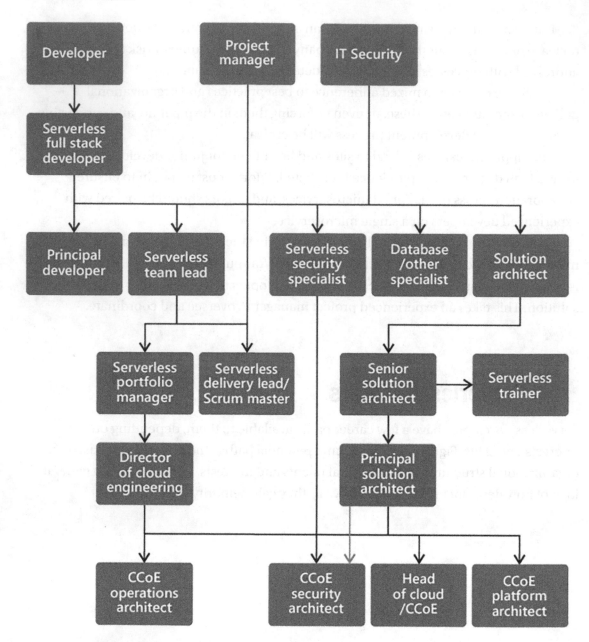

Figure 5-4. *Potential Serverless career paths*

Many developers will want to remain hands-on with code and simply progress through full-stack seniority levels or specialize in security, purpose-built databases, or other similar areas. Security specialists could also come from a security background, adapting to fully understand security in the cloud and the tighter permissions that can be achieved with Serverless architecture.

Some developers may have a talent in mentoring, leadership, and communication. This path can go all the way to enterprise executive, or they might branch off to focus on project delivery and stakeholder management. While some developer background can help, those with a project management or agile background can specialize and also go down the Serverless project delivery path.

For team members who are more interested in cloud infrastructure, strategy, and big picture design, the architect path might be suitable. This path has levels of seniority up to executive, or it can branch off to focus on training.

Many of the career paths can ultimately lead to senior Cloud Center of Excellence roles.

Key Performance Indicators (KPIs)

KPIs – or, for some organizations, objectives and key results (OKRs) – will invariably be different in a Serverless organization. This applies to both team member KPIs and project KPIs.

KPIs especially relevant to Serverless team members can include the following:

- Minimizing the use of servers and long-running containers, though this should not come at the cost of application quality.

- KPIs around cost reduction and sustainability, which will drive proactive rightsizing of microservices and optimization of code and other components.

- KPIs around security and PoLP, which will push tighter controls on permissions.

- KPIs addressing the accuracy of operational cost estimates in comparison with the actual operational costs.

- The quantity of relevant reusable assets submitted, approved, or available – depending on the person's role.

- KPIs related to training, upskilling, and certifications, which can also be considered to drive continuous learning.

- A KPI around the quantity of components can be interesting. Often, there is a concern of quantity overruling quality with such a KPI, but with Serverless architecture, we generally prefer multiple smaller microservices over fewer large microservices. The KPI should use *components,* not *microservices,* because the preference should be serviceful – fully managed services over custom code where appropriate. This can also help drive multiple purpose-built database components, instead of one large relational database.

Operational KPIs for projects can include the following:

- KPIs that reduce latency. These are more important than uptime KPIs because modern deployment practices and fully managed redundancy make the latter less likely to happen.

- Similar to the team member KPIs, project KPIs that address cost reduction, sustainability, and security. These will help drive continuous improvement and optimization of the application.

- KPIs for the number of issues addressed *before* they were reported by end users and the time that was taken to address the issues. This will drive good proactive logging behavior.

More ideas for KPIs should become apparent over the next few chapters.

Borrowing a Team: Working with Serverless Vendors

Some organizations consistently use vendors for their application development needs. Other organizations use vendors or freelancers to temporarily augment small teams or fill gaps when team members are on leave. Either way, taking a multi-repo split team approach will make it easier to manage individual contributors and the overall security of the application.

Multi-repo, shown in Figure 5-5, provides a higher degree of control over access. Individual microservices can each be assigned to a specific developer, and they will only have access to the relevant part of the code. We also have the option to include the full, partial, or no infrastructure configuration in the assigned repository.

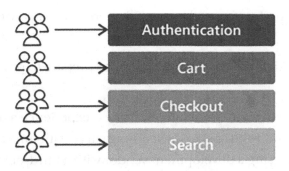

Figure 5-5. *A multi-repo split team approach offers security benefits*

Each microservice can have a narrow scope and clearly defined input and output requirements. The scope and brief should include best practices and non-functional requirements that need to be adhered to. Such bite-sized pieces of work make it easier to brief developers and receive more accurate estimates. Scope creep is also far less likely to happen at this level, though additional microservices may need to be added to the larger project scope based on new insights and unforeseen issues later in the project.

A challenge with multi-repo split teams – and we will cover this in more detail in Chapter 6 – is if best practices and non-functional requirements are not sufficiently briefed and enforced. This can lead to varying coding approaches and standards across the different microservices, which can make it considerably harder to update or maintain the application in the future.

Manually reviewing and enforcing standards and compliance will add considerable overheads to the project. Instead, we use automated CI/CD pipelines that can validate for standards and compliance and perform different types of automated testing on all submitted code and infrastructure templates.

A challenge with Serverless is the lack of experienced developers in the market. This applies to vendors as much as it does to job candidates. The few vendors that have sufficient experience tend to be more expensive than vendors without. However, as covered in Chapter 3, we need to consider the Total Cost of Ownership. The significantly reduced operational costs of Serverless, lower maintenance and overheads, shorter development timelines, and the ease of operation gained from modern DevOps practices can usually make up for the higher one-time cost of development.

There are two approaches for working on a Serverless project with outsourcing vendors:

1. Find an experienced Serverless vendor and prepare to pay a bit more.

2. Find a vendor who does not have Serverless experience and be prepared to cover the cost of the learning curve with time and money. Partnering a development vendor with a third-party Serverless consultant can be considered a way to reduce the learning time at the higher cost of a specialized consultant.

Experienced Serverless Vendors

There are vendors who are *able* to do Serverless architecture and development and even those who *specialize* in Serverless. For example, the AWS Partner site lists preferred vendors with a Serverless capability. Searching for relevant terms such as *"Serverless Lambda developer agency"* can also return some useful results, but make sure to vet them to confirm they have the right experience and capabilities. An experienced Serverless vendor should have several cloud certifications in their team, and, typically, I would expect a blog with Serverless-related articles and public whitepapers relevant to Serverless. Some Serverless open source projects or contributions on GitHub can also be a good sign.

In my experience, Serverless vendors tend to be booked well in advance, so we may need to wait a while before the project can kick off. These vendors also tend to have very well-thought-out development pipelines and automated testing capabilities, and they will have hard requirements on using languages such as TypeScript instead of plain JavaScript. These are all excellent practices, but for those unfamiliar with them, it might be a bit overwhelming. Their level of due diligence and attention to detail can drive the total cost up further, but, in my opinion, it is better to know up front what the real cost is than to have what initially seems like a good deal, but ends up costing a lot more. Tech debt from bad practices early in a project is relentless, and the longer we live with it, the more it will cost to resolve.

Capable Vendor

Finding a capable vendor who may not have much or any experience in Serverless is considerably easier, and they will typically cost less. They may even jump at the opportunity to learn and deliver a Serverless project as most developers will be excited about the technology. However, the downside is that there will be a steep learning curve for them, with many lessons learned the hard way, and they may not have the well-oiled automated development and testing practices in place nor a library of reusable Serverless components that an experienced Serverless vendor would have.

At a bare minimum, a vendor should be experienced with NodeJS or Python. For a web application, they should have experience with JavaScript or ideally TypeScript. Having past projects that include REST APIs will be helpful. Any microservice experience, even if not strictly Serverless, will also be very beneficial. Experience with NoSQL databases is harder to find, but will be an asset to a Serverless project. General experience with the cloud can be reasonably expected from all development vendors at this point, though we might want to consider if their preferred cloud provider aligns with the one used by the organization.

The risks of working with a vendor with limited Serverless experience can be somewhat mitigated by involving a Serverless consultant. They can design the architecture for the solution, provide some training to the vendor, and review and support the team as needed during implementation. It can also be beneficial if they can advise on setting up an automated development and testing pipeline for Serverless if the organization does not already have one. The benefits to the vendor of Serverless education that we are paying for cannot be understated, and we can consider negotiating the vendor's fee with this in mind.

An experienced Serverless consultant capable of managing and training a vendor will come with a price tag, but given the lower cost of the vendor and the potentially reduced development timeline, the total development cost may still work out to be lower than using an experienced Serverless vendor.

Serverless consultants can be found via the cloud providers. For example, the AWS's Partner team can usually recommend a freelancer or consultancy. Depending on the organization's size and the project, one of AWS's solution architects might even be able and willing to help directly.

With the right keywords, LinkedIn and Google Search can potentially provide some leads. For example, searching for "*Serverless consultant*" (with quotes) results in a few freelancers. Some experienced Serverless vendors may also be willing to help with designing the architecture even if they don't get the development work – it's certainly worth asking.

If you are not technical and decide to work with a Serverless-experienced vendor, a third-party independent Serverless consultant can still be beneficial. They can help ensure that the vendor has the right skill set and experience, and they can provide a neutral perspective on the proposed designs and implementation.

The Three Pillars

A triangle of three pillars is a common and often used concept in technology. The basic premise is that there are three desirable traits – the three pillars – but, under normal circumstances, we can only pick two traits.

The 3 pillars of application development are shown in Figure 5-6. Vendors saying they can deliver all three may have a different view of one of the three pillars. Our assessment of a vendor should aim to discover which pillar is not fully being met to our expectations. Having two out of three pillars is not a bad thing; it depends on which pillar is missing and if that is acceptable for our solution and goals.

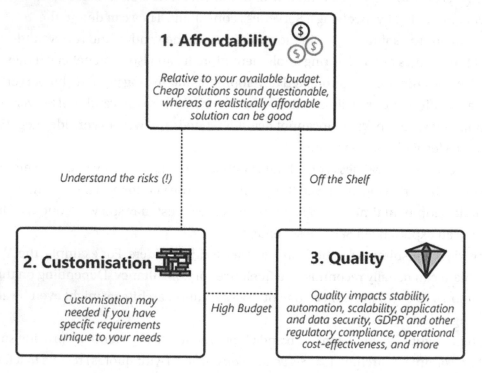

Figure 5-6. *The three pillars of vendor traits (pick two)*

With sufficient budget, we can achieve *customization* and *quality*, but the solution will likely be considered relatively less *affordable*. Note that payment need not always be cash. For startups, shares could be part of the deal, but these still have some agreed value, which can be used to determine if a solution is considered relatively more or less affordable.

Off-the-shelf products and SaaS solutions will often provide *affordability* and *quality*, but there will be minimal *customization* options, so compromises may be needed. This can be a good option for initially trialing a concept and confirming that it solves the problem or that there is a market before putting a budget toward a more custom solution – if that is even needed. A common example is to test a concept or product in the market using Shopify before investing in a custom ecommerce solution.

Less technical clients are often presented with the pillars *affordability* and *customization* in a proposal. *Quality* tends to be minimally addressed so that the desired *customization* can be delivered for the available budget. This results in a solution that will inevitably be a problem in the future. It could be susceptible to a security breach; it might not scale with the business; or any number of other quality-related issues. Over time, this can make the solution less *affordable* than initially thought, and it's why it's so important to assess the vendor properly – especially on the *quality* pillar. Understand which compromises are being made and decide if that is acceptable, given the budget and requirements of the solution.

General Best Practices

Outsourcing always has challenges and risks, but there are a few things we can do to mitigate them:

Practice due diligence.

Practicing diligence and making an informed decision before hiring external vendors is essential. Getting recommendations from credible sources, tapping into our network, and assessing vendor portfolios for technical competency are all critical steps to perform before signing a contract.

Analyze the business and technical needs, and then decide what vendor type would be suitable for outsourcing. Also, make sure the vendor has at least some prior experience with the cloud provider that we want to use.

Then, search for vendors and do some background research by looking for reviews on LinkedIn or Upwork, for example. Once shortlisted, we can send an RFI (Request for Information) and subsequently an RFQ (Request for Quotation) to the selected vendors. This quotation should have the terms and conditions listed. Price should not be the only criterion for selection. Relevant experience, timeline, security, support, communication, testing, project management, and how they handle change requests and priority changes should be taken into consideration too.

Think about security.

Before hiring any vendor, their in-house policies for ensuring the security of a client's data should be investigated. It is important to know that they will be able to safeguard sensitive information and take the appropriate security measures. Assessing their current infrastructure will also provide an idea of the security protocols they have in place. Do they understand how to implement encryption and apply PoLP in the cloud, for example?

Communicate frequently.

Keeping the channel of communication open helps build a strong relationship with vendors and lets them understand our vision for building apps in the best way possible. Effective communication eradicates many hurdles and loopholes that might arise during the entire development process.

Generally, I recommend having daily 15-minute meetings to talk about what was completed, what will be done next, and any blockers. A 1-hour session should be had at least every 2 weeks or at the start of a new set of features. Lastly, there is nothing quite like a good whiteboarding session to make sure everyone is on the same page.

Provide a clear project brief.

Providing a detailed scope of work is important. For example: What are the project goals? What issues are we trying to solve? Are there time or pricing constraints? What are the main features and functions of the application we are trying to build? Having this info in our project brief will ensure that the vendor understands the needs and can provide realistic quotes and timelines.

Proof of concept (POC).

A POC is a common approach to solving questions in the process of designing complex applications. It can be an opportunity to evaluate the vendor's capabilities and set realistic expectations before committing to a larger project. Once the POC is completed, have an open review discussion with the vendor touching on the following:

- Do the results match the communicated requirements? If there are many differences, what caused those changes, and how can they be reduced in the next engagement?

- Did they meet the estimated deadline and deliver a quality result? Is there a shared understanding of what quality means, or are there different views that need to be clarified?

- Was communication sufficient on both sides? Does it need to be more or less frequent, and do discussions need to be more or less technical?

- What were the lessons learned, and how can they be implemented in a larger project?

Look for an agile mindset.

Microservices need to be developed in small agile teams. Go with a vendor that has adopted the agile culture. If we already have a big team working on the project, break it down into several agile teams and make them more independent. Make sure the project manager(s) can synchronize the work of all teams and increase the team size when required.

Use online project management and collaboration tools.

Project management tools are quite effective at streamlining collaboration and software projects. They allow a platform for both clients and vendors to visually interact, share documents, and keep track of projects and deadlines. Investing in a reliable project management tool will give the project a head start.

One final tip: If you decide to work with a vendor with little Serverless experience, ask them to read this book first!

 # Vetting Serverless Capabilities

Earlier in this book, we touched on the fact that Serverless is still relatively new compared with other software architectures. The scarcity of experienced talent applies to vendors, freelancers, and job candidates alike. Even those familiar enough with Serverless to talk about it have often only used it for secondary or minor tasks, not for critical production-level solutions. Depending on expectations for the talent, this may not be relevant, but it's something to keep in mind.

Asking the right questions during an interview can be challenging if the interviewer is not familiar with Serverless architecture. In this section, I wanted to share some technical questions I ask in interviews to get an idea of the real-world experience a Serverless talent may have. These questions are suitable for external vendors, freelancers, and job candidates. I don't ask about specific skills or facts, as such knowledge can be easily learned from the documentation. I try to ask questions that will provide an insight into the candidate's mindset and how they view broader topics such as security and cost-effectiveness. The answers are not a simple case of right or wrong, and there are often multiple valid answers with different nuances. Also, note that most of these questions are very AWS-specific, and while they are relevant at the time of writing, changes in cloud technology could cause them to lose relevance over time.

Can you briefly describe the challenges and benefits of going Serverless?

I like to start these questions with something high level and general to make sure they understand the main selling points and challenges of Serverless before diving into more specific technical questions.

Their response should generally include that Serverless reduces both development times and operational costs and frees up the developers from worrying about provisioning and scaling the infrastructure resources. When it comes to challenges, they might mention latency being the biggest challenge, vendor lock-in, architecting for statelessness, working with NoSQL databases, and more complex access permissions due to the granularity.

What is the relevance of a VPC to Lambda?

Not knowing could indicate a lack of experience with production Serverless solutions. Of the possible answers, there is not really a right or wrong answer; it really depends on the type of architecture they have experience with and the environment they work in.

For pure Serverless solutions, a VPC is not needed, and security can be managed at a policy level. However, some industries or projects might require strict network separation, in which case a VPC has to be used with Lambda.

If a solution has both server components and microservices, a VPC may be needed to ensure these two components can communicate with each other. This includes using certain types of databases with microservices.

With this in mind, answers could include any of the following:

- It is best practice and recommended to use a VPC for Lambda microservices in regulated industries or for highly sensitive applications.

- A VPC is not necessarily required if we have a fully Serverless solution and do not need to interface with EC2, RDS, or other server or container components. Even if we do, there are options such as PrivateLink that might be better.

- Lambda microservices without a VPC are still very well protected through IAM roles. Some regulated industries, such as finance, may require the use of subnets to separate layers of an application.

When placing Lambdas into a VPC, what are some things you need to consider?

This is a follow-up question to the previous one, depending on how detailed their answer was. Any mention of the following items is a good sign. The more they can call out, the better.

- The VPC needs a NAT or IGW for the Lambdas to be able to access the Internet. This includes other cloud services unless we use PrivateLink or VPC endpoints.

- Lambda microservices in a VPC can still be accessed by Lambda microservices outside of the VPC as long as they have the right IAM policy permission.

- Using a VPC will slightly increase latency, though far less than it used to.

- It is no longer the case that we need to ensure a sufficiently sized pool of IP addresses. If they mention this, then their knowledge is outdated.

What is an alternative way for a Lambda microservice to interact with an EC2 instance, relational database, or container without the Lambda being in a VPC?

With this question, we want to see if the candidate knows how to architect hybrid solutions without having to put Lambdas into a VPC when not needed.

One way of achieving this is through decoupling and using an asynchronous approach. A microservice can write a task to SQS that an EC2 instance or container is polling. The EC2 only needs outgoing Internet access or a private link to be able to reach SQS. Another way is by using SNS or just polling a database directly so that the microservice can update with tasks. Lambda now also supports PrivateLink, enabling EC2 instances to communicate with Lambda microservices outside of a VPC.

It's possible to use RDS proxy and Aurora Serverless Data API to avoid putting Lambdas into the VPC just to be able to communicate securely with the database. But this may mean code changes or non-standard ways of interacting with the database.

What should be considered if a Lambda microservice needs to process a really large file?

Start with *really large*, but depending on their response, we can clarify it to at least 11 GB later.

- Lambda microservices have a maximum of 10 GB temporary storage, so anything larger cannot be stored there. Note that temporary storage was increased from 512 MB in 2022.

- Up to 10 GB of data can be stored in memory. In this case, the Lambda microservice should be given sufficient memory to store the file. While not wrong, this method can get expensive because the per-millisecond fee for Lambda is based on the assigned amount of memory.

- For certain use cases, such as reading supported formats, encryption, and compression, we can stream the file from S3. The file is streamed into Lambda bit by bit, where we can read it or process the data and stream the result to S3. Only a bit of the file is in Lambda memory at a given time, so memory and cost are low.

- Use a container instead of a Lambda. For some use cases, this may be the only option, and it adds some overheads to manage the provisioning and termination of a container. For Serverless, the Fargate service would be preferred for this, and the container should be launched on demand and just long enough to process each task.

You are using a Lambda microservice to manage steps in a pipeline, and one of the steps involves shutting down a particular service, which can take up to 10 minutes to complete. You have more steps in the pipeline after the service has shut down. There is an API request to check if the service has terminated, but this needs to be polled as the service does not support any callback notifications. What would be a suitable way to handle that?

This is testing the candidate on how to best handle the fact that it's bad practice to have long-running Lambda microservices and it's not cost-effective to have them idle waiting. Possible answers could include any of the following:

- Run the terminate command and wait for the service API to return to Lambda. The Lambda microservice will run for up to 15 minutes while waiting for the service to shut down and then be able to continue with the next step in the pipeline. This is a valid way of doing it, but it is not very cost-effective to let Lambda run for 10 minutes doing nothing but waiting.

- Run the shutdown command, then add a task to an SQS queue with a 10-minute visibility delay, and end the Lambda. SQS will trigger the Lambda microservice in 10 minutes so it can confirm the service has terminated and continue the pipeline. SQS can delay a task for a maximum of 15 minutes, but this is usually the best option for most use cases.

- As the previous one, but using EventBridge instead of SQS to schedule a trigger in 10 minutes. Like SQS, this is a great Serverless option. The main reason to pick EventBridge over SQS would be to avoid being constrained to a maximum 15-minute delay; an EventBridge schedule can be any future date and time.

- Use Step Functions to orchestrate the pipeline. For use cases with many different steps or steps that require human action, this will be the best option. However, this is a complete service in its own right that will add complexity to the solution.

- For some services, it might also be possible to create a custom CloudWatch alert that triggers a Lambda when the service terminates.

How would you make a third-party service API key or password available to your Lambda microservice?

This is a cybersecurity question and quite an important one to test that the candidate knows how to properly handle sensitive parameters.

Bad answers would include the following:

- *Add it in the code*: This is a major security concern and very bad practice.

- *Add it to the Lambda environment parameters*: This is quite a common option, but it's bad practice to store sensitive data in these parameters.

Acceptable answers would include the following:

- *Store in a secure S3 bucket*: This option is acceptable but more prone to leaking compared with the other following options. It is also more manual to manage, so certainly not ideal.

- *Store in a password manager running on a container or server*: While not wrong, we would need to provide the microservice with access to the manager, and we then have a server-based solution to manage. It is not uncommon for enterprises to have such a solution already, so simply reusing it for a new application can make sense in those cases.

- *Add them to the AWS Secrets Manager service*: This is a good option, but it has a cost attached to it. The main benefit of this service is that it can rotate the sensitive data (if this is supported by the service it's granting access to).

- *Add them as a secure string to the Systems Manager Parameter Store (SSM parameters)*: This is the most cost-effective option for most use cases as described in the question. SSM is secure and completely free to use, although it lacks some of the advanced options that Secrets Manager has.

What is your typical process for developing and testing Lambda microservices?

This is a bit of a double question. I'm looking for a general idea and any insights into their day-to-day process, tools they might use, and libraries or strategies they are familiar with. I also want to understand if the candidate tends to test in the cloud after deploying or if they are familiar with local testing of Lambda and other services using SAM.

Testing in the cloud is common for independent developers and especially if we are close to an AWS data center, as the latency will be fairly minimal. But for larger teams or if they are quite far from an AWS region, then the ability to do local testing is really important for productivity. I also want to understand if they know how to set that up and how they deal with services that are not supported by SAM (all of this is covered in more detail in Chapter 6, "CDK Technical Considerations").

How do you deploy Lambda microservices into the cloud?

This is really about DevOps and CI/CD pipelines, and it's not strictly Serverless, as the process applies to any development. However, given the many microservices a Serverless solution will typically have, it is best to have team members who are familiar with this kind of automation.

Less ideal answers would include the following:

- *Paste or upload directly into the AWS Lambda GUI*: While this will work, and it can be an acceptable approach for quick experimentation, this is not a practice that should be applied to production environments.

- *Directly to Lambda through the AWS CLI*: This is using a scripted approach, but it is still very similar to the previous one. It's acceptable for quick testing/debugging something but not good production practice.

Good answers could include the following:

- *Through CloudFormation templates, deployed via the AWS UI or AWS CLI*: While the deployment step is still manual, having CloudFormation templates at least makes it more scalable, and it will be easier to automate this for production.

- *Via CDK or some other Serverless framework that deploys directly into the cloud or deploys via CloudFormation into the cloud*: Note that this answer is about frameworks, not deployment services. There are a few such frameworks available for developing and deploying Serverless solutions into the cloud in a scalable and automated manner. This works well for individual or small teams in the same location but can prove challenging for larger or distributed teams.

- *Through a DevOps/CI/CD pipeline involving GIT/CodeCommit,
  CodeDeploy, CodePipeline, or similar third-party or AWS services*:
  Deployment can be entirely automated using these kinds of services –
  a must for large or distributed teams but generally best practice for
  teams of any size. CodePipeline orchestrates continuous deployment
  pipelines. CodeDeploy comes with a deployment capability that is
  fully integrated into Lambda. There are other ways to achieve this
  with third-party services, but using native services means it can be
  fully Serverless and it is more secure to keep the code within a single
  platform.

How do you use Lambda layers?

Lambda layers can be a bit divisive. On the one hand, they help reduce code duplication, but, on the other hand, they can make an application more tightly coupled or even monolithic in nature due to the shared dependencies in the layer. This may be appropriate for some use cases, but often it's just an easier choice for those with less experience designing independent microservices.

The candidate's answer to this will reflect how much of a Serverless purist they are. Responses can include the following:

- "I am familiar with them but generally avoid them or use them only
  sparingly." This answer likely means that they are very committed
  to having independent and decoupled microservices in their
  architecture.

- "I only use them for public or third-party libraries and tools." This is
  a fair use case. While it does create a dependency, the benefit is the
  separation of third-party code from the microservices' code, making
  it easier to update these libraries and test new versions without
  touching the live microservices.

- "I use them for shared/common functions between multiple
  microservices." This shows that the candidates are more committed
  to minimizing duplicate code than strict microservice separation. It is
  likely that their solutions are more monolithic than decoupled, even
  if they are using microservices.

- It is also possible that they don't know what layers are. To me, this would indicate that they have not worked much with Lambda as it is not a new feature, and there are several references to it within the service.

How do you optimize the cost of Lambda microservices?

Being cost-aware can make developers more effective Serverless developers, so questions that ask about cost optimization or cost estimation can indicate the developer has experience outside of code and infrastructure. Responses could include the following:

- *Lambda rightsizing*: This is the process of cycling through different memory configurations to find the right balance of memory and execution time. Rightsizing can result in the lowest cost for an acceptable performance or a higher cost for the best performance but without paying for unutilized resources.

- *Code optimization, reducing or removing bulky libraries and frameworks not suitable for a Lambda environment*: Making the code run faster means less execution time, which means lower cost.

- *Splitting large microservices into smaller ones*: Creating smaller and faster microservices can reduce cost as we only pay for execution time, not storage or quantity of microservices. However, if a single request ends up needing multiple microservices instead of just the single large one, then this could increase the cost as Lambda does have an execution quantity fee.

- *Network optimization*: Egress to the Internet is the most expensive data transfer fee. In some cases, the network can be optimized to keep more traffic within the AWS network and so reduce costs.

CHAPTER 6

DevOps and Tooling

The advance of technology is based on making it fit in so that you don't really even notice it, so it's part of everyday life.

—Bill Gates, Co-founder of Microsoft

What Is DevOps?

The word *DevOps* is simply short for *development* and *operations*, and this also pretty much sums up what DevOps is. If DevOps were to be explained, it would be more appropriate to call it a cultural movement by development teams than a framework or methodology. This cultural movement aims to enhance the collaboration between, or even merge, two major departments involved in digital projects, so changes get into production faster and more frequently while maintaining and even improving sustainability and scalability.

Organizational culture and mindsets are key targets of DevOps efforts, helping team members consistently think about how they could automate and make it easy to replicate each step in the development pipeline – from maintaining a history of code, to procuring infrastructure, and to writing, testing, optimizing, deploying, and improving the code.

T. Smart, *Serverless Beyond the Buzzword*, https://doi.org/10.1007/978-1-4842-8761-3_6

Principles and Practices of DevOps

1. **Flow**

   The first principle of DevOps is *flow*, and it focuses on global optimizations of business value in IT instead of going for optimizations that are local and usually of lower value. According to this principle, the flow of value is from left to right, and every project needs to follow this flow starting from an idea, requirement, experiment, or improvement ending up in the hands of the user.

2. **Feedback**

   The second principle of DevOps is perhaps the most crucial one the development and operations teams can follow. DevOps culture stresses the importance of feedback loops. The flow of feedback is opposite to that of value, which is from right to left, that is, from the customer to design teams. It is needed to continuously improve a given solution.

3. **Continual learning**

   The third principle of DevOps is that the learning phase is not complete once a project ends or a product is finished. Instead, the teams learn something new every time they get feedback and improve the solution. An organization setting out to build a DevOps culture needs to track lessons learned and knowledge, as well as cultivating an interest in experimenting with new ideas and technologies as these can lead to new insights and lessons too.

Problems Solved by DevOps

1. **Continuous deployment**

   Companies of all shapes and sizes with a software product in their portfolio have proven that continuous deployment greatly increases productivity. DevOps ensures that small, independent, and self-sufficient teams can deliver many deployments each and every day. Large teams working on a single large monolithic code base with infrequent deployments can lead to problems not being identified until a lot of the code has been written. A smaller team, focusing on one microservice at a time with continuous deployment, will identify issues and incompatibilities far sooner and can adjust before much code has been written. A close collaboration between the development and operations teams is important to carry out this continuous deployment and ensure automated checks are in place.

2. **Organizing teams around a mission**

DevOps revolves around collaborations between development and operations teams. This means that people from both teams come together for each project to ensure efficiency and contribute value to the solution. This places a much higher burden on picking the right people for the team and project. Similarly, a discussion is welcome on the approach, but team members should be aligned on the end goals.

3. **Built-in quality and monitoring**

DevOps requires efficient feedback loops to be built into the pipeline, and a feedback loop is directly proportional to the amount of quality that a team can deliver and receive. When a team gets customer feedback, they can focus on what the customer needs and how the product should tend to those needs, instead of sticking to the initial product assumptions. This whole process of continuous improvement is what a quality product promises. This feedback loop also allows the project managers and top management to efficiently monitor a team and escalate bigger decisions when needed and with the facts in hand.

Evolution of DevOps

DevOps is not a new buzzword. In fact, it has been around since 2009, and, like any other concept, it has gone through its fair share of improvements. It started as a simple automation strategy but became a complete culture movement with many available tools and solutions that guide organizations in every step of the software development process, from commitment to deployment.

DevOps is especially popular with Serverless teams where there are far more independent components to manage. DevOps can ensure effective communication, automation, and consistency, and controls are in place for every microservice within a larger solution. Most fully managed services are built with DevOps in mind so they can easily be integrated into a DevOps pipeline.

 # Infrastructure-as-Code

Infrastructure-as-Code (IaC) has been around since the beginning of DevOps. Some would claim that modern DevOps would not even be possible without it. IaC automates the creation and maintenance of cloud infrastructure, allowing the organization to develop, set up, and scale cloud solutions with less risk, higher speed, and decreased cost.

It's no secret that cloud computing has made a significant impact on the way companies build, compute, and maintain their technology products. Never before have we seen such advancements in developer productivity in such a short time. The cloud has made it possible to log into a UI and launch a service in seconds. This can be repeated for each service the solution needs. For a server-based solution, we may only need three or four services, so the effort, compared with developing the solution, is quite small.

However, with Serverless, we might be using 20 or 30 different services with less code development, so the effort of manually launching services through the UI will be a considerable part of the total effort. Consider also launching the same solution in a different region or separate development and production environments. For each of those deployments, we would need to go through all that manual work again with a significant chance of human errors or unintentionally introducing differences in each one.

Automation is the only way to minimize these mistakes, and IaC is the answer to automate launching cloud environments by enabling us to create typed templates. The idea behind IaC is based on programming scripts that are used for automating IT processes. These scripts are mainly used for automating a series of static steps that need to be repeated a couple of times across many servers – such as installing a base operating system or performing repetitive updates or security tasks.

IaC, on the other hand, uses a more complex language for coding functional deployments. For example, using IaC on AWS, we can provision several microservices, an API Gateway, a database, and storage for an entire Serverless web application in a matter of seconds – including configuring the services, adding parameters, and setting up permissions. Once the IaC template has been created, it can be repeated with the exact same outcome across multiple regions and accounts.

In Figure 6-1, we have a simple illustration to show how IaC works.

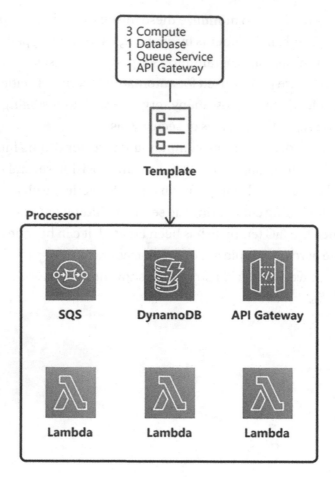

Figure 6-1. *A simplified example of Infrastructure-as-Code (IAC)*

At the top of Figure 6-1, we have an IaC template, and, within the template, we list the services we want to provision with their configuration. The template is then submitted to a processor, which reads the specifications defined and provisions the necessary cloud resources.

Key Values of IaC

- *Speed and simplicity*: With IaC, we can spin up an application's entire infrastructure simply by uploading a template. We can also easily deploy the same infrastructure in different regions or accounts and expect the same result.

- Developers can quickly make changes to the infrastructure and code at the same time and test and rapidly deploy them together and in stages. This makes the whole development and iteration process more efficient and raises the team's productivity.

- Automate deployments, validation, testing, and rollbacks. By reducing or even removing manual actions, we can greatly reduce the chance of mistakes being made and reduce the time and cost of deploying new solutions and maintaining existing ones. An added benefit is increased developer capacity, allowing them to focus on more critical higher-value tasks that cannot be automated.

- *Auditability*: Like code, templates can be versioned. So we have a history of changes that can be audited according to who made the changes and when they were made. And we can roll back to a previous configuration, which is especially useful when a configuration change breaks the application.

- *Consistency in configuration and less "drift"*: Consistency drift happens when manual changes are made to an existing cloud service, which can cause issues in a solution and discrepancies between different deployments. IaC avoids drift by ensuring the same configuration and templates are run for each environment. Drift can lead to problems with deployment, risks while developing apps and services, and security vulnerabilities.

- *Cost-effective*: Using IaC in the cloud, we can lower the cost of infrastructure management by automating and controlling which services are needed when. Because we are not manually setting everything up, it becomes simple to launch on-demand development or testing environments, for example.

- *Cleaning up*: Besides provisioning cloud services, these templates can also be used to remove an environment entirely. This results in fewer chargeable services being forgotten, for example, after a proof of concept has run its course, resulting in less wastage.

IaC Tools and Frameworks

There are several tools and frameworks we can use to design and manage AWS infrastructure. Some are provided by AWS and others by third-party vendors. This list is not exhaustive, but it includes the most popular options.

All-purpose options provide broad access to the full range of AWS services. These tools are not built for any particular type of use case or architecture; they can support any project in the cloud. They do tend to require the most work to explicitly codify every detail of the architecture. As such, they often have the steepest learning curve.

For example, if we want to deploy an API solution, in that case, we will need to define and configure several API Gateway components, every integrated Lambda function, and all of the required permissions.

In this category, two popular IaC tools are CloudFormation, a fully managed service provided by AWS, and Terraform, a cloud-agnostic option provided by HashiCorp. They are often self-managed, but there is also a managed enterprise version available.

Purpose-built IaC tools and application frameworks are often abstracted to reduce the amount of effort needed to create the templates. However, they may be more limited as they are often intended for specific use cases or types of architecture. These tools will generate standard CloudFormation, which can then be deployed as normal, or they will work directly with the cloud service APIs to provision resources.

Going back to our API solution example, with purpose-built tools, we might only need a few lines to create and configure a best-practices API Gateway and the attached Lambda functions. The tool will add the remaining details needed for the final CloudFormation template.

Although the developer may have less control over how services are configured or even which services are available, it simplifies the process, and the abstraction makes templates cleaner and easier to read.

Examples developed by AWS include Serverless Application Model (SAM), Cloud Development Kit (CDK), and Amplify. A third-party and cloud-agnostic option is Serverless Framework.

⚙ AWS CloudFormation

IaC on AWS is typically done with CloudFormation, which is a fully managed service as well as a templating language. The service is free to use, but we do pay for the services provisioned by the CloudFormation templates.

While it can have a learning curve, understanding CloudFormation will make you a better Serverless developer. Even if you are typically using CDK, AppSpec, or a similar abstraction, understanding the foundations and what happens behind the scenes with these frameworks will help better understand the limits, capabilities, and optimizations of AWS IaC.

CloudFormation templates can be written in either JSON or YAML script. Reusable templates can be created for provisioning cloud services and deploying them across multiple accounts, regions, and environments with predictable and consistent results. When a template is run through the CloudFormation service, it creates a stack. This is what contains all the associated resources that have been provisioned.

Besides services and their configuration, CloudFormation offers several supporting features:

- **Condition checks**

    A condition can check the value of a parameter and then perform or not perform a particular action. For example, we can check an environment parameter and then apply different configurations for production and development. Note that changing a condition will not result in a stack update. To update conditions, we must include a resource addition, modification, or deletion in the change. Supported condition types are

    - And

    - Equals

    - If

    - Not

    - Or

- **Creation policy**

  Wait for an external policy (with a configurable timeout) before continuing the deployment.

- **Update policy**

  Create a rolling update that executes the change in small batches, providing time to catch errors before all components are updated.

- **Deletion policy**

  We can specify "*retain*" on a resource such as a database so that we don't lose our data when the stack is deleted or a configuration change requires the resource to be recreated.

- **Functions**

  CloudFormation also supports several useful functions. These are all prefixed with Fn:: to indicate function:

  - Base64: Encode a string to Base64.

  - Cidr: Return an array of CIDR address blocks.

  - FindInMap: Return a value from a mapping.

  - GetAtt: Return an attribute.

  - GetAZs: Return an array of availability zones for a region.

  - ImportValue: Return an output from another stack.

  - Join: Join multiple values into a single value.

  - Select: Return an object from an array of objects.

  - Split: Split a value into a list of values.

  - Sub: Insert values into a string, usually values that are only available after creating or updating a stack.

While not a CloudFormation feature, *cfn-lint* can locally check if a CloudFormation template has any problems with it before it is deployed. This handy tool can be found here: *https://github.com/aws-cloudformation/cfn-lint*.

There are several reasons a deployed stack can fail. When this happens, CloudFormation automatically rolls back the changes to the previous working version of the stack. This prevents a deployed application from breaking. However, automatic rollback can be turned off so that we can troubleshoot the failed state, fix the root cause in the template, and deploy the stack again.

When updating a template and stack, CloudFormation is able to scan and compare the stack against the already deployed resources and their configuration. Any difference between the two, also called *drift*, can be detected. Drift can happen if changes are made to the deployed resource outside of the template, for example, changes that are made directly in the cloud UI or via the service API instead of via the template and stack. While we can configure automatic notification of drift, there is no *undrift* option in CloudFormation, and resolving it typically involves manual remediation such as redeploying the template and forcing an update by changing the relevant parts.

A great benefit of CloudFormation templates is the ability to delete a stack and, with it, all the associated resources. This is especially useful for teams that frequently build temporary projects for learning, rapid prototyping, or testing. Cleaning up afterward can be done with a simple command, which will keep the account neat and reduce the chance of unexpected costs from forgotten resources.

Declarative vs. Imperative

Infrastructure-as-Code tools can be declarative or imperative. Declarative style describes the *what*. It defines the intended or desired state of the infrastructure by listing out all the resources that need to be launched into it. Imperative style describes the *how*. It specifies the specific commands needed to create the resources and get the infrastructure to the desired state.

AWS CloudFormation templates are written declaratively, and the AWS command-line interface (CLI) is imperative. Tools such as Chef can be used in both declarative and imperative manner.

The following is a comparison between those methods for the AWS S3 storage service. In the declarative style, we say which resources we want with any desired properties:

```
S3Bucket:
  Type: AWS::S3::Bucket
  Properties:
    BucketName: my-media-assets
```

With the imperative style in AWS CLI, we specify the command to be run:

```
aws s3api create-bucket --bucket "my-media-assets" --region ap-southeast-1
--create-bucket-configuration LocationConstraint=ap-southeast-1
```

Both commands will give the same result; a single S3 bucket will be created with the name "*my-media-assets*." The imperative style seems simpler, but the magic happens if we were to run both commands again. The CloudFormation template would confirm that there is a bucket with that name and that the configuration still matches the template. The output would be a success state. The AWS CLI command will return an error because it will just run the command again and run into the problem that a bucket with that name exists already:

```
An error occurred (BucketAlreadyOwnedByYou) when calling the CreateBucket
operation: Your previous request to create the named bucket succeeded and
you already own it.
```

Further benefit can be seen when we make a change to the properties. If we add a new tag to the CloudFormation template and run it again, that tag will be added to our existing bucket. The AWS CLI command will fail again because a bucket with the same name already exists.

CloudFormation Example

```
AWSTemplateFormatVersion: "2010-09-09"
Description: "CloudFormation demo template"
```

Parameters to pass into template	```Parameters:
S3Bucket:
Type: String
S3Key:
Type: String
LambdaRoleARN:
Type: String```

```
Resources:
```

Create S3 bucket: • Name • Encryption method • Tags Set deletion policy to *retain* the resource when stack is being deleted	```DemoS3Bucket:
Type: "AWS::S3::Bucket"
DeletionPolicy: Retain
Properties:
BucketName: "demo-bucket"
BucketEncryption:
ServerSideEncryptionConfiguration:
- ServerSideEncryptionByDefault:
SSEAlgorithm: "AES256"
Tags:
- Key: "environment"
Value: "test"
- Key: "project"
Value: "demo"```

Create Lambda function: • Description • S3 code location • Lambda handler • Lambda runtime • IAM role • Timeout	```DemoService:
Type: AWS::Lambda::Function
Properties:
Description: "Demo lambda service"
Code:
S3Bucket: !Ref S3Bucket
S3Key: !Ref S3Key
Handler: "index.handler"
Runtime: "nodejs12.x"
Role: !Ref LambdaRoleARN
Timeout: 300```

Figure 6-2. *CloudFormation template example*

At the top of Figure 6-2, we have the parameters where the service will accept input values from the developer. In this example, we require the name to use for an S3 bucket, the name of an S3 object, and an IAM role for a Lambda function. The S3 bucket name and object actually refer to a Lambda function zip file that we will be deploying with this template.

We then proceed to create an S3 bucket with a deletion policy of retain to preserve it when we delete a stack. We then specify the name of the bucket, the encryption method to use, and some tags to help identify and track it.

At the bottom, we specify a Lambda function. We use the S3 bucket parameters we configured previously to indicate the location of our function code. The handler specifies our entry point for the code. Then we configure the programming language, the IAM role, and, lastly, the timeout.

Once we deploy a stack using CloudFormation, we get back some outputs, as seen in Figure 6-3.

CloudFormation Stack - Events

Timestamp	Logical ID	Status	Status reason
2021-06-07 17:51:00 UTC+0800	HelloCdkStack	⊘ CREATE_COMPLETE	-
2021-06-07 17:50:59 UTC+0800	logSubscriptionDemoServiceLambdaCanInvokeLambdaE37F73FC	⊘ CREATE_COMPLETE	-
2021-06-07 17:50:51 UTC+0800	logSubscriptionDemoServiceLambda68B87443	⊘ CREATE_COMPLETE	-
2021-06-07 17:50:51 UTC+0800	logSubscriptionDemoServiceLambda68B87443	ⓘ CREATE_IN_PROGRESS	Resource creation initiated

CloudFormation Stack - Resources

Logical ID	Physical ID	Type	Status
DemoCloudWatchMonitorLambdaLogRetention2E45C511	/aws/lambda/HelloCdkStack-DemoCloudWatchMonitorLambda8AF12BAE-DHQT3a4Bvlyh	Custom::LogRetention	⊘ CREATE_COMPLETE
DemoCloudWatchMonitorLambdaServiceRole62838DCB	HelloCdkStack-DemoCloudWatchMonitorLambdaServiceRo-OE91TU6S6TPQ ☑	AWS::IAM::Role	⊘ CREATE_COMPLETE
DemoServiceLambda729A830C	HelloCdkStack-DemoServiceLambda729A830C-H4hY4nortGu8 ☑	AWS::Lambda::Function	⊘ UPDATE_COMPLETE
DemoServiceLambdaLogRetention85D377FB	/aws/lambda/HelloCdkStack-DemoServiceLambda729A830C-H4hY4nortGu8	Custom::LogRetention	⊘ CREATE_COMPLETE
DemoServiceLambdaServiceRole0E5F664F	HelloCdkStack-DemoServiceLambdaServiceRole0E5F664F-14C4VDRFZQG8S ☑	AWS::IAM::Role	⊘ CREATE_COMPLETE

Figure 6-3. *CloudFormation events and resources. Source: AWS website* https:// aws.amazon.com/ *2022, Amazon Web Services Inc. or its affiliates. All rights reserved*

At the top of Figure 6-3, we have an overview of what's happening with the stack deployment. This will continuously update until deployment completes successfully or fails. In this example, we can see that the resources have been created successfully. In the event of a failure, we will see the changes that did complete being reverted to the previous deployment before it completes.

At the bottom of Figure 6-3, we have a list of resources that were successfully created and are now active in this stack.

CloudFormation Challenges

Like any technology, CloudFormation is not perfect. Working with the JSON or YAML markup language is frustrating for many developers. The many, frequently inconsistent but always detailed configuration options can be incredibly confusing. Besides spending a good amount of time reading the CloudFormation documentation, there are steps we can take to help tackle some of the challenges.

CloudFormation limits are one of the most frustrating challenges. Read the documentation to know and understand these limits and use multiple stacks and sub-stacks to avoid some of them:

1. Each stack in CloudFormation is limited to a maximum of 500 resources. This sounds like a lot, but it is quite possible to run into this with large Serverless applications. For example, a Serverless CRUD API with just five actions adds up to 70 CloudFormation resources. To avoid hitting this limit, it is recommended to modularize stacks by creating smaller templates and utilizing nested stacks and modules – more on those shortly. An added benefit of modularizing is it reduces the blast radius during infrastructure changes and smaller stacks deploy faster and are easier to debug.

2. Each CloudFormation account is limited to 2000 stacks, but this is a soft limit, so we can submit a service request to ask for an increase.

3. Another easy-to-hit limit is a maximum of 4096 characters for parameter field values. To avoid this limit, we can split the value across multiple parameters in the template and then leverage CloudFormation's join function to merge the different values into the original value before using it.

4. There is a maximum of 200 parameters per stack. To avoid running into this limit, we can put multiple values into a single list-type parameter. Elements of a list can be individually referenced in the template using a CloudFormation function.

5. And there is a maximum of 200 outputs per template. This can
    especially be a problem with abstracted IaC solutions, as we may
    not be able to control the outputs that are created. Best way to
    avoid this is to keep stacks small. Fewer resources usually mean
    fewer outputs.

There is generally increased risk of running into these limits when using abstracted
IaC tools, as there is just less visibility, and often less control, over the CloudFormation
being generated.

Gaining a better understanding of CloudFormation will enable us to better manage
this risk when using such tools. Here are some other challenges to keep in mind:

1. Not all cloud services or their options may be available in
    CloudFormation. We always review the documentation of the
    services that will be used so that we are aware of their availability
    and limitations. We can create custom resources that help manage
    missing services or configurations using Lambda microservices.

2. Use Parameter Store and exported values for common
    configuration parameters and references. Use Parameter Store
    for passwords and other credentials too, and make sure to
    encrypt them.

3. Use Secrets Manager to generate new or temporary passwords so
    we can void including them in the IaC template as plain text.

4. Use comments and descriptions where possible. Like
    documentation, these will help other team members quickly
    understand what a template or resource is doing and why.

5. Moving and renaming resources is often complicated. Some
    resources can't be updated in place and will be deleted entirely
    and recreated. This can be especially troublesome for services that
    store data, such as databases, user authentication, and storage.
    Note that there is a CloudFormation parameter that enables us to
    keep the old version of a service and just add the new version. We
    can then migrate the data from the old service and ensure nothing
    is accidentally deleted. The data migration can potentially be
    automated using a custom resource, but sometimes manual effort
    will still be needed to update any code references to the resource.

6. Use modern development tools that have built-in features
    or plugins to help manage IaC templates. This is easily
    underestimated, but having CloudFormation references on hand
    and with autocomplete can greatly increase productivity and
    reduce frustration for the team.

⚙ AWS CloudFormation Planning

When dealing with CloudFormation, it can be productive to plan the stacks and
resources in advance. For example, we can separate the core components of an
application from other parts of the architecture. These components often have a
different lifecycle than microservices or interfaces and have far fewer updates as a result.

Microservices could be grouped into a single stack, or there could be an independent
stack for each one. The latter fits well with the multi-repo approach, but it can have its
own challenges, such as running into limits and managing infrastructure dependencies
between components. Deployment speed is not necessarily impacted by placing
multiple microservices in a single stack, as only the changed microservices will be
deployed. However, in a multi-repo environment, the pipeline will need to bring the
different infrastructure configurations together into a single logical stack.

Nested stacks provide a means to reuse a particular resource configuration in
multiple parent stacks. When designing stacks, ensure a complete understanding of the
infrastructure dependencies across multiple resources that may be in different stacks.
It is important to deploy the resources and stacks in the correct sequence. For example,
Lambda microservices must be deployed *before* an API Gateway so that the Lambda
integrations exist when the API Gateway is created.

Stacks without dependencies on each other can be deployed in parallel. This can
greatly speed up deployments the first time and after significant changes.

To help others understand the organization of stacks, we can make logical groups.
For example, we can group independent Lambda microservices into one stack and
create a different stack for Lambdas that will integrate with API Gateway. This will help
keep similar resources together while avoiding the resource limit per stack and is the
main reason it's so important to plan stacks ahead of time.

Nested Stacks

Nested stacks enable us to reuse a stack template in multiple parent stacks. This can be useful in situations where the configuration of a service or group of services is repeatedly used within one or more applications.

Like a regular CloudFormation stack, we can define one or more resources with their configuration in a nested stack. However, nested stacks are not deployed to CloudFormation but stored in S3. One or more parent stacks can then embed the nested stack to include the resources defined in the nested stack. The individual resources within the nested stack do not count toward the 500-resource limit of the parent stack; the entire nested stack only counts as *one* resource in the parent stack.

A nested stack can contain nested stacks themselves, creating a hierarchy of stacks. For example, in Figure 6-4 we have a nested stack for a default Lambda template, which is used in a nested stack for a common internal API design. This stack can then be included in various application stacks that need an internal API.

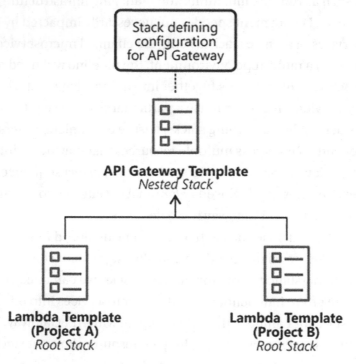

Figure 6-4. *Simple nested stack example*

Nested stack resource attributes can be overridden by the parent stack via parameters – if permitted by the nested stack. The outputs of a nested stack can be referenced and used by the parent stack with the GetAtt function.

Changes can be made to nested stacks and updated to S3. This will *not* trigger a new deployment of the parent stack. To update the deployed resources, the parent stack will need to be deployed again, at which point it will use the latest version of any included nested stacks.

While unchanged stacks will usually be skipped in CloudFormation, stacks with nested stacks will *always* update, even if there have been no changes to the parent or any of the nested stacks. This update won't actually change any infrastructure because nothing has changed in the template. Presumably, this happens because CloudFormation does not know if the nested stack on S3 has changed its configuration. So, to be safe, it just deploys it. This can make the deployment of applications containing many nested stacks slow as it takes time to iterate through the nested stacks, checking if there are changes.

A nested stack is intended to be reused in multiple locations. As such, certain resource attributes will likely need to be customized for each use. For example, if a nested stack is for an S3 bucket configuration, we should be able to define a bucket name each time we include it in a stack.

There are different ways the nested stack can determine how to deal with such attributes using standard CloudFormation parameters, as visualized in Figure 6-5.

1. The nested stack can decide that a particular attribute is fixed. The value will be hardcoded into the nested template, and the parent stack will not be able to override this.

2. The nested stack can implement a parameter used for the attribute value. The parent must then provide the input for this parameter. If the parent does not provide the parameter, then stack deployment will fail.

3. The parameter is set but with a default value configured. So, if the parent does not set the parameter, then the nested stack will use the default instead of the deployment failing.

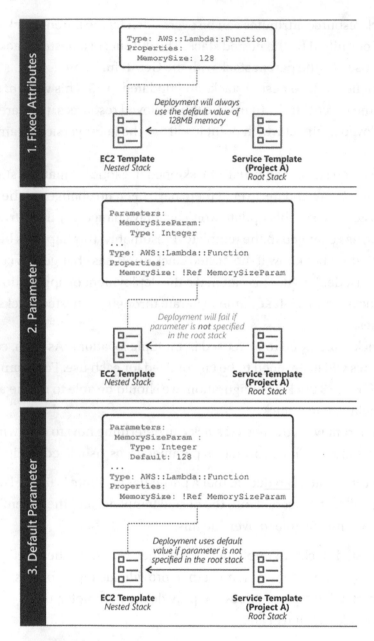

Figure 6-5. *Controlling access to nested attributes*

CloudFormation can validate parameters that we can use in the nested stack template to enforce a particular format or specific set of permitted values on the parameter value provided by the parent stack. For example, we could permit the parent to configure the memory of a Lambda microservice, but only up to 1 GB.

However, note that parameter values are passed to nested stacks as a **string**. So pseudo-variable types such as *id* are not supported, and lists must first be split – using the *Fn::split* function – in the nested stack template before the individual elements can be used.

The ability to reuse nested stack templates, manage them separately from the application scope, and control which attributes can be accessed means such templates could be shared in a central library. Additionally, particular templates could be created and owned by a compliance or cloud team to help application teams follow organizational best practices and security policies.

However, keep in mind that nested stacks can be downloaded, modified, and deployed directly by application teams – if the CI/CD pipeline doesn't prevent this or enforce the configuration set in the nested template.

In the following I provide a quick comparison of nested and separate stacks to help decide on which is the best option for a particular use case.

- **Exports**

  Exports such as the names and IDs of created resources can be kept private with a nested stack, so only the parent would know them. With separate stacks, these exports are essentially available to anyone with access to the AWS account.

- **Lifecycle**

  The lifecycle of separate stacks will be separate; they can be independently updated or deleted if there are no dependencies between them.

- **Ownership**

  Resources in a nested stack will be automatically deleted when the parent stack is deleted, and updates to the nested stack will only take effect after deploying the parent stack. Nested stacks can be owned by a different team to manage a particular resource configuration while still making certain parameters available to application teams.

While this could, in theory, also be done with multiple stacks, the team would either need to own the deployed stack for each application or do a manual review of the stack template for each application's changes. Either way, not very pragmatic.

- **Independence**

  As nested stacks become part of a parent stack, the latter has to be deployed for any changes in the nested stack to take effect. With separate stacks, either stack can be deployed separately from the other, though dependencies between them can force a particular deployment order.

Modules

Another way to manage CloudFormation stacks is with modules.

Modules function similarly to nested stacks. They can include multiple resources, help avoid running into limits, and be included in multiple parent stacks. There can be modules within modules to create hierarchies, and modules can be managed by another team to enforce a particular service configuration.

While nested stacks are intended for repeat use of a particular service configuration within one or more applications, modules are designed to be managed by a separate team to enforce best practices or compliance on cloud infrastructure configuration.

CloudFormation has a feature called Change Sets. These enable us to review changes that will be made to resources before we deploy the stack. They can help ensure we didn't miss or forget anything in our configuration. Change Sets provide visibility into the resources provisioned by *modules* but are unable to do so for *nested* stacks.

Modules do have some challenges. They are still a relatively new feature, and new features on AWS often need a while to settle as they work through user feedback. Modules need to be deployed into a region in an AWS account before applications can use them; this can be a lot of work for organizations with many AWS accounts. Versions are tracked as simple integers, and consumers must use the version specified as *default*. Neither of these is guaranteed to be consistent across deployments or accounts, which can lead to undesired deployment differences between development and production environments, for example.

Macros

The last CloudFormation feature we will look at is macros. These extend the capabilities of CloudFormation, enabling us to run Lambda microservices that can programmatically process a submitted CloudFormation template.

Some use cases for macros include the following:

- Using the capabilities of a programming language to reduce the effort of manually creating IaC templates. For example, we can loop and duplicate parts of a template or retrieve and inject shared variables or sensitive parameters.

- Perform pre-deployment infrastructure validation to reduce the time taken to get an error result.

- Implement custom quality, security, or compliance controls.

In Figure 6-6, we create a *count* macro that supports a new attribute, also called *count*, in the CloudFormation template.

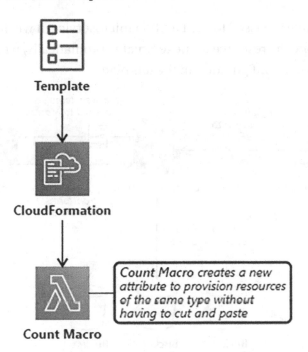

Template

CloudFormation

Count Macro creates a new attribute to provision resources of the same type without having to cut and paste

Count Macro

Figure 6-6. *CloudFormation macro example Source: https://github.com/aws-cloudformation/aws-cloudformation-macros/tree/master/Count*

The template code is as follows:

```
AWSTemplateFormatVersion: "2010-09-09"
Transform: AWS::Serverless-2016-10-31
Resources
  Macro:
    Type: AWS::CloudFornation::Macro
    Properties:
      Name: Count
      FunctionName: !GetAtt CountMacroFunction.Arn
  CountMacroFunction:
    Type: AWS::Serverless::Function
    Properties:
      CodeUri: src
      Handler: index.handler
      Runtime: python3.6
      Timeout: 5
```

When the template is passed to the Lambda microservice, it will look for the count attribute and replicate the resource in the template automatically, without us having to copy-paste the resource configuration in the template.

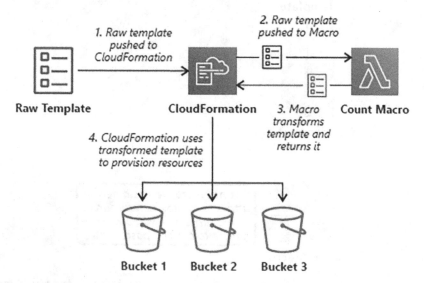

Figure 6-7. *CloudFormation macro execution example Source: https://github. com/aws-cloudformation/aws-cloudformation-macros/tree/master/Count*

The raw template looks like this:

```
AWSTemplateFormatVersion: "2010-09-09"
Transform: Count
Resources:
  Bucket:
    Type: AWS::S3::Bucket
    Properties:
      Tags:
        - Key: TestKey
          Value: my_bucket_%d
    Count: 3
```

And the processed template looks like this:

```
AWSTemplateFormatVersion: "2010-09-09"
Resources:
  Bucket1:
    Type: AWS::S3::Bucket
    Properties:
      Tags:
        - Key: TestKey
          Value: my_bucket_1
  Bucket2:
    Type: AWS::S3::Bucket
    Properties:
      Tags:
        - Key: TestKey
          Value: my_bucket_2
  Bucket3:
    Type: AWS::S3::Bucket
    Properties:
      Tags:
        - Key: TestKey
          Value: my_bucket_3
```

After the macro is deployed, we submit our CloudFormation template, which has the new attribute *count* in one of the resources, seen in Figure 6-7. CloudFormation will pass the submitted template to the macro to transform it and convert the count to three actual instances of that resource in the template. The macro will then return it to CloudFormation, which will process the updated template and provision the three S3 resources.

⚙ Terraform

Terraform is a third-party open source IaC tool that is cloud-agnostic. Terraform works with any of the cloud providers, as well as other platforms and SaaS solutions such as Datadog, VMWare, Kubernetes, and Heroku.

While Terraform is cloud-agnostic, a common misconception is that this means the IaC templates created in Terraform are also cloud-agnostic. They are not; a template will need to be created for each service for each cloud provider that needs to be supported. It makes sense to use Terraform in a multi-cloud organization so that a consistent tool and template language can be used for each cloud provider. However, Terraform will **not** reduce the effort of designing and running an application on multiple cloud platforms.

Terraform uses a state file to track deployed resources and their configuration. With the open source version, the state file needs to be self-managed locally or in the cloud. All developers working on the infrastructure will need to be able to access this state file, either directly or indirectly, via an advanced deployment pipeline. In the enterprise version of Terraform, there is an option to have the state file fully managed in their platform.

When Terraform is used for provisioning AWS resources, it deploys them by interacting directly with the service APIs; it does not generate or deploy CloudFormation – no stacks will appear in the CloudFormation service after deploying Terraform.

Terraform uses a custom syntax called HashiCorp Configuration Language or HCL. It also supports the JSON format.

In Figure 6-8, we have an HCL template that creates an API Gateway, a Lambda function, and an IAM role – the Lambda invoke policy – which we then attach to the API Gateway.

Create API Gateway	```resource "aws_api_gateway_rest_api" "MyDemoAPI" { name = "MyDemoAPI" description = "This is my demo API" }```

Create Lambda function	```resource "aws_lambda_function" "example" { function_name = "ServerlessExample" filename = "lambda_function_payload.zip" handler = "main.handler" runtime = "nodejs10.x" role = aws_iam_role.lambda_exec.arn }```

Create Lambda invoke policy	```resource "aws_iam_role" "lambda_exec" { name = "serverless_example_lambda" assume_role_policy = <<EOF // IAM policy here EOF }```

Attach policy to API	```resource "aws_lambda_permission" "lambda_permission" { statement_id = "AllowMyDemoAPIInvoke" action = "lambda:InvokeFunction" function_name = aws_lambda_function.example.function_name principal = "apigateway.amazonaws.com" source_arn = "${aws_api_gateway_rest_api.MyDemoAPI.execution_ arn}/*/*/*" }```

Figure 6-8. Terraform template example

Terraform has a feature called the Terraform graph, which provides a visual representation of our infrastructure. CloudFormation has something similar called CloudFormation Designer.

Terraform offers preconfigured templates in the Terraform Registry, which can be easily shared and reused by users within the community.

299

Lastly, Terraform supports modules. Like the CloudFormation equivalent, cloud teams can use these to create approved resource templates that can help application teams follow best practices and compliance policies.

Unlike CloudFormation, Terraform has the ability to *undrift* or revert unauthorized changes made to the infrastructure outside of the IaC templates, as shown in Figure 6-9.

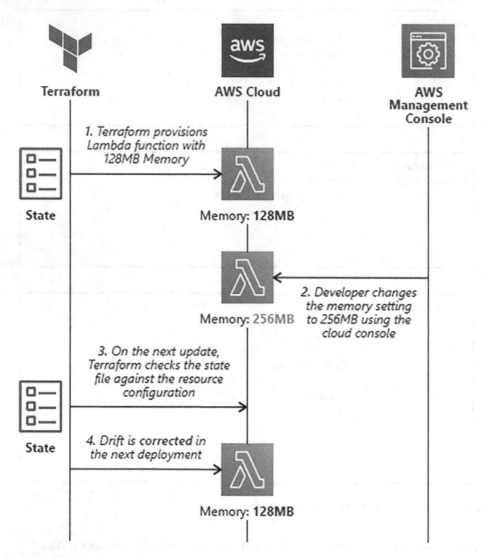

Figure 6-9. Terraform architecture example

Status output indicates a state that needs to be fixed:

```
Terraform will perform the following actions:

  # aws_lambda_function.test_lambda will be updated in-place
  ~ resource "aws_lambda_function" "test_lambda" {
      id                         = "terraform-demo"
    ~ memory_size                = 256 -> 128
      tags                       = {}

      # (19 unchanged attributes hidden)
      # (2 unchanged blocks hidden)
  }
```

A Terraform template is used to create a Lambda function with 128 MB of memory configured. The template is deployed, and the new resource with its live configuration is tracked in the state file.

Later, a developer uses the management console to change the memory configuration to 256 MB. On the next template update, Terraform will compare the resource configuration in the state file with the actual deployed resource configuration. The memory difference between these is flagged for review. On the next deployment, Terraform will replace the changed memory setting with the value stated in the template, correcting the drift.

If Terraform is unable to update the resource, which could happen if the resource was deleted or if the parameter is one that cannot be updated, then Terraform will recreate the resource entirely. This could potentially lead to loss of data or some downtime, depending on the resource and environment.

Challenges

As with all technologies, Terraform also has some challenges.

With CloudFormation, the state is entirely managed by AWS, for free and in the cloud, easily accessible by authorized users wherever they are. With Terraform, the state file must be self-managed unless using the enterprise version or third-party management services. For a larger team, the state file will need to be stored somewhere centrally, where all team members who need access can access it. Terraform's more advanced features, such as team management, Single Sign-On, and audits, will also incur an additional cost.

Terraform has no automatic rollback to a previous working state after a deployment failure happens. If a stack fails to deploy, a previous template version first needs to be retrieved and then deployed again to revert the infrastructure to a working state.

As with CloudFormation, managing Serverless architecture with Terraform can be challenging as it offers no abstraction. The configuration details of all resources, their integrations, and permissions will need to be codified in the template to ensure successful and secure deployments.

AWS Serverless Application Model (SAM)

The AWS Serverless Application Model (SAM) is an open source framework for building Serverless applications on AWS. It is an abstraction of CloudFormation that is intended to make it easier to provision Serverless architecture.

SAM IaC templates are smaller, with fewer details needed to configure each resource. SAM will add the remaining attributes using best practice defaults to create the full CloudFormation template that is submitted to the service for deployment. Like CloudFormation, SAM is free to use; we pay only for the provisioned resources.

In Figure 6-10, a Lambda microservice is provisioned and integrated with a new API Gateway with only a few lines of code.

```
AWSTemplateFormatVersion: "2010-09-09"
Transform: AWS::Serverless-2016-10-31
Description: "CloudFormation demo template"
Resources:
```

Creates a Lambda Function	```HelloWorldFunction: Type: AWS::Serverless::Function Properties: CodeUri: hello_world/ Handler: app.lambda_handler Runtime: python3.8 Timeout: 3```

```
      Events:
```

Creates an API Gateway	```HelloWorld: Type: Api Properties: Path: /hello Method: get```

Figure 6-10. *SAM template example provisioning a Lambda and API Gateway*

Behind the scenes, SAM adds the missing service attributes from best practice defaults, the necessary integration configuration, and the IAM role and policy required for API Gateway to be able to call the Lambda microservice.

Another SAM capability, and, for many, the only capability that is used, is that it can help with local testing. Using Docker containers and mock data, SAM can simulate trigger events from most cloud services to execute a Lambda microservice locally. Doing so without needing to deploy anything to the cloud is great for developer productivity. To further improve productivity, SAM Globals can be specified in templates and reused across many resources.

SAM can also help debug deployed applications. It can stream CloudWatch logs to the local machine, making it easier to troubleshoot issues without having to log in to the console.

SAM is backward compatible with CloudFormation. So, in situations where services need to be provisioned that are not supported by SAM or a specific configuration is required for a service, standard CloudFormation syntax can be used in the SAM template.

Serverless Application Repository

The Serverless Application Repository is a SAM community where anyone can publish, share, and download SAM templates for different pieces of architecture and service configurations. As with SAM, the service and templates are free; we just pay for the provisioned resources after the template is deployed.

Through the repository, we can leverage existing patterns or pre-build templated components for the organization. This can help reduce reinventing the wheel, set organizational best practices, and get applications to market faster.

Challenges

SAM does not support all cloud services, not even all Serverless cloud services. Not supporting a service means that SAM does not have the default best practices. However, we can still fall back to standard CloudFormation in the same template to provision the unsupported services.

For the supported services, SAM uses an opinionated approach to configure them with best practice defaults. This means developers will have less control over the configuration, and the configuration might not align with organizational or industry-specific regulatory policies. To configure services in a particular way, we will need to fall back to standard CloudFormation again.

Lastly, SAM is still primarily a templating solution. While it can simplify things for specific types of projects, it does not offer many of the benefits of a more comprehensive IaC abstraction framework.

 # AWS Amplify

Amplify is another AWS approach to provisioning cloud resources. Amplify provides a cloud service, code libraries, UI components, and a command-line tool (CLI) that simplifies adding sophisticated cloud back ends to mobile and web applications by provisioning back-end resources with the help of AWS CloudFormation.

Compared with the other tools, Amplify is less technical, with more of the infrastructure configuration completed with default settings. It's largely targeted at front-end and mobile developers, providing an easy means to create Serverless back ends for their applications.

There are three key components:

1. Open source set of UI components and code libraries to simplify integrating cloud-enabled capabilities such as authentication and synchronization into web and mobile interfaces

2. A command-line tool for creating and managing applications through simple commands to add services and survey-like questions to configure them

3. The Amplify cloud service for deploying and hosting full-stack Serverless web apps

```
C:\Users\            \Projects\amplify-demo>amplify init
Note: It is recommended to run this command from the root of your app directory
? Enter a name for the project amplifydemo
The following configuration will be applied:

Project information
| Name: amplifydemo
| Environment: dev
| Default editor: Visual Studio Code
| App type: javascript
| Javascript framework: none
| Source Directory Path: src
| Distribution Directory Path: dist
| Build Command: npm.cmd run-script build
| Start Command: npm.cmd run-script start

C:\Users\KangZhengLi\Projects\amplify-demo>amplify add auth
Using service: Cognito, provided by: awscloudformation

 The current configured provider is Amazon Cognito.

 Do you want to use the default authentication and security configuration? Default configuration
 Warning: you will not be able to edit these selections.
 How do you want users to be able to sign in? Username
 Do you want to configure advanced settings? No, I am done.
Successfully added auth resource amplifydemo6c0061e4 locally
```

Figure 6-11. *Amplify commands and response. Source: Amplify CLI*
https://aws.amazon.com/ 2022, Amazon Web Services Inc. or its affiliates.
All rights reserved

To start a new project, we use the command-line tool to initiate it in the folder we want to use – *amplify-demo* in Figure 6-11. Amplify will guide us through a series of questions to configure a few things and create a directory structure for the project. Once the project is set up, we can add resources to the project and configure them with a similar series of questions. Amplify does not provide individual cloud services but rather named blueprints such as *auth* that can consist of one or more cloud resources that provide a particular purpose – in this case, a Cognito user pool, an identity pool, and the required IAM roles and policies.

Once the *auth* blueprint has been provisioned, we can use the available libraries and UI components to integrate it into an application and enable a login capability for users. Here, we have a sign-in code snippet example using the Amplify JavaScript Auth library. Using just a few lines of code, we can authenticate a user with a provided *username* and *password*:

```
import { Auth } from 'aws-amplify';
async function signIn() {
  try {
    const user = await Auth.signIn(username, password);
  } catch (error) {
    // login failed
    console.log('error signing in', error);
  }
  // login succeeded
}
```

The complexity of setting up the back end is completely abstracted for the user, and this greatly lowers the barrier of entry for developers who are less comfortable with cloud or back end. Instead of having to configure Cognito from scratch, Amplify does it automatically based on a few simple questions. Of course, this also makes Amplify considerably less flexible and difficult to customize. As such, it is not a great option for complex applications, nor is it usually the preferred choice of experienced back-end developers and cloud architects.

It can be especially problematic for projects that start simple, but as they scale and gain complexity, it becomes harder and harder to manage them within Amplify. The only option at that point will be to rebuild the application in a more flexible framework.

Amplify is a good fit for simple web or mobile applications that are unlikely to grow in complexity over time. Plug-and-play features are provided out of the box for

- A scalable API back end with microservices

- Authenticating users

- Storing data securely

- Authorizing access to data

- Integrating simple machine learning services

- Analyzing application metrics

Amplify supports DevOps efforts with capabilities for code testing, version control, and production deployment. Parts are open source, which provides a means to extend some functionality with custom plugins.

Given the level of abstraction and the question-based approach to provisioning services, there is no learning curve for CloudFormation or the details of complex cloud services. Not all cloud services are supported, but those typically needed for a simple web or mobile application are covered. These include Lambda microservices, API Gateway, different types of databases, and fine-grained access and user management controls.

The supported services are all fully managed, so developers can focus on code and don't need to worry about managing servers, patching, maintenance, or other overheads. Similarly, backups, redundancy, and scaling are all automated and fully managed.

Amplify provides a complete solution for making and operating iOS and Android apps natively as well as through Ionic and React Native. Web applications are fully supported with JavaScript, React, Angular, and Vue. It is the only solution that provides development support for the back end and front end of applications.

For mobile, Amplify maintains on-device data storage with built-in synchronization to the back-end data store. Amplify allows apps to write data locally when offline, and it will automatically synchronize with the cloud when connected again.

Like SAM, Amplify CLI can emulate supported cloud services locally for testing and development without needing to first deploy them to the cloud. This improves developer productivity and enables rapid iteration.

AWS Cloud Development Kit (CDK)

In July 2019, AWS released Cloud Development Kit (CDK). This open source software development framework enables developers to model and provision cloud resources using programming languages they are already familiar with.

Provisioning cloud resources can be a challenging and time-consuming task. When done via the AWS web interface, it includes many manual tasks. While using CloudFormation – AWS's Infrastructure-as-Code templates – makes it far easier to repeat and automate infrastructure provisioning, creating these templates in JSON or YAML can be confusing and often frustrating.

CDK uses the power and the familiarity of common programming languages to create application infrastructure, provision resources, and deploy code. As CDK is effectively a layer on top of CloudFormation, it can do everything CloudFormation can and more:

- Make infrastructure deployments predictable and repeatable across multiple regions. Avoid manual steps and drastically reduce the chance of human error.

- Provision and configure any AWS service that CloudFormation supports. For those not supported, developers can use a custom resource – a Lambda microservice that runs at the end of a deployment to perform any action supported by service APIs.

- Group collections of resources together in a stack, making it easy to monitor for any changes or to clean everything up again when we are finished with a project.

- Create reusable service configurations and entire blueprints that can be shared with the organization.

CDK provides code functions called *constructs* to easily provision services with any required dependencies and default settings. This greatly reduces the amount of coding needed compared with CloudFormation. We can extend constructs and design our own reusable constructs that meet organizational best practices and compliance requirements. As with any open source software library, we can create an organization-specific build that can be shared to rapidly bootstrap new projects with best practices and required settings enabled by default.

Because CDK uses real programming languages instead of template markup, we can use the language's built-in capabilities such as loops, objects, classes, and functions to further automate tasks and design patterns that may be unique to a given project or organization. Requirements such as security policies or privacy settings in resources can be defined at an organization level and implemented in CDK to make it easier for development teams to comply. The following use cases can be considered:

1. The enterprise cybersecurity team creates classes that sit on top of CDK to enforce security services and settings. Developers must use these classes and cannot change the settings. For example, when a developer creates an API, a cybersecurity function could automatically add a Web Application Firewall to the API with the desired set of security rules that the firewall should enforce.

2. Further simplification of common internal design patterns by creating classes or functions that sit on top of CDK and set the defaults for each service, as well as string together multiple services for a common cloud design. For example, a CDK function that, with one line of code, can create a build-test-deploy pipeline for a microservice.

3. Create microservices or even entire applications as a reusable and shareable template. This template can be modified as needed by other teams and then rolled out in their region or for their particular use case. Microservice templates can be added and reused in multiple projects. The entire baseline of a new project could even be pre-scripted for each type of project. For example, if a developer indicated to CDK that they are going to create a new API project, this could automatically add the components needed for a typical API project.

For these types of use cases, it should be noted that CDK constructs are local and ambitious developers can easily change the code and overrule any required security settings. This is why CDK constructs should be considered *directive* controls – they *inform* but do not *enforce* – and need to be supported by preventive and other controls in the deployment pipeline that can provide the necessary enforcement.

CDK also helps accelerate the onboarding of team members who may be new to AWS. They can apply their existing programming skills to quickly understand how a project's infrastructure has been provisioned without having to learn CloudFormation.

Besides generating CloudFormation templates, CDK can also deploy solutions into the cloud. For example, it can

- Compile microservice code and deploy it to Lambda.

- Compile user interfaces, such as React web applications, and deploy them to S3. CDK can even invalidate an integrated CloudFront CDN cache, so the latest changes are immediately available to the users after deployment.

- Compile Docker containers and deploy them to ECR, where they can be scanned for vulnerabilities and used by ECS, EKS, and Fargate.

For rapid prototyping or development environments, CDK can deploy infrastructure and code directly from the command line to CloudFormation and individual cloud services. This makes it easier for small teams to get started.

However, best practice is to use a proper deployment pipeline, especially for larger teams and production environments. CDK can deploy through a build-test-deploy pipeline using DevOps services such as AWS CodeCommit, CodeBuild, and CodePipeline. There are different approaches to this; in my opinion, allow developers to push their CDK project to an appropriate branch in a CodeCommit repo. From there, we can trigger a deployment workflow to build the CDK project, provision infrastructure, and deploy code. This approach can support pipelines with cloud controls and limits the access needed by developers to the cloud.

With CDK, we can construct the cloud architecture of Serverless web applications using only a few lines of code, relying on the defaults to fill in the rest. However, we do have full access to all the configuration settings – for many services via the simplified approach of constructs or for all services through base functions that support all of the settings available in CloudFormation templates.

CDK generates standard CloudFormation templates, but the programming language approach makes it easier and a better experience for many developers. Project code will be more manageable and readable, especially for developers unfamiliar with CloudFormation.

More information about the Cloud Development Kit can be found on the product page here

https://aws.amazon.com/cdk/

and on the GIT repo here:

https://github.com/aws/aws-cdk

Differences Between Amplify and CDK

While there are certainly overlaps and they can be used together in some cases, there are some crucial differences, especially in terms of the scale and scope of a project.

CDK is preferred for large-scale custom solutions and those that are predominantly a back-end pipeline using many different cloud services.

Amplify is a better option for smaller projects requiring minimal customization to the infrastructure and settings provided by Amplify.

CDK will need more experienced developers and is very code-focused. Amplify is simple to use, even for less technical people who just want to get a simple back end up and running.

One other advantage that Amplify has, and where it can work *within* a CDK project, is a great front-end library of features for interacting with API Gateway, Cognito, and other services.

CDK is more suitable for the long-term plans of an organization. It can be used as a strategic framework for organizational cloud enablement, while Amplify is a single project framework. With CDK, we can build reusable infrastructure templates specific to an organization's needs and communicate best practices and compliance policies.

⚙ CDK Technical Considerations

As CDK is a programming layer built on top of CloudFormation, it can achieve many things that CloudFormation alone cannot. However, there are still some common challenges and limitations inherited from CloudFormation that CDK is not yet able to solve.

For all its complexity, CloudFormation can sometimes be a bit of a *dumb* template system. If we are developing a complex project with multiple stacks, it's common to run into dependency issues when trying to deploy deletes or changes to resources. The -e argument for *exclusively* in CDK deploy can be very helpful as it deploys only the named stack(s) without any dependent stacks. This can speed up the deployment process and help resolve dependency issues in some cases.

One example of this is with Lambda layers. Suppose we have a Lambda layer in one stack and a Lambda microservice in another stack that uses that layer. We will not be able to make changes to the layer and deploy it without CloudFormation throwing an error because CDK will attempt to delete the old layer when updating it. Deleting is not possible in this case because the Lambda microservice in the second stack is referencing it. The approach to achieve this without an error is as follows:

1. Remove the layer from the Lambda configuration.

2. Deploy the Lambda stack with -e *nameOfLambdaStack*.

3. Make the changes to the layer.

4. Add the layer back to the Lambda configuration.

5. Deploy the Lambda stack without -e.

Step 5 will automatically first deploy the layer stack as it is a dependency of the Lambda stack. Once the layer is deployed, CDK will attach the deployed layer to the Lambda configuration and deploy the second stack.

CloudFormation's 200-resource limit per stack is easier to hit with CDK because it is easy to miss how many individual resources are being created behind the scenes. We can use CDK synth to generate the CloudFormation template and see the number of resources. This will help determine when we need to split a project across multiple stacks. However, doing this in the middle of a project can be quite challenging. So it is best to plan ahead and split the project into logical stacks at the start of the project.

Large API Gateway projects with many resources and methods can be split across multiple stacks too. More information about that here:

https://docs.aws.amazon.com/cdk/api/latest/docs/aws-apigateway-readme. html#breaking-up-methods-and-resources-across-stacks

Local Dev and Testing

As we covered earlier, the AWS SAM command-line interface (CLI) can test Lambda microservices locally before deploying them.

When we invoke a Lambda microservice in debug mode within the SAM CLI, we can attach a debugger that lets us step through the code line by line. We can see the values of variables and fix issues the same way we would for any other application. More information about setting SAM up and debugging can be found in the documentation here:

https://docs.aws.amazon.com/serverless-application-model/latest/ developerguide/serverless-getting-started.html

One more thing to highlight: SAM can trigger different events for local Lambda microservices. It can simulate events from DynamoDB, S3, SQS, and others. More information about that can be found here:

https://docs.aws.amazon.com/serverless-application-model/latest/ developerguide/sam-cli-command-reference-sam-local-generate-event.html

Existing CloudFormation Projects

There are three ways to convert existing projects using CloudFormation templates to CDK:

1. Rewrite the application in CDK. This is the most work-intensive, but it can provide a good introduction to CDK through a managed learning curve where the outcomes or requirements are very clearly defined in the existing project.

2. CDK has a feature to include existing CloudFormation templates. This is the quickest way to convert an existing project; however, it won't enjoy some of the benefits of CDK, such as the infrastructure being represented in a standard programming language.

3. Use the disassembler tool to convert CloudFormation templates to CDK code. Note that, at the time of this writing, this is not recommended by AWS, as it is an experimental tool. It can provide the legwork for some templates, but the result will certainly need manual reviewing and cleaning up to get something that is production-ready. The tool and more information can be found here:

    https://github.com/aws/aws-cdk/tree/master/packages/ cdk-dasm

Extending CDK

CDK ships with many built-in constructs we can use to provision infrastructure, but, as mentioned earlier, there are several reasons to create our own. Creating reusable constructs for specific service configurations or more complex patterns commonly needed within an organization is a great way to increase the development team's productivity. Either way, learning how to make a reusable construct provides excellent benefits for CDK productivity.

Custom constructs can be created for single service configurations to complex end-to-end pipeline designs. Constructs can easily be reused across multiple projects and shared between different teams. Before developing anything, it is important to fully understand the services that will be used, how well they are supported in CloudFormation, and how well they are already supported in CDK. This will indicate if it is possible and the amount of effort needed. If something is impossible in CloudFormation, then an alternative approach might be with a custom resource – a Lambda microservice that can perform actions through the AWS SDK and APIs.

In large enterprises, compliance requirements and limitations imposed on the AWS account that could impact CDK must be understood. For example, a common challenge with regulated industries is that the desired cloud service may be unavailable and it will require a lengthy attestation process before it is approved.

This blog has some great examples of extending CDK
https://garbe.io/blog/2019/10/01/hey-cdk-how-to-write-less-code/
and this one, which also shows how to publish a public construct:
https://matthewbonig.com/2020/01/11/creating-constructs/

CDK DevOps

Once the architecture is defined, we can run the synth command in the CDK CLI to generate the corresponding CloudFormation templates. The templates can be uploaded to the CloudFormation service using the deploy command, which will provision the resources. The CLI displays any errors and the final result locally for easier troubleshooting.

CDK also supports custom pipelines. It can deploy to an existing pipeline, or we can create one in the project itself using a pipeline construct, as shown in Figure 6-12.

The CDK pipeline is a high-level construct with many opinions built in. When this construct is deployed, it automatically creates a CodePipeline with the defined stages to test and deploy the application.

The pipeline construct can reside with the project code, meaning that we can simply edit the same CDK file and deploy it if we want to build additional capabilities into the pipeline. This is especially helpful when we want to recreate the entire infrastructure in a different AWS account or region with confidence that resources will be consistently deployed.

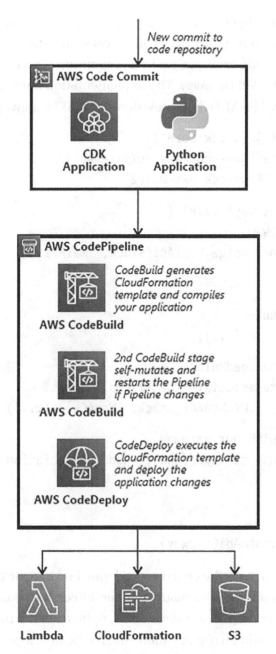

Figure 6-12. *CDK cloud-native pipeline example*

The use of programming languages opens up many possibilities to employ CDK for other use cases – for example, using CDK constructs as directive controls as mentioned earlier. In the following code example, we have a common class that defines the implementation for AWS API Gateway. The implementation automatically integrates a Web Application Firewall (WAF) when provisioning an API Gateway:

```
const cdk = require('@aws-cdk/core');
const apigw = require('@aws-cdk/aws-apigateway')
const waf = require('@aws-cdk/aws-wafv2')

function createApiGateway(stack) {
  // Create API Gateway
  let apiGateway = new apigw.RestApi(stack, 'WafAPI', {...});

  let wafRules = [];

  // 1 AWS Managed Rules
  let awsManagedRules = {...};

  wafRules.push(awsManagedRules)
  // Create WebACL to associate the firewall rules
  let webACL = new waf.CfnWebACL(stack, 'WebACL', {...});

  // Associate WAF with our gateway
  new waf.CfnWebACLAssociation(stack, 'WebACLAssociation', {...})

  return apiGateway
}

module.exports = {createApiGateway}
```

Developers simply include the construct with one line of code to provision the pre-approved service configuration and ensure their architecture is compliant. This can help speed up the onboarding of new developers, reduce the learning curve for complex compliance requirements in an organization, and let the developers focus more on delivering application requirements and customer value:

```
// Create lambda service
const demoService = new lambda.Function(this, 'DemoLambda' {...});

// Use imported library to create API Gateway
let apiGateway = sgCommons.createApiGateway(this)
```

```
// Create API Gateway resource
const resource = apiGateway.root.addResource('helloworld');

// Lambda integration with API Gateway
let lambdaIntg = new apigw.LambdaIntegration(demoService, {...});

// Add method path to integration
resource.addMethod('GET', lambdaIntg, {...});
```

Another use case is to simplify the provisioning of common service configurations by adding organizational-approved default settings to service constructs. In the following code example, we have a CodePipeline construct with the necessary stages fully configured with common defaults:

```
function createDeploymentPipeline(stack) {
  const code = codecommit.Repository.fromRepositoryName(this,
  'ImportedRepo', 'DemoRepo');

  new codepipeline.Pipeline(this, 'Pipeline', {
    stages: [
      {
        stageName: 'Source',
        actions: [...]
      },
      {
        stageName: 'Build',
        actions: [...]
      },
      {
        stageName: 'Deploy',
        actions: [...]
      }
    ]
  });

  this.lambdaCode = lambda.Code.fromCfnParameters();
}
module.exports = {createDeploymentPipeline}
```

In the application IaC template, the application team can include the entire deployment pipeline with one line of code:

```
// Use imported library to create API Gateway
sgCommons.createDeploymentPipeline(this)
```

Lastly, we can create microservices or even entire applications as reusable and shareable templates within the organization. This approach enables developers to easily reuse code from other developers while still being able to make any changes needed for their particular project. This reduces the need to reinvent the wheel and increases developer productivity.

We can even take this approach one step further and bundle multiple services as a single construct – for example, a reusable API configuration compliant with internal policy and following architectural best practices.

An app team in need of an API pattern can take and modify this construct as needed for their project, again boosting developer productivity by providing a ready-to-use base for the project:

```
const cdk = require('@aws-cdk/core');
const lambda = require('@aws-cdk/aws-lambda');
const logs = require('@aws-cdk/aws-logs');

// Edit these variables for any custom attributes
const LAMBDA_HANDLER = 'index.handler';
const LAMBDA_DESCRIPTION = 'Cloudwatch logs monitor';
const LAMBDA_RUNTIME = lambda.Runtime.PYTHON_3_8;
const LAMBDA_MEMORY = 128;
const LAMBDA_TIMEOUT_SECONDS = 600;
const LAMBDA_CODE_PATH = './lambda_src_path/'
const LAMBDA_ENV = {}
const LOG_RETENTION_PERIOD = logs.RetentionDays.THREE_DAYS;

class HelloCdkStack extends cdk.Stack {
  constructor(scope, id, props) {
    super(scope, id, props);
```

```
    // demo lambda function
    new lambda.Function(this, 'DemoLambda', {
      description: LAMBDA_DESCRIPTION,
      runtime: LAMBDA_RUNTIME,
      handler: LAMBDA_HANDLER,
      code: lambda.Code.fromAsset(LAMBDA_CODE_PATH),
      memorySize: LAMBDA_MEMORY,
      timeout: cdk.Duration.seconds(LAMBDA_TIMEOUT_SECONDS),
      logRetention: LOG_RETENTION_PERIOD,
      environment: LAMBDA_ENV
    });
  }
}

module.exports = {HelloCdkStack}
```

CDK Tips

- The CDK cache folder *cdk.out* – which can easily become several GBs in size – can be safely deleted at any time, for example, when it gets too large, when sharing the project directly, or when the project is archived.

- While keeping CDK up to date is best practice, always read the changelog before doing so:

  https://github.com/aws/aws-cdk/releases

  Especially read the *breaking changes* section. Look for any services used in a given project and understand what the impact might be before updating CDK. At the time of writing, changes are made frequently and often with great new features that can make it easier to achieve certain patterns. So it is recommended to keep an eye on this page for any new changes.

- The JavaScript version of CDK uses a fixed version in the project package.json for core components. When adding CDK modules through NPM, the modules will have a *minimal* version in package.

json. This means that when we run *npm update*, the modules will be updated, but the core components will not. It can cause issues when the versions get too far apart and incompatible. To resolve this, ensure the core components have a ^ character before the version in package.json, allowing them to automatically update with the modules. Alternatively, if we prefer to stick with the older version of CDK, we can install a specific version of each module to match the core module, for example: *npm install @aws-cdk/aws-iam@**1.7.0***.

- Using *cdk deploy* is a simple way to push a project into the cloud, and it can be a good choice when rapid prototyping. However, this is not best practice. We should use a deployment pipeline. When the organization does not provide one, we can create it with CDK in one stack and then deploy all resources and code through that pipeline in later stacks. More information can be found here:

  https://docs.aws.amazon.com/cdk/latest/guide/codepipeline_example.html

- The target audience for CDK is not regulated enterprises. It is usually a great fit for small to medium organizations, but it can face compatibility issues with existing cloud management, landing zone, and deployment strategies for larger ones. While CDK does output standard CloudFormation, not all enterprise pipelines will support that, and changes to the configuration or even customization of the tool may be required to utilize CDK in such environments.

⚙ Serverless Framework

Serverless Framework is an open source tool and framework for deploying Serverless applications. Serverless Framework abstracts some of the complexity of infrastructure configuration, resulting in cleaner and shorter infrastructure templates.

An active GitHub community is dedicated to supporting and maintaining the tool, and it is free to use. There is a paid version for larger teams and enterprises, which also includes some advanced tools such as the Developer Studio.

Serverless Framework is provider-agnostic – meaning it works with all major cloud providers. Like Terraform, individual templates still need to be created for the different cloud providers. So, while it offers a single framework for multi-cloud, it does not reduce the learning curve or make it easier to design and operate multi-cloud applications.

Serverless Framework generates CloudFormation templates to provision AWS infrastructure; it generates Terraform for Azure and GCP.

Figure 6-13 provides an example of how we can deploy an API backed by Lambda using Serverless Framework.

```
service: demo-serverless-service
frameworkVersion: "2"
```

Creates a Lambda function	```functions:
hello:
handler: handler.main
memorySize: 128
description: Say hello world
runtime: python3.8```

```
Events:
```

Creates an API Gateway	``` - http:
path: hello
method: get```

Figure 6-13. Serverless Framework template example

The implementation is simplified and easy to understand, and developers usually only need to provide the settings they want to customize. The remaining ones will be filled in by the framework using opinionated defaults.

The commercial version of Serverless Framework offers additional services, such as a dashboard for a unified view of all Serverless applications. Using the dashboard, we can monitor performance, collect logging metrics, and configure alerts for any issues. If the organization does not provide one, we can create a CI/CD pipeline to test and consistently deploy changes.

Serverless Framework supports plugins, many of which are developed by the community. For example, the *Serverless Offline* plugin provides local testing capability similar to what we covered earlier with AWS SAM.

Plugins can also have some overlap with CDK constructs. They can be used as directives to add best practice or compliant infrastructure configurations and blueprints to an application.

Challenges

Serverless Framework supports only a few cloud services out of the box. Unsupported services will require standard CloudFormation, and mixing different templating syntaxes can make the IaC confusing.

While Serverless Framework provides some abstraction and a supportive community, it can still be a steep learning curve for developers, especially when it needs to be used within a restrictive organization and on top of learning Serverless architecture.

Having to mix different templating formats and approaches for different services, understanding which plugins should be included, and the multi-cloud capability that adds complexity that is not even needed for most organizations can make it challenging for teams to use Serverless Framework.

As with any technology, the recommendation is to try out different options to find the one that is the best fit for the organization, team, and project.

The most touted benefit of Serverless Framework is that it has a huge community, but this does not necessarily make it a good product.

Indeed, its popularity may be a result of not having any suitable competitor for quite some time and a snowball effect from having the domain name *serverless.com* giving it the top position in many search engine results.

For those that are 100% on AWS, I believe CDK is a better solution. It is easier to work with, has better support for cloud services, is more integrated into the AWS ecosystem, and usually has a far shorter learning curve.

However, Serverless Framework may be more suitable for organizations with a multi-cloud requirement that want something more abstracted than Terraform.

Code Repositories

In an agile project world, developers are often collaborative and work on multiple projects throughout their time at the organization. A clearly defined and agreed project structure will help with developer onboarding, application debugging, and making components more reusable across multiple projects. This is even more relevant for Serverless projects, which can consist of tens or hundreds of independent components.

Some decisions faced in establishing a project structure include the following:

- *Deciding on mono- or multi-repo*: Which one is best for Serverless?

- *Separating infrastructure templates from application code*: This is about managing risk; should individual developers – who could be external vendors – have access to both the code and potentially sensitive infrastructure configuration of a component assigned to them?

- CloudFormation stacks have several capabilities related to project structure. What do these capabilities do, and which can help with Serverless applications?

There are two strategies for code repositories, mono-repo and multi-repo.

Mono-repo

A mono-repo is a single repository containing all the project's code and configuration. In some cases, it might even include multiple projects. Monolithic applications use mono-repos because they have many internal dependencies. So splitting them into individual components is too challenging.

In a Serverless project using a mono-repo, all infrastructure configuration, microservices, and interfaces are bundled into a single repository. All developers will work with this single repository and have access to all code and infrastructure configuration within it. While *write* access can be managed through branches and pull requests, the entire team, regardless of rank, internal or external, will at least have *read* access to the entire project.

This approach keeps things simple and can work well for small projects with few developers. However, there are security and code management challenges to consider for larger teams and more complex projects.

An advantage of a mono-repo is that it can foster collaboration and communication among developers. Since everyone is working on the same code base, it discourages developers from working in silos.

With a single repository, commonly used code can be shared through a shared folder structure or similar, and developers can easily reference other developers' code or any shared components they need to interact with.

Mono-repos can simplify dependency management, as the relevant functions and files are together in a single location. Changes can be made and tested locally, and there is a single source of truth.

With a single code base, it can be easier to achieve best practices since there is shared oversight. Any team member can provide feedback, and other parts of the code can be referenced as an example.

A downside of mono-repo is the complication of the CI/CD pipeline. Either the entire code base needs to be deployed, which can be very time-consuming, or we need to be able to partially deploy code, which can be complex to implement, and risk dependencies being missed or not tested properly.

Testing typically needs to remain in place for the entire application if there are dependencies or shared code. Only testing the changed code could lead to missing issues in other parts of the application that might depend on that code.

With a larger code base, version control may see a decline in performance. For example, it may take some time for the tool to respond when checking the status of a repository with a large code base.

Finally, in a collaborative environment, there will be many changes to the repository, and this could increase the likelihood of a broken branch, which will affect future requests until it is fixed.

Multi-repo

In a multi-repo – also called a poly-repo – each component of an application is managed in its own separate repository. Typically, in an organization with a modern approach to the cloud, each repo will have its own attached deployment pipeline. This offers opportunities to optimize the pipeline and its controls for that particular component.

While splitting components may not be possible in a monolith, it is a natural fit for Serverless architecture and is best practice to scope repositories to the microservice or UI level. This is also an AWS recommendation. However, components in this context can actually be four things:

1. A microservice

2. A user interface, such as a React front end

3. The Infrastructure-as-Code template for a single managed service

4. The Infrastructure-as-Code template for a group of managed services

While the first two components should be quite clear and easy to distinguish, the distinction between 3 and 4 is not always straightforward. Context, security requirements, scope, and the integrations of a piece of infrastructure will all play a part in determining if a particular managed service should be treated as a separate component or part of a group of components.

For example, a database could be regarded as a separate independent component. Alternatively, a database could also be considered part of a group of shared infrastructure containing other databases, storage facilities, and support services. There are no hard rules or even best practices for these components, and the organization or project team will need to determine the most appropriate structure to use.

A multi-repo approach is more suitable for complex Serverless projects, especially those with multiple developers involved, as it offers more fine-grained control over access. We can decide who needs access to each individual repository based on their assigned tasks.

Another consideration, especially for microservices, is whether to keep the microservice code and the infrastructure configuration together in a single repo.

1. **Combine infrastructure and code.**

   a. Efficient as it enables the developer to self-manage their component configuration

   b. Suitable if the developer is trusted to manage potentially sensitive infrastructure configuration

325

2. **Separate infrastructure and code.**

   a. Limit inexperienced or external developer access to potentially sensitive infrastructure configuration.

   b. The architect or team lead retains control over infrastructure configuration.

   c. The infrastructure configuration can be stored in a shared resources repository or a separate repo.

3. **Why not both?**

   a. It is also possible to include some infrastructure options with the microservice code. For example, it is productive and poses little risk if the developer can manage the *environment variables* of a Lambda microservice themselves.

   b. The deployment pipeline will need to support this and merge the permitted infrastructure options with the main configuration on deployment.

Figure 6-14 shows the differences between combining infrastructure and code and splitting them.

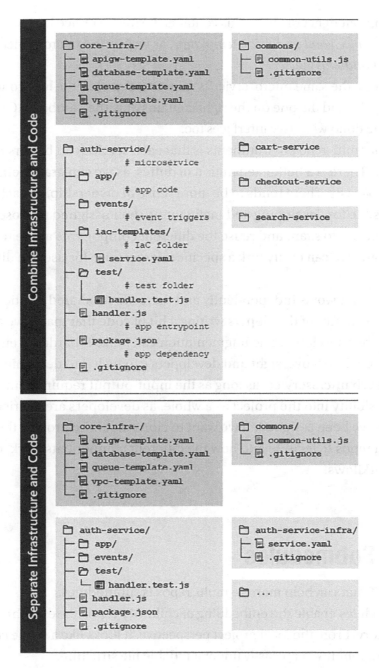

Figure 6-14. *Combine or separate IaC from microservice code*

Note the top-left light gray box. This contains the microservice Lambda configuration *service.yaml* under *iac-templates/*, as well as the microservice code, in this case a NodeJS *handler.js* file.

At the bottom, the same microservice is split. One repo (on the left) contains the microservice code, and the one on the right contains only the Lambda IaC configuration. This split can be done with user interfaces too.

A benefit of multi-repo environments is that each service can be versioned independently. There is a better separation of duties, as we can grant permissions on a per-repository basis. There tends to be more sense of ownership, as each developer is now responsible for developing and maintaining their assigned microservices. It also becomes easier to share and reuse the different components as the repos are independent, and we can easily fork a specific microservice for use in a different project.

Since each team works independently and there are no shared utilities or code, there is a higher chance of developers writing a bit of code that may have already been written by another developer. The fragmentation can make it harder to enforce best practices, as there is less oversight and developers can be left to determine their own approach for each microservice, as long as the input-output requirements are met. There is less visibility into the project as a whole, as developers are restricted to the services they have been assigned. If we want to clone an entire project, then we need to know which repos to include and how the different components work together in the various workflows.

GIT Submodules

A feature in GIT that can help manage multi-repos is submodules.

GIT submodules enable the embedding of child GIT repositories within the main project repository. From the local project perspective, it looks like a single code base with all the components in an easily understandable file structure.

From the repository perspective, each one is independent with its own lifecycle and deployment integration. The sub-repo can be cloned or forked as with other repositories and worked on separately without even needing access to the main project repository. When we add a submodule to a project, GIT creates a *.gitmodules* file in the main repo, which contains a reference to the sub-repo.

A use case for GIT submodules is to manage third-party libraries. This way, there is no need to manually download and merge the external code into the project. This can still be useful for some specific cases but is mostly considered redundant for languages such as Python and NodeJS that include package managers that are more suitable for managing third-party dependencies and their versions – at least for those dependencies that have been registered with the package manager.

For Serverless, GIT submodules have seen some renewed usefulness in mitigating one of the challenges of multi-repo. The challenge in question is relevant to senior team members who want to have the entire project locally in a logical folder structure. Sub-repos can help achieve that, as seen in Figure 6-15.

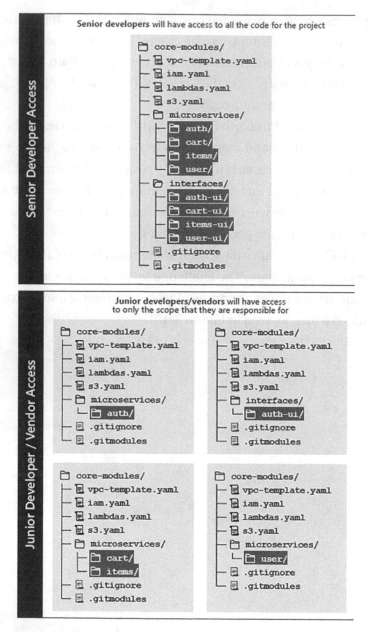

Figure 6-15. *Using GIT submodules to achieve a single project overview locally*

In Figure 6-15, at the top is a *main* repo with the shared infrastructure and submodules for each microservice and UI. An architect or senior project lead can clone the main repo with all submodules, providing a logically structured project on their local system. Individual developers can be given access only to the components they are working on.

Sub-repos make it easier to share reusable components within an organization. When using another team's component, the team can create their own branch of the sub-repo and customize it for the new project that they are working on, as shown in Figure 6-16.

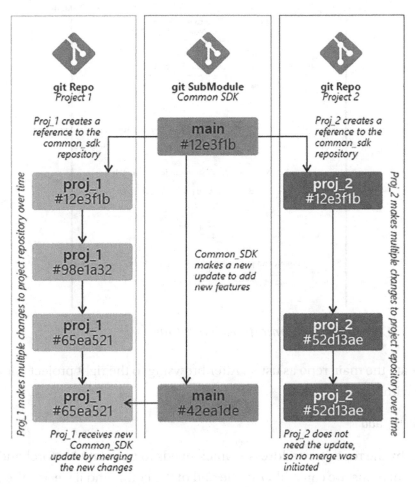

Figure 6-16. *Component version management with GIT submodules*

If the original team releases a new update to the component, the second team can perform a GIT merge with the main branch to retrieve the latest update without losing their customizations.

Of course, unless it is a security update, doing a merge is optional. It will require testing, and the effort might not be justified if the project does not need the new update.

If the second team needs to make significant changes to the component for their project, then forking the original might be a better idea, and updates will need to be handled differently.

Figure 6-17 shows how we can create a repo with submodules.

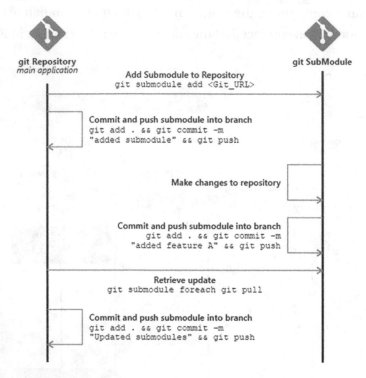

Figure 6-17. *Creating GIT submodules workflow*

First, create the main repo as usual. After browsing to the right project folder, add the submodule with

```
git submodule add
```

followed by the repository address – which needs to be created beforehand. As with cloning normal repos, we can add ./ to the end of the command if we are already in the folder we want to use for the code.

Save the submodule link to the main repo with a standard

```
add *
commit -m "new subrepo"
push
```

The submodule code can then be worked on as per usual and committed/pushed when done. After any external changes, pull the latest update in the submodule folder.

We can update all submodules in the main repo with the following:

```
git submodule foreach git pull
```

Common Challenges

There can be some challenges when working with submodules, but I also have some mitigations that can be considered. When cloning a GIT repo containing submodules, the submodules are not cloned by default. Use the *--recurse-submodules* flag when cloning the main repo to include all linked submodules.

After changes to the local submodule code, both the submodule and the main repo need to be committed and pushed. Some IDEs automate this process, or an alias can be created to make this easier like so:

```
git config alias.spush 'push --recurse-submodules=on-demand'
```

Instead of the *git push* command, we then use *git spush* to push both the main and submodule repo(s).

Lastly, submodules start off with a detached head, so before making any changes, we must make sure to *check out* into an appropriate branch.

Lambda Layers

I also want to touch on Lambda layers in this context. Lambda layers should not be used for shared utilities or other code between deployed microservices as this is an anti-pattern. It creates dependencies between microservices, resulting in a tightly coupled distributed monolith.

Submodules can be used for shared utilities between microservices locally and to reduce duplicate code. As the shared utils are embedded in each microservice code base and so individually deployed, it avoids dependencies between our deployed microservices. As shown earlier, versions can be managed through standard repo capabilities, allowing for different components to include different versions of the utils and only updating those that need the latest version.

A private NPM registry or equivalent for other programming languages can also work for shared code, and we can manage updates via the built-in versioning option.

Developer Tooling

Next, let's look at some other useful tools for developing Serverless applications that have not been covered yet.

AWS Command-Line Interface (CLI)

The AWS CLI is a tool for interacting with AWS services from a command line, avoiding the need for using the visual console. Using the CLI, developers can create scripts to automate certain tasks and streamline workflows.

Because of its ease of use and the reusability of scripts, it is a convenient channel for users to quickly retrieve or add data, run tests, and troubleshoot issues with cloud resources. While we can also provision and configure resources with it directly via the service APIs, this is considered bad practice. Provisioning and configuring resources should be done with CloudFormation templates, which the CLI can deploy to the service.

The CLI is available for Linux, Windows, and MacOS systems. Let's look at two examples:

1. Copy data into an S3 bucket:

```
aws s3 sync ./ s3://my-bucket --region ap-southeast-1
```

2. Invoke a Lambda function and store the output in output.json:

```
aws lambda invoke --function-name demo-function \
    --invocation-type RequestResponse \
    --payload '{"data":"some data"}' \
    output.json
```

LocalStack

A useful tool for testing is LocalStack, an AWS service emulator that can provision mocked AWS services locally. Figure 6-18 shows the free, open source version that supports many common cloud services, such as Lambda, API Gateway, and S3.

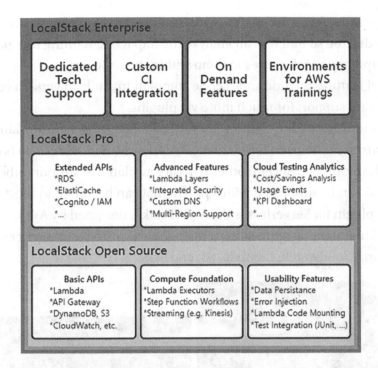

Figure 6-18. *LocalStack features and integrations*

The paid version of LocalStack can emulate more advanced cloud services, such as Cognito and Secrets Manager. A limitation is that not all services or all features are fully supported. We also need to be mindful of changes to services that might take some time to be reflected in LocalStack. For more information and the full list of supported services, visit the LocalStack GitHub page:

https://github.com/localstack/localstack

Integrated Development Environment (IDE)

Next, I want to talk briefly about three IDEs – software used to develop applications. Most developers will have their personal preferences, and some organizations might enforce a particular one. I want to cover these not to promote a particular software but to present certain features that can improve the experience of developing Serverless solutions.

The IDE I use is from JetBrains, which offers a suite of IDEs designed to improve productivity and help write cleaner code. The IDE offers real-time code inspection, flagging unused and duplicated code for review so code can be refactored and optimized. This can help make microservice code more efficient.

It has a powerful refactoring engine, with the ability to flag references to files before they are deleted so that we can analyze the impact. Renaming files or variables automatically updates all references to them within the code base.

Other useful features include smart code completion, built-in version control and database tools, and support for much more via plugins.

JetBrains products are each optimized for a particular programming language. For example, *PyCharm* is optimized for Python development, and *WebStorm* is optimized for JavaScript development. Several other IDEs are available to support other languages. CloudFormation can be supported with a plugin that can be added to most of their IDEs.

One useful plugin for Serverless is the AWS Toolkit, designed by AWS to aid in developing and maintaining applications. It integrates with several services such as CloudFormation, CloudWatch, Lambda, S3, and SQS.

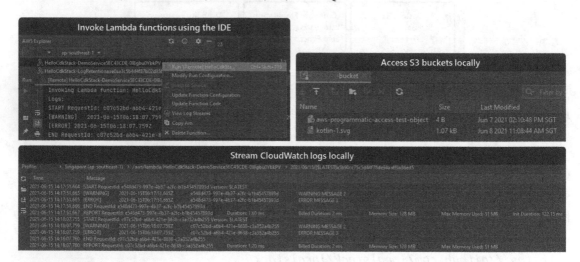

Figure 6-19. *PyCharm with AWS Toolkit. Source: JetBrains application*

In Figure 6-19 at the top, we see how the toolkit can be used to invoke a Lambda microservice from within the IDE. The resulting execution logs are conveniently streamed into the IDE too.

In the second example, we can see how the toolkit can display the contents of an S3 bucket in the IDE, and the third example shows a stream of logs coming from CloudWatch.

The toolkit integrates with SAM to provide local testing of Lambda microservices right from within the IDE. As we covered earlier, SAM includes message templates from many AWS services, which can be used to generate mock events used to invoke the local microservice.

JetBrains provides a suite of testing tools for troubleshooting code. When debugging applications, the IDE can test components directly with an interface supporting breakpoints.

An IDE that is perhaps more common with enterprises is Visual Studio Code (VS Code). Microsoft developed and open-sourced this tool, and unlike JetBrains, Visual Studio Code is free to use.

This IDE offers smart capabilities such as *IntelliSense* for syntax highlighting and auto-completion. It is lightweight and fast to work with, but it has some limitations. It does have a strong community and extensive plug-in library that can help overcome those limitations.

Visual Studio Code, shown in Figure 6-20, works with several programming languages, including JavaScript and Python. CloudFormation can be supported with a plugin. AWS also provides the AWS Toolkit for Visual Studio Code. Similarly, we can invoke Lambda microservices, access S3 buckets, and stream CloudWatch logs locally.

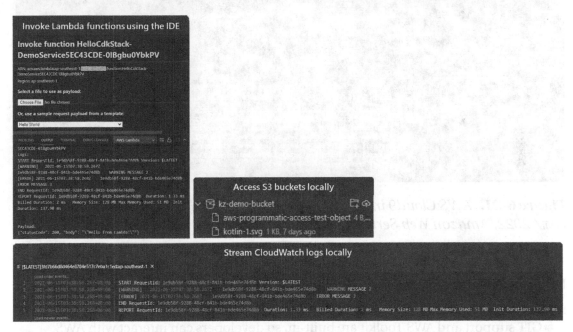

Figure 6-20. *Visual Studio Code with AWS Toolkit. Source: VS Code application*

Visual Studio Code also has testing capabilities to help run tests and troubleshoot any issues.

A slightly different IDE for developers shown in Figure 6-21 is Cloud9 by AWS. This is an online IDE where developers can write, run, debug, and deploy code using a web browser. With Cloud9, developers can work anywhere and on most devices, as long they have a screen and an Internet connection.

Figure 6-21. *AWS Cloud9 interface. Source: AWS console* `https://aws.amazon.` `com/` *2022, Amazon Web Services Inc. or its affiliates. All rights reserved*

Cloud9 supports several popular programming languages, including JavaScript and Python. Cloud9 enables developers to share workspaces with one another, supporting pair programming by allowing them to work together remotely.

GIT support and AWS Toolkit are built-in, so developers can interact with AWS resources such as invoking Lambda functions, viewing CloudWatch logs, and deploying microservice code.

Cloud9 is not a SaaS solution or Serverless. An EC2 instance will be provisioned in our AWS account to host it. It can be configured to automatically hibernate when the IDE is idle to help manage costs.

Other Tools

First, we have Jazz, an open source Serverless development platform designed by the T-Mobile application team. Using Jazz, developers can more easily create Serverless applications such as APIs, microservices, and static websites. The platform automatically configures the necessary services as well as the code repo for developers to work with. It includes a CI/CD pipeline with webhooks to automatically trigger builds and deployments whenever a code change is pushed. Jazz supports both AWS and Azure:

https://github.com/tmobile/jazz

If we want to quickly provision APIs and event-driven microservices, we can consider Claudia.js. Easily installed as an NPM package, it enables developers to define the API endpoint and microservice logic within the code, and Claudia.js automatically provisions and configures the necessary API Gateway and Lambda resources:

https://claudiajs.com/

For Python microservices, Zappa can help provision and configure the necessary Lambda and API Gateway resources. Zappa supports common frameworks such as Flask and Django, minimizing the amount of refactoring required in existing applications:

https://github.com/zappa/Zappa

UP is another tool for deploying API Gateway and microservice solutions. It supports several languages, including NodeJS and Python, enabling developers to easily provision resources without having to interact directly with the cloud. There are two versions of UP available, a free open source version and a paid version that includes additional functionality:

https://github.com/apex/up

The Architect Framework (ARC) is an IaC tool that enables developers to define their cloud services in a simplified syntax using an ARC file. It also supports more traditional templating languages such as JSON and YAML. Using Architect, developers can quickly start a local sandbox environment to host and test APIs and microservices. Out of the box, ARC supports NodeJS, Python, and Ruby:

https://arc.codes/

Code Quality Assurance

Lastly for this chapter, how can we achieve quality assurance in AWS?

AWS Well-Architected Framework

The Well-Architected Framework is an analysis and review framework used to determine how well designed, implemented, and operated a given AWS solution is. It is an approach to learn, measure, and improve the solution. More information can be found on the AWS website page shown in Figure 6-22.

Figure 6-22. *AWS Well-Architected introduction. Source: AWS website*
`https://aws.amazon.com/` *2022, Amazon Web Services Inc. or its affiliates.*
All rights reserved

It consists of five pillars that identify areas of a solution that are to be reviewed: operations, security, reliability, performance, and cost.

For each pillar, there is a series of questions to be answered about the solution, which can result in recommendations for improvement. The Well-Architected tool is available to help interview the application team, note the answers, and return the insights and recommendations in a nice report.

Performing the assessments and following the recommendations is a relatively straightforward way of improving the quality of Serverless applications. We will cover this in more detail in Chapter 9.

AWS Trusted Advisor

Trusted Advisor is a service that can inspect a cloud environment and make recommendations for saving money and improving system performance, availability, and security. The summary output is shown in Figure 6-23.

Figure 6-23. *AWS Trusted Advisor insights. Source: AWS console* `https://aws.amazon.com/` *2022, Amazon Web Services Inc. or its affiliates. All rights reserved*

All AWS accounts have access to the core security checks and checks for service limits and quotas. For example, it will find any security groups, allowing unrestricted access to risky ports.

Other checks, such as cost optimization and system performance, will require an AWS business or enterprise support subscription.

AWS CodeGuru

CodeGuru is a code analysis tool - an overview of its capabilities can be seen in Figure 6-24. Currently, it supports Java and Python – though I'm hopeful JavaScript support will be added. It automates code reviews and optimizes an application's performance using machine learning to identify critical defects and any deviation from coding best practices.

It scans through CodeCommit code repos to find lines of code that are *expensive* –
that take more time than necessary to execute – and suggests ways to optimize code and
reduce resource requirements and cost.

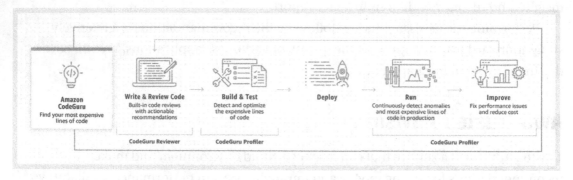

Figure 6-24. *AWS CodeGuru overview. Source: AWS website* https://aws.
amazon.com/ *2022, Amazon Web Services Inc. or its affiliates. All rights reserved*

CodeGuru only scans CodeCommit repos. If the organization prefers a different repo
provider, we can consider mirroring from that provider into CodeCommit. This is done
automatically and offers a way to use CodeGuru and more easily integrate with other
DevOps services such as CodePipeline.

CodeGuru can also be used for continuous monitoring to detect any operational
issues and provide recommendations on how to resolve them. For currently
unsupported languages, there are similar third-party tools such as SonarQube that
can be considered, though these will need to be self-managed and more work may be
needed to integrate them.

Amazon CodeWhisperer Preview

This is a new service, released while I was working on this book and, at the time of
writing, only available as a preview. It is a machine learning service that proposes best
practice code snippets. It integrates into several IDEs, including the ones covered in this
chapter.

To use it, developers simply write a comment in their code, and CodeWhisperer
will determine a matching cloud service and propose a snippet of code to interact
with it. More information is found here: https://aws.amazon.com/about-aws/whats-
new/2022/06/aws-announces-amazon-codewhisperer-preview/.

CHAPTER 7

Data

The technology you use impresses no one. The experience you create with it is everything.

—Sean Gerety, User Experience Manager at The Home Depot

 ## Data Is a Valuable Asset

These days, data is one of an organization's most important assets. Expectations around its usage and protection are high. Modern organizations can generate or collect an enormous amount of data daily, and knowing how to manage it effectively increases their ability to generate value from it.

In the past, database options were limited, and most organizations would opt for a relational database since it was widely available and well supported. Consider also what we covered in Chapter 4. With a monolithic architecture application, the entire application and server have access to the whole database. So, for this architecture, it makes sense to use an all-purpose database to cover the needs of the entire application.

However, with the advancement of technology, wide adoption of the cloud, and modern distributed architectures, more specialized database types were developed to cater to specific use cases. Options such as NoSQL, time series, graph, and ledger databases, when combined with the right type of data, significantly improve the cost-effectiveness, scalability, and efficiency of managing that data.

AWS has both general and purpose-built database services for a wide range of use cases. In Figure 7-1, I have categorized the services by their different data types and noted some of their use cases, if they are managed or Serverless, and their billing model.

© Thomas Smart 2023
T. Smart, *Serverless Beyond the Buzzword*, https://doi.org/10.1007/978-1-4842-8761-3_7

Database	Type	Use Cases	Service	Billable
RDS	Relational	Traditional applications, Enterprise Resource Planning (ERP), Customer Relationship Management (CRM), e-commerce	Managed	Instance type
Aurora			Managed	Instance type
Aurora Serverless			**Pseudo**	Capacity unit
Redshift		Data warehouse for analytical workloads	Managed	Instance type
Redshift Serverless			**Serverless**	Utilized capacity
DynamoDB (on demand)	NoSQL	Key-value database for high-traffic web applications, e-commerce systems, gaming applications, in-memory caching	**Serverless**	Reads and writes
DynamoDB (Provisioned)			Managed	Read and write capacity unit
DocumentDB		Document database for content management, catalogs, profiles, gaming applications	Managed	Instance type
Keyspaces (on demand)		Wide column database for high-scale industrial apps for equipment maintenance, fleet management, and route optimization	**Serverless**	Reads and writes
Keyspaces (provisioned)			Managed	Read and write capacity unit
Neptune	Graph	Graph database for fraud detection, social networking, recommendation engines	Managed	Instance type
ElastiCache for Memcached	In-memory	Caching, session management, leaderboards	Managed	Node type
ElastiCache for Redis			Managed	Node type
MemoryDB for Redis		Web and mobile applications, online games, media streaming	Managed	Node type
Timestream	Time series	IoT applications, DevOps applications, analytics applications, industrial telemetry	**Serverless**	Reads and writes
QLDB	Ledger	Systems of record, supply chain, registrations, banking transactions	**Serverless**	Read and write I/O

Figure 7-1. *An overview of AWS database services*

Database Selection

Before we dive into the different database services, we must first understand some of the different types of databases available today.

Relational databases should be known to most people in IT. They have long been the default option with fixed columns and rows of data. They are general-purpose, suitable for both OLTP (online transaction processing) and OLAP (online analytical processing) use cases. Relational databases are still the most common database type. They can store a lot of data and perform all kinds of complex search queries, but they are often considered relatively slow and difficult to scale.

NoSQL generally refers to anything that is not relational, though it is usually associated with more general-purpose **key-value** databases where the columns are not fixed. Each data record can have the same or a different set of columns. The columns are defined in the record as keys, and the values are the data. This structure makes them very scalable and fast to interact with, but less suitable for complex search queries.

Document databases store data as documents. They support formats such as JSON, YAML, and XML. A benefit is that data is stored in the same format as the application uses, reducing the conversion overhead. They are suitable for use cases where records can be thought of as documents, such as pages in a CMS or products in a catalogue.

Wide-column databases are ideal for analytics workloads. Like relational databases, wide-column databases use columns and rows to store data. The difference is that relational databases store *rows* of data together, which makes sense because usually we want to retrieve a particular record with all of its fields. Wide-column databases store *columns* of data together, which makes sense for analytics workloads where we want to retrieve the same field from many records so that we can plot a line on a graph. Like other NoSQL databases, the columns in a wide-column database are flexible for each record.

Graph databases focus on the relationship between data. For example, in a social network, it would track connections or friends. Who is linked to who in the network, and who is the next layer connected to? Thousands upon thousands of connections within a single data set. These databases store data as nodes (the entities) and edges (the connections between nodes). This design allows for efficient chaining and consolidating of complex data relationships within a single query.

Ledger databases provide immutable, transparent, and cryptographically verifiable records. They are a good fit for storing sensitive transactions such as finances and logistics. Ledger databases do not overwrite existing data when updating a record but add a new record with the updated value. The current record and all previous versions remain available and linked in a chain, making it very difficult to tamper with the data.

Time series databases are used to store data that is tightly bound to a time or date. They can handle huge volumes of data in a format that allows for fast insertion and retrieval. These databases are fast and scalable and have capabilities to automatically fill any data gaps between entries. Time series databases are commonly used for IoT and operational applications.

In-memory databases are not for any specific type of data. The term refers to how the database *operates*; they store and query their data in RAM memory. This makes them extremely fast, but also quite expensive to run. Typically, these types of databases are used for caching use cases, where only the active records are stored in memory and the rest of the data is stored in another, more affordable type of database.

The **use case** can often help determine an appropriate database for a given data set:

- For OLTP or transactional use cases, we might want something fast with low latency, such as a NoSQL key-value type.

- If we are looking at OLAP or analytics use cases, we can probably accept a bit more latency but will often want easily scalable storage, which some relational databases and wide-column types can provide.

- If we want to improve application performance with caching, we are more likely to choose an in-memory database type.

With Serverless architecture, each microservice requiring a data store can, potentially, have its own dedicated database, as seen in Figure 7-2. This can be an exclusive relationship, with any other microservices having to go via the owner to interact with that data, or it can be a shared database.

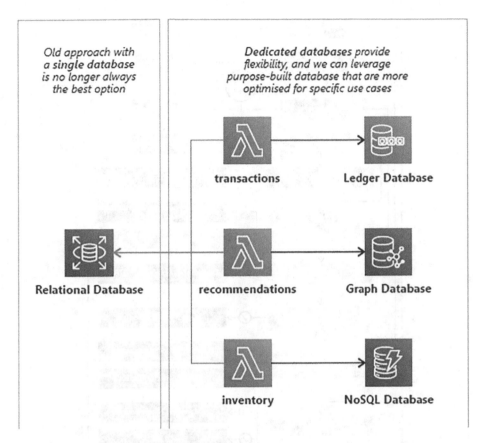

Figure 7-2. Using a dedicated database for a particular microservice

These options give application teams considerable flexibility in determining the ideal type of database, data schema, and query design for the different data sets within their applications. Rather than relying on a less efficient general-purpose database, we can use purpose-built databases optimized for each data set.

The flowchart in Figure 7-3 offers a way to identify the right database for a given use case.

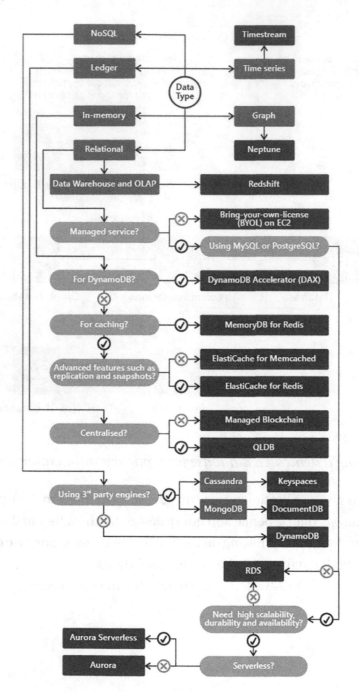

Figure 7-3. *AWS database decision flowchart*

We start with determining the type of data we are going to store. If we have relational data that can't be converted to NoSQL, we can look at the relational database options at the top.

Following this path, if our use case is OLAP or data warehouse, we end up at Redshift, but if we are looking for an application database, we need to decide if we want self-managed or cloud-managed. The latter will have lower operational overheads, while self-managed provides more flexibility and control.

We will go with cloud-managed, and the next question is whether we want to use MySQL or PostgreSQL. If we are not using either of those, then our options are Oracle and MS SQL in RDS. However, if we can use PostgreSQL and need high scalability and availability, we have the Aurora database options. For Serverless applications, *Aurora Serverless* would usually be the most suitable database option.

Knowing the application's target users can also help in making a decision. For *external* users, we might prioritize *performance* for a better user experience. So Aurora would again be a good option as it provides the fastest experience for relational data.

If the users are *global*, Aurora offers global databases. Alternatively, for NoSQL data, we could consider DynamoDB global tables. Both support multi-region deployment to ensure minimal latency around the world.

For *internal* users, *lower operational cost* might be a priority. RDS MySQL could be a good fit for relational data as it supports smaller servers than Aurora. For NoSQL data, DynamoDB would usually be the best option.

⚙ Event Sourcing

Most databases will store, log, back up, and restore changes only for themselves. An architecture with multiple databases can lead to multiple sources of truth, especially when there is overlap in the data.

For example, in Figure 7-4, we have three databases. Each has its own audit log.

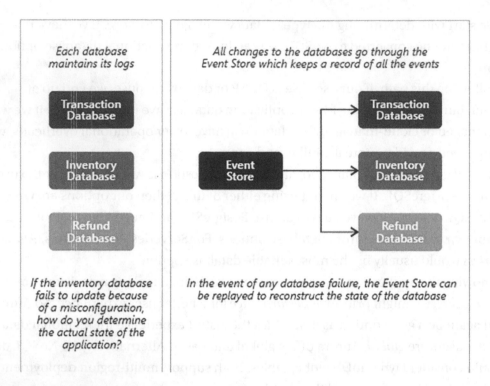

Figure 7-4. *Standard workflow vs. Event Sourcing comparison*

The inventory database is updated right after the transaction database whenever a new transaction occurs. In the event of an error, we could end up with a data discrepancy between the two databases, and the inventory database would no longer reflect the actual warehouse inventory.

So how can we determine what the correct state should be of the data? To resolve this, we would need to analyze the failed updates using the inventory database logs and then refer to logs of both databases to reconstruct the state. Done manually, this will be a slow and tedious process. This can make ensuring data consistency a challenge in Serverless applications.

One approach to addressing this is using an architectural pattern called Event Sourcing. We use events that have happened within the architecture to automatically determine the state of the data at any point in time.

Event Sourcing uses a centralized event store containing an immutable list of events. For each transaction, the system publishes a new event into the event store, resulting in the databases being updated with the latest information. Event stores can be implemented using managed services such as EventBridge.

All changes that need to be made to any database must go through the event store, which keeps a record of each event and can even include metadata such as description or user ID. If there are any errors that impact data, the event store should have replay capabilities that can execute failed events again to reconstruct the data. Of course, microservices and databases that processed the event correctly will need to be able to identify and ignore duplicate events if they are replayed.

Let's go through an example using Figure 7-5 that shows how we can implement Event Sourcing in a given architecture.

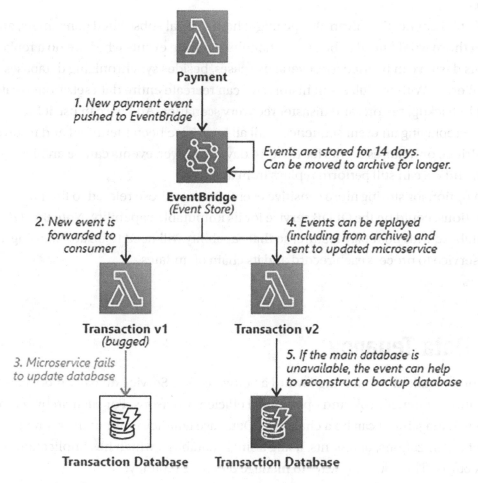

Payment

1. New payment event
pushed to EventBridge

Events are stored for 14 days.
Can be moved to archive for longer.

EventBridge
(Event Store)

2. New event is
forwarded to
consumer

4. Events can be replayed
(including from archive) and
sent to updated microservice

Transaction v1
(bugged)

Transaction v2

3. Microservice fails
to update database

5. If the main database is
unavailable, the event can help
to reconstruct a backup database

Transaction Database   **Transaction Database**

Figure 7-5. *Simple Event Sourcing architecture example*

From the top, we have a payment microservice that issues a new event into EventBridge each time an order is confirmed and paid for. EventBridge stores the event and forwards it to the subscribed consumers – in this example, initially only the transaction v1 microservice.

This microservice performed a database update. However, the update failed due to a bug, and no data was stored. We resolve the bug and deploy an updated transaction microservice – v2 in Figure 7-6. We can use EventBridge to replay the past event, which is successfully processed by the fixed transaction microservice, and the database is updated.

In a real application, EventBridge might have several subscribed consumers, and each of those would need to be able to handle duplicate events when we do a replay.

This design can be used for several use cases, besides synchronizing databases after an error. With the full event history, we can recreate entire data sets from scratch, aiding in backup, restore, and disaster recovery scenarios. And we can use it for testing – replaying an event sequence until all bugs have been identified and resolved. EventBridge only stores events for up to 14 days. However, events can be archived for far longer, and we can still perform replays from archives.

An option for storing more sensitive events, such as those related to financial transactions, could be the QLDB service for its immutable capability. Note that QLDB is a database with no replay feature, so that capability will need to be added using a microservice to process each record and its chain of updates.

Data Tenancy

Many organizations are moving toward a Software-as-a-Service delivery model for their applications, often for cost and operational efficiency reasons. For such architectures, tenancy management can be a challenge. Database tenancy is about the number of distinct organizations, or tenants, using a single database, which has implications for data security. There are two ways to manage database tenancy:

1. Pooled database tenancy (Figure 7-6)

All of the tenants use the same shared database. This is the most common option, especially for public SaaS offerings.

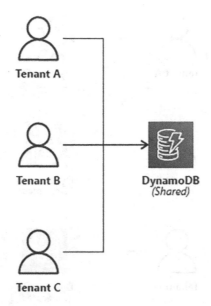

Figure 7-6. *Pooled database tenancy*

Scaling is done based on the total user base, making it the most cost-effective option enjoying significant economies of scale. However, as everyone uses the same database, the individually owned data sets will be mixed within it. This has security implications and can raise accountability concerns with the individual tenants.

2. Siloed database tenancy (Figure 7-7)

This uses dedicated databases for each tenant, making it significantly more secure and minimizing the chance of data leaking between tenants.

Dedicated databases come at the cost of being less scalable, as each one will need to be scaled independently. This also makes it less cost-effective, as it increases the chance of underutilization, and there are now many more distinct databases to manage. Such costs will usually be passed on to the customers, making the service more expensive.

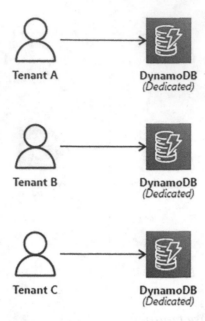

Figure 7-7. *Siloed database tenancy*

An advantage with Serverless resources, such as DynamoDB on demand used in the two examples, is that we only pay for *actual utilization*. So, in terms of cloud operational cost, there is unlikely to be much difference between the two tenancy options. The cost aspect really lies in managing the number of resources and potentially having to deal with limits. For example, DynamoDB has a soft limit of 2500 tables per account and per region. This effectively limits the application to 2500 siloed tenants until an increase is requested from AWS, which will need to be justified.

From a security perspective, most tenants will prefer siloed tenancy when it comes to SaaS services shared with strangers, but the added cost might be difficult to justify outside regulated industries. With Serverless, this might be more about perception than fact. There is always a risk, but DynamoDB has incredibly fine-grained access controls – as I mentioned in Chapter 4.

For example, in Figure 7-8, we have an IAM policy condition that only permits the *current user* to access database records associated with them with their ID. Any requests from *other users* for the same record will be rejected.

Remember that IAM permissions are implemented at an infrastructure level, meaning that even if a bad actor compromises the API and microservice, they are still unable to retrieve more data than the permissions allow.

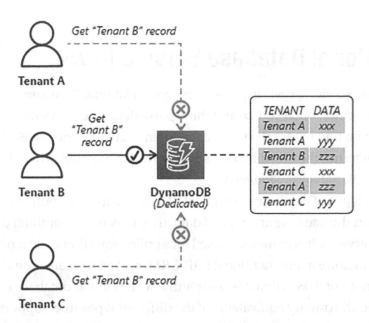

Figure 7-8. *Pooled database tenancy secured with an IAM policy*

With the DynamoDB partition key containing the user_id value, the following IAM policy condition can achieve this:

```
"Condition": {
  "ForAllValues:StringEquals": {
    "dynamodb:LeadingKeys": ["${www.amazon.com:user_id}"]
  },
  "StringEqualsIfExists": {
    "dynamodb:Select": "ALL_ATTRIBUTES"
  }
}
```

This assumes the application's user authentication is achieved with an IAM user or role or that one of those is attached to each logged-in user before they perform a database query directly. If a Lambda microservice does the queries, it will need to assume the user's IAM role before querying the database. This can be achieved in an API Gateway–Cognito–Lambda architecture as described here:

https://aws.amazon.com/premiumsupport/knowledge-center/cognito-user-pool-group/

Relational Database Service (RDS)

The first database service we will explore is Amazon Relational Database Service (RDS). RDS includes common open source and third-party databases as well as AWS's proprietary Aurora databases. The service has been available since 2009. Perhaps surprisingly, it was not the first database service. That distinction is held by the now deprecated NoSQL database *SimpleDB*.

The various types of databases offered by RDS are all general-purpose and relational. So, depending on the use case and type of data, they may be less optimal than one of the purpose-built services. It is commonly used for applications that need a relational data schema. These include many traditional ERP, CRM, and ecommerce solutions.

A major benefit of RDS is that it is compatible with popular database engines – the open source and third-party equivalents of the different types RDS supports, such as Postgres, MySQL, and others. Only minimal refactoring will be needed for existing applications migrating to the cloud, and common relational libraries and tools will be compatible too.

With the exception of Aurora Serverless, the available types of databases are offered as managed services. Hardware, operating systems, and software are managed by AWS. There may be some downtime during maintenance windows, and some administrative overhead should still be expected. We will need to configure and maintain the size and quantity of database servers, networking, access, scaling, and disaster recovery. RDS is highly scalable and available, with features such as read replicas and multi-AZ deployments, but these do need to be configured. The monthly bill will be determined by the type of database and the type and quantity of servers running that month, regardless of actual utilization.

RDS offers automated backups and point-in-time recovery, reducing data loss to under 5 minutes. This will also need to be configured when provisioning the database, and they are not intended for global workloads.

RDS Proxy

A challenge with using RDS databases for Serverless applications is that SQL databases were built for long-lived connections, such as those maintained by servers and often containers. This is not possible with Lambda microservices, as each invocation is temporary. As such, every invocation needs to establish a new connection with the database, and multiple microservices may have multiple connections open in parallel. This can lead to performance degradation, and it affects the microservice response time.

RDS Proxy aims to address these challenges.

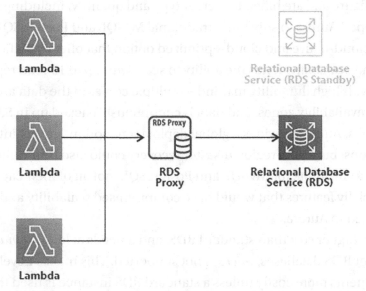

Figure 7-9. *RDS Proxy architecture example*

The proxy sits between an application and RDS, as shown in Figure 7-9, acting as a gateway for the microservices. RDS Proxy maintains a pool of database connections, so the microservices don't need to make or manage them, and new microservices can quickly reuse existing connections instead of having to constantly create new ones.

A downside of RDS Proxy is that it can only connect to one database server at a time. Additional database servers in the same cluster are listed as hot standby targets. This means that if the database is only used via RDS Proxy, then one or more entire servers will not be utilized. Alternatively, if we configure only one database server, we risk a single point of failure, which is not a best practice design.

Note that RDS Proxy does not support Aurora Serverless version 1 at this time, but there we have Data API, which we will look at in a moment. RDS Proxy does support Aurora Serverless version 2.

Amazon Aurora

Amazon Aurora is a proprietary database engine developed by AWS and available through the RDS service. As with other RDS types, Aurora is an SQL relational database and offers a MySQL-compatible version and a PostgreSQL-compatible version. With Aurora, we configure and are billed for server type and quantity, including idle time.

AWS developed Aurora to substitute traditional MySQL and PostgreSQL database engines with a cloud-native and cloud-optimized option that offers significantly better performance and scalability. It has the ability to scale with up to 15 read replicas. Aurora is built with high durability in mind – multiple copies of the data are stored across multiple availability zones, and data is continuously backed up in S3. Unlike other RDS options, Aurora provides a global deployment option, mostly intended for global applications, but multi-region disaster recovery could also be a valid use case. While Aurora is a substitute for MySQL and PostgreSQL, not all of their capabilities are available. Especially features that would have compromised scalability and performance have been omitted in Aurora.

Aurora has a higher cost than standard RDS, and it needs at least a *small* instance size. Unlike other RDS databases, *micro* is not supported. This makes development and testing environments more costly unless a standard RDS instance is used there instead. As with other RDS types, Aurora is billed based on the configured server type and quantity, and being billed for idle time and underutilization is inevitable.

Aurora Serverless

Note that this section is based on Aurora Serverless version 2, which has been generally available since April 2022. While there is some overlap with version 1, there are many differences, and it is recommended to use the latest version.

Aurora Serverless is a different implementation of RDS Aurora, where AWS takes on the cluster and server responsibilities. Operational overheads are reduced by AWS managing the underlying server cluster and automatically scaling resources as needed without any disruption. Automatic scaling makes it ideal for applications with an unknown or unpredictable workload. Like Aurora, it is highly durable due to its architecture, built-in redundancy, and backups.

Aurora Serverless bills based on Aurora capacity units (ACUs). As the name indicates, ACUs determine how much memory and CPU capacity the database will have, impacting the number of requests that can be supported.

While *Serverless* is in its name and no servers need to be managed, there is still a minimum amount of billable reserved capacity, regardless of actual utilization. The minimum is 0.5 capacity units, which is about $72 per month today. As such, it does not entirely satisfy my definition of Serverless, where the *minimum billable* should be zero if there is no utilization. Note that Aurora v1 had a minimum capacity of 1 ACU for MySQL and 2 ACUs for PostgreSQL. However, v1 charges less per ACU, resulting in about $72 and $144, respectively, per month.

Aurora Serverless v1 has an *autopause* feature. This can be used to automatically stop the cluster after a configurable amount of idle time – 5 minutes to 24 hours. This sounds great and very Serverless, but it has a terrible cold start latency of 20–60 seconds, which makes this option impractical for most production applications. It can be a good option to help manage the cost of non-production environments. Version 2 does not have autopause but supports the standard start-stop cluster capability that Aurora offers. This can be automated to provide the same experience as autopause. While slightly faster, the cold start latency is still too significant for most production workloads.

A challenge of Aurora Serverless is that it can be quite expensive for high-load applications. There is a break-even point where it can make sense – at least from a cloud operational cost perspective – to switch to a standard Aurora cluster.

Aurora Serverless only allows for VPC traffic. To connect from a local machine, we need to use Direct Connect or a VPN, and Lambda microservices will need to be deployed into the VPC to connect directly.

I mentioned just now how the architecture makes Aurora quite durable. Under the hood, it separates the storage from the database software.

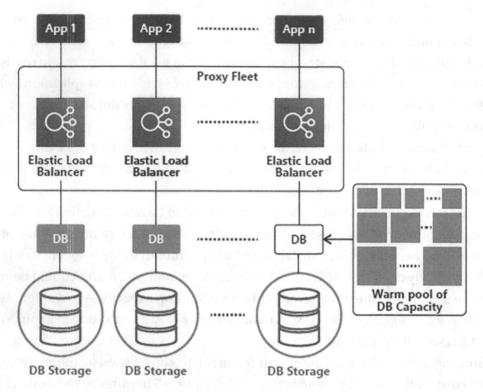

Figure 7-10. *Aurora Serverless architecture*

Storage space scales automatically based on the amount stored, up to 128 terabytes per database, and six copies of the data are stored across three availability zones. It can continue to operate even if an entire zone goes down.

The compute layer – with the database software – can autoscale based on demand within a configurable range of ACUs. We configure the minimum and maximum ACUs that are needed in increments of 0.5. Aurora bills for active ACUs. If there is no activity, then it only bills for the minimum assigned ACU.

In version 1, scaling between ACUs can take up to a few minutes. So databases might struggle with sudden bursts of new users if they are configured with only 0.5 minimum ACU. In version 2, scaling is near-instant, resolving this issue.

Version 2 also supports many of the standard Aurora features that were not included in Aurora Serverless version 1, such as global databases, IAM authentication, Lambda triggers, and others.

Aurora Serverless Data API

Aurora Serverless Data API is another way for applications to connect to an Aurora Serverless cluster. Similar to RDS Proxy discussed earlier, it manages the SQL connections and sits between Lambda and the database, as shown in Figure 7-11. Note that as of the time of this writing, Data API **only** supports Aurora Serverless version 1, though RDS Proxy does support Aurora Serverless version 2.

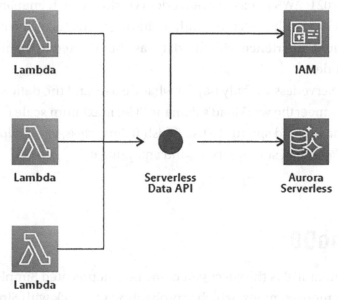

Figure 7-11. *Aurora Serverless Data API architecture example*

Data API removes the complexity and overhead that comes with traditional SQL connection management. It also gets around the limitation of only being able to connect to Aurora Serverless within a VPC, and database requests can be authenticated using IAM.

Compared with RDS Proxy, the Data API is an entirely different interface and does not use standard SQL protocols. As the name implies, it offers an HTTPS API interface that we can interact with through the AWS SDK, CLI, or directly. As a result, existing applications will need to be refactored, and most common database libraries are unlikely to support it at this time.

Redshift Serverless

Redshift is a data warehousing solution built by AWS for big data use cases. It's not only a database but a database management platform that can handle exabytes of data from different sources and can be queried using standard SQL. Redshift is a managed service that is used mainly for online analytical processing (OLAP) workloads.

In November 2021, AWS released a Serverless version, which enables users to gather insights from their data within seconds without having to manage any infrastructure. I have only had limited experience with this database but wanted to mention it for this new Serverless mode.

With Redshift Serverless we only pay for what we use, and the data warehouse can seamlessly scale to meet the workload's demand. The maximum scale (RPU) can be configured to manage cloud spend. To use Redshift Serverless, we can load the data using the console and then start querying and analyzing it.

DynamoDB

In many ways, DynamoDB is the successor of the now deprecated SimpleDB database. However, it is a lot more complex, which is probably why I stuck with SimpleDB for quite a while before finally making the switch. Now it is my favorite database, and it is generally considered the preferred *all-purpose* database for Serverless applications. For a time, it was the *only* (non-deprecated) Serverless database available. It is NoSQL and similar to a *document*-type database, but it requires us to follow a specific structure. As such, it is more suitable to call it a key-value database service.

DynamoDB offers two billing models, *provisioned* and *on demand*. The *provisioned* model is considered a managed service. We have to predict the application's read and write capacity needs and configure the database to provision that. DynamoDB will then bill for the provisioned amount regardless of how much of it is actually utilized. If the application needs more read or write capacity than is provisioned, then some requests could be blocked, though autoscaling can also be configured to avoid this scenario.

DynamoDB *on demand* is a Serverless billing model that automatically manages capacity based on current demand, and only actual utilization will be billed at the end of the month.

Both billing models have minimal administrative overheads. The service takes care of the underlying servers, the cluster, scaling, backups, data retention, redundancy, and the operating systems and software powering it. It is highly scalable, can handle millions of requests per second, and stores petabytes of data. It is also very fast, providing single-digit millisecond performance or even microseconds with the optional DynamoDB Accelerator (DAX), though this option is not Serverless. DynamoDB is integrated with several AWS services, such as S3 for exporting data and Lambda, which can be triggered when a record is added, updated, or deleted.

A challenge with DynamoDB is the need to properly plan and configure the database and schema design. Bad configurations can make DynamoDB considerably less cost-effective. There are several factors to consider in the design and configuration, such as the keys, indexes, caching, consistency, and billing model. The queries that the application needs to make will help to determine most of these and if DynamoDB is even suitable for the application. As a NoSQL database, it will not be suitable for all types of data, especially those with many relationships.

Existing relational data sets will need to be redesigned for NoSQL, a process called *denormalizing*, which I will cover in more detail later in this chapter. Another consideration when determining suitability for a particular data set is that each record in DynamoDB has a maximum size of up to 400 KB.

Billing Models

Let's look in more detail at the two billing models. Bear with me here as there are a lot of numbers and some math, but for anyone intending to work with DynamoDB, this is critical to understand. It is also a topic that features on the AWS Certified Database – Specialty certification. Note that I focus on billing models and how utilization is calculated; for the latest dollar prices, please check the AWS DynamoDB pricing page.

First, in **provisioned** mode, DynamoDB uses *capacity units* as a kind of currency for buying read and write operations. The number of capacity units requested when configuring the database determines the number of operations per second that can be executed. The cost of the requested capacity units can be reduced by paying up front for 1 or 3 years. This approach requires an accurate estimate of how much capacity a given application will require, certainly if paying up front.

There are two types of capacity units: **write** capacity units (**WCUs**) and **read** capacity units (**RCUs**). Each write operation, such as *put*, *update*, and *delete*, will consume WCU. The precise amount will depend on the size and type of the operation:

- For *standard* write operations, a single 1 KB block of data requires **1** WCU.

- Writing a larger block will require more WCUs. For example, a 4 KB block of data will require **4** WCUs.

We can also opt for *transactional* write operations. With these, we write a group of related queries in a single transaction:

- *Transactional* writes are more expensive, requiring **2** WCUs for every 1 KB block of data.

- Our previous example of a 4 KB block would cost **8** WCUs.

RCUs are used for read operations, such as *query* and *get*. Similarly, the precise number of RCUs depends on the size and type of the operation:

- A read can be *strongly consistent*, where the returned data will be the most up to date. A single 4 KB block of data costs **1** RCU.

- *Eventually consistent* operations could return *stale* data – data that was very recently updated but not propagated to all database instances yet. It is a cheaper option where a single 4 KB block of data costs **half** an RCU.

- Like transactional writes, *transactional* reads batch a group of related read operations into a single transaction. A single 4 KB block of data costs **2** RCUs.

DynamoDB **on-demand** mode uses a Serverless pricing model. We don't need to estimate and provision capacity that may or may not be used. We are billed after the fact, based on the actual number of read and write requests that we used. This is a simpler model, and DynamoDB will automatically adjust the available capacity units in response to the current demand.

On-demand mode is the default choice for most Serverless projects that use DynamoDB – at least until the utilized capacity can be calculated and predicted. Then we can determine if utilization has crossed the break-even point where provisioned capacity is more cost-effective. It is always suitable for unknown, unpredictable, or highly variable workloads and for organizations or applications prioritizing minimal operational overheads. DynamoDB supports toggling between the two modes once every 24 hours.

DynamoDB on demand bills for actual read and write requests. As with provisioned, the precise number depends on the type and size of the operation:

- Up to 1 KB of *standard* write data is billed as **one** write request.

- Up to 1 KB of *transactional* write data is billed as **two** write requests.

- Up to 4 KB of *strongly consistent* read data is billed as **one** read request.

- Up to 4 KB of *eventually consistent* read data is billed **half** a read request.

- Up to 4 KB of *transactional* read data costs **two** read requests.

Note that the **Up to X KB** wording is important to remember. For example, an *eventually consistent* read operation with **1** KB of data instead of 4 is still billed **half** a read request. Going the other way, **one** read request would be billed for 8 KB of data.

Transactional Operations

Each transactional operation costs twice as much for the same amount of data as a standard read or write operation. To add, transactional requests succeed or fail based on *all or nothing*. We can group up to 25 operations in a single transactional request, which all need to succeed; if even one fails, then none of the operations will be executed, and the entire request will fail.

As the operations are grouped within a single transaction, fewer individual requests need to be sent to DynamoDB. This can reduce latency, but we should ensure that latency is sufficient justification for double the costs. Another approach to minimize latency is to perform parallel requests in the application code using standard transactions.

Transactional requests certainly can be more cost-effective if we are using them to consolidate updates that are smaller than the minimal billable for a standard request. For example, we have a request size of 100 bytes, and we need to perform ten write requests. Using *standard* write requests, we would simply be billed for ten of them.

With a *transactional* request, the ten operations can be combined into a single transactional request – 10 × 100 bytes = just under 1 KB, within the size limit. This means we are also only billed for **one** *transactional* request. As we saw previously, the cost for a transactional request is equal to **two** *standard* requests, making this approach 80% cheaper than using individual standard requests for this particular example.

Comparison of DynamoDB Billing Models

Figure 7-12 compares the two modes. Prices are in USD and based on the Singapore region pricing at the time of this writing. We can calculate a break-even point when it makes sense to change from on-demand to provisioned capacity. These comparisons assume a database without any global secondary indexes.

	Provisioned		On Demand	
Unit	Write capacity unit (WCU)	Read capacity unit (RCU)	Write request units	Read request units
Cost	$0.00074/hour	$0.000148/hour	$1.4231/million ($0.0000014231/write)	$0.285/million ($0.000000285/read)
On Demand More Cost-Effective				
Assuming 100,000 read and 100,000 write requests spread out evenly across the month (140 reads and 140 writes per **hour**)				
	WCU cost	RCU cost	Write requests cost	Read requests cost
	0.00074 × 24 × 30 = $0.5328	0.000148 × 24 × 30 = $0.10656	1.4231/10 =$0.14231	0.285/10 = $0.0285
	$0.64		**$0.17**	
Break-Even Point				
Assuming 370,000 read and 370,000 write requests spread out evenly across the month (520 reads and 520 writes per **hour**)				
	WCU cost	RCU cost	Write requests cost	Read requests cost
	0.00074 × 24 × 30 = $0.5328	0.000148 × 24 × 30 = $0.10656	1.4231/10 × 3.7 = $0.526547	0.285/10 × 3.7= **$0.10545**
	$0.64		**$0.63**	
Provisioned More Cost-Effective				
Assuming 12,960,000 read and 12,960,000 write requests (5 reads and 5 writes per **second**)				
	WCU cost	RCU cost	Write requests cost	Read requests cost
	§0.00074 × 24 × 30 = $0.5328 $0.5328 × 5 = $2.664	§0.000148 × 24 × 30 = $0.10656 $0.10656 × 5 = $0.53	§12.96 × 1.4231 = $18.44	§12.96 × 0.285 = $3.69
	$3.19		$22.13	

Figure 7-12. *Comparing DynamoDB billing models*

The first price comparison shows that at 100,000 reads and writes, on demand is more cost-effective. The middle price comparison shows the break-even point, which is when the DynamoDB database is consistently making about 520 writes per hour and 520 reads per hour. The last price comparison shows that after the break-even point, on demand gets significantly more expensive, $3.19 for provisioned vs. over $22 for on demand, so switching over should be considered at this point.

These comparisons are for a DynamoDB database without global secondary indexes because such indexes require their own capacity in provisioned mode. In the on-demand billing model, only requests are billed, including on global secondary indexes. As such, if we perform a request against a secondary index instead of the primary index, the net total billable remains the same. However, if we convert the billing model to provisioned, then the additional index will require its own estimated provisioned capacity, which could easily double the break-even point.

Keys and Queries

The partition key is the primary key for the database. It's important to carefully consider which field is used for this key, as it will also be used to select subsets of data. If only a partition key is defined, then the value of this key in each record must be unique.

Sort keys are required when the partition key values are not unique. It is joined to the partition key to form a composite key for each record that must be unique. As the name implies, the sort key is also used to sort data in some operations.

When both keys are defined, both values will be needed to retrieve a particular record from DynamoDB. A common mistake is to use a predictable partition key and a date for the sort key, but a date is difficult to guess when a single record needs to be retrieved. Client applications will need both values to retrieve the record. Alternatively, we can encrypt and Base64 both keys into a separate attribute and then pass that to a front-end client as the single record identifier. The client uses that when requesting a single record, and the back end decodes and decrypts it to get the two keys needed for a DynamoDB request.

In DynamoDB, there are two ways to request lists of records. One way is with the **scan** command. Scan reads the *entire* database and *then* filters the results based on the request parameters. For small databases with a few hundred records, this will have a limited performance impact. For larger databases, scan will use many capacity units or read requests to retrieve all records before filtering. This approach makes scan operations costly and slow. However, it does support filter options such as text search.

Usually, the preferred method for retrieving lists of records is the **query** command. This reads a subset of the data based on the requested *partition key* value. Then it filters and sorts that subset based on the *sort key* values. Query is usually more cost-effective, and it offers better performance. It does mean that we need to carefully design our database's keys in a way that meets the application's request needs.

Adaptive Capacity

Anyone who might have used DynamoDB in the past may remember that when designing the partition key, the recommendation was to ensure a high level of variety in the key values – also called the key *cardinality*.

DynamoDB splits data across multiple partitions (servers) using the partition key, ideally evenly, as this is good for performance. To match this spread of data, provisioned capacity units were also spread equally across the same partitions.

For example, if there are three partitions to store data and we provision 300 WCUs, each partition would be given 100 WCUs. However, if the partition keys are too similar, the data cannot be partitioned evenly, and an imbalance will be created between data and available capacity units on a particular partition. For example, one of the partitions might be receiving 75% of the data but still only the same 100 WCUs to add that data with. This is called a *hot key,* and it used to result in performance degradation.

To address this issue, AWS created a feature called *adaptive capacity* in DynamoDB. This enables DynamoDB to allocate the required capacity units to each partition based on the *actual workload* – provided this does not exceed the total *provisioned* capacity. In Figure 7-13, we have the three partitions with 100 WCUs each. Partition A experiences a spike in workload, and partitions B and C are underutilized, consuming only 50 WCUs each. Adaptive capacity can take the unused WCUs from B and C and allocate them to partition A, increasing its capacity to handle the demand. While this does not prevent a hot key from happening, it does prevent it from degrading database performance.

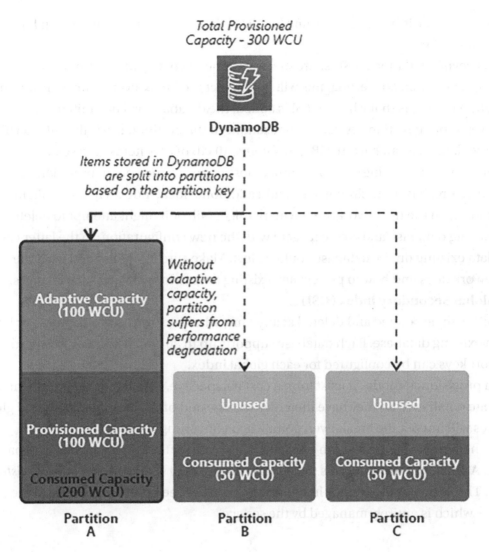

Figure 7-13. *DynamoDB adaptive capacity*

DynamoDB Indexes

Indexes are another aspect that needs to be considered when designing DynamoDB databases. These provide a means to create additional keys, unlocking more ways to select and filter our data using the preferred *query* command.

Local Secondary Index (LSI)

LSIs can only be created when the database is provisioned. They cannot be added to an existing database, nor can they be deleted. Each database supports up to five local indexes. The partition key is the same for all local indexes, but each index can have a different sort key.

In provisioned mode, LSIs share the provisioned capacity units with the main database. So, when converting, this will not impact the break-even point. One important limitation to note is that when an LSI is added, the database will be limited to 10 GB of data stored per partition key value. For example, if the partition key is the *color* attribute, then the database can have 10 GB of *red* items, 10 GB of *blue* items, and so forth.

Note that when using CDK or a similar abstracting framework to provision infrastructure, it is quite simple to just add additional local indexes in the configuration. Depending on the framework, deployment might fail, or it might attempt to delete the existing database and create it again with the new configuration. In the latter case, any data existing on the database could be lost. Make sure to understand what the framework does and how to protect any existing data before making such changes.

Global Secondary Index (GSI)

GSIs can be created and deleted at any time, when we provision a database or later for an existing database. Each database supports up to 20 global indexes. The partition and sort keys can be configured for each global index.

In provisioned mode, at least from a cost perspective, global indexes are essentially separate databases. So they have their own storage and provisioned capacity, and global indexes will impact the break-even point when converting the billing model.

To help manage cost, we can configure which attributes are included in a global index. A challenge to consider is that global indexes only support *eventually consistent* reads. This is due to the latency in replicating data between the main table and the index – which is entirely managed by the service.

⚙ Query Examples

Let's look at some example DynamoDB queries to get an idea of how powerful this operation can be when combined with the right keys and indexes.

In the first example, shown in Figure 7-14, two or more user types will be retrieving records assigned to them. These records could be invoices, orders, approvals, or similar.

user_id (Partition Key)	creation_date (Sort Key)	Data
user_id_1	2021-06-27	bbb
user_id_1	2021-01-30	aaa
user_id_1	2021-07-01	xxx
user_id_2	2021-02-14	yyy
user_id_3	2021-01-30	zzz

Figure 7-14. *Example 1 data set*

We set *user_id* as the partition key and *creation_date* as the sort key. In the following snippet, I am using the AWS command-line interface tool (CLI) to query DynamoDB:

```
aws dynamodb query  \
--endpoint-url https://dynamodb.ap-southeast-1.amazonaws.com \
--table-name ddb_example_1 \
--key-condition-expression "user_id = :user_id and
                      creation_date between :start_date and :end_date" \
--expression-attribute-values '{
                          ":user_id": { "S" : "user_id_1" },
                          ":start_date": { "S": "2021-01-01" },
                          ":end_date": {"S": "2021-06-30" }
                      }' \
--no-scan-index-forward \
--region ap-southeast-1
```

This command will retrieve all of the records for the value *user_id_1* that were created within the provided date range. Note that we use *key-condition-expression* to write the search query, but the values are set in *expression-attribute-values*. We could use *expression-attribute-names* to define the names instead of writing them directly in the condition. Separating them helps avoid any issues with reserved words that might have been used as key names.

That snippet will return the results shown in Figure 7-15.

user_id (Partition Key)	creation_date (Sort Key)	Data
user_id_1	2021-06-27	bbb
user_id_1	2021-01-30	aaa

Figure 7-15. *Example 1 result set*

By default, the results are sorted by the sort key in ascending order. However, we can reverse it by setting the ScanIndexForward attribute to false. In the CLI, we use *no-scan-index-forward*, as seen in the snippet example near the bottom.

Expanding on that first example, we can use a global secondary index to manage records assigned to multiple users. In Figure 7-16 we have added an admin user that created the records for the users, and in an admin back end, we want to retrieve all records that a particular admin created.

user_id	admin_id (Partition Key)	creation_date (Sort Key)	Data
user_id_1	**admin_id_1**	2021-06-27	bbb
user_id_1	**admin_id_2**	2021-01-30	aaa
user_id_1	**admin_id_1**	2021-07-01	xxx
user_id_2	**admin_id_1**	2021-02-14	yyy
user_id_3	**admin_id_2**	2021-01-30	zzz

Figure 7-16. *Example 2 data set*

We add a global secondary index, the sort key remains as *creation_date*, but we set the partition key to the *admin_id* attribute. In our query, we configure the secondary index name that we want to use, and we change the key to reflect the *admin_id* key and value *admin_id_2*:

```
aws dynamodb query
--endpoint-url https://dynamodb.ap-southeast-1.amazonaws.com
--table-name ddb_demo
--index-name admin_index
```

```
--key-condition-expression "admin_id = :admin_id and creation_date between
:start_date and :end_date"
```

```
--expression-attribute-values '{
                        ":admin_id": { "S" : "admin_id_2" },
                        ":start_date": { "S": "2021-01-01" },
                        ":end_date": {"S": "2021-06-30" }
                              }'
```
```
--no-scan-index-forward
--region ap-southeast-1
```

Figure 7-17 shows our admin records resulting from that snippet.

admin_id (Partition Key)	creation_date (Sort Key)	Data
admin_id_2	2021-01-30	aaa
admin_id_2	2021-01-30	zzz

Figure 7-17. *Example 2 result set*

Another example: We have multiple record types in a single database – pages for a multilingual CMS in this particular example. Figure 7-18 shows the data set with partition key *language_pagetype*. The values for this key in each record are copied directly from *language* and *page_type* in the same record and joined with a dash.

language_pagetype (Partition Key)	file_name (Sort Key)	language	page_type
en-infopage	UniqueFileName1	en	infopage
en-blogpage	UniqueFileName2	en	blogpage
fr-infopage	UniqueFileName3	fr	infopage
en-infopage	UniqueFileName4	en	infopage
en-infopage	UniqueFileName5	en	infopage

Figure 7-18. *Example 3 data set*

The sort key *file_name* contains a unique file_name for each page record. This is important because the partition key will contain duplicate values, so the combined partition and sort keys must be unique. A creation date might not be suitable for the sort key because it's not impossible that two pages could be created simultaneously by two different admins.

Compounding multiple attributes in a partition key provides a means to query smaller groups of records, but this needs to make sense for the application. If we think of a typical CMS interface, we will be looking at one language at a time and then switching between lists of a particular page type to manage the contents. So, for this use case, grouping by language and page type this way makes sense.

In our query snippet, we are requesting all of the English (en) *infopage* types:

```
aws dynamodb query
--endpoint-url https://dynamodb.ap-southeast-1.amazonaws.com
--table-name cms_ddb
--key-condition-expression "page_type = :page_type"
--expression-attribute-values '{":page_type": { "S" : "en-infopage" }}'
--region ap-southeast-1
```

We only need to define the partition key in our condition. The sort key is omitted as its purpose is to be a unique key, not a filter for our results. DynamoDB will still use it to sort the results, giving us a list sorted by page filename shown in Figure 7-19, which is probably appropriate for display in the CMS interface.

language_pagetype (Partition Key)	file_name (Sort Key)	language	page_type
en-infopage	UniqueFileName1	en	infopage
en-infopage	UniqueFileName4	en	infopage
en-infopage	UniqueFileName5	en	infopage

Figure 7-19. *Example 3 result set*

If the CMS has a feature to generate a sitemap, then we might want to query all pages of a particular language – regardless of page type. A global secondary index can help with this. We set *language* as the partition key and *file_name* as the sort key. We can define which attributes to include in a GSI. So, to reduce cost, we can omit most of them for this use case as a sitemap would usually only need *title*, *file_name*, and *last_update* attributes.

Other DynamoDB Features

DynamoDB supports time to live (TTL), where an attribute with timestamp value can be used to manage data expiry. Once the attribute has been configured as TTL, DynamoDB will automatically delete records shortly after their timestamp value has been reached. This provides a means to automatically remove stale data or manage the retention of sensitive data. There is no charge for configuring this feature or the resulting record delete actions.

DynamoDB Accelerator (DAX) is an in-memory cache for DynamoDB that sits between an application and a DynamoDB database. DAX can improve performance up to ten times, dropping latency from milliseconds to microseconds. DAX also offers a means to offload read capacity from DynamoDB, reducing the number of billable reads. However, note that DAX is not Serverless. It runs on fully managed databases for which we can configure type and quantity. These servers also determine the billable amount and inevitable underutilization.

A cost optimization feature is the standard infrequent access tier. This tier can help save up to 60% on DynamoDB storage costs. However, note that the throughput cost increases by 20%. As the name indicates, this makes the infrequent access tier an ideal option for data that is not requested very often, such as a customer's order history for an ecommerce site, old social media posts, or application logs.

DynamoDB streams create a time-ordered series of modification events that were made to a database. The events can be used to extend the capability of DynamoDB by streaming them through a Lambda microservice. For example, we could run a fraud detection model in Lambda that analyzes all new records or changes and then triggers notifications for any suspicious activity.

DynamoDB global tables replicate a database to other AWS regions. This feature requires streams to be enabled. With global tables, we can provide high-performance, minimal-latency database interactions to users around the world. This feature also ensures the availability of the database in the event of a regional failure.

While the query command with the right keys and indexes is very powerful, there remain situations where more complex queries such as text searches, weighted results, data analytics, and aggregates may be needed. In these situations, we can integrate DynamoDB with the OpenSearch service.

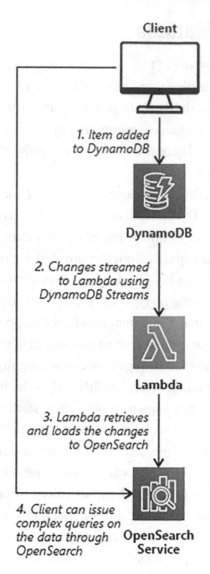

Figure 7-20. *Integrating OpenSearch to enable free text searches in DynamoDB*

OpenSearch was forked from ElasticSearch version 7.10, and features have diverged from that point. OpenSearch on AWS can index DynamoDB data and provide powerful search capabilities. The architecture in Figure 7-20 demonstrates how we can achieve this at a high level.

When a record is added to DynamoDB, streams – which must be enabled – can send the event immediately to a Lambda microservice, which loads the new data into the

OpenSearch service. Once the data is loaded, the client can use OpenSearch to perform the complex queries needed for the application. OpenSearch is not Serverless; we configure and are billed for instance type and quantity.

AWS DynamoDB Checklist

As a NoSQL database, DynamoDB is not suitable for all use cases. AWS offers a checklist to help determine the suitability of DynamoDB for an application's needs. Many of the questions promote DynamoDB capabilities, and others are about technical limitations. Let's have a look at them.

The checklist questions can be found here: *https://aws.amazon.com/blogs/database/how-to-determine-if-amazon-dynamodb-is-appropriate-for-your-needs-and-then-plan-your-migration/*. I will address them by referencing question numbers in the following.

Q1 is talking about DynamoDB being NoSQL. So the application should be using NoSQL or be able to convert to using it for DynamoDB to be a viable choice.

Similarly, Q2 is about organizing data into hierarchies or aggregating data to one or two tables. This refers to *denormalizing* relational data (which we will cover in the next section) and avoiding the multi-table structure typically seen with relational data.

Q3 talks about the challenge that not all queries can be achieved in DynamoDB, or at least not without integrating it with OpenSearch. If there are many requirements for such queries, then DynamoDB might not be the best choice. Either way, we need to make sure our TCO includes any supporting services such as OpenSearch.

Q4's requirement for global distribution refers to DynamoDB global tables, a capability only Aurora can offer on AWS for relational data.

Q5 I don't really understand. In my view, data protection and capabilities such as encryption are **always** important.

I believe Q6, which talks about *traditional backups*, is referring to DynamoDB streams and the fully managed backup capabilities in this service.

Lastly, the remaining questions about varying workloads, high-traffic peaks, millisecond response time, and terabytes of storage suggest that DynamoDB performs and scales better than traditional server-based databases.

NoSQL

In a relational database, data is stored in a normalized format. Consider, for example, a simplified ecommerce website. We will have a different table for each topic within the data set: users, carts, and items. Each entity has its own defined attributes, and there will be many links between tables. For example, each cart has one linked user and one or more linked items. Users might also be linked to one or more items to indicate their favorites.

Two limitations of a normalized database are scaling and the fixed schema of each table. Relational databases are typically designed for queries and relationships between records, not for speed or scaling. Usually, when we need a particular data response to display in an interface, the back end needs to first join multiple tables together in a single query. Such complex queries can be compute-intensive and hard to scale.

Many relational databases were created before the cloud; as such, the approach to scaling is usually to increase the size of the server. This type of scaling, called vertical scaling, can only go so far before it runs into hardware limitations. This is why the preferred scaling method in the cloud is to add more servers and distribute the load. This type of scaling, called horizontal scaling, is not supported by most relational databases, adding to the difficulty of managing the increasingly large data sets of modern organizations.

Schemas can also be thought of as the columns with headers of a table. A value for each column is required in all records. If a record does not have a need for one of them, then it will still exist in the record with a blank or default value. If the schema is changed and a new column is added, then all records will have the default value that was automatically assigned when it was added. Depending on the application and data, a batch update might need to be performed to set the correct value in each record.

NoSQL databases, on the other hand, are usually designed for speed and scalability. They can easily handle a massive data set and use fewer resources to query it. NoSQL databases tend to scale horizontally – adding more servers instead of increasing server size. This makes it easier, faster, and more cost-effective to scale.

NoSQL does not use a rigid schema (columns); each record can include whichever attributes are needed, and we can often create more complex data structures within a single record.

The process of converting relational data to NoSQL data is called denormalizing. There are three steps to this, which are largely the same when designing a new NoSQL data model:

1. Understand the queries that will be required.

2. Determine if those queries will be possible in the database and how to achieve those, as we covered earlier, usually through keys and indexes and sometimes with integrations.

3. Design the record types using as few databases or tables as possible. Try to make each record represent the entire item and avoid linking to other records.

We design a NoSQL data model fundamentally different from how we would design a relational data model. In a relational database, it is relatively safe to assume all queries will be possible. So we can start simple at the start of the project and adjust the design as requirements evolve. As we saw earlier with NoSQL, we need to clearly understand the queries first before we can design the keys and indexes and ensure the database will even support all queries.

The next step is to design the NoSQL data model. If we have an existing data set, then we can use that as input and later convert it to the new design.

When designing NoSQL data models, avoid the need for using JOINS by limiting the data to as few tables as possible. Group closely related entities together. For example, for an *order* record, include all information relevant to the order directly in the record. Consider each order record an independent document containing everything we need to know for that order, such as user information, shipping information, items in the cart, and total cost.

Data duplication is common in NoSQL data sets. In the preceding example, the user details are in the order record but might also be in a user profile database. Data consistency may or may not be an issue, depending on the context. In this case, having static user information in the order record would likely be appropriate. If the user details change in the profile database later, then we still have a record of the user details as they were at the time this order was placed. Either way, it is a good idea to always include timestamps, so we know which is the latest version.

Serverless NoSQL Databases

The following are fully Serverless databases. Each one bills based on actual utilization – usually storage, queries, and data transfer. All Serverless and fully managed databases on AWS are highly scalable, resilient, and secure, so I will only note any exceptions in the following descriptions.

Amazon Keyspaces

Amazon Keyspaces is a wide-column database commonly used for use cases such as fleet management and maintenance. It is especially suitable for organizations looking to migrate from the open source self-managed Apache Cassandra database to a fully managed cloud service in order to minimize operational overheads. Like DynamoDB, it offers two billing modes: managed, with provisioned servers, and Serverless, which bills for actual utilization based on storage and the number of reads and writes per month.

A limitation to consider is that the database Keyspaces is more expensive than DynamoDB, which supports many of the same use cases. Although it is compatible with Cassandra, it does not support all of its features. Keyspaces is a regional database, making it harder to support global traffic and cross-region disaster recovery.

More information here: https://aws.amazon.com/keyspaces/

Amazon Timestream

The Serverless database Timestream is a purpose-built database designed for analyzing data that is stored in a sequential manner and tightly bound to particular dates and times, such as IoT data and logs.

It offers high performance for time series data and up to 1,000× faster query performance at as little as 1/10th the cost of a relational database. It provides high throughput ingestion, rapid point-in-time queries, and fast analytical queries. This can be especially useful when the time order of information is important for data analysis, such as collected sensor data and logs.

Scaling is fully managed and automated, with the capability to process trillions of events and millions of queries per day, and it bills only for the data ingested, stored, and queried. Data lifecycle management is simplified with storage tiering. There are in-memory stores for active data and lower-cost storage for historical data. Timestream automates the transfer of data between these through configurable policies.

With Timestream, data can be analyzed using SQL, and built-in time series functions are available for smoothing, approximation, and interpolation. It also supports advanced aggregates, window functions, and complex data types such as arrays. Alongside this, data on Timestream is always encrypted, both at rest and in transit. This can be done with AWS or self-managed encryption keys.

The challenge is that Timestream is purpose-built, so the database is really only suitable for specific use cases. As of June 2022, it only supports five regions: North Virginia, Ohio, Oregon, Frankfurt, and Ireland.

More information here: https://aws.amazon.com/timestream/

Amazon Quantum Ledger Database

Quantum Ledger Database (QLDB) is a ledger database that provides a transparent, immutable, and cryptographically verifiable transaction log owned by a central trusted authority (AWS). This service can be used when data integrity is critical and any changes to the data have to be verifiable.

Records can be added but not directly changed. Like a financial ledger, to make a change, we add a new record to the end instead of directly changing an earlier record. With QLDB, this immutability of past records is enforced using cryptography.

QLDB is fully Serverless with no resources that need configuring or maintenance. There is also no need to provision or reserve any capacity and no billable idle time. Storage, queries, and data transfer are billable. This makes it a great database to use for all kinds of transactions, but especially those that may be sensitive to fraud, such as financial transactions. As it is a purpose-built database, it is unsuitable for most other use cases.

QLDB is highly durable, with multiple replications within an AZ and across three AZs in a region. QLDB supports the PartiQL query language, which uses a syntax similar to SQL.

A potential limitation is that QLDB does not have a backup and restore capability, as that would conflict with the immutability of the data. Data can be exported to S3, but that can't be used to restore data back into QLDB. For similar reasons, it does not provide support for point-in-time recovery or cross-region replication. This can make it challenging to meet global user and disaster recovery needs.

I mentioned that QLDB uses cryptography to protect the records, but let's look at what that means exactly.

Similar to blockchain networks, QLDB creates a hash of each record that is added to the database. A hash is a unique identifier for the value of the record, mathematically generated and repeatable for the same value. Secure, modern hashes are virtually impossible to decode with current technology (quantum computing may eventually impact that).

As new change records are added for an existing record, a new hash will be created from a combination of the previous hash and the new value.

By creating a hash this way, it links the latest record to all historical records in a chain, protecting the records all the way back to the original.

Every record can be verified by using its hash, making it highly auditable and transparent. To change a past record, one would need to edit all following records and generate new hashes for the entire chain. Besides this being a difficult feat to achieve, QLDB prevents any user from having this level of access to the data.

By comparison, in a traditional database, a user with the right privileges can modify historical data without leaving a trace just by editing a single record.

More information here: https://aws.amazon.com/qldb/

Managed NoSQL Databases

The following databases may be useful to be aware of. They are fully managed, not Serverless, so there is an operational overhead to configure server type and quantity, and the inevitable underutilization will lead to being billed for idle time.

DocumentDB

As the name indicates, DocumentDB is designed for documents. It's a good fit for content management, catalogues, profiles, and similar applications. Built as a MongoDB alternative and fully compatible, DocumentDB would be an easy choice when migrating from a self-managed MongoDB cluster.

There is a minimum storage of 10 GB and a maximum storage size of 64 TB, compared with petabytes in DynamoDB. DocumentDB is a regional database; it does not support cross-region replicas or global workloads.

DocumentDB is compatible with MongoDB, but it is not a direct replacement as it lacks a few MongoDB capabilities.

Amazon Neptune

Amazon Neptune is a graph database that specializes in use cases that require highly connected data sets. Neptune can store billions of relationships and execute queries with millisecond latency. It can execute more than 100,000 queries per second and supports automated backups.

Neptune is a regional service, so there are no cross-region replicas, which makes global and DR use cases harder to implement. There is a minimum storage of 10 GB up to a maximum capacity of 64 TB. Scaling an instance type will result in a few minutes of downtime.

 # NoSQL Databases Comparison

In Figure 7-21 we can compare some of the different types of NoSQL databases we looked at.

	Key-Value	Document	Wide-Column	Graph	Ledger	TimeSeries
What	Simplest type of NoSQL.	Records as documents.	Between a relational and NoSQL.	Focus on relationship between data.	Immutable, verifiable records.	Data that is tightly bound to a particular date/time.
Structure	Dictionary structure. Every value is mapped to a key.	Formats such as JSON, YAML, XML, and BSON.	Uses tables, rows, and columns.	Stores data as nodes (entities) and edges (relationships).	Ledger entries (changes not possible).	Columns and rows of data. Missing rows can be created based on earlier and later data.
Benefits	Most scalable.	Document is understood by apps. Less translation is needed.	Good for analytics.	Efficient in chaining and consolidating related entities within a query.	Cryptographically verifiable and fraud resistant.	Very fast and with several functions specifically for working with this type of data.
Use cases	High-traffic web applications, e-commerce systems, gaming applications, caching.	Content management, catalogs, profiles, games.	High scale apps for equipment maintenance, fleet management, route optimization.	Social networks, fraud detection, recommendations.	Financial and other sensitive transactions.	IoT sensor data.
AWS DB	DynamoDB	DocumentDB	Keyspaces	Neptune	QLDB	Timestream
Other DBs	Memcached, Redis	MongoDB	Apache Cassandra	Neo4j	Modex, Sequence	Aerospike, Akumuli

Figure 7-21. *NoSQL databases compared*

In-Memory Databases

In-memory databases could be NoSQL or SQL. Their purpose is that they run in RAM, so they are incredibly fast, but this also makes them expensive. I mentioned the in-memory database DynamoDB Accelerator earlier, but that is only available as a DynamoDB integration, so we won't include it here.

ElastiCache

ElastiCache offers microsecond latency for high-performance applications. ElastiCache is typically used as a buffer for regular databases, where it can cache and return popular query results. This can significantly reduce the load on the underlying database and greatly speed up the user experience. ElastiCache is run as a scalable cluster, where we can scale the nodes horizontally and vertically to handle the demand. ElastiCache can also support global workloads.

ElastiCache is a managed service, so the instance type and quantity must be configured for the cluster. This will also determine the billable amount – and billable underutilization is expected. Like many other solutions that have been assimilated into the cloud and offered as a managed service, ElastiCache does not include all of the original features.

ElastiCache supports two equally fast engines, Memcached and Redis.

Memcached is designed for simplicity and is ideal when we only need a basic caching service without any unnecessary features.

Redis is a full-fledged database with a suite of capabilities such as snapshots, persistence, replications, publish-subscribe, and support for multi-AZ.

Unlike DynamoDB Accelerator, ElastiCache does not seamlessly integrate with the source database. There is no automatic synchronization of data or any cache management. All of this needs to be developed and handled in the application.

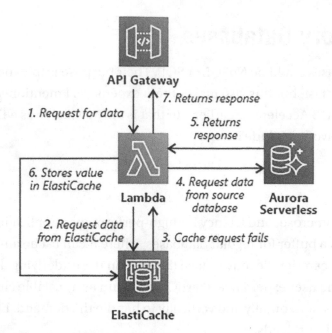

Figure 7-22. *ElastiCache simple architecture example*

In Figure 7-22, we have a user request arriving from API Gateway. The request is asking for data that the Lambda microservice needs to retrieve. The microservice must first query ElastiCache. If it has a valid cached record, it can be quickly returned to the user, ending this request. If ElastiCache does not have the data, then the microservice must query the source database. The retrieved record can then be returned to the user, and at the same time, the microservice must store a copy of the data in ElasticCache so that the next user request can return the cached result faster with only one back-end query needed.

Cache invalidation also needs to be considered in the application. Like *adding* data to ElastiCache, the application must also determine when the cached data has expired or when the source data has changed. In either of those cases, the application will need to *replace* the cached data in ElastiCache with the most recent response from the source database.

MemoryDB

Released in August 2021, MemoryDB is the latest addition to this group. MemoryDB is a Redis-compatible database, providing high durability and ultrafast performance. Unlike ElastiCache, MemoryDB has been positioned as a database instead of a supporting cache service.

The compatibility with Redis means that existing code and libraries for Redis are usually compatible. Like DynamoDB streams, MemoryDB provides transaction logs stored across multiple AZs. These can help achieve high availability, fast failover, and data recovery.

At the time of this writing, I have not used the service yet, and there is not much support or discussion online either. As a managed service, we need to configure instance type and quantity, and idle time will be billable. It can run on a small general-purpose server, which is great as it will help manage costs in a development environment. Production environments will likely need one of the more expensive high-memory server types to avoid performance issues.

 AppSync

AppSync is a GraphQL API service, mostly intended for mobile applications. While it is not a database or store, I have included it in this chapter as it is still quite relevant to data in Serverless projects.

AppSync is a Serverless GraphQL API that integrates with a few different services behind the scenes. AppSync handles most aspects of the integration with data sources such as DynamoDB and Aurora. This helps reduce the operational overhead of configuring and provisioning infrastructure and writing code. Scaling is similarly fully managed by AWS.

AppSync uses caching to reduce response latency and load on the integrated services. Caching is configured with server types and quantity, so it is not Serverless, and billable idle time should be expected.

AppSync provides several support features that web and mobile applications commonly need in a back end, for example, real-time messaging for use cases such as collaboration, chat, and dashboards. It also includes a front-end library with capabilities such as storing data locally in the application and automatically synchronizing it with the back end when connectivity is restored.

Under- and Over-fetching

Like REST in API Gateway, GraphQL is a query language for APIs, but it's a bit different from the traditional REST format. GraphQL aims to address the challenges of REST, specifically under- and over-fetching of data.

Under-fetching happens when a single API call to a particular path does not return all the data the application needs. So additional requests must be made to retrieve data from other API paths. For example, on a user profile page, we might want to show a user's profile information and a promoted product. A typical REST API, shown in Figure 7-23, would require two requests: one to the profile path and one to the product path.

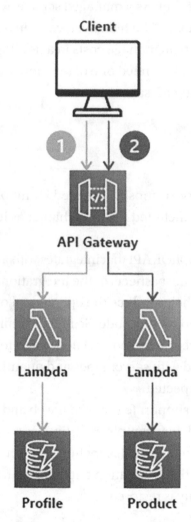

Figure 7-23. *REST needs two requests to get the information needed*

Over-fetching is when an individual API request includes data the application does not need. In our user profile example, the REST API profile path might include profile statistics or delivery addresses that we don't want to show on the current page. The full data set is returned because it is usually easier to develop it this way. Different pages that need different parts of the profile data can access it all in the same location and cherry-pick the attributes they want to use.

GraphQL addresses these issues by asking the client to define the data and structure it wants in the initial request. The GraphQL API will then gather all the required information from the connected databases and return it to the client in a single response, as shown in Figure 7-24.

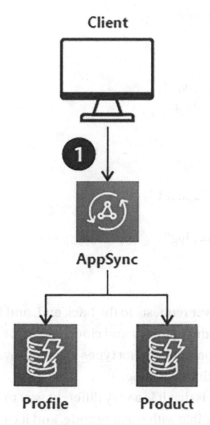

Figure 7-24. GraphQL needs one request to get the information needed

GraphQL request example

```
query {
  user (1d: 1) {
      full_name
      preferred_name
      age
  },
```

```
product (id: 1) {
     name
     price
     image
}
}
```

GraphQL response example

```
{
  "user": {
       "full_name": "John Doe",
       "preferred_name": "John",
       "age": 32,
  },
  "product" : {
       "name": "Awesome Product",
       "price": 100,
       "image": "abcd1234.jpg"
  }
}
```

This approach needs fewer requests to the back end, and less data needs to be transferred. Both of these reduce latency and cloud spend for the application. Defining the expected response and parameter data **types** also improves consistency and reduces the chance of missing bugs during testing.

A challenge of GraphQL is that it is a very different way to interact with a back end. This often makes it incompatible with existing code, and it can pose a considerable learning curve for developers more familiar with REST APIs.

AppSync APIs are public by default, and, at the time of writing, it is not possible to deploy the service into a private subnet. For enterprises where this is a hard requirement, we can consider running Apollo GraphQL in Lambda. More information about this can be found here: www.apollographql.com/docs/apollo-server/deployment/lambda/.

API Gateway can be deployed in a private network and proxy requests to Lambda running Apollo to provide a GraphQL experience. It will be easier to switch from this setup to AppSync when they add support for private subnets in the future.

If running AppSync in a public subnet is acceptable, there are a number of built-in security features to harden this against misuse:

- AppSync has D-DoS protection, enabling the service to remain available even in the event of an attack.

- There are different implementations available to secure endpoints with authorization:

  - API keys

    Suitable for granting guest access, can be easily disabled if compromised

  - Cognito user pools

    Can include user and profile management, supports integrations with social media platforms and Active Directory

  - OpenID

    Can include user and profile management, supports integrations with social media platforms and Active Directory

  - Identity and Access Management (IAM) service

    Can grant AWS services, such as Lambda, access to the AppSync API

A custom authorizer implemented with a Lambda microservice is supported too. This microservice can then authorize the user with a third-party service or internal user management system.

AppSync provides a means to hide data fields based on the authorization method used. For example, in the following snippet, we have a GraphQL schema that exposes two fields: ID and description. The tag added to the end means that access to the description is only permitted if the user is authorized with Cognito:

```
type Post @aws_api_key @aws_cognito_user_pools {
    id: ID!
    description: String @aws_cognito_user_pools
}
```

Simple Storage Solution (S3)

S3 should be familiar to anyone who has used AWS. It is a storage service where we can store really any kind of data in any format. Within the S3 service, we create buckets; these are each given a unique name, and it's where we store our files, manage access, and configure options such as logging, versioning, and static website hosting. Files stored in a bucket are referred to as *objects*, and the paths to the objects are called *prefixes*. This is because they are not really paths; they just look like what we would consider a path in an operating system. We should actually think of S3 as a key-value database. The prefix and the object name together are the *key*, and the file contents make up the *value*. S3 is well known for its availability, security capabilities, performance, and extreme, practically unlimited storage scalability.

Here are some things to note:

- There are different storage classes; each has different attributes and fees (which we covered extensively in Chapter 3).

- The maximum size for a single file is 5 TB.

- The maximum request size is 5 GB – use *multipart upload* to add files larger than this.

- Storage, requests, and data transfer are billable, but there is a generous free tier available.

- S3 is suitable for use cases such as storing documents and media, user uploads, logs and archives, hosting static files and web application front ends, data lakes, and backups.

S3 Events

Events are a very useful feature in S3 for event-driven Serverless architecture. S3 sends out notifications for all activity within the bucket, such as when a file is uploaded or deleted. The notification includes information about the object, its prefix, any metadata, and the event. We can configure the notifications to be sent to another service such as SNS, SQS, or Lambda. In an event-driven architecture, these notifications can trigger a response and react to events without polling or similar inefficient solutions to monitor for changes.

A common use case for S3 events is starting file processing workflows automatically in response to a new file upload. For example, we can automatically scan new files for malware or sensitive data, or we can automatically process an uploaded video file to transcode it for streaming (we cover this example in more detail in Chapter 10).

Signed URLs

S3 buckets are private by default, and there are several ways to set permissions (as we covered in Chapter 4). Signed URLs have been mentioned a few times so far, but let's look at them in more detail.

S3 signed URLs offer a way to create unique links with an optional expiry to private files in a secure S3 bucket. Signed URLs can be shared with users or systems to retrieve or upload files. The files don't need to exist in S3 as the process does not verify if the file exists when it generates the URL. This is especially relevant for signed **upload** URLs, but there are cases where we might want to generate a download URL first and add the file to be downloaded later.

Signed URLs help avoid making an entire bucket public or having to move files to a public bucket just so that external users can download them. Similarly, it helps applications meet the Principle of Least Privilege by only providing an entity access to the file or upload location that it needs at that point in time.

Besides the configurable expiry date, we can also configure an IP allowlist, a maximum upload size, and an encryption requirement.

Some common use cases for signed URLs include getting around the 6 MB request size limit in API Gateway and Lambda. When handling potentially larger user uploads, the application generates a signed upload URL. The client then uses the URL to upload the large file directly to S3 instead of via API Gateway.

Another common use case is when working with containers running open source software to process video, images, or similar. We can lock down the container and prevent all external access to limit the potential impact of compromised open source libraries. Then, instead of providing access to the entire bucket containing the files it needs to process, we include two signed URLs with each request. We provide a signed GET URL to the specific file it needs to process and a signed POST URL where it can store the result. This approach can also work well with third-party services, SaaS, and containers with a different cloud provider.

Multipart Upload

Using multipart upload for large files is a recommended best practice from AWS. This feature splits a large file into smaller parts, which are then uploaded to S3, usually multiple in parallel. This enables us to upload files larger than the request limit of 5 GB. It has the added benefit of increasing the upload speed on a sufficiently robust connection since, with parallel transfers, more data can be transferred within the same period of time. When all the small parts are uploaded, S3 reconstructs the large file and stores it in the bucket.

There are two things to keep in mind with multipart uploads:

1. If a multipart upload is cancelled, the uploaded parts will be retained on S3, and storage for them will be billed. Incomplete multipart uploads can be automatically deleted with a lifecycle policy that can be added to the bucket.

2. The upload request for each part is billable as a *put* request, as well as the initial *CreateMultipartUpload* and the final *CompleteMultipartUpload*. These additional requests will increase the one-time cost of uploading a file that would otherwise fit within the 5 GB limit as a single upload. While it is a minimal amount for a single upload, this can add up if uploading many files or if using a small part size relative to the total file size.

AWS developer tools such as Boto3 and CLI support multipart upload out of the box and apply it automatically on all files above a certain size (usually 5 MB).

S3 Object Lambda

We covered this S3 feature from a data protection perspective in Chapter 4. Here, we will look at the architecture in more detail.

To summarize what we previously covered, S3 Object Lambda can be thought of as a proxy Lambda microservice that sits between the requester and the objects stored in an S3 bucket. The microservice can process objects after the user requests the file but before the file is returned to the user. With this approach, manually moderating files to identify sensitive data is no longer needed, and only one copy of the data needs to be stored, which can be transformed on request.

Like S3, this feature accepts a standard GET request, so only the URL to the object will need to be changed in any existing application code. Let's walk through the S3 Object Lambda workflow in Figure 7-25.

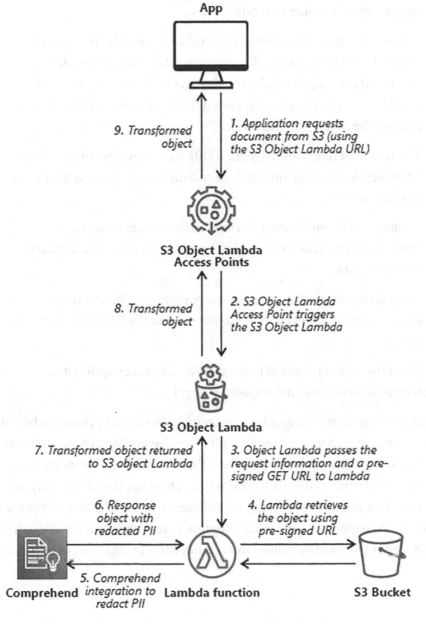

App

9. Transformed object

1. Application requests document from S3 (using the S3 Object Lambda URL)

S3 Object Lambda Access Points

8. Transformed object

2. S3 Object Lambda Access Point triggers the S3 Object Lambda

S3 Object Lambda

7. Transformed object returned to S3 object Lambda

3. Object Lambda passes the request information and a pre-signed GET URL to Lambda

6. Response object with redacted PII

4. Lambda retrieves the object using pre-signed URL

5. Comprehend integration to redact PII

Comprehend   **Lambda function**   **S3 Bucket**

Figure 7-25. *S3 Object Lambda architecture and flow*

1. An application is attempting to retrieve a document from S3. It uses the S3 Object Lambda URL instead of the standard S3 URL for the object.

2. An S3 Object Lambda access point receives the request and triggers the S3 Object Lambda service.

3. The service generates a pre-signed GET URL for the requested object. It will then invoke the configured Lambda microservice. The event message includes the signed GET URL, the user request and identity information, and any additional optional information that can be defined in the service.

4. The microservice uses the signed URL to retrieve the object from S3, which it can read and analyze and on which it can perform the desired actions.

5. Actions can be performed through custom code or service integrations such as Comprehend, which can detect and redact sensitive data.

6. Once all needed actions have been completed, the microservice returns the modified object as a response to the S3 Object Lambda service.

7. From there, it is returned to the user via the access point as a response to the original request in step 1.

This workflow is entirely a synchronous request, so latency needs to be considered from the network, as well as the time the microservice and any integrated services need to process the object. Benchmarks show that the average base latency without integrated services is 600 ms, compared with 100 ms when retrieving the file directly from S3. The Lambda in our test was only retrieving a 450-byte file from S3 and returning it right away without any processing. In a real-world situation with integrated services, the latency could easily reach 1 second or more, which is not ideal for the user experience.

Avoiding Size Limit Issues in Lambda

Another data use case for S3 is to help get around the size limit in Lambda. Lambda offers temporary storage of 10 GB for every invocation. This used to be 512 MB, which was often too little. Still, for those use cases where multiple GBs are needed, the time needed to copy it to the temporary space can lead to undesirable latency being added to the request. For some such use cases, it may be possible to stream data from S3 instead.

Some examples are shown in Figure 7-26. For these architectures, we stream data from a source S3 bucket to a destination S3 bucket. This works for compression, encryption, and some other use cases. Streaming also works for line-by-line reading of data from file formats that support this, such as CSV and JSON, if formatted in a particular way.

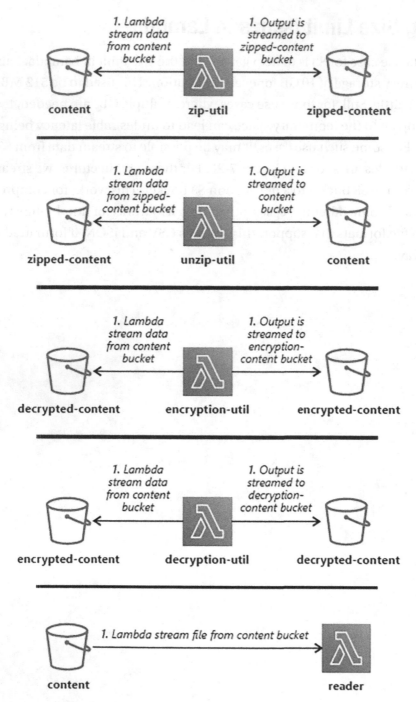

Figure 7-26. *S3 and Lambda data streaming*

📋 Elastic File System (EFS)

Elastic File System, or EFS, is a centralized storage service for compute instances. Using EFS, we can share files between multiple instances, containers, or microservices using the NSF-v4 protocol. It uses traditional file permissions, has file locking, and has a standard directory structure. Unlike S3, EFS is what an operating system would consider *standard* file storage. This makes it easier to mount and use the drive like any other storage space.

EFS automatically scales storage capacity, up or down, as data is added or removed, with minimal latency and without disrupting the application. Like S3, we only pay for the storage we actually use, though the cost per GB is higher than the S3 storage tiers.

Data on EFS is persisted separately from the containers or microservices it is mounted in, providing a way to get around the limited temporary storage available in Lambda and its ephemeral nature. We can store files larger than 10 GB in EFS and do not need to copy them to temporary storage each time the Lambda executes. Lambda microservices can mount the EFS with minimal latency and immediately start using the large file directly on EFS.

Similar to S3, with EFS lifecycle management, we can automatically move data that is accessed less frequently to a more cost-effective storage option.

CHAPTER 8

Logging and Testing

Just because something doesn't do what you planned it to do doesn't mean it's useless.

—**Thomas Edison, Inventor**

 Logging

Logging is an important aspect of any application and, like many other topics covered by this book, certainly not a concept unique to Serverless architecture. However, the distributed and often asynchronous nature of Serverless means that activities such as troubleshooting are particularly difficult in this architecture without a comprehensive logging strategy in place.

Logs provide valuable information for application teams to monitor resource usage and behavior. They help troubleshoot application errors and other issues. Metrics can help optimize performance and resolve bottlenecks, and audit logs can help prove compliance and investigate security events.

Traditionally, applications took a more reactive approach to application issues, namely, waiting for an issue to be reported before responding and searching through logs to uncover the root cause. While there is nothing wrong with passively browsing logs looking for any insights and inspiration (I even encourage it), doing so when trying to resolve a bug in a production application can be time-consuming and frustrating, not to mention that delay in resolving bugs is bad for the user experience. This is compounded in Serverless, where we use multiple services and microservices, all of which generate hundreds of logs, often in different formats.

A better approach to logging, and an essential one for Serverless, is a **proactive** logging strategy. With this approach, our environment analyzes relevant logs in near real time and can automatically determine and take action before a user reports an issue.

401

Proactive logging can be achieved using cloud services and custom microservices for more advanced options. In this chapter, we will look at how to achieve proactive logging, how this can increase productivity and improve user experience, and why it is so essential for Serverless applications.

Reactive Logging

To better understand the value of *proactive* logging, we must first understand the more common *reactive* logging.

Creating logs in the cloud is easy, and it's usually turned on by default or via a simple configuration option. For example, NodeJS console and Python print output from Lambda microservices will be written to CloudWatch logs. API Gateway can write user requests to CloudWatch logs, S3 can generate logs for activity on stored files, and many other cloud services have similar logging capabilities.

With *reactive* logging, developers will react to user feedback, bug reports, and support tickets **after** the issue has inconvenienced a user. For example, if the microservice for processing a contact form has a bug that causes an error only when a particular phone number format is submitted, then this would go unnoticed until a user attempts to submit the contact form with that format number and promptly calls in to complain about it not working.

The application team will need to further inconvenience the user to get the exact data they submitted so the error can be recreated. The team will then analyze the logs, identify the root cause, fix the bug, and deploy an update.

The problem with this approach is that remediation only happens *after* the damage has been done and issues may go unnoticed for quite some time. In the case of the phone number format, many users may not have had the issue, and others might have run into it but not reported it and simply moved on to a competing organization.

This raises the question: How can we react faster to application issues and, ideally, entirely remove the dependency on users reporting issues in the first place? The answer is, of course, *proactive* logging.

📋 Proactive Logging

With proactive logging, we automate the analysis of logs within our environment to take action instantly according to what is being reported in the log, without waiting for user reports or support tickets.

Most developers will be familiar with autoscaling; this is the same principle. We don't wait for a user to complain that an application is slow before scaling. The metrics are monitored, and additional resources are added automatically when certain thresholds are crossed.

Logging services such as CloudWatch will capture logs, often in near real time, and store them securely and indefinitely for browsing at our leisure. These services often have filter or search capabilities and perhaps even some visual dashboarding. Automated reactive capabilities are not enabled by default and must be configured according to preferences – again, much like autoscaling, where we must define the thresholds and scaling steps we want for the application.

Besides third-party solutions, there are two common approaches to achieving this automation within AWS.

The first is the easy option: using CloudWatch alarms, a feature of CloudWatch that can be configured to send a notification in response to a log.

The second approach uses CloudWatch subscriptions, a more advanced feature that passes logs to a custom microservice. This provides greater control and more options for reacting to a given log.

Proactive logging helps reduce the time needed to respond to an issue. Improving our previous bugged form example, the log generated by the bug in the microservice automatically sends a notification to the developer. This happens almost instantly and without needing to wait for any bug report from the user. The log can contain details about the submitted data that triggered the bug, which microservice, and where in the code it happened. So the developer has the relevant information on hand and can quickly get to the right location to start debugging.

General Considerations

Before we delve into logging services and custom microservices, there are a few considerations I want to mention.

When we generate custom logs – from microservices, for example – we must ensure that useful information is captured in the log. It can also help to ensure that logs are consistently formatted, making it easier to automate analysis and responses later.

Cloud services can generate many logs. For example, besides logs generated by microservice code each time a Lambda microservice is executed, the service generates at least two informational logs about that execution. Public-facing interfaces such as API Gateway or Web Application Firewall can generate an immense volume of access logs. As part of our strategy, we need to decide which logs we want to analyze and which will be ignored. For example, we don't need the default Lambda logs if we are focused on monitoring for errors, but we will need one of them if we are monitoring for cost tracking. In a production environment, we might want to spend a bit more on logging activity related to sensitive data. In the development environment, we only use test data, making logging a lower priority.

There is a risk of sensitive data ending up in logs. Based on the data classification, we may need to consider appropriate protection of such logs, such as encryption or tokenization. Similarly, data retention of logs could be driven by any sensitive data contained in them – especially personal data, which will have regulatory implications. If there is no sensitive data, retention will usually be driven by cost factors. For example, for Lambda microservices, it is common to track memory usage, which drives rightsizing decisions for performance. The increasing storage costs are unlikely to be justified by the value of storing those logs beyond the time needed to do the rightsizing analysis.

There are different types of actions that we can take in response to different logs. Part of a logging strategy is to determine levels of criticality and associate one or more actions with each level. Typically there will also be some special cases that fit in a category of their own.

Lastly, we need to determine how we want to implement our proactive logging capabilities. Do we want to use managed cloud services, augment with custom microservices, or rely on a third-party solution?

Logging Format and Content

Log format and the contained information are important and really the first step in the journey of a log, so let's look at that in a bit more detail.

Note that this section concerns the logs generated in our microservices where we can control the format and content. We are usually unable to influence the structure of logs generated by managed cloud services, which can differ significantly depending on the service.

For our microservice-generated logs, there are two ways to structure them. One is simple line format logs, also called string, flat, or CEF logs. Each log is a single line of values, usually spaced with tabs or bar characters.

Tab spacing example

```
1636596485  35261afc-4294-11ec-803253629336  CUST_70855  SUCCESS
1636596485  35261afd-4294-11ec-803253629336  CUST_70604  SUCCESS
1636596485  CUST_70842  SUCCESS
1636596485  35261aff-4294-11ec-803253629336  CUST_52633  ERROR
1636596485  35261b00-4294-11ec-803253629336  CUST_76849  SUCCESS
1636596485  35261206-4294-11ec-803253629336  CUST_12895  SUCCESS
```

Bar spacing example

```
1636596485|35261207-4294-11ec-803253629336|CUST_35016|SUCCESS
1636596485|35261208-4294-11ec-803253629336|CUST_69494|SUCCESS
1636596485||CUST_33241|SUCCESS
1636596485|3526120a-4294-11ec-803253629336|CUST_64063|SUCCESS
1636596485|3526120b-4294-11ec-803253629336|CUST_45645|ERROR
1636596485|3526120c-4294-11ec-803253629336|CUST_63084|SUCCESS
```

This format is commonly used by services such as Web Application Firewall for access logs. No special libraries are needed for this format, nor is there any conversion, so it has minimal overhead and latency. There are no attribute names or other special characters other than the tab between each value, so logs are concise and require little storage space.

However, this format is usually less flexible, and it can be harder to read the raw logs. We need to be familiar with the included attributes and their order. In the preceding simplified examples, there are only four attributes:

```
timestamp - log ID - user ID - status
```

Actual logs could have many more attributes per row. This format expects each line to have all attributes in the same order, even if an attribute has no value for a particular log. This is more noticeable in the bar spacing example, where two bars next to each other indicate an empty value. In the tab spacing example, it can be much harder to see which attribute is missing, certainly when there are many more attributes.

It can be difficult to filter this type of log without specific keywords being added. Processing the individual values often requires a full programming language to split the lines and turn them into arrays.

Another format is structured logging, where we have attribute names followed by their values:

```
{"timestamp":1636596485,"log_id":"35261afc-4294-11ec-803253629336","user_id
":"CUST_70604","status":"SUCCESS"},
{"timestamp":1636596485,"log_id":"35261afd-4294-11ec-803253629336","user_id
":"CUST_70842","status":"SUCCESS"},
{"timestamp":1636596485,"user_id":"CUST_52633","status":"SUCCESS"},
{"timestamp":1636596485,"log_id":"35261aff-4294-11ec-803253629336","user_id
":"CUST_52633","status":"ERROR"},
{"timestamp":1636596485,"log_id":"35261b00-4294-11ec-803253629336","user_id
":"CUST_76849","status":"SUCCESS"},
{"timestamp":1636596485,"log_id":"35261206-4294-11ec-803253629336","user_id
":"CUST_12895","status":"SUCCESS"}
```

This example uses the JSON format. Each log is still on a single line, but we can clearly see that the first attribute is *timestamp*. It's easier to read the raw logs and understand what they are about without needing any processing first. Similarly, tools such as CloudWatch can read such formats, making searching for keywords and automating responses easier.

Structured logs are more flexible because we indicate each attribute by name. Attributes can be in any order, and we can omit attributes that don't have any value or are not relevant to a particular log to save space. This can be seen in the third line of the preceding snippet, where the *log_id* has been omitted because it has no value.

406

However, structured logs typically need some library or programming function to generate and convert them between the original format and a basic string version that can be stored in a log. This adds overheads and latency. Because of the attribute names, quotes, and other characters, these logs are often larger, despite being able to omit attributes. However, the repetitive key names mean structured logs can be significantly compressed, which should certainly be considered when archiving.

Service Logs in the Cloud

Let's look at some common service logs available in the cloud that may be relevant to Serverless projects.

First, we have application logs, which are the logs generated from within our microservices using the standard logging functions associated with the programming language we are using, for example, console.log in NodeJS and print in Python. As we covered, the content and structure of these logs can and should be explicitly designed. It's important to use a consistent format and to include the information needed to troubleshoot or understand the purpose of the log. Besides error handling, application logs can be used for timing events and tracking identities and user activity for security or cost tracking.

Second, access logs track user and system interactions with cloud services such as Web Application Firewall, API Gateway, Application Load Balancer, and S3. Access logs are useful for security audits as they can provide visibility into the movement of users and data within a system. We can also use these logs to analyze and predict traffic patterns, such as determining peak periods.

Third, resource logs are metrics usually collected by the AWS platform. While we have limited control over their contents, we can use them to monitor and automate things. An example would be Lambda memory metrics, which we can use for rightsizing and performance optimization.

Next, profiling logs collect timing metrics for services and service integrations, for example, tracking service and network latency (which can be visualized) to help developers identify and locate bottlenecks that can be addressed.

Lastly, we have event logs. Managed services typically generate these in response to changes happening within the service. We can also create custom events from within our microservices. For example, when a file is uploaded to S3, an event log is generated that can be used to trigger a Lambda microservice to process the new file. Event logs are used extensively in Serverless, where we ideally want to use event-driven designs to automate processes.

Cloud Logging Services

Here, we have an overview of some AWS services that log activity. For some, logging is enabled by default; for others, it needs to be enabled in the configuration. Some services have additional, more detailed logs that can be enabled – note that usually these are billable. Whatever the situation, the creation, format, and content of these logs are handled entirely by each service. We can only read the logs looking for insights or use them to automate workflows.

Logs are typically stored in S3 or CloudWatch directly. In some cases, we can configure Kinesis Data Firehose to move logs to their destination.

Most logging operations are free, but associated charges such as storage and data transfer need to be considered to determine the Total Cost of Ownership. Optional logs that contain more details or more frequent measurements may have additional charges associated with them.

API Gateway collects access logs that contain information such as who used the service. Debug logs provide useful information for troubleshooting, such as the response code and authorization state from custom Lambda authorizers. With detailed logging, we get additional metrics, such as the number of API calls, the latency, and the number of errors.

The default CloudWatch metrics of Application Load Balancer provide information such as the number of requests and errors. Access logs must be enabled and include information such as the client's IP address, latency, and request and response information.

CloudTrail logs all the API management events made by users in an AWS account. This includes requests from the console, CLI, and SDKs. CloudTrail provides a full record of what was changed at what time and by whom. By default, logs are stored in S3. There is also an option to store them in CloudWatch.

VPC Flow Logs collects traffic metrics about network interfaces in a VPC. They can be useful for uncovering networking bottlenecks, for example.

Route 53 query logs contain information such as the requested DNS record, the date and time, and the response code.

S3 access logs need to be enabled and contain information about all requests made to objects in a bucket. The logs can include the object name, time, and date. While these logs are still available, it is recommended to use CloudTrail data events instead. These are easier to configure, have lower latency, and contain more detailed information.

CloudFront access logs contain information such as date and time, viewer IP, and response information. Standard CloudFront logs are usually delivered within an hour but may be delayed up to 24 hours. However, we can enable real-time logs to receive logs in seconds instead.

Web Application Firewall provides logs on the traffic that a security rule has evaluated. It includes information such as the client's IP address, the rules applied, and the result of the rule.

CloudWatch

CloudWatch is the most common AWS service used for logging and is integrated with more than 70 AWS services. Out of the box, CloudWatch handles application and metric logs, stores the logs encrypted at rest, and provides features such as filters and dashboarding to help analyze logs. CloudWatch is, for the most part, a storage facility with some search capabilities, and achieving a *proactive* strategy will require some additional features to be configured.

CloudWatch Metrics

CloudWatch metrics are usually managed and handled by AWS, sometimes only after they have been enabled for a given service. We use metrics to monitor utilization, identify bottlenecks, and improve performance. With Serverless architecture, we are most interested in metrics such as Lambda memory utilization and concurrency. Metrics such as CPU utilization, uptime, and disk storage are usually less relevant.

High-resolution metrics are published to CloudWatch in intervals of less than 60 seconds and will be available for 3 hours. Metrics that are initially published as high resolution are later aggregated for longer-term storage.

For example

1. After 3 hours, the metrics are aggregated into 1-minute intervals, available for 15 days.

2. After 15 days, the metrics are aggregated into 5-minute intervals and are available for 63 days.

3. The last step is after 63 days when the metrics are aggregated into 1-hour intervals and available for 15 months.

To keep higher-resolution metrics, export them to S3 before they are aggregated. This can be automated using a schedule and a Lambda microservice.

CloudWatch Logs

CloudWatch logs store application logs, which are typically used for debugging and tracking what is happening in microservices. Application and service logs are stored indefinitely by default. This is not ideal as the costs can increase rapidly if the application generates many logs. CloudWatch has a configurable retention period, after which the logs are automatically deleted. The configured retention period can be up to 10 years.

Although CloudWatch is a useful service for analyzing and visualizing logs, it is not a cost-effective option for storing logs. If we want to archive logs, are unable to delete them, and no longer need to use the filter and dashboard features, it is more cost-effective to move them to S3.

Storing logs in S3 standard storage is about 16% cheaper, and we can still use the Serverless Athena service to perform search queries on the data if needed. Storing logs in S3 Glacier is about 67% cheaper, but this is considered cold storage, and there can be a delay and additional cost when retrieving data.

CloudWatch Alarms

In CloudWatch alarms, we can configure thresholds on a maximum limit and minimum limit, average and mathematical formulas such as percentiles, trimmed mean, and windowed mean.

For example, we can set a metric that monitors the runtime duration of a Lambda microservice. Based on previous executions, the duration averages around 700 ms and does not exceed 900 ms. We set a threshold to trigger the alarm when the Lambda microservice takes more than 900 ms to run, which could indicate that something has changed in our environment, causing additional latency.

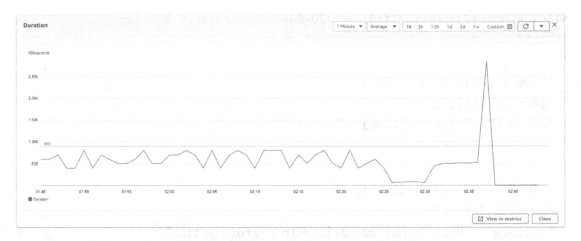

Figure 8-1. *Amazon CloudWatch graph. Source: AWS console* `https://aws.` `amazon.com/` *2022, Amazon Web Services Inc. or its affiliates. All rights reserved*

In Figure 8-1, there is a spike in execution time where it took more than 2.8 seconds for the microservice to complete its task. As a result, an email notification is sent to the application team so they can determine the cause and make any necessary adjustments to the code or configuration.

CloudWatch alerts also offer a dashboard, where we can create a custom layout using alarms and metrics to get immediate performance insights without having to search through the logs.

CloudWatch Metric Filter

As the name suggests, a metric filter is where we can search and filter logs. We can create custom metrics using the filters and use them in alarms and dashboards. This helps simplify the process of analyzing logs without needing to code anything. By integrating alerts, we can achieve a simple proactive logging strategy with automated email notifications triggered by our custom metrics.

Here we have a structured log generated by our microservice:

```
START RequestId: 0bed9741-0741-44f0-8950-954fccdfac69 Version:
$LATEST
{
  "time": 1634004072.1578627,
  "level": "info",
  "message": "Starting Lambda function"
}
{
  "time": 1634004873.6210654,
  "level": "error",
  "message": "User is not authorized to perform action"
}
END RequestId: 0bed9741-0741-44f0-8950-954fccdfac69
```

Each log contains the time, log level, and log message, as defined in the microservice.

To create a metric filter, we first need to identify a filter pattern and then configure the details. For this example, we could create a filter pattern that looks for any logs with the *level* attribute set to **error**. We then create a metric for this pattern to count the number of error logs over a period of time.

Once the metric is created, we can use it in CloudWatch dashboards and alarms. We can reference the metric and set a threshold for a given maximum number of errors. Once the threshold is reached, it will trigger an email notification to let us know something is wrong.

This is also a common metric to use for automating deployment rollbacks when the latest update introduces a new issue. Besides sending an alert, we would trigger the relevant deployment pipeline to return the updated application to the previous version. The application team can then debug the issue and deploy again once the issue has been resolved. This helps minimize the amount of time that a missed bug is in the live application.

⚙ Exporting Logs to S3

In Figure 8-2 is an architecture example showing how we can automatically export logs from CloudWatch to S3.

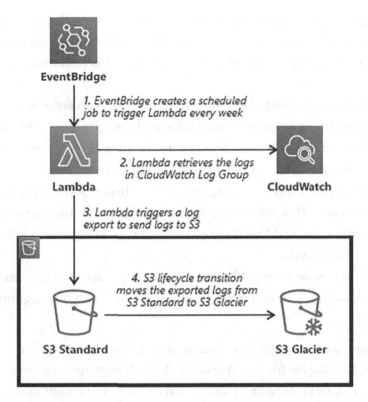

Figure 8-2. *Exporting logs to S3*

From the top, we create a weekly recurring schedule in EventBridge that invokes a Lambda microservice. The microservice will call CloudWatch to retrieve the metrics and export them into standard S3 for storage.

On our S3 bucket, we can configure a lifecycle policy that will automatically move the logs from standard storage to infrequent access and Glacier storage after some time to save costs.

⚙ CloudWatch Subscriptions

CloudWatch subscriptions enable developers to achieve near-real-time analysis of log files. Once configured, CloudWatch will stream incoming logs to a Lambda microservice where we can develop all kinds of custom processing and follow-up actions.

The microservice can read the log to determine what type of log it is, the context, and which users, services, and data may be involved. For example, we can identify an error log, see if it is related to a user or a system, and determine if the error impacts any sensitive data.

This immediate assessment of the logs is where it can help enforce consistent formatting, making the log structure predictable and easier to read. After the initial assessment, we have the option to perform more complex analyses in a microservice, such as detecting personal data or potentially fraudulent behavior.

To manage cost, filters can be configured in the subscription to only forward *relevant* logs to the microservice. This will reduce the number of times the microservice is invoked. For example, we could limit the subscription to only forward logs that contain the keyword *error* to Lambda.

Once the microservice has established what the log is about, it can determine a suitable course of action. This can really be any action that can be programmed into a microservice:

- In some cases, it might just discard the log or store the log in an aggregated log file for that day or week. Such aggregations are more cost-effective to store and can be easier to search through using the Athena service.

- We can opt for benign actions such as a notification to a Slack channel, email address, SMS, or another messaging platform.

- We can integrate with ticketing systems or collaboration platforms such as Jira and automatically create a ticket from a log.

- More aggressive or impactful actions can also be considered, for example, banning user accounts, disabling encryption keys, blocking IP addresses, locking down a data source, rolling back a code or IaC update, or even taking an entire application offline and replacing it with a maintenance page.

Let's look at a simple example in Figure 8-3. At the top, a user tries to insert malicious data (1) into a microservice. The microservice detects the invalid data (2) and logs the event to CloudWatch (3).

A subscribed microservice is triggered and sent the log contents (4). It determines that the data was indeed malicious and takes two courses of action:

1. It sends a notification to the application team via Slack, informing them of the data, microservice, and user ID (5).

2. As a precaution, it locks the user account in IAM (6).

The application team can review the event, determine if the user account was compromised, and take any necessary follow-up action.

A more detailed overview, including code examples for CloudWatch subscriptions with Lambda microservices, can be found in Chapter 10.

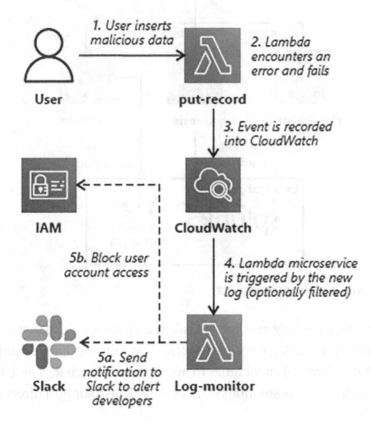

Figure 8-3. *CloudWatch subscription architecture*

⚙ Managed Services for Proactive Logging

CloudWatch alarms and subscriptions require manual configuration, and log processing microservices need to be developed, managed, and maintained to achieve a proactive logging strategy. This might not be an ideal option for organizations with few Serverless developers.

Another option is to integrate a full-featured service that can offer similar capabilities. In Figure 8-4, we can see three options for integration.

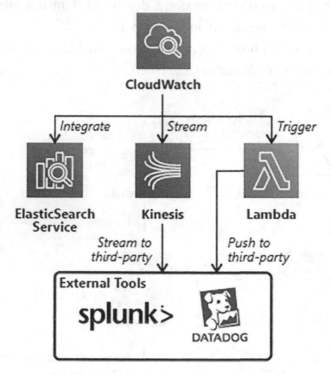

Figure 8-4. *CloudWatch integrations*

At the top, we have the fully managed ElasticSearch AWS service that can ingest data directly from CloudWatch using the CloudWatch Logs Subscription Consumer library. ElasticSearch offers advanced capabilities to monitor and search logs and design custom dashboards. Some third-party solutions such as Splunk also support direct integration with CloudWatch.

In the middle, we can use Kinesis to stream logs to third-party tools that support streams, such as Splunk and Datadog. Both provide a host of features for monitoring and logging. These tools also accept logs from other cloud providers and SaaS solutions, providing a unified view of the organization's application and infrastructure logs.

Lastly, instead of *processing* logs in Lambda, we can use Lambda to push, publish, or post logs to third-party tools that don't support direct integration or Kinesis streams. An added advantage is that we can remove or tokenize any sensitive content in the logs before they are sent to a third-party solution.

Error Monitoring

In the following sections, we will look at four common use cases for logging and how we might implement them. We will start with error monitoring, where we want our system to automatically respond to application errors.

There are three steps to take to achieve proactive error monitoring.

The first is to **collect logs**. If we are monitoring for issues in our cloud resources, then CloudWatch monitors and collects these by default without needing to code anything. Depending on the service, there may be an optional setting to enable advanced or more detailed logging.

If we are monitoring application issues, they will also be collected into CloudWatch, but we need to ensure our code is outputting logs with useful data and that we use a consistent log format.

Second is to **process and analyze logs**. We can use CloudWatch metric filters to create custom filters to monitor only the events of interest. For example, we could set a threshold for the number of *error* logs within a period of time.

If we want a custom log processor in a Lambda microservice, we can use a CloudWatch subscription. A microservice can process logs really in any way that we can program. For more stateful analysis, such as events over a period of time, a data store such as DynamoDB or Timestream will be needed to track the events.

If we are using third-party tools, we can use CloudWatch Metric Streams or Lambda as a forwarder to send the logs to the tool where they can be processed.

Third, we then decide the best course of **action** for each log. This might be to do nothing at all if the log is not important:

- If we are using filters and CloudWatch alarms, then our options are limited to a notification or event trigger.

- For microservices, we can take any action that we are able to program.

- For third-party tools, it will depend on the capabilities of the tool.

The following pseudo-code snippet creates a structured JSON log, with the log information included as key-value pairs. This snippet should be wrapped with a function such as `console.log()` in JavaScript or `print()` in Python to send it to CloudWatch:

```
{
  "time": date.getTime(),
  "level": "info",
  "message": "Successfully executed DynamoDB request",
  "item_count": response.Count,
  "more": response.LastEvaluatedKey != null
}
```

- The *time* field denotes the time that the log was created. The function *date.getTime()* gets the current timestamp.

- *level* is used to mark the type of log, such as debug or error. Here we have used *info* to indicate that it is an informational log. Logs created in a `try-catch` or similar construct can have type set to *error* to indicate an error happened and was caught.

- *message* provides some human-readable context about the log. In this case, we want to log that a DynamoDB request was successful. Combined with the timestamp, this log could provide information about how long it took for the DynamoDB request to run, helping us track down any bottlenecks.

- *item_count* and *more* are additional fields specific to this particular log. In this case, they tell us how many records were returned and if there is another page of results that can be retrieved. Because we are using a structured log, we can have these arbitrary additional fields as needed for each log. Keep in mind that the log processor will need to know what to do with them.

Once the log is generated, we can use CloudWatch to analyze it, as shown in Figure 8-5.

Figure 8-5. *Amazon CloudWatch log events. Source: AWS console* `https://aws.`
`amazon.com/` *2022, Amazon Web Services Inc. or its affiliates. All rights reserved*

We can perform a keyword search on logs with key-value pairs to filter our logs. Here, we extracted all logs related to a successful connection to DynamoDB using the message field. Another approach would be to use a log code and filter by that. This does require maintaining a dictionary of codes and their meaning, however.

In Figure 8-6, we have another example using CloudWatch Logs Insights. This graphing tool allows us to create graphs based on the metrics we have defined.

Figure 8-6. *Amazon CloudWatch Logs Insights. Source: AWS console* `https://` `aws.amazon.com/` *2022, Amazon Web Services Inc. or its affiliates. All rights reserved*

The query in Figure 8-6 again uses each log's key-value pairs to search for specific ones and extract the information we need.

CloudWatch Events

CloudWatch Events delivers a near-real-time stream of changes made within an AWS environment. For example, Events can capture API events, such as new objects created in an S3 bucket, and then use this event to trigger other services, such as Lambda, to process the newly uploaded file.

In Figure 8-7, we configure CloudWatch Events to monitor a Step Function workflow's state changes looking for any FAILED status, as configured top right.

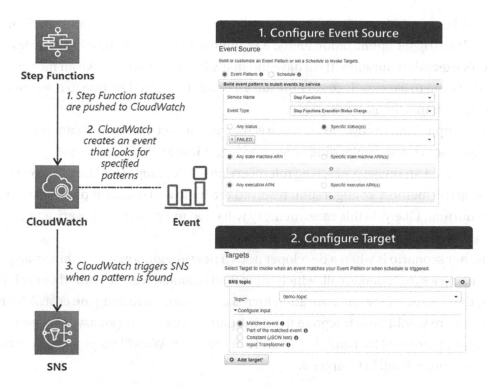

Step Functions

1. *Step Function statuses are pushed to CloudWatch*

2. *CloudWatch creates an event that looks for specified patterns*

CloudWatch   Event

3. *CloudWatch triggers SNS when a pattern is found*

SNS

Figure 8-7. *Reacting to Step Function failed state changes*

Any failure of a workflow step will now trigger an event that sends a message to an SNS topic – the configured *target* – that will notify the application team about the failure in near real time.

 # Performance Optimization

AWS tracks the performance metrics of most cloud services, and we can use these logs to optimize our architecture. For example, CloudWatch alarms can be configured to send an alert when specific logs are identified in a service:

- Many dropped request logs might mean that we need to adjust the throttling configuration in API Gateway.

- High execution duration on a Lambda microservice could indicate that we need to split our microservice into smaller ones or adjust the memory configuration.

- Latency can be tracked, which can identify bottlenecks in our architecture that we can prioritize for optimization.

With filters and CloudWatch alarms, we can monitor performance and configure thresholds to trigger optimization alerts. A common metric to monitor in Serverless is Lambda's execution duration. If we have too many invocations that take an increasing amount of time to execute, it could indicate an issue. This could be due to a recent code change or a change in user behavior.

An example from my own experience is that as Internet speeds and cameras improved, users started uploading larger and larger image files.

This caused an image processing microservice to take longer and longer to execute. Increasing the memory configuration resolved the issue and returned processing time back to normal. Likely, in this case, memory will need to be increased every few years, so runtimes need to be actively monitored.

Another scenario is when a developer adds a new integration with a third-party service using a synchronous call, which waits for a response. As the Lambda now has to wait, the duration for each invocation increases, in turn increasing the cost. A better approach here would be to integrate the third-party service using an asynchronous call, avoiding the need for Lambda to wait for a response. We will cover asynchronous patterns in more detail in Chapter 9.

Lambda Rightsizing

When we rightsize Lambda microservices, we are talking about adjusting the memory setting. Because the cost of a Lambda execution is relative to the amount of assigned memory, a common assumption is that less memory means lower cost. However, that is not always the case, as Lambda is also billed based on the time taken to execute, and the amount of memory can impact this in some cases.

This is because the number of virtual CPUs assigned to a microservice is proportional to the amount of assigned memory, at a ratio of 1,769 MB of memory to one (virtual) CPU. Less memory means partial CPU availability. Without getting into the weeds of CPU sharing science, it's something like timesharing. This article does a pretty good job of explaining the details:

https://engineering.opsgenie.com/how-does-proportional-cpu-allocation-work-with-aws-lambda-41cd44da3cac

Where Lambda rightsizing is concerned, for certain microservices, an increase in memory and CPUs could lead to a reduction in execution time and cost. Alternatively, if the goal is not necessarily reducing the cost, then better performance could be achieved at the same cost.

Rightsizing is a common term originally used for selecting the right-size server to meet the expected demand. With servers, the *right size* will depend on the number of expected requests or jobs that a single server will execute, but not so with Lambda microservices. With Lambda, each request has its own private microservice instance, so the only consideration for rightsizing is what resources the microservice code requires to run a single execution. The number of potential users or requests is irrelevant in this case.

By default, CloudWatch doesn't publish these memory usage metrics, nor does it provide cost metrics for developers to determine which is the most cost-effective option.

However, with a bit of work, there is a way to track this with a CloudWatch metric filter. As mentioned earlier, for each Lambda execution, besides any code logs, at least two logs are generated by the service. One of those logs is a report at the end of every execution that includes the run duration and memory usage.

Here's an example of such a log, which is stored in CloudWatch logs:

```
REPORT RequestId: fef1d62b-8a8b-456d-9bf4-5821affc6f3b Duration: 1658.16 ms
Billed Duration: 1659 ms
Memory Size: 128 MB
Max Memory Used: 71 MB
Init Duration: 412.33 ms
```

Billed duration and *max memory used* are the relevant parts of this log that we are interested in. Using a metric filter, we can create a custom metric that can extract this information from the log. We can use this custom metric to monitor resource usage for each microservice execution, as shown in Figure 8-8.

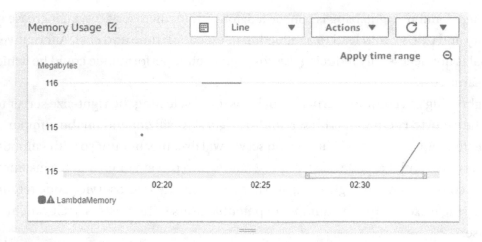

Figure 8-8. *AWS Lambda memory usage metric. Source: AWS console* `https://` `aws.amazon.com/` *2022, Amazon Web Services Inc. or its affiliates. All rights reserved*

With the metric and graph in place, we run a few more tests using different memory configurations to find the most optimal one for the microservice. The thing to look out for after each change of the memory setting is how it affects the *billed duration* and the *max memory used*. Usually, we want to find the configuration that gives us the lowest *billed duration* and where *max memory used* is closest to *memory size*.

Once optimized, we can use the final memory setting and average duration to determine the run cost of each execution – keep in mind that Lambda bills based on *assigned* memory, not *used* memory. We can also create an alarm that monitors the memory usage to alert us if an average threshold is breached. This could be due to changes in the microservice code, in the environment or service, or in user behavior.

Lambda Insights

Another way to monitor Lambda memory usage is through Lambda Insights. This optional feature must be manually enabled, but it avoids the need to create a custom metric.

Like standard CloudWatch metrics, Insights metrics can be used to trigger CloudWatch alarms. But Insights provides a lot more information and metrics for Lambda executions, such as the function cost, duration and memory usage, errors, and other metrics. All of these could potentially help optimize Lambda microservice configurations.

To help automate the process of cycling through and testing different memory configurations, the open source script *aws lambda power tuning* is available on GitHub. This project uses Step Functions to coordinate multiple executions of multiple Lambda microservices using different configurations.

We can specify the microservices and the different configurations that we want to test. At the end, it provides a nice visual report for each tested microservice.

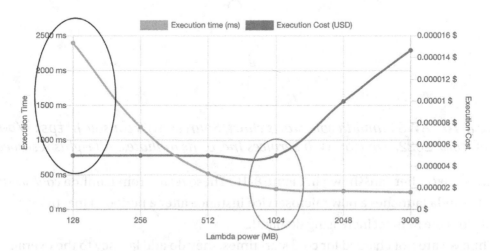

Figure 8-9. *AWS Lambda rightsizing chart. Source: Lambda Power Tuning*
`https://aws.amazon.com/`

In Figure 8-9, we can see that if we configure this microservice with 128 MB of memory, it will take about 2.4 seconds to execute the microservice, which costs about $0.000005 per execution. If we increase the memory to 1 GB, it executes eight times faster and, despite the additional memory, at the same cost, providing a great boost in performance.

One thing that might stand out in Lambda metrics are certain outliers, especially for duration metrics.

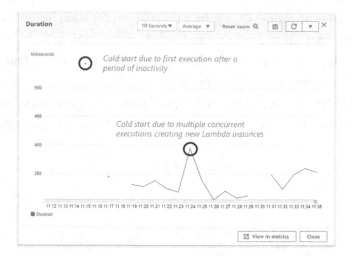

Figure 8-10. *AWS Lambda cold starts chart. Source: AWS console* https://aws. amazon.com/ *2022, Amazon Web Services Inc. or its affiliates. All rights reserved*

Two such outliers are shown in Figure 8-10. These result from Lambda *cold starts*, where Lambda launches a new microservice instance after a period of inactivity or when it needs to scale to meet increasing demand.

While we are not charged for cold start times, they do add latency to the overall request. As such, it is certainly worth optimizing these when possible to improve performance and user experience. Too little memory or a large code base can also increase cold start latency, and some programming languages have a higher cold start latency than others.

X-Ray

Another optimization technique is to monitor Serverless architecture using the X-Ray service. This service provides information such as latency and response codes for the various components and their integrations in a workflow. These metrics can help discover bottlenecks and inefficiencies in the architecture and code.

X-Ray can be enabled in services such as API Gateway and Lambda, as well as embedded in microservice code using the X-Ray SDK.

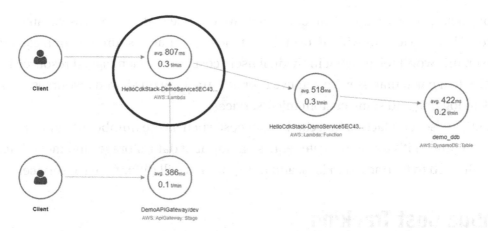

Figure 8-11. *AWS X-Ray chart. Source: AWS console* `https://aws.amazon.com`
2022, Amazon Web Services Inc. or its affiliates. All rights reserved

Figure 8-11 is a map generated by X-Ray after several executions of a Lambda
microservice. We can see that the request made its way through the different
components in the workflow. Each component indicates the average amount of time it
needs to run, and it seems that the microservice takes the longest, with an average of 800
milliseconds. Based on this, we can consider flagging the microservice for rightsizing or
code optimization efforts.

⚙ Cost Tracking

If configured, logging can help provide an accurate cost per user. This enables several
use cases, such as billing users or departments based on actual usage at the end of each
month and tracking what a user, department, or organization is costing us in a given
application. One easy option to note first: If the use case is the transfer of data to another
party with an AWS account, then we can consider the *requester pays* feature in S3. With
this feature enabled, the requesting account will be charged for the data request and
transfer instead of the source account.

For example, if we have a large data set that we would like to make available to
another department or organization but we want to avoid getting billed for the cost of
transferring the data set, with requester pays, the other party will use their AWS account
to retrieve the data set, and that account will be billed for the associated costs.

427

For tracking costs at an architecture level, we can use tags to group associated services. This provides us with an overview of the cost for all resources within each tag. However, this won't tell us what individual users cost unless each tagged resource is exclusive to a particular user. To achieve user cost tracking on shared resources, we need to look to logging and some custom microservices.

There are several factors that can impact cost, such as the number of requests, execution time, if it's a read or write request, amount of data, storage, and more. Each of these will need to be tracked in logs, and the approach will differ for each service.

Lambda Cost Tracking

Let's start with Lambda microservices. There are two parts to this.

As we saw earlier, Lambda will log a report at the end of each execution containing the duration billed for that execution. The problem is that this report contains no information about *who* executed the function, so we need to make the link.

One approach is to find the fastest way to identify the user in the Lambda, for example, using a hash of the API key or Cognito ID that API Gateway could pass to Lambda in the event message. We use a hash to avoid accidentally including any personal data in logs.

Our microservice can then log an *identification* event that contains the identity hash and request ID, which can be retrieved from the Lambda context variable. Then we can connect the identification log with the report log using the request ID and store the duration with the identity hash in a database.

Once we have the duration, we can multiply that by the Lambda-per-millisecond cost for the assigned memory and region. Lambda request quantity is also a cost factor. Once we have linked the report with a user ID, we can get the total execution cost by simply adding the regional request cost.

Figure 8-12 shows a high-level architecture for achieving that.

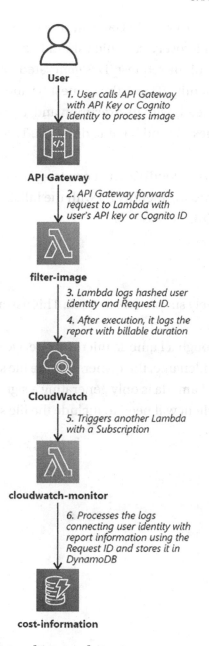

User

1. User calls API Gateway with API Key or Cognito identity to process image

API Gateway

2. API Gateway forwards request to Lambda with user's API key or Cognito ID

filter-image

3. Lambda logs hashed user identity and Request ID.

4. After execution, it logs the report with billable duration

CloudWatch

5. Triggers another Lambda with a Subscription

cloudwatch-monitor

6. Processes the logs connecting user identity with report information using the Request ID and stores it in DynamoDB

cost-information

Figure 8-12. *Lambda cost tracking architecture*

At the top, we have a user calling API Gateway. We can use a feature in API Gateway that generates unique API keys for end users. Alternatively, we can use an integrated Cognito identity pool.

When the user executes the call, API Gateway must forward the API key or Cognito identity ID to our Lambda microservice, which should hash or tokenize it. At the start of each Lambda execution, a unique request ID is generated for it. The microservice should create a log with both the identity ID and the request ID and store it in CloudWatch. Then, the microservice proceeds with its execution and, at the end, will produce a report with the same request ID and billable duration. This report is also sent to CloudWatch logs.

Once the information is in CloudWatch, it can trigger another Lambda microservice, which reads the logs, matches the identity ID with the billable duration using the request ID, and adds it to DynamoDB.

S3 Cost Tracking

S3 storage is another relatively simple one to track. This assumes that the users upload or create files to be stored in the system.

If files are uploaded through a Lambda microservice, we can simply write a log to CloudWatch, including the filename, the owner, and the file size, as shown in Figure 8-13. This can also be done if the Lambda is only generating a signed URL to be used for the actual upload, though the client will need to include the file size when requesting the signed URL.

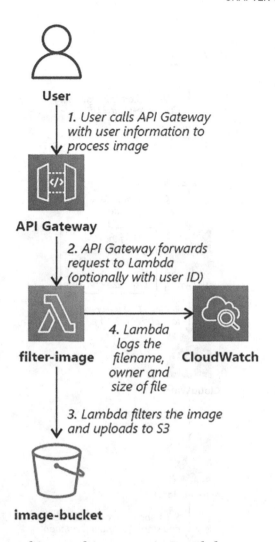

User

1. User calls API Gateway with user information to process image

API Gateway

2. API Gateway forwards request to Lambda (optionally with user ID)

filter-image

4. Lambda logs the filename, owner and size of file

CloudWatch

3. Lambda filters the image and uploads to S3

image-bucket

Figure 8-13. *S3 cost tracking architecture via Lambda*

If files are uploaded without Lambda, such as via AWS CLI or a signed URL from another source, we need to first enable CloudTrail data events or S3 access logging. S3 access logs are not guaranteed, and there can be long delays, so CloudTrail data events are the better option.

Either way, we can trigger a Lambda microservice to process the logs as they are written to S3 and extract the information we need to track cost, such as the requester's IAM username and the object size, as shown in Figure 8-14.

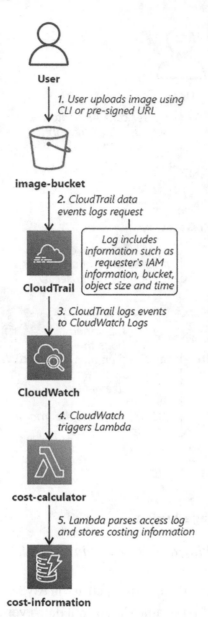

Figure 8-14. *S3 cost tracking architecture for direct interactions*

Another advantage of using CloudTrail data events is that they will also include state changes. So, if we have a lifecycle policy that moves files to deep storage or deletes files, we will also be able to find when that happens in the logs and track the associated cost. There is currently no entry for these events in S3 logs.

Tracking the Cost of Other Services

In Serverless architecture, a Lambda microservice will typically be used at some point in a workflow. As such, the microservice can create the logs necessary to track the cost of integrated services. Besides some form of user ID, we include the service name and its billable metrics.

For example, the image analysis service *Rekognition* is initiated from a microservice that passes it an image to analyze. Rekognition bills per processed image, so simply including the service name in the log will suffice for calculating the cost. For DynamoDB, we should also track the size of the data we pass to it. Other services may have additional metrics that influence their cost.

In cases where the microservice does not have access to all billable metrics, we might be able to store an execution ID returned from the service. This ID can be used to retrieve the missing information from the logs of that service after the task completes. Note that additional logging may need to be enabled on the service to give us the information we need.

For other services, we might include a task ID, time to get a response, the size of the data passed to it, or any other metric that influences the execution cost for that particular service.

When there is a need to create temporary resources such as servers or containers, we can use tags to link them to the user they were created for. For example, if there is a need to spin up a Fargate container to execute a long-running task, Lambda can be used to launch the container, log the request, and add tags to the container that identify the user. We can also include tags for any configured parameters that influence the cost, such as assigned memory and CPUs. A centralized microservice can run on a schedule to read the tags and retrieve the associated runtime to calculate the total cost for that execution and link it to the user.

Service integrations that are done outside of Lambda, such as when S3 directly triggers SQS, are more challenging to track. Advanced logging or CloudTrail can provide a means to get the required information, but these cases usually need a bit of research to figure out, especially to link the event to a particular user.

An often-overlooked cost when calculating estimates are data transfer charges. For tracking data transfer charges from S3, we can use signed URLs and API keys that have been used to download the file. This data can be found in the logs that are stored in CloudWatch if the logging infrastructure is in place.

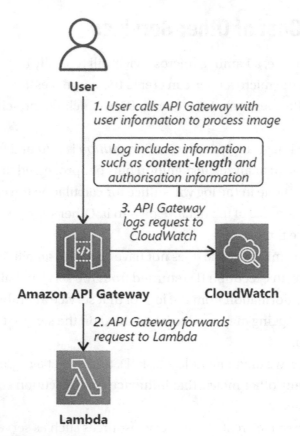

Figure 8-15. *Tracking data transfer costs in API Gateway*

For calls to other services, we can use API Gateway to track the data transfer costs, as shown in Figure 8-15. API Gateway logs helpful information such as the requester's details, which can be used to identify the user, and headers, such as *content length*, which can provide the size of the payload that is being transferred. Using this information, we can determine the data transfer charges associated with each invocation.

For requests that don't require authentication, it will be much harder to link the activities to a particular individual. In some cases, the client interface might be able to include an ID parameter, but that will be sensitive to fraud.

⚙ Security Monitoring

Using the right services, we can achieve clear visibility of who, when, and how someone accesses our services and data. Ensuring accountability and transparency is crucial for organizations seeking to demonstrate compliance with privacy regulations such as the EU's GDPR or Singapore's PDPA. Security monitoring can help ensure that sensitive data is stored securely and any violations can be remediated swiftly through automation.

Macie

AWS provides detective services to help detect data risks. One such service is Macie, a machine learning service that can scan the content of S3 buckets looking for sensitive information. When it identifies something, it can send an alert or trigger a microservice for a response.

For example, if a user accidentally uploads a file containing credit card information, Macie will identify that and trigger a microservice to automatically delete the file or move it to a secure bucket for further analysis and action. This minimizes the risk and exposure of the sensitive data to other users.

Figure 8-16 shows the architecture of Macie monitoring for sensitive data uploaded to S3.

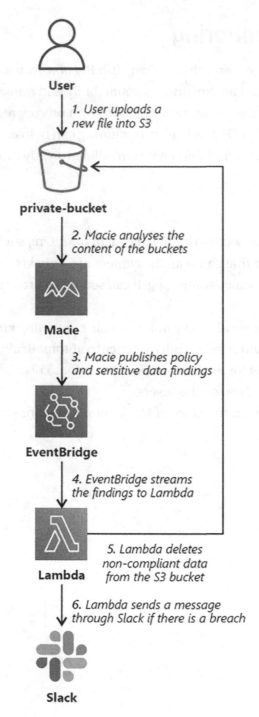

Figure 8-16. *Macie monitoring architecture example*

Besides credit card numbers, Macie can monitor and detect many forms of personal data (PII). In our example, a user uploads a file to an S3 bucket. Macie analyzes it and determines that it contains PII data. Macie will then publish a security event to EventBridge, which can be configured to trigger a Lambda microservice. In this example, the microservice will delete the offending file from S3 and send a notification to the security team via Slack.

GuardDuty

Logs generated by services and microservices can be fed into GuardDuty for analysis. GuardDuty can identify anomalies that could suggest a compromise of the environment or accounts, log them, and send a notification. For example, if there is a new request in the management console originating from a country that is not usually seen in this account, then a notification can be automatically sent to the security team to assess the event.

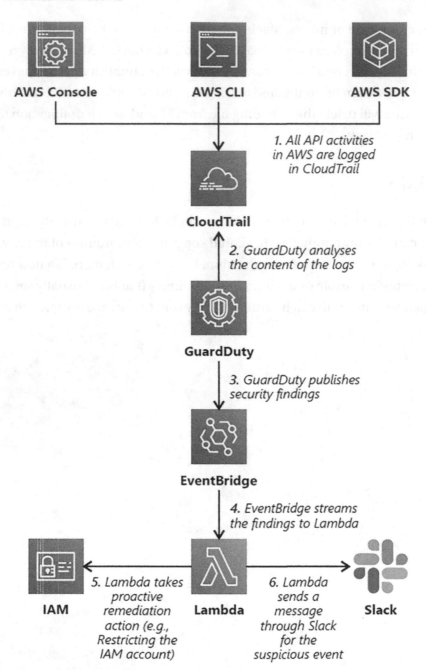

Figure 8-17. *GuardDuty monitoring architecture example*

CloudTrail keeps a record of all activity by users in the AWS console, CLI, and SDKs. In Figure 8-17, we have a compromised AWS user account that a bad actor is abusing from another country. They attempt to launch an EC2 instance using the console – an activity that is recorded in CloudTrail.

GuardDuty is configured to analyze CloudTrail logs in this account and recognizes that the *launch EC2* request originated from a country not typically used. This triggers a new security finding that is published to EventBridge. Upon receiving the new event, EventBridge invokes a Lambda microservice that calls IAM to block the user account and sends a message to the security team via Slack.

With this design, we can quickly detect suspicious behavior and quickly remediate it to minimize the potential impact.

CloudWatch Subscription

One more way to monitor for unauthorized behavior is with a CloudWatch subscription. In Figure 8-18, a bad actor attempts to access an API endpoint without proper authorization.

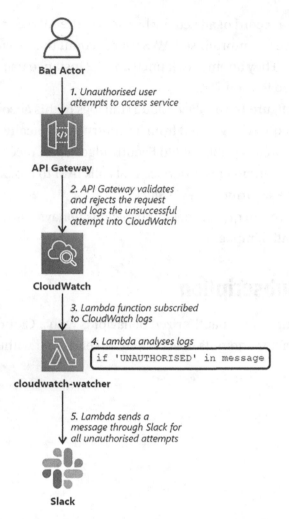

Figure 8-18. *CloudWatch subscription architecture example*

API Gateway validates the user request but rejects them. The request details are logged into CloudWatch with the rejection status. CloudWatch triggers a microservice with the log details. Recognizing a failed authorization attempt, the microservice logs the event with Slack. Alternatively, and to avoid reporting simple login mistakes, it could track the number of attempts within a short amount of time and only log it to Slack if it hits a certain threshold, indicating it may be a brute-force attack.

Note that Web Application Firewall can be used to automatically block IP addresses attempting a brute-force attack.

⚙ Logging Best Practices

There are many possible reasons an application could fail, such as unexpected customer behavior, device incompatibility, resource shortage, or invalid input from the user. This is why error handling is such a vital part of applications.

Centralized Logging

A best practice for logging is to have a centralized logging account for the organization, where logs from CloudWatch, CloudTrail, and other sources, and from all of the AWS accounts, can be stored.

By consolidating all the logs, they can be more easily managed, and restrictions can be put in place to ensure only authorized people can access, modify, or delete logs. For example, we can allow developers to view the logs for their respective projects but not change or delete the logs. This helps ensure log integrity and auditability.

We can also have a centralized approach to backups and log retention, reducing the administrative overhead of managing this across multiple accounts and reducing the chance of unnecessary logs piling up and causing excessive storage costs.

Error Messages

When informing an end user about an error, we should limit the amount of information shared and ideally provide actionable steps for anything they can do to get past the error, even if the advice is only to *wait and try again a bit later*.

If it is an issue with the application, we can inform the user that a developer has been notified to give them the assurance that the issue will be swiftly addressed. In Figure 8-19, a Lambda microservice is experiencing throttling due to concurrency limits being hit. This will cause some user requests to fail, but it is an error that typically resolves itself if the user tries again after a few seconds.

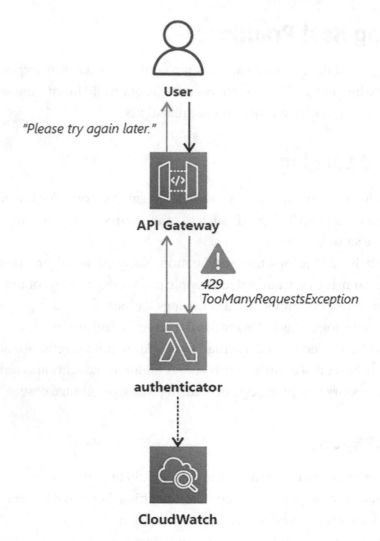

Figure 8-19. *Error reporting best practices*

Instead of showing the HTTP response code that API Gateway returns, which could confuse the user with unnecessary information, we create a generalized message asking them to try again later.

For this type of temporary issue, there is also an opportunity for the client application to try and handle it. For example, a waiting animation and message could be displayed to the user, and the client could automatically retry a few seconds later for two or three attempts before asking the user to try again at a later time.

Another example in Figure 8-20 is a user who entered the incorrect username when attempting to log into the system.

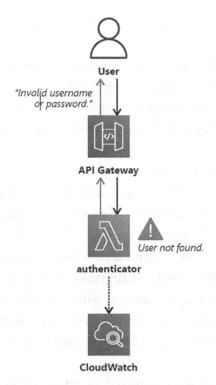

Figure 8-20. *Error reporting security considerations*

Instead of returning a *user not found* error message, it is best practice to instead return a less specific error. In our case, we inform the user that the username and password combination is incorrect. This is a better message because knowing if a user exists or not can help a malicious actor brute-force a confirmed user account with a dictionary list of passwords.

Keep in mind that it is best practice to put a Web Application Firewall (WAF) in front of any public API Gateways and configure it to block brute-force attacks.

Sensitive Data in Logs

Sometimes logs may contain sensitive user data or configuration details that could be exploited. Ideally, we should avoid putting sensitive data into logs, as often, at least read access to logs needs to be provided to application teams to aid in troubleshooting.

It is crucial to always ensure that logs are well protected. When storing logs, they should be encrypted. This is done automatically in CloudWatch. By default, it uses an

AWS-managed encryption key, but this can be configured to use a customer-managed key instead.

When using a different storage service or exporting logs to a service such as S3, it is important to ensure that encryption at rest is enabled in the target service. For exporting, we should also confirm that encryption in transit, such as TLS, is configured for any integration points. Where that is not possible, client-side encryption should be considered.

Keep in mind that putting personal data into logs will complicate meeting privacy regulations such as GDPR and PDPA. Logs containing personal data will need additional auditing and security measures to ensure compliance, which may hamper troubleshooting more than tokenization would.

If it is unavoidable to include sensitive attributes in logs for troubleshooting an application, we can anonymize the data using tokenization so that the logs don't expose the sensitive data. In some cases, the tokenized data may be sufficient to troubleshoot. In other cases, limited access can be provided to the tokenization map. A map tracks which original data was replaced with which token and can be used to restore the original data for authorized users.

By tokenising data, we replace sensitive data in logs with randomly generated values. The token by itself does not give any clue as to what the original data was, nor can it be decoded to identify the original value.

If we always replace the same value with the same token, any relationships that might exist between logs will be maintained. This is especially useful when we want to perform analysis on the logs, such as understanding user patterns or when we want to trace activities leading up to an event but do not necessarily need to know the user's identity.

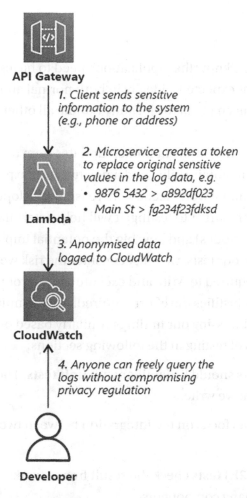

API Gateway

1. Client sends sensitive information to the system (e.g., phone or address)

2. Microservice creates a token to replace original sensitive values in the log data, e.g.
- *9876 5432 > a892df023*
- *Main St > fg234f23fdksd*

Lambda

3. Anonymised data logged to CloudWatch

CloudWatch

4. Anyone can freely query the logs without compromising privacy regulation

Developer

Figure 8-21. *Tokenizing sensitive data in logs*

In Figure 8-21, we log an issue with a customer request that includes sensitive information, such as their phone number or address.

Before the microservice logs the error, it generates a token to replace the original sensitive values in the data.

Application team members can freely review the logs to troubleshoot issues without compromising privacy compliance. If there is a need for authorized individuals to access the original data, then the tokenizer can create and securely store a map of the tokens to the original data.

Testing

Most developers intuitively know that applications need to be tested. Testing ensures that the system behaves as expected – ideally in both normal and edge use cases – and that there is a *catch* mechanism to elegantly handle all other situations that were not tested.

Automated testing can help prevent broken updates from deploying. This contributes to long-term maintainability and a positive user experience. The automation reduces the amount of manual work needed, increasing developer productivity.

Risk assessment is a precursor to testing; it will help determine what could go wrong (also called failure modes) and how big the potential impact will be if the failure happens. When we create our tests, we must consider the risk we want to mitigate and estimate the effort required to write and execute the appropriate test. We can then determine if the risk justifies the effort required. After running our test cases, it is important to prioritize addressing our findings similarly based on criticality and effort.

I will cover four types of testing in the following sections:

1. Most developers should be familiar with **unit tests**. These focus on the code that we write.

2. **Integration tests** focus on the integration between two or more components.

3. **End-to-end (E2E) tests** check the result from a workflow consisting of many components.

4. Less common, **contract tests** are similar to integration tests but focus more on the messages passed between the components in a given integration.

Testing Challenges in Serverless

Testing can be challenging for any architecture. Compared with monoliths, Serverless microservices are both easier and harder to test. Easier in that independent microservices have a narrow scope and clearly defined input and expected output. Harder in that the architecture style typically integrates many fully managed cloud services operated by the provider and outside our direct control. Serverless also frequently uses asynchronous and parallel processing in workflows, which are hard to test because we need a test to start the workflow and one or more separate but linked tests that validate the different exit points and outputs of the workflow.

Testing Environments

Understanding *where* we test is important to understanding some of the challenges. Figure 8-22 shows there are generally three environments where we test.

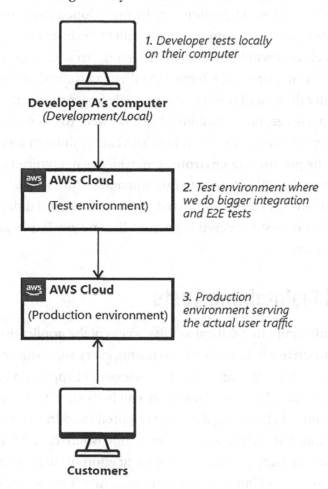

Figure 8-22. The environments we test in

Testing starts in the **local development environment**. The more that can be done here, the faster the developer can get feedback from tests because the time needed for deployment and network latency can be avoided. With Serverless architecture, which has a high dependency on cloud services, it is important to use tooling and service emulators to help achieve as much testing as possible in the local development environment.

Next are the **cloud development and testing environments**, also called *non-prod environments*. To test here, we need the infrastructure to be provisioned and code to be deployed to the cloud. Some tests can be automated in a sufficiently capable deployment pipeline. For example, unit tests can be run in a build service such as CodeBuild. We can perform integration and end-to-end testing in these environments using custom Lambdas microservices and Step Functions on the provisioned cloud services.

For effective testing, this environment should reflect the intended production environment as closely as possible, at least while testing. An advantage of Serverless architecture is that it is far more cost-effective to mirror a production environment, as we don't need to consider the cost of running the typically larger production servers. Billing is also based on actual usage, not availability, but if we want to use temporary testing environments, deploying one is fully automated and can be done in seconds.

Lastly, we have the **production environment**, which is not typically a place where we want to do much testing. We do need to monitor and ensure we pick up on any errors as quickly as possible so they can be addressed. I also recommend doing automated spot tests in production just to ensure everything is running and any issues are caught well before users notice them.

Creating and Maintaining Tests

This is time-consuming but often critical to the success of the application. When writing unit tests, we need to strike a balance between testing every single line of code and pragmatic use of available project time. The risk assessment approach I mentioned earlier, which we will look at in more detail soon, can help identify the test cases that pose a more significant risk, justifying the effort required to address them.

Tests require as much attention as application code when there are updates to the application, considerably adding to the development effort of such updates. We need to schedule time to assess and implement new tests as new features are introduced and additional edge cases are uncovered. The more tests we add, the more confidence can be gained that the system will be stable. However, more tests significantly increase development time for the initial creation and documentation and future application updates.

We need to plan carefully and strike a balance between the different test types. Determining what type of test will be most effective for a given risk will help us minimize unnecessary overlap. Integration and end-to-end tests are harder to write and automate but more reflective of actual user behavior.

Single-purpose microservices will make writing and maintaining tests easier as they are small in scope, but this is not always pragmatic. Sometimes it might be overengineering a problem, and creating a single *CRUD* Lambda instead of four single-purpose Lambdas will be a better use of project time. We should still be careful to avoid developing mini-monoliths.

Local Testing

The biggest challenge when testing Serverless applications is that it is difficult or even impossible to do full testing locally. Projects will always need an amount of testing after resources and code have been deployed to the cloud. This is largely due to the dependency on fully managed cloud services. While many of them can have emulated events locally, not all of them support this. Emulations are also not the same as testing with the actual service. Such emulators might not support some edge cases or be missing recent capabilities of the service and have different event messages or error responses as a result.

Some options to consider for emulation include

- AWS SAM, a Serverless development tool provided by AWS, which can mock many different events to trigger and test Lambda microservices locally

- aws-sdk-mock on GitHub, a JavaScript and TypeScript library

- LocalStack, local container-based emulation of AWS services

- Moto, a tool for emulation of AWS services in Python

Besides emulation challenges, the time needed to deploy resources, as well as network latency in the cloud, can add considerable time to testing, decreasing developer productivity. Ideally, all tests should run in a deployment pipeline, allowing developers to remain productive while the deployment and tests execute automatically.

Integrated Managed Services

Another challenge lies in the architecture we use, especially those areas related to integrations with fully managed services. We hope the service documentation covers the different possible responses, including any edge cases and error messages. However, some research is often needed to look for undocumented cases that others have come across. Alternatively, we can do a proof of concept (POC) and try to uncover different scenarios.

Fine-grained permissions are one of the best security benefits of Serverless architecture, but from a testing perspective, they are a major challenge. For example, Lambda's running integration tests on multiple components will need access permissions for all of the involved components. Not only is this a challenge to configure, but such broad access can also pose a security risk. Strategies such as only enabling the permissions during test runs and finding ways to limit the access to a particular context or condition need to be designed and implemented to manage this risk.

Another challenge related to managed services is that there is little consistency between the different services in AWS. Schemas not only contain different values but can even be structured in radically different ways. Services have different hard and soft limits, throttle, capacity or resource configurations, and relevant metrics. All of this means that each integration test usually needs to be unique and custom-created specifically for each integration.

Additionally, for end-to-end tests, a request could enter at different points in a complex workflow, and decision trees with parallel paths can mean multiple variants of an end-to-end test need to be created.

Debugging Failed Tests

Our next challenge is finding out where a test is failing. It's important to keep this in mind when designing tests. If they are too broad, like end-to-end tests, we will need to look through many logs to find the issue. On the other hand, fine-grained testing can be costly to develop and potentially take a long time to run.

Let's consider a relatively simple Serverless API where we perform an end-to-end test after a change is deployed. The test fails, and the output only indicates that there was an error. There are at least seven places where this could have gone wrong:

1. The API Gateway configuration, settings such as the path, parameters, method, validation, CORS, throttling, or authentication.

2. The API Gateway and Lambda integration with the Lambda reference, IAM permissions, and integration configuration.

3. The underlying Lambda configuration, timeout, memory, environment variables, or concurrency.

4. The Lambda code, perhaps the expected event structure, mapping, permissions, some error in the code, or insufficient error handling.

5. It could also be caused by integrations between Lambda and another service, such as S3 or DynamoDB. IAM permissions again, the format of the request, or service-specific errors.

6. The response path, starting with the integration from Lambda back to API Gateway, integration settings, or a missing or wrongly formatted response message.

7. There can always be changes outside of our control, service outages, or some recent changes made by the provider to any of the components, encryption, or supporting services

This complexity shows the importance of having multiple types of tests working together. End-to-end tests will tell us something is wrong in a given workflow, but they won't tell us in any detail *where* or *why* it went wrong. Cloud services typically don't return errors back through the chain of integrated components. For example, a Lambda code error will see API Gateway return the same error message as a service permissions error. Integration tests will take more effort to create for an entire workflow, but they will indicate where the issue is happening more precisely. Proactive logging can also help and may be more cost-effective than integration tests in supporting end-to-end tests. Automated alerts can be sent for errors that happen within a workflow, indicating the location, cause, and stack trace, for example.

Unit tests are intended for testing lines of code. As such, in a Serverless back end, they are really only relevant to the microservice code – a relatively small part of the overall solution, only one of the seven potential problem areas.

From the earlier example, it should be clear how critical *integration* tests are for Serverless architecture – three of the seven potential problem areas. Not only do they cover a more significant portion of a Serverless application but they are also more fine-grained, more precisely identifying the root cause of an issue.

What to Test

The final challenge I want to touch on is how we decide *what* to test when we deploy our code. Automated tests during development are typically triggered by pushing updates to the code repository, which kicks off a deployment pipeline with built-in automated tests.

For new deployments, it's simple; we just run all of the tests. When deploying changes to an existing application, it can be difficult for the pipeline to know what changed and what should be tested. If it was an infrastructure change, we need to run IaC tests on the templates and integration tests after deployment. For code updates, we only need to run unit tests. If the code change impacted any integrated components, then we would need to run integration tests too. If this component is part of a workflow, we might have to run end-to-end tests to ensure the workflow is still working as expected.

All that sounds complicated to configure and prone to error. So perhaps we do not need to care about what specifically changed and just run every test after every deployment to be safe. But running all tests on a large application can take time, which is bad for productivity.

For applications with larger teams, integration and end-to-end tests might fail because another team member has not yet completed a component on which the integration or workflow is dependent. In an automated deployment pipeline, a failed test due to a missing component would result in the deployment being rejected, blocking the component and leading to frustration and reduced productivity.

The multi-repo approach to Serverless that we covered earlier can help mitigate this. Each repo has its own deployment pipeline, and the tests only cover that deployment and its integrations. A separate repo contains integration tests between components from different team members and the end-to-end tests for entire workflows. These run less frequently and only after the individual repos have passed all their own tests.

Another possible solution is personal development environments. While not unique to Serverless, this is relatively easy and cost-effective with a fully Serverless solution, as we are billed only based on actual utilization. A private environment enables team members to run tests without interference or dependencies on other developers. In this case, the deployment pipeline should be configured to deploy each repo branch to its own unique environment.

 Types of Tests

Next, we will look at the different types of tests available and the differences between synchronous and asynchronous testing.

First, the general structure of a test. A common approach is to follow arrange-act-assert or similar variations. This approach works for unit, integration, and end-to-end tests, so it is quite versatile.

```
Documentation  def test_lambda_handler():
                   """
                   Test default Lambda handler with a mock Event
                   and assert response to be successful
                   """

Arrange            # Arrange: Create a mock API gateway event
                   gateway_event = {
                       "resource": "/{proxy+}",
                       "requestContext": {
                           "resourceId": "123456",
                           "apiId": "1234567890",
                           "stage": "prod"
                       },
                       "httpMethod": "POST",
                       ...
                   }

Act                # Act: Trigger Lambda to run
                   ret = app.lambda_handler(gateway_event, "")
                   data = json.loads(ret["body"])

Assert             # Assert: Check results
                   assert ret["statusCode"] == 200
                   assert "message" in ret["body"]
                   assert data["message"] == "hello world"
```

Figure 8-23. *Breakdown of a test*

Arrange is about getting everything ready to perform the test. This could be deploying cloud services or creating local mock events to emulate the services. Arrange also covers getting code ready to test and any input data needed.

Act is the execution of the code and, with it, the test.

Assess is where we confirm that the result meets expectations. Depending on the test, this could be a successful result or that an intended error is handled appropriately.

If we want to test a Lambda function, we start by preparing the code to run based on a mock SQS event triggered by SAM. We then execute the trigger. The function reacts to the mock SQS message, performs some processing on the data, and returns the transformed data. The testing framework confirms that the result matches the configured expectation. If it does, the test was a success, and it will continue to the next test. If it fails, feedback can be provided to the developer to resolve matters and try again.

Tests should be well-documented. Typically we would do this in-line as part of the test code, as seen at the top of Figure 8-23. We want to explain what we are testing, which services may be involved, if we need the actual service or can emulate it, and if we are looking for a valid result or an error being handled.

Unit Tests

Most developers should be familiar with unit tests, and there are many libraries, tools, and resources that support this type. This should help reduce any learning curve as well as development effort. Unit tests are fast, can be fully automated, and typically run locally for instant feedback without needing to deploy anything.

The following is an example of a simple synchronous unit test:

```
import lambda_src_path.index as handler
def test_lambda():
    """

    Validate add method
    """

    # Arrange
    num_1 = 1
    num_2 = 2
```

```
# Act
ans = handler.add(num_1, num_2)

# Assert
assert ans == 5
```

Unit tests can also be used to verify Infrastructure-as-Code templates before deployment. As with code tests, this will depend on the accurate assessments being created for the templates. It will not guarantee the validity of the template, but it may decrease the chance of common issues during the more time-consuming cloud deployment.

For comprehensive code coverage, many tests are needed, typically doubling the development effort. Additional effort will be needed if we need to develop and maintain mock responses for the tests. Given the reduced value of unit tests in a Serverless application, it may be difficult to justify this.

With Serverless, microservices interact with many external cloud services, such as DynamoDB. While unit tests focus on the code and not directly on interaction with other services, the code, and test, may fail if those services are unreachable when testing locally. One way to overcome this challenge is to mock or fake the service response locally.

Common microservice languages have third-party libraries or tools to achieve this. Such solutions intercept calls to external services and return a hardcoded response instead. This way, the code does not need to be changed, and it will not fail when it can't reach the actual service. This approach requires regular maintenance to update the third-party solution and our hardcoded response whenever changes are made to the cloud service.

Integration Tests

Integration tests look at how two or more services interact with one another to ensure that they are doing so correctly and with the expected requests and responses. A high-level example between Lambda and DynamoDB is shown in Figure 0-24.

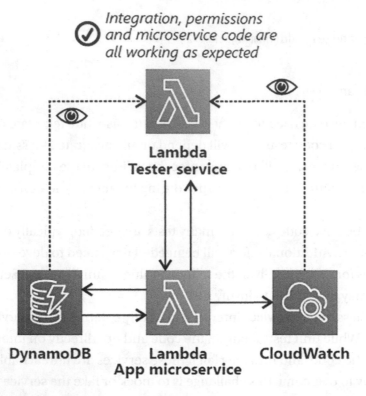

Figure 8-24. *Integration testing architecture*

To conduct the test, we create a tester service that interacts with the components within the application. First, our tester service will invoke the Lambda microservice. The microservice will store a record in the integrated DynamoDB service. The response from DynamoDB is logged to CloudWatch. This response also determines the response of the microservice.

Our tester can assess the microservice response to determine if the test passed or failed. A successful result will mean that the integration, permissions, and microservice code are all working as expected.

Optionally, a more advanced tester could also verify the record in DynamoDB or even check CloudWatch logs for the DynamoDB response the microservice received.

Integration tests are critical to Serverless architecture, given how much of the architecture relies on integrations with a variety of cloud services.

Besides testing for errors, integration tests can also test for performance, latency, and bottlenecks to help prioritize optimization efforts.

Though harder to do, integration tests can be automated. To do so, supporting microservices should be developed, and additional services such as X-Ray or Synthetics need to be configured and added to the architecture. Doing this for each project can be considerable work, so I recommend establishing a shared testing framework attached to the deployment pipeline. Individual projects can create integration tests that are executed by the framework. Often, these tests will be reusable for the same integrations in other projects, so sharing them internally can greatly improve productivity.

It is possible to run integration tests locally using mocks. However, the value of this is usually questionable, and it should be considered a high-level validation at most. Generally, integration tests have to run on deployed cloud infrastructure to ensure the integrations are being tested with factual and up-to-date responses and error messages from the live services.

Besides the time needed to deploy infrastructure and code changes, integration tests will have latency from service runtimes, network speeds, trigger delays, and other factors that can add to the total execution time needed to run them.

Lastly, as these tests are running on deployed cloud infrastructure with Serverless architecture, each run will incur a cost for each service that is utilized as a part of the test.

End-to-End Tests

End-to-end tests are high-level assessments of an entire workflow. These tests simulate actual user behavior more closely than other types, and they offer the convenience of covering an entire workflow with just one test.

An end-to-end test kicks off a workflow, such as sending a request to an API Gateway endpoint, and then waits for the response from API Gateway. The test does not monitor the components within the workflow, only that an expected response is eventually provided – which could be assumed to mean that the components are doing what they are supposed to.

Any errors that happen in the workflow – which can include a variety of errors in any of the components – will typically result in the same standard error message returning from API Gateway. For example, the error *"internal server error"* would be returned for a wide range of issues happening in the Lambda microservice or any of its integrations. While it tells us that the workflow is broken, it does not tell us where. This is why end-to-end tests must be combined with component tests or proactive logging to make it easier to find and troubleshoot any issues causing the end-to-end test to fail.

In Figure 8-25, we have a requirement that the workflow should not exceed a given runtime. This type of requirement must be tested in the cloud because network and cloud service latency will be key factors.

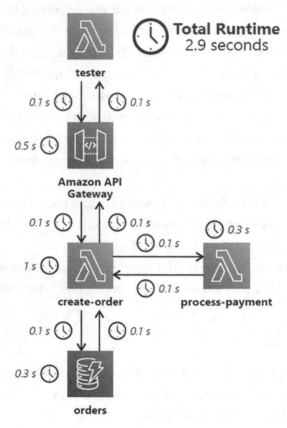

Figure 8-25. *Timing with one end-to-end test vs. multiple integration tests*

We can run a single end-to-end test that will return the total runtime of the workflow, or we can implement individual integration tests between each component to provide a detailed breakdown of all the timings. The latter provides more detail, but the effort would be considerable. Conversely, the end-to-end test will tell us if we exceed the total runtime requirement, but it will not tell us *where* the bottlenecks are.

Sometimes, it might be more cost-effective for tests to be augmented with proactive logging instead of adding more fine-grained tests. In the Figure 8-25 example, we can include a profiling service such as X-Ray or even simple time logs from our microservices. Running the end-to-end test will cause logs to be created that we can review to find the bottleneck if the total time exceeds the target.

User Simulation

I mentioned that end-to-end tests more closely emulate actual user behavior, and this can even extend into the user interfaces. Tools such as Appium, Selenium, and Katalon can start end-to-end tests in a browser or mobile application. These tools mimic human behavior to automate the interaction in visual interfaces, such as clicking buttons and filling out forms. After the interaction, the tools can assess the content displayed on the result page to complete the test.

For example, if we have a service that extracts text from uploaded images, we can test it by using the tool to simulate a user uploading an image via the UI. After the UI processes the upload, the tool will check the result page to validate that the correct text was extracted from the image. This being an end-to-end test, it provides input and waits for a result. It will tell us very little about the actions in the workflow of components between those two events.

As we are testing the entire workflow, this needs to be deployed in its entirety, including any dependencies. Like integration tests, we are billed for all components that are utilized in the course of running the test. For accurate results, it is recommended that the test environment replicates the production environment as closely as possible, including full data sets or at least realistic fake data.

Lastly, for complex workflows with decision trees and parallel processing, we will need multiple variations of the test to ensure all possible paths are covered, including any edge cases.

Contract Testing

Components, such as a microservice or an API, are created by a developer to help a consumer fulfil its task. Typically, a consumer is another component – which could have been created by a different developer. Each component provides a particular function, such as authentication or data processing, as part of a larger workflow.

When a developer updates a particular component, we need to test it to ensure that the change does not break any integrated consumers. For a test to pass, all dependent components must be available and updated to handle the new changes. Commonly, integration and end-to-end tests are used to test each integration after an update, but this requires a lot of coordination between the different developers. They must update all relevant components and deploy them before the tests can be completed.

In a given Serverless application, there can be many integrations to test. For example, if we have ten connected components, there could be up to 45 integrations that need to be tested. For each of those, communication could be one or two-way. Realistically, for event-driven microservices, the number of integrations will be lower since each microservice is likely to interact with only one or two microservices in a one-way communication. Nevertheless, coordination between developers is still required to ensure compatibility between the components and a successful end-to-end workflow.

Contract testing addresses these challenges by using a broker and a contract to test the integration points, as shown in Figure 8-26.

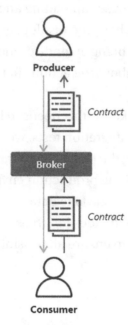

Figure 8-26. *Contract testing with a broker*

A contract defines the structure of an expected request and response for a given component. This can include parameters, transport protocol, and body. Once defined, the contract is sent to the broker for validation and storage. Instead of components messaging each other, they will message the broker, which validates the request and responds with the expected response.

In many ways, contract testing is similar to integration testing. However, the broker helps us avoid dependencies on target components by responding instead. Each component is, in effect, isolated from the workflow, and we can avoid components that don't need testing, such as fully managed services and components that are not yet ready to test.

Contract testing avoids developers waiting for each other or having to match their deployment schedule. The contract can be agreed on beforehand and requests and responses tested through a broker instead of the actual components.

Pact

One way to do contract testing is with an open source tool called Pact. Pact helps provision the broker and database. Pact also provides code libraries that can be used to interact with the broker and run tests. It supports various programming languages, including JavaScript, Python, and Java.

For enterprises, Pactflow is a commercial version that provides advanced features such as Single Sign-On, user management, an advanced interface, and a service for managing application secrets.

Pact is not a functional testing framework; it is not intended to test the quality or ability of written code. It verifies the requests and responses between components. The workflow in Figure 8-27 visualizes how contract testing with Pact works in practice.

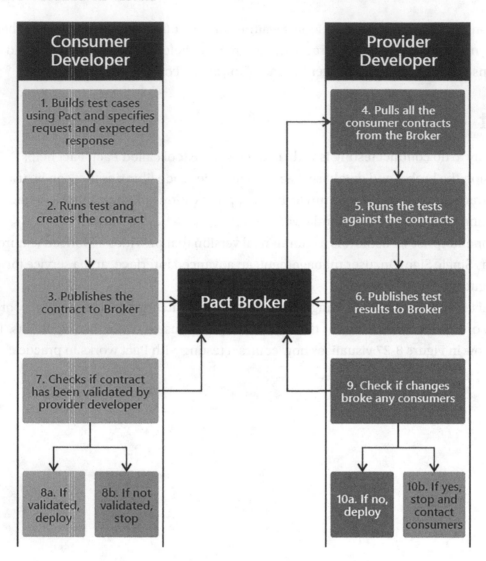

Figure 8-27. *Contract testing workflow with Pact*

On the left of Figure 8-27, we have our consumer components. The developer of these components creates test cases using the Pact library. Once the tests are created, the developer generates the contract and publishes it to the Pact broker. This is repeated for all of the consumers of a particular service.

The service developer can pull all the contracts published by all consumers from the broker. The developer can test against these contracts to ensure that a new update will not break any existing integration. The new update can be deployed to production if there are no issues. Once testing is completed, the results are published back to the broker.

Each consumer's developer can similarly check with the broker if there are broken integrations with any providers before deploying a change.

Comparing the Types of Testing

The difference between **unit** and **contract** tests is that the former tests pieces of code and functions within a microservice. Mocks used in unit tests help us avoid cloud deployment and keep the tests local. Contract tests don't test code but will indirectly verify the microservice via the request and response messages. If there is a bug in the code, the response is unlikely to match the contract.

The difference between **integration** and **contract** testing is that the former needs to run on deployed infrastructure and all components in an integration need to be available to complete the test. Contract testing performs multiple tests against the different integration points in our application. We can decide which components to include in the test and which will be mocked.

Contract Testing with Pact for Serverless

I should point out that contract testing using Pact was not necessarily designed for Serverless architecture but for container-based microservices. With container architecture, it's not uncommon for two microservices to talk directly to each other, but that is an anti-pattern in Serverless, where we should always include a decoupler such as SQS or SNS between them.

To add, Serverless architecture minimizes custom code, preferring fully managed cloud services where possible. Strict contract testing requires testing both sides, but there's little value in writing contract tests for managed services that we can't change.

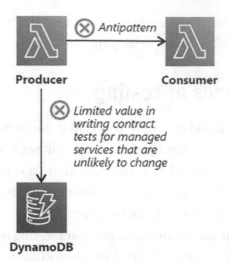

Figure 8-28. *Contract testing Serverless architecture*

Contract testing can add value to Serverless architecture with a few changes to how we implement it. Microservices will have a managed decoupler between them, and there is little value in testing such a managed service.

For example, in Figure 8-29, instead of writing contract tests between component A and SQS, our tests should focus on the data that is indirectly being exchanged between the two components.

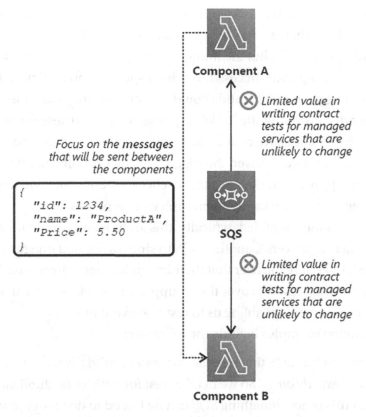

Figure 8-29. *Contract testing the data exchanged between components*

Here, a contract is formed that states that component B requires the ID, name, and price fields to be included in the request. The underlying messaging technology could be implemented using SQS, EventBridge, or anything else. While the contract will not test the specific technology, it will need to factor in any changes the technology makes to the message structure.

Asynchronous Testing

As we saw in the previous examples, with synchronous testing, we submit our test input and await a response. Writing tests for this is relatively straightforward, but Serverless often makes considerable use of asynchronous requests. With these requests, the first response only indicates that a request was received. The actual result is sent back via a different channel – if at all.

An event-driven architecture is a common example. We can use the earlier example of triggering a Lambda when a new file is added to an S3 bucket. A synchronous end-to-end test could upload a file, but the immediate response from S3 only indicates that the upload was completed successfully. The response won't tell us if the Lambda microservice was triggered or if Lambda could process the image because these events happened asynchronously after the initial response. To assess these events, we need additional tests. For example, we could add a test to verify the processed image. This would indicate that Lambda received the trigger and successfully handled the task. A more fine-grained approach might see a test to check for an invocation log and a test that simulates the trigger to get the Lambda microservice response.

This example is quite simplified; typically, this architecture would include SQS to store the incoming image events, another SQS to store processed image events, and WebSockets or SES to notify the user that their image has been processed. We can expand on the preceding tests to cover these supporting services. Note that SES can be configured to receive emails, enabling us to test that event too.

Other challenging examples include the following:

- Services such as SQS that have an "*at least once*" delivery guarantee and not "*exactly once.*" So we need to test for accidental duplicates, though this is not something SQS can be forced to do on demand.

- Some services, such as SQS, have a dead letter queue (DLQ), which stores failed events after a few attempts were made to process them. Here, we need to test multiple failures, the DLQ failover event, and sometimes follow-up actions to the DLQ event, such as alerts.

- With batch jobs, partial processing of the batch should be tested. Are the successful items duplicated on the next run, or are the failed items lost, for example?

- Testing Lambda concurrency limits with too many parallel requests can be difficult to achieve, at least without significantly reducing the limits.

- Step Functions is challenging to test with its capabilities for mixing sequential and parallel paths and splitting and merging data for the latter. Often we need to have several tests to validate each of the possible outcomes of a workflow.

Figure 8-30 has an architecture for the earlier asynchronous testing example.

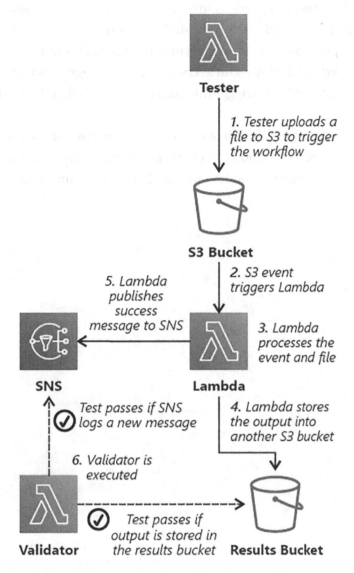

Figure 8-30. Asynchronous testing architecture

A file is uploaded to S3, which triggers a Lambda to process it. After processing, it stores the result in a second S3 bucket. The Lambda then publishes a success message to SNS. In a real solution, this SNS topic might trigger the next step in a workflow. Here, it only notifies the test validator microservice.

Given what we have covered so far, it should be clear that unit tests will not be very helpful with this async example. A mix of end-to-end and integration tests will be needed. We use an end-to-end test to kick off the upload process; this could be done with a Lambda, as per our example, or via a user interface. This test will only assess that the file was uploaded successfully. Our second test is an integration test sitting in the validator microservice. SNS will trigger this, and it can assess that the file is indeed in the results bucket.

To automate this process in a deployment pipeline, we would use Step Functions , as shown in Figure 8-31. Step Functions can launch the end-to-end test and then wait for the validator to indicate that the test is completed. If it fails or times out, the deployment will be rejected.

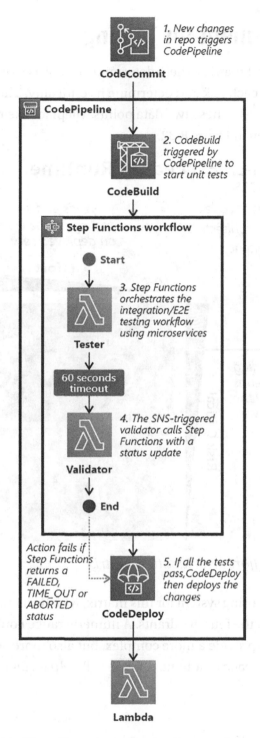

Figure 8-31. *Using Step Functions to orchestrate asynchronous testing*

Risk Assessment for Testing

We can use a risk vs. effort matrix to help determine if a risk is worth testing and how to best proceed. We assess each risk and determine its criticality. Then we determine the effort needed to test the risk. These two data points will place the risk somewhere in the two-by-two matrix shown in Figure 8-32.

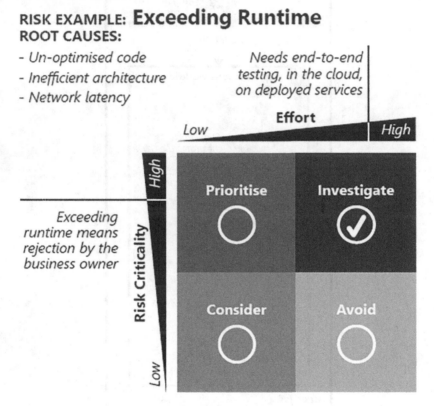

Figure 8-32. *Risk vs. effort prioritization matrix*

We use a low-high scoring system for this matrix, which will provide a simple result, placing the risk in one of the four quadrants. A numeric range could also be used, such as one to ten: this would provide a more complex, but also more accurate, result across a range of positions within each quadrant. A range will help further prioritize items within a given category.

To decide the criticality of a risk, we first need to understand it.

- What could go wrong? What is the issue we want to test for?

- What could be the potential root cause? Keep in mind that visible issues are often symptoms of an underlying cause.

- What impact, financial or otherwise, could this risk have on our business, application, or users?

To determine the effort, we focus on the test itself.

- How will we test this? A unit test or a more complex end-to-end test, for example?

- Can this test be run locally, or do we need to first deploy the application to the cloud? If so, then we must consider the associated costs of running the test on billable infrastructure.

- Can the test be automated, and where in the pipeline would this test sit? What tooling, custom microservices, or cloud services will we need to run the test?

With the criticality rating and effort estimate, it's fairly straightforward to determine the risk's position in the matrix. In the example noted in Figure 8-32, the risk lands in the *Investigate* quadrant because we should ensure that the criticality justifies the effort before committing resources to address it.

Risks in the *Prioritize* quadrant, with its low-effort-high-criticality rating, should be prioritized and implemented first.

Those in the *Consider* quadrant would likely be placed in a *phase 2* list. They are low effort but also low criticality, so they are not an immediate concern.

It is usually not justified to address the high-effort-low-criticality risks. Comprehensive error handling and proactive logging are likely a more practical way to address them and prevent issues.

Test Pyramid vs. Test Honeycomb

In monolithic architecture, developers tend to favor a framework called the Test **Pyramid**, shown in Figure 8-33. The pyramid shape indicates the ratio in terms of the importance and quantity of each type of test in a typical application.

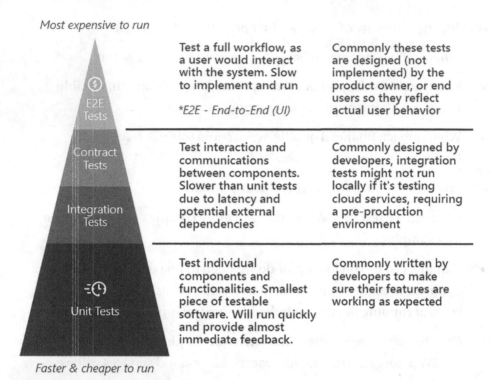

Figure 8-33. *Test Pyramid testing strategy*

As we move up the pyramid, the cost and effort required to create and maintain the tests increase, so the quantity decreases. At the bottom and largest part of the pyramid are the unit tests, followed by integration and contract tests and, lastly, end-to-end tests at the top.

The pyramid strongly emphasizes the relatively lower-cost unit tests at the bottom.

While this balance has been proven effective for monolithic applications, for the far more distributed nature of Serverless architecture, having a lot of unit tests does not provide sufficient coverage to confidently state that the application will work as expected.

With Serverless, developers need to shift and focus more on integration tests. Instead of a pyramid, we have the **Honeycomb** framework shown in Figure 8-34 that places the necessary emphasis on integration tests instead of unit tests.

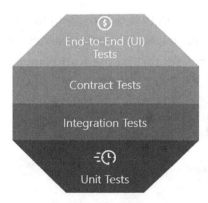

Loss of speed during testing but the increased speed of development and ease of maintenance can make up for it

Verify the correctness of the individual components as well as the interaction between them

Figure 8-34. *Honeycomb testing strategy*

Since many services and microservices interact with one another in Serverless architecture, we need to ensure that these interactions are working as intended. End-to-end tests are similarly important in ensuring that workflows work as intended. However, given the lack of detail, they will still be secondary in quantity to integration tests. While contract tests are not specifically mentioned in this framework, I would combine them with integration tests, picking the appropriate type based on a given situation.

⚙ Deployment Pipeline

The following is a basic Serverless deployment pipeline architecture using cloud-native AWS services. While different organizations will have their own approach to such pipelines, at least conceptually, they will all have similar components.

Figure 8-35 visually shows where different types of tests can be executed. Let's walk through it and see where we can achieve some automation. Starting at the top, we have our local development environment, where we can run unit tests and integration tests for services we can run or emulate locally.

Code that completes local testing is deployed to the repo.

Here we can run code quality and analysis tools such as CodeGuru, which can detect bugs, inefficiencies, and other insights.

The deployment pipeline is then triggered, kicking off a build service that, similar to our local environment, can run automated unit tests and integration tests for services that can be emulated. However, a build service runs in the cloud, so it can perform tests with cloud services that are generally available, such as Rekognition, and cloud services that are already provisioned in the environment.

Once these tests are concluded successfully, infrastructure deployment follows. Built-in checks in the CloudFormation service provide a final automated review of the infrastructure configuration before the cloud services are provisioned, and our code is deployed.

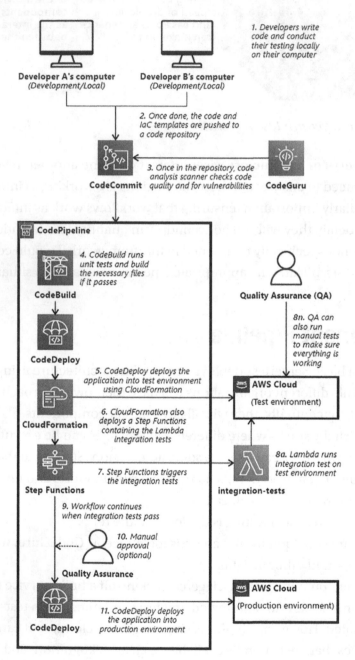

Figure 8-35. *Architecture example of a cloud-native deployment pipeline*

At this stage, we can insert integration testing capabilities. In this architecture, we are using Step Functions and Lambda microservices to perform custom integration tests between the provisioned cloud resources and our microservices. This can be fully automated if we can codify the tests with the deployment to be executed by a shared testing framework that is part of the pipeline.

Once our integration tests pass, we have a fully tested solution in our dev-test environment. Manual approvals, user testing, and quality reviews could be done at this point before the changes are promoted to the production environment as the final step.

A test failure in any of these steps will see the process halted and feedback returned to the developer so they can resolve the issue and attempt the deployment again.

AWS Testing Services

AWS has several tools and services that can help test Serverless architecture.

Serverless Application Model (SAM)

While SAM is intended as a full Infrastructure-as-Code solution for Serverless applications, its capability for testing microservices locally without needing to deploy anything likely sees more usage. SAM creates a container and hosts microservice code locally to emulate the Lambda service.

SAM then generates an event trigger using one of the many built-in mocked service event messages. For example, it can mock an S3 new file uploaded event or an SQS pull message. SAM will invoke local microservices using this trigger so we can test how the microservice responds to it.

SAM can also retrieve and display CloudWatch logs locally to help troubleshoot a deployed microservice.

For teams using AWS CDK, SAM is often already used for local testing. However, previous versions required some effort to set it up in a way that was nicely integrated with a CDK project. The latest version of SAM fully integrates with CDK out of the box, enabling developers to test CDK-defined microservices far easier.

LocalStack

LocalStack is not an AWS service or product, but it does emulate AWS services locally, greatly helping local testing efforts. For example, we can create a local S3 bucket that our microservices can execute API calls against, avoiding the need to deploy the services or wait for network latency during testing.

A challenge is that not all services and features are fully supported. We should also be mindful of recent changes to services that might not be reflected in the emulations yet. Still, being able to at least do preliminary testing locally can greatly boost developer productivity.

LocalStack supports CloudFormation and CDK, and we can use the same IaC templates to provision mocked services locally instead of in the cloud.

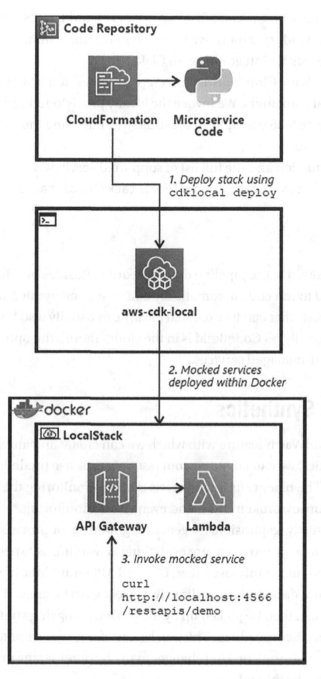

Figure 8-36. *LocalStack example architecture*

To use LocalStack with CDK, we first install Docker and LocalStack (in Docker). When the project is ready to deploy, we use the *aws-cdk-local* library – a wrapper provided by LocalStack for integrating with CDK.

This library reads the CloudFormation template generated by CDK to provision the services in local containers. We invoke the locally provisioned services, such as API Gateway in the Figure 8-36 example, in the usual way but using the container hostname instead of an AWS one.

For more information and the full list of supported services, visit the LocalStack GitHub page here: `https://github.com/localstack/localstack`.

CodeBuild

I mentioned CodeBuild in the pipeline example earlier. Besides building code, we can also use CodeBuild to test code automatically and ensure everything works before deployment. Any tests that can be executed locally can usually also be executed in CodeBuild. Additionally, as CodeBuild is in the cloud, there's the option to test against deployed and cloud-managed services.

CloudWatch Synthetics

Synthetics is a CloudWatch feature with which we can create and automate end-to-end tests. With Synthetics, we can create custom test scripts or use predefined blueprints provided by AWS. The blueprints include tests such as monitoring the availability of a service, error responses, broken URLs, and even visual monitoring.

Though not directly responsible for generating, storing, or processing logs, it can trigger events within a system to ensure everything is working as expected. Such triggers can be scheduled to run on microservices, UIs, and API endpoints. It emulates user requests, can capture data, and can indirectly cause logs to be created.

These outputs can then be picked up by the proactive logging strategy to report any errors before a user discovers them. This can be a useful way to monitor a production environment and catch any breaking changes made by other teams or the cloud provider that might otherwise be missed.

Synthetics can run on demand, in response to an event in an environment, or on a fixed schedule. Several useful metrics are provided, such as the number of failures and latency. Alerts can be configured to notify of any insights or issues via SNS or a CloudWatch event, which can, in turn, trigger a Lambda for a proactive response.

Another useful capability of Synthetics is its ability to conduct tests on services that are behind a private endpoint without having to expose them to the Internet.

Figure 8-37 provides an example of using Synthetics that can be considered for production environments.

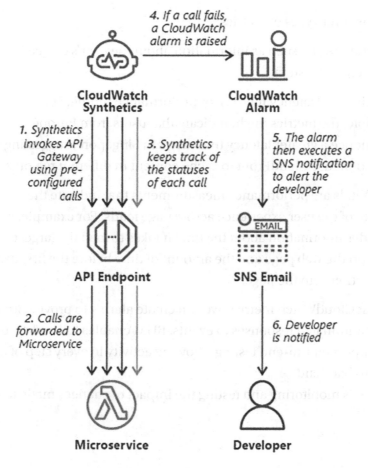

Figure 8-37. *Synthetics architecture example*

In Figure 8-37, Synthetics is configured to test an API Gateway endpoint using a mix of valid and invalid calls to assess different scenarios. The valid calls that make it past API Gateway are forwarded to the microservice. When a test fails, Synthetics can trigger an SNS notification to inform the developer.

CloudWatch Real User Monitoring (RUM)

With RUM, developers can insert code into web front ends to collect metrics from user interactions. It can also be used for monitoring front-end metrics, performance, and user experience.

RUM collects three types of metrics:

1. General metrics such as information about the user's device, browser, and system.

2. Location and latency metrics for performance tuning. For example, the metrics might indicate that users from Europe experience a greater latency than users in Singapore, suggesting we should use CloudFront to cache content in different regions.

3. Web Vitals are performance measurements that indicate the quality of the user experience across page loads. For example, it provides information about the time it takes to load the largest asset on the web page and the amount of time before the first user interaction with the page.

As with most CloudWatch metrics, we can create alarms to provide immediate notifications or automated responses to events. RUM enables full end-to-end logging capability to support end-to-end testing, showing activity in every step of a request flow from front end to back end.

One use case is monitoring and testing the impact of changes made to front ends.

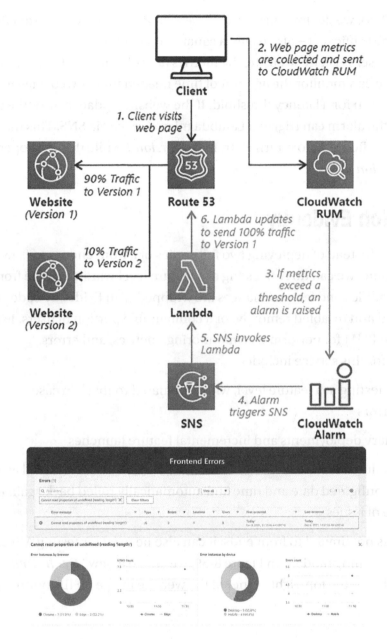

Figure 8-38. *Real User Monitoring (RUM) architecture example*

In Figure 8-38, we deploy a new website *version 2* and have configured Route 53 to send 10% of the traffic to it – also called a canary deployment.

When our users visit the website, the metrics are collected and sent to CloudWatch for analysis. We can monitor the amount of time needed for the web page to load and configure an alarm for a latency threshold. If the website update causes the threshold to be breached, the alarm can trigger a Lambda microservice via SNS. This microservice can then update Route 53 to return all traffic to *version 1* while the developer works on optimizing *version 2*.

CloudWatch Evidently

With Evidently, instead of deploying two full copies of a front end, as we saw in our previous example, we can do A-B testing at a feature level within a single front end.

New capabilities and feature changes are wrapped with Evidently code so that they can be enabled and disabled remotely for a configurable portion of users. Evidently integrates with RUM for performance monitoring, metrics, and errors.

Use cases for this service include

- A/B testing at a feature level, with automated rollback in case of errors

- Canary deployments and incremental feature launches

- Scheduled feature launches that can be automatically released at a preconfigured date and time and automatically rolled back again in case of issues

Evidently is not limited to front ends; it can also be used for testing API endpoints and machine learning models. In Figure 8-39, we create a new "*Get In Touch*" button on a website, visible in the top-right corner of the website image on the bottom right.

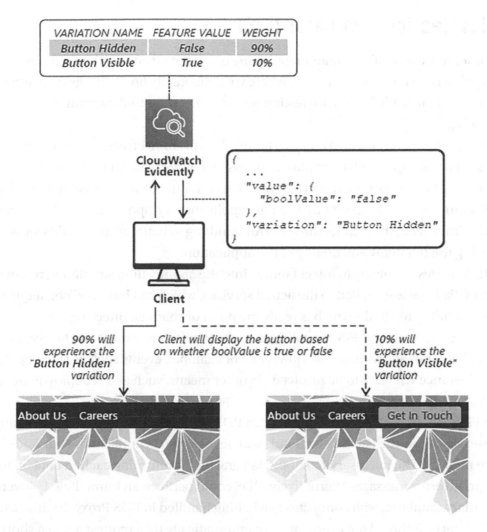

Figure 8-39. *Evidently A/B testing example*

We add the button as a new feature in Evidently, with two variations.

The first variation is "*Button Hidden*" (the new feature will not be displayed). We set the *weight* to 90%, which will result in 90% of the visitors experiencing this variation. The second variation is "*Button Visible*" with 10% weight, which, predictably, will result in the button being shown to 10% of the visitors in our A/B test.

When a new user arrives, the front-end script will check with Evidently if it wants to show the button to the user or not. Evidently processes the request and returns the decision in line with the defined weights. The front end then hides or shows the button based on the response. RUM will track the decision and the usual metrics that it supports.

Fault Injection Simulator (FIS)

FIS is a service that enables chaos engineering on deployed applications. Chaos engineering is an approach to testing where we deliberately break things to observe how the solution reacts. It's focused on testing traits such as redundancy, fault tolerance, and self-healing.

Tests include events such as service failure, loss of connectivity, and overwhelming requests. For example, will the application crash if connectivity fails to a third-party non-essential service such as analytics, or will it continue running since this loss does not affect the user's workflow? Based on the application's response to a fault, we can consider improving the architecture or error handling to better deal with this situation, improving the reliability and quality of the application.

FIS provides the ability to inject failures into the architecture, simulating real-world disasters. Failures are applied to the actual services, which can have real consequences if we are not fully prepared – which is really the point of chaos engineering.

If the test goes wrong, FIS can roll back to the previous working state *for certain events*. This is not always possible, however. For example, events such as shutting down an EC2 instance will have to be resolved via other means, such as a redeployment of the IaC.

In Figure 8-40, we use FIS to simulate an RDS service failure, used here by a Lambda microservice. How the Lambda responds will be recorded in application logs and service metrics. The microservice should fail gracefully, returning cached data or an appropriate error message. Alternatively, RDS could perform an immediate failover to a secondary database, with connection switching handled in RDS Proxy. In this case, the microservice should not even notice or automatically try a request again a short while later.

FIS is a relatively new service launched in December 2020. It does not support Serverless services at the time of this writing, but this is definitely a service worth keeping an eye on.

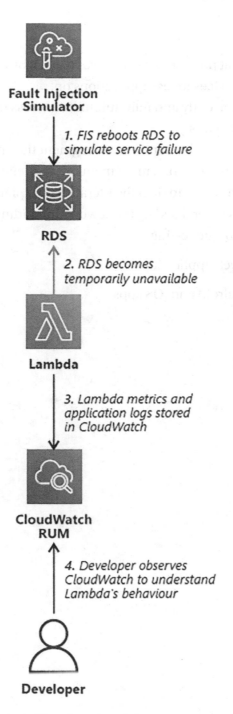

Figure 8-40. Fault Injection Simulator architecture example

Device Farm

This is a testing service that provides an extensive range of browsers and both virtual and remote physical mobile devices to test applications on.

Tests can be run concurrently and fully automated across multiple platforms and operating systems simultaneously.

The service can generate videos and logs to augment the application logs and help identify and troubleshoot issues. For a more manual experience or as part of debugging efforts, we can use remote access to directly interact with a platform via our browser.

Device Farm supports several testing frameworks, including a couple I mentioned when talking about end-to-end testing:

- Selenium, for web applications

- Appium, for Android and iOS apps

CHAPTER 9

Architecture

As an architect, you design for the present, with an awareness of the past for a future which is essentially unknown.

—Norman Foster, Architect (of Buildings)

⚙ Challenges and Mitigations

We covered several challenges in the introduction with some high-level mitigations. However, there are a few more challenges and many more mitigations that are quite technical. As such, I kept them for this chapter.

Vendor Lock-In

It is possible to make a cloud-agnostic solution that can run on different clouds, but to achieve this, it needs to be built for the lowest common denominator using only the services and features available across both cloud providers.

Infrastructure provisioning templates will need to be uniquely created for each cloud provider. However, the microservice code should be largely reusable with only minor changes in how the microservices communicate with the different cloud services.

Given the likely limitations on services and features, it will mean more custom work is needed, for example, the creation and management of containers as an alternative to managed services not available with either of the cloud providers.

Typically, a multi-cloud Serverless solution will be considerably less cost-effective than a single-cloud Serverless solution. A cost-benefit analysis should be done to compare Serverless with a container strategy that is a better fit for applications that need to be cloud-agnostic.

© Thomas Smart 2023
T. Smart, *Serverless Beyond the Buzzword*, https://doi.org/10.1007/978-1-4842-8761-3_9

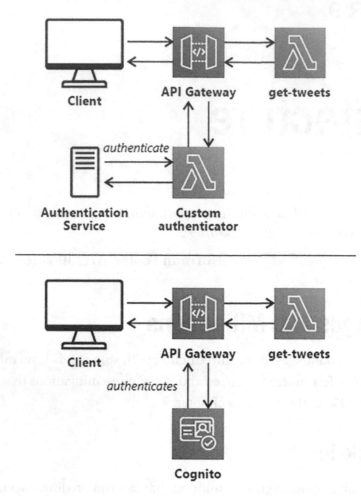

Figure 9-1. *Multi-cloud solutions may need to use self-managed components*

Figure 9-1 compares a third-party cloud-agnostic authentication solution running in a container against the fully managed but proprietary AWS Cognito service. In the former, the container (or server) will need to be maintained and patched. Scaling and redundancy need to be managed, as well as secure integration with the authentication service. All of that is built-in for a simple per-active-user fee with Cognito.

Cross-cloud is another approach to take. Here we are not seeking to make the entire solution run on different cloud providers but rather to accept that different providers have different strengths and weaknesses and design a solution accordingly. There are two strategies here:

1. The best of both worlds

2. Reduced capability failover

With the best of both worlds, we have the main solution running on one provider and specific services being utilized from another cloud provider. This might be because the services are better, more cost-effective, or unavailable from the main provider.

Keep in mind that multi-cloud requests will have additional latency, which is already a challenge in Serverless architecture, and data transfer costs can be high if there is a lot of traffic or large files being moved around.

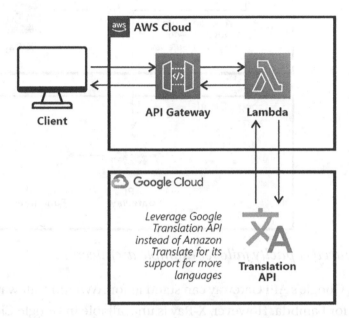

Figure 9-2. *Best of both worlds multi-cloud architecture example*

In Figure 9-2, we use the Google translation service in our Serverless AWS application. At the time of writing, the Google service works out slightly cheaper, and it supports a few more languages – either of those could be a reason to opt for this approach despite the latency challenge.

A reduced capability failover is a simplified version of an application running on a second cloud provider. This version provides a disaster recovery option in the event of the primary cloud provider suffering a complete service or region outage. While the reduced version might not have the full functionality, it still offers a functional fallback that may be preferable over a static maintenance page for certain critical applications.

The main point is that this achieves multi-cloud availability without compromising the architecture of the primary application. How *reduced* the failover is depends on the availability of compatible services with the second provider and the available development budget for what is essentially a second version of the application.

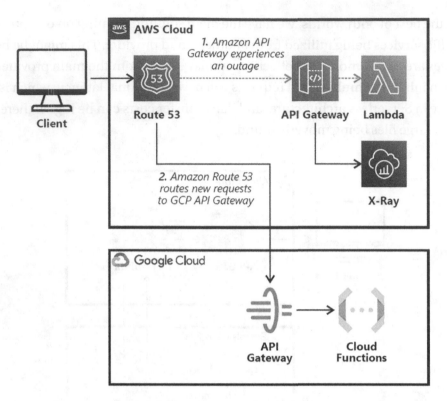

Figure 9-3. *Reduced capacity failover example architecture*

In Figure 9-3, Google's API Gateway can stand in for AWS API Gateway and Google's Cloud Functions for Lambda. However, X-Ray is unavailable in Google Cloud, so this capability will need to be dropped from the failover or replaced with a self-managed third-party solution.

Assuming both solutions remain fully Serverless within the capabilities of each cloud provider, there is a benefit compared with attempting the same with a server application. For Serverless, while storage will always be billable, the operational and maintenance costs of the failover will be negligible as there will only be billable utilization in the event of a failover.

A challenge is the cost of developing and maintaining a second version of the application and any minimal operational cost needed for storage and fully managed services. It should also be noted that in the event of a severe failure, the Route 53 service might also be unavailable, which means it will take some time before users can be switched to the failover provider. DNS redundancy should be considered with a failover outside of AWS preconfigured with the domain registrar.

Service-Level Agreements (SLAs)

In some cases, SLAs can be improved by using multi-region architectures, as seen in Figure 9-4. However, this will not be possible for applications using sovereign data that must remain in the organization's region.

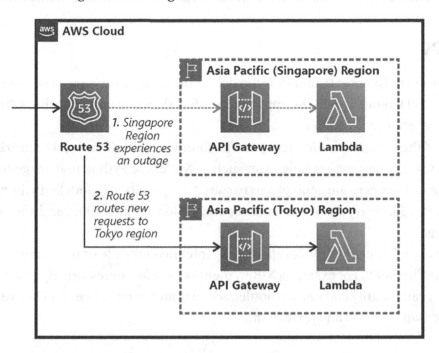

Figure 9-4. *Using multi-region to improve SLA guarantees*

An advantage of Serverless is, of course, that it's billed based on utilization, so besides storage costs, multi-region deployments on Serverless services don't necessarily cost much more than a single-region deployment.

Stateless Microservices

In traditional applications, sessions can track a user across multiple requests and share information between different parts of the application. This makes it easier to know who the user is and their past actions, which may be relevant to a new request. This is also called stateful.

Serverless microservices are temporary and do not retain any information from past requests, so each request needs to be treated as a new one, like a blank slate. This is called stateless, and it means we need to rethink the application structure and how to pass information between different requests. This can be especially challenging for developers new to Serverless. We will look at this in more detail later in this chapter.

Latency

As mentioned in Chapter 1, latency is the delay until a response is received after sending a request. Bad latency causes the application to feel slow and unresponsive, which is a bad user experience.

Most of the mitigations for latency can be found in code efficiency. Optimizing code and using programming languages such as NodeJS or Python that are generally faster for microservices are good places to start. Compared with NodeJS, Python can be more efficient for heavy-duty tasks, such as encryption, compression, and complex file processing.

There are a few cloud services specifically intended for code optimization, as we covered in Chapter 8. For example, X-Ray, mentioned a few times already and shown in Figure 9-5, can identify and resolve bottlenecks within microservices and between the different components of an application.

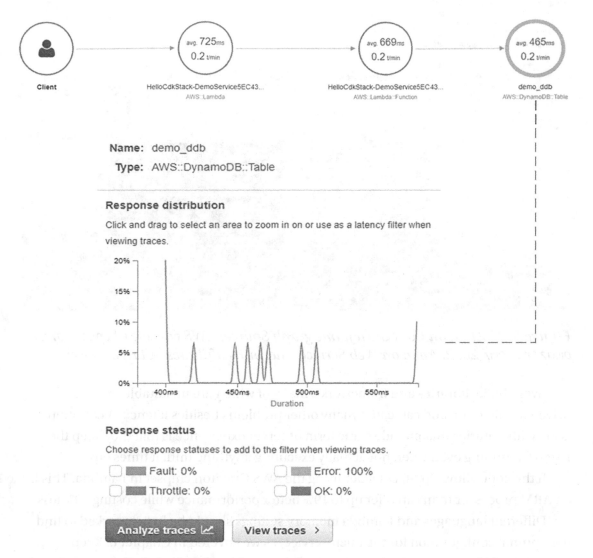

Figure 9-5. *Identifying bottlenecks in AWS X-Ray Source: AWS console* `https://aws.amazon.com/` *2022, Amazon Web Services Inc. or its affiliates. All rights reserved*

CodeGuru Profiler can be considered for Python microservices. It can analyze application CPU utilization, heap usage, and latency metrics. It will identify what is using the most time and resources in an application to debug and improve performance. CodeGuru does not yet support NodeJS, but there are similar third-party SaaS and self-managed tools available, such as SonarQube. An example output can be seen in Figure 9-6.

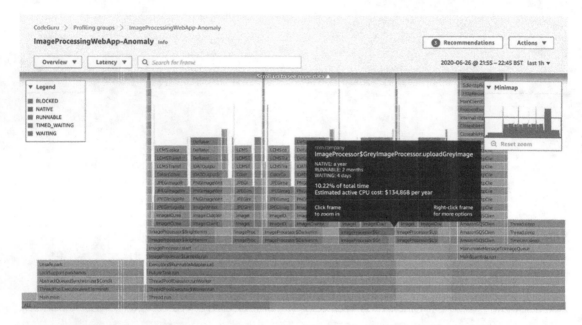

Figure 9-6. *Amazon CodeGuru flame graph Source: AWS console* `https://aws.` `amazon.com/` *2022, Amazon Web Services Inc. or its affiliates. All rights reserved*

Avoid bulky libraries and frameworks, many of which are unsuitable for an event-driven architecture and can cause many other problems besides latency. A common issue with libraries that provide some form of server experience is that they keep the Lambda running even when not actually executing anything until it times out.

If the code allows for it, consider using the AWS Graviton chipset in Lambda. This is an ARM processor than can offer up to 19% better performance while costing 20% less.

Different languages and Lambda memory settings should be benchmarked to find the optimal configuration for the microservice, as we covered in Chapter 8. Keep in mind that unlike server rightsizing, Lambda rightsizing is entirely based on what the microservice code needs for a single execution and not the total number of users.

Note that public benchmarks for languages and other aspects of Lambda tend to be narrow in focus and not indicative of the performance of a real-world microservice. While they can provide a rough idea, benchmarks should be done using actual microservices before making a decision.

Use parallel requests when possible, such as the following example in NodeJS that uses promises.

These are two arbitrary functions that return a promise:

1. Upload a file to S3:

```
function uplToS3File(fileName) {
  const file_path = `${__dirname}/${fileName}`;

  const fileContent = fs.readFileSync(file_path);

  let s3 = new AWS.S3();
  const params = {
    Bucket: 'likz-demo-bucket',
    Key: fileName,
    Body: fileContent
  };

  console.log("Uploading to S3");
  return s3.upload(params).promise();
}
```

2. Create file metadata:

```
function createFileMeta(name) {
  let docClient = new AWS.DynamoDB.DocumentClient();

  let params = {
    TableName: 'demo_ddb',
    Item: {
      name,
      url: `s3://${BUCKET_NAME}/${name}`
    }
  };

  console.log("Adding a new item...");
  return docClient.put(params).promise();
}
```

We initiate the promise functions, which execute at the same time, and store the returns in a list. This could easily be many more promises if needed:

```
let myPromises = [];
const file_name = 'demofile.txt';
myPromises.push(uplToS3File(file_name);
myPromises.push(createFileMeta(file_name);
// ... etc. for more promise functions
```

We use `Promise.all()` to wait for all promises to complete before we continue with our next step. The *result* in Promise.all is a list containing the outputs from all promises, in the same order that they were initiated:

```
Promise.all(myPromises).then(result => {
  const s3_success = result[0];
  const ddb_success = result[1];

  if (s3_success && ddb_success)
      console.log('all success');
  else
      console.log('error');
});
```

Using such asynchronous designs in applications can be a good way to manage unavoidable latency on certain types of requests. We will look at this in more detail later in this chapter.

Fully Managed Scaling

As mentioned, automatic scaling is one of the benefits of Serverless. Still, it can cause a budget shock if no limits are applied in the application infrastructure or code.

In API Gateway, we can create a unique API key for each user and assign it to a usage plan. A usage plan applies throttling limits to all assigned API keys. A *maximum number of requests per second* can be configured, as well as a *maximum number of requests within a given time period*, such as per month.

In S3, as we covered a couple of times, we can generate a pre-signed URL for each upload to manage the number of uploads and shown in Figure 9-7. Each URL has a default maximum upload limit of 5 GB. By adding a *content-length-range* parameter to the pre-signed URL, we can configure an arbitrary minimum and maximum size limit within 5 GB.

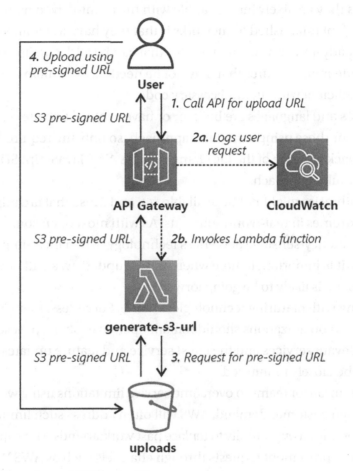

Figure 9-7. *Using signed URLs in S3*

In Serverless, we can track individual users through the application relatively easily, enabling us to implement a system to monitor user activities and limit overuse of any resources. We can also use this to track the incurred costs so we can do user or cross-department billing based on actual usage of our application.

Maturity of the Technology

While microservices can be created in several programming languages, the traditional mature web application frameworks in those languages are often not supported. Nor would it be advisable to use them if they are developed for always-on server or container environments, as they are likely incompatible with the event-driven nature of Serverless.

The advantage of established frameworks is that they have a significant community and libraries of ready-to-use, proven functions that can be added to an application. But these often include many features that may not be needed, and microservices need to be lightweight and efficient without unnecessary code.

Some libraries and languages are built for or have evolved to better support Serverless. Look for those using a modular approach, so only the required features are included in the package. One of the big changes in the AWS JavaScript SDK version 3 was to switch to a modular approach.

Many niche libraries might not be available yet, and those that are might not have been tested to extremes in real-world solutions. As with most open source but especially fast-moving and latency-sensitive Serverless technology, when including such functions in microservices, it is important to note when the last update was and how actively maintained the code is likely to be going forward.

When working with maturing technologies such as Serverless, there is often a high pace of change, and organizations should remain open to evolving past solutions. The changelogs of relevant services and the latest service and feature updates from the cloud provider should be closely monitored.

It is not uncommon for teams to overcome service limitations using workarounds and hacks. With enough customer demand, AWS will often address such limitations with new capabilities, presenting an opportunity to replace past workarounds with supported features.

AWS accepts improvement requests through channels such as AWS Wishlist on Twitter that can influence road map priorities. AWS partners can also reach out to their account managers with such requests.

Organizations can monitor new capabilities and feature announcements through the AWS blog. There is an RSS feed that can be integrated into a Slack channel for easy access. From there, further automation can be considered, such as tagging or notifications triggered by specific service mentions.

Besides released changes and services, organizations should consider participating in previews. A preview is early access to a new cloud service, usually without any SLA but suitable for proof of concepts. Previews offer organizations the opportunity to gain early experience and evaluate if the service may be useful to them. It can also be a fun exercise in digital innovation.

Lastly, one of the benefits of becoming an AWS Ambassador is that we gain access to service road maps, enabling us to plan ahead, though we do need to plan quietly, as this early information is provided under NDA.

Service Limits

As Lambda is a core service for Serverless, let's look a bit deeper at its limits shown in Figure 9-8.

Memory Allocation	Timeout	Request and Response Sizes	Code Size	Temp Storage
128 MB—10 GB	900 seconds (15 minutes)	6 MB (synchronous)	250 MB	10 GB
Rightsizing is important. Assigned CPUs are relative to memory.	Set a higher timeout. Avoid idle waiting.	Use S3 and pass reference. Return signed S3 URL.	Up to 10 GB in customer container.	Use S3. Connect EFS.

Figure 9-8. *Lambda service limits*

Memory can be from 128 MB to 10 GB. Lambda is billed per GB-milisecond. That means the more memory assigned, the more expensive the per-millisecond rate. So it's important to pick the right amount, monitor memory usage, and adjust as needed. The number of CPU cores assigned to the microservice is relative to the amount of memory being assigned, so there might be a trade-off between cost and speed of execution for the microservice.

Keep in mind that it is not a server; memory usage is not going to change based on the number of users. It is tied to what the microservice is doing for each request. As such, it's usually possible to find the ideal amount of memory through up-front testing for a tightly scoped microservice.

If a microservice requires more than 10 GB of memory or the associated CPUs, we should consider using a container instead.

Microservice code can be a maximum of 50 MB zipped and 250 MB unzipped. This includes any Lambda layers that are configured in the microservice. Generally, microservices should be kept small – one to five agile user stories as a general guideline. Larger microservices should be split into smaller ones to avoid mini-monoliths.

However, some use cases are justified in needing more storage, such as machine learning models or search indexes, either of which can be several GBs in size. To stay with the event-driven and Serverless model, we can use a Lambda container image, which can be up to 10 GB in size. Internal caching helps manage larger container latency, but note that the 15-minute execution limit still applies.

Another limit can be mitigated with container images. Lambda microservices support these programming languages: C#, Go, Java, NodeJS, PowerShell, Python, and Ruby. In a Lambda container image, we can add custom binaries and support any language.

Lambda has a hard maximum timeout of 15 minutes. However, if the microservice code finishes sooner, then execution stops, and with it, the billing. So it is usually safer to set a higher timeout to ensure it doesn't end the microservice prematurely. The risk is that some bugs and frameworks not intended for this kind of environment can cause the microservice to seem operational when it's not actually doing anything, preventing execution from stopping and leading to being billed for idle time until the timeout is reached.

This limitation, coupled with the fact we are billed per millisecond, will impact how microservices are designed. They need to be fast and tightly scoped, and idle time or waiting is to be avoided.

If a microservice needs more than 15 minutes to run, there are two mitigations that can be considered. If most of that time is idle waiting for another component to complete, then that is an anti-pattern – a bad way to use Lambda. Instead of making the microservice wait, we could split the application into smaller steps and use Step Functions to create a multistep workflow with waits, retries, and error handling. Waiting in Step Functions doesn't cost anything.

For simpler workflows, SQS or EventBridge can be used to avoid Lambda waiting time. In this case, the microservice will start the long-running process, add a task to SQS or EventBridge, and then terminate. In SQS, we can configure a *visibility delay* to provide the time needed before the next step. In EventBridge, we can schedule a task at a future date and time to provide the delay. In either case, a follow-up Lambda will be triggered after the delay to continue the process.

Alternatively, a container might be a better approach if a microservice needs more than 15 minutes of actual execution time. Containers are not limited by any service timeout and can be always on. If an event-driven approach is possible, we can consider using Lambda to launch an on-demand container. The container performs the task and terminates when it completes, minimizing idle time billing and wastage.

Request and response sizes are limited to 6 MB. This is usually more than enough for event messages and JSON data. There are cases where a larger request is needed – such as when dealing with media files.

One mitigation would be for the client to upload the file directly into an S3 bucket using a signed URL, as shown in Figure 9-9.

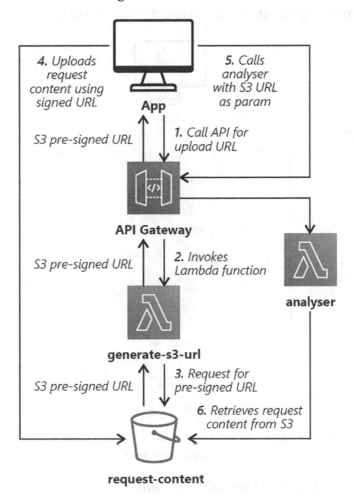

Figure 9-9. *Secure direct uploads to S3*

When the client establishes that a large file needs to be sent, it requests an upload URL via an API Gateway endpoint. The attached Lambda microservice creates and returns a signed S3 POST URL with an expiry date and optional minimum and maximum file size range. The client uploads the file directly to the bucket via the signed URL. Lastly, the client can submit the file metadata and any user input to the API; the attached Lambda microservice can then handle the new file as needed.

Similarly, but in reverse, S3 can be used to overcome the 6 MB limitation for response size. In this case, the Lambda microservice generates a signed GET URL for a file on S3 and returns this to the client instead of the actual file, as shown in Figure 9-10. The client uses the URL to download the file before it expires. Such URLs can also be shared with end users via channels such as email to download files.

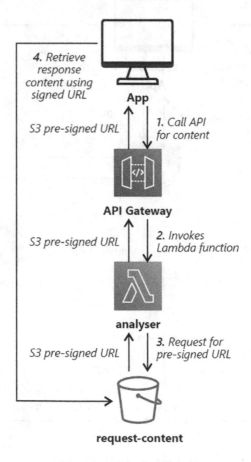

Figure 9-10. *Securely retrieve files directly from S3*

Lambda temporary storage was increased to 10 GB in 2022. However, if more storage is needed or if we need something that is more permanent, we can use S3 or attach an EFS to Lambda. EFS is an NFS-compatible network drive that can be mounted into a Lambda microservice providing considerably more storage capacity.

Besides the size limit, Lamba's writable storage is ephemeral. The data is often deleted when the execution ends. If the next invocation needs the same data, then the repeated loading of data into the temporary storage will add considerable latency. EFS can both solve the size limit and offer a persistent storage option. It supports multiple concurrent clients and file locking and can scale to accommodate petabytes of data. Internal caching will make repeat reading of the same files across multiple microservice instances much faster.

EFS has lower latency than S3 but higher latency than using the local temporary storage option. EFS is more expensive than S3, and the Lambda temporary storage is included with the execution cost. Interestingly, EFS does not add any significant latency to Lambda's cold start.

Another potential mitigation for specific use cases is to stream the data through Lambda. Usually, we would stream from a source S3 bucket to a destination S3 bucket. This works for compression, encryption, and line-by-line reading of data from file formats that support this, such as CSV.

Learning Curve

A common challenge faced by application teams when adopting Serverless is in realizing that Serverless architecture can be quite different from traditional approaches to cloud applications. It differs from a server architecture where instances are provisioned and running 24/7. In Serverless, the microservice essentially does not exist between requests.

Serverless applications scale up very quickly; each request is given a single microservice instance. As such, resources are determined only based on the needs of the code, without any consideration for the potential number of users.

There are some common anti-patterns to avoid in Lambda microservices:

- For example, having a too large microservice or trying to do too many different things. Keep the scope of microservices small; one to five agile user stories are a good guideline. Use event storming to break up large monoliths.

- Shared code in Lambda layers is to be avoided. Layers are for separating third-party code from custom code for a single microservice. If duplicate code must be avoided, this should be done locally before deployment. Versioning can be used to manage shared code changes to avoid monolithic code issues.

- Idle waiting in Lambda for long-running jobs to complete increases the cost and chance of running into the 15-minute execution time limit. Instead, take an asynchronous approach using services such as SQS, EventBridge, or Step Functions and let them handle the waiting instead of the Lambda.

- Avoid creating dependencies on less scalable services, resulting in a bottleneck. For example, DynamoDB and Aurora Serverless are preferred over RDS because they can match the speed and extent of Lambda scaling.

Database Strategy

In Serverless, we prefer fully managed databases to match Lambda microservices' redundancy, scalability, and speed. For a long time, only DynamoDB was available, which has led to many Serverless examples and best practices leaning toward that database. However, other options are available today – purpose-built databases intended for a particular use case and Aurora Serverless as a more familiar relational database.

Traditionally, relational databases such as RDS MySQL or Oracle were the go-to database of choice for most applications. When we pair Lambda with a less scalable service, we limit the capabilities of Lambda and often remove the benefits of having a Serverless architecture. Consider upskilling in NoSQL and learning techniques in converting relational data models to NoSQL – also called denormalizing.

Besides DynamoDB, consider more purpose-built databases such as Neptune, Timestream, or QLDB if they are a good fit for the use case. These databases can offer far better performance than an all-purpose database. If the application requires a relational data model, consider using Aurora Serverless to minimize operational overheads and match Lambda scalability. To further improve performance, consider the Data API if Aurora Serverless version 1 is used (version 2 does not yet support it).

Other Challenges

Some other challenges have been covered in detail in previous chapters already. These include Lambda rightsizing, proactive logging, integration or contract testing, and estimating the cloud operational cost of Serverless architecture.

⚙ AWS: Microservices and APIs

In Amazon Web Services, the managed service Lambda is used to host our microservices. Lambda is what we call *Function-as-a-Service (FaaS)* because we upload function code and everything else, such as redundancy and scaling, is fully managed. We are billed for each request and for the milliseconds that the function is running. On AWS, we sometimes also call microservices *Lambdas* or *Lambda functions*.

Lambda has tight integrations with many other AWS services, such as DynamoDB, CloudWatch logging, API Gateway, and many more. Access is typically managed through IAM policies.

The fully managed service *Fargate* can host container-based microservices that exceed Lambda limits. This makes them suitable for use cases such as long-lived connections. While the service is fully managed, we should expect to be billed for idle time, so it should only be considered if Lambda is unsuitable.

Lambda Scalability and Cold Start

After publishing a microservice to Lambda, AWS will make an instance of the microservice available to each incoming request. This could be a new instance or an existing one if the previous request has been completed already. Each instance will only process one request at a time. Multiple requests at the same time are processed in parallel by multiple instances. The default limit, called Lambda concurrency limit, is up to 1000 microservices running at the same time. This is a soft limit and can be increased with a service request. The longer a microservice needs to run, the higher the chance of hitting this limit.

Each launched instance will remain available for 5–7 minutes. We are only billed for actual execution time, not this available time. Any requests handled by an available instance will have a faster, or *warm*, start. Requests handled on a new instance will have a slower *cold* start.

The difference can be a couple of hundred milliseconds. A larger microservice with more code can increase this difference, and there are differences between the different programming languages that Lambda supports. JavaScript and Python have the smallest difference and Java and C# the largest. The amount of assigned memory does not usually impact start latency, except for C# microservices, where they can make a considerable difference, and a minimum of 2 GB is recommended.

Reserved Concurrency

The Lambda concurrency limit is shared among all Lambda functions within the account and region. Once the limit is hit, Lambda invocations will be throttled, and users will have to wait until the concurrency space is freed up.

However, we can assign *reserved concurrency* to a particular Lambda microservice to ensure that it is not throttled. Concurrency space not allocated is known as *unreserved* concurrency; this remains shared among all Lamda microservices without reserved concurrency.

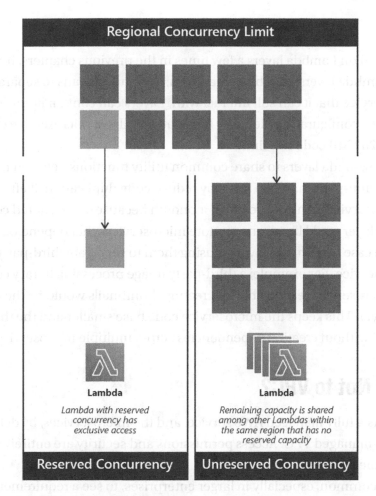

Figure 9-11. *Lambda concurrency limits*

Reserved concurrency also works as a limiter, limiting the number of instances that the function will be able to run to the amount reserved. For example, if reserved concurrency is set to 10, then a maximum of ten instances of the microservice can be executed at any one time, regardless of any available unreserved concurrency. As with the total concurrency limit, running into the reserved maximum will mean additional requests are throttled and users will have to wait.

Layers

We have touched on Lambda layers a few times in the previous chapters, but let's summarize. Lambda layers are a bit contentious; they are a means to separate code from a microservice that it can still interact with. Layers can contain libraries, a custom runtime, data, or configuration files. Any layers attached to a microservice count toward the maximum 250 MB code size limit.

Relying on Lambda layers to share common utility functions between multiple functions is an anti-pattern. While this may reduce code duplication, it effectively turns the microservice architecture into a monolith because of the shared code. Future changes to the layer could break one or more microservices that depend on it.

A good use case for Lambda layers is using them to segregate third-party code from a single microservice. For example, a third-party image processing library could be kept in a layer. A microservice responsible for creating thumbnails would be the only one to include that layer. This keeps the microservice code base smaller and the third-party code separated without creating dependencies across multiple microservices.

To VPC or Not to VPC?

Lambda runs as a fully managed AWS service, and the microservices, by default, will run in an AWS-managed VPC. Access permissions and security are entirely managed through IAM role policies.

It is not uncommon, especially in larger enterprises, to see a requirement for Lambda microservices to run in a VPC managed by the organization. Typically, this is related to security policies requiring subnet segregation. However, adding Lambdas to a VPC creates some additional complexity. There is a slightly higher cold start latency, security groups need to be configured and managed, and a proxy or NAT may be required – neither of which is Serverless.

AWS recommends defense-in-depth, meaning multiple layers of security protection, including subnet segregation. Ultimately, the use case and organizational requirements will determine if the added complexity is worth it.

Lambda microservices that need to talk to resources in a VPC may also need to run in a VPC to be able to access them. However, other ways can be considered first, such as an asynchronous approach using SQS (Figure 9-12) or SNS or, for RDS databases, using RDS Proxy.

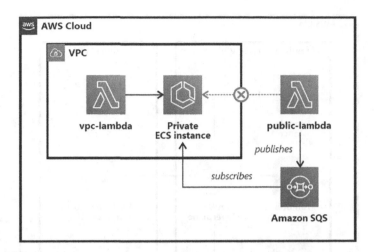

Figure 9-12. *Using SQS to talk to a Lambda microservice in a VPC*

Let's look a bit closer at how AWS manages the running of Lambda microservices in a VPC. This used to be a lot more complex, and we had to manage IP pools and connections. AWS then simplified it by adding a Hyperplane, which is a kind of load balancer, shown in Figure 9-13. When a Lambda microservice is launched within our VPC, an Elastic Network Interface (ENI) is created in the VPC. The Lambda service creates an AWS Hyperplane, and a network connection is established between the two.

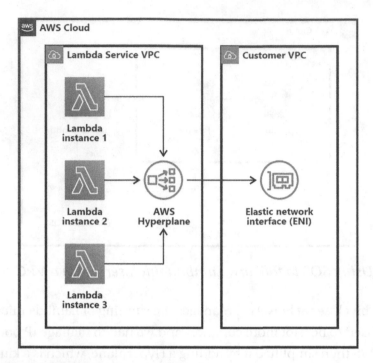

Figure 9-13. *Lambda Hyperplane architecture*

Previously, one ENI had to be created per Lambda function instance, which had many challenges. For example, the number of Lambdas that could be provisioned was limited by the number of ENIs supported by the VPC and the number of IP addresses available in the configured range. There was also a considerably longer cold start time because each instance needed to be attached to an ENI before it was available.

With the new Hyperplane approach, multiple microservice instances can be attached to one Hyperplane. Cold start time is greatly reduced because a tunnel can quickly be created to establish a connection to the VPC. Since the number of ENIs is greatly reduced, we are also less likely to run out of them, and we don't need to worry about managing IP address pools anymore.

When we first create or update a Lambda microservice in a VPC, the initial setup of a Hyperplane can take up to 90 seconds. Once set up, the Hyperplane remains available and ready for launching future instances of that microservice. However, if the Lambda microservice is unused for a few weeks, the Hyperplane could be decommissioned. To counter this for less utilized microservices, schedule a weekly invocation using EventBridge.

Lambda DevOps

Lambda integrates with AWS-native deployment services such as CodePipeline to quickly test, build, and deploy new microservice versions. CloudFormation, or at least another IaC templating language, can and should be used to configure a Lambda microservice and any integrations and permissions.

Lambda supports versioning, providing a record of previous deployments. This enables us to roll back any changes quickly when needed. Aliases help direct traffic to the microservice version that we want to use. For example, in Figure 9-14, we deploy a new version of the microservice and update the *DEV* alias to point to it while keeping a TESTING alias pointing at the previous version.

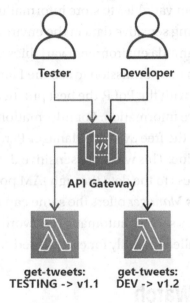

Figure 9-14. Lambda versioning and aliases

There are several deployment techniques available, but the two most relevant to Serverless, and especially to Lambda microservices, are *blue/green* deployment and *canary*.

The blue/green approach deploys a new version of an application entirely in a new *green* environment. Developers test the new functionality, and then traffic is routed from the old *blue* environment to the new *green* one. If issues start appearing in the *green* environment, then traffic can be moved back to the *blue* environment fairly quickly. A risk with blue/green is that 100% of the traffic is moved over. So, in case of issues, potentially everyone will experience them.

511

Canary deployments are like blue/green, but instead of shifting all the traffic at once, canary only moves a small configurable portion into the new environment. If there are no issues, the remaining traffic will then be shifted over, either all at once or in increments over a period of time.

As with blue/green, if there are any issues with the new deployment, the moved portion of traffic can be shifted back to the old environment. This can be entirely automated by reacting to CloudWatch event error logs. Canary reduces the number of users potentially exposed to issues and minimizes the time spent in an error state.

Lambda Environment Variables

Lambda supports environment variables to store information such as SQS URLs or S3 bucket names. However, storing sensitive data in the environment variables is not a best practice. Even though Lambda environment variables are encrypted at rest, they are still visible to anyone who has permission to see the Lambda microservice in the AWS console or CLI. To align with the PoLP, the best practice is to separate Lambda access from access to sensitive information. For information such as passwords and other credentials, we can use the free Systems Manager Parameter Store service with a "*secure string*" type for the value. This will store sensitive data fully encrypted, and we can manage fine-grained access to the data through IAM policies for users or services. Another service called *Secrets Manager* offers the same capability. This is a more advanced service with features such as automatic password rotation. However, Secrets Manager is not free; we are billed monthly for each stored secret.

Lambda and CloudWatch

We covered Lambda-CloudWatch integrations extensively in Chapter 8. Here, I just wanted to add that to start using CloudWatch for Lambda, the first step is to grant Lambda access to CloudWatch logs. In CloudWatch, logs are organized in groups. These provide a means to distinguish between logs from different services, applications, and microservices.

Once a log group has been created, the Lambda microservice needs permission to write logs to it. If we create a specific log group that we want to use, we only need to give the Lambda two permissions: *logs:CreateLogStream* and *logs:PutLogEvents*. This approach is recommended as it also provides an opportunity to configure the retention setting of the logs. If we do not create the log group beforehand and want Lambda to create it automatically the first time it executes, the microservice will also need the *logs:CreateLogGroup* permission. Keep in mind that to align with the PoLP, the microservice only needs this permission the first time it runs or if the log group is deleted.

What Metrics to Monitor for CloudWatch and Why?

Besides memory, which we covered in detail earlier, the following are some more key Lambda metrics to watch and why:

- **Concurrency limit**This can be either concurrent executions or a combination of concurrent executions and unreserved concurrent executions, depending on whether some of the functions have reserved concurrencies. This region-wide metric determines whether the Lambda microservice will soon start to throttle requests. It is important to track for systems that have many simultaneous events.

- **Errors (standard Lambda failure errors)**Error in a Lambda microservice can cause problems for other microservices if it is part of a workflow. Alerts should be configured to notify the app team of such events for speedy follow-up. Note that whether or not this type of error appears depends on the code. If we are diligent in handling errors, such as using try/catch, we will be able to output our own, perhaps more meaningful error messages and status codes, and these standard catch-all Lambda errors might never occur.

- **DeadLetterErrors**This metric is all about data loss. It arises when failed events cannot be written to a safe backup location to be debugged and rerun. An alert is recommended so that teams can address the issue immediately.

- **Duration**Lambda microservices should be small and fast. It is important to track the execution duration and have an alarm when they reach an unacceptable threshold. It allows teams to debug and find the cause of events that are often edge cases slowing things down and driving up costs.

The documentation on all the Lambda metrics can be found here: $https://docs.$
$aws.amazon.com/lambda/latest/dg/monitoring-metrics.html$.

Lambda and API Gateway

API Gateway is possibly the most commonly used service with Lambda, at least user-facing solutions. It acts as the front door for applications to access microservices and provides a means to manage, monitor, and secure access to APIs. API Gateway is a fully managed cloud service that does not require code development, meaning that developers can leverage Serverless capabilities for significant productivity gains while reducing operational overhead costs.

API Gateway supports three types of interfaces.

WebSocket APIs are used for real-time bidirectional communication between a backend and front end – commonly used in chat apps and games, but especially relevant in Serverless as they can enable the back end to update the front end when an asynchronous request has been completed. To achieve this, WebSocket connections remain open, allowing them to be used at any time without needing to initiate a connection for each request.

The ***HTTP*** and ***REST*** **APIs** both create RESTful APIs. *HTTP* APIs are more simple but offer lower latency and cost. The name is misleading; connections are still secured with SSL over *HTTPS*. REST is a type of API design for two systems to communicate using the same HTTP we use when browsing websites. Like standard HTTP requests, API requests are open for the duration of the request – just enough time for the back end to process the request and provide a response.

The ***REST*** **API** provides more features such as usage plan, caching, and firewall integration. Most importantly, the *REST* API supports data validation, which means this does not need to be done in the microservices, and I recommend using this type for all but the simplest of APIs. While it is called an API service, it is also possible to directly serve dynamic HTML pages with this service and Lambda.

WebSockets

HTTP was created for the Internet, but in certain situations, it is not an ideal protocol - especially for applications that need to process streams of data or need to be able to push data from the back end to the front end without the front end asking for it.

In 2011, the WebSocket protocol was standardized to address these needs. This protocol enabled flexible data transfers along with peer-to-peer (P2P) or direct communication between browsers. In contrast to HTTP, WebSockets connect to the server and stay open for communication until the client or server issues a termination request. This enables data to be pushed to the browser when the back end needs it instead of waiting for the front end to ask for it.

With API Gateway WebSockets, we can create an open connection between a web client and the API. API Gateway maintains the open connection with the client and passes individual requests through to the microservice. Importantly, the Lambda microservice is initiated for each request, and it does not need to remain running between requests.

Figure 9-15 shows how we can implement and use WebSockets. As mentioned, it is a bidirectional API service ideal for real-time applications such as chats and collaboration services.

A chatbot service retrieves the order status for a customer. When a client initiates a request to the API Gateway, it uses a WebSocket protocol instead of a regular HTTP call. The connection between the client and API Gateway remains open, and API Gateway generates a connection ID that uniquely identifies it. API Gateway then sends all future requests with the connection ID to our back-end service, initiating the Lambda for each request.

Our back-end service processes the request before sending the results back to the API Gateway using its connection URL and the connection ID. API Gateway identifies the appropriate socket connection using the connection ID and sends the response to the client.

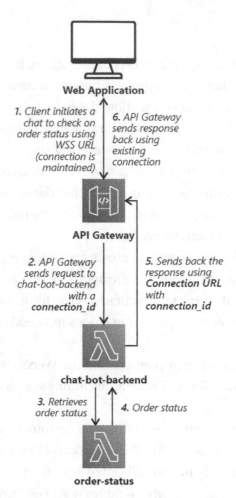

Figure 9-15. *API Gateway WebSockets architecture example*

The following is a high-level overview of setting up WebSockets with Lambda:

1. Using CDK, create a new API using CDK's apigatewayv2 module with the protocol type WEBSOCKET.

2. Create a role that permits the API *lambda:invokefunction* access to the socket-handling microservice. (Remember to create the Lambda microservice first.)

3. Add a Lambda integration using CfnIntegration. This is needed three times, one for each: $connect, $disconnect, and $default (or $message). For WebSockets, the integration type is always proxy.

4. Then we create three routes, again one for each – $connect, $disconnect, and $default – using CfnRoute. The targets are the integrations we created in step 3.

5. Lastly, we create the deployment (CfnDeployment) stage (CfnStage). To ensure that the resources are loaded in the correct order, we need to use ConcreteDependable to make the three routes a dependency of the deployment.

The API Gateway service will provide a wss:// URL to use to connect to the WebSocket. We can do so with plain JavaScript as follows:

```
// connect
const mySocket = new WebSocket(api_socket_url);

// listen for incoming messages
mySocket.onmessage = function(message) {
  // handle message
}

// send a message
app.socket.send(message);
```

The Lambda microservice handles sockets as follows:

```
// connect, disconnect or default
let action = event.requestContext.routeKey;

// this client's ID
let cid = event.requestContext.connectionId;

// new connection
if(action === '$connect') {
  // optionally store the session in a DDB
}

// new incoming request
if(action === '$default') {
  // handle the requests
}
```

```
// send a message to the client
const apigwManagementApi = new AWS.ApiGatewayManagementApi({
  apiVersion: '2018-11-29',

  // retrieve from API GW, the link that starts with https://
  endpoint: <SOCKET_URL_FOR_MESSAGES>
});

apigwManagementApi.postToConnection({
  ConnectionId: <RECIPIENT_CLIENT_ID>,
  Data: <MESSAGE>
}).promise();
```

Proxy vs. Non-proxy Integration

The API Gateway REST API offers two types of integration with Lambda: proxy and non-proxy.

For proxy integrations, all requests and responses are forwarded as is to the destination Lambda with no modifications. With proxy integrations, we lose access to many great features in API Gateway. However, there are a couple of use cases where proxy integration is unavoidable:

1. Third-party service libraries running in Lambda expecting to receive the full unmodified API request – common with sensitive services such as PayPal

2. Server libraries, such as Apollo, a GraphQL API that can run in Lambda

Non-proxy integrations can leverage API Gateway functions to analyze, validate, and transform the content of both requests and responses. This is really the recommended approach for Serverless as it decouples the payload and HTTP status information from the application logic. Importantly, this enables us to perform parameter validation on user input, which we covered in Chapter 4 Note that if we do these operations in Lambda, we are not only reinventing the wheel but also billed per millisecond for something API Gateway provides for free.

Request Transformation

Another useful feature of API Gateway is request transformation.

```
1 #set{$header1Override = "foo")
2 #set{$header3Value =
  "$input.params('header1')$input.params('header2')")
  $input.json("$")
3 #set($context.requestOverride.header.header1 =
  $header1Override)
4 #set($context.requestOverride.header.header2 =
  $$input.params('header2'))
5 #set($context.requestOverride.header.header3 =
  $header3Value)
```

Headers
{helloworld}

header1:hello
header2:world

*Incoming request from
the client is transformed
in the API Gateway
before being forwarded
to our backend services*

```
Endpoint request headers: {
        header1=foo,
        header2=world,
        header3=helloworld,
        X-Amz-Date=20211005T020031Z,
        x-amzn-apigateway-api-id=xxxxx,
        Accept=application/json
        ...
}
```

Figure 9-16. *Transforming request headers in API Gateway*

In Figure 9-16 at the top, we define a mapping template that can change and remap request attributes before they are sent to the back-end service. In this example, we update the header1 value of the request to "*foo*," make no change to header2, and create a new header3 that combines the original header1 and header2 values. Our test request has a header1 value of "*hello*" and header2 value of "*world*." As we can see from the resulting endpoint request header, API Gateway has transformed the values of all three headers before forwarding the request to the back-end service.

Dynamic HTML

Lambda microservices are typically used to handle back-end events and API endpoints, but Lambda microservices can return virtually anything. This also includes returning HTML markup with dynamic content directly. API Gateway can be configured to pass that through to the user, resulting in a dynamic website instead of an API-based website. This is one approach to achieving SEO-friendly dynamic pages. However, the latency is not great.

Error Reporting

Error reporting in API Gateway is not great, but two tips to slightly improve that are as follows:

1. Make sure to add the following header to the standard 400 and 500 responses in API Gateway "Gateway Responses":

    `Access-Control-Allow-Origin: '*'`

    This will ensure that the client can receive the error response instead of just failing on CORS.

2. Add the following code to the "application/json" request body for the Gateway Response error type "BAD_REQUEST_BODY":

    `,"error":"$context.error.validationErrorString"`

    This will provide a bit more information with the standard error code, which can help find the issue, but it is still not great and may need some trial and error to find the exact cause.

Other Integrations

Besides Lambda, API Gateway integrates with several other services that can process incoming requests and provide responses. For example, we can integrate with ECS and Fargate containers, as well as directly with EC2 servers.

Direct integrations with some AWS service APIs are also possible. For example, we can allow a user to start a Step Functions workflow simply by opening a URL instead of the more complex approach of interacting directly with the Step Functions API. With

API Gateway in front of the service, we can determine which service capabilities can be utilized and control the validation of the requests.

Lastly, API Gateway supports what we call *mock* integrations. These are fake integrations with a fixed response. Mock integrations are commonly used for testing and simulation while the actual back end is still being developed. The API can provide a fixed response that reflects what the actual response might be when the back end is ready. This enables the front-end developers to work in parallel with the back-end developers without needing the latter to finish development first.

Lambda and Application Load Balancer

Another way to front Lambda for user access is with Application Load Balancer, as shown in Figure 9-17. This is the preferred approach for serving dynamic pages from Lambda, but it does require a VPC.

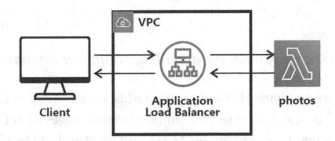

Figure 9-17. *Application Load Balancer (ALB) fronting a Lambda microservice*

While it initially appears to perform the same role as an API Gateway, the ALB lacks useful features such as handling HTTP headers and request and response transformation. If such capabilities are required, they will need to be developed as part of the microservice code, adding unnecessary complexity. The ALB can integrate with Cognito for user authentication and to enforce access control.

The ALB works on a per-hour pricing model based on the Load Balancer Capacity Unit (LCU) that is defined. This LCU defines the number of new connections supported per second, the number of active connections per minute, and the number of bytes that can be processed per hour. Each LCU can evaluate up to 1,000 rules per second. To increase the limit, we need to increase the number of LCUs configured in the ALB.

	API Gateway		Application Load Balancer
Requires a VPC	No.		Yes, ALB is deployed in a VPC.
Timeout	Hard limit of 30 seconds.		Default: 60 seconds Max: 4,000 seconds *(Lambda max execution time: 900 seconds)*
Protocol	HTTPS only.		HTTP and HTTPS.
Payload Size	6 MB *(sync)*	256 KB *(async)*	1 MB
Features	More robust AuthN and AuthZ features, WebSockets, request validation, payload transformation, etc.		Path-based forwarding, authentication with Cognito, and OIDC IdP and health checks.
Decoupling	Automatically handles and parses HTTPS request and response.		Microservice must set Base64 encoding status, status code, and headers for HTTP response.
Cost	*Pay per request*: Tiered pricing *(Straightforward, pay-as-you-go)*		*Hourly rate*: Per load balancer and per Load Balancer Capacity Units (LCUs) *(More complicated, needs predicting)*

Figure 9-18. *API Gateway vs. Application Load Balancer comparison*

In Figure 9-18 we compare API Gateway with ALB. We can see that the ALB approach is quite limited and best suited for serving simple dynamic pages from Lambda. From a Serverless perspective, having to predict LCU is not ideal and will inevitably lead to being billed for idle time. The VPC requirement may also be a concern for some.

However, the cost comparison between the **REST** API Gateway and the ALB approach in Figure 9-19 is quite interesting. Here we are using 100 requests per second to do a comparison in cost for different request sizes and find the break-even point. Pricing is for the Singapore region and in USD. ALB pricing is based on 1 LCU.

REST API Gateway				Application Load Balancer	
Pay per request (tiered pricing)				Hourly rate	
First 333 mil	Next 667 mil	Next 19 bil	> 20 bil	$0.0252 per ALB	$0.008 per capacity unit (LCU)
$4.25/mil	$3.53/mil	$3.00/mil	$1.91/mil		
Assuming 100 requests per second (259.2 million requests per month) in ap-southeast-1					
*If average size of request is **large** (~512KB) | 0.000512GB × 100 requests × 60 seconds × 60 minutes = 184.32 GB/hour*					
$1,101.60/month				$2,709.47/month	
*If average size of request is **small** (~14 KB) | 0.000014 GB × 100 requests × 60 seconds × 60 minutes = 5.04 GB/hour*					
$1,101.60/month				$91.98/month	
***Break-even** (~209.6 KB) | 0.0002061 GB × 100 requests × 60 seconds × 60 minutes = 74.196 GB/hour*					
$1,101.60/month				$1,101.66/month	

Figure 9-19. *API Gateway vs. Application Load Balancer cost break-even point*

The size of each request is a crucial parameter in this. API Gateway charges the same for any request between 0 and 512 KB. For ALB, the size greatly impacts cost as it charges based on LCU, and each LCU supports 400 MB *per hour*.

As such, we can see when comparing them that if the application expects large requests, API Gateway will be considerably cheaper to run than ALB. But if the requests are small, then ALB will be the cheaper option. The break-even point for this example with 100 requests per second is a request size of around 210 KB.

This comparison also indicates that API Gateway may be easier to predict monthly costs for. ALB fluctuates a lot more depending on the different sizes and number of requests.

For the API Gateway HTTP API, we would see a similar result. However, the cost is lower for HTTP APIs, which reduces the break-even request size for this calculation to about 62 KB.

⚙ Design Patterns

Serverless is not the end-all/solve-all architecture for modern cloud applications. It is a type of architecture that may or may not work for any given use case. Rarely are large complex solutions 100% Serverless. Applications with complex or legacy data models tend to make a relational database unavoidable. As such, applications, especially migrated ones, tend to be hybrid with a mix of Serverless, fully managed, and containers or servers. Similarly, sometimes a monolithic approach just makes more sense for a given application or team. A good architect should not force an inappropriate solution into Serverless.

In my experience, the following types of Serverless projects are most common:

1. Simple stand-alone functions like a trigger function that reacts to a new image uploaded to S3 and creates a thumbnail for it or microservices with exclusive access to a specific DynamoDB database to add a layer of security and auditing.

2. Pipelines where the Lambda microservices are the glue between services like video processing (video analytics for faces and objects + extract audio and transcribe + analysis of text). Step Functions is often a suitable service to manage pipelines.

3. IoT and similar edge computing cases. There is strong support for these types of use cases with a range of fully managed and Serverless services.

4. Simple one-page websites with basic interaction such as processing a contact or registration form.

Complex solutions with many different resources and features tend to be hybrids, mixing Serverless and other architectures. Hybrid is a very common approach in real-world projects. It helps meet the requirements and limitations of complex cloud-based solutions while ensuring each section has been designed as cost-effectively and efficiently as possible. It is important to get away from thinking that one project means one approach. A project can be broken down into parts, and each can be individually assessed for the best approach.

For example, we might have a collection of microservices working with data in a relational database. It could make sense to create a section for these that are a bit more monolithic, using a Lambda layer to reduce the amount of duplicate code. Another part of the solution might be a single microservice performing a very specific task and using a NoSQL database. This can be a separate section using an independent microservice approach.

Each section can be treated as a discrete project with its own IaC, repo, and documentation. Parameters can be shared between stacks or through services such as Parameter Store. The following section designs can be considered:

a. *Fully Serverless*: Where each Lambda microservice or Fargate container is independent and we exclusively use Serverless services such as DynamoDB. While very cost-effective, this can be hard to achieve, and it should not be forced if it is not in the best interests of the project.

b. *Monolithic Serverless*: We still use Lambda microservices, but most of the functions are in a single Lambda or a shared layer. This may be a good approach to reduce code duplication in situations where there would otherwise be several very similar microservices, such as API CRUDs.

c. *Container- or even server-based*: There are valid cases where a particular problem cannot be solved with a Lambda microservice or even a Fargate container, for example, machine learning and other GPU-dependent tasks – neither Lambda nor Fargate has access to GPUs at the time of writing. In these circumstances, we will need to use a container, server, or server-based service. Where possible, it should be launched by a microservice, perform its task, and terminate once finished. This will minimize risk and billable idle time exposure.

When Not to Use Strict Microservice Architecture

For a simple API service that isn't going to grow over time, it might make more sense to have a single microservice per API resource doing the create/retrieve/update/delete rather than splitting that into four distinct microservices per resource.

In situations where we have significant code similarity between the different components, we might want to consider if microservices are the right approach, as we will end up with lots of near-identical microservices. This is again a common situation for simple API back ends where each API path is doing very similar CRUD activities. A single microservice that can handle different data schemas might be a better approach if the remaining actions on that data are all the same.

If low latency is a critical factor, splitting a request across multiple microservices might not be the right approach, as each step will add latency to the request.

Serverless microservices are event-driven and not intended for long-lived connections; containers are more suitable if the request cannot be converted to an event-driven design.

⚙ Microservice Example Architectures

Basic CRUD API

An API microservice is a simple processing function that can do "create/retrieve/update/delete" (CRUD) actions on a specified database table, storage facility, or another service. In some cases, it makes sense to use the same microservice for multiple tables, especially as data validation is done in API Gateway, so there might only be limited differences in the code between multiple microservices. Figure 9-20 shows a simple API microservice that gets tweet records from a database in response to an API request.

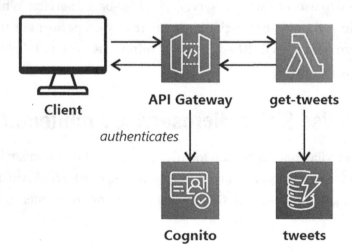

Figure 9-20. *Architecture example: basic CRUD API*

CRUD microservices offer a quick response to the user, but they lose some resilience compared with decoupling them. A microservice for managing WebSocket connect, request, and disconnect events would also fall into this category.

Triggered or Decoupled

Triggered or decoupled microservices run in the background and react to events in a cloud environment. Another service or microservice could trigger them directly or add tasks to a queue that triggers them. A decoupled microservice is usually asynchronous, meaning it runs in the background, and any front end should continue and not wait for a response.

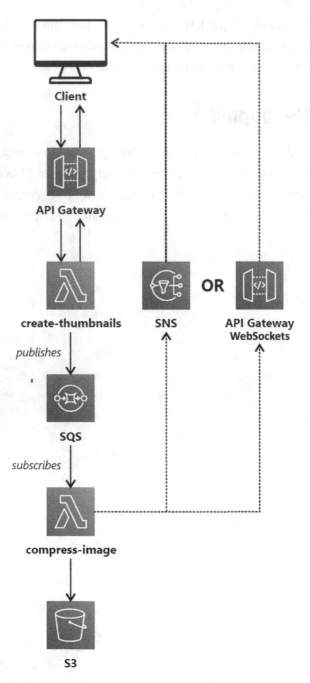

Figure 9-21. *Architecture example: triggered or decoupled microservices*

If a response is needed at the end of the request, it can be pushed to the front end via WebSockets, or the user could be informed directly via email or similar channel. An example use case for a decoupled microservice is shown in Figure 9-21. The *create-thumbnails* microservice receives a request via API Gateway to process an image. The microservice adds a processing task to an SQS queue and then returns a message to the user that the request was received. Meanwhile, the SQS triggers the *compress-image* microservice to process the image, and, when completed, it notifies the user via WebSockets or an SNS message. Another approach would be to add a task to SQS when a new image is uploaded to an S3 bucket, as we saw in some earlier examples.

Gatekeeper

Gatekeepers are what I call microservices that have exclusive access rights to a specific database, storage facility, or other resources. We saw this in our first example with the personal data microservice and another example can be seen in Figure 9-22.

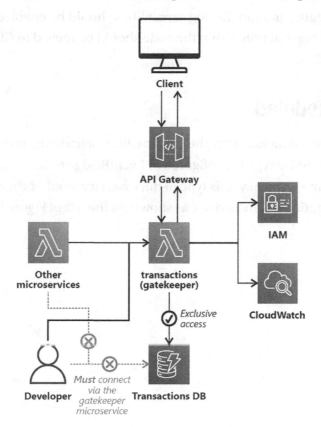

Figure 9-22. *Architecture example: secure gatekeeper microservice*

Any microservice, application, or user wanting to do anything with this data must go via the gatekeeper microservice. This provides a single location where the request can be validated, formatted, and logged. This ensures consistency for data going in and out of the database, and it provides an audit trail for all actions related to this data. Gatekeeper microservices are especially useful for protecting sensitive data such as PII, medical, finance, or security data.

To create a gatekeeper, we assign it a role with access to a specific DynamoDB table, S3 bucket, or other relevant services. We must then make sure no other microservice is given the same access. Any other microservice that wants to perform any activity with this data must retrieve it from, or pass it to, the gatekeeper microservice. In some cases, a target service supports incoming access policies, and we can add one that only permits access from the gatekeeper. Alternatively, most data storage facilities support KMS keys for encryption. We can leverage the fine-grained security option of KMS keys to provide exclusive access to the gatekeeper microservice. This way, even if another service gains access to the data store, it won't be able to decrypt the data.

All available logging and monitoring capabilities should be enabled for these microservices, and every action within the code should be logged to CloudWatch with the user ID for auditing.

CRON or Scheduled

A CRON microservice is named after the classic CRON scheduling application on Linux servers. This microservice type is configured in EventBridge to run at intervals or at a specific date and time. Typically, this type of microservice would be used for scheduled cleanup and aggregation microservices, as shown on the left of Figure 9-23.

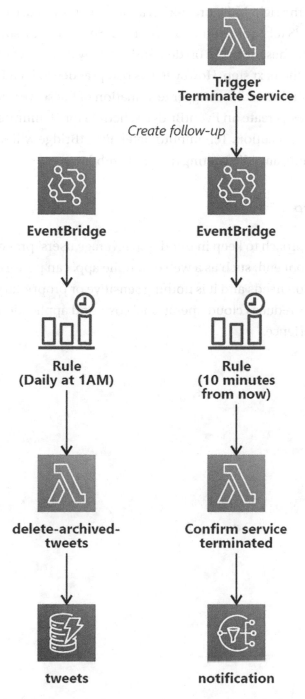

Figure 9-23. *Architecture example: recurring and scheduled one-off events*

The example on the right in Figure 9-23 is another common use case. Many server-based services on AWS take some time to terminate. So, if we are using a microservice to launch and terminate these services on demand, we may need to wait for confirmation before moving on to the next step. However, it is bad practice to let a Lambda microservice idle wait. Instead, we trigger termination of the server-based service (which will take 5–10 minutes), create an EventBridge schedule for 10 minutes later, and then end the microservice execution. Ten minutes later, EventBridge will trigger the next step in the process, avoiding any idle waiting time in Lambda.

Edge Compute

One more design approach to keep in mind is to leverage users' processing power where appropriate. If the front end, such as a web or mobile app, can perform some of the actions the application needs and it is nothing sensitive or proprietary, move that to the front-end scope. This reduces cloud operational costs and application latency, resulting in a better user experience.

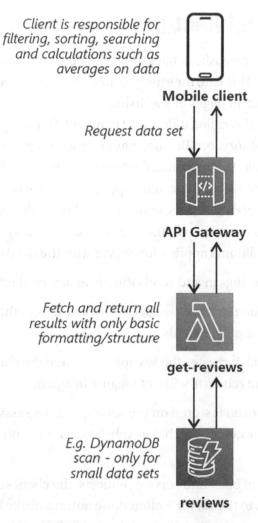

Client is responsible for filtering, sorting, searching and calculations such as averages on data

Mobile client

Request data set

API Gateway

Fetch and return all results with only basic formatting/structure

get-reviews

E.g. DynamoDB scan - only for small data sets

reviews

Figure 9-24. *Architecture example: using client devices for compute*

In Figure 9-24, we leverage the client to perform the search, ordering, and light analysis of the data. This will only work for smaller data sets, but it can offload a significant number of queries to the front end. This greatly reduces latency for the user and the cloud operational cost for the organization.

⚙ Stateless Architecture

In a typical application or website, a back end will keep a record of the user data relevant to their current session. This can, for example, help achieve a seamless experience when navigating through different pages of a website.

This session data is also called a *state* and can contain information such as authentication status, history, profile information, and current activity.

In traditional monolithic applications, information is stored locally on the application server, which is called a stateful application. This is a common pattern since the server offers easily accessible persistent storage. State information can be stored and retrieved very quickly, and any part of the application can easily access it. Let's consider the session flow of a traditional application server with the database on the same server:

1. First, the client logs in and sends the necessary credentials.

2. The application retrieves the user information from the database and validates the credentials.

3. Once validated, it creates the session token that the client can use for subsequent requests without logging in again.

4. This session token is stored on the server, and the session token is returned to the client, which, for websites, is then typically stored in a cookie.

5. For subsequent back-end service requests, the client sends the session token to the server – often done automatically by the browser using the cookie. The application validates the token and retrieves the state needed for the request.

While this design worked and was the gold standard in the days of single-server applications, there are some challenges when migrating such solutions to the cloud. A stateful design works with a single-server application, but in the cloud, there is a drive for scalability, and applications should be run on a cluster of servers (EC2 instances).

When stateful legacy applications are migrated to the cloud, we must ensure that a particular user's requests are always sent to the same server that created their session. If they are sent to a different server, it will not have their session, and they will be forced to log in each time.

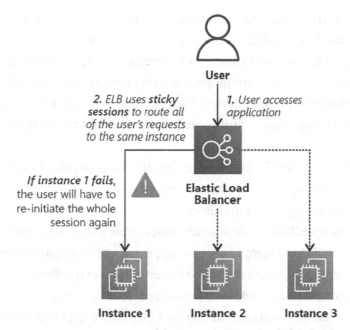

Figure 9-25. *Stateful architecture with sessions example*

When we need to scale the cluster and add more servers, existing users will still be sent to the old servers, making it harder to distribute the load, and the user experience will suffer. If a server fails, the session data on that server will be lost. The cluster will redirect users to a working server, forcing them to log in again so a new session can be created.

Instead of stateful, a stateless design is more suitable for modern cloud applications. The term *stateless* can be a little misleading. It does not mean the absence of sessions; it's about where the session data is stored. In a stateless design, sessions are stored in an external storage solution, such as a database.

If we look at Figure 9-25 again, but we move the sessions to an external database service, then, after receiving the credentials from the user, the application will still retrieve the user information, validate the credentials, and generate a session token. However, in our new architecture, the token is sent to the external database instead of stored locally, and, similarly, for subsequent requests the session is retrieved from the external database.

Multiple servers in an autoscaling infrastructure now all have access to the same sessions, and the load can be distributed evenly when it scales. Similarly, server failures should go unnoticed by the users as another server will simply take over. Centralized sessions also make it easier to manage sessions and perform visitor analytics. A downside to this design is added latency. Time is needed for an additional database query for every incoming request and sometimes two if data needs to be added to a session.

While I have used servers in these examples, the same applies to containers. They can support both stateful and stateless designs, but the latter will be needed for scalability and redundancy in our architecture.

With Serverless, specifically Lambda microservices, a stateful approach is not possible. Microservices have temporary storage, but there is no guarantee that it will be available or even the same microservice instance between different requests. With microservices, we can take a stateless approach, preferably using the fast DynamoDB database to store sessions (as shown in Figure 9-26). However, even with the speed of DynamoDB, there is still added latency for the additional requests. As we covered, latency is generally a challenge with this architecture, so there is a drive to reduce it as much as possible.

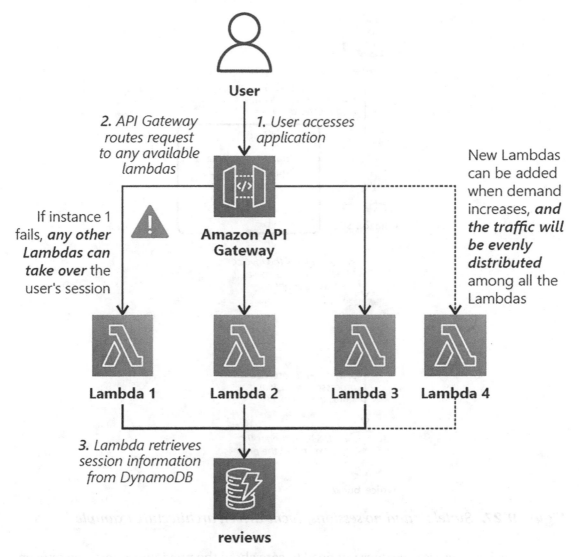

User

2. API Gateway routes request to any available lambdas

1. User accesses application

New Lambdas can be added when demand increases, *and the traffic will be evenly distributed* among all the Lambdas

If instance 1 fails, *any other Lambdas can take over* the user's session

Amazon API Gateway

Lambda 1   **Lambda 2**   **Lambda 3**   **Lambda 4**

3. Lambda retrieves session information from DynamoDB

reviews

Figure 9-26. *Stateless Lambda architecture with sessions in DynamoDB*

Using a database for sessions is relatively similar to traditional session management, making it quite comfortable for developers still adjusting to Serverless. However, given the latency, it's not the ideal way to approach Serverless architecture. Instead, we want to get away from sessions and switch to thinking of applications more in terms of events, as shown in Figure 9-27.

For example, a microservice that creates an invoice does not need a session; it needs to be triggered by an event with data that it injects into an invoice template and then saves as a PDF to be further handled by the next step in the process.

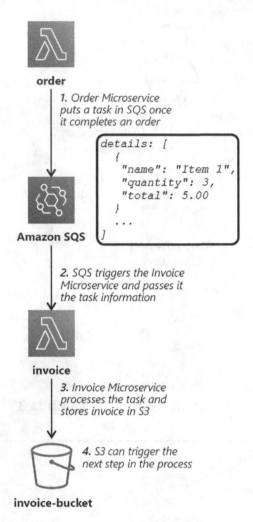

order

*1. Order Microservice
puts a task in SQS once
it completes an order*

```
details: [
  {
    "name": "Item 1",
    "quantity": 3,
    "total": 5.00
  }
  ...
]
```

Amazon SQS

*2. SQS triggers the Invoice
Microservice and passes it
the task information*

invoice

*3. Invoice Microservice
processes the task and
stores invoice in S3*

*4. S3 can trigger the
next step in the process*

invoice-bucket

Figure 9-27. *Stateless and no sessions, event-driven architecture example*

An invoice microservice does not need to care about the previous or next step or even about the data itself – at least not more than where each parameter goes in the invoice template. Its only concern is receiving some data, doing its task, and returning a result.

⚙ Decoupling Microservices

Coupling is the relationship between two components in an application that defines how closely they work together and are dependent on each other. Decoupling is when we seek to reduce that dependency without impacting the output or quality of the component. This is something that microservices are especially suited for as they are by nature independent and self-contained.

The reason for decoupling is to improve fault tolerance and enable each component to perform its respective tasks independent of the performance of other components in a workflow. Self-healing and automated error reporting can be designed into a decoupled workflow by monitoring each component and responding to events such as failures.

Decoupling Started with Servers

Decoupling a request from the processor is not new to Serverless architecture; it was traditionally an approach to buffering requests hitting a scaling cluster of servers – giving them time to catch up to demand and process a backlog. Administrators deployed message brokers using services like RabbitMQ or Apache Kafka, as shown in Figure 9-28. This often involved a second cluster of servers that needed to be managed and maintained.

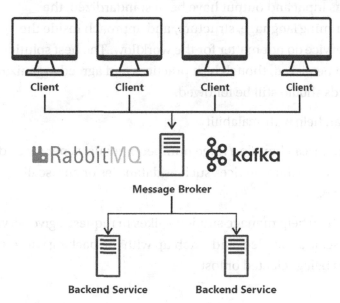

Figure 9-28. *Decoupled architecture without cloud services*

Such systems were considered critical, and considerable effort was required to ensure that the message brokers could scale as needed, perform reliably, and remain available.

Benefits of Decoupling

Decoupling further improves the independence of microservices:

- Independence makes it easier to update microservices as the trigger, input, and output are standardized.

- Similarly, decoupled microservices are easier to scale independently from other components.

- Decoupling makes it easier for multiple applications to use a single shared microservice and for multiple developers to work on different microservices in parallel.

- Workflows become more flexible; it is easier to develop decision trees with dynamic sequences and add or remove steps to or from the workflow.

- Lastly, as input and output have been standardized, the programming language, structure, and approach inside the microservice do not matter for the workflow. The best solution for the task can be picked, though best practices and agreed organizational standards should still be followed.

Decoupling can help with scalability:

- A job queue can handle a huge number of requests per second, typically more than services such as databases or autoscaling containers.

- A queue can help manage sudden spikes in requests, give services time to scale as needed, and catch up with the backlog without requests being rejected or lost.

Challenges of Decoupling

Decoupling is always an asynchronous process that will add latency to the total request time:

- This makes it ill-suited for some use cases, and there needs to be a way to push an update to the client once the request has been completed.

There are also additional costs to be considered:

- The job queue service is chargeable for each job and interaction.

- While individual charges are low, they can add up at scale.

The architectural complexity increases:

- Distributed, asynchronous, and parallel patterns come with their own challenges and often a steep learning curve.

- Eventual consistency instead of guaranteed needs to be considered in applications handling data.

- Duplicate events may happen, which will need to be identified and appropriately handled by components.

- Fan-out decoupled patterns mean there will be multiple recipients of event messages, which can also bring new challenges.

Decoupling Example

In Figure 9-29, we have three coupled microservices. As each microservice completes its task, it passes the output directly to the next microservice in the workflow. If any microservice fails in this architecture, the entire request will fail because the previous microservices expect a positive response to be able to complete the request.

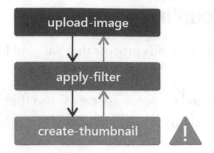

Figure 9-29. *Coupled microservice flow*

When an error occurs, it is not the expected response, so only an error can be returned to the user, despite the fact that at least partial processing was completed. The request and any file data are also lost and need to be resubmitted by the user after the issue has been resolved.

Decoupling can improve this workflow significantly, as shown in Figure 9-30.

Instead of each microservice sending its output directly to the next microservice, it sends the output to a job queue. This queue will, in turn, trigger the next step in the workflow. When the next microservice successfully completes its task, it removes it from the queue and passes the output to the next step and so forth.

If a microservice fails, the task will not be removed from the queue and become active again after a short while. The queue will try to trigger the microservice again, auto-recovering from any temporary issues. If that does not work, then a notification can be sent to the application team to manually resolve the issue.

Once the issue is resolved, the task can be sent back to the queue for the workflow to continue where it left off. The request, and the file data, will not be lost, so it does not need to be resubmitted by the user.

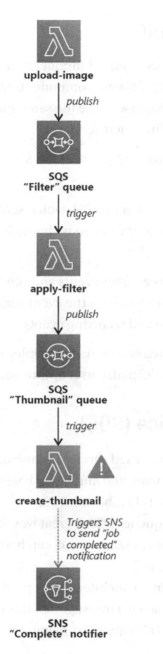

Figure 9-30. *Decoupled microservice flow*

⚙ AWS: Decoupling

The main requirements for decoupling components are that the producers (components sending a result event) and subscribers (components triggered by the event) agree on a standard schema for the messages and use the same message broker. AWS commonly uses four services for decoupling microservices:

1. Simple Queue Service (SQS), where tasks are added to a queue for processing.

2. Simple Notification Service (SNS), which sends notifications in various formats and over various channels to one or more endpoints.

3. EventBridge, which can filter events and send notifications to specific AWS services based on the event content. EventBridge can also schedule future and recurring events.

4. Step Functions, which can manage complex workflows with multiple steps, parallel paths, user approvals, and more.

Simple Queue Service (SQS)

SQS is likely the most frequently used service for microservice decoupling. It is easy to set up and is Serverless (fully managed and billed based on actual usage). SQS integrates with many AWS services such as Lambda and S3.

Besides decoupling, SQS queues offer a great way to buffer cloud services that need to scale – such as databases or containers. SQS can hold the tasks while the service scales up to meet the increased demand.

We create an SQS queue in the architecture. A producer, such as a microservice, can create and send a task – also called a message – to this queue, while a consumer retrieves and processes the message. SQS is many-to-many. A queue can have multiple producers and multiple consumers.

After a consumer retrieves a message from the queue, it will be hidden from other consumers for a while. The consumer can permanently delete the message once it completes successfully. In the case of an error, the message will not be deleted and will return to an active state for another consumer to pull and attempt processing.

When a producer sends a message to the queue, it can configure a delay of up to 15 minutes before it is available to consumers. How long a message is hidden from other consumers can be configured up to 12 hours – this is typically linked to how long it takes for the message to be processed. How long a message is retained in the queue when no consumers retrieve it can be configured up to 14 days.

We can configure how many message retries are permitted by consumers before the task is considered permanently failed. It can then be deleted or moved to a second queue called a dead letter queue for failure handling.

SQS Message Delay and Visibility Timeout

Sometimes, when we add a new message to a queue, we might need to introduce a delay before the message is available to the consumers. This can be useful in scenarios such as service termination, where we may want to ensure the service was terminated before continuing the workflow.

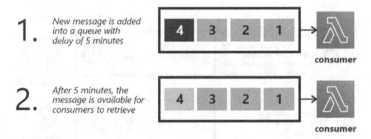

Figure 9-31. *Adding an SQS message with visibility delay*

We can achieve this by configuring the visibility delay to the time we expect the service needs to terminate, 5 minutes in Figure 9-31. Only after this delay will consumers be able to retrieve the message.

When a consumer retrieves a message from the queue, the message is hidden from the queue for the visibility timeout.

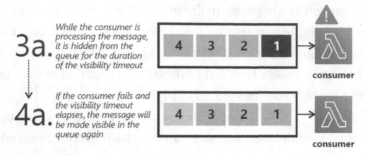

Figure 9-32. *SQS message returns to the queue after the visibility timeout*

In Figure 9-32 the message is returned to the queue again after the visibility timeout. If the consumer is unreachable or fails to process the message, then the message can be picked up by another consumer or the same one if the issue was temporary.

For this reason, the consumer must delete the message from the queue when it does process it successfully to avoid the same task being processed again after the visibility timeout, as shown in Figure 9-33.

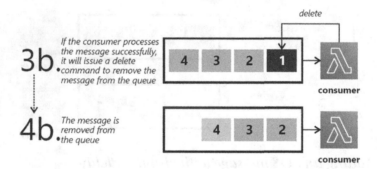

Figure 9-33. *Deleting an SQS message after it is successfully processed*

This is also why the timeout is usually configured slightly higher than the expected time needed to process a message. This is even enforced when adding a Lambda microservice as a consumer; SQS will not permit the visibility timeout to exceed the configured Lambda timeout.

SQS supports two types of queues: standard and FIFO (first-in-first-out), shown in Figure 9-34.

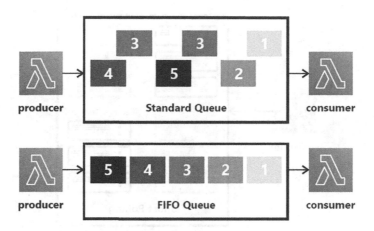

Figure 9-34. *SQS standard and FIFO queue types*

In standard queues, the messages are not ordered, and there is a chance of messages being duplicated or pulled twice by consumers, which will need to be addressed in the consumer code.

If the order of messages is critical and duplication is not acceptable, then the first-in-first-out or FIFO queue type can be considered. For a slightly higher fee, this queue ensures that the order of messages is strictly preserved and that there will be no duplication.

SQS offers two polling methods: short and long, shown in Figure 9-35.

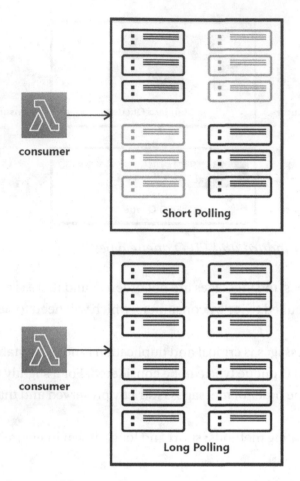

Figure 9-35. *SQS short and long polling*

With short polling, SQS retrieves messages from a small subset of SQS instances. We get a near-instant response using short polling, even if there are no messages on those particular instances.

Usually, long polling is preferred as it is more cost-effective, but it does introduce a latency. With long polling, we can configure up to 20 seconds to wait for new messages to be visible, and all SQS instances are checked. This approach can reduce the number of requests needed, making it more cost-effective as each request is chargeable.

SQS and Lambda Integration

In Serverless architecture, the most common design pattern with SQS will be with Lambda microservice consumers. Lambda, and much of this integration, is fully managed, making it easier to set up but also providing less control over the integration.

When the integration is initially created, or when messages arrive after a long period of inactivity, Lambda will automatically poll the SQS queue using five parallel long-polling connections. The polling is handled entirely by the Lambda service; nothing needs to be coded for this in the microservice. There is no Lambda polling charge, but it results in around 650,000 SQS requests per month, costing a total of 26 cents.

Lambda monitors the number of incoming messages for the SQS queue. When it detects that the number of messages is increasing, it will adjust the polling frequency, adding 20 additional requests and 60 concurrent microservice instances.

As long as the number of messages keeps increasing, it will continue to scale the polling and concurrent microservices until it hits Lambda's concurrency soft limit – 1000 by default. As the number of incoming messages decreases, Lambda will reduce the polling frequency by ten requests and the concurrency by 30 each step.

The fact that Lambda scales until it hits the concurrency limit is a considerable risk. It means this one microservice is taking up all of the concurrency available in this account and region, potentially blocking other microservices from executing. This makes it important to carefully manage the concurrency of microservices triggered by SQS. We could increase the regional concurrency limit, though this may only be delaying the inevitable. Alternatively, we can configure reserved concurrency on the microservice handing the SQS queue. However, this can result in Lambda being unable to handle some SQS messages if there are more pollers than microservice instances (we have no control over the number of pollers created by the Lambda service).

In this case, the unhandled messages will get sent back to the queue. Depending on the queue settings, this could result in messages being discarded as failed before they have even reached the microservice. However, in practice, this outcome is less likely to occur, and it at least limits the impact even if it does.

If we control the producer, there might also be an option to limit the speed at which messages are added to the queue. However, I would not usually recommend this as it can cause issues in the future when scaling or if the limit is removed.

An approach to optimizing queue handling and potentially managing concurrency issues is **batch processing**. When we integrate SQS with Lambda, we can indicate the batch size – the number of messages to send to Lambda with each request. For many use cases, just one message would likely make sense, guaranteeing the least latency.

However, the batch size can be up to 10,000 for a standard queue. This means a poll could result in up to 10,000 messages being delivered in a single microservice trigger.

The batch window – the time the poller will wait to fill the batch – can be up to 300 seconds. With a batch size of one, it will return as soon as it has one message. For larger batch sizes, it will wait until it reaches the batch size target or for the request to expire after the batch window before returning the result to the Lambda poller.

Another area outside our control is that messages will be automatically deleted from the SQS queue if the Lambda response is a success. This can cause problems if the microservice responds with an error message but not an actual error response code. The SQS message will be deleted in that case, even if something went wrong in the microservice code that it was trying to report in the error message.

In the past, batches would succeed or fail as a whole, which meant partial failures needed to be manually addressed in the microservice code. However, in November 2021, AWS introduced a new partial batch response. Microservices can now return a list of failed message IDs, and SQS will only return those messages to the queue.

Figure 9-36 offers a visual representation of Lambda's integration with SQS. At the top left, we have the five default polling instances, sending long-poll requests to the SQS queue. When we configure Lambda to use a batch size of two and a batch window of 10 seconds, Lambda will wait for 10 seconds **or** until two messages appear in the queue – whichever comes first – and then pass the result to the microservice.

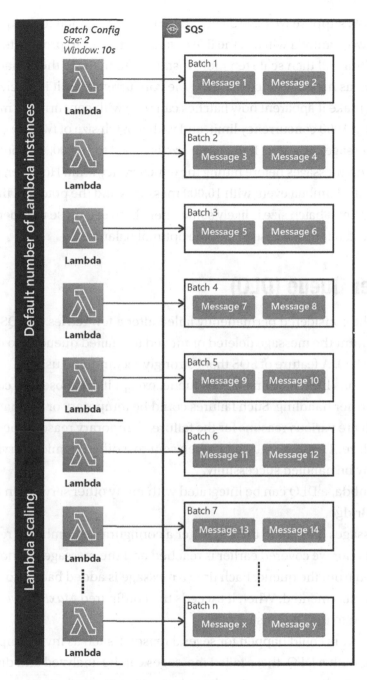

Figure 9-36. *Lambda and SQS integration*

In Figure 9-36, suppose we have 30 messages that were added to the queue. With a batch size of two, Lambda will use the five default instances to process ten of the messages. Lambda will then scale ten more instances to manage the remaining batches of two and so on, as messages increase until the concurrency limit is reached.

This should make it apparent how batches can help with concurrency management. Within the default 1000 concurrency limit, and with a batch size of two, we can effectively manage 2000 messages at a time. If the batch size is raised to 10,000, we could potentially manage 10 million messages before hitting the concurrency limit. However, given the likely overhead of a Lambda event with 10,000 messages and the potential time to process that, the most optimal batch size is likely somewhere between those numbers – something that should be tested for each case to find the optimal balance.

Dead Letter Queue (DLQ)

A message can be considered permanently failed after a few retries. In SQS, we can configure if we want the message deleted or moved to a failed queue, also called a dead letter queue or DLQ. A feature of SQS that I strongly recommend using.

A DLQ functions like an ordinary SQS queue, except its purpose is to collect failed messages for further handling. Such failures could be temporary or permanent in nature, and within each are various reasons for the failure. Temporary reasons include network or hardware failure. The same message, when sent to a different microservice instance, could potentially be handled successfully.

Besides Lambda, a DLQ can be integrated with many other services in AWS, such as SNS and EventBridge.

In SQS, messages are sent to the DLQ after a configurable number of retries – when the visibility timeout we covered earlier is reached and the message has not been explicitly deleted from the queue. Each time a message is added back into the queue, *ReceiveCount* is incremented. When it exceeds the configured *MaxReceiveCount*, the message is moved to the DLQ instead.

Permanent errors could happen for several reasons, such as invalid input data or a bug in the code. With a DLQ, these failed messages can be analyzed and discarded or republished back to the source queue after a bug has been fixed.

To visualize this, Figure 9-37 provides an architecture example for an image upload pipeline.

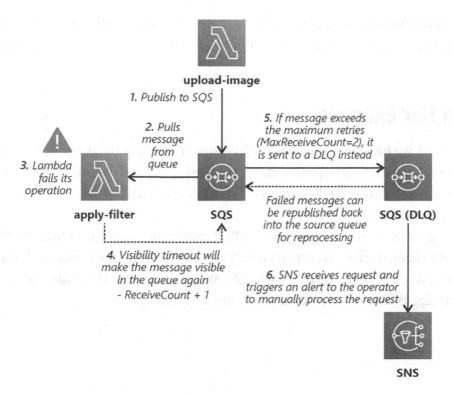

Figure 9-37. *Decoupled image upload and processing architecture*

When a user submits a new request, the Lambda microservice *upload-image* creates a message in the SQS queue. A separate microservice, *apply-filter,* retrieves the message from SQS for processing.

Ideally, the *apply-filter* microservice will succeed, and the workflow will continue as planned. However, *apply-filter* could also fail. A common cause of image functions failing is the **format** of the uploaded file. Because *apply-filter* fails the request, the message is not deleted and, after the visibility timeout, is added back into the queue, and *ReceiveCount* is increased by 1.

Since the uploaded format is unsupported, all subsequent processing attempts will predictably also fail until *ReceiveCount* exceeds *MaxReceiveCount,* and the message is promptly sent to the DLQ.

In Figure 9-37, we configured the DLQ to trigger an SNS notification when a new failed task message is added to it. The application team can then follow up, investigate, and decide if it's simply an invalid format or a valid image format for which support could be added in a future update.

If it is an issue with the application code, the developer can choose to republish these failed messages back to the source queue after the bug is fixed to reprocess the failed messages.

SQS Buffer Example

In Figure 9-38, we have an object recognition container where users can submit images. The container will identify objects in the images using machine learning. Typically I would recommend using the Rekognition service for this activity instead of a container, but bear with me for this example.

We use S3 to host the front end – typically, CloudFront would be in front of this, but we wanted to keep the architecture simple. We are using a Fargate container for the object recognition service as it might feasibly run for more than 15 minutes on large complex images – the model prioritizes quality over speed.

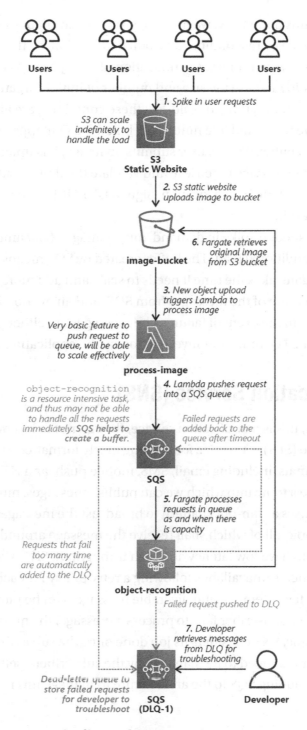

Figure 9-38. *Using SQS to buffer scaling operations*

As the service gains popularity, we need to ensure the availability of the back end. Fargate containers scale by responding to resource utilization, so this is a step-by-step process with some delays to monitor the utilization of newly scaled containers before adding more. We could increase the size and number of initial Fargate instances, providing more capacity and time to scale. But these containers are always on, which will result in considerable waste and idle time being billed for. Our approach in Figure 9-38 is to use SQS to create a buffer.When a user submits an image, it is uploaded into S3. This triggers a Lambda microservice to retrieve and validate the image and publish a new SQS message containing the image location (signed GET URL) and a destination (signed POST URL) for the result.

In the event of a sudden spike in demand, fully managed S3, Lambda, and SQS will scale to handle any additional load. The buffer created by SQS means that messages can wait there while Fargate takes the time it needs to scale and add more containers. As it scales, it will take on more of the messages from SQS, and an overload from the sudden peak can be avoided. In the event of failures, the messages are either added back into the SQS queue or go to a DLQ for further investigation by the application team.

Simple Notification Service (SNS)

As the name implies, this is a notification service, though not to be confused with Simple Email Service (SES) – a service for sending nicely formatted emails to users. SNS supports several formats, including email, SMS, mobile push, and HTTP endpoints.

In SNS, we create a topic into which we can publish messages, much like SQS. However, SNS uses a "fan-out" pattern to broadcast the messages to one or more subscribers of the topic, all of which shall receive the message around the same time.

SNS is designed to have low latency and high throughput. SNS will attempt to redeliver if a subscriber is unavailable, following a retry policy for each endpoint type.

Like SQS, after a few attempts, undeliverable messages can be moved to a DLQ for review. Unlike SQS, if a subscriber fails to process a message, the message cannot be added back to the topic. SNS considers its job done once the subscriber has received the message. Errors after that need to be managed by the subscriber itself.

We can consider adding SQS to the architecture to manage this risk, as shown in Figure 9-39.

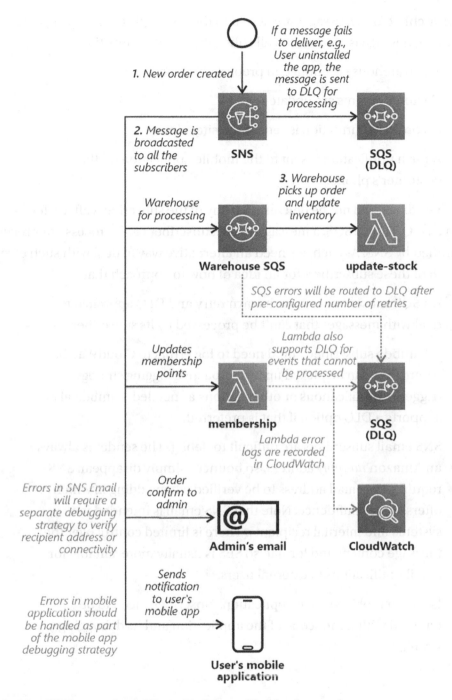

Figure 9-39. *SNS error handling on the available channels*

In this architecture, messages are added to the SNS topic at the top, a new order in this case. The message is then sent to all subscribers at the same time:

1. The warehouse is notified to prepare the order.

2. Customer points are updated.

3. An order confirmation is sent to the site admin.

4. A push notification is sent to the mobile application on the customer's phone.

Messages that could not be **delivered** to any of the subscribers after a few retries are moved to a DLQ. Unlike SQS, a message that a subscriber can't process after receiving it is **not** handled by SNS. As such, we need an alternative way to deal with such errors. Let's look at each of these subscribers for an idea of how to approach that:

1. An SQS subscriber can use its own retry and DLQ approach to deal with messages that can't be processed by its subscribers.

2. A Lambda subscriber would need to log errors to CloudWatch, where they can be picked up by a proactive logging strategy, triggering notifications or other actions as needed. Lambda also supports a DLQ option if that is preferred.

3. SNS email subscribers are difficult to debug. The sender is always an Amazon *no-reply* address, so bounces simply disappear. SNS requires the email address to be verified when adding it, which offers some confidence. Note that SNS email is intended for systems and internal recipients. There is limited control over the message content and format, so SES is usually more suitable for email notifications to external users.

4. Issues in mobile or web application subscribers need to be handled within the scope of the application and its debugging strategy.

EventBridge

This service is a successor to CloudWatch Events, it was split off, and new capabilities have since been added. If we need a notification solution for AWS service targets, EventBridge is usually a better choice than SNS.

EventBridge is a Serverless event bus for building event-driven applications. Using EventBridge, we can set up rules to filter events and specify the targets to send the events. Event sources can be cloud services, scheduled events, custom events, or even some third-party SaaS applications.

EventBridge can transform data between the event source and the event targets. This can be useful, among other things, for formatting a message in a way that a recipient might require.

If a message fails to deliver, EventBridge will retry up to 185 times within 24 hours. Like other services we have covered, undeliverable messages are moved to a DLQ.

Another interesting feature of EventBridge is the ability to retain and *replay* events. We can archive older events and replay them in the event bus. This is especially helpful for testing and debugging.

On the surface, SNS and EventBridge seem quite similar. They are both used to decouple publishers from subscribers and capable of filtering messages and result in a fan-out broadcast to recipients. However, there are some important differences between these services, so it pays to pick the right one for a given use case.

Events

EventBridge is generally intended for events and notifications within a cloud application, while SNS is aimed at external targets, though more technical targets than end users. And this is reflected in many of the attributes of each service.

Integrations

EventBridge is integrated with over 35 target AWS services, compared with the three offered by SNS – Firehose, Lambda, and SQS.

Number of targets

SNS supports millions of subscribers, compared with up to 1,500 for EventBridge, clearly reflecting that SNS is intended to be used for many external users, while EventBridge is for fewer internal components.

Message routing

Recipients are configured in EventBridge by the person provisioning the service. SNS recipients subscribe to an available topic with a required confirmation step. For example, email recipients must click a link in a received confirmation email, while HTTP recipients must respond to a confirmation query with an appropriate response.

Input transformation

EventBridge can transform message data between a source and destination, avoiding the need to do so in a microservice. It can also transform a message to match a particular input schema of a recipient that is outside of our control.

Message filtering

They can both filter messages, but EventBridge can also filter events based on IP addresses.

Pricing

EventBridge costs a dollar for every million requests, compared with 50 cents for SNS. SNS also enjoys 1 million free-tier requests per month.

Other features

EventBridge has additional capabilities such as Schema Registry and event sequence replay.

In Figure 9-40, we have another architecture example. This is again a back-end flow for an ecommerce application, but this time we are using *EventBridge* to pass messages around.

EventBridge has been implemented much like SNS was in Figure 9-39. However, there is one key difference. The submitted order message sent to EventBridge contains a lot of information. In EventBridge, we can transform this to retain only the relevant information in our notification to the recipients. The rest of this architecture remains mostly the same, and the notification is sent to all recipients simultaneously. Failed deliveries are retried and sent to a DLQ after repeated failures. Message processing failures need to be dealt with by the recipients. There is one new addition to the architecture, a unique capability of EventBridge that allows us to schedule an event at a recurring interval or a specific time and date in the future.

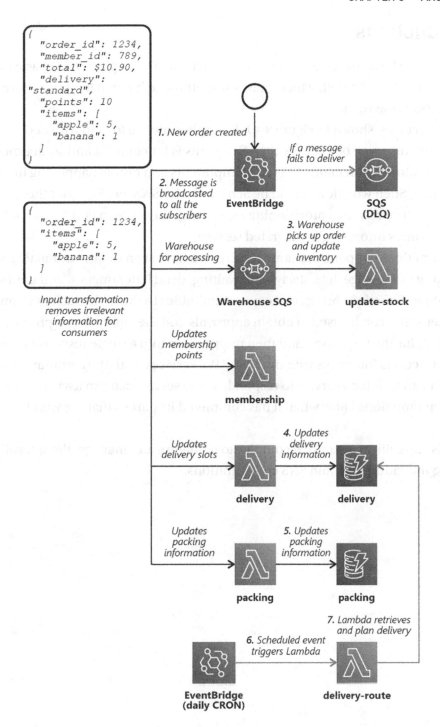

Figure 9-40. *Decoupling architecture with EventBridge*

Step Functions

The services we have looked at so far have been relatively simple in their basic premise: an event happens on the left, which causes something to happen in one or more components on the right.

Step Functions, shown in Figure 9-41, is another service to help with decoupling, but for a very different type of use case. Step Functions is for complex and sometimes long-running workflows, with many different components and events happening in linear and parallel paths. Such workflows could be achieved with SNS and SQS, but there would be significantly more resource provisioning and configuration. Step Functions packages all those capabilities into a single integrated service.

Step Functions supports the same features we have seen so far: automatic retries, transforming of message data, delays and waiting, dead letter queues, and notifications. However, Step Functions brings some new capabilities to the table, such as manual request steps that can be used to obtain approvals and the ability to run processes in parallel, wait for the responses, and then merge them into a single response object.

Step Functions integrates with over 200 AWS services, with the communication often two-way. It can wait for a service to respond, or the service can run asynchronously and let Step Functions know when it has completed its part so that the workflow can continue.

All this capability can make it complex to configure and manage, though still easier than using individual SQS and SNS configurations.

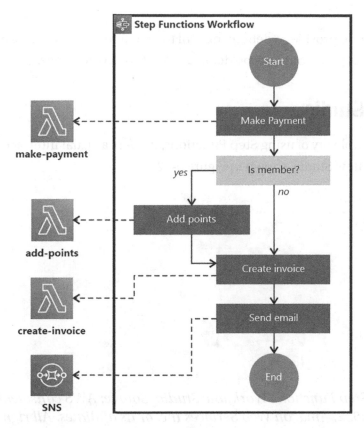

Figure 9-41. *Decoupling architecture with Step Functions*

Step Functions has two run modes: standard and express.

Processing guarantee

Standard enforces exactly-once processing, while express has at-least-once. This means it might accidentally process the same task twice, so the components will need to be able to deal with that accordingly.

Workflow duration

Standard mode can be used for very long-running workflows, up to a year even. The state of the steps can be persisted in a data store or Step Functions, and we can download the execution history for up to 90 days, making it quite auditable. Express, as the name implies, is intended for short-running workflows of up to 5 minutes.

Executions

Standard mode is limited to about 800 executions (jobs) per second, while the main use case for express is high-volume processing, with around 6000 executions per second. These are soft limits per account, which can be increased with a service request.

Debugging

Standard mode provides a debugging tool to help find and resolve issues in the workflow. Express mode can only be debugged via CloudWatch logs.

Workflow Studio

To aid in the complexity of using Step Functions, it offers a visual interface option: Step Functions Workflow Studio, shown in Figure 9-42.

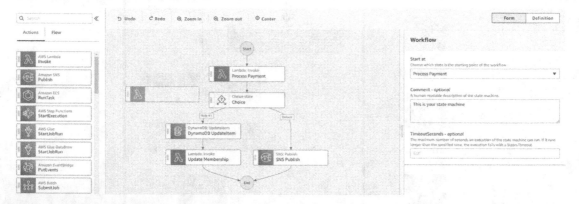

Figure 9-42. *Step Functions Workflow Studio Source: AWS console* `https://aws.` `amazon.com/` *2022, Amazon Web Services Inc. or its affiliates. All rights reserved*

The tool offers drag-and-drop building blocks to design, prototype, and experiment with workflows. It will validate the design and the service API request parameters, but not the existence nor any valid response from the target components.

The tool can export the necessary Step Functions configuration for the completed workflow design. In line with good DevOps practices, provisioning and configuring cloud services, including Step Functions, should be done with CloudFormation or a similar Infrastructure-as-Code (IaC) solution. The exported configuration can be copied into a CloudFormation template to make that easier.

⚙ Event-Driven Architecture

Event-driven architecture is a different way of designing Serverless microservices that is more aligned with the business view of a solution than the technical one. We touched on this briefly at the end of the "Stateless Architecture" section with the invoice PDF microservice that didn't need a session. That microservice was triggered by an event instead.

Microservices in an event-driven architecture represent steps in the business flow or process instead of technical features. The differences may seem subtle, but it makes microservice architecture considerably more easy to understand and to map the user stories or business requirements to technical requirements.

Before diving deeper into event-driven architecture, let's look at service **orchestration** in Figure 9-43, a common way of designing our monolithic applications.

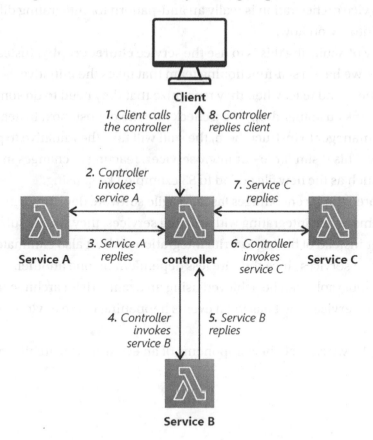

Figure 9-43. *Service orchestration example with Lambda microservices*

In service orchestration, we have a controller that is responsible for coordinating all the instructions and movement of data between the components of a workflow. This can be visualized as an overly zealous micro-manager who insists on being involved in every part of the decision-making process.

With this design, services within the architecture wait for instruction from the controller, which will invoke each service one by one and expects a response before proceeding to the next step. If the manager doesn't give the instruction to start working, the workers will simply sit there and do nothing.

Effectively, we end with a distributed monolith. The services are tightly coupled with one another through the controller, and services must wait for one another before they can proceed with their task. If there is a failure, the entire workflow stops.

This design also introduces a single point of failure that the developers will need to address. If our controller fails, like our manager being on leave, the whole process stops. Thus, service orchestration is really an anti-pattern for integrating different microservices into a workflow.

A better way of achieving this is to use the service **choreography**. Instead of having a micro-manager, we have a self-functioning team that takes the initiative. Services listen to the environment and react when they recognize that they need to do something.

Imagine a bank customer dropping a check into the deposit box. Instead of waiting for the manager to instruct them, the staff will take the initiative to process it automatically. This is similar to our microservices, reacting to changes in the environment, such as the new file added to S3 example I keep using.

Service choreography encourages fast and agile software development. For application teams, when integrating with existing services, they simply subscribe to the event router instead of having to write integration code. It also eliminates the tight coupling between services since they are less dependent on one another.

Service choreography can be achieved using an event-driven architecture. In this architecture, our services react based on events happening in the environment that have been broadcast.

In Figure 9-44, we can see the components of an event-driven architecture.

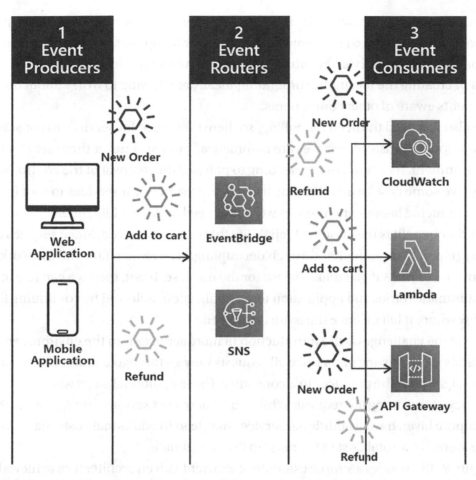

Figure 9-44. *Service choreography architecture example*

First, we have the event producer, which is responsible for the initial trigger or request, for example, a user uploading a file to an S3 bucket or a microservice signaling the completion of their task.

Next, we have the event router, the backbone of this architecture. Routers are responsible for routing the events generated by producers to the consumers. Within the router, we may also be able to apply event transformation actions such as removing certain information from the original event.

Lastly, the event consumer is the recipient of messages broadcast by the router. Consumers will determine if they need to respond to a given event message and then process it.

A benefit of this approach is the increased scalability achieved through decoupling. Since we removed the need for a controller, it is easier for application teams to extend the capabilities of our service by subscribing new services into the environment instead of creating the integration programmatically and having to worry about making components aware of other components.

We also removed the need for polling, so there is no need for services to constantly check for updates. Instead, services are automatically told whenever there are changes in the environment. As a result of not needing to poll and the removal of the controller, we can achieve some cost savings. We can also remove the need for services to wait for one another, reducing latency and the fees we would need to pay for idle time.

Another benefit is the improved reliability that can be achieved. Since services are now less reliant on one another through decoupling, services can fail, and the workflow will continue to run – if that makes sense for the use case. If not, then we can rely on the usual automatic retries and application team notification, followed by continuing the workflow where it left off once the issue is resolved.

One of the challenges is the introduction of more services into the environment, which adds more moving parts since all requests now go through a router instead of going straight from the producer to a consumer. These additional steps will also increase the latency of executing the request. While we achieve cost savings through optimizing our compute layer, having additional services may lead to additional costs that need to be considered in a Total Cost of Ownership (TCO) estimate.

Figure 9-45 provides a simple example of an event-driven architecture achieved using SNS. This video processing workflow allows users to submit their videos to S3 for processing.

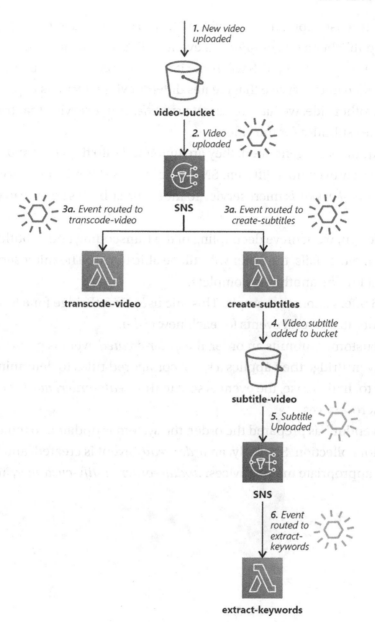

Figure 9-45. *Event-driven video processing workflow*

From the top, a user uploads a new video file into our S3 video bucket. Once completed, S3 publishes a *video-uploaded* event to SNS to indicate a successful upload. Upon receiving the new event, SNS will route it to its subscribers. On one side, we have the *transcode-video* microservice that creates different video formats to play on different devices. On the other side, we have the *create-subtitles* microservice that transcribes the audio and creates subtitles for the video.

Once the subtitles are generated, they are uploaded into the *video-subs* S3 bucket, which creates a new event in a different SNS topic. This SNS topic then forwards the new event to the *extract-keywords* microservice to index the subtitles so we can use the data for searches.

With this design, we achieve decoupling of the transcoding and subtitle microservices. If either fails, the other will still be able to run. The microservices also do not have to wait for one another to complete.

Figure 9-46 offers another example. This one uses EventBridge for a food ordering service that generates several events for each new order.

When the customer submits an order, the *order-created* event is published to EventBridge. EventBridge then applies a set of configured rules to determine where to send the event to. In this case, the event is sent to the *create-order*, *notify-vendor*, and *assign-rider* microservices.

When the vendor has prepared the order, the system is updated to indicate that the order is ready for collection. Similarly, an *order-ready* event is created, and EventBridge routes it to the appropriate microservices: *update-order*, *notify-customer*, and *notify-rider*.

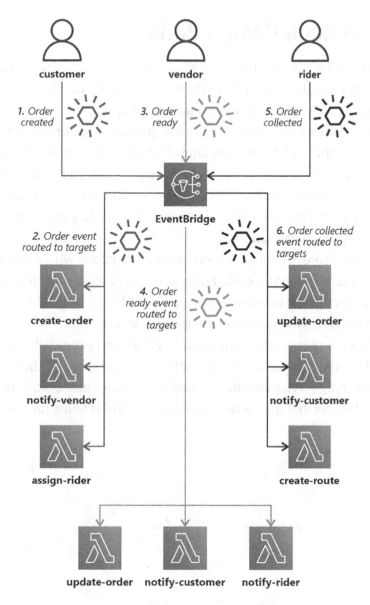

Figure 9-46. *Event-driven food ordering service architecture*

When the rider collects the order, the same things happen again. The *order-collected* event is generated and is routed by EventBridge to the relevant microservices.

While this architecture may look like a service orchestration architecture seen earlier, there is an important difference. Instead of waiting for a reply from each microservice, EventBridge is only responsible for forwarding the events to them.

With this design, if any of the services fail, the workflow will still be able to continue; just that one component may need to be retried or handled via error handling.

⚙ Asynchronous Design Pattern

Usually, API services use a synchronous (sync) design, which receives a request, processes it, and returns the result within the same connection. If the request takes a while to process, the client will have to wait until it is done.

An asynchronous (async) design receives a request, can optionally perform some validation on it, responds to let the client know that the request was successfully **received**, and then ends the connection. The client does not wait on the connection for the actual request result. The back end will process the request and take the time it needs. Any response that may be required will be returned via a new connection, which could be an entirely different channel.

This design can improve the user experience for workflows where users don't necessarily expect an immediate result. For example, a process such as generating an invoice PDF that can then be emailed to the user would work well, while confirming a payment would not be a good candidate for asynchronous.

In Figure 9-47, the user sends a request to API Gateway, which validates the sent parameters and forwards the request to a Lambda microservice. The microservice invokes a long-running service by adding a task to SQS and then quickly returns a confirmation to the user that the request was received and is being processed.

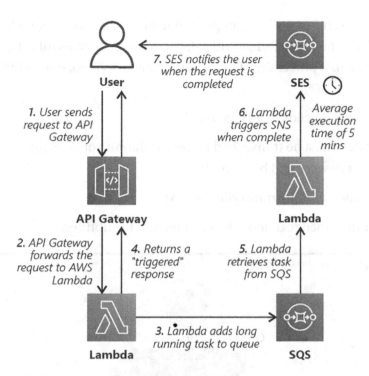

Figure 9-47. *Asynchronous architecture example*

Once the confirmation is returned, the user can proceed with other tasks while the request is processed in the background. When processing completes, the user is notified by an email from SES and can take any follow-up action that may be needed.

Parallel Processing

The fact that asynchronous requests run independently in the background also makes them great for parallel processing. With parallel processing, we split a request into multiple smaller requests and execute them simultaneously. Typically, results are merged once all parallel processes complete.

One example would be a request for which data needs to be retrieved from multiple sources. Each retrieval can be split off and run in parallel. Once all retrievals are done, the data is merged into a single data set before the workflow proceeds to the next step.

Another example would be for requests that consist of multiple sub-requests. For example, when generating thumbnails for a batch of images, each image task can be split off and run in parallel.

Figure 9-48 presents a similar example, but instead of processing multiple images, it performs multiple tasks on a single video file. Use cases such as this often combine parallel and sequential processing. Before publishing the video, four activities need to happen:

1. A thumbnail needs to be generated.

2. The video must be transcoded to three different versions for different devices and bandwidths.

3. The audio has to be transcribed to text.

4. The transcribed text needs to be converted to subtitles.

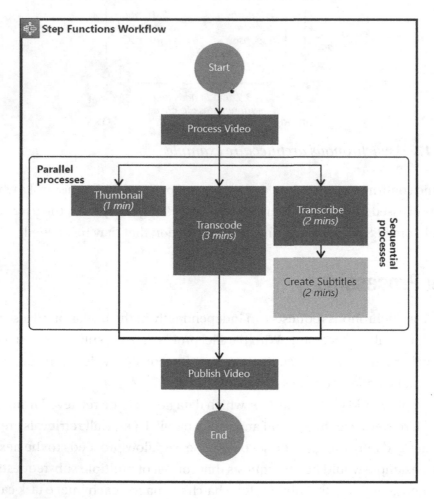

Figure 9-48. *Step Functions parallel processing example*

The first three actions can start simultaneously, though they will take different amounts of time to complete. Action 4 – generating subtitles – can only happen after action 3 – transcribing the text. So these two actions need to be sequential. Still, we can see that by running three of the actions in parallel, the total runtime for this workflow is 4 minutes. If we were to run all actions sequentially, the total runtime would be 8 minutes. Step Functions is a great service for designing and managing this kind of complex parallel and sequential process and merging the results within the same workflow.

Asynchronous design will reduce the initial waiting time for a given request by responding quickly with a "*request received*" status. That does not mean reduced **processing** time; the user will still need to wait for the background process to complete before receiving the final result. However, doing the processing in the background and allowing the user to leave or do other activities can be a better user experience for certain workflows.

If the request can be split and run in parallel, it can also mean reduced processing time. However, this might not lower cloud **costs**. For example, it will still be the same execution time, number of database queries, or other service activities; it will just be running at the same time.

A potential challenge of asynchronous design is that it could increase processing time – if parallel processing is impossible. The request is handled in a separate process, typically with multiple steps that will add to the total latency.

Another challenge is in managing and merging parallel processes. Like any other process, parallel processes can experience errors, so error handling and retries must be considered. Waiting for all processes to successfully complete and merging the different results into a consistent final output can be complex too.

Lastly, reporting results back to the client after processing completes will require a new connection. This can be achieved in various ways depending on the requirements. Common is to send a notification or email if we only need to inform the client or user of the completed status. When follow-up steps are necessary by the client, we can use WebSockets, as we covered earlier in this chapter. Figure 9-49 shows how we can use an API Gateway WebSocket response with a Step Functions workflow.

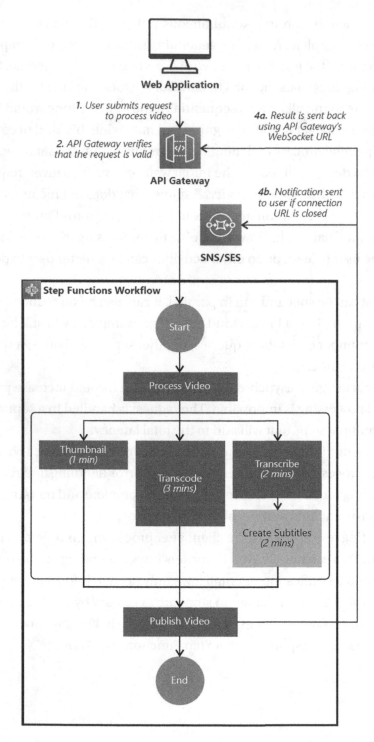

Figure 9-49. *Asynchronous Step Functions with WebSocket response*

As we covered earlier, API Gateway WebSockets establishes a two-way connection between the client and the back end. This allows us to push messages from the back end to the client – without the client needing to ask for them first.

Extending the earlier example, once the processing of the video completes, the *publish video* microservice can construct a completion message with the necessary details, such as a streaming URL for the transcoded video. This message is sent to API Gateway WebSockets, which sends it to the client, where it can be displayed in the UI.

If the connection was dropped, such as the user closed the application, then the microservice can fail over to SNS or SES to send a notification instead. This is a common scenario, so such a failover should always be considered when using WebSockets.

⚙ Containers

The idea of containerizing was born in the bare-metal era, but, at the time, implementing it was not easy. The first commercial container was introduced as a feature of the Solaris 10 UNIX operating system with the name *Zones*.

Containers are similar to virtual machines because both provide a segregated, secure, independent space for software programs to execute while giving the impression of an independent system. However, where virtual machines have their own operating system and so need some time to boot, containers are launched from within an operating system and can boot within seconds or even milliseconds.

The technology eventually found its way to Docker in 2013, changing the notion that containerizing was hard to do. Docker became popular because of its ease to bundle an application with all of its dependencies, enabling it to run the same way on different machines.

The emergence of containers led to cloud providers developing new services to host and manage them, which eventually got the name Container-as-a-Service (CaaS). Google was especially active in this area with a service that eventually got split off into an open source project called Kubernetes. AWS has Elastic Container Service (ECS) and Elastic Kubernetes Service (EKS), which are examples of CaaS.

Lambda vs. Containers

Under the hood, Lambda is essentially a container platform. The function code gets bundled and packaged as a container and then launched on demand within the Lambda service. Its container management platform is called Firecracker, which is available as open source here: `https://github.com/firecracker-microvm/firecracker`.

The main difference between Lambda and other container services is that Lambda is more managed and, therefore, more limited. Sometimes, those limits get in the way of solving a particular problem, for example, any workload that needs to run for more than 15 minutes. If it can't be solved with Lambda, then a container might be the next best option.

Serverless Containers

Until the end of 2017, containers on AWS were not considered Serverless because Elastic Container Service (ECS) and Elastic Kubernetes Service (EKS) services required managing the underlying EC2 instances the containers were launched onto. These servers also needed to be paid for per hour, regardless of utilization.

While this option is still suitable for applications that have larger fleets of containers, AWS launched Fargate in 2017 for those with smaller needs. With Fargate, AWS fully manages the underlying cluster and its instances, so we can just run containers when we need them and only pay for the time the container is available. Note that *available* is not the same as *utilized*, so this billing model is closer to that of EC2 instances than Lambda microservices.

On-demand tasks are the best use case for Fargate, for example, video conversion, machine learning models, and certain data aggregation tasks that need to run longer than a Lambda microservice would support. When only considering the operational service fee, it is not cost-effective to run a Fargate container 24/7. However, if we factor in maintenance and other operational costs and risks, it may still be worth it, as the only responsibility is the contents of the container.

The "True Serverless Containers" section in Chapter 10 details how to implement a fully Serverless task container in ECS Fargate. It does this by only launching the Fargate container when needed and terminating the container again when it is no longer utilized.

Lambda Custom Containers

Launched in 2020, Lambda Custom Containers runs actual containers as a Lambda function. The containers are run in their own isolated environment and were introduced as an alternative to Lambda functions that can be limiting for certain use cases.

We can package and deploy our own container images up to 10 GB in size that can support many more programming languages, tools, and other runtimes than Lambda functions. However, the containers are still bound by the 15-minute execution time limit, so similarly to microservices, these containers should be part of an event-driven architecture.

Lambda Custom Containers helps developers easily build and deploy larger workloads that rely on sizable dependencies, including data-intensive workloads such as machine learning (if no GPU is required). They benefit from the same operational simplicity, automatic scaling, and high availability of Lambda functions.

⚙ AWS: Edge

At the time of writing, Figure 9-50 shows that AWS has over 200 CloudFront edge locations across 47 countries, with several more announced for the coming years. *Regions* offer a full suite of cloud services, while *edge locations* are primarily intended for content delivery.

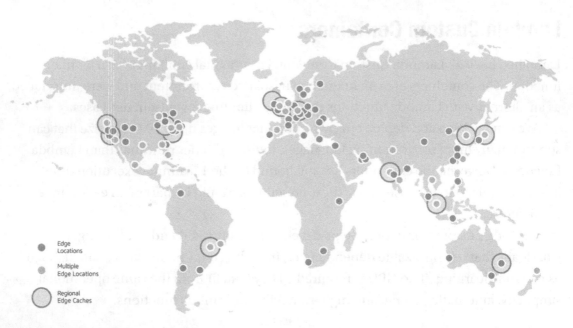

Figure 9-50. *AWS locations Source: AWS websitehttps://aws.amazon.com/*
2022, Amazon Web Services Inc. or its affiliates. All rights reserved

Amazon CloudFront is a content delivery network (CDN) that taps into this global
presence. Using CloudFront, requests for content such as web pages, images, and
videos are cached at edge locations closest to the viewer. Besides providing low-latency
access to content, CloudFront is also useful for reducing the compute demand on back-
end resources. By serving content from the edge, fewer requests are sent to Lambda,
databases, and other services, reducing the cloud cost.

CloudFront is commonly connected to S3, which can host static websites and web
application interfaces. CloudFront integrates with several other AWS services to extend
its capabilities, for example, Web Application Firewall for monitoring traffic and blocking
anything malicious.

Lambda@Edge

Lambda@Edge is a feature of CloudFront that brings Lambda microservices into edge
locations. As with Lambda, there is no infrastructure or software to manage.

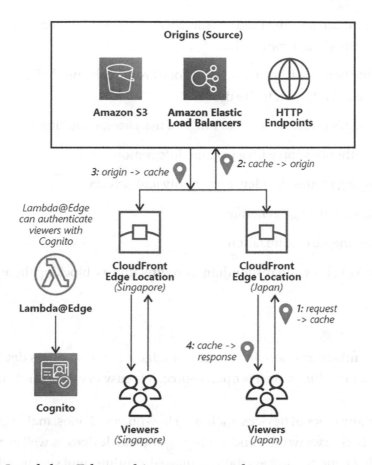

Figure 9-51. *Lambda@Edge architecture example*

With Lambda@Edge, our microservice is deployed and runs at an edge location, minimizing the latency for users. It can be run at four points in a request lifecycle, as seen in Figure 9-51. Once we configure it for a point, the microservice is automatically triggered for each request as it passes through. At each point, the service passes the request to the microservice and continues to the next step using the microservice output as the updated request:

1. The first trigger point is after the request is received but before it is passed to the CloudFront cache.

2. The next point is triggered if no cache is available but before the output is sent to the origin.

3. Then, we can take the origin response and process it before it is sent to the CloudFront cache.

4. Finally, there is a trigger after the CloudFront cache but before the response is returned to the user.

Lambda@Edge is useful for a broad range of use cases, including

- User authentication with a Cognito integration

- Modifying request headers for security and privacy

- Dynamic web page generation

- Search Engine Optimization

- Identifying bots and responding to, redirecting, or blocking them

FreeRTOS

FreeRTOS is essentially an operating system for edge and on-premises devices such as IoT and industrial machines. As it is open source, it is easy to extend and customize for bespoke devices.

It runs on many types of devices, including low-powered ones, making it very versatile. FreeRTOS eases writing and deploying code to devices as well as managing them. It can collect and preprocess data, manage downtime, and synchronise it to the cloud. Local capabilities include data analysis, displaying insights on a screen, and taking action such as triggering alarms or shutting down an integrated system.

Use cases for FreeRTOS include managing monitoring and quality devices in industrial settings, utility monitors used in commercial and residential buildings, and a range of smart devices such as locks, lights, cameras, and more.

IoT Greengrass

Another offering of note is IoT Greengrass, a framework for running scripts, machine learning, and data management. For certain devices running FreeRTOS, it can be installed as a feature. However, Greengrass usually runs on a gateway, with multiple IoT devices connecting to it.

Greengrass can run Lambda functions and Docker containers. Its machine learning capabilities support the deployment and running of cloud-trained machine learning models. This is especially useful for use cases that require minimal latency, such as visual analytics or safety. Greengrass also works offline, useful in locations where connectivity may not be stable, such as the maritime sector.

Greengrass helps simplify managing and scaling an IoT network, with capabilities to deploy over-the-air updates, bug fixes, new features, and local and cloud messaging support. The Greengrass cloud service is Serverless. We pay each month for the number of devices connected to the cloud service. An example architecture is shown in Figure 9-52.

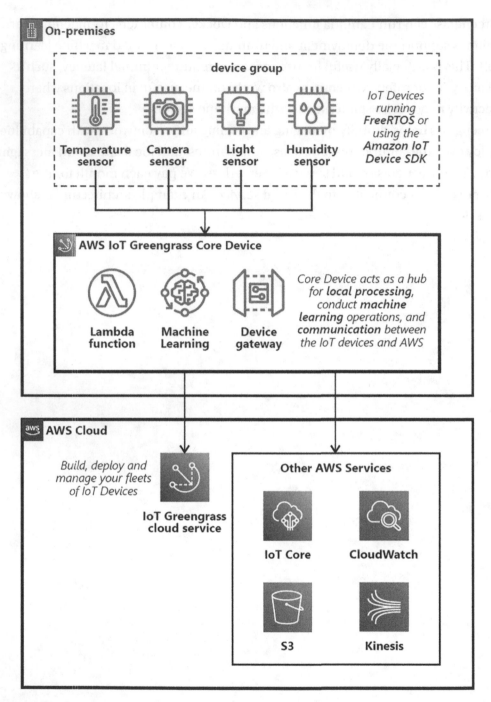

Figure 9-52. *IoT Greengrass architecture example*

Snowball

Snowball is a physical storage device that can be temporarily rented from AWS to transfer large volumes of data into the cloud. The main purpose of Snowball is to overcome network transfer speed limitations. Even on multi-GB connections, it may be faster to use a physical device when transferring petabytes of data to the cloud.

Once our data is loaded onto the Snowball device, we ship it back to AWS, where the data is imported into an S3 bucket in our account. Snowball charges a job fee and a fee for each day that we have the device. Snowball is available in several sizes, though this may vary per region. There is no charge for data transfer, but there is a charge for the S3 upload requests and the resulting storage amount, which will initially be on the standard tier.

Snowball Edge is a version of the device that includes some compute capabilities, allowing it to run Lambda Python microservices. There is even a version with a GPU for processing visual data and running complex machine learning models at the edge. The microservices can preprocess the data being added to the device. We can perform activities such as filtering, cleaning, aggregating, converting, or even visual processing of image and video data.

Outposts

AWS Outposts is another approach to hybrid cloud architecture, enabling organizations to extend the capabilities of the cloud into their on-premises data centers.

AWS Outposts can support many compute, networking, and security services such as EC2 servers, ECS and EKS containers, S3 storage, and RDS databases. Outposts are physical products for installation in an on-premises data center.

There are two types of outposts. The Outpost 42U rack allows us to configure the included server types and storage. Outpost Server is available as a 1U or 2U rack-mounted server. The available cloud services can be managed via the outposts UI in the AWS console and can be interacted with in much the same way as standard AWS services.

Racks are installed and fully managed by AWS. Servers are shipped to the location for self-installation and then managed and supported remotely by AWS.

Use cases for outposts include workloads with sensitive data sets not yet approved for cloud and ultralow-latency applications. They can also offer a potential solution to data sovereignty challenges in countries that do not yet have an AWS region.

⚙ AWS: Internet of Things (IoT)

The Internet of Things refers to the billions of physical devices globally connected to the Internet (either via a private network or public Internet). Each device collects and shares data for monitoring, production, and offered services. The purpose of connecting the devices to the Internet is usually to bring the data back to a central location or for remote control or management of the device.

IoT devices have become ubiquitous over the last couple of years, many becoming part of our day-to-day lives. Any device with *smart* in its name can be considered an IoT device, including smart home assistants, smart watches, smart thermostats, and smart utility monitors. IoT is also common in security, covering Internet-connected cameras, door locks, and alarm systems.

The cloud can be utilized for IoT to provide organizations a head start in managing the complexities of operating a global IoT network and significantly reducing overheads.

Common requirements in IoT projects include

1. Control software running on the IoT devices

2. Authentication and authorization to securely include devices in a network

3. Ability to remotely monitor, manage, and update devices

4. Data collection, verification, and storage

5. Analytics and visualization to derive insights

6. User and profile data management

7. Remote control and APIs to interact remotely with devices

IoT is well supported on AWS, with a range of mostly Serverless and fully managed services and tools that can support IoT projects end to end. For example, Greengrass, which I mentioned earlier, can be run on the devices or gateways to manage processing and communication at the edge and provide authorization and monitoring capabilities.

Once the IoT devices are connected to the cloud, they can integrate with many other cloud services and custom microservices to achieve many unique requirements.

The heart of the AWS IoT cloud services is IoT Core, shown in Figure 9-53. It is this service that potentially billions of IoT devices globally can connect to. Connectivity, authorization, monitoring, messaging, rules, and shadowing for IoT devices are key capabilities of this service. It is also Serverless, which means we only pay for what we use with no idle fees or minimum utilization requirements.

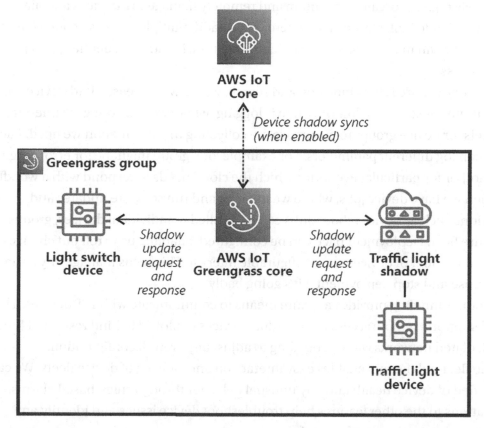

Figure 9-53. *IoT Core service in the cloud works with Greengrass at the edge*

Rules in IoT Core are used to perform actions on incoming messages and data from the devices. These actions can include passing the data to another cloud service as an event, triggering notifications, or kicking off a workflow in the cloud.

Shadowing creates a virtual copy of an IoT device that can remember and restore its state. For example, a shadow of an IoT light can receive a command to make the light red – even when the physical light is disconnected. When the physical device connects again, the virtual copy will remember that the light state is supposed to be red and update the physical light automatically.

For those familiar with technical specifics of IoT, Core supports LoRaWAN or low-power-long-range-wide-area-network devices. This capability enables us to connect these types of devices to the cloud, and we can avoid the need for developing such a network.

AWS IoT Device Management offers a dashboard overview and capabilities to securely register, organize, monitor, and remotely manage IoT devices at scale. Features include bulk registration, where we can add multiple devices at once into the network. We can manage each device's authorization, identity, credentials, and policy-based access.

Another feature is fleet indexing and search, where we can easily find devices based on attributes or state. In addition, there is logging, where we can configure fine-grained log levels for device groups to ensure we are collecting the information we need. Each group can log different parameters. For example, one group might be for error logging and another for particular events for which the cloud needs to respond with a workflow.

Then we have device jobs, where we monitor and run software updates and operations such as device reboot. Jobs can be applied to individual devices, groups, or the entire fleet. Deployment pace can be configured, enabling us to roll out changes to a specified number of devices at a configurable interval. This helps manage any issues that might arise and stop deployment if it's going badly.

Secure tunneling provides a secure means to communicate with IoT devices. The tunnel supports remote access to individual devices deployed behind restricted firewalls or on isolated networks without needing to adjust any firewall configuration.

The fleet hub feature enables easy interaction and viewing of device fleets. We can be notified of device health and any unusual behavior through rules-based alarms. Integrations to the other features help troubleshoot device issues and identify any corrective actions that may be needed.

A related IoT service is Device Defender – a security suite specifically developed for IoT. It continuously assesses devices against compliance and security best practices. Device Defender is Serverless and bills for the number of devices being audited in a given month.

A capability of Device Defender is audit, shown in Figure 9-54. This compares device resources such as certificates, policies, and device IDs against AWS's IoT security best practices. It will report non-compliance issues such as multiple devices using the same identity or overly permissive policies not following the PoLP.

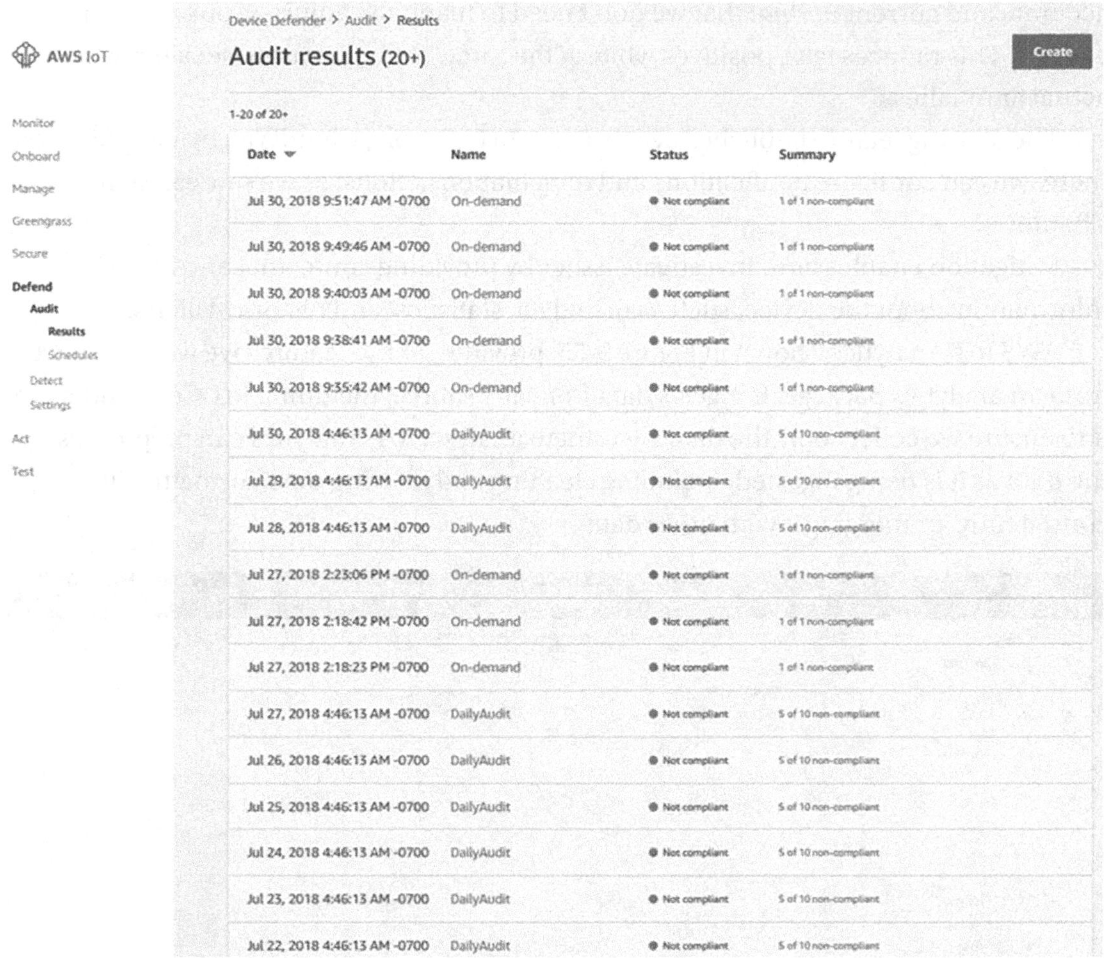

Figure 9-54. *AWS IoT Device Defender audit results Source: AWS console* `https://aws.amazon.com/` *2022, Amazon Web Services Inc. or its affiliates. All rights reserved*

Another capability is Rules Detect, where we can define what *normal* looks like by configuring rules for different metrics. It will then detect unusual device behavior that may indicate a compromise or other issue, for example, high numbers of failed authorization attempts or sudden changes to open ports or logging configuration.

Where we must manually configure *normal* in Rules Detect, **ML** Detect automatically configures a device *normal* based on common or past behaviour. ML Detect is also continuously learning and fine-tuning the expected *normal* daily based on real device data. The key benefit of ML Detect compared with Rules Detect is that it provides a more accurate and current *normal* that we don't need to manually adjust as our solution evolves. This reduces false positives while at the same time increasing sensitivity to actual anomalies.

The alerting feature publishes events to the IoT console, CloudWatch, and SNS. From there, we can configure notifications and remediation actions, as we saw earlier in Chapter 8.

Mitigation enables us to investigate issues by providing contextual and historical information about the device, such as metadata, statistics, and historical alerts.

AWS IoT Analytics, shown in Figure 9-55, provides all the features we would expect from an analytics package. It ingests data from any source, including IoT Core, and filters it to ensure we collect only the data we want to analyze. IoT Analytics can preprocess the data as it is being ingested, including cleaning and filtering data, formatting it consistently, or merging it with other data.

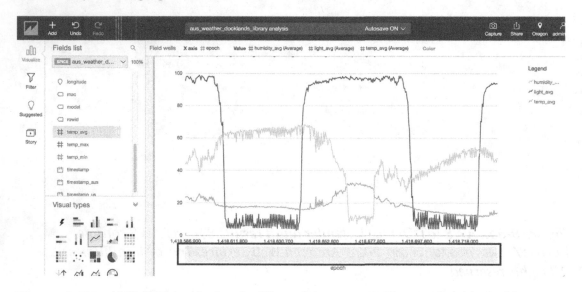

Figure 9-55. *AWS IoT Analytics dashboard Source: AWS console* `https://aws.` `amazon.com/` *2022, Amazon Web Services Inc. or its affiliates. All rights reserved*

IoT Analytics is Serverless; we pay for execution time and the amount of stored data. Any integrated services will have their own pricing models.

Data is stored as time series data; both processed and original data can be stored. Ad hoc and scheduled SQL queries can be run on the data for analysis. Standard time series analysis and incremental data capture with customizable time windows are supported, as well as hosted Jupyter Notebooks. In addition, custom containers for more bespoke analytics and machine learning can also be deployed, and IoT Analytics integrates with QuickSight to provide visualization.

IoT Events is an important service that monitors changes, alerts, and data from devices so that we can assess and determine if a response is needed and what that response should be. Events can trigger actions to AWS services, such as a Lambda microservice to perform any programmable action. IoT Events is Serverless, billed per evaluated message and for each active alarm. Additional fees may be incurred for integrated services such as SNS or Lambda.

An example use case can be found in security. A connected camera can be streamed to the cloud and analyzed. Insights are published to IoT Events, which can respond to logs indicating detected motion. It will determine if an alert should be sent or if the perimeter IoT lights should be switched on based on configured rules.

Events can also evaluate incoming signals from multiple devices before taking one or more actions, for example, taking temperature readings from three or four sensors in a room before taking action to change the thermostat setting, log the change, and send an email notification to inform the occupant that the thermostat has been adjusted.

The last service for IoT that we will cover is the AWS IoT Things Graph service, shown in Figure 9-56, which helps build IoT applications by taking a visual approach to IoT solution design. We can create drag-and-drop models and draw connections and actions between them.

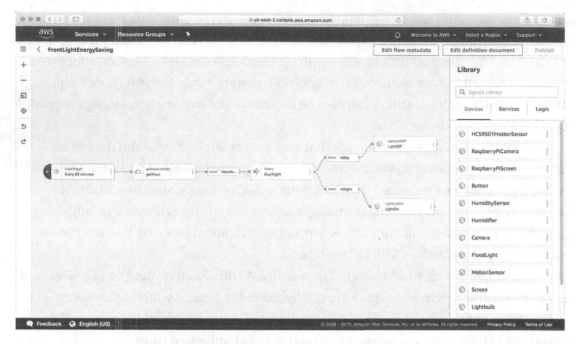

Figure 9-56. *AWS IoT Things Graph interface Source: AWS console* `https://aws.`
`amazon.com/` *2022, Amazon Web Services Inc. or its affiliates. All rights reserved*

The models are digital representations of devices we can create and reuse across
many applications and workflows. Mappings convert the output of one device to the
input of another device. Like models, these mappings can be created and added to a
library so we can easily reuse them.

Activity in applications and workflows is monitored, and logs include result status
and execution time, which enable us to analyze the performance and address any issues.

A Things Graph application can run at the edge in any Greengrass-enabled device or
gateway. Being close to the action, it can respond to local events with minimal latency
and even when connectivity is lost.

AWS Robotics

Another area where most AWS-offered services are Serverless is robotics. Advancements
in cloud connectivity, IoT, and machine learning have paved the way for new
opportunities in this space. The cloud, and its provided services, can help address
previously hard-to-resolve challenges in robotics.

Amazon Robotics is the team responsible for automating Amazon's fulfilment centers to improve efficiency and workplace safety. Their robots are powered by AWS cloud services, such as IoT Core (manages the devices and data) and SageMaker (a machine learning service).

It can be difficult for organizations to start with robotics due to the high barrier to entry. They will need all the required hardware, resources, and space needed to develop solutions. In addition, it can be challenging to find robotics engineers who need to be experienced in domains such as mechanical engineering, electronics, and machine learning.

In 2021, AWS partnered with MassRobotics and launched the AWS Robotics Startup Accelerator, which helps organizations adopt AWS cloud for their robotics development efforts. It is only available to startups in their early stages with less than $10 million in revenue and less than $100 million in investment raised. The accelerator is a four-week program where startups get the opportunity to work with and learn from AWS and MassRobotics' experts.

AWS DeepRacer is a simulation service to help train autonomous vehicles and devices. It is also a great advocacy and education tool, providing developers with a fun and engaging way to learn more about this type of machine learning. Besides the cloud service, a one-eighteenth-scale physical race car can be purchased to see the training results in the real world. The learning experience is gamified through leaderboards, and AWS provides the support needed to get started with training autonomous models in SageMaker. The models can be deployed and tested in the simulator or deployed to the physical car to race on real-world tracks.

AWS RoboMaker is another simulation service where engineers can create virtual environments to test solutions. Instead of owning and creating a physical space and infrastructure, which is an expensive and slow process, with RoboMaker, engineers can quickly build environments that resemble physical spaces. This lets them run repeatable and consistent test simulations and train and orchestrate devices in diverse environments.

Multiple tests can be run in parallel to tweak settings and fine-tune device performance before testing it in the real world. RoboMaker is Serverless, so we don't have to worry about provisioning, configuring, or managing any of the infrastructure or software required for the simulations. No specialized 3D modeling or simulation code knowledge is needed to use the service and reap the benefits; engineers can focus entirely on their devices and ML models.

RoboRunner was announced during 2021 re:Invent. Robot vendors tend to use their own custom management system for their devices, making it difficult for organizations to orchestrate workflows of multiple robots working together. RoboRunner solves that challenge by providing a centralized independent management platform that devices from different vendors can be connected to. We can then integrate the different devices and make them work together productively. Tools are provided to help create workflows, improving operational efficiency and ease of use. RoboRunner also offers a dashboard view of the robotics and their status, helping to quickly identify and locate errors and other issues.

Industrial Internet of Things (IIoT)

This is a sub-category of IoT that is specific to industrial environments such as manufacturing plants and warehouses. The IoT services we covered already are relevant here too, but there are cloud services available that cater specifically to the needs of industrial environments. These services focus on *predictive quality, predictive maintenance, and asset management.*

The Industrial Internet of Things (IIoT) brings the capabilities of IoT devices into industrial facilities. By leveraging the capability of these devices, it opens up new capabilities for organizations to improve their product and increase the productivity of their processes.

Predictive Quality

Predictive quality uses machine learning to analyze data from devices integrated into the manufacturing process. Derived insights can identify defects earlier and pinpoint possible process faults that can be addressed to reduce operational impact. Predictive quality has been shown to improve customer satisfaction, largely because instead of the usual random sample checks, all products can be checked before they reach the customer. This approach has also been shown to reduce the number of recalls, resulting in less wastage.

Amazon Lookout for Vision is a machine learning service that detects visual flaws in photos taken of the process and final product. For example, when manufacturing computer chips, Lookout for Vision can identify defects, such as damage and missing components, in a photo of the chip. Insights trigger an automated response to pull the chip from the process and prevent it from being shipped. Lookout for Vision can also detect recurring issues and any subtle changes over time, potentially indicating a process fault or degradation that must be addressed.

The machine learning model that powers it can be trained with just 30 images, and its continuous learning ability increases its accuracy over time.

AWS Panorama is another predictive quality service that includes a hardware device. An example architecture is shown in Figure 9-57. A major advantage is that it can add computer vision capabilities to existing standard on-premises cameras. The service analyzes the video streams for different use cases. For example, it can monitor camera feeds in the manufacturing process to evaluate the quality of the products and detect manufacturing or process defects.

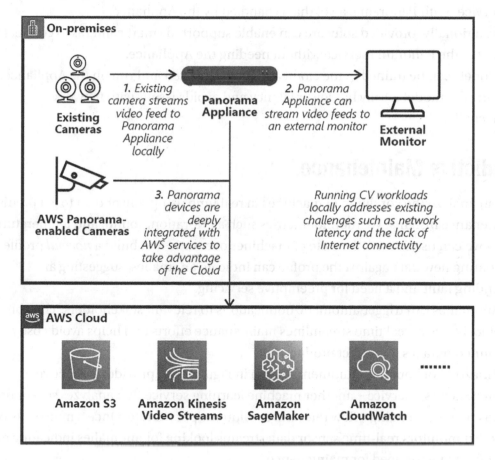

Figure 9-57. *High-level architecture for the Panorama Appliance*

Panorama can also be used to monitor CCTV feeds covering the workplace to detect potential health and safety compliance issues, such as workers with incomplete protective gear or exhibiting dangerous behavior around machinery. A use case that is less industrial but still interesting can be found in retail environments to monitor and track *footfall*. This is a common metric used to optimize staff scheduling and improve sales.

The hardware device included with Panorama is called the *Panorama Appliance*. It processes the video feeds of any on-site cameras connected to it. A monitor can be attached to view the streams and events locally in real time.

The main difference between this approach and Lookout for Vision is that with the latter, we need to develop a process for capturing and sending photos or video frames to the service. With Panorama, all of that is handled by the Appliance.

Additionally, provided software can enable supported smart cameras to connect directly to the Panorama service without needing the Appliance.

Models can be trained in the cloud and then deployed and run on the Appliance. Running the model locally has lower latency and avoids issues with network connectivity.

Predictive Maintenance

We can analyze the condition of machines in real time using sensor data to get predictive maintenance insights. We monitor metrics such as vibration, sound, and temperature, which we can use to track the state of machines over time and build a *normal* profile. Comparing new data against the profile can indicate anomalies, suggesting an impending fault and a need for preemptive servicing.

Anomalies can trigger automatic notifications to relevant stakeholders. The ability to detect issues in real time streamlines maintenance efforts and helps avoid costly unplanned outages that affect productivity.

Amazon Lookout for Equipment, shown in Figure 9-58, provides predictive maintenance as a service – another machine learning service that analyzes sensor data such as pressure readings, flow rate, and revolutions per minute. Once a model has been trained, it monitors real-time sensor data streams looking for anomalies indicating an impending fault or need for maintenance.

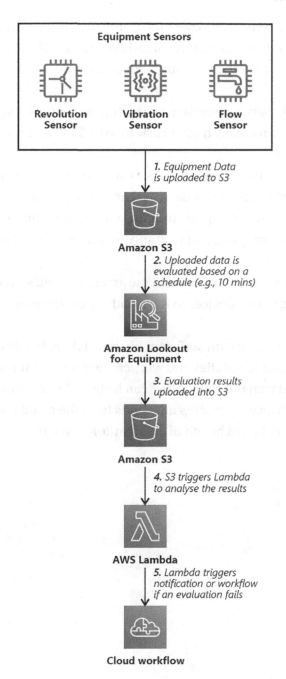

Figure 9-58. *Predictive maintenance with Lookout for Equipment*

When an anomaly is detected, Lookout for Equipment can pinpoint the sensor providing the data to guide support staff to the maintenance area and potential root cause.

Like its Vision counterpart, Lookout for Equipment has a training stage where we feed it historical sensor data and maintenance information. The service analyzes the data to train a model and uses continuous learning to improve the model's accuracy over time.

The trained model analyzes new sensor readings and stores insights in an S3 bucket. From there, we can automatically trigger custom workflows and notifications depending on the desired response.

Amazon Monitron, shown in Figure 9-59, is another predictive maintenance service. This service includes physical sensor devices that can be purchased and attached to industrial assets. The sensors monitor vibration and temperature. The service and devices are simple to set up, plug, and play and do not require coding or machine learning experience.

Once the sensor devices are attached to the asset, they will start collecting data that is securely sent (via a gateway device) to the cloud, where the predictive maintenance model is trained.

Once the model is trained with sufficient historical data, Monitron will analyze the incoming data looking for anomalies and will generate insights for any identified. A mobile app is included with the service that can be linked to the devices attached to the assets. The app will receive insights and alerts from the cloud service and provide a dashboard view of the data and health of the monitored assets.

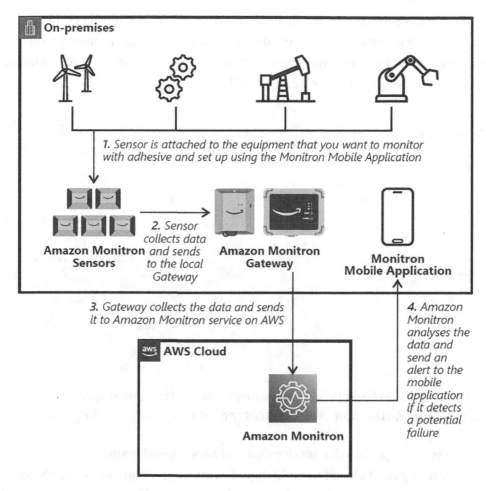

Figure 9-59. *High-level architecture for the Monitron devices*

Asset Management

There is value in providing visibility into industrial assets such as machines, vehicles, and factories and capturing metrics such as state, location, and history to indicate an asset's health, maintenance cycle, and remaining lifespan. This data can help identify possible bottlenecks, potential optimizations, and gaps in processes that the organization can address. This enables them to better manage and optimize the use of their assets.

The service AWS IoT SiteWise helps manage physical assets. It is a centralized dashboard, shown in Figure 9-60, where data from industrial equipment can be collected, organized, analyzed and visualized. It enables organizations to understand and improve processes across one or more facilities.

Figure 9-60. *AWS IoT SiteWise dashboard Source: AWS console* `https://aws.` `amazon.com/` *2022, Amazon Web Services Inc. or its affiliates. All rights reserved*

SiteWise is a comprehensive service that includes several features.

Asset modeling can be used to build digital twins of physical assets. Attributes and relationships for the assets can be included in the model to define entire facilities. This provides a more contextual understanding of the data being collected, where it sits in the workflow, and how it relates to different parts of the facility.

Asset metrics include data streams and fixed or calculated equipment properties that can be defined. Keeping them all in one place makes them readily available for analysis.

SiteWise Edge runs on-premises to facilitate the collection, organization, and processing of data locally before sending it to the cloud. This can help streamline data transfer volume and meet compliance requirements. SiteWise supports several other data ingestion methods, including common messaging and IoT protocols.

With SiteWise Monitor, we can create no-code, fully managed web applications for visualizing and interacting with the operational data being collected. Alarms can be defined to respond to equipment behavior and potential performance issues.

Applications can use the service's API to easily retrieve asset data and computed metrics from SiteWise. It is also possible to subscribe to a stream of near-real-time data to power custom dashboards.

SiteWise is Serverless and billed based on utilization. The various features have different fees, so review the documentation for details.

⚙ AWS: Managed Machine Learning (ML)

AWS offers several fully managed machine learning services. No machine learning experience is required to use them; for most, we simply provide the input and receive the result.

Rekognition

The most well-known managed AI service is Rekognition, shown in Figure 9-61 it is a visual analysis service for images and videos. It is Serverless and billed per analysis request. The image detection features include object and scene recognition, inappropriate content detection, and text and facial recognition. All of these can be used on images and some on video. It is also possible to create a custom analysis model by training a base model with just a few images specific to the use case – significantly less than training a new model from scratch.

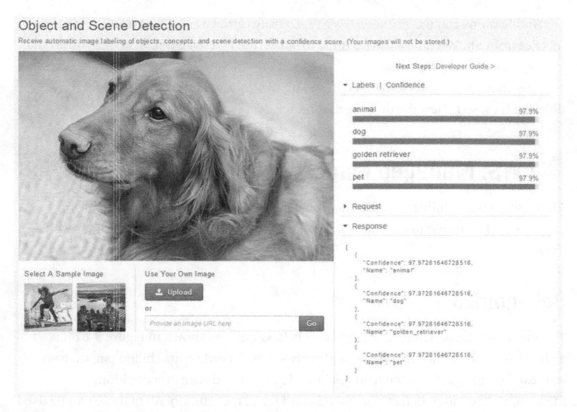

Figure 9-61. *Amazon Rekognition interface Source: AWS console* `https://aws.` `amazon.com/` *2022, Amazon Web Services Inc. or its affiliates. All rights reserved*

The use cases for this service include platforms with large volumes of user-generated content, such as social media, gaming, and matchmaking.

In these cases, we can use Rekognition to proactively moderate large volumes of media data to keep users safe from inappropriate or illegal content. The same capability can be used for compliance in media and ecommerce solutions. Here, we can use Rekognition to identify potentially unsafe content and assign the appropriate age and content ratings for different geographies. Similarly, we can ensure that third-party product listings or classifieds do not violate the policies on ecommerce or other digital platforms.

Brands advertising on news, media, or ecommerce platforms may not want to be associated with certain types of sensitive content, such as alcohol or violence. We can identify and filter out unwanted associations for each brand using Rekognition's insights.

DeepLens

This is a commercially available high-definition camera with built-in compute capability, bringing computer vision capabilities closer to the hands of developers. We can deploy SageMaker models directly to DeepLens, and video analysis is done on the device itself, avoiding the need for connectivity or additional hardware once the model has been deployed.

DeepLens includes several tutorials and sample projects, and there are community projects available that can be easily deployed and experimented with.

DeepLens services can be used for object detection, object classification, face identification, sentiment analysis, and activity recognition. It supports SageMaker and Lambda integrations, providing ways to tap into more custom capabilities and behaviors.

Textract

AWS's machine learning service that extracts text and retains the layout of complex forms and tables, as shown in Figure 9-62. This makes the service particularly adept at extracting usable content from scanned invoices and reports. The service does remarkably well with different handwriting styles, making it great for use cases such as extracting data from site reports and written receipts.

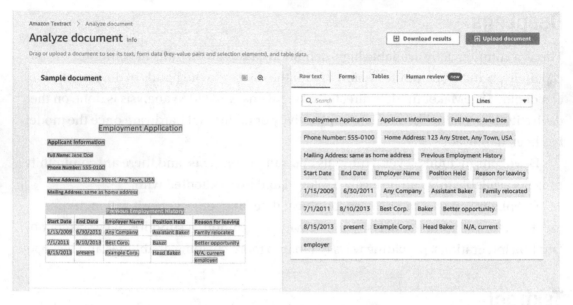

Figure 9-62. *Amazon Textract interface Source: AWS console* `https://aws.` `amazon.com/` *2022, Amazon Web Services Inc. or its affiliates. All rights reserved*

Textract is intended for pages of content, which is not something that Rekognition supports. Textract supports PNG, JPEG, and PDF file formats, and we are charged for each processed image or PDF page.

Polly

AWS's text-to-speech service is aptly named *Polly*. It converts written text to spoken voice. There are *standard* voices, which all sound a bit robotic, and modern *neural* voices trained with machine learning techniques that sound hauntingly human.

This service supports a range of languages, accents, and genders. With Polly, it is possible to create a custom voice. However, currently this is a bespoke and costly service working directly with the Polly product team, who handle most of the model training. Given recent advancements in synthetic voice training, this will hopefully become a more affordable, self-managed process in the future.

Polly bills for each processed character of text. Replays of the same body of text are cached for a time and are free. Polly is considerably cheaper than hiring a voice talent, and results are immediately available on demand. This approach is suitable for several use cases, including

- Low-cost multilingual voice-overs for online content

- Videos and announcement systems

- Dynamic on-demand voices for virtual avatars, such as those available in the Sumerian service

- Audio responses in applications to make them more inclusive

Sample	SSML
This is how I speak normally.	(none)
I can also speak in a Newscaster style, as if I were reading a news article or delivering a flash briefing.	`<speak><amazon:domain name="news">I can also speak in a Newscaster style, as if I were reading a news article or delivering a flash briefing.</amazon:domain></speak>`
I can speak in a higher pitched voice, or I can speak in a lower pitched voice.	`<speak>I can speak in a <prosody pitch="high">higher pitched voice</prosody>, or I can speak <prosody pitch="low">in a lower pitched voice</prosody></speak>`
I can speak really slowly, or I can speak really fast.	`<speak>I can speak <prosody rate="x-slow">really slowly</prosody>, or I can speak <prosody rate="x-fast">really fast</prosody></speak>`
I can also speak very loudly, or I can speak very quietly.	`<speak>I can also speak <prosody volume="x-loud">very loudly</prosody>, or I can speak <prosody volume="x-soft">very quietly</prosody>. </speak>`
I can whisper.	`<speak>I have a secret to tell you, I will whisper it to you.<amazon:effect name="whispered">'<prosody rate="x-slow"> <prosody volume="loud">I am not human. </prosody></prosody></amazon:effect>Can you believe it?</speak>`

Figure 9-63. *Amazon Polly SSML Source: AWS Polly documentation* `https://aws.amazon.com/` *2022, Amazon Web Services Inc. or its affiliates. All rights reserved*

Besides the text-to-speech capability, the service supports advanced customization features with which we can configure talking style, breathing, pausing, intonation, pronunciation, and more – all geared toward making the result more natural and human. Some examples can be seen in Figure 9-63.

Transcribe

Transcribe is a speech-to-text service. It can convert a recording of speech in an audio file, video file, or live stream to text. Besides the plain text, the output includes the exact timing of each word or character, confidence level, and any alternative interpretations. Transcribe supports several audio and video formats, including FLAC, MP3, MP4, OGG,

WebM, AMR, and WAV. Domain- or industry-specific vocabulary can be configured to help Transcribe recognize words, acronyms, or abbreviations that it might not be familiar with.

A common use of this service is creating video subtitles. The output includes the exact timing and speaker identification, providing everything we need to create subtitles. There are third-party libraries available in several programming languages that can do this out of the box, taking the direct output from Transcribe and converting it to a common subtitle format such as SRT. Transcribe can also be integrated with the Translate service to automatically generate subtitles in multiple languages.

Transcribe output

```
"items": [
  {
    "start_time": "1.15",
    "end_time": "1.35",
    "alternatives": [
      {
        "confidence": "1.0",
        "content": "How"
      }
    ],
    "type": "pronunciation"
  },
  {
    "start_time": "1.35",
    "end_time": "2.05",
    "alternatives": [
      {
        "confidence": "1.0",
        "content": "about"
      }
    ],
    "type": "pronunciation"
  }
  ...
]
```

Output converted to SRT subtitle format

```
1
00:00:01,150 --> 00:00:03,899
How about language?

2
00:00:03,899 --> 00:00:05,112
Several languages can be transcribed.
```

Another common use case for AWS Transcribe is extracting analytics and insights from recorded conversations. Transcribe call analytics is a feature within the service specifically for this use case. It will transcribe the call recording and then use natural language processing to uncover conversation insights. These insights include sentiment analysis, detected issues, and speech characteristics such as talk time, speed, and interruptions. The insights can be used for reports, driving service improvements, and call center automation, such as automatically matching issues with possible solutions.

Another great feature is its ability to detect and redact personal information in call transcriptions. It can do this in the resulting text transcript and the audio file – returning a redacted audio file with the personal data blanked out.

Transcribe bills for each second of audio transcribed, with a minimum fee of 15 seconds. It currently supports 38 languages and variations.

Lex

This is a service for building chatbots, the same technology powering Amazon Alexa devices. It features a conversational AI that can be programmed using intents, values, and desired outcomes, as shown in Figure 9-64. The AI can recognize natural language in written and spoken text and respond appropriately to obtain all necessary information.

It is best at order workflows, where known inputs are required from the user that can then be converted to a specific order. For example, when booking a flight, the chatbot can get user inputs for origin airport, destination airport, date, time, and class. We would configure the desired user inputs, limited to a type or set of values for each one, and Lex will figure out everything else needed to get that information from the user.

This service makes it easier to build and deploy a chatbot, and while considerably easier than developing one from scratch, building a successful Lex bot still requires some expertise. In particular, a deep understanding of the intended users, how they might interact, and the kind of language they might use will be essential to delivering an effective chatbot that offers a good user experience.

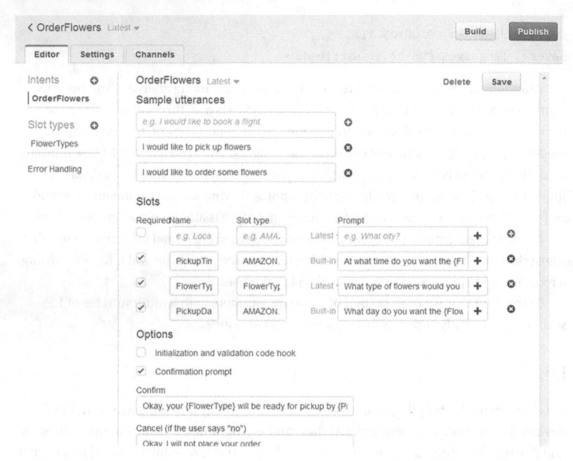

Figure 9-64. *Amazon Lex builder interface Source: AWS console* `https://aws.` `amazon.com/` *2022, Amazon Web Services Inc. or its affiliates. All rights reserved*

Lex supports various content types, input values, and other features to help guide a conversation. Behind the scenes, each step in the discussion can be fed to a custom microservice to enable more complex interactions and integrations with third-party systems.

Use cases can include order and booking workflows for web, mobile, and call center integrations, as well as some support and productivity use cases. Lex bills for each text and speech request.

QnA Bot

QnA Bot is an open source, multi-channel, multi-language conversational chatbot built on Amazon Lex. Developers can curate a list of questions and answers, which the bot will use to answer customers' questions.

It integrates machine learning tools such as Translate to offer multi-lingual capabilities. For example, a chatbot may be curated with a list of questions and answers written in English. When a customer asks the chatbot a question in French, it

1. Automatically translates the question to English

2. Matches it to a question in the data bank

3. Translates the answer to French

4. Returns the translated answer to the customer

Besides the curated list of questions, we can integrate resources such as documents on S3, SharePoint, Salesforce, and content management systems (CMSs). All of these the bot can use as a source for answers to customer queries, enabling it to answer questions that might not have been included in the curated list.

QnA Bot can also ask questions. This can help improve the user experience by capturing customer feedback.

Comprehend

This is a natural language processing (NLP) service that can analyze bodies of text to provide insights. Many of the features will be recognizable from Transcribe call analytics as Comprehend is powering those analytics under the hood. The insights include language recognition, key phrase extraction, syntax, and sentiment analysis.

The service can generate keywords and descriptions from text such as website pages and product catalogue entries. It can understand the sentiment, meaning, and intent of text from social media, reviews, feedback forms, and other sources.

It can detect and redact personally identifiable information (PII), helping to meet privacy regulation compliance. It is also possible to create custom NLP models to categorise text and extract custom entities for new use cases or specific industries.

Comprehend currently supports 12 languages, but it is possible to run a text through the Translate service before passing the result to Comprehend, indirectly supporting additional languages. Some relevant uses of this service include generating descriptive metadata for content, archives, and other data sets, as well as analyzing social media, support tickets, and other posts or user messages for sentiment, intent, or category.

Comprehend bills for each analysis category on every 100 characters, with a minimum spend of 300 characters per request.

⚙ AWS: Ledger Technology

As technology and the cloud mature, providers develop new services to address more specific use cases. Ledger technology is one area where support has been growing over the last couple of years, developed for its ability to verify data integrity.

In a traditional database, data can be stored, edited, and deleted. When an item of data is edited, it replaces the previous value. While previous values may still be present in backups, such sources are ill-suited for verifying data integrity, requiring manual work to compare and detect accidental or malicious changes and restore a backup.

With ledger technology, existing records are not changed. Instead, a new record that represents the update is added. Old records remain available, allowing a history of all changes to be audited – much like an accountant's ledger.

A one-way cryptographic hash is generated for each new record. This represents the data with a unique set of characters, like an ID or certificate that proves the data has been unchanged. The update records are hashed to using the previous record hash and the new data, chaining them together in blocks – hence the name *blockchain*. This is what prevents previous records from being changed directly. Any unauthorized attempt to modify existing values directly will break the chain, and the record will be flagged as compromised. Such changes are blocked entirely, or valid data can be automatically restored.

Amazon provides two services related to ledger technology: *Managed Blockchain* and *Quantum Ledger Database* (QLDB).

Managed Blockchain

A lot of overhead is involved in building a blockchain network, including acquiring the right software and hardware and managing the network connectivity and access controls. This fully managed service manages those overheads, making it easier for organizations to use public or private blockchain networks. A high-level architecture is shown in Figure 9-65.

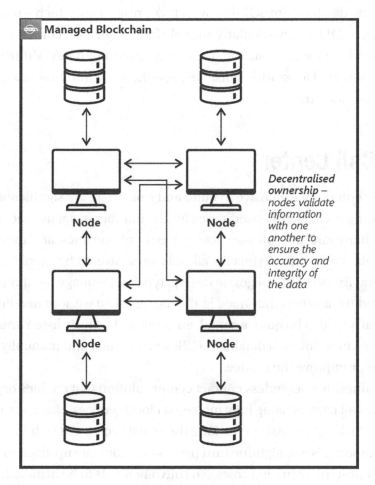

Figure 9-65. *Managed Blockchain service*

The service uses a decentralized approach, where each node keeps a record of all changes. The fully managed nodes talk to one another to validate the accuracy and integrity of their data. AWS Managed Blockchain supports two popular open source blockchains, Ethereum and Hyperledger Fabric. This service is suitable for any use case that works on either blockchain network.

Quantum Ledger Database (QLDB)

As the name indicates, QLDB is a database service more than a managed blockchain network. Unlike a network, QLDB is centralized, owned and operated by AWS.

QLDB ensures that stored data is immutable and cryptographically verifiable. It is highly available with multiple replications and continuous backup, and it is a Serverless service, so we are billed on actual usage of storage and queries.

Queries on the database are SQL-like with JSON responses, which should be familiar to most developers. QLDB is particularly suitable for system-of-record and similar use cases and financial or other transactional ledger-type requirements within applications. It can also be considered for storing sensitive logs where the immutable aspect will help ensure a verifiable audit trail.

⚙ AWS: Call Center

Traditional call centers are expensive to build and run. There are significant costs to consider, including a sufficiently sized space for the number of agents needed to answer incoming calls, hardware and software license needs, phone lines, and much more to manage, maintain, and pay for. Typically, all calls are answered by agents, even if it goes via a digital menu first to help categorize the call type and manage the queue. Only rarely might callers find the answers they need in the digital menu without needing to talk to an agent. The calls tend to be quite manual; an agent will actively listen and search for possible solutions in scripts or a database. Calls are recorded and manually reviewed to assess the agent or improve the service.

Amazon Connect is a Serverless contact center solution that enables organizations to set up remote call centers using fully managed cloud services. Using the cloud means that agents can work from anywhere, as long they have access to a web browser and the Internet. The setup is a straightforward process without any up-front investment or committing to long-term recurring costs. No software needs to be installed, and agents can be onboarded within 20 minutes.

Organizations pay for the customer-connected minutes. This helps organizations in enabling agents to work flexible hours. There are no minimum monthly fees, licensing charges, or long-term commitments. This makes it easier for organizations to scale their call centers according to demand.

Call recordings, reports, and transcripts are generated and stored in a secure S3 bucket. Managers have a dashboard view to track the performance of the call centers, listen to past recordings, generate reports, and manage their service levels. The AWS Connect service includes a suite of features and integrations with other cloud services that help improve the agent and customer experience.

Contact Lens provides conversational analysis for the agent to automatically uncover crucial insights and feedback about the product or services, as shown in Figure 9-66. It allows call center managers to quickly identify trends and issues such as price discrepancies across different sales channels or the number of times customers ask agents to repeat themselves. The latter could flag a need for training or a need to improve the call script for a particular region.

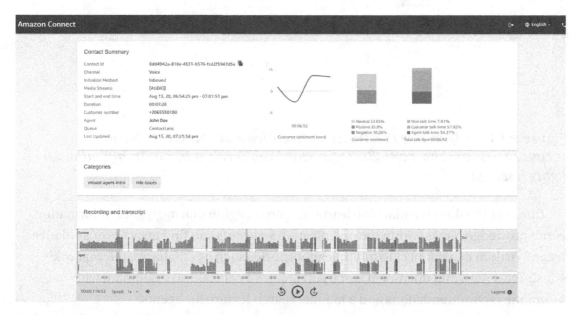

Figure 9-66. *Analytics and sentiment with Contact Lens Source: AWS console* `https://aws.amazon.com/` *2022, Amazon Web Services Inc. or its affiliates. All rights reserved*

Contact Lens also provides real-time transcripts of conversations, including alerts when certain words or phrases are used. For example, if a customer says the word *cancel*, a manager can be instantly alerted and jump in to assist in helping the agent resolve the customer's issues. In transcripts, all personally identifiable information or PII, such as names, ID numbers, and addresses, can be automatically redacted to protect the customer and ensure compliance with privacy regulations.

Connect Voice ID enables agents to do real-time caller authentication, as shown in Figure 9-67. This is an opt-in service for callers and avoids the need for agents to ask the caller multiple questions to confirm their identity before assisting them. Connect Voice ID analyzes the customer's speech attributes and creates a digital voice print. With the digital voice print, agents no longer need to ask callers as many identity questions, saving time for both the agent and customer.

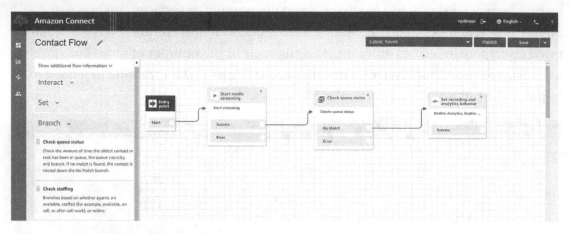

Figure 9-67. *Self-service IVR (voice) authentication Source: AWS console* `https://aws.amazon.com/` *2022, Amazon Web Services Inc. or its affiliates. All rights reserved*

Connect Wisdom is a machine learning search engine that aggregates information from knowledge banks within the organization so agents can find answers or guidance faster. Wisdom can connect to multiple repositories such as databases, internal wikis, Salesforce, FAQs, and document storage. It creates a centralized dashboard with automatic recommendations and a manual search feature for agents.

Wisdom continuously learns, so agents can rate the recommendations and answers provided to improve future matches.

There are a few more Connect features that are worth highlighting:

- Connect Tasks helps agents track and prioritize a list of tasks that they need to do following a call. Tasks are managed using the same interface as Connect, so agents do not have to toggle between multiple applications.

- Connect Customer Profiles consolidates the customer's information from different sources, including third-party applications such as Salesforce or Zendesk. The information is then displayed in a unified dashboard where we can view all previous interactions with the caller. Customer Profiles scans the phone number or customer ID when a call is initiated and automatically retrieves their profile for the agent.

- Connect offers a visual dashboard and analytics capabilities to support managers in analyzing trends such as average queue abandonment time and the average call length. Using this information, managers can make data-driven decisions to improve agent productivity and customer experience.

Well-Architected Framework

The AWS Well-Architected Framework is a repository of important guidelines that AWS developed to help cloud architects build highly secure, resilient, and efficient solutions. The framework provides a consistent approach for architects and clients to evaluate their existing architectures against proven solutions and insightful studies that AWS architects have conducted.

The Well-Architected Framework started as a whitepaper that Amazon launched in 2012. It gained immense popularity over time, and Amazon kept expanding and improving it. Now it includes domain-specific versions, hands-on-labs, and the AWS Well-Architected Tool to guide users through the assessment process.

In 2017, AWS extended the framework with the concept of "lenses" to provide more workload-specific advice. Lenses extend the AWS architectural guidance to more industry-specific realms such as Serverless, high-performance computing, the Internet of Things (IoT), and financial services. Lenses are not stand-alone; they should be used together with the Well-Architected Framework.

The framework and its tooling can be applied by architects and organizations to their own solutions or by consultants to client solutions.

The Five Pillars of the Well-Architected Framework

The AWS Well-Architected Framework is based on five core pillars and six design principles. For Serverless projects, some of the specific guidelines in the pillars are less relevant as they become the cloud provider's responsibility. Nevertheless, it is worth understanding each pillar's deeper meaning and applying them appropriately to Serverless architecture.

- **Operational excellence**

  The focus of this pillar is system monitoring to increase business value and continually improve processes. The critical areas under this pillar include automation of changes, responding to events, and the definition of standards for managing daily operations.

- **Security**

  The security pillar acts as a gatekeeper for information and systems. The main topics of discussion under this pillar include integrity and privacy of data, identification of privilege management, safeguarding systems, and establishing processes to detect security-based events.

- **Reliability**

  The reliability pillar ensures that a workload performs correctly and efficiently. A robust workload is quick to recover from failures and restore availability to users. The major topics include distributed system design, recovery planning, and change handling.

- **Performance efficiency**

  The performance efficiency pillar brings attention to using IT and computing resources wisely. The vital topics under this pillar include selecting the right resource types and sizes, performance monitoring, and making well-informed decisions to meet the evolving needs of businesses.

- **Cost optimization**

  As the name implies, this pillar focuses on eradicating unnecessary costs. It helps understand and control where the money is being spent, select the suitable number and types of resources, and scale resources without overspending.

The Design Principles

The Well-Architected Framework identifies a set of six general design principles, based on the five pillars, that help ensure good design practices in the cloud:

1. **Stop guessing capacity needs.**

   There are very few challenges with capacity planning in cloud computing. We can scale up or down automatically instead of paying for idle resources or accepting performance degradation due to limited capacity.

2. **Test systems for production scale.**

   We can create a production-scale, temporary test environment in the cloud. After completing the testing, resources can be deleted to avoid ongoing charges. The cost of running a temporary test environment is a fraction of the cost of doing live testing on-prem.

3. **Automate to make architectural experimentation easier.**

   Automation helps replicate workloads at lower cost and reduces manual effort. Tracking automation changes, auditing the impact, and reverting to previous settings when needed are all straightforward in cloud computing and Serverless solutions.

4. **Allow for evolutionary architectures.**

   With traditional physical infrastructures, architectural decisions cannot evolve rapidly due to expense and time limitations. But in cloud-based Serverless solutions, automation, testing on demand, and deployment strategies such as blue-green and canary are game-changers. They allow systems to evolve quickly without impacting the underlying resources, while businesses enjoy the benefits of innovation.

5. **Drive architectures using data.**

   It is easy to collect data on how architectural choices may affect workloads in the cloud. This means we can make factual choices rather than assumed ones. Since the cloud infrastructure is essentially just code, we can track architecture choices and improve them over time.

617

6.   **Improve through game days.**

Scheduling game days is a great way of simulating live events to test the efficacy of architecture and processes. This helps identify weak links in the infrastructure and improves the organizational experience when dealing with incidents.

Why Use the AWS Well-Architected Framework?

This framework is a complete approach to learn, measure, and improve the cloud journey. It should not be viewed as an audit but rather a collaborative effort to improve processes for solutions and organizations. It is an established and practical advice repository that provides lifecycle support, not just a one-time system check. Here are some key reasons to incorporate the Well-Architected Framework into our infrastructure:

- **Build instantly and deploy rapidly.**

  The Well-Architected Framework helps build a robust and reliable infrastructure, which enables teams to create and deploy apps faster.

- **Reduce risks.**

  Carry out periodic assessments of the entire cloud account, following the Well-Architected Framework's guidelines. This provides the opportunity to assess any bugs, security vulnerabilities, or potential threats and fix them proactively.

- **Make educated decisions.**

  Since the framework provides logical and time-tested advice, we can make educated infrastructure decisions instead of guessing.

- **Learn and implement AWS best practices.**

  The framework offers best practices for cloud architects. If followed correctly, we can ensure stable and secure infrastructure and systems.

AWS Well-Architected Tool

The Tool is a free service offered by AWS that can be accessed from the AWS Management Console. It provides a great way to regularly evaluate workloads, identify high-risk problems, and record enhancements. Customers fill out a form, and, in return, Amazon provides recommendations for their infrastructure and potential risk assessments that align with the core five pillars of the Well-Architected Framework.

The Tool follows five steps:

1. Launch the Well-Architected Tool web page from the console and navigate to "*define workload*." Fill out the workload basics, including industry type, region, and environment. Click "*define workload*" again.

2. The Tool will go through a systematic workload review of the current infrastructure. Depending on our needs, we have the option of configuring pillar prioritization. This aligns the recommendations with the pillars that matter the most to us.

3. Once we complete the review, a PDF report will be generated based on the predefined selection of workloads and pillar priorities.

4. After analyzing the report, we can return to the workloads tab and click an *improvement plan* to receive recommendations for our workloads.

Serverless Lens and Its Layers

The Serverless Applications Lens is a modifier for the Well-Architected Framework that makes it more relevant to Serverless applications. Similar to the pillars, lenses include layers of relevant attributes. The following is a general overview of the layers in the Serverless Lens:

- **Compute**

  The function of the compute layer is to manage workload requests from external systems and control access and proper authorization of requests. Applications such as Lambda, API Gateway, and Step Functions are included in this layer.

- **Data**

  The data layer is responsible for managing persistent storage and provides a safe mechanism to store the states required by the business logic. It also triggers events in response to data changes. Database applications like DynamoDB, DynamoDB Streams, and DynamoDB Accelerator are present here, along with storage and analytics-based apps such as S3, Elasticsearch Service, and AppSync.

- **Streaming and messaging**

  The messaging layer facilitates communication between the different components of a workload. The streaming layer provides real-time analysis and processing of streaming data. Applications such as SQS, SNS, Kinesis, and Kinesis Data Firehose operate in these layers.

- **User identity and management**

  This layer focuses on the identification, authentication, and authorization of workload users. Applications such as Cognito and Federated Identities are present in this layer.

- **Edge**

  This is the layer that connects to external customers. Data can be efficiently delivered to customers in various geographical locations. Snowball Edge and CloudFront are present at this layer, as well as Greengrass.

- **Monitoring and deployment**

  The monitoring layer continuously checks systems through metrics and observes their behavior over time. The deployment layer manages changes through a release process. Tools such as CloudWatch and X-Ray are present in this layer.

Any organization that cares deeply about architecting a reliable, secure, scalable, and resilient AWS cloud-based infrastructure should endeavor to follow the Well-Architected Framework. By implementing the best practices and guidelines in this framework, we can ensure continuous improvement of our applications and deliver high-quality solutions.

Read more about the AWS Well-Architected Framework, the hands-on labs, and the AWS Well-Architected Tool or explore the AWS Management Console here:

- *https://aws.amazon.com/architecture/well-architected/*

- *www.wellarchitectedlabs.com/*

- *https://aws.amazon.com/well-architected-tool/*

- *https://console.aws.amazon.com/wellarchitected/*

⚙ Serverless Tips

The following are a final list of tips and lessons to consider as you embark on your Serverless journey. They are mostly minor lessons I have learned over the last few years that we have not covered in earlier chapters.

Uploading Files

One way to upload files to a Lambda-backed REST API is to encode the file as Base64 and pass it as we would any other parameter in the POST or PUT body. API Gateway and Lambda limit the request size to 6 MB. Considering the 1.5 MB required for Base64 encoding, that leaves just over 4.5 MB for the file data. While this is probably sufficient for most standard single-image uploads, it won't be for high-resolution or multiple images, videos, visual PDF files, and many other requirements. Earlier, we covered the solution for that using S3 signed URLs.

Layers of Caching

A common use case for Lambda is automated thumbnail generation. There are two ways this is often used as an example in many Serverless tutorials:

1. One of the most common implementations is for S3 to trigger a Lambda for each new file uploaded. The output variation is typically stored on S3 indefinitely. This works well if the various dimensions are predefined and must be applied to every new image. But this may result in unnecessary processing and stored image variations that may never be used.

2. Another approach is to generate images dynamically on demand by routing the user request through API Gateway to a Lambda. This approach can support custom dimensions, and it ensures that only requested dimensions are generated. The problem is that the result is returned right away via API Gateway, and nothing is stored. Frequently requested images will be generated again and again for every request. This processing can also add significant latency to the request, which can make the solution feel slow.

A better way is to combine the preceding two approaches and add a caching layer using CloudFront CDN. CloudFront is configured to pull requested content from S3 to present to the user. It is then stored or cached for some time geographically near that user on the AWS network so that subsequent requests can be served faster. When a file is not requested for a while, it will be automatically deleted from the cache. The next time an expired file is requested, it will retrieve it again from the S3 origin.

CloudFront has a feature called origin failover, essentially a backup origin from which CloudFront will request the file if it can't find it on the main origin. We can configure the failover origin as our API endpoint and Lambda microservice that will generate the thumbnail. The Lambda microservice will store the output on the S3 and return it to CloudFront in a single request. Because we have this option to regenerate the image variation, we can have a lifecycle policy on the S3 origin to automatically delete variations over a certain age or that have not been requested for a given period.

This way, we minimize data stored unnecessarily, can still serve requests for variations that may have expired, can serve requests very promptly for commonly requested variations through CloudFront, and can support generating custom variations if required.

Multilingual

In our globalized world, I think it's important to remember that not everyone is a native English speaker. Consider adding i18n support to microservices and UIs. There are libraries available that can achieve this relatively easily, and once we get in the habit, it's really not much more work. This doesn't just make it easier to support multiple languages in the future; it also makes it far easier to edit and improve the written content of a solution.

TypeScript

If you are a JavaScript developer, switch to TypeScript. It will make your life so much easier, the code better, and the solution more scalable, readable, and transferable. Python is great too, and it certainly has its place, especially for interoperability with other languages and data science activities. But well-written TypeScript compiled to JavaScript will often run faster than Python in many web application and API use cases.

Pick the Right Tool for the Job

With modern, Serverless microservice-based applications, we are not limited to servers and things that run on servers. Many niche services available in AWS will outperform generic solutions several times over. For each requirement, look closely at the available services to see if one of them can solve the requirement so that you can avoid reinventing the wheel.

- *Encryption/decryption*: KMS

- *Streaming data*: Kinesis

- *Video*: MediaLive suite, Kinesis video streams and WebRTC, Interactive Video Service

- *Ledger and fraud-sensitive transactions*: QLDB

- *Customer purchase recommendations*: AWS Personalize

- *Task queues*: SQS

- *Automated testing of microservices*: CloudWatch Synthetics

- *Application profiling*: X-Ray

- *Storing sensitive information*: Systems Manager Parameter Store or Secrets Manager

...and many more.

Cognito as a User Database

Cognito is a secure service for storing user login information. It can help meet GDPR and other privacy compliance requirements if we keep all of the personally identifiable information in the Cognito user pool and reference it from other databases and services using the ID (called the "sub" in Cognito). With Cognito, we only pay for active users in a given month, so all those test accounts won't be billed after we stop using them.

Tips for using Cognito effectively include the following:

- Retrieve a user from Cognito using their sub instead of a username by using the listUsers function with a Filter:

```
cognito.listUsers({
    UserPoolId: process.env.userpool,
    Filter: 'sub="'+user_id+'"'
}).promise()
    .then(users => {})
    .catch(error => {});
```

- Access and use the standard profile parameters without making them required. Making standard parameters required can cause problems with things like social media integration, so it's best to avoid configuring this in Cognito, and, instead, handle parameter verification in the application. We can add up to 50 custom attributes to a Cognito profile and up to 2048 bytes of data per attribute value.

- One way to manage user access is to include a JSON policy document as a custom parameter in Cognito. This is included in the Cognito token, so it can be accessed both in the web application front end and by a Lambda microservice if we pass it through the API Gateway request in the event (using integration mapping). In the front end, the policy can be used to determine which menus and pages to make visible to the user. In the back end, it can be used to determine if a user should have access to that particular microservice and action.

- Since June 2022, Cognito can query a Lambda on first login and add permissions and other user information to the Cognito session. This avoids the need for individual Lambda functions to query a database to retrieve a user's information and permissions, considerably reducing requests and latency.

- Cognito does not let us export passwords. This can be especially problematic as some configuration changes require the Cognito user pool to be recreated, making migrating existing users a bit difficult. One approach we can consider is creating the new Cognito user pool with the desired settings first and then collecting the users' passwords as they log in to the existing user pool for a period. As we collect each password, we create the full user account, including the password, in the new Cognito user pool. After the collection period, we import the remaining users without their passwords and switch the application to the new user pool. Those remaining users will need to reset their password, but we will have at least saved the more active users from having to do so.

- If the application uses multiple organizations, each with its own users, we could create a Cognito user pool for each organization. However, this can get quite complex. Instead, we could use one of the standard attributes we don't need, such as "family_name," to store the organization ID. Using the Filter option in list users, we can retrieve all users that belong to that organization. Filter only works with standard attributes, which is why we can't use a custom attribute:

```
cognito.listUsers({
    UserPoolId: process.env.userpool,
    Filter: 'family_name="'+organisation_id+'"'
}).promise()
    .then(users => {})
    .catch(error => {});
```

CHAPTER 10

Case Studies

Technology is the campfire around which we tell our stories.

—Laurie Anderson, Artist, Musician, and Film Director

⚙ Introduction

The following is a write-up by Won Jenn Lee, a family member and past intern who worked on some of the following case studies to gain some knowledge about Serverless. His insights should be useful to those new to this type of architecture.

Lack of reference code

One thing I realised after embarking on the project, was that it was difficult to find examples to base my code off. Usually when doing other projects, what I'd do would be to find code for certain components of the project and alter it to fit my case. Even if the code could not be altered to fit the project, I could at least get a sense of how to use the various functions. However, when working with AWS, what I found were usually too general to be of much help. I didn't find examples of the specific components that I was working with, for example CloudWatch. I commonly found examples on how to use the components through the AWS UI, which did not help much when utilizing the CDK. Eventually I learnt to use the AWS CDK documentation to find what I needed, which helped greatly.

Lots of things to learn

Another problem I had was that I wasn't entirely sure of the architecture of the code, and how the services work. I found a video (https://www.you-tube.com/watch?v=Lh-kVC2r2AU) which explained the architecture quite

T. Smart, *Serverless Beyond the Buzzword*, https://doi.org/10.1007/978-1-4842-8761-3_10

clearly, and it helped me better understand how the structure of the code should look like. The sheer number of services that AWS provides was also a bit daunting to me, but by limiting myself to learning one service at a time, I found it more manageable. It also helped to try out the service through the AWS UI first to get a better understanding of what the service provides, before going on to exploring the CDK code.

Lack of experience

After getting more used to the architecture of AWS applications, I relied less on finding code and more on the documentation provided. AWS does provide extensive documentation for CDK on their website, which helped a lot. It was usually the first place I would search for when I got stuck. I still had minor issues such as how to create an event to log, but that was due to my lack of experience with AWS. In the end I created a work around using an SQS queue to send messages, before realizing it was possible to create test events.

Documentation of actions for policy statement

I also thought that some things could be better arranged though, like the list of available actions when creating a policy statement. The valid actions were not searchable through the "aws-iam" section of the documentation, which was where I would expect it to be, given that the roles and policies were there. Instead, I had to go to the API reference document of each service, to find the supported actions, which I thought to be a slight inconvenience. I was also thinking that it would be possible to replace it with an enumerator, which would make it more convenient to see the available actions while coding.

Lack of error logging

At one point I ran into a problem where I wasn't sure why my Lambda microservice wasn't sending any logs. I think it has something to do with the policies, as this problem occurred only after I started adding the policy statements. However, I wasn't sure if it was due to the Lambda microservice not being able to read the input, or not being able to write to the output. I tried allowing both in the actions, but I was not sure if I was doing it correctly. And as the function was not outputting anything to the logs, I did not know where the error lay. In the end I had to look at an example, and realized I was missing a few actions when outputting the logs.

Similarly, when I was trying to upload the logs to S3. Based on the messages I was trying to log, it seemed like the functions for accessing S3 weren't running. I tried to list buckets, list objects in bucket, put objects in bucket, but I wasn't getting any response, not even error messages. This caused me to spend a lot of time trying to figure out where the problem lay. In the end I realised it was due to me only adding the bucket to the resources, and not the objects in it which you can add by adding the S3 bucket arn followed by "/*" (without quotes).

⚙ Proactive Logging

In Chapter 8, I described how Lambda and CloudWatch logs are integrated. All of the console output from Lambda will be written to CloudWatch logs. API Gateway can also write to CloudWatch logs, as can many other services. S3 can store logs in another S3 bucket. In short, creating logs is very easy, and it's often turned on by default or it's a simple configuration option.

With some development, we can go further, not just making logs but reading and reacting to them automatically. A simple architecture is shown for this in Figure 10-1. There are two use cases that I do this for:

1. Error monitoring, so that if an error happens in the back end, it can notify me right away.

2. Cost tracking, so that we can attach the operational cost of each action back to the user that performed it. This enables us to bill users based on actual usage or simply to track what a user or organization costs in a solution.

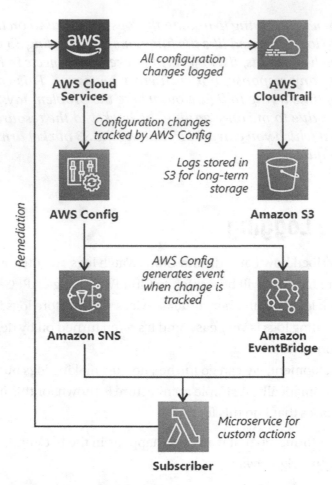

Figure 10-1. *Simple architecture for proactive application logging*

For error monitoring of Lambda microservices, we can do the following. First, create a Lambda microservice in CDK that will be triggered by each log being written:

```
const lambdaTrigger = new lambda.Function(this, "CloudWatchMonitor",{
  description: "Microservice to monitor CloudWatch logs",
  runtime: lambda.Runtime.NODEJS_12_X,
  handler: "index.handler",
  code: lambda.Code.fromAsset("./lambda_src_path/"),
  role: lambdaRole, // at least SNS:Publish
  memorySize: 128,
  timeout: cdk.Duration.seconds(600),
```

```
logRetention: logs.RetentionDays.THREE_DAYS,
environment:{}
});
```

We will also need to create a log destination:

```
const lambdaLogDestination = new logsdestinations.
LambdaDestination(lambdafn);
```

With those in place, we can then create a log group and add a subscription to each Lambda microservice that we create after that:

```
// create the Lambda microservice first
const newLambda = .....
const newLambdaFN = newLambda.functionName;

// add the log group to CloudWatch logs
const newLGroup = new logs.LogGroup(this,"logsFor"+newLambdaFN, {
  logGroupName: "/aws/lambda/"+newLambdaFN,
  retention: logs.RetentionDays.THREE_DAYS
});

// set log monitor subscription
new logs.SubscriptionFilter(this, "logSubscription"+newLambdaFN,{
  destination: lambdaLogDestination,
  logGroup: newLGroup

  // optional, use a filter to only get relevant logs
  filterPattern: logs.FilterPattern.allTerms(""),
});
```

The code of your monitor function will need to do a few things:

1. The messages received from CloudWatch will be zipped, so we need zlib. Decode the message from Base64, unzip it, and then JSON parse it. We want the key .logEvents from that final result.

2. Loop through the raw logs to determine if we need to take action based on the type of log message and content.

3. If action is needed, we can send a notification through SES or SNS, for example.

4. Optionally, we can also write logs to an aggregated JSON file on S3 for long-term storage.

Cost Tracking

We covered this high-level in Chapter 8. One tip to add to that is about getting the user sub from a Cognito authorization header so we can use it to identify the user:

```
let sections = authorization.split('.');
let buffc = Buffer.from(sections[1], 'base64');
claims = JSON.parse(buffc.toString('ascii'));
```

The user sub can be found in claims.sub.

Here's a NodeJS Lambda snippet for decoding the CloudWatch log from the trigger event

```
const zlib = require('zlib');
let payload = Buffer.from(event.awslogs.data, 'base64');
let unzipped = zlib.unzipSync(payload).toString();
logevents = JSON.parse(unzipped).logEvents;
```

and checking if it's a report log:

```
let isreport = logevents[1].message.substr(0,6)  === 'REPORT';
```

Split the log into parts:

```
let parts = logevents[1].message.trim().split("\t");
```

The request ID is

```
requestid = parts[0].substring(18);
```

Create the full log in a usable format:

```
let rlog = {"report":true,"requestid":requestid};
for(let p in parts){
  if(!parts.hasOwnProperty(p)) continue;
  if(p == 0) continue;
```

```
// report key/values
let q = parts[p].trim().split(':');
if(typeof q[1] == 'undefined') continue;

// key
let k = q[0].replace(/\s/g,'_').toLowerCase();

// value
rlog[k] = parseInt(q[1].substring(0,q[1].length-2).trim());
}
```

After that, we can store it on S3 as JSON or in DynamoDB.

Parsing S3 Logs

This has some pitfalls, so here are some tips to help with it.

Here are columns that we can extract from the log:

```
const columns = [
  'Bucket_Owner','Bucket','Time','Remote_IP','Requester', 'Request_
ID','Operation','Key','Request_URI','HTTP_status', 'Error_Code','Bytes_
Sent','Object_Size','Total_Time', 'Turn_Around_Time','Referrer','User_
Agent','Version_Id'
];
```

First, retrieve the S3 logs. We can read them all into memory, read them one by one, or stream them, whichever suits the use case (mostly driven by the number of files being processed in one sitting). Whatever the preferred method, we will need to read in a single log's data and then parse it:

```
// split and loop through rows
let rows = S3_log_data.split("\n");
for(let r in rows){
  if(!rows.hasOwnProperty(r)) continue;

  // parse the row (function is below)
  let cols = getDataFromCSVLine(rows[r]);

  // skip if invalid
```

```
  if(cols.length < 10) continue;

  // skip if not relevant to use case, I only needed get requests
  if(cols[7] !== 'REST.GET.OBJECT') continue;

  // fix date field, it's annoyingly spread over 2 columns, merge into the
  first, delete the 2nd
  cols[2] = cols[2].substring(1)+' '+cols[3].substring(0, cols[3].length-1);
  cols.splice(3,1);

  // create timestamp, because thats more useful to work with
  let dp = cols[2].split(' ')[0]; // 0: date+time, 1: offset
  dp = dp.split(':'); // 0: date, 1:hour, 2: minute, 3:second
  let dd  = dp[0].split('/'); // day, month, year
  cols[2] = new Date(
                  dd[2],
                  months.indexOf(dd[1]),
                  dd[0],
                  dp[1],
                  dp[2],
                  dp[3]).getTime();

  // create nice key-value object log
  let newLog = {};
    for(let c in cols){
      if(!cols.hasOwnProperty(c)) continue;

      // the last couple of columns don't seem to fit into the
      // column names, but i didn't need them so I just made this
      // quick fix
      if(typeof columns[c] === 'undefined'){
       columns[c] = 'column '+c;
      }

      newLog[columns[c]] = cols[c];
    }

    // add "newlog" to a collector object, db or json file
  }
```

This is a simple CSV-parsing function to parse the S3 log row:

```
function getDataFromCSVLine(line) {
  let dataArray = [];
  let tempString="";
  let lineLength = line.length;
  let index=0;

  while(index < lineLength) {
    if(line[index]=='"') {
      let index2 = index+1;
      while(line[index2]!='"') {
        tempString+=line[index2];
        index2++;
      }
      dataArray.push(tempString);
      tempString = "";
      index = index2+2;
      continue;
    }

    if(line[index]!=" ") {
      tempString += line[index];
      index++; continue;
    }

    if(line[index]==" ") {
      dataArray.push(tempString);
        tempString = "";
        index++;
        continue;
    }
  }

  dataArray.push(tempString);
  return dataArray;
}
```

Parsing API Gateway Logs

To set API Gateway up for logging, create a role that API Gateway can use to write logs to CloudWatch. Then, enable CloudWatch logs in the stage configuration. Log level should be "info," and check "Log full requests/responses data."

Create a Lambda microservice (NodeJS) that retrieves the CloudWatch logs to process them. This could also be a trigger, but I found a daily batch approach more suited to my use case. API Gateway creates a whole bunch of streams with hash names for writing its logs too. This is a bit different from Lambda logs with time-based naming. Which stream gets written to seems to be random. There are a few steps to go through to parse the API Gateway logs into something useful:

1. Get all the streams for the API Gateway log group that was created using describeLogStreams. Make sure to configure this request to orderBy 'LastEventTime', and the descending param should be true. This means that the response will be first the stream with the most recent log and then older logs until it gets to streams that have no logs. This may need to be a looping CloudWatch request if a nextToken is returned.

2. Check each returned stream to create an "active stream" array. If data.logStreams[s].lastEventTimestamp is undefined, then it does not have any logs. Note that because of the orderby config that we are using, once we get to a stream that has no logs, we can stop looping through the streams as nothing after it will have any logs either.

3. Loop through the active streams using getLogEvents to retrieve all the logs in the stream. As with streams, this may need to be a looping request until no more nextToken is returned.

4. Parse each log message and pull out the useful information.

5. Store the logs in daily segments so they can be included with a log aggregator later on.

Parsing the logs themselves can be a bit tricky. Each message consists of a timestamp and a message param. The timestamp is valid and can be used as is. How to parse the message will depend on what type of message it is.

Get the log ID from the message:

```
let logID = /\((([^)]+)\)/.exec(message)[1];
// note: error check logID to make sure it's not undefined
```

Get the HTTP method and path:

```
let search = 'HTTP Method: ';
let searchIndex = message.search(search);
let message = let m = message.substring(searchIndex+search.length).trim();

let parts = message.split(',');
let method = parts[0];
let path  = parts[1].substring(15);
```

Most other data will likely be JSON or JSON-like. Some fixes are needed to be able to read most messages, but all of this will need to be tweaked for our configuration (user input/JSON schema/API Gateway transforms/etc.):

```
// get a Cognito sub to link action to the user
let search = 'Cognito User Pool Authorizer claims from JWT:';

// Get the response size, this is the data transferred to the
// user that has a cost attached to it
let search = 'Endpoint response headers: ';
let searchIndex = message.search(search);
let message = message.substring(searchIndex+search.length)
                     .trim();

// fix truncated json (the details of this are dependent on
// how you have configured json input coming in from the user
if(message.search('[TRUNCATED]') !== -1){
  message = message.replace('[TRUNCATED]','"}}');
}

// result
let result = {};
```

```
// try this, it will work for some messages
try{
  result = JSON.parse(message.replace(/\\n/,''));

// else we need to clean some more
}catch(e){

  // disclaimer: this is the quick and easy option

  // cut brackets from string
  message = message.substring(1,message.length-1);

  // add quotes and the brackets back on
  message = '{"'+message.replace(/=/g,'":"')
                      .replace(/, /g,'", "')+'"}';

  // fix dates
  message =  message.replace('"Date":"Mon", "','"Date":"Mon, ')
  .replace('"Date":"Tue", "','"Date":"Tue, ')
  .replace('"Date":"Wed", "','"Date":"Wed, ')
  .replace('"Date":"Thu", "','"Date":"Thu, ')
  .replace('"Date":"Fri", "','"Date":"Fri, ')
  .replace('"Date":"Sat", "','"Date":"Sat, ')
  .replace('"Date":"Sun", "','"Date":"Sun, ');

  // fix X-Amzn-Trace-Id=root=
  message = message.replace('root":"','root:')
                  .replace(';sampled":"',';sampled:');

  // try again
  try{
    result = JSON.parse(message);

  }catch(e){
    // debug and add more fixes until resolved
    console.log('COULD NOT PARSE: ',message);
    return false;

  }
}
```

Similar approaches are possible with the logs of many other services, but each service will have its own format and way of doing things that will need to be researched first.

⚙ Serverless Data Lake

Organizations collect an enormous amount of data across their business functions and store this data in various databases and file systems. The data is stored in different file formats and data schemas.

With such a diverse spread of methods, it is very difficult to analyze the data as a whole, making it difficult to extract business value. To address this challenge, organizations can build a data warehouse where the many sources of data can be combined and analyzed and value can be extracted. A data warehouse functions differently from a traditional database. It is optimized for fast queries, batch processing, and advanced analytics. Data warehouses are often used as a central data repository and a *single source of truth* for organizations.

While data warehouses have enabled organizations to generate value and insights from their data, a significant amount of preprocessing must be done to curate and standardize the diverse data sources into a single structure. The time and effort needed to preprocess data make real-time analysis difficult and expensive. Any changes to the agreed structure in the future are similarly high effort and cost.

Organizations evolved their data strategy to address these limitations, developing data *lakes*. A data lake is a centralized repository where organizations can store data from diverse sources **as is** while providing the capability to analyze the data using common big data analytics, machine learning, and visualization techniques.

With data lakes, data in different databases and file formats can be analyzed as if it were a single consistent data set. Once the sources have been registered, the data lake automatically crawls, catalogues, and indexes the data to make it possible to analyze it as if it were a single large data set. By removing the need to curate and preprocess the data, data scientists have easier access to a larger data pool, and they can work with new data much faster, sometimes even in real time.

Figure 10-2 presents a generic data lake using the open source platform Hadoop. It runs on servers on-premises or in the cloud and can import data into its own storage facilities or simply connect to the external source. Either way, the data is indexed, and we use Spark to perform queries on the indexes. As shown in Figure 10-2, other systems can connect to Spark to perform analytics and gain insights that can be presented to business users.

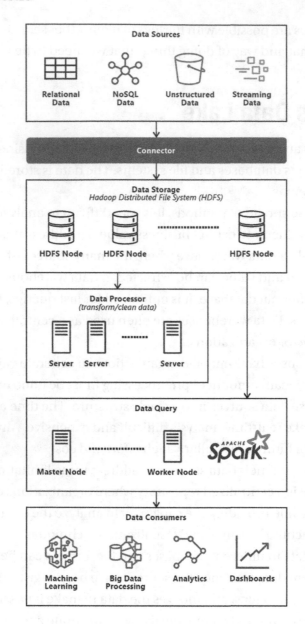

Figure 10-2. *Generic Serverless data lake design*

Hadoop requires managing a cluster of servers that require maintenance and will result in resource underutilization and billable idle time. However, that is not the only approach to a data lake; AWS offers a range of services we can use to build a **Serverless** data lake.

First, we have data ingestion and storage services.

We have covered S3 extensively in this book, so I won't go into detail here. S3 makes a great storage facility for our data lake. It is Serverless, is cost-effective, has great access controls, and supports several ways to add data. Users and external systems can upload any type of data into buckets. Uploading can happen in batches directly to S3, via an API, or through streaming.

A common workflow is to ingest raw data to one bucket where it can be assessed before being moved to a second bucket for cleaned and verified data. This second bucket is the data lake storage facility that is registered with the analytics services. We can also leverage features like versioning, backups, and lifecycles to help manage our data.

Kinesis is used to ingest real-time data streams such as customer click streams, logs, and data from IoT devices. Kinesis also supports audio-video streams. The service is fully managed and integrates with other services, avoiding the need for custom development. However, it is billed based on the availability of the ingestion streams we create, so we will be billed for idle time if the streams are not active.

If near real time is sufficient for the use case, Kinesis Firehose might be a better option. Firehose is Serverless; we pay based on the amount of ingested data. It integrates with cloud services that can support converting, cleaning, or otherwise processing the incoming data stream before storing it in an S3 bucket.

There are two Serverless databases relevant to data lakes where we pay for actual utilization. The first is DynamoDB, which we covered extensively in Chapter 7. DynamoDB is highly performant and has a lifecycle management feature called time to live, which can automatically delete stale data. This makes it a great option for file metadata, aggregated analytics for reports, and current data used in dashboards. The second database is Timestream. It is relevant to most data that is ingested in real time or near real time, such as logs and IoT data.

AWS Glue is an extract, transform, and load (ETL) service. Glue crawls and analyzes the files in S3 buckets, extracts the data, can transform it to be more efficient for analytics, and loads the necessary data into an index. AWS Glue can convert between formats and merge multiple small files into a single large file, as shown in Figure 10-3, greatly reducing data lake cost and query latency. Glue is fully Serverless, billing for job runtime and similar metrics.

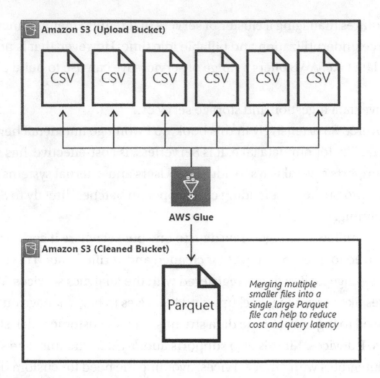

Figure 10-3. *File optimization with Glue to reduce cost and query latency*

We can use Lambda – another service already covered extensively – for custom data processing. Common use cases for integrating Lambda include compression, encryption, malware and virus scanning, and metadata extraction.

Moving on to analysis and visualization, the first AWS service of note is Athena. This service enables technical users to query all Glue-indexed data in the data lake, seamlessly integrating without the need to manage anything other than access permissions.

Athena uses standard SQL as the query language, which should be familiar to developers, data scientists, and even some business users. This makes it easy to integrate into other cloud services and some third-party analytics tools that work with SQL, such as Microsoft BI. Athena is Serverless, billing for the amount of data scanned by the queries.

For visualization, AWS offers QuickSight – a business intelligence dashboard. QuickSight is a bit different from other AWS services in that it is intended for non-technical end users and is a SaaS offering, billed per user per month.

QuickSight integrates with Athena, which performs the queries and provides the data to be visualized. QuickSight can also integrate with other SQL databases in the cloud or external and third-party SaaS solutions such as Salesforce and Jira.

It supports a wide range of visualizations, graphs, tables, and other components, easily used and configured into dashboards and reports by non-technical business users. There are standard and enterprise versions available. The enterprise version supports features such as Active Directory integration and machine learning for advanced analytics.

Data lakes are typically created manually as it provides the flexibility to add custom processing or meet specific compliance requirements. However, AWS Lake Formation is a service that can quickly create a simple and standard data lake deployment in minutes. Using this service, we define the data sources, and it will automatically collect and catalogue them and then clean and classify the data. It also offers powerful security features such as column- and row-level permissions.

Creating and using a Serverless data lake has benefits and limitations compared with a self-managed solution such as a Hadoop cluster. A significant benefit is that with a data lake, there are no servers, operating systems, or software to manage and maintain, nor do we need to configure or manage redundancy, scaling, or backups. This means we pay only for what we use and not idle time. Similarly, there are no licenses to manage or pay for, it's both easy and fast to create or delete a data lake at any time, and any licenses are included in the fees for the time we use it. S3 offers virtually unlimited storage, and we are not limited by hardware procurement or having to manually swap out or add new drives.

As with any technology, there are limitations to a Serverless data lake. There will be less control compared with a self-managed system. For example, we cannot select or configure the underlying operating system, and the services will only have some software configurations available.

For regulated industries, in particular, there may be policy or other compliance challenges in storing certain types of data in the cloud. Data classification and policies should be in place and referenced before committing to a Serverless solution.

It is also important to note that Serverless solutions in the cloud can have higher latency when compared with an on-premises solution. This will depend on the distance from the cloud data center, but it should certainly be considered for real-time use cases.

Figure 10-4 provides an example architecture of a Serverless data lake. Beginning with the data sources at the top left, these could be a web app, mobile app, IoT devices, or industrial machines. Streams of data can be fed into the cloud using Kinesis, Firehose, or IoT Core. Other ingestion methods include posting data to an API or batch uploads directly to S3 using the AWS CLI or SDK.

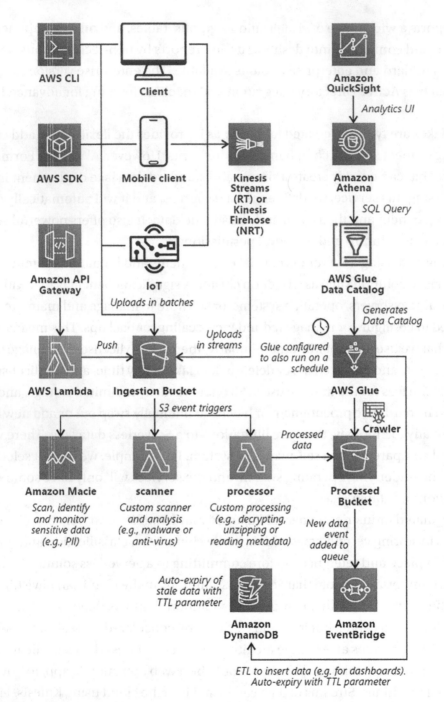

Figure 10-4. *Architecture example of a Serverless data lake*

All data ends up in the S3 ingestion bucket in the data lake. In this example, we use Macie to scan the data for any personal or sensitive data we want flagged. We can also integrate a Lambda virus scanner or any number of custom scanners running in microservices.

Once any initial processing completes, the files are added to a processed bucket in the data lake. As files are added, the S3 event can automatically trigger a Glue crawler to start running, which indexes new data into a search index table. We can also schedule regular crawls of the data lake to make sure the index is updated with any deleted or changed files.

As part of the indexing process, we can use scripts to copy parts of the data into DynamoDB. This could be used for analytics, a dashboard, or reports. We can configure the *time to live* parameter with a date to automatically delete data. This ensures that only the latest data is used in our dashboard or reports.

Our index, called a Glue Catalogue, can be queried using standard SQL with the Athena service. QuickSight can be added in front of Athena to offer a more visual interface to less technical users.

This architecture provides a basic searchable data lake, but there are many other capabilities we could add to this based on the needs of the organization.

⚙ Serverless Video

Traditionally, video studios require significant up-front investment to set up video processing servers and transcoding farms. With the pace of change in video technology and the matching expectations of the users, studios may find it hard to keep up with new technologies, resolutions, and formats that require additional investment to support.

The cloud can support video studios and content creators with a range of services in this space to store, process, and deliver both recorded and live video content.

The cloud provides capabilities for transporting and sharing footage, transcoding video into different formats for a range of devices, live streaming, secure storage for media content, and even ways to monetize videos by embedding advertisements within them during distribution.

Elemental Media Services

The AWS solution suite Elemental includes six distinct media services.

One challenge for video production studios is securely moving data between locations; expensive private networks are typically created to achieve this. Elemental **MediaConnect** is a service that enables us to securely move video files into, within, and out of the AWS global network, reducing the need for private networks. Large media files can be shared with a specific organization or individual, and fine-grained security controls enable us to be very selective about who has access, under which conditions, and for how long.

Larger studios can consider adding Direct Connect for the last mile – a private connection between AWS and the studio's physical location.

Another use case for MediaConnect is ingesting live video streams or raw footage into AWS for processing and packaging before distribution.

Video transcoding is the process of converting large studio-quality footage into common streaming and distribution formats. This process requires considerable computing power and is often done in transcoding farms – data centers full of servers built for video processing. These farms require a considerable investment to build and maintain, with capacity planning and scaling presenting challenges.

The Elemental **MediaConvert** service was created specifically for converting various source video formats to on-demand formats for distribution. It can create common Internet streaming formats supported by a range of mobile and other devices, video-on-demand (VOD) formats used by video subscription organizations such as Netflix to distribute their content, and video file formats commonly used by social media and learning management systems.

Elemental **MediaLive** does something similar but for live video. It encodes high-quality source video in real time to lighter formats more suitable for online streaming.

Sometimes studios want to create the various formats themselves to retain control over quality and other aspects. However, the challenge of *distributing* on demand or live video content remains. For this challenge, there is the Elemental **MediaPackage** service, which does not modify the video but simply packages it for distribution.

Given the size of media data, storage has several challenges, especially given the high expectations around latency, availability, and durability.

The Elemental **MediaStore** service is a storage solution optimized for media content. It integrates with the other media services for fast processing, moving media files between services, and distribution to viewers.

Besides storage, MediaStore functions as a media sharing platform where users can upload content and share it with others across many supported devices. Studios can use the same capability to distribute their content if the files have been suitably packaged.

While there are third-party solutions available to help with monetization, they typically need to be installed, managed, and maintained on servers. This requires time to be spent on server provisioning, scaling, and management. Elemental **MediaTailor** provides monetization capability for media content without all the overheads of managing the software or servers running it. MediaTailor enables producers to inject advertisements into video content. The advertisements are seamlessly stitched into the videos, and we can personalize them for individual viewers.

Making the Media Services More Serverless

While the Elemental media services are fully managed, they are not Serverless, as we are billed for idle time when they are running but not used. We can manage this and make Elemental slightly more Serverless by automating the provisioning of the services *on demand* and removing them again when no longer needed.

Figure 10-5 shows how we can create an on-demand live streaming workflow to minimize underutilization and billable idle time. We start the workflow with the broadcaster, who will request a new live video event. This request reaches API Gateway via our WAF and is then forwarded to a Lambda microservice to handle.

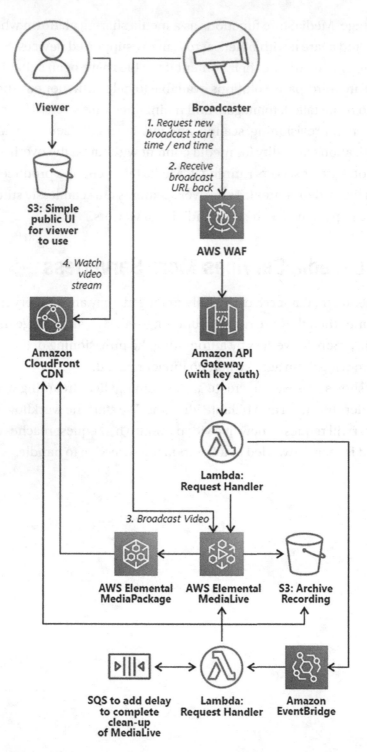

Figure 10-5. *Architecture example for an on-demand live streaming workflow*

Lambda will launch the MediaPackage and MediaLive services and create a CloudFront CDN to distribute the content. Lastly, the microservice will create an EventBridge schedule for the event end time that the broadcaster would have indicated in their request. The broadcaster then connects to MediaLive and starts sending their video stream, it is encoded to suitable formats for streaming, and a copy is recorded to S3. The stream is passed to MediaPackage, which packages it for live video distribution, making the packages available to CloudFront. Meanwhile, the viewers connect to the broadcasting web page on S3, which loads the live video stream packages from CloudFront.

The EventBridge schedule created earlier will trigger soon after the live event ends. This will launch a cleanup Lambda that will terminate MediaLive, MediaPackage, and the CloudFront CDN. MediaLive consists of two components, and the second can only be terminated after the first one finishes terminating, which can take a couple of minutes. To avoid Lambda idle waiting for the first to terminate, we use SQS to trigger the cleanup microservice after a 10-minute visibility delay. This time, the microservice will terminate the second component.

Video Processing and Analysis

Our next case study shown in Figure 10-6 is a simple video processing pipeline that can help automate common processes and generate more value from media. New video files are stored in S3 from any number of sources. For example, this could be the MediaLive recording we saw in the previous case study.

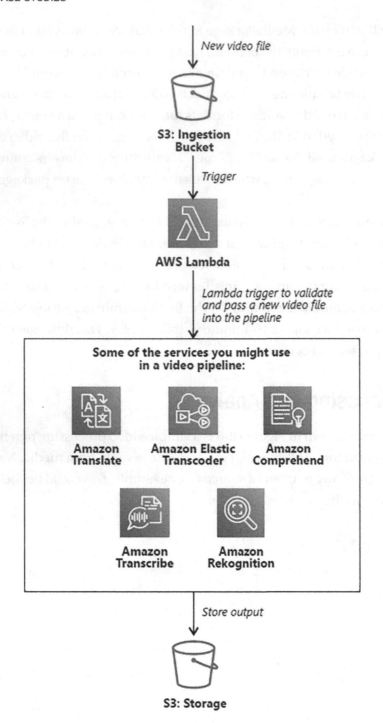

Figure 10-6. *High-level architecture for event-driven video analysis*

S3 can be configured to trigger a Lambda microservice for each newly added file. The microservice can validate the file to ensure it is a video and then pass it to a number of processing services that can analyze it and generate useful outputs – for example, generating subtitles in several languages or identifying keywords, phrases, objects, people, or scenes to power advanced search capabilities.

The output of the different processing services can be stored in S3.

Such outputs can automatically trigger the next step in the workflow. For example, the Transcribe service output can trigger a microservice to send the resulting text to the Translate service.

⚙ Serverless Minecraft

This case study shows how we can use Serverless to achieve an on-demand Minecraft server that is reliable and cost-effective for casual players. This case study leverages the public GitHub project *minecraft-ondemand*, created and maintained by Ray Gibson (doctorray117) and licensed under the Apache License 2.0. It's a fun project for introducing people to Serverless and comparing different architectures. The open source project and further instructions can be found here: *https://github.com/ doctorray117/minecraft-ondemand*.

Developed by Mojang Studios and released in 2011, Minecraft is one of the best-selling video games of all time. Microsoft acquired it in 2014, and, as of 2022, it has over 170 million active users. Minecraft can be played locally or by joining a game server, hosted by another player or commercially.

Connecting to a server provides a multiplayer experience, enabling players to interact with one another and form communities. Anyone can start their own Minecraft server simply by downloading and configuring the software provided by Mojang.

Tech-savvy parents like to maintain a measure of control over the Minecraft environment their children play in. Having a personal server allows us to set our own rules, customize game play, and determine who joins the server. Hosts can also create communities and monetize the server by selling in-game items and experiences.

Traditionally, there are two popular ways to host a Minecraft server. We can host it locally on any laptop or desktop that meets the requirements. If we do not have a gaming PC – not uncommon as many players use a tablet to play Minecraft – then an up-front fee will be needed to buy a suitable machine. The running cost of the personal server is minimal; we need to maintain the PC and pay for the electricity. If we want the server to be available to external users, there will also be an Internet connectivity cost. It varies per region, but the yearly Total Cost of Ownership (TCO) would be around $160. In industry terms, this is what we call *on-premises infrastructure* – we are responsible for purchasing and maintaining the hardware, networking, and computer's operating system and software.

Another common method is to use a commercial Minecraft hosting provider. These providers offer an all-in-one service that includes hosting and maintaining a Minecraft server. There are no up-front fees; we pay a fixed monthly or yearly cost regardless of how much the server is actually used. This option is very stable as the provider manages everything and we do not have to worry about maintenance or redundancy. In industry terms, this is what we call *fully managed infrastructure*. Depending on the provider, and despite having no maintenance overheads, the TCO is similar to self-hosted due to economies of scale.

But what about casual players just looking to have a server available for the family? It's probably not worth investing in a gaming PC, and we might not want to commit to recurring monthly bills for a commercial server. In this case, we can consider using Serverless architecture to host a Minecraft server on AWS. This is a highly cost-effective approach, as we only pay for what we use, and the server is automatically shut down when there are no players. One consideration is the cold start latency with this approach. When we want to start playing, we will need to wait a short while for the Minecraft server to become available – though this shouldn't be longer than a minute or so.

An average play time of 20 hours a month would cost about $1.50. This is at least ten times cheaper than the commercial offering. If we want a Minecraft server running 24/7, using an EC2 instance instead of an on-demand Fargate container will likely be slightly more cost-effective. However, EC2 requires more technical capability in cloud infrastructure. For the less technical, running this project 24/7 will still be more cost-effective than a commercial fully managed server.

Let's look at the AWS services used in Figure 10-7:

- Route 53, a Domain Name System (DNS), allows us to use minecraft.example.com to connect to our game, which is easier to remember than an IP address.

- CloudWatch is used to react to requests for our Minecraft server and store error and status logs from the server.

- Simple Notification Service (SNS) notifies us when the Minecraft server starts and shuts down and when there are any errors.

- Lambda is used to respond to Route 53 events and launch the Minecraft server – if it's not already running.

- In Fargate, we configure a task that includes a Minecraft server container. Lambda would not be suitable as we may want to play for longer than Lambda's 15-minute execution time limit.

- Elastic File System (EFS) is a storage service that can be shared among different compute services. EFS is an ideal service for keeping the Minecraft gaming files. The EFS storage will remain available, retaining our files after the Fargate container is terminated.

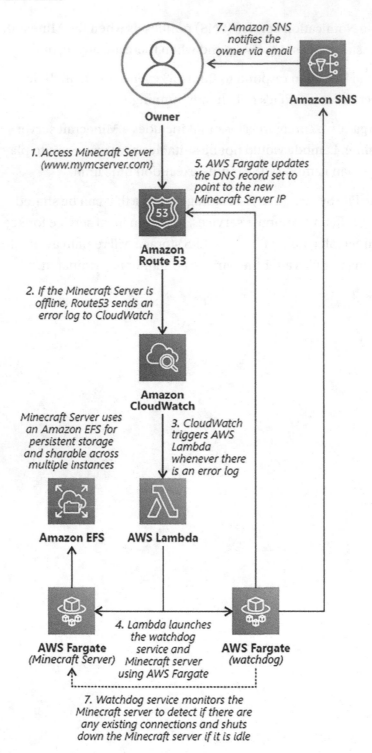

7. Amazon SNS notifies the owner via email

Amazon SNS

Owner

1. Access Minecraft Server (www.mymcserver.com)

5. AWS Fargate updates the DNS record set to point to the new Minecraft Server IP

Amazon Route 53

2. If the Minecraft Server is offline, Route53 sends an error log to CloudWatch

Amazon CloudWatch

Minecraft Server uses an Amazon EFS for persistent storage and sharable across multiple instances

3. CloudWatch triggers AWS Lambda whenever there is an error log

Amazon EFS   **AWS Lambda**

AWS Fargate (Minecraft Server)

4. Lambda launches the watchdog service and Minecraft server using AWS Fargate

AWS Fargate (watchdog)

7. Watchdog service monitors the Minecraft server to detect if there are any existing connections and shuts down the Minecraft server if it is idle

Figure 10-7. *Architecture for Serverless Minecraft*

Fargate tasks can include multiple containers at no additional cost. Here, our Fargate task also includes a Watchdog. This tool monitors the Minecraft server container utilization.

Fargate has both standard and spot pricing. Spot pricing can often be used at a far lower cost – about 30–40% of standard pricing. However, the risk with spot pricing is that the container is provided based on availability and could be taken away at any point. We do receive a 2-minute notice, which is enough time to shut down and save any changes to our Minecraft world. The risk of this happening really depends on the region, time of day, and other factors.

We begin by connecting to our domain name from a Minecraft game on a PC or tablet. If the Minecraft server is not running, it will return an error to our game, indicating that it failed to connect.

In the background, Route 53 will log an error to CloudWatch. CloudWatch will trigger the subscribed Lambda microservice that will launch the Fargate task containing the Minecraft and Watchdog containers. When the Minecraft container launches, it will connect to the EFS drive with the game files and launch the Minecraft server. The Watchdog container will wait for the server to be available and then update the Route 53 record to point our domain to the server container's IP address.

All of this should take no more than a minute. At this point, the Minecraft server is available, and SNS will send an email notification to let us know. We can now try to connect the game to our domain name again, which should work this time.

Minecraft Server Setup

The following are the high-level steps to deploy this project. More details can be found in the readme files of the GitHub project:

1. We will need an AWS account and a user with programmatic access and associated credentials. Locally, install AWS CLI and configure it to use the AWS user account – more detailed directions for this can be found in the CLI documentation.

2. Download and install the CDK CLI. To test and confirm it is set up correctly, run `cdk bootstrap` in a command line. This should prepare the cloud account for working with this framework. More detailed directions and troubleshooting options for this can be found in the CDK documentation.

3. Create a Route 53 hosted zone for the game domain. Note that we can also buy a new domain in Route 53.

4. Download and configure the project from GitHub (after installing GIT). Clone this project repository:

   git clone *https://github.com/doctorray117/minecraft-ondemand.git*

5. Head into the CDK folder, and copy or rename *.env.sample* to just *.env*:

   ```
   cd cdk/
   cp .env.sample .env
   ```

6. Open and edit the *.env* file to reflect the preferred settings. At a minimum, we need to enter our domain name at the top:

   ```
   # Required
   DOMAIN_NAME = minecraft.example.com
   ```

7. Install NodeJS with NPM, and then run the following command:

   ```
   npm run build && npm run deploy
   ```

8. The following bootstrap error might be encountered during the build and deploy step, even if the bootstrap command was run earlier:

   ```
   X minecraft-domain-stack failed: Error: minecraft-domain-
   stack: SSM parameter /cdk-bootstrap/hnb659fds/version not
   found. Has the environment been bootstrapped? Please run
   'cdk bootstrap' (see https://docs.aws.amazon.com/cdk/latest/
   guide/bootstrapping.html)
   ```

One of the following steps might be able to resolve the issue:

1. Add

   ```
   "@aws-cdk/core:newStyleStackSynthesis": true
   ```

   to the file *cdk.json* as a new row within the *context* section. Remember to add a comma to the end of the previous line.

2. Execute the following bootstrap command. Note that this can take 10–15 minutes to execute!

```
cdk bootstrap --cloudformation-execution-policies
arn:aws:iam::aws:policy/AdministratorAccess
```

Once the project is successfully deployed, visit the URL generated by CDK. The default behavior creates a Minecraft subdomain under the configured domain, such as *minecraft.example.com*. If we open this subdomain in the browser, we will see an error message. This error is what the Minecraft game will see if it tries to connect to the server before it is available.

Notes

It is important to note that this is not scaling infrastructure. Minecraft will be running on a single container that must be large enough to support all expected users. We can configure the resources in the .env file.

Any request to the domain name will trigger Minecraft to be launched. This can result in false positives from bots that commonly test public domain names. While the container will automatically be shut down again by the Watchdog, if this happens frequently, the costs could add up. Using a random subdomain can help with this; certainly avoid using the root domain for the server.

⚙ SEO-Friendly Website and CMS

There are different approaches to developing websites. For the sake of simplicity, the term *website* here can include basic information websites, web applications, and ecommerce websites. Three common approaches are as follows:

1. **Static website**

    A website without any back end or interaction, a one-way information flow. It's the simplest method consisting of HTML, CSS, and perhaps some JavaScript. The HTML files contain all the content, and there is no latency due to database communication. This makes the pages very fast, and search bots can easily index the content.

2. **Dynamic page website**

   There is a back end that provides database content and processing. The content and processing results are combined with HTML templates to generate the pages seen in the browser. Depending on the page content, the pages are generated for every request or every request from a particular user. Pages might also be cached for a period, depending on how frequent the page content is expected to change.

3. **API website**

   This is how modern websites are typically built. The UI is completely separate from the back end. The UI can put and retrieve data through the API, which is the interface for the back end. The API response is then injected into the HTML templates in the front end and presented to the user.

Serverless Websites

Serverless can use all three of these approaches. Static websites can be stored on S3 and served directly or via CloudFront CDN. This is a common way to serve simple websites that are only providing information to visitors. The problem with static websites is that they are a fixed point in time. There is no database for the site owner to manage content, typically requiring a developer to make changes to the site.

Dynamic page websites are less commonly developed with Serverless architecture. It is possible to generate and serve HTML with Lambda – directly, with API Gateway, or with Application Load Balancer. However, these services are not really designed for this and add considerable latency to the user experience.

APIs are the most common approach used in Serverless websites, especially for more complex web applications with a lot of interaction between the user and the back end. The problem with the API approach is that most search bots struggle to index API content. While this does not usually matter for web applications, websites often depend on good search engine rankings to attract visitors.

A typical API website needs to retrieve its content from the API before it is displayed in the browser. This means that when a typical search engine crawler indexes an API website, it will see no content, just lots of code. You can combine some static content pages with API pages, but then you are back to the problem with static pages, where it's harder to manage the contents.

Over the last couple of years, search engines have made progress with indexing API-driven websites, so some may be able to see the retrieved content. However, the result is still not as good as when the search engines index a static website, and there may be penalties for additional latency or complex code structures.

Another Approach

Figure 10-8 shows the architecture of another approach that can be considered. On the left, we have an API-driven content management system (CMS). A CMS is a web application, and SEO is not important here, so an API approach is a good fit. API Gateway can secure the CMS with Cognito and WAF integrations, and the Lambda back end can manage content in a DynamoDB database.

The *Page Builder* microservice generates the public-facing website on the right of Figure 10-8. It combines data from the DynamoDB database and HTML templates stored on S3 to generate static HTML pages that are then stored on S3 and distributed by CloudFront CDN. Whenever a page is changed in the CMS, it will ask the *Page Builder* microservice to regenerate the page for the website. At the same time, the microservice can force a cache reset in CloudFront.

Interactive website pages, such as a contact form, can combine the static generated HTML with a public API to submit and retrieve information. Interactive pages with content unique to a particular user would be behind a login and can be API-driven, as SEO would not be a requirement.

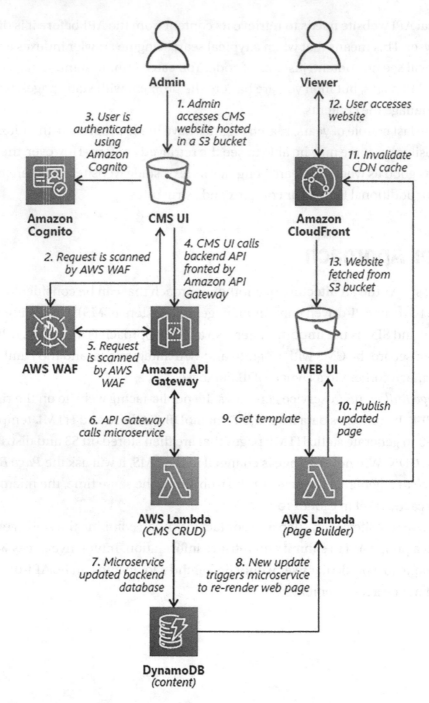

Figure 10-8. *Serverless CMS with static site generation*

This architecture gives us the benefits of the different approaches while avoiding the challenges:

1. A non-technical site owner can manage the website's content through a user-friendly CMS interface.

2. Search engines experience the website as static, with all the content embedded and easily indexed.

3. Interactive capabilities can be supported through a public API where needed. The pages can be static, and the few necessary dynamic parts would not impact SEO.

4. The website will be incredibly fast, rapidly delivered through the closest CDN endpoint and without the delays typically caused by communicating with a back end or database.

Serverless Website Tips

Here are a few tips from my own experience that might be helpful for this approach:

- Consider carefully how the output pages will be rendered from data and an HTML template. There are existing libraries such as EJS (`https://ejs.co/`) to achieve this, or a custom one can be developed. Factor in potential future needs, not only the currently known requirements, as changing the render engine can be a lot of work.

- Figure 10-8 uses an automatic trigger on the DDB to generate changed pages. However, some site owners may prefer a manual publish approval step.

- Consider an option to regenerate all pages for a given template as well as the entire public website; this will be very helpful when there are template changes.

- Make sure to invalidate the CDN after publishing new website files, or the updates won't be visible to the content manager.

- Keep the generated pages separate from static content such as JavaScript, CSS, and image files used by the website templates. A separate bucket can be used, which will make it easier to clean up or regenerate all HTML pages.

- The Page Builder microservice can be a single microservice to handle all templates, or there could be a unique microservice for each template. In practice, I have found that most publishing steps are the same for different templates, so it made more sense to use a single microservice. This is run in parallel for each job triggered by the DynamoDB or a publish request.

- Include a config.json file with the HTML templates that contains information about which data should be loaded from the database for each template. This will make retrieving data in the render engine more efficient.

- For content, I use a single DynamoDB, with partition keys to separate the different languages and types and the range keys to uniquely identify a given page. For ecommerce, additional DynamoDBs can be added for product inventory and orders. QLDB can be used for transaction records. Keep in mind that only the site admin will be working with the content database as the public website is static.

⚙ Virtual Host

Creating a virtual host is quite fun and a great case study for education. We use Amazon Sumerian – a Serverless browser-based 3D engine service – to create a 3D environment with a 3D avatar (the virtual host). We then make the host interactive using speech and some reaction behaviors.

We covered Polly in Chapter 9; it does text-to-speech and integrates well with the avatars in Sumerian, making them seem to speak. For user input, we can use speech recognition in the Chrome browser or touch input. The experience works great on a large, portrait-oriented touch screen TV, making the avatar appear almost life-size.

For additional impact, we can include a camera to capture the user's face for facial and expression recognition by passing it to the Rekognition service. The API Gateway and Lambda in Figure 10-9 are to facilitate these interactions and store any session data and activity logs. We use WebSockets to facilitate two-way communication.

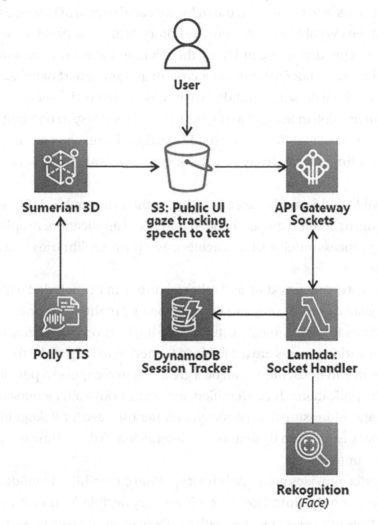

Figure 10-9. *Serverless 3D environment and talking host*

In the browser, we can also capture video from a camera and use it to track the user as they move via gaze tracking implemented with JavaScript. Be warned, though, that this can be a bit creepy. One such tracking library can be found here: *https:// webgazer.cs.brown.edu/*.

To implement this use case, we start with Sumerian. For it to access Polly and use this service as the voice of the avatar, it needs a Cognito user pool with roles for *authorized* and *unauthorized* that have the appropriate Polly permission configured. The Cognito user pool ID is then configured in Sumerian under *AWS Configuration*, which can be found in the settings panel on the right. We can design a 3D scene as a backdrop and pick one of the available avatars from the library. Sumerian provides several such avatars in different genders and ethnicities, though most have a similar, somewhat cartoonish, style. It does not currently offer custom avatars as part of the services, though they have created them for some brands as a bespoke (and costly) service.

The Polly integration in Sumerian is seamless and very easy to configure. Select the voice and apply the text that the avatar should speak in the text box or through a script. Lex integration is similarly relatively straightforward if we want to achieve a full chatbot experience.

The final published Sumerian scene can be reached via a public URL, suitable for early prototyping, or secured and embedded into a web application. Amplify can make this embedding process much easier to achieve as it provides libraries specifically for Sumerian scenes.

API connectivity, gaze tracking, and other features can be included within Sumerian using JavaScript, or they can be implemented in the web application, and we create functions to communicate with the web application in Sumerian. Hooks and notifications for various events are available in Sumerian to help make this a bit easier.

A web camera and Rekognition can be a great way to recognize a person from their profile in a web application. Once identified, the avatar could offer a personalized welcome message addressing them directly. Another use case for Rekognition could be to monitor a user's expression throughout an interaction to determine their mood about certain activities or topics.

The Lex service provides great speech recognition capabilities to guide a user through a particular order flow. However, it is not very flexible for non-order flow use cases. The Chrome browser comes with similarly powerful speech recognition capabilities without being tied to any particular flow or use case. Using the Chrome option does mean that we need to develop the logic around the recognized text, but it provides a lot more flexibility to achieve a given application's specific requirements. An added advantage is that it has far lower latency compared with Lex. Most other browsers do not offer similar capabilities at this time, so we need to ensure that the users are using Chrome if the avatar is publicly accessible via the Internet.

In an education setting, I like to include IoT light bulbs in the mix so users can ask the avatar to turn the lights on or off. These kinds of physical elements can greatly enhance the learning experience.

⚙ True Serverless Containers1

In 2017, AWS launched Fargate, a fully managed container service. The cloud provider fully manages the underlying server clusters, operating systems, and platform software. We create and launch our Docker containers into it and only pay for the resources that those containers are assigned while running, *regardless of utilization*. Fargate supports long-running and on-demand task containers.

Task containers have a higher latency than Lambda microservices, so I prefer using Lambda for my Serverless back end. However, there are cases where Lambda limits get in the way, such as Lambda's 15-minute time limit, which can be a problem when working with video.

As mentioned, Fargate's billing model is not Serverless; we pay for runtime, not execution time. As such, it will include underutilization and billable idle time. However, like the live video case study, we can use Lambda to make Fargate containers on demand and minimize the amount of idle time that we need to pay for.

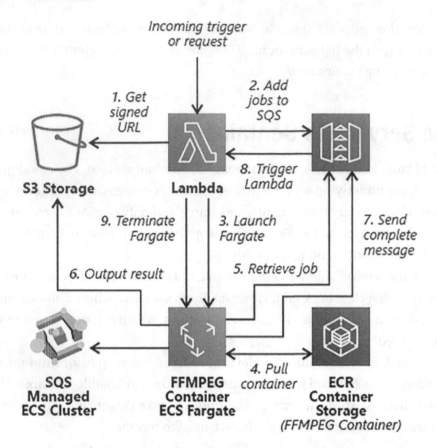

Figure 10-10. *Serverless-managed Docker container tasks*

In the example shown in Figure 10-10, I aim to have an FFMPEG container that I can pass a job to, which it then executes. I have also included some directions for running a service that needs to be externally accessible.

I use CDK to write all the fixed infrastructure and a Lambda microservice to load the on-demand services I need. Before copying my CDK instructions, please check out the CDK GIT page, especially the changelog, as there are frequent changes. I created the following in version 1.38. The CDK GIT page can be found here: *https://github.com/ aws/aws-cdk.*

For the container to be truly Serverless, I should only be paying for storage, requests, and container time spent executing the job. To avoid giving the container full access to my S3 buckets, I will generate signed GET and POST S3 URLs in the Lambda and pass these to the container via an SQS message.

The container will retrieve the video file(s) from the signed GET URL(s) and store the result on the signed POST URL. Once the job completes, the container will report out via another SQS message, triggering a Lambda that can confirm the job and terminate the container. The SQS queue approach means I can keep the Lambda microservices out of a VPC and completely decoupled from the containers in a VPC.

Here are the components that go into getting a container up and running:

1. Create, configure, and build the Docker container.

2. Put the container in a registry.

3. Enable long ARN names in ECS (if resource tags will be used).

4. Create support services for the use case.

5. Create the policies and roles.

6. Create a task definition.

7. Add the container to the task definition.

8. Create the cluster (and VPC) that the task will run in.

9. Launch the container.

Let's look at each of these with the associated options and pricing. Note that all pricing here is for the Singapore region. The USA region tends to be cheaper, and I am also not factoring in the free tier that would be available to new accounts.

1. Create, Configure, and Build Our Docker Container

This is fairly straightforward, and we can follow any guide for building and testing a Docker container locally. For this example, I was using a modified version of this container, *https://hub.docker.com/r/jrottenberg/ffmpeg/*, and adding bash scripts to handle the interactions with SQS and execute my video jobs.

AWS cost: $0 – this can be done locally

2. Put the Container in a Registry

I used AWS's Elastic Container Registry (ECR) service as it makes it easier to automate with CDK and integrate with other AWS services. I put my container config and files into a /src folder in my CDK stack and use *ecrassets.DockerImageAsset()* to build and deploy the container to ECR.

After including @aws-cdk/aws-ecr-assets, we need one line of code:

```
const ffmpegContainer = ecrassets.DockerImageAsset(this, "ffmpeg", {
directory: __dirname +"/src" });
```

This will add the container to a CDK-managed repo in our AWS account; it does not create a unique repo for the container. If we want our own unique repo, we can achieve it using the appropriate functions in the ECS module for CDK, but it takes a few more lines of code.

AWS cost: $0.10/GB/month storage and $0.12/GB data transfer

The total cost depends on the size of the container, and we will be billed for data transfer out (each time we launch the container). I consider this Serverless because we are paying only for usage.

3. Enable Long ARN Names in ECS

I didn't realize this was needed until my Lambda threw an error later on. ECS has a default and a long format for ARNs, and if we want to use tags (which we should), we must enable the long format. We can do this with three commands in the AWS CLI:

```
aws ecs put-account-setting-default --name serviceLongArnFormat --value
enabled
```

```
aws ecs put-account-setting-default --name taskLongArnFormat --value
enabled
```

```
aws ecs put-account-setting-default --name containerInstanceLongArn
Format --value enabled
```

Remember to add --profile [profile name] to the commands if the workstation has multiple AWS profiles.

AWS cost: $0

4. Create Any Support Services

For this example, I need two SQS queues, one for new jobs for the container to execute and one for completed jobs for the container to report out. Creating SQS queues is just another one-liner with CDK:

```
// new task messages
const sqsNew = new sqs.Queue(this, "ffmpegJobNew", {
  visibilityTimeout: cdk.Duration.seconds(7200)
});
```

```
// completed task messages
const sqsDone = new sqs.Queue(this, "ffmpegJobDone", {
  visibilityTimeout: cdk.Duration.seconds(300)
});
```

The container will be getting and putting video files from S3. I didn't include that capability here, as it is specific to my use case. Using SQS is a common pattern, which is why it is included.

AWS cost: $0.0000004 per message. This is, again, a truly Serverless service where we only pay for what we use.

5. Create the Policies and Roles

Using CDK, we can create the necessary policies and attach them to the roles. We need two roles:

1. An execution role that can load the container from the CDK-managed ECR repository

2. A task role that will be used by the container to access roles

```
// execution policy
const policyExecution = new iam.PolicyStatement({
  effect: iam.Effect.ALLOW,
  resources:[
    ffmpegContainer.repository.repositoryArn // from step 2
  ],
  actions: [
    "ecr:BatchCheckLayerAvailability",
    "ecr:GetDownloadUrlForLayer",
    "ecr:BatchGetImage"
  ]
});
```

```
// execution role
const erole = new iam.Role(this, "roleEcsExecution", {
  assumedBy: new iam.ServicePrincipal("ecs-tasks.amazonaws.com")
});
```

```
// attach policy to role
erole.addToPolicy(policyExecution);
```

For my use case, the container will need access to the two SQS queues:

```
// sqs access policy
const policyNew = new iam.PolicyStatement({
  effect: iam.Effect.ALLOW,
  resources:[sqsNew.queueArn],
  actions: [
    "sqs:GetQueueAttributes",
    "sqs:ReceiveMessage",
    "sqs:DeleteMessage"
  ]
});
```

```
const policyDone = new iam.PolicyStatement({
  effect: iam.Effect.ALLOW,
  resources:[sqsDone.queueArn],
  actions: [
    "sqs:SendMessage"
  ]
});
```

```
// task role
const role = new iam.Role(this, "roleEcsTask", {
  assumedBy: new iam.ServicePrincipal("ecs-tasks.amazonaws.com")
});
```

```
// attach policies to task role
role.addToPolicy(policyNew); // new sqs policy
role.addToPolicy(policyDone); // done sqs policy
```

AWS cost: $0. AWS does not bill for policies and roles.

6. Create a Task Definition

An ECS task definition defines the resources (CPU and memory) assigned to the container. As there is no cost attached to the definition itself, this is another step we can safely do in CDK:

```
const ecstask = new ecs.FargateTaskDefinition(this, "ecstask", {
  cpu: 1024, // 1 cpu... yes, this is confusing
  memoryLimitMiB: 2048, // 2gb memory
  executionRole: erole, // the above execution role
  taskRole: role // the above task role
});
```

AWS cost: $0. AWS does not bill for task definitions.

7. Add the Container to the Task Definition

This step simply adds a specific container to use to the task definition. Again, there's no cost attached to it as we are not launching anything yet, just providing the configuration. The CDK function *addContainer* can be used on the created ECS task. This also assumes that our container is in ECR as per step 2:

```
// get the container tag, ecrassets doesn't provide it so we
// have to get it from imageUri
let imageTag = ffmpegContainer.imageUri.split(':').pop();
ecstask.addContainer("ffmpeg", {
  image: ecs.ContainerImage.fromEcrRepository(
                        ffmpegContainer.repository,
                        imageTag
  ),
  environment:{
    INPUT_QUEUE_URL: sqsNew.queueUrl, // queue for new tasks
    OUTPUT_QUEUE_URL: sqsDone.queueUrl // queue for done tasks
  },
  workingDirectory: "/app"
});
```

I don't need these for my FFMPEG use case, but if we were creating a container service that we need to access externally, this is also where we would add port mappings. They can be added to the end of the *addContainer* function:

```
// continued from above
.addPortMappings({
  containerPort: 1234,
  // host port will be automatically assigned
  protocol: ecs.Protocol.TCP
});
```

AWS cost: $0. AWS does not charge for this definition.

8. Create the Cluster (and VPC) That the Task Will Run In

This is where things stop being so straightforward.

If we want to run a container that is running 24/7, we can follow the documentation for launching a Fargate service. I would not consider this Serverless because while we would not need to manage any servers or OS, we would be paying for idle time. In my case, I want to run a task on demand and not pay anything when no task is running.

If I go ahead and create a cluster in CDK, this will create a default VPC with two private subnets and NAT gateways. Those gateways will be costing $80+/month for doing nothing most of the time – NOT Serverless.

There are three approaches to consider:

1. Use an existing VPC.

If we already have a VPC with a public subnet or private subnet with a NAT, then we could use that. There would be no additional cost in using the existing VPC for the container, so this new feature could still be considered Serverless (though the overall solution would not be).

In CDK, create an ECS cluster and refer to the existing VPC:

```
const myCluster = new ecs.Cluster(this, "ecscluster", {
  clusterName:"myCluster",
  vpc: <EXISTING_VPC>
  // this needs to be an ivpc object in CDK, not an ARN string
});
AWS cost: $0 (on top of what we are already paying for the VPC)
```

2. Use a public subnet.

If we don't mind containers being on a public network or if we need them on a public network – as would be the case if we need to access the container externally – we could create a VPC with a public subnet and Internet gateway. This would not include the billable NAT gateway. Note that access to the container can be controlled through a security group and mapped ports.

In CDK, create a VPC with a public subnet, Internet gateway, and no NAT gateway. (Include the EC2 CDK module first.)

```
const myVPC = new stack.services.ec2.Vpc(this, "myvpc", {
  cidr: "10.0.0.0/16",
  natGateways: 0,
  subnetConfiguration: [{
    cidrMask: 24,
    name: "mySubnet1",
    subnetType: ec2.SubnetType.PUBLIC,
  }]
});
```

Then create the ECS cluster and refer to the new VPC:

```
const myCluster = new ecs.Cluster(this, "ecscluster", {
  clusterName:"myCluster",
  vpc: myVPC
});
```

AWS cost: $0. If done right, there should be no billable components in this setup.

3. Dynamically create a VPC and cluster in Lambda.

This is probably the trickiest option, and it has a minute or so of latency to launch the task as it takes some time to launch the NAT. There are also several steps, any of which could go wrong, and the per-minute cost of running a task will be higher than other options. The primary reason I have included this option is that in many enterprises, the use of a private subnet for containers is required. Make sure to have monitoring in place to avoid orphan VPCs from lingering around and driving up costs for unutilized time.

For this case, no further steps are needed in CDK; the rest will be done in the Lambda microservice.

AWS cost: $0.059 per hour or partial hour that each NAT is running (one NAT should be sufficient)

Note 1. Security group

While all preceding options will create a default security group to go with the VPC, I do recommend creating one specifically for the container, so we have some measure of control over it, and in case we need to open ports or provide access. If we are launching a container that needs external access (and we configured port mapping when creating the task definition), then we will need to add the ports needed to this security group. Note that if we picked option 3, then we will need to create this in the Lambda instead of in CDK.

Create a security group in CDK:

```
const secGroup = new ec2.SecurityGroup(this, "secgroup", {
  vpc: myVPC,
  allowAllOutbound: false // enable required ports below
});
```

Add ports to the security group:

```
secGroup.addIngressRule(
  ec2.Peer.ipv4("0.0.0.0/0"),
  ec2.Port.tcp(1234),
  "Example of opening an ingress port for the container"
);
```

```
secGroup.addEgressRule(
  ec2.Peer.ipv4("0.0.0.0/0"),
  ec2.Port.tcp(443),
  "Example of opening an egress port for the container"
);
```

Note 2. VPC Gateways

If we are working with S3 and/or DynamoDB, we can use VPC Endpoint Gateway to connect a VPC to those services for free and avoid sending data over the public Internet. This free option only supports those two services. The alternative is via PrivateLink, which has an hourly fee, so this would only be considered Serverless if we added the PrivateLink from Lambda for the duration of the task. As Fargate requires the Internet to load the container image and reach CloudWatch, we can enable PrivateLink if we are using a private subnet to avoid using the public Internet for those connections. If we want to avoid using a NAT, then we MUST use PrivateLink for these services for Fargate to work.

Note 3. CloudWatch logs

We can enable console output to CloudWatch logs on the Fargate container. Like Lambda microservices, we can then write out statuses, errors, and any other kind of information from the container. This is useful for debugging, proactive monitoring, and cost or activity tracking.

First, create a new LogGroup using CDK (this will need the CDK module logs):

```
const logGroup = new logs.LogGroup(this,"ecslogs-abc", {
  logGroupName: "/aws/ecs/groupname",
  removalPolicy: cdk.RemovalPolicy.DESTROY,

  // destroy logs after 3 days
  retention: logs.RetentionDays.THREE_DAYS
});
```

Add this *logging* parameter in the *addContainer* function params (step 7):

```
logging: new ecs.AwsLogDriver({
  streamPrefix: "MYSTREAM",
  logGroup: logGroup, // created above

  // destroy logs after 3 days
  retention: logs.RetentionDays.THREE_DAYS
});
```

Note that we can opt to use the same *LogGroup* for multiple containers and just indicate the container name in the *streamPrefix*, or we can create a unique LogGroup for each container.

This will also need the following permissions in the execution task role

```
"logs:CreateLogStream",
"logs:PutLogEvents"
```

and this resource (the bold part should match the name given to the preceding log group):

```
"arn:aws:logs:"+region+":"+account+":log-group:/aws/ecs/groupname/*"
```

675

Note 4. Elastic Load Balancer (ELB)

AWS recommends putting an Elastic Load Balancer in front of Fargate containers that need to be publicly accessible. I did not need it for my use case, but it makes sense for public containers. Keep in mind that load balancers have a per-time cost, so to keep it truly Serverless. The load balancer would need to be created and attached in the Lambda microservice. This will add latency to the availability of the container and require the Lambda microservice to run a bit longer.

9. Launch the Container

This will be done in the Lambda microservice as we will be billed for the time the container is running. As my use case can be interrupted and it's not time-sensitive, I will be using Fargate spot pricing, which is quite a bit cheaper than on-demand pricing.

AWS cost of running the container: $0.015168/CPU hour + $0.001659/GB memory hour

For the FFMPEG container, we have one CPU and 2 GB, so the total cost is $0.018486/hour.

The grand total of all of these will be

- ECR

    $0.01/month storage for the container (my FFMPEG container is just under 100 MB)

    $0.012 data transfer per FFMPEG job

- Lambda

    $0.0000004 per job (there will be two requests for each job)

    Options 1 and 2 (if the VPC and cluster are created in CDK):

    $0.000031245 per job (1.5 seconds at 128 MB)

    or

    Option 3 (if the VPC and cluster are created in Lambda):

    $0.000007291 per job (35 seconds at 128 MB per FFMPEG job)

- SQS

    $0.0000008 for two SQS messages per FFMPEG job

    VPC (for option 3: the VPC and cluster are created in Lambda with a NAT)

    $0.059/hour (depends how long the FFMPEG job needs)

- ECS

    $0.018486/hour (depends how long the FFMPEG job needs)

- S3

    Data transfer between S3 and EC2/Fargate in the same region should be free, especially if we are using an Endpoint Gateway for S3, as it remains on the internal network.

For example, if we would run five FFMPEG jobs per day, with videos an average of 1 GB, and each job takes 1 hour to complete, the total average cost per month would be For options 1 and 2 (existing VPC created in CDK without a NAT):
$ 4.59/month (+ existing VPC cost for option 1)

For option 3 (VPC created in Lambda with a NAT):
$ 13.43/month

The Lambda Microservice

This is not my full Lambda microservice code, but I have put the key parts in basic JavaScript or pseudocode in the following to make it easier to understand. Generally speaking, the flow would be to create the services – some in parallel, some in a specific order. For some services, we may need to wait a short while. I use JavaScript *promises* followed by a *Promise.all* for the items that can happen in parallel and loop *setTimeOut* when I need to wait for some previous step to complete.

I also suggest having a cleanup function in the Lambda microservice. This function can undo every completed step if something goes wrong to avoid leaving orphaned services running and costing money.

The goal is to minimize idle time in Lambda, so do as much as possible in parallel and only wait when there is no other option. Luckily, a NAT launches in around 30 seconds. If it needs longer, use SQS with a visibility delay or an EventBridge schedule.

First are the access and environment variables needed for the Lambda microservice. Resources:

- The task and execution role ARNs that were created in step 5

- arn:aws:ecs:"+region+":"+account+":service/CLUSTER_NAME/*

Actions:

- "ecs:CreateService",

- "ecs:DeleteService",

- "ecs:TagResource",

- "iam:PassRole"

For option 3 we will also need these actions (with appropriate resources):

- "ecs:CreateCluster",

- "ec2:TagResources",

- "ec2:CreateVpc",

- "ec2:CreateInternetGateway",

- "ec2:AttachInternetGateway",

- "ec2:AllocateAddress",

- "ec2:CreateSubnet",

- "ec2:CreateRouteTable",

- "ec2:CreateNatGateway",

- "ec2:CreateRoute",

- "ec2:CreateSecurityGroup",

- "ec2:AuthorizeSecurityGroupIngress",

- "ec2:AuthorizeSecurityGroupEgress",

- "ec2:AssociateRouteTable",

- "ec2:DisassociateRouteTable",

- "ec2:DeleteSecurityGroup",

- "ec2:DeleteRouteTable",

- "ec2:DeleteNatGateway",

- "ec2:ReleaseAddress",

- "ec2:DetachInternetGateway",

- "ec2:DeleteInternetGateway",

- "ec2:DeleteSubnet",

- "ec2:DeleteVpc"

Environment variables:

- "ecs_taskdefinition": ecstask.taskDefinitionArn,

- "ecs_cluster": myCluster.clusterArn,

- "ecs_subnet": myVPC.publicSubnets[0].subnetId,

- "ecs_secgroup": secGroup.securityGroupId

(Option 3 would only have the taskdefinition variable.)

Launching a VPC and Cluster (If We Went with Option 3)

I have noted in the following the function names needed from the AWS SDK and some of the params. Please see the documentation for more details and other options.

Start with these in parallel.

- Get an elastic IP address:

  ec2.allocateAddress

- Domain: "vpc"

  - Create NAT.

- Create IGW:

  ec2.createInternetGateway

- no params

  - Attach IGW.

- Create VPC:

  ec2.createVPC

CidrBlock: "10.0.0.0/16"

- Attach IGW.

- Create a subnet:

ec2.createSubnet(

CidrBlock: "10.0.1.0/24", VpcId: vpcresult.Vpc.VpcId

  - Create NAT.

- Create Route Table:

ec2.createRouteTable

VpcId: vpcresult.Vpc.VpcId

  - Create Route.

These steps are dependent on some of the preceding steps:

- Attach IGW.

Dependent on: VPC and IGW

ec2.attachInternetGateway

InternetGatewayId: igwresult.InternetGateway.InternetGatewayId,
VpcId: vpcresult.Vpc.VpcId

  - Create NAT.

- Create NAT.

Dependent on: VPC, elastic IP, subnet, IGW

ec2.createNatGateway

AllocationId: eidresult.AllocationId, SubnetId: subnetresult.Subnet.SubnetId

  - Create Route.

- Create security group.

Dependent on: VPC

ec2.createSecurityGroup

GroupName: "my-security-group", VpcId: vpcresult.Vpc.VpcId

- Add rules (if needed):

    ec2.AuthorizeSecurityGroupIngress and ec2.
    AuthorizeSecurityGroupEgress

    See documentation for details.

The Create NAT step will need around 30 seconds. The result will come back right away, but the NAT will not have launched yet, so we need to wait for it to do so. I set a timeout for 30 seconds. Then I try to run Create Route. If it fails with an err.code "InvalidNatGatewayID.NotFound", I wait for another 5 seconds and then try again. This keeps looping until it succeeds (or Lambda times out if something went wrong).

- Create Route.

    Dependent on: Route Table and NAT

    ec2.createRoute

    DestinationCidrBlock: "0.0.0.0/0", NatGatewayId: natresult.NatGateway.
    NatGatewayId, RouteTableId: routetableresult.RouteTable.RouteTableId

- Associate Route Table with the subnet.

    Dependent on: Route Table and subnet

    ec2.associateRouteTable

    RouteTableId: routetableresult.RouteTable.RouteTableId, SubnetId:
    subnetresult.Subnet.SubnetId

Once all of this has been completed, we have a running VPC that we can use for our cluster and Fargate service. Creating a cluster does not require a VPC, so we can run it in parallel with VPC creation. See the latest documentation for creating an ECS Fargate cluster in CDK.

Launching a Fargate Service

This service manages the task and ensures that the container is running and available. If we went with option 1 or 2, we would only need this step in Lambda, and it will start costing money once it's running. See the latest documentation for creating an ECS service in CDK.

Retrieve the Container IP

There is one more step we will need to do in Lambda after the one earlier if we have a container that needs to be externally accessible: get the public IP address.

The steps are as follows:

1. Use setTimeout to wait a short while before calling the next function. How long exactly depends on the size and complexity of the container. For my example, I needed to wait about 6 seconds.

2. List the task ARNs using *ecs.listTasks* and provide the params for the cluster ARN, launchType FARGATE, and service name. This will return an array parameter called *taskArns*. If the length is 0, we need to wait another couple of seconds and try again:

   ```
   listTasksResult.taskArns.length > 0
   ```

3. Once we have the array with the *taskARN* in it, we can call *ecs. describeTasks* with the cluster ARN and the *taskARN* array. Make sure the response has a non-empty *tasks* param, and, inside the first task in that array, a non-empty *attachments* array. In the first *attachment* array, we should check the status param to see if it's *ATTACHING*. If not, wait a couple of seconds and try the request again:

   ```
   describeTasksResult.tasks[0].attachments[0].status
   === "ATTACHING"
   ```

4. When the attachment status is *ATTACHING*, we can loop through its *details* array to find an object with the param *name* set to *networkInterfaceId*. The value param in that object will be the ENI ID we need for the next step.

```
res.tasks[0].attachments[0].details[i].name ===
"networkInterfaceId"
res.tasks[0].attachments[0].details[i].value
```

5.   We can call *ec2.describeNetworkInterfaces* with the ENI
     ID set as the first element in an array value for the param
     NetworkInterfaceIds. If everything is correct, we will find the IP
     address here:

```
describeNetworkInterfacesResult.NetworkInterfaces[0].
Association.PublicIp
```

Finished

And that's it; we can now launch Serverless containers for tasks and long-running
services. Terminating the service when we are done is a matter of calling *ecs.deleteService*
at the right time. For my FFMPEG case, the container will send a *job done* message
(which includes the task ARN) to the output SQS queue that triggers my Lambda so
that it can terminate that particular service. Another solution might be to have an
EventBridge CRON that calls a Lambda microservice to terminate it. We can also
have a recurring CRON triggering a Lambda microservice to list all of the services and
terminate those that have expired (checking the *expire* tag we used previously).

One other thing I bumped into that may be relevant to some use cases: Fargate does
not permit the *privileged* param on containers, so existing containers that need to run
something as a service may not work without some changes.

Epilogue

There are only two ways to influence human behavior: you can manipulate it or you can inspire it.

—Simon Sinek, Author and Motivational Speaker

Never stop learning is a mantra I try to live by. I enjoy writing because it is a way for me to share knowledge and gain a deeper understanding of the subject. For a few years now, I have been almost exclusively involved in Serverless projects, but there are always gaps and more things to learn, especially because the pace of change is so fast. New services are launching, existing ones are evolving, and keeping up with everything, while fun, is a challenge, to say the least.

I hope reading this book has been a great learning experience for you and that it will inspire you to consider a Serverless approach for a next suitable project. Please connect on LinkedIn and feel free to ask any questions or engage in discussion on any of the topics I've covered here.

Now that you are a newly minted Serverless pro, if you are looking for some Serverless swag to show off your new knowledge, please check out my e-store here: `https://swag.binarythinktank.com.`

All proceeds go toward writing my next book!

Happy learning, and check out this fun video about Serverless:
`https://youtu.be/zMuaOcuhFnc`
Thomas Smart
`www.linkedin.com/in/thomasjsmart`

© Thomas Smart 2023
T. Smart, *Serverless Beyond the Buzzword*, https://doi.org/10.1007/978-1-4842-8761-3

References

The following are resources referenced, quoted, or just good to read to delve deeper into the subjects covered in this book:

- Thomas Smart's blog, `www.binarythinktank.com/blog`.

- Amazon Web Services, `https://aws.amazon.com/` (April 2020).

- M. Roberts and J. Chapin, *What Is Serverless?*, p. 56.

- S. A. El-Seoud, H. F. El-Sofany, M. A. F. Abdelfattah, and R. Mohamed, "Big Data and Cloud Computing: Trends and Challenges," Int. J. Interact. Mob. Technol. IJIM, vol. 11, no. 2, p. 34, April 2017, doi: 10.3991/ijim.v11i2.6561.

- M. Armbrust et al., "A view of cloud computing," Commun. ACM, vol. 53, no. 4, pp. 50–58, April 2010, doi: 10.1145/1721654.1721672.

- T. Dillon, C. Wu, and E. Chang, "Cloud Computing: Issues and Challenges," in 2010 24th IEEE International Conference on Advanced Information Networking and Applications, April 2010, pp. 27–33, doi: 10.1109/AINA.2010.187.

- G. McGrath and P. R. Brenner, "Serverless Computing: Design, Implementation, and Performance," in 2017 IEEE 37th International Conference on Distributed Computing Systems Workshops (ICDCSW), June 2017, pp. 405–410, doi: 10.1109/ICDCSW.2017.36.

- Amazon annual revenue 2018, `www.statista.com/statistics/266282/annual-net-revenue-of-amazoncom/` (accessed April 2020).

- `https://hackernoon.com/websockets-api-gateway-9d4aca493d39` (accessed April 2020).

- `www.pubnub.com/blog/websockets-vs-rest-api-understanding-the-difference/` (accessed April 2020).

© Thomas Smart 2023
T. Smart, *Serverless Beyond the Buzzword*, https://doi.org/10.1007/978-1-4842-8761-3

REFERENCES

- https://docs.aws.amazon.com/apigateway/latest/developerguide/api-gateway-request-validation-set-up.html (accessed April 2020).

- https://lumigo.io/blog/tackling-api-gateway-lambda-performance-issues/ (accessed April 2020).

- M. Kiran, P. Murphy, I. Monga, J. Dugan, and S. S. Baveja, "Lambda architecture for cost-effective batch and speed big data processing," in 2015 IEEE International Conference on Big Data (Big Data), October 2015, pp. 2785–2792, doi: 10.1109/BigData.2015.7364082.

- Red Hat's "What is virtualization," www.redhat.com/en/topics/virtualization/what-is-virtualization (accessed April 2020).

- Engdahl, S. (2008). Blogs. From https://aws.amazon.com/blogs/security/how-to-protect-data-at-rest-with-amazon-ec2-instance-store-encryption/ (accessed May 2020).

- New Amazon S3 Encryption & Security Features. https://aws.amazon.com/blogs/aws/new-amazon-s3-encryption-security-features (accessed May 2020).

- Aviv Degani, N. (2020). Amazon S3 Encryption: How to Protect Your Data in S3. https://cloud.netapp.com/blog/amazon-s3-encryption-how-to-protect-your-data-in-s3 (accessed May 2020).

- How to improve LDAP security in AWS Directory Service with client-side LDAPS. https://aws.amazon.com/blogs/security/how-to-improve-ldap-security-in-aws-directory-service-with-client-side-ldaps/ (accessed May 2020).

- How do you protect your data in transit? AWS Well-Architected Framework. https://wa.aws.amazon.com/wat.question.SEC_10.en.html (accessed May 2020).

- Erich, Floris & Amrit, Chintan & Daneva, Maya. (2017). A Qualitative Study of DevOps Usage in Practice. Journal of Software: Evolution and Process. 00. 10.1002/smr.1885.

- Mali Senapathi, Jim Buchan, Hady Osman, Capabilities, Practices, and Challenges: Insights from a Case Study.

- www.datamation.com/cloud-computing/top-serverless-vendors.html (accessed May 2020).

- https://techbeacon.com/enterprise-it/serverless-vendor-lock-should-you-be-worried (accessed May 2020).

- www.iheavy.com/2017/04/15/top-amazon-lambda-questions-hiring-serverless-expert-interview/ (accessed May 2020).

- https://venturebeat.com/2017/10/22/the-big-opportunities-in-serverless-computing/ (accessed May 2020).

- www.cio.com/article/3183504/why-your-cloud-strategy-should-include-multiple-vendors.html (accessed May 2020).

- https://mediatemple.net/blog/cloud-hosting/serverless-benefits-and-challenges/ (accessed May 2020).

- www.onlineinterviewquestions.com/aws-lambda-interview-questions/ (accessed May 2020).

- https://dashbird.io/blog/companies-using-serverless-in-production/ (accessed May 2020).

- https://raygun.com/blog/best-practices-microservices/ (accessed May 2020).

- https://aws.amazon.com/cdk/ (accessed May 2020).

- https://github.com/aws/aws-cdk (accessed May 2020).

- https://docs.aws.amazon.com/serverless-application-model/latest/developerguide/serverless-sam-cli-using-invoke.html (accessed May 2020).

- https://garbe.io/blog/2019/10/01/hey-cdk-how-to-write-less-code/ (accessed May 2020).

- https://docs.aws.amazon.com/cdk/latest/guide/constructs.html (accessed May 2020).

- https://matthewbonig.com/2020/01/11/creating-constructs/ (accessed May 2020).

- https://docs.aws.amazon.com/cdk/latest/guide/stack_how_to_create_multiple_stacks.html (accessed May 2020).

- How to Earn a Top Paying AWS Certification & Salary. www.globalknowledge.com/us-en/resources/resource-library/articles/how-to-earn-a-top-paying-aws-certification-salary/ (accessed June 2020).

- AWS Certification - Validate AWS Cloud Skills - Get AWS Certified, https://aws.amazon.com/certification/ (accessed June 2020).

- M. Andersson, "Which AWS certification is right for me?", https://info.acloud.guru/resources/which-aws-certification-should-i-take (accessed June 2020).

- AWS Certified Cloud Practitioner 2020 (Certification Course), www.udemy.com/course/aws-certified-cloud-practitioner/ (accessed June 2020).

- Introduction to Serverless, www.udemy.com/course/introduction-to-serverless/ (accessed June 2020).

- AWS Serverless APIs & Web Apps - A Complete Introduction, www.udemy.com/course/aws-serverless-a-complete-introduction/ (accessed June 2020).

- Basic AWS Architecture Best Practices - 1 Hour Crash Course, www.udemy.com/course/awsbestpractices/ (accessed June 2020).

- Serverless Framework Bootcamp: Node.js, AWS & Microservices, www.udemy.com/course/serverless-framework/ (accessed June 2020).

- Azure Serverless Functions and Logic Apps, www.udemy.com/course/azure-serverless/ (accessed June 2020).

- Cloud Computing Basics (Cloud 101), www.coursera.org/learn/cloud-computing-basics (accessed June 2020).

- Introduction to Cloud Computing, `www.coursera.org/learn/introduction-to-cloud` (accessed June 2020).

- AWS Fundamentals: Building Serverless Applications | Coursera, `www.coursera.org/learn/aws-fundamentals-building-serverless-applications` (accessed June 2020).

- Learning Path – Serverless Computing – Linux Academy, `https://linuxacademy.com/learning-path/serverless-computing/` (accessed June 2020).

- AWS Global Summit Program, `https://aws.amazon.com/events/summits/` (accessed June 2020).

- 2019 re:Invent, `https://aws.amazon.com/new/reinvent/` (accessed June 2020).

- ServerlessDays, `https://serverlessdays.io/` (accessed June 2020).

- `www.devops-certification.org/` (accessed June 2020).

- `https://docs.aws.amazon.com/wellarchitected/latest/serverless-applications-lens/welcome.html` (accessed June 2020).

- `https://aws.amazon.com/blogs/aws/new-serverless-lens-in-aws-well-architected-tool/` (accessed June 2020).

- `https://morioh.com/p/00b367a81251` (accessed June 2020).

- `https://aws.amazon.com/blogs/apn/the-5-pillars-of-the-aws-well-architected-framework/` (accessed June 2020).

- `https://docs.aws.amazon.com/IAM/latest/UserGuide/best-practices.html` (accessed June 2020).

- `www.skyhighnetworks.com/cloud-security-blog/13-aws-iam-best-practices-for-security-and-compliance/` (accessed June 2020).

- `http://techgenix.com/iam-security-best-practices/` (accessed June 2020).

- www.skyhighnetworks.com/cloud-security-blog/skyhigh-research-finds-password-insecure-reuse-cloud/ (accessed June 2020).

- www.freecodecamp.org/news/how-to-secure-microservices-on-aws-with-cognito-api-gateway-and-lambda-4bfaa7a6583c/ (accessed June 2020).

- https://techbeacon.com/app-dev-testing/8-best-practices-microservices-app-sec (accessed June 2020).

- https://medium.com/@bluesoft/getting-started-with-microservices-on-aws-lambda-2d45762b439e (accessed June 2020).

- https://d1.awsstatic.com/whitepapers/architecture/AWS-Serverless-Applications-Lens.pdf (accessed June 2020).

- https://news.ycombinator.com/item?id=24091257 (accessed June 2020).

- www.1strategy.com/blog/2018/06/19/tips-for-creating-iam-policies/ (accessed June 2020).

- www.1strategy.com/blog/2020/03/10/ten-tips-for-improved-iam-security/ (accessed June 2020).

- https://engineering.upside.com/s3-antivirus-scanning-with-lambda-and-clamav-7d33f9c5092e (accessed June 2020).

- https://aws.amazon.com/premiumsupport/knowledge-center/s3-bucket-policy-for-config-rule/ (accessed June 2020).

- https://aws.amazon.com/blogs/security/iam-policies-and-bucket-policies-and-acls-oh-my-controlling-access-to-s3-resources/ (accessed June 2020).

- www.codemotion.com/magazine/dev-hub/security-manager/how-to-comply-with-gdpr-in-a-serverless-world/ (accessed June 2020).

- https://gdpr.eu/ (accessed June 2020).

- www.endpointprotector.com/blog/data-protection-legislation-around-the-world-in-2020/ (accessed June 2020).

- `https://aws.amazon.com/blogs/security/all-aws-services-gdpr-ready/` (accessed June 2020).

- `https://azure.microsoft.com/en-gb/blog/protecting-privacy-in-microsoft-azure-gdpr-azure-policy-updates/` (accessed June 2020).

- `https://nuvalence.io/intro-to-lambda-monitoring-with-cloudwatch-alarms-and-cloudformation/` (accessed June 2020).

- `https://docs.aws.amazon.com/lambda/latest/dg/services-cloudwatchevents.html` (accessed June 2020).

- `https://lumigo.io/serverless-monitoring-guide/how-to-monitor-lambda-with-cloudwatch-metrics/` (accessed June 2020).

- `https://docs.aws.amazon.com/lambda/latest/dg/monitoring-metrics.html` (accessed June 2020).

- `https://github.com/jonrau1/ElectricEye` (accessed September 2020).

- `https://dzone.com/articles/microservices-event-driven-architecture-and-kafka` (accessed September 2020).

Back Cover

This book is for anyone interested in Serverless, regardless of their technical level. I share the strategic approach to modern cloud management for entrepreneurs and executives; planning, budget, and team insights for project managers; and technical deep dives for architects and team leads. The intent is to provide a deep and broad understanding of Serverless architecture and how it could impact your organization and projects.

Index

A

Access Control Lists (ACLs), 143, 181
addContainer function, 673, 677
Agile methodology, 233, 236, 243
Amazon, 15, 181, 617
Amazon Aurora, 360
Amazon CloudFront, 36, 582
Amazon Connect, 614
Amazon Keyspaces, 382
Amazon Lookout, 596, 598
Amazon Neptune, 11, 385
Amazon QLDB, 11
Amazon QuickSight, 125
Amazon Robotics, 595
Amazon Timestream, 11, 382–383
Amazon Web Service (AWS), 507
Amplify, 306–309, 313, 666
API-driven content management system (CMS), 661–663
API Gateway, 32, 36, 96, 104, 138, 142, 172, 178–180, 182, 186, 188, 291, 300, 305, 314, 318, 341, 388, 392, 404, 409, 423, 430, 431, 436, 453, 459, 481, 498, 516, 517, 519–525, 528, 531, 574, 623, 624, 631, 638, 661
API Gateway Model Schemas, 188
API Gateway service, 178, 519
API Gateway's Model Schema, 96
API Gateway WebSockets, 517, 518, 577, 579
API reference document, 630

Application Load Balancer (ALB), 177, 182, 409, 410, 523–525, 660
Application security, 70, 164, 165, 182
AppSync, 182, 389, 392, 393, 622
Architect Framework (ARC), 341
Artifacts and schemas, 86, 98, 104
Asset metrics, 602
Asset modeling, 602
Asynchronous approach, 268, 506, 510
Asynchronous design pattern
    API Gateway, 574
    design, 574
    example, 575
    parallel processing, 575, 577–579
Asynchronous testing, 455, 467–471
Athena, 412, 416, 644, 647
Aurora, 245, 351, 358, 360–363, 379, 389
Aurora capacity units (ACUs), 361, 362
Automated testing, 227, 259, 260, 448, 454, 625
Autoscaling, 2, 23, 63, 114, 122, 123, 126, 176, 364, 405, 538
AWS API Gateway, 164, 318, 492
aws-cdk-local library, 480
AWS cloud-based infrastructure, 622
AWS Config, 57–59, 175, 207, 245, 666
AWS Global Summits, 251
AWS-managed VPC, 138, 150
AWS Pricing Calculator, 145
AWS Security Hub, 165, 202, 214, 217

Printed in the United States
by Baker & Taylor Publisher Services